# THE ETERNAL KINGDOM

*Living Under Christ*

WILLEM J. OUWENEEL

AN EVANGELICAL INTRODUCTION TO
REFORMATIONAL THEOLOGY
VOL IV/3

PART IV: CONSUMMATION:
THE LIVED SHAPE OF THEOLOGY

# AN EVANGELICAL INTRODUCTION TO REFORMATIONAL THEOLOGY

*Part I: Scripture: The Revealed Source For Theology*
  I/1 *The Eternal Word*: God Speaking To Us
  I/2 *The Eternal Torah*: Living Under God

*Part II: God: The Personal Source Behind Theology*
  II/1 *The Eternal God*: God Revealing Himself To Us
  II/2 *The Eternal Christ:* God With Us
  II/3 *The Eternal Spirit*: God Living In Us

*Part III: Redemption: The Christ-Centered Heart of Theology*
  III/1 *The Eternal Purpose*: Living In Christ
  III/2 *Eternal Righteousness*: Living Before God
  III/3 *Eternal Salvation*: Christ Dying For Us
  III/4 *Eternal Life*: Christ Living In Us

*Part IV: Consummation: The Lived Shape of Theology*
  IV/1a *The Eternal People*: God in Relation To Israel: Israel in the Tanakh and the New Testament
  IV/1b *The Eternal People*: God in Relation To Israel: Post-New Testament Israel
  IV/2 *The Eternal Covenant*: Living With God
  IV/3 *The Eternal Kingdom*: Living Under Christ

*Part V: Method: The Comprehensive Foundation of Theology*
  V/1 *Eternal Truth*: The Prolegomena of Theology

# The Eternal Kingdom:

*An Evangelical Theology of Living Under Christ*

Willem J. Ouweneel

*The Eternal Kingdom: An Evangelical Theology of Living Under Christ*

This English edition is a publication of Paideia Press, a publishing imprint of the Cántaro Institute (Jordan Station, Ontario, Canada L0R 1S0). Copyright © 2026 by Paideia Press. All rights reserved. Except for brief quotations in critical publications or reviews, no part of this book may be reproduced in any manner without prior written permission from Paideia Press at the address above.

Unless otherwise indicated, Scripture quotations are from the ESV® Bible (The Holy Bible, English Standard Version®). Copyright © 2001 by Crossway, a publishing ministry of Good News Publishers. Used by permission. All rights reserved.

Scripture quotations or references marked as NKJV are taken from the New King James Version®. Copyright © 1982 by Thomas Nelson, Inc. Used by permission. All rights reserved.

Scripture quotations or references marked as NIV are taken from the Holy Bible, New International Version®, NIV®. Copyright © 1973, 1978, 1984, 2011 by Biblica, Inc.™ Used by permission of Zonderan. All rights reserved worldwide. www.zonderan.com. The "NIV" and "New International Version" are trademarks registered in the United States Patent and Trademark Office by Biblica, Inc.™

Book Design: Paul Aurich

ISBN 978-1-998711-42-0

Printed in the United States of America

*Your kingdom is an **eternal kingdom**,*
  *and your dominion endures through all*
  *generations.*
Ps. 145:13 (NET)

*How great are his signs,*
  *how mighty his wonders!*
*His kingdom is an **eternal kingdom**;*
  *his dominion endures from generation to generation.*
Daniel 4:3 (NIV)

*... His kingdom shall be an **eternal kingdom**,*
*and all the dominions shall serve him and hear him.*
Daniel 7:27 (JUB)

*... [I]n this way there will be richly provided for you an entrance into the **eternal kingdom** of our Lord and Savior Jesus Christ.*
2 Peter 1:11 (ESV)

# Table of Contents

| | | |
|---|---|---|
| Series Preface | | xxiii |
| Author's Preface | | xxvii |
| Abbreviations | | xxxi |
| Chapter 1 | Introduction to the Kingdom | 1 |
| Chapter 2 | The Hope of the Kingdom | 51 |
| Chapter 3 | The Parables of the Kingdom (I) | 101 |
| Chapter 4 | The Parables of the Kingdom (II) | 143 |
| Chapter 5 | The Adversaries of the Kingdom | 193 |
| Chapter 6 | The Disciples of the Kingdom | 241 |
| Chapter 7 | The Kingdom and the Church | 289 |
| Chapter 8 | The Spreading of the Kingdom | 319 |
| Chapter 9 | Faith, Hope, and Love in the Kingdom | 377 |
| Chapter 10 | Early History of Kingdom Theology | 425 |
| Chapter 11 | Later History of Kingdom Theology | 475 |
| Chapter 12 | Early Dispensationalism and Kingdom Theology | 529 |
| Chapter 13 | Later Dispensationalism and Kingdom Theology | 569 |
| Bibliography | | 615 |
| Scripture Index | | 567 |
| Subject Index | | 567 |

# Table of Contents Expanded

| | |
|---|---|
| Series Preface | xxiii |
| Author's Preface | xxvii |
| Abbreviations | xxxi |
| 1. Introduction to the Kingdom | 1 |
|   1.1 Basileology | 2 |
|     1.1.1 The Centrality of the Theme | 2 |
|     1.1.2 New Testament Voices on the Kingdom | 7 |
|     1.1.3 Pre-Easter Saints Expecting the Kingdom | 10 |
|   1.2 The Kingship of God | 12 |
|     1.2.1 Divine Rule in the Old Testament | 12 |
|     1.2.2 Conservation and Providence | 15 |
|   1.3 God's Kingship and Israel | 18 |
|     1.3.1 "King of Jacob" | 18 |
|     1.3.2 King and Messiah | 21 |
|     1.3.3 Universal and Mediatorial Kingship | 23 |
|   1.4 God's Kingship and the Nations | 26 |
|     1.4.1 The *Missio Dei* | 26 |
|     1.4.2 The Ultimate Goal | 28 |
|   1.5 The Kingdom under Humans and Satan | 30 |
|     1.5.1 The Kingdom under Humans | 30 |
|     1.5.2 Eve As Queen | 31 |
|     1.5.3 Crowned Rulers Surrender to Satan | 33 |

|       |       |                              |     |
|-------|-------|------------------------------|-----|
|       | 1.6   | The Meaning of Satan         | 36  |
|       |       | 1.6.1 Satan and Devil        | 36  |
|       |       | 1.6.2 Justice and Power      | 38  |
|       | 1.7   | Satan and His Powers         | 40  |
|       |       | 1.7.1 The World Rulers       | 40  |
|       |       | 1.7.2 Romans 8:20            | 43  |
|       | 1.8   | Satan's Fall and Power       | 44  |
|       |       | 1.8.1 His Fall               | 44  |
|       |       | 1.8.2 Ongoing Conflict       | 47  |
| 2.    | The Hope of the Kingdom      |                | 51 |
|       | 2.1   | Kingdom Prophecies           | 52  |
|       |       | 2.1.1 *Mashiach*             | 52  |
|       |       | 2.1.2 David                  | 55  |
|       |       | 2.1.3 Other Prophecies       | 58  |
|       | 2.2   | The Typology of the Kingdom  | 60  |
|       |       | 2.2.1 Introduction           | 60  |
|       |       | 2.2.2 Pre-Davidic Types      | 62  |
|       |       | 2.2.3 Davidic Types          | 64  |
|       |       | 2.2.4 Other Types            | 66  |
|       |       | 2.2.5 Moses?                 | 67  |
|       | 2.3   | The Kingdom: Present and Future | 68 |
|       |       | 2.3.1 The "Kingdom of Heaven" | 68 |
|       |       | 2.3.2 The "Presence" Passages | 70 |
|       |       | 2.3.3 "Within You" or "Among You" | 74 |
|       | 2.4   | Two Sevens                   | 77  |
|       |       | 2.4.1 Seven Stages           | 77  |
|       |       | 2.4.2 Seven Proofs           | 79  |
|       | 2.5   | The King's Self-Presentation | 82  |
|       |       | 2.5.1 The Son of Man         | 82  |
|       |       | 2.5.2 The Messiah            | 85  |
|       |       | 2.5.3 Jesus' Claims          | 87  |
|       | 2.6   | Recapitulation               | 89  |
|       |       | 2.6.1 Whose Kingdom?         | 89  |

|        |       | 2.6.2   | Ambiguity                              | 91  |
|--------|-------|---------|----------------------------------------|-----|
|        | 2.7   | Pilgrims of the Kingdom                          | 94  |
|        |       | 2.7.1   | The Goal of Israel's Journey           | 94  |
|        |       | 2.7.2   | Israel On Its Pilgrimage               | 96  |
|        |       | 2.7.3   | Pilgrim Songs                          | 99  |
| 3.     | The Parables of the Kingdom (I)                            | 101 |
|        | 3.1   | Matthew's Parables                               | 102 |
|        |       | 3.1.1   | Introduction                           | 102 |
|        |       | 3.1.2   | Survey                                 | 105 |
|        |       | 3.1.3   | Seven Types                            | 107 |
|        | 3.2   | Why Parables?                                    | 110 |
|        |       | 3.2.1   | The Secrets of the Kingdom             | 110 |
|        |       | 3.2.2   | What Exactly Was "Hidden"?             | 113 |
|        |       | 3.2.3   | Five Aspects                           | 115 |
|        | 3.3   | Three Parables of a General Nature               | 116 |
|        |       | 3.3.1   | New and Old Treasures                  | 116 |
|        |       | 3.3.2   | The Fluting and Wailing Children       | 118 |
|        |       | 3.3.3   | Pollution                              | 119 |
|        | 3.4   | Two Positive Parables                            | 121 |
|        |       | 3.4.1   | Two Interpretations                    | 121 |
|        |       | 3.4.2   | Arguments                              | 122 |
|        |       | 3.4.3   | The Treasure in Heaven                 | 124 |
|        | 3.5   | Kingdom Parables and the Messianic Torah         | 128 |
|        |       | 3.5.1   | The Wise Man and the Foolish Man       | 128 |
|        |       | 3.5.2   | The Lost Sheep                         | 129 |
|        |       | 3.5.3   | The Unforgiving Servant                | 132 |
|        |       | 3.5.4   | The Laborers in the Vineyard           | 136 |
|        |       | 3.5.5   | The Two Sons                           | 138 |
|        | 3.6   | Epilogue                                         | 140 |
| 4.     | The Parables of the Kingdom (II)                           | 143 |
|        | 4.1   | The Tenants                                      | 144 |

|       |       | 4.1.1 | The King's Vineyard, the King's Servants | 144 |
|       |       | 4.1.2 | New Tenants | 147 |
|       | 4.2   | The Wedding Feast |       | 149 |
|       |       | 4.2.1 | The Invitations | 149 |
|       |       | 4.2.2 | Judgment | 151 |
|       |       | 4.2.3 | Bad and Good | 153 |
|       |       | 4.2.4 | The Man Without a Wedding Garment | 155 |
|       | 4.3   | Comparable Passages |       | 158 |
|       |       | 4.3.1 | Again Matthew 13 | 158 |
|       |       | 4.3.2 | The Sons of the Kingdom | 160 |
|       | 4.4   | The Kingdom: A Mixture |       | 162 |
|       |       | 4.4.1 | The Sower | 162 |
|       |       | 4.4.2 | The Wheat and the Weeds | 165 |
|       |       | 4.4.3 | "The Field Is the World" | 169 |
|       |       | 4.4.4 | The Mustard Seed | 172 |
|       |       | 4.4.5 | The Leaven | 174 |
|       |       | 4.4.6 | The Woman | 176 |
|       |       | 4.4.7 | The Net | 177 |
|       | 4.5   | Parables of the Olivet Discourse |       | 179 |
|       |       | 4.5.1 | The Fig Tree | 179 |
|       |       | 4.5.2 | The Two Servants | 181 |
|       |       | 4.5.3 | The Ten Virgins | 185 |
|       |       | 4.5.4 | The Talents | 189 |
|       |       | 4.5.5 | Contrasts | 191 |
| 5.    | The Adversaries of the Kingdom |       |       | 193 |
|       | 5.1   | The Powers in Jesus' day |       | 194 |
|       |       | 5.1.1 | The Battle Against Satan | 194 |
|       |       | 5.1.2 | A Kingdom Taken Violently | 196 |
|       |       | 5.1.3 | A Kingdom of Suffering | 198 |
|       | 5.2   | Suffering and Triumph |       | 200 |

|       |       |       |                                              |     |
|-------|-------|-------|----------------------------------------------|-----|
|       | 5.2.1 |       | A Kingdom of Power                           | 200 |
|       | 5.2.2 |       | First Suffering, Then Glory                  | 203 |
|       | 5.2.3 |       | Two Types of Christians                      | 206 |
| 5.3   |       | The Announcement of Triumph                  |     | 210 |
|       | 5.3.1 |       | The *Palingenesia*                           | 210 |
|       | 5.3.2 |       | The Olivet Discourse                         | 211 |
|       | 5.3.3 |       | Two Other Events                             | 213 |
| 5.4   |       | Far Off Or Imminent?                         |     | 216 |
|       | 5.4.1 |       | Far Off                                      | 216 |
|       | 5.4.2 |       | Imminent?                                    | 217 |
|       | 5.4.3 |       | Paul and Peter                               | 219 |
| 5.5   |       | Seven Conditions for Entrance                |     | 221 |
|       | 5.5.1 |       | Regeneration                                 | 221 |
|       | 5.5.2 |       | Righteousness                                | 223 |
|       | 5.5.3 |       | Inner Sincerity                              | 225 |
|       | 5.5.4 |       | Childlike Simplicity                         | 226 |
|       | 5.5.5 |       | Renunciation                                 | 228 |
|       | 5.5.6 |       | Spiritual Power                              | 229 |
|       | 5.5.7 |       | Perseverance                                 | 230 |
| 5.6   |       | Responsibility and Grace                     |     | 232 |
|       | 5.6.1 |       | Dimensions of the Twofold Gospel Compared    | 232 |
|       | 5.6.2 |       | No Responsibility Without Grace              | 233 |
| 5.7   |       | The Conditions Contained in the Beatitudes   |     | 235 |
|       | 5.7.1 |       | The Principle of Righteousness               | 235 |
|       | 5.7.2 |       | Mercy and Love                               | 237 |
|       | 5.7.3 |       | The Last Two Beatitudes                      | 239 |
| 6.    |       | The Disciples of the Kingdom                 |     | 241 |
| 6.1   |       | Subjects of the Kingdom                      |     | 242 |
|       | 6.1.1 |       | Permeated with the Torah                     | 242 |

|       |       |       |                                         |     |
|-------|-------|-------|-----------------------------------------|-----|
|       |       | 6.1.2 | Becoming Like the Master                | 245 |
|       |       | 6.1.3 | Teacher, Torah, Trainees                | 248 |
|       | 6.2   | King and Teacher                                | 250 |
|       |       | 6.2.1 | Subjects and Disciples                  | 250 |
|       |       | 6.2.2 | Friendship                              | 253 |
|       | 6.3   | Conditions for Discipleship                     | 255 |
|       |       | 6.3.1 | Becoming a Disciple                     | 255 |
|       |       | 6.3.2 | Denying One's Family                    | 257 |
|       |       | 6.3.3 | Denying Oneself                         | 260 |
|       |       | 6.3.4 | Renouncing One's Possessions            | 262 |
|       | 6.4   | The Way (New Testament *Halakhah*)              | 264 |
|       |       | 6.4.1 | Disciples, Christians, "Those of the Way" | 264 |
|       |       | 6.4.2 | Peter and *Halakhah*                    | 268 |
|       |       | 6.4.3 | The Other Apostles                      | 271 |
|       | 6.5   | Discipleship and Kingdom                        | 273 |
|       |       | 6.5.1 | The Disciples' Question                 | 273 |
|       |       | 6.5.2 | Jesus' Response                         | 275 |
|       | 6.6   | The Message of the Kingdom                      | 278 |
|       |       | 6.6.1 | Thessalonica                            | 278 |
|       |       | 6.6.2 | Other Opposition                        | 281 |
|       |       | 6.6.3 | Ephesus                                 | 283 |
| 7.    | The Kingdom and the Church                              | 289 |
|       | 7.1   | From Matthew to Paul                            | 290 |
|       |       | 7.1.1 | Introduction                            | 290 |
|       |       | 7.1.2 | "I Will Build My Church"                | 292 |
|       |       | 7.1.3 | A Future Matter                         | 293 |
|       |       | 7.1.4 | Significance of Christ's Glorification  | 296 |
|       | 7.2   | Church and Kingdom                              | 298 |
|       |       | 7.2.1 | General Relationships                   | 298 |
|       |       | 7.2.2 | Societal Relationships                  | 299 |

|  |  | 7.2.3 | The Church Over Against the Kingdom? | 301 |
|---|---|---|---|---|
|  | 7.3 | The Church and the Coming Kingdom | | 304 |
|  |  | 7.3.1 | "*In* the World" | 304 |
|  |  | 7.3.2 | The Scope of the Kingdom | 306 |
|  |  | 7.3.3 | "Not *of* the World" | 308 |
|  | 7.4 | Various Views | | 310 |
|  |  | 7.4.1 | Roman Catholic | 310 |
|  |  | 7.4.2 | Reformed | 312 |
|  |  | 7.4.3 | Others | 314 |
|  | 7.5 | Final Remarks | | 315 |
|  |  | 7.5.1 | Summary of Kingdom Teaching | 315 |
|  |  | 7.5.2 | The Twofold Gospel | 317 |
| 8. | The Spreading of the Kingdom | | | 319 |
|  | 8.1 | Church, Kingdom, and Spirit in Paul's Ministry | | 320 |
|  |  | 8.1.1 | *Trait d'Union* | 320 |
|  |  | 8.1.2 | The Spirit and Sonship | 322 |
|  |  | 8.1.3 | Sons and Heirs | 324 |
|  | 8.2 | The Coming Kingdom | | 327 |
|  |  | 8.2.1 | Eternal Life and the Inheritance | 327 |
|  |  | 8.2.2 | Moral Characteristics | 329 |
|  |  | 8.2.3 | The Present and the Future | 331 |
|  | 8.3 | The Present Kingdom | | 334 |
|  |  | 8.3.1 | Colossians 1:12-13 | 334 |
|  |  | 8.3.2 | 1 Corinthians 4:19-20 | 336 |
|  |  | 8.3.3 | Romans 14:17-18 | 338 |
|  | 8.4 | Jesus' Lordship | | 341 |
|  |  | 8.4.1 | The Lordship of the King | 341 |
|  |  | 8.4.2 | Confessing the Lord | 343 |
|  |  | 8.4.3 | Other Examples of Lordship | 346 |

| | 8.5 | Disavowing Jesus' Lordship | 349 |
|---|---|---|---|
| | | 8.5.1 Ryrie and Hodges | 349 |
| | | 8.5.2 Refutation | 351 |
| | | 8.5.3 The Opponents | 353 |
| | 8.6 | The Kingdom in Other Letters | 357 |
| | | 8.6.1 The Kingdom in Hebrews 12:28-29 | 357 |
| | | 8.6.2 The Kingdom in James 2:5 | 359 |
| | | 8.6.3 The Kingdom in 2 Peter 1:10-11 | 361 |
| | 8.7 | The King in Revelation | 364 |
| | | 8.7.1 God and Christ as King | 364 |
| | | 8.7.2 Revelation 1:5-6 and 5:9-10 | 365 |
| | | 8.7.3 Revelation 1:9 and 20:4-6 | 367 |
| | 8.8 | The Messianic Kingdom in Revelation | 369 |
| | | 8.8.1 Revelation 11:15-18 | 369 |
| | | 8.8.2 Revelation 12:10 | 371 |
| | | 8.8.3 Revelation 19:6 | 372 |
| | | 8.8.4 Revelation 22:3-5 | 374 |
| 9. | | Faith, Hope, and Love in the Kingdom | 377 |
| | 9.1 | The Kingdom and Practical Faith | 378 |
| | | 9.1.1 Sight and Faith | 378 |
| | | 9.1.2 Believing in Jesus | 380 |
| | | 9.1.3 Powerful Believing | 383 |
| | 9.2 | A Threefold Cord | 385 |
| | | 9.2.1 Seeking the Kingdom | 385 |
| | | 9.2.2 Great Faith | 387 |
| | | 9.2.3 Miracle-Working Faith | 390 |
| | 9.3 | Kingdom Hope in the Old Testament | 393 |
| | | 9.3.1 Genesis | 393 |
| | | 9.3.2 Asaph and Solomon | 396 |
| | | 9.3.3 Old Testament Hope | 399 |
| | 9.4 | Kingdom Hope in the New Testament | 401 |

|  |  | 9.4.1 | The Intermediate State | 401 |
|---|---|---|---|---|
|  |  | 9.4.2 | Waiting and Longing | 403 |
|  |  | 9.4.3 | Living in Hope | 406 |
|  | 9.5 | The Beloved King | | 408 |
|  |  | 9.5.1 | Colossians 1:13 | 408 |
|  |  | 9.5.2 | Vertical Love | 411 |
|  |  | 9.5.3 | Horizontal Love | 413 |
|  | 9.6 | Characteristics of Love | | 416 |
|  |  | 9.6.1 | Tolerance | 416 |
|  |  | 9.6.2 | Mercy | 418 |
|  |  | 9.6.3 | The Law of Love | 420 |
| 10. | Early History of Kingdom Theology | | | 425 |
|  | 10.1 | Jewish Basileology | | 426 |
|  |  | 10.1.1 | A Future Jewish Kingdom? | 426 |
|  |  | 10.1.2 | Restoring the Kingdom to Israel | 429 |
|  |  | 10.1.3 | Küng on the Kingdom | 431 |
|  |  | 10.1.4 | All Too Earthly | 433 |
|  | 10.2 | The Constantinian Turn | | 436 |
|  |  | 10.2.1 | Consequences | 436 |
|  |  | 10.2.2 | Militarism | 438 |
|  |  | 10.2.3 | Supersessionism | 440 |
|  | 10.3 | Anti-Millennialism | | 442 |
|  |  | 10.3.1 | Church Buildings | 442 |
|  |  | 10.3.2 | The "Last Day" | 444 |
|  |  | 10.3.3 | Augustine | 446 |
|  | 10.4 | The Way of Augustine | | 448 |
|  |  | 10.4.1 | Israel and the Church | 448 |
|  |  | 10.4.2 | The First Group | 449 |
|  | 10.5 | The Battle Against Spiritualism | | 451 |
|  |  | 10.5.1 | The Second Group | 451 |
|  |  | 10.5.2 | Jacobus Koelman | 452 |
|  |  | 10.5.3 | William à Brakel | 454 |

|  |  |  |  |
|---|---|---|---|
| | 10.6 | Further Openness to Israel | 458 |
| | | 10.6.1 Van der Groe and Cocceius | 458 |
| | | 10.6.2 Other Voices | 459 |
| | | 10.6.3 An Important Hermeneutical Rule | 461 |
| | 10.7 | Millennialism: Historical-Theological | 463 |
| | | 10.7.1 Terminology | 463 |
| | | 10.7.2 Church Fathers | 466 |
| | | 10.7.3 Other Views | 469 |
| 11. | Later History of Kingdom Theology | | 475 |
| | 11.1 | Protestant Premillennialism | 476 |
| | | 11.1.1 The Reformers | 476 |
| | | 11.1.2 The Revival of Premillennialism | 479 |
| | 11.2 | Protestant Postmillennialism | 481 |
| | | 11.2.1 A Confused Picture | 481 |
| | | 11.2.2 Critical Questions | 483 |
| | 11.3 | Old-Liberal Basileology | 486 |
| | | 11.3.1 What Is Liberal? | 486 |
| | | 11.3.2 Ritsch and Harnack | 488 |
| | 11.4 | "Consistent" Basileology | 489 |
| | | 11.4.1 An Illusion? | 489 |
| | | 11.4.2 A Delayed Parousia | 492 |
| | | 11.4.3 The Necessity of a Delayed Parousia | 494 |
| | 11.5 | Realized Basileology | 497 |
| | | 11.5.1 Focusing on the Present | 497 |
| | | 11.5.2 A Delicate Balance | 499 |
| | 11.6 | Transcendent/Existential Basileology | 501 |
| | | 11.6.1 Barth, Bultmann, Moltmann | 501 |
| | | 11.6.2 Liberation Theology | 502 |
| | 11.7 | Newer Views | 504 |
| | | 11.7.1 The Jesus Seminar | 504 |
| | | 11.7.2 Dominion Theology | 506 |

|  |  | 11.7.3 | Prosperity Theology | 508 |
| --- | --- | --- | --- | --- |
|  | 11.8 | Basic Misunderstandings | | 510 |
|  |  | 11.8.1 | Spiritualization | 510 |
|  |  | 11.8.2 | Kingdom and Church | 512 |
|  |  | 11.8.3 | The Parousia Already Fulfilled? | 513 |
|  | 11.9 | Materialist and Secularized Views | | 516 |
|  |  | 11.9.1 | Material Aspects | 516 |
|  |  | 11.9.2 | Secularization | 519 |
|  |  | 11.9.3 | The Premillennial View | 521 |
|  | 11.10 | Summary of Dilemmas | | 524 |
| 12. | Early Dispensationalism and Kingdom Theology | | | 529 |
|  | 12.1 | Terminology | | 530 |
|  |  | 12.1.1 | Dispensation | 530 |
|  |  | 12.1.2 | Dispensationalism | 532 |
|  | 12.2 | Types of Dispensationalism | | 533 |
|  |  | 12.2.1 | Biblical Hints | 533 |
|  |  | 12.2.2 | Forms of Dispensationalism | 535 |
|  |  | 12.2.3 | Periodizing Is Unavoidable | 536 |
|  | 12.3 | Are We Living in Some "Third Era"? | | 539 |
|  |  | 12.3.1 | Many Calculations | 539 |
|  |  | 12.3.2 | The *Dictum Eliae* | 541 |
|  | 12.4 | Other Views | | 543 |
|  |  | 12.4.1 | Playing with Numbers | 543 |
|  |  | 12.4.2 | Joachim of Fiore | 545 |
|  | 12.5 | Are We Living in Some "Fourth" or "Fifth Era"? | | 548 |
|  |  | 12.5.1 | The "Fourth Era" | 548 |
|  |  | 12.5.2 | The "Fifth Era" | 551 |
|  | 12.6 | Are We Living in Some "Sixth Era"? | | 553 |
|  |  | 12.6.1 | The "Friday" of Redemptive History | 553 |
|  |  | 12.6.2 | Early Millennialism | 555 |

|  |  |  |  |
|---|---|---|---|
|  |  | 12.6.3 Augustine | 557 |
|  | 12.7 | Periodizing in the Reformed Tradition | 559 |
|  |  | 12.7.1 Cocceius | 559 |
|  |  | 12.7.2 Sibersma and Van der Groe | 561 |
|  | 12.8 | Are We Living in Some "Seventh" or "Eighth Era"? | 562 |
|  |  | 12.8.1 The "Seventh Era" | 562 |
|  |  | 12.8.2 The "Eighth Era" | 565 |
| 13. | Later Dispensationalism and Kingdom Theology | | 569 |
|  | 13.1 | Classical Dispensationalism | 570 |
|  |  | 13.1.1 John N. Darby | 570 |
|  |  | 13.1.2 Cyrus I. Scofield | 573 |
|  |  | 13.1.3 Comments | 576 |
|  | 13.2 | Deviant Forms of Dispensationalism | 579 |
|  |  | 13.2.1 Ultradispensationalism | 579 |
|  |  | 13.2.2 Cessationism | 581 |
|  |  | 13.2.3 Refutation of Cessationism | 583 |
|  | 13.3 | Newer Forms of Dispensationalism | 586 |
|  |  | 13.3.1 "Revised" and "Progressive Dispensationalism" | 586 |
|  |  | 13.3.2 Traditional Dispensationalism Outdated | 589 |
|  | 13.4 | The Stages of the Kingdom | 591 |
|  |  | 13.4.1 The First Four Stages | 591 |
|  |  | 13.4.2 The Fifth Stage | 595 |
|  |  | 13.4.3 The Last Two Stages | 598 |
|  | 13.5 | Chiastic Structure | 599 |
|  |  | 13.5.1 First Similarity | 599 |
|  |  | 13.5.2 Second Similarity | 600 |
|  |  | 13.5.3 Third Similarity | 601 |
|  | 13.6 | The Nine World Empires | 603 |

|  |  |  |
|---|---|---|
| 13.6.1 | Framework | 603 |
| 13.6.2 | Earlier Millennial Kingdoms | 604 |
| 13.7 | The Middle Stage | 606 |
| 13.7.1 | The Old Testament Solomon | 606 |
| 13.7.2 | The Glory of Solomon | 609 |
| 13.7.3 | The New Testament and the Future Solomon | 611 |

| | |
|---|---|
| Bibliography | 615 |
| Scripture Index | 647 |
| Subject Index | 663 |

# Series Preface

BY MEANS OF THIS Preface, the editor and publisher of this series wish to help the reader both understand and process the content of these volumes.

The capacities and erudition of Dr. Willem Ouweneel need no demonstration or defense from us. His voluminous work and prodigious writing stand as a testimony to his love for the Lord Jesus Christ, God's Word, and God's people.

But these volumes present ideas that will surprise some, anger others, and possibly confuse still others. Both the editor and publisher disagree with some of Dr. Ouweneel's assertions and conclusions, but this is not the place for offering our counter-arguments. That requires an altogether different venue. Nevertheless, discerning readers will legitimately wonder why this editor and publisher invested effort and resources in putting these volumes into print.

At least three reasons justify that investment. Each of them is very sensitive.

The first reason is: *self-examination*. Some of our readers may conclude that, in presenting his exegetical, doctrinal, and historical case, Dr. Ouweneel is "coloring outside the lines" of what they have come to believe. He challenges deeply and firmly held convictions and beliefs, like those associated with Israel, with the law of God, with election and reprobation, with infant baptism, with covenant theology, and with justification. At each point, his challenges call us readers to self-examination, regarding our love for Scripture, for the God of Scripture, and for the Truth revealed and incarnated personally in Jesus Christ. One of Ouweneel's challenges is for us believers in Jesus Christ who are Reformed and Presbyterian church members to recognize that there are millions, even billions, of Jesus-believers who disagree with us *and are nevertheless genuine Christians.* And they ought to be acknowledged as such.

The second reason is: *repentance.* Coming, as they do, from one who lives and teaches outside the orbit of many of our readers, Dr. Ouweneel's observations about the state of our (numerous) churches and of our (interminable) doctrinal squabbles ought to embarrass us Reformed and Presbyterian church members. Our incessant polemicizing, our cantankerous stridency, and our offenses against the unity of Christ's church seriously compromise the gospel's witness to the watching world. Brothers and sisters, we must repent of these, for the sake of the gospel, for the sake of the church's witness, and for the sake of our children.

The third reason is: *ecumenicity.* This reason may indeed strike you as strange, but one of the salutary outcomes of reading Dr. Ouweneel's arguments can be this: *not* that you surrender your commitments and convictions that are being challenged, but instead that you come to *respect* and *love* those Jesus-believers who don't share them with you. These Christians are those whose spiritual pilgrimage and gospel-guided history have not brought them to the same place on the road, but who nonetheless are walking the same road as we.

You may well be asking: How, then, is this different from advocating doctrinal relativism? If these distinctive features of Reformed confession and theology are biblical, then why is Dr. Ouweneel being given a microphone for proclaiming his criticisms and rejections of these distinctive emphases of Reformed teaching? The short answer is this: So that from this brother in Christ, this close cousin in the faith, this fellow pilgrim-soldier, we may learn how to lock arms with other Jesus-believers as we face unbelief in our day, even if we can't hold hands. So that we may learn what it means to be Jesus-believers *first*, Reformed or Presbyterian confessors *second*, and only then, *thirdly, theological advocates*.

So we leave you with this challenge: Why do you believe what you believe? What is your biblical warrant? Dr. Ouweneel presents fairly the various positions prevalent within Christianity. The reader will learn why others believe what they believe, and why they don't emphasize certain teachings in the same way that we do.

These books, then, are *not* for the faint of faith. But they *are* for those wanting to grow up and mature into the unity of faith in our Lord Jesus Christ (John 17: 20–23; Eph. 4:13).

Nelson D. Kloosterman, editor
John Hultink, publisher

# Author's Preface

THIS BOOK IS A re-working and expansion of a part of Volume IX of my *Evangelical Dogmatic Series*, which is published by Medema, Heerenveen [the Netherlands] and comprises a total of twelve volumes.[1] My intention was, and is, to offer an Evangelical analysis of various subjects that traditionally have played a great role in Reformational—especially Reformed—thinking: the law, the covenant, and justification, and to a lesser extent, the kingdom. At present, I have planned an additional fifth volume: *The Eternal Purpose: An Evangelical Theology of Living In Christ.*

By the term "Reformational" I mean all that refers to the sixteenth-century Protestant Reformation. "Reformed" refers to one specific brand of Reformational thinking, namely, Calvinist. Unless specified otherwise, the word "Reformed" also encompasses "Presbyterian," not referring to a specific type of church government but to Calvinist thought of Scottish and English origins. "Reformed" in the narrower sense refers to Calvinist thought of German and especially Dutch origins.

---

1. Ouweneel (2011a, chapters 9–14).

In these volumes, "Evangelical" means little more than orthodox Protestant (in which "orthodox" refers to Protestants rooted in the Apostolic and Nicene Creeds, as well as in the sixteenth-century Reformation). I use the term Evangelical to indicate that I am neither a Lutheran, nor a Calvinist, and that I feel more at home with pre-scholastic Christianity. This Christianity apparently did not yet feel constrained to develop what I call an "inferential theology": an elaborate thought system built upon inferences drawn from inferences derived from inferences (inferentialism). These matters have been explained in the second volume of this series.

The subject of the kingdom seems to be less characteristic of Reformational theology than subjects like covenant, justification, and election (predestination). Yet, in my work, *The Heidelberg Diary*,[2] I have tried to point out the importance of the kingdom of God in the Heidelberg Catechism; see especially Day 76, 96-97, 101, 158, 252-260, 267, 299, 334-335, 337, 344-347, and 362 (Q&A 26, 31-32, 50, 82-85, 87, 103, 119, 123, 128). And to strike a different note: if, in recent decades, interest in the subject of God's kingdom has grown, we must credit first and foremost the great work by the Reformed theologian Herman N. Ridderbos, *The Coming of the Kingdom*.[3]

Bible quotations in this book are usually from the English Standard Version.

I thank Dr. Nelson D. Kloosterman again very warmly for his expert editorial work on the manuscript of this

---

2. Ouweneel (2016a).
3, Ridderbos (1962; original Dutch edition: 1950).

*Author's Preface*

book. And I am again deeply thankful to my publisher, John Hultink, for his constant encouragement in this entire project.

Willem J. Ouweneel
Huis ter Heide, Netherlands
January, 2016

# Abbreviations

**Bible Versions**

| | |
|---|---|
| AMP | Amplified Bible |
| AMPC | Amplified Bible, Classic Edition |
| ASV | American Standard Version |
| CEB | Common English Bible |
| CEV | Contemporary English Version |
| CJB | Complete Jewish Bible |
| DLNT | Disciples' Literal New Translation |
| DRA | Douay-Rheims 1899 American Edition |
| ERV | Easy-to-Read Version |
| ESV | English Standard Version |
| ESVUK | English Standard Version Anglicised |
| EXB | Expanded Bible |
| GNT | Good News Translation |
| GNV | 1599 Geneva Bible |
| GW | God's Word Translation |
| HCSB | Holman Christian Standard Bible |
| ICB | International Children's Bible |
| ISV | International Standard Version |
| JUB | Jubilee Bible 2000 |
| KJ21 | 21st Century King James Version |
| KJV | King James Version |

| | |
|---|---|
| LEB | Lexham English Bible |
| MEV | Modern English Version |
| MSG | The Message |
| NABRE | New American Bible (Revised Edition) |
| NASB | New American Standard Bible |
| NBG | Nederlands Bijbelgenootschap (1951) |
| NCV | New Century Version |
| NET | New English Translation |
| NIRV | New International Reader's Version |
| NIV | New International Version |
| NLV | New Life Version |
| NKJV | New King James Version |
| NLT | New Living Translation |
| NOG | Names of God Bible |
| OJB | Orthodox Jewish Bible |
| RSV | Revised Standard Version |
| TLB | Living Bible |
| VOICE | The Voice |
| WE | Worldwide English (New Testament) |
| WEB | World English Bible |
| YLT | Young's Literal Translation |

## Other Sources

| | |
|---|---|
| BT | Kelly, W., ed. *The Bible Treasury*. Winschoten: H. L. Heijkoop. |
| COT | Gispen, W. H. and N. H. Ridderbos. *Commentaar op het Oude Testament*. Kampen: Kok. |
| CR | *Corpus Reformatorum*. 1st series and 2nd series. Vols. 1–87. Brunswick: Schwetschke, 1834–1900. |

| | |
|---|---|
| CW | Darby, J. N. N.d. *The Collected Writings of J. N. Darby*. Kingston-on-Thames: Stow Hill Bible and Tract Depot. |
| EBC | Gaebelein, F. E., ed. *The Expositor's Bible Commentary*. 12 vols. Grand Rapids, MI: Zondervan. |
| EDR | Ouweneel, W. J. *Evangelische Dogmatische Reeks*. 12 vols. Heerenveen: Medema. |
| EGT | Nicoll, W. R., ed. 1979 (repr.). *The Expositor's Greek Testament*. Grand Rapids, MI: Eerdmans. |
| KV | *Korte Verklaring der Heilige Schrift*. Kampen: Kok. |
| NICNT | Bruce, F. F., ed. *The New International Commentary on the New Testament*. Grand Rapids, MI: Eerdmans. |
| NICOT | Hubbard, R. L. Jr., ed. *New International Commentary on the Old Testament*. Grand Rapids, MI: Eerdmans. |
| NIGTC | Hagner, D. A. and I. H. Marshall, eds. *New International Greek Testament Commentary*. Grand Rapids, MI: Eerdmans. |
| TNTC | Morris, L. L. *Tyndale New Testament Commentaries*. Leicester: IVP. |
| WA | *Luthers Werke* (Weimarer Ausgabe). Wimar: Böhlau Verlag, 1883–2009. |

# Chapter 1
# Introduction to the Kingdom

*The time is fulfilled,*
 *and the kingdom of God is at hand;*
*repent and believe in the gospel.*

Mark 1:15

*The kingdom of the world has become*
 *the kingdom of our Lord and of*
 *his Christ,*
*and he shall reign forever and ever.*

Revelation 11:15

**Summary:** Basileology (the doctrine of kingdom of God) is tremendously important because, aside from divine persons, the "kingdom of God" is probably the most important subject in the Bible. It was the central theme in the ministry of both Jesus and the apostles. The kingdom of God has first a general meaning: the universal rule of God over his creation, including important notions such as conservation and providence. Second, more specifically, God was King of

*Israel; but this kingship became increasingly identified with his earthly representative: David, and after him the Davidic kings. These kings pointed forward to a figure that gradually emerges from the mist of history: the Messiah, the anointed King of Israel and the world, who at the same time is the Last Adam. God had placed the kingdom under the feet of the first Adam, but after his Fall, the kingdom would ultimately be placed under the authority of the Last Adam. In the meantime, between the Fall and the consummation, Satan is the prince of this world. The chapter ends with an extensive summary of Satanology.*

THE DOCTRINE OF THE kingdom of God is sometimes referred to as *basileology*.[1] This word is derived from the Greek words *basileus*, "king," *basileia*, "royalty, kingdom," and *basileuō*, "to reign" (the latter English word is derived from Latin *rex*, genitive *regis*, "king," and the cognate verb *regnare*). The kingdom of God is one of the most significant theological topics, but one that has been rather neglected in systematic theology. This is a pity, for, apart from divine persons of the Holy Trinity, the kingdom is the primary subject in God's entire Word revelation. We can only be thankful that, during the last decades, interest in the truth of the kingdom has obviously increased quite substantially.

## 1.1 Basileology

### 1.1.1 The Centrality of the Theme

Herman Ridderbos says, "The central theme of Jesus' message, as it has come down to us in the synoptic gos-

---

1. Joe Boyd claims that he has coined the term (rebelpilgrim.blogspot.com/2010_04_01_archive.html). But Claus Petersen invented it as well (www.reich-gottes-jetzt.de/presse2.htm)—as did everyone who needed a scholarly term for "kingdom doctrine.

pels, is the coming of the kingdom of God. . . . [F]or insight into the meaning and the character of the New Testament revelation of God, it is hardly possible to mention any other theme equal in importance to that of the kingdom of heaven"[2] And Otto Weber says, "The Kingdom of God stands at the center of all Christian expectation and it comprehends everything which must be said about it in detail. . . . [T]he proclamation of the Kingdom, . . . is the content of the message of the pre-Easter Jesus, and at the same time the whole thrust of the message which was uttered by the Community of the Resurrected One . . . ."[3]

Joseph Ratzinger (pope Benedict XVI) writes, "The 'kingdom of God' is a theme that runs through the whole of Jesus' preaching."[4] In my view, this statement could be extended to all Scripture. As John Bright says, the concept of God's kingdom truly encompasses the total message of the Bible, not only the teaching of Jesus.[5] He even suggests that, if we should give one title to the entire Bible, it should be, "The Book of the Coming Kingdom of God."[6] Herman Hoyt similarly says that, apart from the theologian's specific eschatological conviction, if he undertakes a serious attempt to explain the Scriptures, he has to admit without hesitation that the Bible is a doctrine of the kingdom of God.[7]

---

2. Ridderbos (1962, xi).
3. Weber (1981, 2:675).
4. Ratzinger (2007, 62).
5. Bright (1953, 197).
6. Bright (1953, 197).
7. H. A. Hoyt in Clouse (1977, 64).

A Reformed theologian would probably call himself first and foremost a federalist, that is, an adherent of the covenant idea as the most central notion of Scripture. I would call myself in the first place a basilealist (if the reader permits me the term). At best, one could sympathize with Gordon Spykman's thesis that covenant and kingdom are two sides of the same coin.[8] Personally, I see the kingdom as a far more central notion than the covenant, certainly in the present dispensation. As Reformed (!) theologian Herman Ridderbos says, "[T]he idea of the kingdom *in se* is wider and more universal than, e.g., that of the divine covenant, or that of justification of the sinner through faith, . . . ."[9] He admits that there is a connection between the kingdom, on the one hand, and covenant and justification, on the other, but he adds: "Yet, neither the idea of the covenant, nor that of justification . . .can represent the entire thought of the kingdom of God, . . . . The idea of the kingdom of God is more comprehensive exactly because it is not only oriented to the redemption of God's people, but to the self-assertion of God in *all* his works. Not only does it place Israel, but also the heathen nations, the world, and even the whole creation, in the wide perspective of the realization of all God's rights and promises."[10]

It is not difficult to substantiate this statement. As far as has been reported to us, Jesus used the word "covenant" only once (Matt. 26:28; Mark 14:24; Luke 22:20), but the word "kingdom" (in the sense of the kingdom of God) appears in Matthew alone some forty-seven times.

---

8. Spykman (1992, 11, 258).
9. Ridderbos (1962, 22).
10. Ridderbos (1962, 23).

The term "covenant" occurs in the entire New Testament thirty-two times, of which seventeen appear in Hebrews. But the term "kingdom" in its spiritual sense occurs some one hundred thirty times in the New Testament, of which more than one hundred occur in the Gospels (the precise numbers depend on manuscripts and translations). This does not tell us everything, but it does give us an indication.[11]

As to the covenant, it is questionable whether Scripture knows of a covenant before Noah, not to mention whether it speaks of a covenant from eternity.[12] Such a covenant does exist in federalist thinking, but not in Scripture, as far as I can see. However, we do know for sure that the kingdom of God, in the broad sense of God's rule over all creation, has existed from the beginning of creation (and in a sense, from eternity). Certainly the covenant is of great significance, especially in the Old Testament, but also in the eschatological sense. However, its significance is always subservient to that of the kingdom. Therefore, as a systematic-theological topic, basileology is more fundamental than federology.

Moreover, no subject is so clearly interwoven with virtually every other topic in systematic theology. Russell Moore speaks of a kingdom eschatology, a kingdom soteriology, and a kingdom ecclesiology,[13] and that is no wonder: the world is en route to the Messianic kingdom in the *eschaton*, salvation is realized not only individual-

---

11. Just as it is significant that, e.g., Reformed author Kersten (1947) uses the word "covenant" many times, but "kingdom of God" not once (at least according to the index).
12. See extensively, Ouweneel (2016c).
13. Moore (2004, chapters 2–4).

ly but also within the framework of God's kingdom, and the kingdom is closely intertwined (though not identical) with the church. Similarly, basileology overlaps with the doctrine of God (it is *God's* kingdom, involving *his* kingship, *his* rule), with Christology (it is *Christ* who has been made King in God's kingdom), with anthropology (it is to *humans*, who have been created as royal beings, that God entrusts his kingdom: initially to the "first man," then to the "second Man"), with hamartiology (the Fall into *sin* also implied that God's kingdom had fallen into the wrong hands), and satanology (since the Fall, *Satan* is the prince of this world; see §§1.7 and 1.8). In this enumeration we are leaving aside the tremendous significance of basileology for a Christian view of the nation state, of politics, and of society.[14]

It is therefore a reason for joy to see that so many Christian authors are occupied today with the doctrine of God's kingdom. In the Netherlands, already in 1950 the important book by Herman Ridderbos was published, which appeared in an English edition as *The Coming of the Kingdom*.[15] At about the same time, several other works on the kingdom were published in the Anglo-Saxon world.[16] As to more recent times, I would mention at this point the work of Russell Moore and Derek J. Morphew,[17] in addition to sev-

---

14. This is the actual meaning of Moore (2004); also see Ouweneel (2014a).
15. Ridderbos (1962).
16. Bright (1953); Beasley-Murray (1954); Ladd (1959); McClain (1959).
17. Moore (2004); Morphew (2011).

eral useful overviews of twentieth-century interpretations of the kingdom.[18]

## 1.1.2 New Testament Voices on the Kingdom

Jesus, who mentioned the covenant only once, spoke dozens of times about the kingdom of God. The essential element in the life and teaching of Jesus was this very kingdom of God,[19] as illustrated in this summary of Jesus' proclamation by the earliest Gospel writer, Mark: "Now after John was arrested, Jesus came into Galilee, proclaiming the gospel of God, and saying, 'The time is fulfilled, and the kingdom of God is at hand; repent and believe in the gospel.'" Interestingly, the gospel of God's kingdom is here described as the "gospel of God" (Mark 1:14–15; cf. Matt. 4:23; 9:35; 24:14).

Jesus' first message, as registered in the Gospels, like that of John the Baptist (Matt. 3:2), was indeed: "Repent, for the kingdom of heaven is at hand" (4:17). His last message on earth, after his resurrection, is found in Acts 1: "[Jesus gave] commands through the Holy Spirit to the apostles whom he had chosen. He presented himself alive to them after his suffering by many proofs, appearing to them during forty days and speaking about the kingdom of God" (vv. 2–3). For forty days, he spoke about one and the same topic: the kingdom of God! What could underscore more clearly the significance of this subject?

As far as has been recorded, the apostle Peter explicitly mentioned the covenant only once (Acts 3:35), but he referred to the kingdom many times. Of course, his

---

18. Willis (1987); Saucy (1997).

19. G. R. Beasley-Murray in Saucy (1997, xiii).

first address, on the Day of Pentecost, was primarily about the Holy Spirit being poured out, but it was also about God's kingdom connected with it: "Let all the house of Israel therefore know for certain that God has made him both Lord and Christ [Messiah, i.e., the anointed King], this Jesus whom you crucified" (2:36). That is, the crucified Jesus is none other than the very King whom God has installed over the universe.

In Peter's second address, he referred to the coming kingdom as well: "Repent therefore, and turn back, that your sins may be blotted out, that times of refreshing may come from the presence of the Lord, and that he may send the Christ [Messiah] appointed for you, Jesus, whom heaven must receive until the time for restoring all the things about which God spoke by the mouth of his holy prophets long ago" (3:19–21). The coming (again) of the anointed King is here associated with the "times of refreshing" and "restoring all the things," which refers to the Messianic kingdom of peace and justice.

Peter's last recorded words deal with the kingdom as well: "...For in this way there will be richly provided for you an entrance into the eternal kingdom of our Lord and Savior Jesus Christ" (2 Pet. 1:11). "Since all these things are thus to be dissolved, what sort of people ought you to be in lives of holiness and godliness, waiting for and hastening the coming of the day of God, because of which the heavens will be set on fire and dissolved, and the heavenly bodies will melt as they burn! But according to his promise we are waiting for new heavens and a new earth in which righteousness dwells" (3:11–13).

In his New Testament letters, Paul mentions the covenant eight times (Rom. 9:4; 11:27; 1 Cor. 11:25; 2 Cor.

3:6; Gal. 3:15, 17; 4:24; Eph. 2:12), but speaks about the kingdom nineteen times (Rom. 14:17; 1 Cor. 4:20; 6:9-10; 15:24, 50; Gal. 5:21; Eph. 5:5; Col. 1:13; 4:11; 1 Thess. 2:12; 2 Thess. 1:5; 2 Tim. 4:1, 18), apart from the times he mentioned the kingdom in the book of Acts (Acts 14:22; 19:8; 20:25; 28:23, 31). The first message he preached—in Damascus—was: "[Jesus] is the Son of God." "Saul increased all the more in strength, and confounded the Jews who lived in Damascus by proving that Jesus was the Christ," that is the Messiah, the anointed King of Israel (Acts 9:20, 22). Later, he explained by way of a summary that he had "gone about proclaiming the kingdom" (20:25). His last message in Acts was this: "When they [i.e., the Jewish leaders in Rome] had appointed a day for him,...he expounded to them, testifying to the kingdom of God" (28:23). "He lived there two whole years at his own expense, and welcomed all who came to him, proclaiming the kingdom of God and teaching about the Lord Jesus Christ with all boldness and without hindrance" (vv. 30-31). And his last recorded message was this: "I charge you in the presence of God and of Christ Jesus, who is to judge the living and the dead, and by his appearing and his kingdom . . ." (2 Tim. 4:1-2). "The Lord will rescue me from every evil deed and bring me safely into his heavenly kingdom" (v. 18).

The latter expression, "his heavenly kingdom," is not a kingdom somewhere in heaven, but a *heavenly* kingdom *on earth* or, if you like, within visible creation, as it will be manifested at the parousia of the Lord.[20] It is no different than the expression "kingdom of heaven" that we find so often in Matthew's Gospel. "Heaven rules," Daniel told Nebuchadnezzar—but here on earth (Dan.

---

20. Cf. Towner (2006, 647).

4:26). The MSG ("keeping me safe in the kingdom of heaven") and the NLV ("He will bring me safe into His holy nation of heaven") are mistaken here because the reference is to the kingdom in its future state (note the verb: "save unto," Greek *sōsei eis*). The Voice ("carry me safely to His heavenly kingdom") smacks too much of "carrying me to heaven."[21] I will discuss this subject more extensively later.

## 1.1.3 Pre-Easter Saints Expecting the Kingdom

Several times in the Gospels we hear about those who expected the kingdom of God, such as "Joseph of Arimathea, a respected member of the council, who was also himself looking for the kingdom of God" (Mark 15:43). When we read of Simeon, "waiting for the consolation of Israel" (Luke 2:25), and of Anna and other Jews "waiting for the redemption of Jerusalem" (v. 38), this was essentially the same expectation. In the Messianic kingdom, in the day when it will be manifested in power and majesty, Israel will be consoled and Jerusalem will be redeemed.

The criminal on the cross said, "Jesus, remember me when you come into your kingdom" (23:42). This is an interesting expression. The Greek has *eis tēn basileian sou*, "into your kingdom," but there is an important variant reading, *en tēi basileian sou*, "in your kingdom," which may be viewed as a Semitism for "in your kingship (royalty, kingly dignity)," or simply, "as King."[22] That is, let me be in your company (by raising me from

---

21. This is indeed the mistaken interpretation of Bouma (1937, 185).
22. Marshall (1978, 872).

the dead) when you return as King.²³ The former reading has some preference;²⁴ in this case, the criminal prayed, "Jesus, think of me when you enter into your kingdom," namely, at your parousia, or: "when you accept your royal dignity." Jesus' response amounts to this: You will not have to wait for centuries until my kingdom will appear in majesty—already *today* you will be with me in Paradise, and dwell *there* in the blessed expectation of the kingdom as it will arrive one day in power and glory.

The criminal's prayer was very special. He was, as Joel Green put it, "the first to recognize that Jesus' crucifixion is a precursor to his enthronement (cf. Acts 5:30-31), and thus he anticipates in his request Jesus' kingly rule."²⁵ This very man, in *his* situation, was thus *the* prototype of the godly Jew, longing for the coming of the Messiah and the establishment of his kingdom. His prayer was in line with that of his distant ancestor, Jacob, who proclaimed in the blessings over his sons: "The scepter shall not depart from Judah, nor the ruler's staff from between his feet, until tribute comes to him [Hebrew: until Shiloh comes]; and to him shall be the obedience of the peoples. . . . I wait for your salvation, O LORD" (Gen. 49:10, 18). To Jacob, the beginning of Shiloh's rule and the breakthrough of full salvation coincided; the Messiah is the great bringer of salvation, the Redeemer of Jacob's entire posterity, even of the whole world. Jacob's latter

---

23. See Morris (1974, 328-29); Bruce (1979, 41); Liefeld (1984, 1044 note).
24. Metzger (1975, 181).
25. Green (1997, 823).

statement has absolutely nothing to do with the expectation of some heavenly paradise.[26]

Entirely parallel with this are the prophetic words of the priest Zechariah: "Blessed be the Lord God of Israel, for he has visited and redeemed his people and has raised up a horn of salvation [cf. Ps. 132:17] for us in the house of his servant David [i.e., granted us a Davidic king], as he spoke by the mouth of his holy prophets from of old, that we should be saved from our enemies and from the hand of all who hate us; to show the mercy promised to our fathers and to remember his holy covenant, the oath that he swore to our father Abraham, to grant us that we, being delivered from the hand of our enemies, might serve him without fear, in holiness and righteousness before him all our days" (Luke 1:68–75).

## 1.2 The Kingship of God

### 1.2.1 Divine Rule in the Old Testament

Alva McCain has pointed out that, if we consider the biblical material on the kingdom, this notion refers to an encompassing situation that includes at least three elements: first, a ruler with sufficient authority and power; second, a domain of subjects that have to be ruled; and third, the factual exercise of the function of rulership.[27] The first meaning of God's kingdom in which this description is valid is the universal rule ("rulership") of God (the "ruler") over his creation (his "domain"), from the foundation of the world unto all eternity. By definition, the Creator of the universe is also its ruler, or king, or sovereign, even if this is never explicit-

---

26. See Ouweneel (2012a, §2.5.2).
27. McClain (1959, 17).

*Introduction to the Kingdom*

ly stated in Genesis (perhaps apart from 14:19, 22, "God Most High, Possessor [Heb. *qonēh;* others translate, Maker] of heaven and earth").

As soon as the redeemed people reach the other side of the Red Sea, they make this confession: "The LORD will reign [or, will be King, or, is King] forever and ever" (Exod. 15:18). The verb used, Hebrew *m-l-k*, from which *melek*, "king," was derived, means "to be king" or "to reign, to rule." Entirely apart from the Messianic idea, God is King of the world, as it is expressed in so many orthodox Jewish prayers, *melek ha'olam*, "king of the world (or, universe)." More specifically, he is the King of Israel (see §1.3). In Revelation 15:3, God is called "King of the nations," in line with Jeremiah 10:7.[28]

Elsewhere it is said implicitly that God is "King of the world": "The LORD sits enthroned over the flood; the LORD sits enthroned as king forever" (Ps. 29:10). "[T]he LORD, the Most High, is to be feared, a great king over all the earth. . . . Sing praises to God, sing praises! Sing praises to our King, sing praises! For God is the King of all the earth; sing praises with a psalm! God reigns over the nations; God sits on his holy throne" (47:2, 6-8). "The LORD reigns; he is robed in majesty; the Lord is robed; he has put on strength as his belt. Yes, the world is established; it shall never be moved" (93:1; cf. 96:10). "The LORD reigns, let the earth rejoice; let the many coastlands be glad!" (97:1). "Make a joyful noise to the LORD, all the earth; break forth into joyous song and

---

28. Some manuscripts have "King of the ages" (cf. 1 Tim. 1:17; Tob. 13:4; 1 Henoch 9:4); [N]KJV and others have "King of the saints," which finds hardly any support in the Bible manuscripts; see Metzger (1975, 753-54).

sing praises! . . .With trumpets and the sound of the horn make a joyful noise before the King, the LORD!" (98:4, 6). "[T]he LORD is the true God; he is the living God and the everlasting King. At his wrath the earth quakes, and the nations cannot endure his indignation" (Jer. 10:10). "I am a great King, . . .and my name will be feared among the nations" (Mal. 1:14).

Also in Babylon (Marduk) and Canaan (Baal), the godhead was presented as being enthroned as a king. In opposition to this, Israel made the confession that not the gods of the pagans but YHWH is King, with some unique specifications by which Israel's faith distinguished itself from that of the neighboring nations.[29] On the one hand, the people confessed YHWH as the absolutely only One, as the First Commandment expressed: "You shall have no other gods before me" (Exod. 20:3); "the LORD is God; there is no other besides him" (Deut. 4:35; cf. 32:39). On the other hand, Israel confessed him as the "God of gods,"[30] that is, the one true God, who triumphs over all that are called "gods" by the nations but are nothing but either mute idols, or fallen angelic powers.[31] Yahweh triumphs over the gods, but at the same time he is the *only* God, because the others are no true gods.

God is King over *all* creatures, which includes fallen angels, who are worshiped by the nations as "gods": "[T]he LORD is a great God, and a great King above all gods" (Ps. 95:3). Thus, Isaiah calls him "the King, the LORD of hosts," that is, the God of all earthly and especially heav-

---

29. Verkuyl (1992, 442–43).
30. Deut. 10:17; Josh. 22:22 (KJV, etc.); Ps. 50:1 (EXB, etc.); 136:2; Dan. 2:47; 11:36.
31. See extensively, Ouweneel (2016d, 23–37).

enly hosts (or armies) (Isa. 6:5; cf. Zech. 14:16-17). Compare Palm 89:5-8: "Let the heavens praise your wonders, O LORD, your faithfulness in the assembly of the holy ones [i.e., angels]! For who in the skies [or, heavens] can be compared to the LORD? Who among the heavenly beings [lit., sons of God, i.e., angels] is like the LORD, a God greatly to be feared in the council of the holy ones [i.e., angels], and awesome above all who are around him? O LORD God of hosts, who is mighty as you are, O LORD, with your faithfulness all around you?"

## 1.2.2 Conservation and Providence

From the notion of God's universal rule over the entire universe, theological notions such as "conservation" (upholding) and "providence" have been derived. God rules all things, everything is in his hand, nothing could ever slip from his fingers. The breath of all creatures is in his hands (Job 12:10; Ps. 104:29; Dan. 5:23). In him all creatures live and move and have their being (cf. Acts 17:28).

Of course, the same thing can also be expressed without using the notion of "kingship," as in Psalm 104, where God's glory in his world government is described. Of the Son it is said that "he upholds the universe by the word of his power" (Heb. 1:3), and "in him all things hold together" (Col. 1:17). This does not refer to his Messianic glory or any other human glory of his, but to his divine power with which he keeps all things in his hand, sustains and steers them. As time-bound as Jesus' Messianic kingship is—it involves his human nature, and thus dates from his incarnation—so timeless is this universal world dominion of the Triune God. However, where the two aspects become intertwined, an element of expectation and therefore of time-conditionedness ("there is something still to come") arises, also where God's universal world dominion is concerned (Isa. 24:23; 33:22; Obad. 1:21; Zeph. 3:15; Zech. 14:16-17).[32]

Elsewhere I have written about the way God reveals himself as King in his work of creation.[33] In Genesis 1, we do not find so much the "building" God (in spite of the "making" in vv. 7, 16, 25; cf. Job 38:4-11), nor the planting God (cf. Gen. 2:8-9), nor the fighting God (apart perhaps from vv. 2-3; cf. Ps. 18:13-15; 77:16, 19-20),[34] but the commanding God. Here, God is not so much the Architect, the Farmer, or the Warrior, but the King. No building material, no agricultural or military or any other utensils are needed; God's spoken command is sufficient to get the work done. Genesis 1, in which the words "sun" and "moon" do not even occur, shows that these celestial bodies, the "greater" and the "lesser light," do rule (see §1.5.1), but only as servants of God, appointed "to separate the day from the night" and to "be for signs and for seasons, and for days and years" (v. 14). The "great sea monsters" (v. 21 EXB, NASB, etc.), which were a threat to Israel, especially Rahab (Job 26:12; Ps. 89:10; Isa. 51:9) and Leviathan (Ps. 74:14; Isa. 27:1), turn out to be nothing but creatures of God, called forth merely by his voice, and completely under his dominion.

Genesis 1 opens with *bereshith*, "in [the] beginning," a well-known term to indicate the start of a king's rule (Jer. 26:1; 27:1; 28:1; 49:34; cf. Gen. 10:10: "the beginning of his kingdom was. . ."). In other words, "in the begin-

---

32. Cf. Von Rad (1964, 568-69).
33. Ouweneel (2008a, §2.4.5).
34. Ouweneel (2008a, §§2.4.2-2.4.4).

ning," God created for himself a kingdom over which he could rule. No chaos power (v. 2, *tohu wabohu* [the "formless and void"], "darkness"; cf. Jer. 4:23) can threaten this kingdom, no matter how strongly Satan and his angels may try. Merely with his voice, the King commands each of his creatures to emerge and take the place assigned to it. And as befits his sovereignty, he gives each of his creatures an appropriate name (vv. 5, 8, 10). In line with this, Adam too, God's viceroy (see §1.5.1), gives names to the animals that God had created (2:19–20), and after his fall, he also names his wife (3:20), an expression of the authority bestowed upon him. (This does not minimize the fact that his wife is involved on equal footing in world rule; vv. 26, 28; see §1.5.1.)

The exalted position of Adam and Eve, destined to rule the world on behalf of God, is expressed here in their having been created "in the image of God," that is, as God's representatives on earth.[35] In Egyptian and Mesopotamian societies the king or a high ruler was sometimes called the "image of God";[36] here, this royal designation is applied to humanity in general. Just like the pagan king represents his deity, who is the true king of the nation, Adam and Eve functioned as viceroys representing God the King.

The calling of the first humans to subdue the earth and have dominion over it (1:26, 28), whereby they would serve as viceroys, indirectly refers back to God himself, who as King was entitled to put humans in this office. It is as if he speaks to them the words of the Pharaoh: "You shall be over my house, and all my people shall order

---

35. Ouweneel (2008a, §§5.1.2 and 5.2); also see Dumbrell (1994, 20).
36. Hamilton (1990, 135).

themselves as you command. Only as regards the throne will I be greater than you" (Gen. 41:40; cf. Mordecai in Esther 10:3, "Mordecai the Jew was second in rank to King Ahasuerus"). Many Israelites lived in fear with regard to the other nations, and even more so with regard to the spiritual powers *behind* these nations. However, in a comforting way, Genesis 1 testified to them that the almighty God is in control, that all things are under his feet, and that all creatures are at his disposal. In creation as described in Genesis 1, all the signs of his "eternal power and divine nature" are present (Rom. 1:20).

## 1.3 God's Kingship and Israel
### 1.3.1 "King of Jacob"

In a special way, God's universal rule turns out to be connected with Israel: "The LORD their God is with them, and the shout of a king is among them" (Num. 23:21). "The LORD reigns; let the peoples tremble! He sits enthroned upon the cherubim; let the earth quake! The LORD is great in Zion; he is exalted over all the peoples" (Ps. 99:1–2). God is the King of his chosen people in a way he is not of any other people. This more specific character of God's kingship—King of his people of Israel—is stated many times. God is the "King of Jacob" (Isa. 41:21): "I am the LORD, your Holy One, the Creator of Israel, your King" (43:15), "the King of Israel and his Redeemer" (44:6), "the King of Israel" (Zeph. 3:15). At Sinai, God calls his people a "kingdom of priests" (Exod. 19:6)—a kingdom, not so much because the Israelites would be kings themselves (different from New Testament believers, Rev. 20:4, 6; 22:5; cf. 1:6; 5:10), but rather because God is their King. The Israelites are priests, that is, a community of worshippers.³⁷ And one Dutch translation (*Groot Nieuws Bijbel*) puts it this way: "[Y]ou will serve me as priests, and I will be your King." The Lord is King of a kingdom whose subjects are priests to him.

God is King; as yet, there is no reference in the Torah to some earthly king, except in this law: "When you come to the land that the Lord your God is giving you, and you possess it and dwell in it and then say, 'I will set a king over me, like all the nations that are around me,' you may indeed set a king over you whom the Lord your God will choose. One from among your brothers you shall set as king over you" (Deut. 17:14-15).³⁸ When Israel asked Gideon: "Rule³⁹ over us, you and your son and your grandson also," Gideon replied, "I will not rule over you, and my son will not rule over you; the Lord will rule over you" (Judg. 8:22-23). His son Abimelech thought otherwise.⁴⁰ His name may mean, "My father is king" (!), or more likely,⁴¹ "father of a king" (as if a dynasty is envisioned). He made himself king in Israel (9:6), though he was nothing more than a bramble (v. 15); he met his miserable destiny.

When some time later, the people asked again for their own, human king, the Lord told the prophet Samuel: "[T]hey have not rejected you, but they have rejected me from being king over them" (1 Sam. 8:7). The

---

37. Dumbrell (1994, 45).
38. As to whether Deut. 33:6 might be a reference to Moses, see §9.4.2.
39. From Heb. *m-sh-l*; see §1.5.
40. Dumbrell (1994, 57-58).
41. In Abimelech it is *abi* with patach (= status constructus of *ab*, "father"), not *abi* ("my father").

Lord confirmed his kingship every time he drove foreign nations out of the land of Israel: "The Lord is king forever and ever; the nations perish from his land" (Ps. 10:16). It is said of the King who triumphantly enters into his city Jerusalem: "Who is this King of glory? The Lord of hosts, he is the King of glory!" (24:10).[42] Certainly there are Messianic overtones here, yet it is the Lord God whose kingship is being affirmed here. The same is true of Psalm 48:2, where Jerusalem is called "the city of the great King" (cf. Matt. 5:35). "Let Israel be glad in his Maker; let the children of Zion rejoice in their King!" (Ps. 149:2). "The Lord will reign forever, your God, O Zion, to all generations. Praise the Lord!" (146:10). *Your* God, therefore *your* King.

In this sense, the Lord, in a very personal way, is the King of every Israelite, from whom the latter expects his redemption: "Give attention to the sound of my cry, my King and my God, for to you do I pray" (Ps. 5:2). "You are my King, O God; ordain salvation for Jacob!" (44:5). "Yet God my King is from of old, working salvation in the midst of the earth" (74:12; see further 68:24; 84:3; 145:1; 149:2). "For the Lord is our judge; the Lord is our lawgiver; the Lord is our king; he will save us" (Isa. 33:22).

In Isaiah 6, it was no coincidence that the prophet beheld his throne vision in the year that king Uzziah died (v. 1), that is, at a time when there was a brief governmental hiatus. Therefore, the prophet said, "I saw the Lord," that is, *Adonai*, not *YHWH*: *Adonai* is the true

---

42. The reference is probably to the ark being brought into the city (2 Sam. 6:17), and later into Solomon's temple; since the *Shekhnah* was connected with the ark, it was as if the Lord himself was entering.

Sovereign over heaven and earth. Isaiah also exclaimed: "[M]y eyes have seen the King, the LORD of hosts!" (v. 5).[43] The death of an earthly king of Judah was a good moment to realize again that YHWH is the true Sovereign and King of his people, even of the entire world and of all the heavenly hosts.

From the beginning of Israel's national existence, God has been the King of his people. Certain Old Testament passages, however, refer to God's kingship over Israel in a future sense: "Then the moon will be confounded and the sun ashamed, for the LORD of hosts reigns [or, is King; or, will be King] on Mount Zion and in Jerusalem, and his glory will be before his elders" (Isa. 24:23). This is a reference to the Messianic kingdom, as is clear from what immediately follows in Isaiah 25 (see especially vv. 6-9).

### 1.3.2 King and Messiah

Zechariah 14:9-11 refers is to some future time as well: "And the LORD will be king over all the earth. On that day the LORD will be one and his name one. . . . Jerusalem shall dwell in security." Here, God's kingship and Messiah's kingship are clearly interwoven. The chapter speaks of the new and definitive establishment of God's kingship, this time in the person of the Messiah.

Such passages referring to God's future kingship always have Messianic overtones. Sometimes, it is explicitly indicated that God's kingship over Israel is a mediatorial kingship: from the time of David, God ruled over Israel through David or the Davidic king: "Why do the nations rage and the peoples plot in vain? The kings of

---

43. Oswalt (1986, 176-77, 183).

the earth set themselves, and the rulers take counsel together, against the LORD and against his Anointed, saying, 'Let us burst their bonds apart and cast away their cords from us.' He who sits in the heavens laughs; the Lord [*Adonai*] holds them in derision. Then he will speak to them in his wrath, and terrify them in his fury, saying, 'As for me, I have set [44] my King on Zion, my holy hill'" (Ps. 2:1–6). Such passages show that the kingdom, also in its eschatological sense, though thoroughly Jewish, is universal in its extent.[45]

It is in this Jewish-Davidic context that we find the few instances in which the Old Testament speaks explicitly of the kingdom of God, which actually is the kingdom of Israel:[46] "I will confirm him [i.e., Solomon] in my house and in *my kingdom* forever, and his throne shall be established forever" (1 Chron. 17:14). David says, "And of all my sons . . . he has chosen Solomon my son to sit on the throne of the *kingdom of the* LORD over Israel" (28:5; cf. 29:11; 2 Chron. 13:8). The "kingdom [CEB: royal rule; cf. GNT, MSG, NET] of the LORD" is here Hebrew *malkut*, from *m-l-k*, "to reign, to be king." In this connection, there is also reference to the "throne of the LORD" (*kissē' YHWH*) in 1 Chronicles 29:23, just as Jerusalem will one day be called the "throne of the LORD" (Jer. 3:17; cf. Ezek. 43:7 in regard to the new temple).

We thus find a twofold view of God's throne:

---

44. AMP and YLT have "anointed." The verb *n-s-k* means "to pour out," here: "to consecrate" (through the pouring out of anointing oil, or through a drink offering).
45. J. R. Michaels in Willis (1987, 114); also see Odendall (1970).
46. Chia (2005, 31).

(a) It is both in heaven (1 Kgs. 22:19; 2 Chron. 18:18; Ezek. 1:26, on which God is seated) and on earth, namely, in Jerusalem, on which is seated the human representative of God: David, or the Davidic king (1 Kgs. 2:12, 24, 45; Jer. 22:2), and in the end, the Messiah (Isa. 9:7; Luke 1:32).

(b) It is connected with both the ark and the royal throne. In 1 Chronicles 29:23, the point is the contrast with the ark of the covenant (implied in v. 16), which was once the place where God was enthroned (1 Sam. 4:4; 2 Kgs. 19:15; Ps. 80:1; 99:1; Isa. 37:16). As with David, both the kingdom and the LORD's throne coincide with Israel and the Davidic kingship over Israel, respectively.

In Psalm 45, God's rule and Messiah's rule merge beautifully: "Your throne, O God [i.e., the Messiah; cf. Heb. 1:8-9!], is forever and ever. The scepter of your [i.e., God's] kingdom is a scepter of uprightness; you have loved righteousness and hated wickedness. Therefore God, your God, has anointed you [i.e., again the Messiah] with the oil of gladness beyond your companions" (vv. 6-7).

### 1.3.3 Universal and Mediatorial Kingship

When the reference is to the future kingdom of God, the focus is upon *the* Davidic son: "Behold, I, I myself will judge between the fat sheep and the lean sheep.... I will rescue my flock; .... And I will set up over them one shepherd, my servant David [i.e., the Messiah], and he shall feed them: he shall feed them and be their shepherd. And I, the LORD, will be their God, and my servant David shall be prince among them.... And they shall know that I am the LORD, when I break the bars of their yoke, and deliver them from the hand of those who enslaved them. . . . And they shall know that I am the LORD their God with them, and that they, the house of Israel, are my people. . . . And you are my sheep, human sheep of my pasture, and I am your God" (Ezek. 34:20–31).

Here we find something we will expand later: *mediatorial* kingship. That is, God exercises his kingship through (the mediation of) the "man after his own heart" (1 Sam. 13:14): David, and in the end, the Messiah, the "true David" (note how the Messiah is called "David" in Ezek. 34:23–24; 37:24–25; Hos. 3:5). However, this mediation actually began not with David but with Adam; to him we will pay attention in §1.5. First, I will summarize the differences between what Herman Hoyt calls "universal kingship" and "mediatorial kingship."[47]

(a) Universal kingship is from eternity or from the beginning of creation (cf. Ps. 145:13). Mediatorial kingship has a beginning in time (Adam, David, Christ, respectively), and is fully realized only in the future Messianic kingdom.

(b) Universal kingship encompasses all creation (1 Chron. 29:12). Mediatorial kingship is all-encompassing, too, but with the focus on Israel as the center of the Messianic kingdom.

(c) Universal kingship is almost entirely part of providence (i.e., through secondary causes; Exod. 14:21; Ps. 29:3; Isa. 10:5–15), sometimes through miracles (Exod. 11:9; Deut. 4:34–35; Ps. 78:12; Dan. 6:27). Mediatorial kingship is based on supernatural intervention by God:

---

47. H. A. Hoyt in Clouse (1977, 73).

he "breaks in" into cosmic reality through his human instrument in order to establish the kingdom.

(d) Universal kingship functions independently of the subjects' attitude (Ps. 103:20; Dan. 4:35; Isa. 40:13-14; Acts 14:15-17). Mediatorial kingship functions with dependence on its subjects: if they are unfaithful, they can lose the kingdom, as happened with Adam (see §1.5) and with the house of David (Jer. 21:11-14). And if they sincerely confess their sins, the kingdom may be restored to them (cf., e.g., Acts 3:17-26).

Please note that the difference between universal kingship and mediatorial kingship is gradual: even God's—the Triune God's!—universal kingship never exists apart from the Son. It is the Son who is "before all things, and in him all things hold together" (Col. 1:17). It is the Son who "upholds the universe by the word of his power" (Heb. 1:3). One important way to make the proper distinction is as follows: the universal kingship is realized in and through *God* the Son; the mediatorial kingship is realized in and through the *Man* Jesus Christ, who at the same time *is* the eternal Son. Some views, such as premillennialism and dispensationalism, place strong emphasis on mediatorial kingship. More traditional views (a- and postmillennialism, federalism) strongly emphasize universal kingship; that is, the continuity of God's rule from the beginning and his ultimate conquering of the powers in and through Christ.[48]

The universal kingship is a purely divine matter, in which "divine" refers to Father *and* Son *and* Spirit. The mediatorial kingship always involves mediation through a male *human being*: Adam, David, Christ.

---

48. Hoekema (1979, 45).

Therefore, Abraham Kuyper was wrong when he separated God's kingship over the world (exercised partially through earthly authorities) from Christ's kingship, with the consequence that, for instance, the official prayer in the city council ought not to bear a Christian character.[49] This matter is linked with many other questions—which we are not going to discuss at this time—such as the question whether God's "common grace" is "in Christ," and is even founded upon his work on the cross.[50]

## 1.4 God's Kingship and the Nations

### 1.4.1 The *Missio Dei*

We can distinguish one special aspect of God's kingship in the Old Testament in which all nations are involved, without the Messianic dimension of God's kingdom being at the forefront. In the Old Testament, God's rule over the nations seems to have quite an explicit missionary goal. The *missio Dei*, "God's mission" (missionary aim), consists of this: especially through Israel, and from Acts 2 through the church, but also independently of them, by the power of his Holy Spirit, all nations on earth will come to know and fear God as King. Merely as Creator and Upholder of the world, God is already King of all nations. But when his name and nature are made known throughout the earth, all nations, or at least a substantial part of them, will learn to worship and serve him as such.

The goal of the *missio Dei* is that God's kingship be established concretely and practically throughout the

---

49. Ridderbos (1947, 77–78); cf. Van Genderen (2008, 303).
50. Cf. Ouweneel (2008b, 44–45, 54–56, 281–84).

## Introduction to the Kingdom

entire world.[51] He himself brings this about. Seen from this viewpoint, God's kingship over the world is not a static notion but a very dynamic concept. In this we see that, humanly speaking, God must deal with the power of Satan, who, since the fall of humanity, holds the world dominion in his hands (though always within the framework of God's permission) (see §§1.5-1.8). Although this is not mentioned, we may assume that it was Satan who, in Genesis 11:3-4, urged humanity to build a city and a "tower with its top in the heavens." God "came down" (v. 5) to oppose Satan and to bring humanity under his own rule. No human has any mediatorial role here; it is God's personal intervention. Today, too, God may act in this way (see below).

Later Judaism has never developed great missionary zeal. However, in New Testament times, Jesus could still say to the religious leaders: "For you travel across sea and land to make a single proselyte" (Matt. 23:15). Indeed, to some extent Israel was always involved in the *missio Dei*; as Paul puts it: "But if you call yourself a Jew and rely on the law and boast in God and know his will and approve what is excellent, because you are instructed from the law; and if you are sure that you yourself are a guide to the blind, a light to those who are in darkness [i.e., the Gentiles; cf. Isa. 42:6-7], an instructor of the foolish, a teacher of children, having in the law the embodiment of knowledge and truth—you then who teach others, do you not teach yourself? . . .For, as it is written, 'The name of God is blasphemed among the

---

51. See C. J. H. Wright (2006, especially chapter 14: "God and the Nations in Old Testament Vision").

Gentiles because of you [Isa. 52:5; Ezek. 36:20-23]'" (Rom. 2:17-24).

## 1.4.2 The Ultimate Goal

Throughout the centuries, this *missio Dei* continues until Revelation 14:6-7: "Then I saw another angel flying directly overhead, with an eternal gospel to proclaim to those who dwell on earth, to every nation and tribe and language and people. And he said with a loud voice, 'Fear God and give him glory, because the hour of his judgment has come, and worship him who made heaven and earth, the sea and the springs of water.'" Here, God's kingship is not mentioned explicitly, but it is implied in his creatorship. If God's mission, described here as the "eternal gospel," is reduced to its essential core, it is this: Honor and worship God the Creator, and recognize his rights over you!

In many Psalms, we clearly hear this appeal to all nations to acknowledge YHWH's kingship, often with obvious eschatological overtones (a few examples: Ps. 22:27-28; 33:8; 47:6-7; 66:3-4; 67:2-4; 68:32-33; 98:4-6; 145:10-13). I could also mention examples from the prophetic books, but here the historical-Messianic dimension is always far more evident. Of course, in some of the Psalms just enumerated we hear clearly Messianic overtones as well. But apart from them, it is an authentic biblical given that YHWH presents himself continually as the God not only of Israel but of all nations, the God who wants to be acknowledged, praised, and served as such. This is not just an eschatological command—it is a spiritual reality even today. In the present time, too, God is entitled to the recognition, worship, and obedience of *all* nations worldwide. The essence of his gospel message is not only salvation for the nations themselves, but also that to which *God* is entitled: that all nations will honor and serve him. He is not only the "God of Israel" (so many times in the Bible, from Exod. 5:1 to Luke 1:68), but also the "God of (all) the earth" (Gen. 24:3; cf. Josh. 3:11, 13; Ps. 97:5; Zech. 6:5; Rev. 11:4).

God makes this clear not only through preaching but also through his interventions in nature and history. There is a "speech" going forth from nature (cf. Ps. 19:1–2), which the nations ignore only to their own loss. Still today, God "makes his sun rise on the evil and on the good, and sends rain on the just and on the unjust" (Matt. 5:45), and still today, God does "good by giving you rains from heaven and fruitful seasons, satisfying your hearts with food and gladness" (Acts 14:17). Still today, he leads the history of all nations, even if they hardly know him (cf. Amos 9:7; Hab. 1:6–11). He still uses nations, especially their rulers, as "rods," "staffs," "axes," and "saws" (Isa. 10:5, 15), or as his "shepherds" (44:28; cf. 45:1–3). He does so in order not only to realize his plans with Israel, but also so that these nations themselves would come to know him. He does this through his blessings, but also through his judgments: "[W]hen your judgments are in the earth, the inhabitants of the world learn righteousness" (Isa. 26:9). "Hear, you peoples, all of you; pay attention, O earth, and all that is in it, and let the Lord God be a witness against you, the Lord from his holy temple. For behold, the Lord is coming out of his place, and will come down and tread upon the high places of the earth" (Mic. 1:2–3).

## 1.5 The Kingdom under Humans and Satan

### 1.5.1 The Kingdom under Humans

We would not understand very much of God's kingdom in Scripture if we limited this notion to the universal rule of God, God's providence, his upholding the world, his general government throughout the centuries, whether over the world in general or over Israel in particular. It belongs to the essence of biblical basileology that *God entrusts his rule over the world to humans*, initially to the "first Adam," and finally to the "last Adam" (cf. 1 Cor. 15:45), and in the meantime to some who are types of the coming "last Adam," especially David and Solomon. As to the latter, notice the universal scope of passages such as 1 Kings 4:34 ("And people of all nations came to hear the wisdom of Solomon, and from all the kings of the earth") and 10:24 ("And the whole earth sought the presence of Solomon to hear his wisdom, which God had put into his mind"). Solomon is also a type of the Messiah: "The queen of the South will rise up at the judgment with this generation and condemn it, for she came from the ends of the earth to hear the wisdom of Solomon, and behold, something greater than Solomon is here" (Matt. 12:42; see more extensively §13.6).

In Genesis 1, we find a description first of the preparation of the kingdom, so to speak, and then at the end, the king and queen themselves make their appearance: "Then God said, 'Let us make man in our image, after our likeness. And let them *have dominion* over the fish of the sea and over the birds of the heavens and over the livestock and over all the earth and over every creeping thing that creeps on the earth.' So God created man in his own image, in the image of

God he created him; male and female he created them. And God blessed them. And God said to them, 'Be fruitful and multiply and fill the earth[52] and *subdue* it, and *have dominion* over the fish of the sea and over the birds of the heavens and over every living thing that moves on the earth'" (vv. 26-28).

It is only the earth that is entrusted here to the dominion of humans. A bit earlier, we read: "And God made the two great lights—the greater light to *rule* the day and the lesser light to *rule* the night—and the stars. And God set them in the expanse of the heavens to give light on the earth, to *rule* over the day and over the night, and to separate the light from the darkness" (vv. 16-18). Thus, we find five different rulers in Genesis 1: in addition to God, these are the sun, the moon, Adam, and Eve. The sun rules the sky by day, the moon by night, and the first human couple ruled the earth and all that was upon it. There is a distinction between the verbs used, though. In verses 16-18 it is the root *m-sh-l*, "to rule," which is also used for earthly kings (Gen. 37:8; Josh. 12:5; Judg. 8:22; 9:12; 2 Sam. 23:3) and for God's dominion (Ps. 22:28; 59:13; 89:9; 103:19; Isa. 63:19). The Hebrew word for "have dominion" in Genesis 1:26 and 28 is *r-d-h*, which is used several times for royal dominion (Num. 24:19; Ps. 72:8; 110:2; Ezek. 29:15).

## 1.5.2 Eve As Queen[53]

Not only Adam, but Adam as well as Eve, were called to royal dominion "over the fish of the sea and over the

---

52. The phrase "all the earth" in Gen. 1:26 (cf. v. 28) refers to the dry land in distinction from the sea and the heavens (the sky) (cf. v. 10).
53. Ouweneel (1998, 81-82).

birds of the heavens and over the livestock and over all the earth and over every creeping thing that creeps on the earth." In both verse 26 and verse 28, the imperatives are in the plural: the dominion over the world is entrusted to the man and the woman on equal footing.[54] Already the rabbis had difficulties with this; Rashi tried to rob especially the plural form of the first imperative ("subdue it") of its force.[55] However, it was not Adam alone who was creation's head—Adam and Eve were this together. This should be considered by those who, on the basis of 1 Timothy 2:12 ("I do not permit a woman . . . to exercise authority over a man"), assert that, "according to the creation order," women are not entitled to dominion. Later we will see that this matter is of vital importance in view of the future Messianic kingdom: there will be no Messiah without a bride at his side.

The most royal term here, also in reference to Eve, is *r-d-h*, "to rule" (see §1.5.1). This verb can have other meanings, too ("to oversee," or even "to oppress"). However, in a number of cases it clearly refers to royal dominion. This applies especially to Solomon (1 Kgs. 4:21; Ps. 72:8). After humanity's fall into sin, no Old Testament king radiated the splendor of Adam and foreshadowed the Messiah as clearly as Solomon. We see this most clearly in Psalm 72:7-11, "In his days may[56] the

---

54. Oveneel (2008a, 100; 2010b, 419).
55. Cen (1983, 7); Heb. *vekibshuah*, "subdue it," is written in the defective form (i.e., without the *vav*), and could therefore be read as a singular. The subsequent *urdu* ("and have dominion"), however, can be read only as a plural.
56. Others translate this as indicative, e.g., NKJV: "In His days the righteous shall flourish. . . . He shall have dominion also from sea to sea," etc.

righteous flourish, and peace abound, till the moon be no more! May he have dominion from sea to sea, and from the River to the ends of the earth! May desert tribes bow down before him, and his enemies lick the dust! May the kings of Tarshish and of the coastlands render him tribute; may the kings of Sheba and Seba bring gifts! May all kings fall down before him, all nations serve him!"

In a parallel psalm, we find alongside this "new Adam" also a "new Eve": "[D]aughters of kings are among your ladies of honor; at your right hand stands the queen in gold of Ophir. Hear, O daughter, and consider, and incline your ear: forget your people and your father's house, and the king will desire your beauty. Since he is your lord, bow to him" (Ps. 45:9-11). Just as Adam is the prototype of the Messiah, Eve is the prototype of this eschatological queen. A line connects this prophetic "queen in gold of Ophir" to that mysterious "land of Havilah," in the neighborhood of the Garden of Eden, "where there is gold. And the gold of that land is good" (Gen. 2:11-12). In that land, Eve was the queen, alongside king Adam.

### 1.5.3 Crowned Rulers Surrender to Satan

Because of the first humans' special, royal position, Scripture says of them: "Yet you [i.e., God] have made him a little lower than the heavenly beings and *crowned* him with glory and honor. You have given him *dominion* over the works of your hands; you have put all things under his feet, all sheep and oxen, and also the beasts of the field, the birds of the heavens, and the fish of the sea, whatever passes along the paths of the seas" (Ps.

8:5–8). Here, "given dominion" (v. 6) is *m-sh-l*, as in Genesis 1:16–18.

Verse 5 has always drawn much attention: "[Y]ou have made him a little lower than the *elohim*," that is, according to some, "lower than God" (ASV, NASB, RSV, etc.), or "less than God" (HCSB), or "less than divine" (CEB, ISV). The Septuagint has: "a little lower than the angels [Greek *angeloi*, cf. Vulgate, [N]KJV, NIV, etc.), and thus it is quoted (and sanctioned) in Hebrews 2:7. In my view, the latter rendering is far preferable to the former one, which comes close to the lie of Genesis 3:5 ("you will be like God").[57] Possibly we ought to translate here: "little lower [or, less] than the gods," that is, the "heavenly hosts" (cf. ESV, LEB, NET: "heavenly beings"), angels who are venerated as gods by the pagans (cf. Ps. 82:1; 86:8; 89:6; 95:3; 96:4; 97:7, 9; 135:5; 138:1).[58] Humanity with its royal dominion is so exalted that it almost equals the heavenly powers, which have royal features too (cf. "angels, rulers, powers, authorities, dominions, thrones"; Rom. 8:38–39; Eph. 1:21; 3:10; 6:12; Col. 1:16; 2:15).

All the worse, then, that already in Genesis 3, the first humans surrendered their dominion into the hands of Satan—a matter to which Western exegesis has paid little attention. This problem is related to the one-sided Western emphasis on the problem of sin, both at the Fall and in redemption, and less emphasis on the problem of Satan and its solution.[59] In Genesis 3, the empha-

---

57. Very exceptionable is Luther's rendering: "You will, for a little while, make him to be forsaken by God" (Du wirst in lassen eine kleine zeit von Gott verlassen sein).
58. See Ridderbos (1955, 74–75); Van Gemeren (1991, 113).
59. Cf. Ouweneel (2009a, 181–99).

sis is indeed on the transgression of God's command, and the consequences thereof for humanity and the world. Yet, there is also a reference to the superiority that, according to verse 15, the "serpent"—that is, the devil, Satan (Rev. 12:9; 20:2)[60]—apparently had and has. God foretells that the serpent's offspring will repeatedly bruise the heel of the woman's offspring (ERV, GNT, etc.: bite its heel/foot). At the same time, it is foretold that, in the end, the woman's offspring will prevail.

Conservative exegetes invariably see in this verse a Messianic prophecy: the Messiah is the offspring (lit., seed) of the woman, and thus of Adam (cf. Luke 3:23-28). They even go so far as to capitalize the word "Seed" (AMP, NKJV, KJ21). Jewish and modernist expositors do not see any Messianic prophecy here at all, and claim that conservative Christians read far too much into the verse. With the latter point we can certainly agree: Josh McDowell and Francis Schaeffer even assumed that this verse contained a reference to the virgin birth of Christ.[61]

First, the text clearly refers to two progenies in the literal sense: serpents and humans (cf. Isa. 65:25). Secondly, the text refers on the one hand, to the figurative offspring of Satan (cf. John 8:44, "your father, the devil"; 1 John 3:10, "children of the devil") and on the other hand, to that of the (reborn) woman (Eve = *Havvah* = "life," Gen. 3:20). The text is about the ongoing conflict between the wicked and the righteous. These are the two progenies of death and life, respectively, of darkness and light, of hatred (cf. Gen. 4:8; 1 John 3:11-12) and love

---

60. See Ouweneel (2008a, §9.3).
61. McDowell (1972, 116); Schaeffer (1982, 73-74); see Ouweneel (2007b, 162).

(cf. Col. 1:3, from "darkness" to "love"; Acts 26:18, "from darkness to light [cf. 1 Pet. 2:9] and from the power of Satan to God"). In the end, Satan's head will be bruised, and this implies his definitive destruction. The One prevailing over Satan is the Messiah (Col. 2:15; Heb. 2:14; 1 John 3:8; cf. Rev. 20:1, 10). In this sense, one may call Genesis 3:15 an indirect, hidden Messianic prophecy.[62]

Of greatest interest right now is that this verse points to the power which, from that moment on, Satan would exercise in human history. This power is explicitly a *royal* power, and his domain is a true kingdom, as Jesus said: "Every kingdom divided against itself is laid waste, and no city or house divided against itself will stand. And if Satan casts out Satan [as the spiritual leaders had accused Jesus of doing], he is divided against himself. How then will his kingdom stand?" (Matt. 12:25-26). In contrast with this, Jesus presents God's kingdom: "But if it is by the Spirit of God [instead of by Beelzebul] that I cast out demons, then the kingdom of God has come upon you" (v. 28). From this manifestation of God's kingdom until the end of the present age, there is and will be a continual battle between the kingdom of Satan and the kingdom of God. We will now consider this matter a little more closely.

## 1.6 The Meaning of Satan
### 1.6.1 Satan and Devil

The word *satan* comes from the Hebrew root *s-t-n*, which means "to resist," especially in the sense of "to accuse" (Ps. 38:20; 109:4; Zech. 3:1). The participle *soten* means "adversary," especially in the sense of "accuser" (Ps.

---

62. Ouweneel (2007b, 162).

71:13; 109: 20, 29), and this is also true of the noun *satan*. This word may refer to a person who is someone's adversary in war (1 Sam. 29:4; 1 Kgs. 5:18; 11:14, 23, 25), or someone's accuser before a court (Ps. 109:6) or a personal adversary (Num. 22:22, 32; 2 Sam. 19:23). Together with the article, *hassatan*, apparently the word always refers to one specific angelic being, who incites humans to sin (1 Chron. 21:1), or accuses them before God (Job 1:6-8; 2:1-7; Zech. 3:1-2). Zechariah 3:1 combines verb and noun: "Satan [*hassatan*, the accuser or adversary] standing at his right hand to accuse him [*lesitno*]." The most remarkable verse is 1 Chronicles 21:1, where the very accuser (*satan*, without the article) incites his victim to sin, in order to have a reason to accuse him in the heavenly courtroom. Here, Satan clearly is an evil being.

Especially in Job 1 and 2, Satan is still hardly the wicked person that we know from the New Testament, in which the Hebrew word has been adopted in the Greek as a loanword (from Matt. 4:10 to Rev. 20:7). In Job, *hassatan* is the "public prosecutor" of the heavenly counsel.[63] Presumably, this is a parallel to the royal household of a great empire, in which the king (or emperor) had secret servants who patrolled the empire in order to observe the behavior and loyalty of the subjects. In the Persian world, they were known as "the eyes and ears of the king."

In the Septuagint, *hassatan* is translated as *ho diabolos*, which occurs in the New Testament many times as well (from Matt. 4:1 to Rev. 20:10), and which in English has become "devil" (cf. *duivel, Teufel, diable, diabolo*).

---

63. Hartley (1988, 71-72, including n7).

The terms "Satan" and "devil" are entirely exchangeable; they refer to the "great dragon," the "ancient serpent, who is called the devil and Satan, the deceiver of the whole world" (Rev. 12:9; cf. 20:2). The Greek word *diabolos* comes from the verb *diaballō*, literally "to throw over," here "to accuse" (Luke 16:1, "to bring charges"), usually, "to accuse falsely (slanderously)." We must be careful with etymology here. From the literal meaning, "to throw over," it does not follow that in the Bible the devil is the one "throwing over," the "confuser," the "bringer of chaos."[64] In the Bible, the "devil" is always the "accuser" in a court.

Satan is the "accuser [Greek *katēgōr*] of our brothers" (Rev. 12:10), the one who tries time and again to show believers in a bad light before God. He "sifts" Jesus' followers "like wheat" (Luke 22:31), not in order to keep the wheat and let the chaff blow away (cf. Prov. 20:26; Isa. 30:28), as Jesus would do, but to smuggle the wheat away, and triumphantly hold up the chaff before the judge.[65] He is a false prosecutor, who ignores all the positive evidence and emphasizes the negative evidence. The notions of "adversary" and "accuser" are combined in 1 Peter 5:8, "Your adversary [Greek *antidikos*, prosecutor before a tribunal; *dikē* means "justice"] the devil prowls around like a roaring lion, seeking someone to devour."

## 1.6.2 Justice and Power

The terms "Satan" and "devil" are primarily judicial terms, which refer in particular to someone's prosecu-

---

64. As in the story by Edgar Allen Poe, *The Devil in the Belfry*.
65. Cf. Geldenhuys (1983, 566).

tor in a court. In the New Testament, however, we encounter a conceptual transition from justice to power. Satan is not only an accuser, who tries to have his way before a judge, but he himself is a power, a ruler, who is able to impose his own will. If he is an accuser, he is so as a viceroy before a king. He has command of his own angelic army (Matt. 25:41; Rev. 12:7), which consists of fallen angels, just like he himself apparently is a fallen angel (cf. 2 Cor. 11:14, where Satan "disguises himself as an angel of light").[66]

Acts 26:18 speaks of the power of Satan; the Greek word used is *exousia*, "authority," as we also find in Luke 4:6, where the devil told Jesus: "To you I will give all this authority [*exousia*] and their glory, for it has been delivered to me, and I give it to whom I will." He also held the "power [*kratos*] of death" (Heb. 2:14), which seems to mean something like he was the ruler of the realm of death (Hades). Satan can destroy people by assaulting their bodies (1 Cor. 5:5; cf. Job 2:6-7; Acts 10:38; 1 Tim. 1:20). He knows how to incite people to sin (Matt. 4:1-11; John 13:2; 1 Cor. 7:5; Eph. 6:11; 1 Tim. 3:7; 5:15; 2 Tim. 2:26; Rev.12:9; 20:10; cf. Eph. 4:26-27; James 4:7; 1 Pet. 5:8; 1 John 3:8). He can stop God's ambassadors (1 Thess. 2:18), even overpower them (Rev. 2:10). He knows how to disrupt the work of Christ (Matt. 13:39; Luke 8:12; John 6:70). He "was a murderer from the beginning, and does not stand in the truth, because there is no truth in him. When he lies, he speaks out of his own character, for he is a liar and the father of lies" (John 8:44; cf. 1 John 3:8). In a believer's life, a "messenger [angel, DRA, etc.]

---

66. Cf. Ascensio Isaiae II.2; Vita Adae et Evae XVI.

THE ETERNAL KINGDOM: LIVING UNDER CHRIST

of Satan" can be a "thorn in the flesh," to "harass" him or her (2 Cor. 12:7).[67]

For our purpose, especially those passages are important that refer to the *royal* power of Satan. I quoted Matthew 12:25-26, in which Jesus explicitly pointed out the contrast between the kingdom (Greek *basileia*) of Satan and the kingdom of God. This makes it very clear: Satan is a king. Jesus calls him the "ruler [*archōn*] of this world" (John 12:31; 14:30; 16:11), the "rulers of this age" probably being his servants (1 Cor. 2:8).[68] *Archōn* is a more general term for a leader (John 3:1; 7:26, 48; etc.), but can also refer to royal dominion: the kings are the "rulers [*archontes*] of the Gentiles" (Matt. 20:25). In Acts 4:26, Psalm 2:2 is quoted, where "kings of the earth" and "rulers" are parallel. Jesus is the "ruler of the kings of the earth" (Rev. 1:5).

## 1.7 Satan and His Powers
### 1.7.1 The World Rulers

Ephesians 6:11-12 says that believers must "put on the whole armor of God . . .against the schemes of the devil," for their battle is "against the rulers [*archai*], against the authorities [*exousiai*], against the cosmic powers [one word: *kosmokratores*] over this present darkness, against the spiritual forces [one word: *pneumatika*] of evil in the heavenly places." For the "rulers" and "authorities," see also 3:10 and Colossians 1:16 and 2:15.

Especially important here is the phrase "world powers of this darkness" (*kosmokratores tou skotous toutou*), freely rendered as "the powers of this dark world" (NIV,

---

67. See Ouweneel (2005a, 181-82, 200-201).
68. See Ouweneel (2016d, 33n25, 42-43).

etc.).⁶⁹ In the Greek, world, the term *kosmokratores* was used, among other things, for the gods. It is not impossible that, in this term, there is still some echo of the notion of (evil) angelic princes, each having a certain territory of the cosmos under them. The idea was that this domain was allotted to them by their *archōn* ("ruler"), that is, Satan.⁷⁰ Compare here the "morning stars" (Job 38:7; Isa. 14:12), which are heavenly beings. Ancient nations connected the planets with angelic powers by giving them the names of their gods; we still identify the planets by the Roman names of Mercury, Venus, Mars, Jupiter, etc. (Babylonian names: Nebo, Ishtar, Nergal, Marduk, respectively).

This sheds light on Deuteronomy 4:19, which says that the celestial bodies have been allotted to all the peoples on the earth. This verse finds its striking parallel in 29:26, where we read that Israel served other (i.e., foreign) gods, "gods whom they had not known and whom he had not allotted to them." This implies that they had been allotted to the foreign nations. Look at this parallel: God had allotted celestial bodies to the nations, and he had allotted gods to them. This suggests a relationship between these celestial bodies and these gods.⁷¹ (The main difference is that here God, not Satan, makes the allotment.) Amos 5:26 seems to imply the same connection between planets and gods: "You shall take up Sikkuth [i.e., the Babylonian god Sakkut, possibly Saturn] your king, and Kiyyun your star-god [Heb. *kokav*

---

69. See Ouweneel (2016d, 42–43).
70. Cf. Eph. 2:2, "the prince [archōn] of the power of the air [i.e., sky]."
71. See far more extensively, Ouweneel (2016d).

*elohēkhem*, i.e. Saturn]—your images that you made for yourselves." [72]

According to a Midrash,[73] God said to the angel of death, that is, Satan (cf. Heb. 2:14), that, although God had made him *kosmokratōr* ("world ruler") over humans, he was not allowed to have anything to do with the Israelites anymore, for they were *his* (God's) children (cf. Deut. 14:1; Hos. 1:10). This corresponds with Deuteronomy 32:8-9, "When the Most High gave to the nations their inheritance, when he divided mankind, he fixed the borders of the peoples according to the number of the sons of God [i.e., the angelic princes].[74] But the Lord's portion is his people, Jacob his allotted heritage." The *kosmokratores* have no say over the Israelites because they are the Lord's.

In Job 1–2, Satan is one of these same *benēy haelohim*, the "sons of God," that is, virtually "members of the divine realm." These are the "angelic princes" (Hebrew *sarim*) of this world, such as the "*sar* of (the kingdom of) Persia" and the "*sar* of Greece" (Dan. 10:13, 20; note v. 21 and 12:1, where the archangel Michael is the *sar* of Israel). These *sarim* are worshiped as gods by the Gentiles.[75] Thus, Satan is the "god of this world [NIV, NKJV, etc.: of this age, Greek *aiōn*]" (2 Cor. 4:4), an expression that is related to "rulers [sing. *archōn*] of this age [KJV: world]" (1 Cor. 2:6, 8; see above). Thus, Satan is a god, an angelic prince (*sar*), namely—in the evil sense—the

---

72. Ouweneel (2016d, 26–29).
73. Lev. R. 18.3 (Exod. 24:7); see also Exod. R. 51.8.
74. This is the reading of the Septuagint and a Dead Sea Scroll; the idea is that he divided the nations according to the number of angelic princes, but that he kept Israel as his own portion (see Ouweneel [2016d]).
75. See Ouweneel (2016d, §2.1 and passim).

greatest prince known in the present age, that is, the world in its present course (ways, mentality; Greek *aiōn*, Eph. 2:2). Satan is the head of all apostate national angelic princes (*sarim*), for he can say that he has authority over all kingdoms of the world, and can even add, "[I]t [i.e., this power] has been delivered to me, and I give it to whom I will" (Luke 4:5-6). It is to be noted that Jesus did not contradict this claim! Satan *was* indeed the prince of this world, and to a certain extent he still is.

### 1.7.2 Romans 8:20

One could say that the power over the earth has been surrendered to the devil by the first humans, even if unintentionally. This took place under God's providence, of course.[76] In this context, Romans 8:20 is striking: "For the creation was subjected to futility, not willingly, but because of him who subjected it." Who is this "him"? Bible versions like KJ21, AMP, HCSB, and others capitalize this pronoun, apparently thinking it refers to God. Some even interject the word "God" (ERV, ICB, etc.). Other translations that capitalize pronouns referring to God (KJV, etc.), have "him," apparently understanding the pronoun as referring to humanity: it was Adam who caused the creation to be subjected to futility. As the annotation to the Dutch States Translation (*Statenvertaling*, the equivalent of the KJV) says, "That is, because of Man's sin, through which, according to God's righteous judgment, the curse came upon the earth; . . . ." This suggests that it was Adam and Eve who surrendered the creation to the power of Satan.

---

76. Geldenhuys (1983, 160-61); see the fascinating study by Kruse (1977, 50-56).

John Gill (†1771) thought otherwise: "Though they [i.e., the first humans] were willingly vain, yet they were not willingly made subject to vanity; they willingly went into idolatrous and other evil practices, but the devil made them subject, or slaves unto them; he led them captive at his will, and powerfully worked in them, by divine permission, so that they became vassals to him, and to their lusts; for he seems to be designed, 'by him who hath subjected the same', and not Adam, by whom sin entered into the world."[77]

Expositors are quite divided over the matter.[78] Already John Chrysostom, and later Geoffrey W. H. Lampe, Theodor Zahn, and Heinrich Schlier thought that the "him" referred to Adam. John Gill and Frédéric L. Godet (with reference also to Adam) thought that the "him" was Satan. Most other expositors thought that the "him" was God. Douglas J. Moo says, "Reference to Adam . . .is unlikely; as [Johann Albrecht] Bengel says, 'Adam rendered the creature obnoxious to vanity, but he did not *subject* it.' Nor did Satan 'subject' creation (to himself, or otherwise), whatever his role in humanity's fall may have been. Paul must be referring to God, who alone had the right and the power to condemn all of creation to frustration because of human sin."[79]

## 1.8 Satan's Fall and Power
### 1.8.1 His Fall

Since humanity's fall into sin, the ruler of the world is no longer any human but Satan; if one so wishes, Satan

---

77. See biblehub.com on Rom. 8:20.
78. See Moo (1996, 515–16).
79. Moo (1996, 516).

*Introduction to the Kingdom*

is the viceroy, because both human and satanic dominion is always under the supreme rule of God. Until the fall of the first humans, they had served God. Similarly, it seems that, until his own fall, Satan had served God as well. One indirect argument is that all angelic powers were originally created by God (Col. 1:16), and God created all things good (Gen. 1:31), so that, if Satan is an angelic power, he must originally have been good, and must subsequently have fallen into evil.

There has been a lot of speculation about Satan's fall. Many have pointed to Isaiah 14:12–15 and Ezekiel 28:13–19, but these passages obviously refer to the angelic princes (*sarim*) of Babylon and Tyre, respectively. It is possible, however, that especially in the first case the angelic prince must be identified with Satan himself.[80] The passage is quite suggestive: "How you are fallen from heaven, O Day Star, son of Dawn [i.e., the sun]! How you are cut down to the ground, you who laid the nations low! You said in your heart, 'I will ascend to heaven; above the stars of God I will set my throne on high; I will sit on the mount of assembly in the far reaches of the north; I will ascend above the heights of the clouds; I will make myself like the Most High.' But you are brought down to Sheol,[81] to the far reaches of the pit."

In Luke 10:18 ("I saw Satan fall like lightning from heaven") it is unclear whether Satan's fall here refers to some event that occurred in the past or during Jesus' time on earth, or that is still a future event (cf. Rev. 12:10). In the first case, we may indeed think of a refer-

---

80. Ouweneel (2016d, 74–78).
81. Or Hades, the realm of death.

ence to Satan's fall before humanity's fall.[82] In the second case, the reference may be to what happened during Jesus' life: the power of Satan was broken, first by binding Satan (Matt. 12:29) and driving out demons, then through Jesus' work on the cross (Heb. 2:14; 1 John 3:8), as the preparation for Satan's ultimate definitive fall.[83] In the third case, the reference may be to Satan's fall as described in Revelation 12:7-18 (half a "week" before the end; cf. Dan. 9:24-27).[84] At any rate, Luke 10:18 is not an unequivocal reference to Satan's fall in the past.

In 1 Timothy 3:6, a recent convert "may become puffed up with conceit and fall into the condemnation of the devil." The pivotal question here is whether "of the devil" is an objective genitive, that is, whether it is the devil who is condemned here (because of his own conceit; cf. again Isa. 14:12-15).[85] As the AMP says, ". . .fall into the [same] condemnation incurred by the devil [for his arrogance and pride]." The other possibility is that "of the devil" is a subjective genitive: it is the devil who condemns the young puffed up convert. As the CEB says, ". . .fall under the devil's spell" (MSG: ". . .lest the position go to his head and the Devil trip him up").[86]

We find the most extensive description of Satan's fall in 2 Enoch 29:3-4 (cf. 31:3-4). Here, God supposedly said, "And one from out the order of angels, having

---

82. Thus various church fathers; see Bruce (1979, 541); Liefeld (1984, 939).
83. Greijdanus (1955, 270); Ladd (1974b, 157); Hoekema (1979, 46); Geldenhuys (1983, 302).
84. Cf. Green (1997, 419).
85. White (1979, 114).
86. Cf. Towner (2006, 259).

turned away with the order that was under him, conceived an impossible thought, to place his throne higher than the clouds above the earth, that he might become equal in rank to my power. And I threw him out from the height with his angels, and he was flying in the air continuously above the bottomless."[87]

## 1.8.2 Ongoing Conflict

Since Genesis 3, we see a gradual growth in the expectation of God's kingdom, which is to replace Satan's newly acquired kingdom. However, it will only be in the end, at the consummation of the ages, that Satan's kingdom will fall to the ground. Until that time, there is, and there will be, continual battle between the two kingdoms (cf. again Matt. 12:25-26).[88] From the first manifestation of God's kingdom in Jesus' day, the kingdom of *love* opposes the kingdom of hatred (cf. Col. 1:13). The kingdom of *life* opposes the kingdom of death (cf. Heb. 2:14). The kingdom of *light* opposes the kingdom of darkness (cf. 1 Pet. 2:9). God's kingdom opposes Satan's anti-kingdom, God's word opposes Satan's anti-word. In the words of Johan A. Heyns: "The kingdom is a reality that knows an anti-reality . . .an anti-kingdom, which tears up creation and tempts believers with an anti-word."[89]

It sounds almost unfair: in a few moments, Adam and Eve lost their world dominion to Satan. It takes many cen-

---

87. www.scribd.com/doc/301941/The-Book-of-The-Secrets-Of-Enoch.
88. Regarding this, see Kallas (1961, 78-80); Kee (1983, 156-70); Saucy (1997, 324-26).
89. Heyns (1988, 353).

turies to recoup this world dominion, and to re-establish the kingdom of God under the "second man," the "last Adam" (cf. 1 Cor. 15:45, 47). However, this is not an accurate description of God's plan for the cosmos: world history is not simply a return to Paradise.[90] History is not a circle but rather a spiral. The *eschaton* does not imply a simple restoration of the old world, nor a simple replacement by a different (new) world, but the *exaltation* of the present world, as we will see.

The kingdom of God has a double purpose: a negative and a positive one.[91] The negative aim of the kingdom is the destruction of all evil powers that, since humanity's fall, have kept God's world captive for so many centuries. These are the powers of the devil, death, and darkness, which continually oppose the power of life, light, and love. The evil powers exercise their influence through earthly instruments: emperors, kings and presidents, leaders of false religions (including "Christian" cults), politicians and artists, scientists and scholars, journalists and anchormen and -women, and all others who influence public opinion. The positive powers exercise their influence through similar earthly instruments: emperors, kings and presidents, religious leaders, politicians and artists, scientists and scholars, journalists and anchormen and women, and all others who influence public opinion. Every person in the world is basically an instrument either in the realm of darkness or in the kingdom of light.[92]

---

90. In the sense, e.g., of John Milton's *Paradise Regained* (1671).
91. Doyle (1999, 33–34).
92. Cf. Ouweneel (2014a).

## Introduction to the Kingdom

The positive aim of the kingdom of God is the ultimate establishment of peace and justice on earth, and thus the greatest bliss for humanity. The kingdom of God is the rule of God in and through Christ, who destroys everything that is hostile to divine dominion. The first Adam ruined everything, the last Adam restores as well as exalts everything. Satan aims at the ultimate destruction of all things, Christ aims at *his* (Satan's) destruction, and at rebuilding the world for God. World history is the continual conflict between two realms, two kingdoms, a conflict whose end has been established from the outset: "[H]e must reign until he has put all his enemies under his feet [cf. Ps. 110:1]. The last enemy to be destroyed is death. For 'God has put all things in subjection under his feet.' [Ps. 8:6] But when it says, 'all things are put in subjection,' it is plain that he is excepted who put all things in subjection under him. When all things are subjected to him, then the Son himself will also be subjected to him who put all things in subjection under him, that God may be all in all" (1 Cor. 15:25–28).

# Chapter 2
# The Hope of the Kingdom

*For to us a child is born,*
  *to us a son is given;*
*and the government shall be upon*
  *his shoulder,*
  *and his name shall be called*
*Wonderful Counselor, Mighty God,*
  *Everlasting Father, Prince of*
  *Peace.*
*Of the increase of his government*
  *and of peace*
  *there will be no end,*
*on the throne of David and over*
  *his kingdom,*
  *to establish it and to uphold it*
*with justice and with righteousness*
  *from this time forth and*
    *forevermore.*

Isaiah 9:6-7

> *My servant David shall be king over them,*
> *and they shall all have one shepherd...*
> *They shall dwell in the land that I gave to*
> *my servant Jacob,*
> *where your fathers lived...*
> *and David my servant shall be their*
> *prince forever.*
>
> Ezekiel 37:24–25

**Summary:** *The Old Testament is full of types (foreshadowings) of the eschatological anointed King who would come from the house of David, the Savior of Israel and of humanity: Adam, Melchizedek, Joseph, Moses, David, Solomon, Josiah, Cyrus, Mordecai, and includes many prophecies, beginning with Jacob ("Shiloh") and ending with the post-exilic prophets. In fact, the kingdom of the Messiah began with the birth of the Messiah ("Where is the newborn King of the Jews?"), and especially with his glorification at the right hand of God and the pouring out of the Holy Spirit. There is a certain tension here, for today the kingdom exists in a hidden form because the King is hidden, until the time of his return, when the kingdom will be established in power and glory. The tension is that in the Gospels Jesus speaks of the kingdom in both its present and its future form. We ourselves live with joy in the kingdom in its present, hidden form, and we are identified as pilgrims en route to the future public manifestation of the kingdom.*

## 2.1 Kingdom Prophecies

### 2.1.1 *Mashiach*

AT THE MOMENT OF the restoration and the re-acceptance of the first humans after their fall into sin, the hope of

God's kingdom was born. From now on, it would no longer be a kingdom that was put under the feet of the "first man," the "first Adam," but it would be a kingdom that was going to be put under the feet of the "second man," the "last Adam" (1 Cor. 15:45, 47). What the first Adam has ruined, the last Adam must restore. Compare here Psalm 69:5, where the Messiah says: "What I did not steal must I now restore," which is the essence of the guilt offering.[1] From now on, humanity will live by the promise, which begins with the announcement of judgment in Genesis 3:15, a proclamation containing an implied promise: in the end, the woman's offspring will bruise the serpent's head.

The Old Testament Messianic hope is a vast subject,[2] which we can only summarize here. Let us first look at the term "Messiah" itself. It is generally known that the word "Messiah," occurring in the Greek New Testament in John 1:41 and 4:25 (*Messias*), goes back to Hebrew *mashiach*, derived from *m-sh-ch*, "to anoint." The Greek equivalent is *christos*, derived from *chriō*, "to anoint." Thus, the words Messiah and Christ both mean "anointed (one)." In the Old Testament, *mashiach* is a word for *every* anointed one, namely, the "anointed priest" (*hakkohēn hammashiach*, Lev. 4:3; etc.), and subsequently the "anointed one" in the sense of the king, whether Saul (1 Sam. 12:3, 5; etc.), or David (2 Chron. 6:42; Ps. 132:10), or Cyrus the Persian (Isa. 45:1).

Interestingly, in Psalm 105:15 the term "anointed" is also used for the patriarchs (cf. vv. 9-10) in the sense of those consecrated to God's service, even though there

---

1. See Ouweneel (2009a, 167).
2. See extensively, Ouweneel (2007b, chapter 5).

never was any anointing oil on their heads. Abraham, Isaac, and Jacob had, so to speak, that kind of royal, priestly, and prophetic features for which later servants of God were literally anointed (see for the prophets, 1 Kgs. 19:16; Isa. 61:1).

Strikingly enough, *mashiach* seldom has the meaning of "Messiah" in the Old Testament; at best that meaning is indirect, as, for instance, in Psalm 2:2 ("against the LORD and against his Anointed"; cf. Acts 4:25-26); 20:7 ("I know that the LORD saves his anointed [one]"); 132:10 ("do not turn away the face of your anointed one"), 132:17 ("There I will make a horn to sprout for David; I have prepared a lamp for my anointed"). In my view, the clearest passage is Daniel 9:25-26 (NKJV), "[F]rom the going forth of the command to restore and build Jerusalem until Messiah the Prince, [there shall be] seven weeks and sixty-two weeks. . . . And after the sixty-two weeks Messiah shall be cut off, but not for Himself."[3] I do realize, though, that others have seen very different figures in this *mashiach*, If they are right, we must conclude that the term *mashiach* nowhere in the Old Testament has the *direct* meaning of "Messiah" in the sense specified by Jewish and Christian hope.

Whether or not the term *mashiach* in the Old Testament does refer to the Messiah, at any rate, throughout the centuries, the Messianic hope grew stronger and stronger. Already in Genesis, the circle gradually became smaller: from the very general "woman's offspring" (Gen. 3:15) to the "tents of Shem" (9:27), to Eber (10:21-25; 11:10-27), to Abraham (22:18), to Isaac (21:12), to Jacob (28:14; cf. Num. 24:17-19), to Judah: "The scep-

---

3. See Ouweneel (2007b, 188-90).

ter shall not depart from Judah, nor the ruler's staff from between his feet, until tribute comes to him [or, until Shiloh comes]; and to him shall be the obedience of the peoples" (49:10). After this, the line narrowed down through Judah's descendants: Boaz (Ruth 4:18-22), Jesse (Isa. 11:1, 10), and finally David.

### 2.1.2 David

David is the key figure because he is the first true *king* in the long chosen line from Adam. The Messiah is the anointed King of Israel, descendant of the first truly anointed one in Israel. I include here the word "true" to exclude Saul, who is called eight times the "anointed of the LORD" (*meshiach YHWH*) by David (from 1 Sam. 24:6 to 2 Sam. 1:16). Not the Benjaminite running in vain after donkeys (1 Sam. 9:3-5, 20) but the Judean leading the sheep and defending them against the lion and the bear (16:19; 17:34-37) is God's man. Not the man anointed from a fragile jar (10:1) but the one anointed from a strong horn (16:1, 13) turns out to be the man after God's own heart (13:14). (Interestingly, David is called the "anointed of the LORD" only once, but see also Ps. 89:20, "I have found David, my servant; with my holy oil I have anointed him").

It is David who became the forefather of the Messiah, and not only this: he was the model of the entire Messianic idea as such. In some Old Testament passages about David, such as Psalm 2, it is not even clear whether they refer to David himself, or to each Davidic king, or to the greatest son of David, the Messiah, or whether all these three approaches are valid.[4] Of course, there is a deep

---

4. See Ouweneel (2007b, 171-73).

connection between these various explanations, because David is the Old Testament type of Christ *par excellence* (see §2.2.3). This extends to calling the Messiah himself by the name "David": "For the children of Israel shall dwell many days without king or prince, without sacrifice or pillar, without ephod or household gods. Afterward the children of Israel shall return and seek the Lord their God, and David their king, and they shall come in fear to the Lord and to his goodness in the latter days" (Hos. 3:4–5). These last words (JUB: "in the end of the days") are characteristic of (the beginning of) the Messianic era.[5] Therefore, the Targum identifies "David their king" here as the Messiah. Israel "seeking" the Messiah can hardly refer to Christ's first coming; it is to be fulfilled only in the Messianic kingdom (Isa. 12:1–6; 66:23; Jer. 33:11; Ezek. 20:40; etc.).[6]

We find the same name "David" for the Messiah in Ezekiel: "I will set up over them one shepherd, my servant David, and he shall feed them: he shall feed them and be their shepherd. And I, the Lord, will be their God, and my servant David shall be prince among them" (34:23–24). "My servant David shall be king over them, and they shall all have one shepherd. . . . They shall dwell in the land that I gave to my servant Jacob . . . forever, and David my servant shall be their prince forever" (37:24–25). There can be no reasonable doubt that "David" is here a name for the Messiah, the great son of David.[7]

David himself must have had some consciousness of the coming Messiah, no matter how little. Thus he says,

---

5. S. M. Lehrman in Cohen (1980, 13).
6. See Wood (1985, 183).
7. M. C. Mulder in Knevel and Paul (1995, 127–29, 136–38).

"The LORD [*YHWH*] says to my Lord [*Adonai*]: 'Sit at my right hand, until I make your enemies your footstool'" (Ps. 110:1). This thought is supported by the interpretation of this verse that Jesus gives in Matthew 22:42-45, applying it to the Messiah, that is, to himself.[8] In 2 Samuel 23:3-4, David speaks in a clearly Messianic way of the coming ruler, and connects him with his own house (v. 5). If verse 3 refers to a specific person (NASB: "'He who rules over men righteously, who rules in the fear of God") this can be none other than the Messiah:[9] ". . . he dawns on them like the morning light [cf. Mal. 4:2], like the sun shining forth on a cloudless morning, like rain that makes grass to sprout from the earth" (v. 4).

Amos 9:11-12 says, "In that day I will raise up the booth of David that is fallen and repair its breaches, and raise up its ruins and rebuild it as in the days of old, that they may possess the remnant of Edom and all the nations who are called by my name." This prophecy is quoted by James in Acts 15:16-17. He quotes mainly from the Septuagint, with the implication that, in the latter days, David's "booth" or "tent," that is, David's "house" or dynasty, shriveled to almost nothing, will be restored in David's great Son, and that this will have enormous consequences for Israel as well as for all the nations. It suffices to notice here that the perspective of Amos 9:11-15 seems to be clearly Messianic,[10] and that James applies it this way in Acts 15.[11]

---

8. See further, Ouweneel (2007b, §§5.4.2-5.4.3).
9. Goslinga (1962, 417-24), and references.
10. Thus also S. M. Lehrman in Cohen (1980, 123).
11. The peculiar differences between the Masoretic text and the Septuagint, and even between the latter and Acts 15, do not

### 2.1.3 Other Prophecies

In addition to the prophecies just discussed, we could mention here many more Old Testament prophecies with regard to the Messianic kingdom as it will be established one day here on earth in power and glory—that is, as we know now: at Christ's parousia.[12] I have discussed these in a separate volume (in Dutch) that deals with eschatology.[13] Right now, I will limit myself to four striking examples from four prophetic books.

(a) "For to us a child is born, to us a son is given; and the government shall be upon his shoulder, and his name shall be called Wonderful Counselor, Mighty God, Everlasting Father, *Prince* of Peace. Of the increase of his government and of peace there will be no end, on the throne of David and over his *kingdom*, to establish it and to uphold it with justice and with righteousness from this time forth and forevermore" (Isa. 9:6-7).

(b) "It shall come to pass in the latter days that the mountain of the house of the Lord shall be established as the highest of the mountains, and it shall be lifted up above the hills; and peoples shall flow to it, and *many nations* shall come, and say: 'Come, let us go up to the mountain of the Lord, to the house of the God of Jacob, that he may teach us his ways and that we may walk in his paths.' For out of Zion shall go forth the law, and the word of the Lord from Jerusalem. He shall *judge* between *many peoples*, and shall decide for strong nations

---

have to occupy us here; see Bruce (1988, 293-94); J. Mudde in Knevel and Paul (1995, 157-66).

12. Greek *parousia*, "coming"; in the present book this always refers to Christ's second coming.
13. Ouweneel (2012a, especially chapters 5-6 and 13).

far away; and they shall beat their swords into plowshares, and their spears into pruning hooks; nation shall not lift up sword against nation, neither shall they learn war anymore; but they shall sit every man under his vine and under his fig tree, and no one shall make them afraid, for the mouth of the LORD of hosts has spoken" (Mic. 4:1-4; cf. Isa. 2:2-4).

(c) "'I will leave in your midst a people humble and lowly. They shall seek refuge in the name of the LORD, those who are left in Israel; they shall do no injustice and speak no lies, nor shall there be found in their mouth a deceitful tongue. For they shall graze and lie down, and none shall make them afraid.' Sing aloud, O daughter of Zion; shout, O Israel! Rejoice and exult with all your heart, O daughter of Jerusalem! The LORD has taken away the judgments against you; he has cleared away your enemies. The *King* of Israel, the LORD, is in your midst; you shall never again fear evil. On that day it shall be said to Jerusalem: 'Fear not, O Zion; let not your hands grow weak. The LORD your God is in your midst, a mighty one who will save; he will rejoice over you with gladness; he will quiet you by his love; he will exult over you with loud singing'" (Zeph. 3:12-17).

(d) "On that day living waters shall flow out from Jerusalem, half of them to the eastern sea and half of them to the western sea. It shall continue in summer as in winter. And the LORD will be *king* over all the earth. On that day the LORD will be one and his name one.... Then everyone who survives of all the nations that have come against Jerusalem shall go up year after year to worship the *King*, the LORD of hosts, and to keep the Feast of Booths" (Zech. 14:8-9, 16).

## 2.2 The Typology of the Kingdom
### 2.2.1 Introduction

The expectation of the kingdom of God in the Old Testament becomes manifest essentially in two ways: first, through direct Messianic prophecies, and second, through Messianic typology.[14] In the New Testament, typology is quite common. Paul says about Israel's wilderness journey: "[T]hese things took place as examples [*typoi*] for us, .... these things happened to them as an example [one Greek word: *typikōs*, by way of types], but they were written down for our instruction, on whom the end of the ages has come" (1 Cor. 10:6, 11; cf. Rom. 15:4). "Adam ... was a type of the one who was to come" (Rom. 5:14). Where the passage through the Red Sea is a type of spiritual cleansing, there baptism is the *antitypos* (1 Pet. 3:21).

Of special interest is Galatians 4:21-24, "Tell me, you who desire to be under the law [i.e., the Mosaic Law], do you not listen to the law [i.e., the Pentateuch]? For it is written that Abraham had two sons, one by a slave woman and one by a free woman. But the son of the slave was born according to the flesh, while the son of the free woman was born through promise. Now this may be interpreted allegorically [*estin allēgoroumena*. i.e., here, by way of types]: these women are two covenants," etc. In verse 21 the apostle almost seems to blame the Galatian Christians that they themselves had not discerned these types in Genesis. This is an encouragement for us to find such types for ourselves.

---

14. Two general standard works on typology are those by Habershon (1957) and Fairbairn (1975). See also Ouweneel (2000, 34-36; 2007b, §7.6.1); C. A. Evans in Green *et al.* (1992, 862-66).

*The Hope of the Kingdom*

See how naturally this is done, for instance, in Hebrews 7:1-3: "For this Melchizedek, king of Salem, priest of the Most High God, met Abraham returning from the slaughter of the kings and blessed him, and to him Abraham apportioned a tenth part of everything. He is first, by translation of his name, king of righteousness, and then he is also king of Salem, that is, king of peace. He is without father or mother or genealogy, having neither beginning of days nor end of life, but resembling [*aphōmoiōmenos*] the Son of God he continues a priest forever." And see how naturally Stephen presents us Joseph and Moses as foreboders of the Messiah, without using the term "type" (Acts 7:9-38).

I already mentioned David as a special type of Jesus as the Messiah, the anointed King of Israel. David is not only a forefather, he is also a type of the Messiah; these are two different matters. In fact, this Davidic typology becomes manifest in all the prophecies mentioned that speak of "David" or of the "son of David," where actually the Messiah is meant. This typological way of speaking in the Old Testament becomes clearly visible in the New Testament. The latter appeals extensively to the Old Testament to prove that Jesus is the fulfillment of the Messianic predictions, even if in these quotations it is not always the actual grammatical-historical exegesis of the quoted passages that is applied.[15] In some cases, for instances, we are dealing with Messianic applications of Old Testament passages that refer to the Davidic king in general (see Ps. 2:7 and 2 Sam. 7:14 in Heb. 1:5).

In other cases, the relationship is even weaker; they involve midrashic (typological) applications of Old Tes-

---

15. Ouweneel (2007b, 157-58).

tament passages that grammatical-historical exegesis would never have considered (see Hos. 11:1 in Matt. 2:15, or Jer. 31:15 in Matt. 2:18, or Ps. 102:25-27 in Heb. 1:10-12, or Ps. 8:4-6 in Heb. 2:6-8). This is sometimes called a *pesher* interpretation, in which a Jewish expositor taps into a deeper layer in the text than grammatical-historical exegesis does (the term *pesher* overlaps here with *midrash*).[16]

This does not mean that, in such cases, the New Testament does not do justice to the Old Testament passages involved. On the contrary, to exegetes it cannot be insignificant that, in Acts 2:25-31, Psalm 16:8-11 is applied in a Messianic way. The same holds for Psalm 2:5-7 in Hebrews 2:6-9, and for the way Isaiah 6 is explained in a Christological sense in John 12:41. This may encourage us to look for deeper meanings in certain texts than strict grammatical-historical exegesis could ever uncover. (Think again of passages such as 1 Cor. 10:1-11, Gal. 4:21-31, and Heb. 7:1-10.)

### 2.2.2 Pre-Davidic Types

The seven Old Testament persons who, in my view, are unmistakably types of Jesus as the Messiah, the anointed King in the Messianic kingdom of peace and justice, are the following (historically they are five kings and two viceroys).[17]

(a) *Melchizedek.* Where the book of Hebrews connects Jesus with Melchizedek, we find one of the most explic-

---

16. Also see Ouweneel (2007b, §§5.4.1, 5.5.1).
17. See Ouweneel (2007b, §7.6.2; also see §5.1.3 and references concerning Old Testament types); Habershon (1957, 122-42, 165-74).

itly typological passages in the New Testament:[18] "For this Melchizedek, king of Salem, priest of the Most High God, met Abraham returning from the slaughter of the kings and blessed him, and to him Abraham apportioned a tenth part of everything. He is first, by translation of his name [Heb. *malki-tsedek*], 'king of righteousness,' and then he is also king of Salem [Heb. *Shalem*, cf. the related *shalom*], that is, king of peace. He is without father or mother or genealogy, having neither beginning of days nor end of life, but resembling the Son of God he continues a priest forever. See how great this man was" (Heb. 7:1-4a; also see 5:6, 10; 6:20; 7:10-11, 15, 17). The idea is not that Melchizedek was literally without parents, or without beginning and end, but that this is the way he is presented in Genesis. As such he resembles Jesus who, as the Son God, had no (earthly) parents, beginning, or end.

(b) *Joseph*. As viceroy of Egypt (although he is never called this[19]), and thus as savior of his father's house, and especially in his way of suffering that led to his rulership, Joseph is one of the clearest types of Christ in the entire Bible. Evidence for this is the way Stephen points to Joseph (Acts 7:9-14), who was sold by his brothers, as one of the Old Testament examples of God's men who, already in those days, had been badly treated by

---

18. See Ouweneel (1982, 1:86-89).
19. Gen. 41:40-41 comes closest: "You shall be over my house, and all my people shall order themselves as you command. Only as regards the throne will I be greater than you. . . . See, I have set you over all the land of Egypt. . . . I am Pharaoh, and without your consent no one shall lift up hand or foot in all the land of Egypt."

the "sons of Israel" (cf. the application to Christ in v. 52: "Which of the prophets did your fathers not persecute? And they killed those who announced beforehand the coming of the Righteous One, whom you have now betrayed and murdered"). Joseph received from the Pharaoh the name Zafenath-Paneah (Gen. 41:45), which has been variously explained as: "God speaks and he lives," "the god said: let him live" (EXB), "the man who knows things," "the sustainer of life," "sustenance of the land is the [i.e., this] living one."[20] Traditionally, the name has been explained as "the savior of the world" (see DRA, WYC), but this rendering is doubted by many.

### 2.2.3 Davidic Types

(c) *David*. Elsewhere I have quoted many psalms that refer literally to David but in the New Testament turn out to have a Messianic intention.[21] This is the same as saying that in such cases David is a type of Christ. This is no wonder: as the first true king of Israel, he is *the* model of the great son of David, the Messianic King of Israel. This relationship is so intimate that, as we have seen, the Messiah himself is sometimes called "David." Just as in the case of Joseph, there are three stages in his life: the time of prosperity (Joseph in his father's house, David at Saul's court, both being the favorites of their father/father-in-law), the time of rejection and humiliation (Joseph as slave and prisoner, David fleeing before Saul), and the time of exaltation (Joseph becomes viceroy of Egypt, David king of Israel). The first stage corresponds with eternity past, when the Son

---

20. See Hamilton (1995, 507–508).
21. Ouweneel (2007b, chapter 5).

was still with the Father as his beloved (John 17:24). The second stage corresponds with the kingdom of God in its present form (in which Christ was first rejected personally, and subsequently the Spirit of the rejected Christ shares in the humiliation of his people). The third stage corresponds with the kingdom of God in its future form: Christ on the throne of David.

(d) *Solomon.* I will return to Solomon at the very end of this book, so at this point I will limit my comments to a few references to be discussed later (1 Kgs. 4:20-25 [cf. Mic. 4:4]; Ps. 72:8-17 together with Isa. 60:6-10). Solomon was the "beloved of the LORD" (Jedidiah, 2 Sam. 12:24-25). It was about him that God said, "I will be to him a father, and he shall be to me a son"—words that in Hebrews 1:5b are applied to Christ. As son of David he was the foreshadowing of *the* son of David (Matt. 9:27; 12:23; 15:22; 20:30-31; 21:9, 15).

(e) *Josiah.* He was the last good Davidic king over Judah. Lamentations 4:20 says, "The breath of our nostrils, the LORD's anointed, was captured in their pits, of whom we said, 'Under his shadow we shall live among the nations.'" According to the Targum, Rashi, and others, these words refer primarily to Josiah,[22] even though the announced ending of this "anointed" was not fulfilled in Josiah himself but in his son Zedekiah. The words, "Under his shadow we shall live among the nations," sound very Messianic, certainly when compared with similar passages (cf. Song 2:3; Ezek. 17:23; Hos. 14:7; see also Ps. 91:1; Isa. 25:4).

---

22. Quoted by Aalders (1925, 104), who, however, calls this an "absolute impossibility."

## 2.2.4 Other Types

(f) *Cyrus*. Although Cyrus was a Persian king who hardly knew YHWH, God spoke to him in strikingly Messianic language: ". . . who says of Cyrus, 'He is *my shepherd*, and he shall fulfill all my purpose'; saying[23] of Jerusalem, 'She shall be built,' and of the temple, 'Your foundation shall be laid.'" Thus says the LORD to *his anointed*, to Cyrus, whose right hand I have grasped . . . : 'I will go before you and level the exalted places, I will break in pieces the doors of bronze and cut through the bars of iron, I will give you the treasures of darkness and the hoards in secret places, that you may know that it is I, the LORD, the God of Israel, who call you by your name" (Isa. 44:28–45:3). Of a typically Messianic character are also some other references to Cyrus: "I have stirred him up in righteousness, and I will make all his ways level" (45:13), and especially "the man of my counsel" (46:11).

(g) *Mordecai*. The Jew Mordecai, who was threatened with death by his enemies, was exalted in God's time: "For the man whom the king delights to honor, let *royal* robes be brought, which the king has worn, and the horse that the king has ridden, and on whose head a *royal* crown is set. And let the robes and the horse be handed over to one of the king's most noble officials. Let them dress the man whom the king delights to honor, and let them lead him on the horse through the square of the city, proclaiming before him: 'Thus shall it be done to the man whom the king delights to honor'" (Esther 6:7-9). In the end we read of him: ". . . the full ac-

---

23. The ESV seems to suggest that this is God "saying"; others (NKJV, NIV, etc.) place these words on Cyrus' lips.

count of the high honor of Mordecai, to which the king advanced him. . . . For Mordecai the Jew was second in rank to King Ahasuerus, and he was great among the Jews and popular with the multitude of his brothers, for he sought the welfare of his people and spoke peace to all his people" (10:2-3). In this position he was comparable to Joseph, the viceroy of Egypt.[24]

## 2.2.5 Moses?

As the eighth type in this series—or, in chronological order, the third type—Moses would have seemed to fit in very well. At any rate, Stephen says in Acts 7:35 that God had sent Moses as "ruler" (Greek *archōn*) to Israel, which comes quite close to the title of king, as is evident from Matthew 20:25 ("the rulers of the Gentiles lord it over them"), Acts 4:26 ("The kings of the earth set themselves, and the rulers were gathered together"), and Revelation 1:5 ("the ruler of kings on earth"). Just as he did to Joseph (§2.2.2), Stephen pointed to Moses as one of the Old Testament examples of God's men who, already in those days, had been badly treated by the Israelites (cf. again the application to Christ in v. 52: "Which of the prophets did your fathers not persecute? And they killed those who announced beforehand the coming of the Righteous One, whom you have now betrayed and murdered").

According to some, several Old Testament passages imply some royal position of Moses.[25] For instance, in Exodus 4:20 and 17:9, Moses took the "staff of God" (Heb. *mattēh haelohim*), which some rabbis interpreted as a

---

24. See extensively, Ouweneel (n.d.).
25. See extensively, Porter (1963); Lierman (2004, 79-81).

symbol of God's royal dominion, which was here entrusted to Moses (cf. also 17:9).[26] In Ezekiel 7:10, the "rod" (*mattēh*) stands for the royal power of Nebuchadnezzar (other references to the royal significance of *mattēh* are Ps. 110:2; Isa. 14:5; Jer. 48:17).

In Deuteronomy 33:4-5 we literally read: "Moses commanded us a law, as a possession for the assembly of Jacob. And he was king in Jeshurun [i.e., Israel; cf. 32:15]." Many rabbis and Jewish commentators (e.g., Philo, Ibn Ezra, Maimonides[27]), some Talmudic tracts,[28] and some Targums[29] assume that it is Moses who is called here "king," and they are joined in this view by some Christian expositors as well.[30] Modern exegetes, however, reject this, or do not even mention this older interpretation. It can hardly be denied that, in the context, it is more obvious to apply this kingship to God than to Moses.

## 2.3  The Kingdom: Present and Future
### 2.3.1  The "Kingdom of Heaven"

Throughout the earlier books of the Old Testament, we hear the reverberating hope of the coming Messiah, the Lord's Anointed, namely, the anointed King from the house of David, who one day will rule over Israel and

---

26. Midrash Psalms on Ps. 21:2; see royal scepters mentioned in Ezek. 19:11, 14; Ps. 110:2.
27. But not Rashi and Nachmanides; see Cohen (1983, 1177).
28. Zevachim 102a; Jer. Sanhedrin 1:3.
29. Targum Onqelos; Targum Pseudo-Jonathan.
30. E.g., John Wesley (bible.cc/deuteronomy/33-5.htm); John Gill mentions this exegesis as a possibility (www.searchgodsword.org/com/geb/view.cgi?book=deandchapter=033andverse=005).

will establish peace and justice on earth. The great difference with the Gospels is that here the kingdom of God is no hope for a distant future anymore but is described as being "at hand" (Matt. 3:2; 4:17; 10:7; other translations: having "come near").

In Matthew, the kingdom is almost always called the "kingdom of heaven" (exceptions: 6:33; 12:28; 19:24; 21:31, 43), an expression that we also know from later Jewish literature.[31] In almost identical parallel passages (cf., e.g., Matt. 4:17 and Mark 1:15), the expression is always "kingdom of God," so that there is no ground for the idea that the two expressions would have different meanings.[32] The apposition "of heaven" is an obvious euphemism for "of God," as in Matthew 5:34, where people take an oath "by heaven" in order to avoid the name of God. In Daniel 4:26, the prophet says, "Heaven rules," which means: "God rules." In Luke 15:18, the prodigal son says, "I have sinned against heaven," that is, against God. The kingdom of heaven and the kingdom of God are identical.

The kingdom of heaven is certainly not a kingdom *in* heaven (the place where God dwells), as Luther often seems to suggest. His hymn on the Lord's Prayer begins with: "Our Father in the kingdom of heaven [*im Himmelreich*]," where the original text says "heaven." (*Himmelreich* is Luther's rendering of "kingdom of heaven" in his translation of Matthew).[33] Rather, the

---

31. Heb. *malkut shamayyim*; see Ridderbos (1962, 8–13).
32. *Contra* Walvoord (1974, 30), who describes the kingdom of heavenas the domain of external "profession," and the kingdom of God as the domain of the true believers. See extensively Savage(n.d.-a).
33. Unfortunately, Hoek (2004, 128) adopts this expression (Dutch:

"kingdom of heaven" is the kingdom in which "heaven" (i.e., God) rules heaven and earth, that is, the total universe (cf. Matthew 28:18, "Jesus came and said to them, 'All authority in heaven and on earth has been given to me'"). Johan Verkuyl therefore rightly describes the kingdom of heaven as "the kingdom descending from heaven to earth."[34]

In the Gospels, there is no ground for giving the expression "kingdom of God" a spiritual and present meaning, and "kingdom of heaven" a future (millennial) meaning, as some dispensationalists have suggested.[35] Although in Jesus' day, God's kingdom had a form different from the one after his ascension, and will have another form after Christ's parousia, it is essentially one and the same kingdom, for it is the same God who rules in Christ. The "kingdom of heaven" is *now* (e.g., Matt. 12:28), and it is *future* (e.g., 8:11); it is *spiritual* (e.g., 5:10, 19–20) and it is *earthly* (e.g., 5:35).

### 2.3.2 The "Presence" Passages

First it was John the Baptist (Matt. 3:2), then Jesus himself (4:17), and then the disciples whom he sent out (10:7), who announced that the kingdom of God was "at hand" (or, had "come near"). Even shortly before his sufferings and death, when Jesus pointed to the forthcoming destruction of Jerusalem and the temple, he still said, "So also, when you see these things taking place, you know that the kingdom of God is near [i.e., at hand]" (Luke 21:31). That which is "near"

---

*hemelrijk*), and thus perpetuates the confusion.
34. Verkuyl (1992, 444).
35. See the refutation by Carson (1984, 100).

("at hand") has not yet arrived. This is all the more striking because at other moments Jesus clearly presents the kingdom as a present reality, namely, in what German theologians call the *Gegenwartstellen* (I call them the "presence" passages).

There has been much debate on the question whether Jesus describes the kingdom as present or future.[36] This is rather strange because it ought to be evident, as James Dunn says, that *both* lines are well rooted in the Synoptic tradition.[37] The presence of the kingdom in its preliminary form is just as real as the future breakthrough of the kingdom in full glory. As the Heidelberg Catechism puts it (Q/A 123): "'Your kingdom come' means: Rule us by your Word and Spirit . . . until your kingdom fully comes, when you will be all in all." The word "fully" seems to suggest: it is already there, but we are still waiting for its "fullness."

To be sure, the word "present" must be nuanced somewhat. Do the "presence" passages mean that the kingdom of God was already a reality in the time of Jesus' ministry? Or can they also mean that they were to be fulfilled after his ascension and glorification, but before his parousia and the establishment of his kingdom in power and majesty? To investigate this matter, let us look at the most important "presence" passages, which at least also include Jesus' day. They are are the following:

---

36. Cf. Ridderbos (1962, 36-60, 104-106), Meier (1994, chapter 16), Stein (1996, 125-31), Bock (2002, 574-79), Theissen and Merz (2004, 252-78), and Knight (2004, 15-26,105-111) about the present and the future aspect of the kingdom.
37. Dunn (2005, 72).

(a) Jesus says, "[I]f it is by the Spirit of God that I cast out demons, then the kingdom of God has come upon you" (Matt. 12:28; cf. Luke 11:20); that is, the *power* of the kingdom became manifest already at that time because, by the power of God's Spirit, Jesus cast out demons. If the power of the kingdom has arrived, then to some extent the kingdom itself must have arrived as well. The same holds for the healings and other miracles that Jesus accomplished; they were signs of the presence of the kingdom.[38] Even the forgiveness of sins was such a sign according to the Old Testament promises (e.g., Isa. 33:24; Jer. 31:34; Mic. 7:18–20; Zech. 13:1): "the Son of Man has *authority* [Greek *exousia*, or, power] on earth to forgive sins" (Mark 2:10). And supplying the people abundantly with bread (Matt. 14:19; 15:36) is also such a sign (Ps. 132:15, "I will abundantly bless her provisions; I will satisfy her poor with bread"). Food, healing, forgiveness—the kingdom of God encompasses the whole of human life.

To be sure, the fact that the King himself has appeared is in itself insufficient evidence that the kingdom of God has begun. A person can be a king, and still not have actually received the power. The wise men from the east came to see the newborn "king of the Jews" (Matt. 2:2), although it is clear that this baby king as such did not yet exercise any power.[39] There was a sharp contrast between him and Herod, the king who, in those days, possessed the real power (apart from the Roman emperor, whose vassal he was) (vv. 1, 3). This

---

38. Hoekema (1979, 46).

39. I am not speaking here of what Jesus was and did as the eternal Son of the Father, even when he was a human baby.

*The Hope of the Kingdom*

power was so real that Herod could massacre all the baby boys of Bethlehem (v. 16). The moment, however, when the King effectively displayed royal power by feeding, healing, delivering, forgiving, his kingdom had apparently become a spiritual reality, no matter how immature and incomplete.

One peculiar aspect of the situation was that, also in Matthew 12, Jesus did not yet rule Israel or any other part of the world. Instead, he displayed his power in the spiritual world, namely, by prevailing over the kingdom of Satan (vv. 25-26). Apparently, the fact that he really was the predicted and promised King became manifest in his triumph over Satan's empire, rather than in his triumph over human empires. In history, many princes have prevailed over human empires, but lost the battle against Satan, that is, either Satan's power within them or around them. Jesus prevailed over the empire of Satan, so that conquering human empires will turn out to be a trifling matter for him. Once Satan's empire will have been broken, his most important instrument, the Antichrist—a human being—will simply be killed by the breath of the King's mouth (Isa. 11:4; 2 Thess. 2:8).

(b) Related to Matthew 12:28 is 10:7-8, spoken to the twelve disciples: "And proclaim as you go, saying, 'The kingdom of heaven is at hand.' Heal the sick, raise the dead, cleanse lepers, cast out demons." In other words, affirm the reality of the coming kingdom by working miracle signs, as Jesus himself did. Parallel with this is Luke 10:8-9, spoken to the seventy-two disciples: "Whenever you enter a town and they receive you, eat what is set before you. Heal the sick in it and say to them, 'The kingdom of God has come near to you.'" In light of Matthew 12:28 (see [a] above), the phrase "has come near to you" (or, "is at hand")[40] could in fact mean: "is on the brink of breaking in," or even, "has broken in." But apart from Matthew 12:28, it can also mean: "the powers are already there, so the kingdom itself cannot be far away anymore." There is here a parallel with Hebrew 6:5: the "powers of the age to come" are already here, but that does not mean that the "age to come" itself has already arrived. This is the age of the future Messianic kingdom, which will be manifested in glory and power.

(c) The eight parables of the kingdom of heaven in Matthew 13 deal with the present reality of the kingdom, too, not so much with the future form of it (although it is referred to): "The kingdom of heaven is like . . . ," that is, resembles, corresponds to (Matt. 13:24, 31, 33, 44-45, 47; cf. 18:23; 20:1; 22:2). *Today*, the kingdom is a mixture of wheat and weeds, of good and bad fish, of wise and foolish virgins, of good and bad servants (13:24-30, 36-43, 47-50; 25:1-30). Some other parables in Matthew deal with the transfer of God's kingdom in Jesus' day from Israel to the Gentile world (the tenants, the wedding garment; 21:33-22:14). See more extensively the next two chapters.

### 2.3.3 "Within You" or "Among You"

(d) "The kingdom of God is in the midst of you [Greek *entos hymōn*)" (Luke 17:21).[41] Together with the King,

---

40. The ESV inexplicably renders the same Greek phrase in two different ways.

41. Cf. the Gospel of Thomas 3: "Jesus said, 'If your leaders say to you, "Look, the (Father's) kingdom is in the sky," then the birds

the kingdom itself has arrived, even though his actual kingship over Israel, in power and majesty, is still future (see below). There has been much debate on this statement,[42] as can be easily seen in the various translations: "within you" (ASV, NKJV, NIV, etc.), "inside you" (Phillips, WE), "among you" (CEB, CJB, etc.), "in your midst" (ESV, NASB, etc.), "within your reach" (Bengel). The latter translation goes back all the way to Tertullian: *in manu, in potestate vestra* ("in your hand, in your power").[43] The translation "within you" or "inside you" may seem strange, since the kingdom could not have been said to be "inside" the spiritual leaders addressed here by Jesus.[44] However, the kingdom was certainly inside the believing bystanders. Thus, *entos hymōn* refers either to the Jews in general, in whose midst the King now was (John 1:26), or to believers among them, in whose hearts he was erecting his kingdom through his Word and Spirit.[45]

If the verse deals indeed with the King's rule in believers' hearts, the assertion of Reinhold Schneider is valid: "The life of this kingdom is Christ's living on in his own; in the heart that is not fed anymore by the life power of Christ, the kingdom comes to an

---

of the sky will precede you. If they say to you, 'It is in the sea,' then the fish will precede you. Rather, the (Father's) kingdom is within you and it is outside you.'"

42. About this, cf. C. C. Caragounis in Green *et al.* (1992, 423–24).
43. *Contra Marcionem* L.4.35; quoted by Bruce (1979, 594).
44. Cf. Greijdanus (1941, 105). Marshall (1978, 655) sees the *hymōn* as undetermined, i.e., as wider than just addressing the Pharisees.
45. Thus the annotation in the Dutch States Translation (*Statenvertaling*).

end; in the heart that is touched and changed by it, the kingdom begins."[46]

Whether *entos hymōn* means in the hearts of the addressed believers, or in the midst of the addressed people, Jesus is speaking here of God's kingdom as a present reality. And this can hardly mean anything else than that the kingdom was present within, or among, his hearers *because he himself was there*; or a little wider: the kingdom became manifest among them through the miracles that he did: "[I]f it is by the finger of God that I cast out demons, then the kingdom of God has come upon you," says the same Gospel (Luke 11:20). The early Christian theologian Origen called Jesus *autobasileia*,[47] "the very kingdom," "the kingdom himself," and Joseph Ratzinger (pope Benedict XVI), who quotes this, adds: "Jesus himself is the Kingdom; the Kingdom is not a thing, it is not a geographical dominion like worldly kingdoms. It is a person; it is he. On this interpretation, the term 'Kingdom of God' is itself a veiled Christology."[48]

The somewhat cryptic phrase "the kingdom of God is in the midst of you" reminds us of the verse just mentioned: John 1:26, "among you [*mesos hymōn*] stands one you do not know." The kingdom had arrived because the King had arrived. As Seakle Greijdanus says of Luke 17:26, "The Lord refers here to himself and his disciples. He himself is in his own person the kingdom of God."[49] Herman Ridderbos refers here to "a *personal* connotation in the expression 'the kingdom of heaven.' The

---

46. Schneider (1979, 31).
47. *Contra Celsum* (1017).
48. Ratzinger (2007, 49).
49. Greijdanus (1941, 105).

manifestation of the kingdom of heaven cannot be conceived as an impersonal metaphysical event, but as the coming of God himself as king,"[50] namely, in the person of Jesus. A little later: "[T]he real and most profound explanation of the presence of the kingdom is to be sought in the person of Jesus himself. The secret of the presence of the kingdom of heaven lies in Jesus' victory over Satan, in his unlimited miraculous power, his unrestricted authority to preach the gospel, in his pronouncements of blessedness and the bestowal of salvation upon his people."[51]

(e) In John 18:36, Jesus speaks to Pilate of the kingdom as a present reality, which at the same time, as a spiritual reality, is exalted above the earthly kingdoms: "My kingdom is not of this world. If my kingdom were of this world, my servants would have been fighting, that I might not be delivered over to the Jews. But my kingdom is not from the world." Therefore he can say in verse 37: "I am a king," not: one day I will be a king. In this context, Jesus seems to mean that his kingdom is a spiritual empire, which apparently exists especially in the hearts of his followers. It is through regeneration that people share in this kingdom (3:5), and that is not only a future matter.

## 2.4 Two Sevens

### 2.4.1 Seven Stages

By way of summary, I point to two groups of seven items. First, I claim that in the history of God's kingdom it is very useful to distinguish seven different stages (see

---

50. Ridderbos (1962, 25).
51. Ridderbos (1962, 81–82).

further §2.6.2; on the matter of periodizing more generally, see chapters 12 and 13):

*Prologue:* The time God was King over his newly created world, before he entrusted this kingdom to the first humans (the first five days of Genesis 1).

(a) *From the installation of the first humans:* Adam and Eve are the rulers of the newly created world, until they lose this dominion to Satan.

(b) *From the restoration after the Fall:* In Genesis 3:15 (the woman's offspring) and 49:10 (Shiloh), the hope of the kingdom of God begins, as the latter will be resumed again in the "last Adam."

(c) *From David:* David is not only forefather but also model of the coming King; in the great days of David and his son Solomon, the conditions in Israel were a foreshadowing of the Messianic kingdom (see §2.2.3).

(d) *From Jesus' birth:* Where the King is, there is the kingdom. The moment he is born—explicitly as the "King of the Jews"—the kingdom in a certain sense is a fact, even though nothing of it can as yet be perceived.

(e) *From the beginning of Jesus' ministry:* Subsequently, the kingdom becomes manifest in the power of the King that is displayed, namely, first and foremost in the spiritual world: he casts out demons. The kingdom of God is emerging, and the kingdom of Satan has to give way. From this, it is apparent that in a certain sense the kingdom has arrived.

(f) *From Jesus' glorification:* The kingdom of God develops even more clearly after the King has died, has risen, has been taken to heaven, and has been glorified at God's right hand as the One who has all authority in heaven and on earth (Matt. 28:18), and subsequently pours out the Holy Spirit (Acts 2): it is a kingdom of *power* (Acts 1:6–8; 1 Cor. 4:20; Heb. 6:5).

(g) *From Jesus' parousia:* Ultimately, the kingdom will be manifested at its highest when the King returns, establishes peace and justice, and erects his empire in power and glory.

*Epilogue:* The new heavens and the new earth.

## 2.4.2 Seven Proofs

Second, I point to another series of seven points: the proofs that Jesus gives, in addition to his verbal preaching, for the fact that in him the kingdom of God has really arrived. Here I am following Marc Saucy,[52] though I offer my own presentation and elaboration.

(1) Jesus' words find their accurate counterpart in his deeds, his *miraculous signs,* which confirm the Old Testament announcement of the Messiah. Heinz Held distinguishes in Matthew between the "Messiah of the words" and the "Messiah of the acts";[53] thus, Jesus' words in Matthew 5–7 (the Sermon on the Mount) immediately precede an orderly summary of a number of his miraculous signs in Matthew 8–9. In Mark 1:22, the people were astonished at Jesus' teaching, and in verse 27 amazed about his miraculous power. Words and deeds each in their own way testify to the same matter: the kingdom of God has arrived in the person of Jesus.[54]

(2) Matthew places much emphasis on the fact that Jesus fulfilled the Old Testament *Messianic prophecies,* and this comes to expression especially in his miracles.

---

52. Saucy (1997, 321–28).
53. H. J. Held in Bornkamm *et al.* (1963, 246).
54. Cf. Kallas (1961, 77).

For instance, compare Isaiah 26:19, 35:4-6, 42:18, and 61:1-2 with Jesus raising the dead (Luke 7:11-17; 8:40-42, 49-56; John 11:1-44). Compare Isaiah 29:18, 35:5, and 42:18 with his healings of the deaf and the blind (also compare the rendering of Isa. 61:1 in Luke 4:19), and 35:6 with his healings of the paralytic and the cripple. See more generally Isaiah 53:4-5, "Surely he has borne our griefs [CEB, WEB, etc.: sickness] and carried our sorrows . . . with his wounds we are healed" (quoted in Matt. 8:17).[55]

(3) In Jesus' words as well as deeds, the *Holy Spirit* was active: "[I]f it is by the Spirit [cf. Luke 11:20, finger] of God that I cast out demons, then the kingdom of God has come upon you" (Matt. 12:28). This Spirit is also promised to his followers, the subjects of God's kingdom: "[H]e who is coming after me is mightier than I, whose sandals I am not worthy to carry. He will baptize you with the Holy Spirit and fire" (3:11); "the heavenly Father will give the Holy Spirit [cf. Matt. 7:11, good things] to those who ask him" (Luke 11:13).

(4) Jesus' miracles point forward specifically to the Messianic age, among other ways by deliberately performing many miracles on the Sabbath (Mark 3:1-6; Luke 13:10-17; 14:1-6; John 5:1-18; 9:1-14),[56] the harbinger *par excellence* of the Messianic era of peace and harmony. Jesus links his miraculous deeds with the announcement of the "year of the Lord's favor" (Luke 4:19; cf. Isa. 61:2). Not only each seventh day, but also each seventh month (the holy month of the autumn festivals), and each seventh sabbatical year (the year of jubi-

---

55. See Betz and Grimm (1977, 31).
56. Cf. Betz and Grimm (1977, 34-35).

lee), point to the Messianic kingdom of peace and justice. In chapters 12 and 13, we will consider the view that the Messianic kingdom itself is the seventh of a series of redemptive-historical epochs.

(5) Jesus performs his miracles and other deeds not only as signs but also as tokens of his compassion (Matt. 9:36; 14:14; 15:32; 20:34 [cf. 18:27]; Mark 1:41; 9:22; Luke 7:13 [cf. 10:33; 15:20]).[57] This compassion (mercy, loving-kindness, Heb. *chesed*) is an essential feature of the coming kingdom: "'In overflowing anger for a moment I hid my face from you, but with everlasting love I will have compassion on you,' says the Lord, your Redeemer" (Isa. 54:8). "Incline your ear, and come to me; hear, that your soul may live; and I will make with you an everlasting covenant, my steadfast, sure love [NKJV: my sure mercies; Heb. *chasde*] for David" (55:3). "You will show faithfulness to Jacob and steadfast love [one word: *chesed*] to Abraham, as you have sworn to our fathers from the days of old" (Mic. 7:20).

(6) In Jesus' words and deeds, we encounter a continual conflict with, as well as triumph over, the kingdom of Satan (see §1.6), entirely as the Old Testament had predicted: "[H]e shall strike the earth with the rod of his mouth, and with the breath of his lips he shall kill the wicked [one]" (Isa. 11:4; cf. 2 Thess. 2:8). "On that day the Lord will punish the host of heaven, in heaven, and the kings of the earth, on the earth. They will be gathered together as prisoners in a pit; they will be shut up in a prison, and after many days they will be punished" (Isa. 24:21–22; cf. Rev. 20:1). "For the ruthless shall come to nothing and the scoffer cease, and all who watch to do

---

57. Cf. Kelsey (1973, 99).

evil shall be cut off" (Isa. 29:20). "Be strong; fear not! Behold, your God will come with vengeance, with the recompense of God. He will come and save you" (35:4); ". . . to proclaim the year of the LORD's favor, and the day of vengeance of our God" (61:2).

(7) Jesus' words and deeds are addressed to the "pure in heart, for they shall see God" (Matt. 5:8)—a notion linked here with the kingdom of God. Hence the significance of his miracles to the lepers, for they are not so much "healed" as "made clean" (Matt. 8:2-3; 10:8; 11:5; Luke 17:12-17; cf. many times in Lev. 13-14). Jesus' opponents attacked him because he violated various rules for *outward* purity (e.g., Matt. 12:1-8), whereas he attacked *them* because of their *inner* uncleanness (15:11, 18-20; 23:25-27). Sometimes, Jesus' healings were explicitly connected with inner cleansing (9:1-8; John 5:14). Cleansing is a condition for entering the kingdom of God: "'Who among us can dwell with the consuming fire? Who among us can dwell with everlasting burnings?' He who walks righteously and speaks uprightly, who despises the gain of oppressions, who shakes his hands, lest they hold a bribe, who stops his ears from hearing of bloodshed and shuts his eyes from looking on evil. . . . Your eyes will behold the king in his beauty. . . . Behold Zion, the city of our appointed feasts! Your eyes will see Jerusalem, an untroubled habitation" (Isa. 33:14-20; cf. Ps. 15).

## 2.5  The King's Self-Presentation
### 2.5.1  The Son of Man

John the Baptist was the King's herald (Matt. 3:2); that is, he was not the King himself, but he *announced* the

King. Subsequently, however, the striking event took place of Jesus coming forward both as the herald (messenger) of the kingdom and as the King himself. He announced that the kingdom was at hand, and thus proclaimed that his own coming as the King was imminent. Already before that, Matthew 1:1 anticipated this by presenting Jesus from the beginning as the Christ (Messiah, Anointed) and as the Son of David, and thus as the One who was entitled to the throne of David. As the angel Gabriel said, "[T]he Lord God will give to him the throne of his father David" (Luke 1:32; notice that Joseph, Jesus' legal father, was called "son of David," Matt. 1:20).

Moreover, Jesus identified himself by often referring to himself as the "Son of Man" (Greek *huios tou anthrōpou*).[58] In Matthew alone he does so thirty times, with all the Messianic connotations belonging to it.[59] The title "Son of Man" (Hebrew *ben-adam*) must be understood primarily from the Old Testament, especially Daniel 7:13, where we find the Aramaic rendering *bar-enash*, "son of man." Originally, this did not mean anything more than "human being" (thus CEB, ERV, GNT, etc.); here, the term does not yet have the specific meaning that it acquired afterward. Nonetheless we sense immediately that this is not an ordinary human person, and we experience the title this way at other places where it is used in the Bible (cf. Ps. 8:4 [Heb. 2:5]; 80:17).[60]

---

58. See Ouweneel (2007b, §5.3.2), also for the derivation of the expression and further details.
59. See further, Ouweneel (2007b, §§9.1.1, 9.2.3, and 9.4.1, and chapters 13–14).
60. Cf. also the *contrast* with Ps. 144:3, 146:3, and Isa. 51:12, where

"He [Jesus] comes from God and hence establishes the true form of man's being," writes Joseph Ratzinger (pope Benedict XVI).[61] In Daniel 7, this Man of men, this human *par excellence*, came "with the clouds of heaven," and received from God ("the Ancient of Days") "dominion and glory and a kingdom, that all peoples, nations, and languages should serve him; his dominion is an everlasting dominion, which shall not pass away, and his kingdom one that shall not be destroyed" (v. 14).

No wonder that the Jews of old have thought here of the Messiah. The rabbis did sense a certain tension with Zechariah 9:9, though, and wondered: Does the Messiah come with the clouds of heaven, or does he come riding a donkey? Rabbi Joshua explained: "If they [i.e., the Israelites] are meritorious, [the Messiah will come] with the clouds of heaven; if not, lowly and riding upon an ass."[62] Of course, this is a solution arising from embarrassment: where in Scripture do we find such indubitable examples of alternative prophecies?

In the Septuagint, more than in the Targum and in the Greek translation of Theodotion, it is clear that the "Son of Man" does not receive anything less that God's own authority as Judge. It seems that here the idea of a pre-existent Messiah is already implied.[63] Perhaps even

---

it is the human being in his littleness. In Ezek. the term is God's common name for the prophet (perhaps marking him as a type of Christ) (cf. Dan. 8:17).

61. Ratzinger (2007, 334); cf. 335: "The new humanity that comes from God iw what being a disciple of Jesus Christ is all about" (cf. 1 Cor. 15:48-49; Eph. 4:24; Col. 3:9-11).
62. Talmud: Sanhedrin 98a.
63. Hengel (1995, 183-84), and references.

divine features are implied: in verse 13 the Septuagint renders the Hebrew *im* ("with") with the Greek word *epi* ("on," cf. Matt. 24:30; 26:64), which is striking because appearing *on* clouds could normally only be said of God (cf. Ps. 18:11-12; 68:33; 97:2; 104:3; Lam. 3:44; and especially Isa. 19:1).[64]

In Jewish apocalyptic literature, the "Son of Man" developed into an important Messianic figure.[65] In the parables of 1 Enoch, he is the object of the hope of a godly community. He is the chosen one, the righteous one, the representative of God's justice and wisdom, who existed already before the foundation of the world, who enters into the Messianic battle with the evil powers, and emerges as victor (46:3; 48:2; 62:7; etc.). The texts clearly tie in with Daniel 7, but also with the psalms and prophets (especially Isaiah), without the expression "Son of Man" having developed into a Messianic *title* yet. Rabbi Akiva seems to have clearly identified the Son of Man in Daniel 7:13 with the Davidic Messiah; there are more such suggestions in the rabbinic tradition.[66]

### 2.5.2 The Messiah

In liberal theology, it is rather common to assert that, during the time of the book of Acts and afterward, the "preacher" (Jesus) became the "preached one."[67] In this case, this would mean that Jesus proclaimed the king-

---

64. This notion already occurred in Ugarit: Baal was called there the "Rider on the Clouds"; see Schwemer (2001, 443-588).
65. Zwiep (2003, 17-31); Knight (2004, 117-20).
66. Chag. 14a par. Sanh. 38b (see Strack [1986, 1:238; 4:871, 1104-1105]); also cf. Hengel (1995, 194-95).
67. See, e.g., Den Heyer (2003, 91).

dom but his apostles proclaimed the King. It is very questionable whether such a distinction is tenable. Notice, for instance, the connections that Jesus presents between the kingdom and himself as the Son of Man (Matt. 10:23; 13:41; 16:27-28; 19:28) (although I do realize that such passages are often dismissed as inventions of the Gospel writers or the early church). Sometimes Jesus even *calls* the kingdom that of the Son of Man (13:41), that is, *his own* kingdom: God's kingdom is the kingdom of God's Anointed One (cf. Rev. 12:10, "God and his Christ"). A little later (Matt. 13:43), he called that same kingdom the "kingdom of their Father," that is, the Father of the righteous (cf. 26:29, "*my* Father's kingdom").

One way of being able to assert that from the preacher Jesus became the preached one is to claim, as Wilhelm Wrede did, that the passages in which Jesus presents himself as the Messiah, the anointed King of Israel, are not authentic.[68] Thus one is caught in a circular argument: simply dismiss all the evidence that contradicts your thesis! Many expositors believe that, generally speaking, there are no good reasons to doubt the authenticity of the passages concerned.[69]

I already mentioned Jesus' statement to Pilate: "I am a king" (John 18:37). The high priest Caiaphas interrogated him under oath: "'I adjure you by the living God, tell us if you are the Christ [i.e., Messiah], the Son of God.' Jesus said to him, 'You have said so. But I tell you, from now on you will see the Son of Man seated at the right hand of Power [Ps. 110:1] and coming on the clouds of heaven [Dan. 7:13].' Then the high priest tore his

---

68. Wrede (1901); see R. A. Guelich in Green *et al.* (1992, 521-22).
69. See Ouweneel (2007b, 147-48).

robes and said, 'He has uttered blasphemy. What further witnesses do we need? You have now heard his blasphemy. What is your judgment?' They answered, 'He deserves death.' Then they spit in his face and struck him. And some slapped him, saying, 'Prophesy to us, you Christ [i.e., Messiah]! Who is it that struck you?'" (Matt. 26:63-68).

Please note carefully that Jesus' answer—"You have said so"—is *not* evasive. This is evident from the fact that (a) the parallel (presumably oldest) version plainly says, "I am" (Mark 14:62) ("you have said so" means "it is as you say"; cf. Luke 22:70); (b) he added immediately the title "Son of Man" with clear reference to himself (at least this is how the high priest understood it, and correctly so); (c) the Sanhedrin sentenced him to death on the basis of Jesus' confession; (d) they adopted his confession by mockingly addressing him as "Messiah"; and (e) they accused him before Pilate of having made himself the Son of God (John 19:7).

### 2.5.3 Jesus' Claims

There are more New Testament passages that shed light on the very important title "Son of Man," and on the way Jesus appropriated this title, and thus Messiahship. When, for instance, Nathanael said to Jesus, "Rabbi, you are the Son of God! You are the King of Israel!" (John 1:49), Jesus did not contradict this but added: "You will see greater things than these. . . . [Y]ou will see heaven opened, and the angels of God ascending and descending on the Son of Man" (vv. 50-51). In this way, he made this title at least as lofty as that of "Son of God," so that the dignity of the "Son of Man" (Ps. 8:4; cf. Heb. 2:6) is not less than that of "Son of God" in the sense of Psalm 2:7 (cf. Heb. 1:5).[70]

When the Samaritan woman said to Jesus, "I know that Messiah is coming (he who is called Christ). When he comes, he will tell us all things," Jesus responded, "I who speak to you am he" (John 4:25-26). When John the Baptist asked Jesus: "Are you the one who is to come, or shall we look for another?" (Matt. 11:3), Jesus pointed to the Messianic signs that had occurred as evidence of his Messiahship. Jesus did not contradict Peter, when the latter addressed him as "the Christ [i.e., Messiah], the Son of the living God" (16:16). On the contrary, he explained that Peter could have known this important fact only through divine revelation (v. 17). The prohibition of trumpeting around that he was the Messiah (v. 20) did not imply that Jesus denied being such, but only that he did not want to throw pearls before pigs (cf. 7:6).

With obvious reference to himself Jesus challengingly asked the spiritual leaders: "What do you think about the Christ [i.e., Messiah]? Whose son is he?" (22:42). He also called himself his disciples' "Lord and Teacher" (John 13:14), and said, "But you are not to be called rabbi, for you have one teacher, and you are all brothers. . . . Neither be called instructors, for you have one instructor, the Christ" (Matt. 23:8, 10). In the Olivet Discourse, he warned: "[M]any will come in my name, saying, 'I am the Christ,' and they will lead many astray" (24:5). After his resurrection he said in reference to himself: "Was it not necessary that the Christ should suffer these things and enter into his glory?" (Luke 24:26). To those who want to avoid a circular argu-

---

70. Kelly (1966, 36).

ment, by assuming that all these self-references by Jesus to his Messiahship *a priori* cannot be authentic, all these passages speak a clear language.

Interestingly, the demons do not even need explicit statements by Jesus: "Now when the sun was setting, all those who had any who were sick with various diseases brought them to him, and he laid his hands on every one of them and healed them. And demons also came out of many, crying, 'You are the Son of God!' But he rebuked them and would not allow them to speak, *because they knew that he was the Christ*" (Luke 24:40–41). Some people did not need Jesus' affirmation either: "One of the criminals who were hanged railed at him, saying, 'Are you not the Christ [Messiah]? Save yourself and us!' But the other rebuked him, saying, 'Do you not fear God, since you are under the same sentence of condemnation? And we indeed justly, for we are receiving the due reward of our deeds; but this man has done nothing wrong.' And he said, 'Jesus, remember me when you [as the King!] come into your kingdom'" (23:39–42).

## 2.6 Recapitulation

### 2.6.1 Whose Kingdom?

In summary, the kingdom of *God* is God's dominion over heaven and earth, not only in a general sense (see already Exod. 15:18) but very specifically: its essence is the world dominion that he, after the fall of the first Adam, entrusts to the last Adam—all things are put under his feet (Gen. 1:26, 28; 1 Cor. 15:45; Heb. 2:8; cf. Ps. 8:6–7; 1 Cor. 15:27; Eph. 1:22). The fact that it is *God's* kingdom is just as essential as the fact that it is a kingdom entrusted to *Man*.

Jonathan Knight believes that the King of the kingdom that Jesus announced is God.[71] Indeed, this is often the case (Matt. 5:35; 6:10; 13:43; 18:23; 22:6; 26:29), but equally often it is Jesus himself who is the King (2:2; 13:41; 16:28; 20:21; 21:5; 25:34; 27:11, 29, 37, 42). The expression "kingdom of God" does not always necessarily mean that God is the King but it does mean that he is *in charge* of the kingdom, and anoints over it the person he chooses: David and the Davidic kings as precursors, and finally the last Adam. In answer to Nebuchadnezzar, Daniel gives the general principle: "[T]he Most High rules the kingdom of men and gives it to whom he will and sets over it the lowliest of men" (Dan. 4:17; cf. Zech. 9:9, "Behold, your king is coming to you; righteous and having salvation is he, *humble* . . .").

Thus, the kingdom is and remains *God's* kingdom, even though it is sometimes called the kingdom of the Son of Man (Matt. 13:41). In that case, it is the kingdom of God as put under the feet of the Son of Man (cf. Ps. 8:4-6; Heb. 2:6-9). Sometimes it carries a double name: "the kingdom of the Anointed One and God" (thus literally in Eph. 5:5), that is, the kingdom of God that he has entrusted to the anointed King of Israel but that remains *his* kingdom. It is "the kingdom of our Lord and of his Christ [Anointed One]" (Rev. 11:15; an allusion to Ps. 2:2), that is, the kingdom of our Lord God (YHWH), which he has placed under the authority of his Anointed One (cf. Rev. 12:10, "the kingdom of our God and the authority of his Christ").

Psalm 2 is of crucial importance here (cf. Heb. 2:5): "The kings of the earth set themselves, and the rulers

---

71. Knight (2004, 103).

take counsel together, *against the* LORD *and against his Anointed,* saying, 'Let us burst their bonds apart and cast away their cords from us.' He who sits in the heavens laughs; the Lord holds them in derision. Then he will speak to them in his wrath, and terrify them in his fury, saying, 'As for me, I have set[72] my King on Zion, my holy hill.' I will tell of the decree: The LORD said to me, 'You are my Son; today I have begotten you. Ask of me, and I will make the nations your heritage, and the ends of the earth your possession. You shall break them with a rod of iron and dash them in pieces like a potter's vessel" (Ps. 2:2-9).

The kingdom of God is the kingdom that belongs to, and is actually bestowed upon, the Anointed One, and this is in fact the case already from the *protevangelium* of Genesis 3:15. It is the kingdom whose authority was placed in the hands of Christ already during his ministry on earth, and that, as witnessed to by all the Messianic signs and miracles, had unmistakably arrived (see again Matt. 10:7-8; 12:28). It is the kingdom in which, after his resurrection (and in fact after his glorification), he receives all authority in heaven and on earth (Matt. 28:18). Until his parousia this rule remains invisible. But after his parousia on the clouds of heaven, he will actually, and for all visibly (Rev. 1:7), *exercise* all power.[73]

## 2.6.2 Ambiguity

During Jesus' ministry on earth, a certain ambiguity existed in the notion of the kingdom: the kingdom was there, namely, in the sense of (d) (from Jesus' birth) and

---

72. See chapter 1, n47.
73. Knight (2004, 101).

(e) (from the beginning of Jesus' ministry), and at the same time it was not yet there, namely, in the sense of (f) (from Jesus' glorification) and (g) (from Jesus' parousia) (see §2.4.1 for the explanation behind the letters used). As a consequence, Jesus kept speaking of the kingdom in the present as well as in the future sense. Today, this ambiguity still exists: the kingdom is there, namely, in the sense of (d), (e), and (f), and it is not yet there, namely, in the sense of (g).

As clearly as Jesus spoke of the kingdom in its present meaning, so surely did he speak of the kingdom in its future meaning,[74] especially when he linked the kingdom with the Father: "... at the end of the age ... the righteous will shine like the sun in the kingdom of their Father" (Matt. 13:40, 43). This is an allusion to Daniel 12:3 (Septuagint: "shine like the lightbearers/stars of heaven"). At another place Jesus said, "I will not drink again of this fruit of the vine until that day when I drink it new with you in my Father's kingdom" (26:29).

In light of the foregoing, we see one thing clearly: where Jesus is, there is the kingdom, and *vice versa*. From his first presentation on earth, the two have been inseparably linked together. Where Jesus stands among the people, there God's kingdom is in their midst (Luke 17:21). When, in Luke 19:29, Jesus speaks of those who have left everything "for the sake of the kingdom of God," this is the same as what we find in the parallel text: "for *my* sake" (Mark 10:29), or "for my *name's* sake" (Matt. 19:29).[75] Notice as well the link between the King

---

74. This has been emphasized by Ladd (1974b, 218), Hoekema (1979, 51), and many others.
75. Hoekema (1979, 43).

and the kingdom in the following statements: Philip "preached good news about the kingdom of God and the name of Jesus Christ" (Acts 8:12); Paul was "proclaiming the kingdom of God and teaching about the Lord Jesus Christ" (28:31). Johan A. Heyns says it beautifully, "[T]he center of Scripture is God's kingdom, and the center of the center is Jesus Christ."[76]

In §3.2 we will see that the kingdom as Jesus brought it hardly seemed to satisfy Old Testament expectations. In other words, the great majority of the Old Testament predictions concerning the kingdom still have to be fulfilled. However, "hardly" does not mean "not." Also during Jesus' life on earth, some of the royal prophecies were already fulfilled. Here are seven examples (partly of a typological nature), four from Matthew, and three from John.

(a) *The Virgin Birth of the King:* "Therefore the LORD himself will give you [plural, i.e., the royal house of David!] a sign. Behold, the virgin shall conceive and bear a [royal!] son, and shall call his name Immanuel" (Isa. 7:14; fulfillment: Matt. 1:22-23).

(b) *The Birthplace of the King:* "But you, O Bethlehem Ephrathah, who are too little to be among the clans of Judah, from you shall come forth for me one who is to be *ruler* in Israel, whose coming forth is from of old, from ancient days" (Mic. 5:2; fulfillment: Matt. 2:1-11).

(c) *The Dawning of the Light:* In Matthew 4:15-16 ("The land of Zebulun and the land of Naphtali, the way of the sea, beyond the Jordan, Galilee of the Gentiles—the people dwelling in darkness have seen a great light, and for those dwelling in the region and shadow of death, on

---

76. Heyns (1988, 28).

them a light has dawned"), Isaiah 9:1–2 is seen as fulfilled in Jesus and his ministry, and thus indirectly verse 6 as well: "For to us a child is born, to us a son is given; and the *government* shall be upon his shoulder, and his name shall be called Wonderful Counselor, Mighty God, Everlasting Father, *Prince* of Peace."

(d) *Jesus Entering Jerusalem on a Donkey:* "Rejoice greatly, O daughter of Zion! Shout aloud, O daughter of Jerusalem! Behold, your king is coming to you; righteous and having salvation is he, humble and mounted on a donkey, on a colt, the foal of a donkey" (Zech. 9:9; fulfillment: Matt. 21:1–9).

(e) *Jesus Betrayed by a Friend:* King David said (possibly thinking of Ahithophel, 2 Sam. 15:31): "Even my close friend in whom I trusted, who ate my bread, has lifted his heel against me" (Ps. 41:9; fulfillment: John 13:18).

(f) *Jesus Hated by His Own people:* King David said, "More in number than the hairs of my head are those who hate me without cause" (Ps. 69:4; fulfillment: John 15:25).

(g) *Jesus' Garments Divided Among His Enemies:* King David said, "[T]hey divide my garments among them, and for my clothing they cast lots" (Ps. 22:18; fulfillment: John 19:24).

## 2.7 Pilgrims of the Kingdom

### 2.7.1 The Goal of Israel's Journey

Let me return once more to Exodus 15:18, "The LORD will reign [or, will be King, or, is King] forever and ever." Surely this is a general statement concerning the world dominion of God. Yet, it stands in a context that, upon closer consideration, turns out to have an eschatological

*The Hope of the Kingdom*

dimension. We see this especially in verses 13 and 17: "You have led in your steadfast love the people whom you have redeemed; you have guided them by your strength to your holy abode. . . . . You will bring them in and plant them on your own mountain [NIV, etc.: the mountain of your inheritance], the place, O Lord, which you have made for your abode, the sanctuary, O Lord, which your hands have established."

The two verses quoted speak of God's "holy abode" or the "sanctuary." Compare verse 2 as well (KJ21, BRG): "I will prepare Him a habitation" (Heb. *veanwēhu*; cf. Targum, Rashi, Sforno). However, modern translations (even NKJV) translate: "I will praise him," or something similar.[77]

In verse 13, we could view the phrase "you have led" (Hebrew *nehalta*) as a prophetic past tense, which in fact refers to the future (cf. Jude 1:14 NABRE, "Behold, the Lord has come with his countless holy ones"). In Exodus 15, the people had not yet been led to God's "holy abode" at all. In verse 17 (*tebiēmo vetittaʿēmo*, "you will bring them in and plant them"), the verb tenses used in the translations differ: future tense (KJ21, etc.), present tense (GNT), and past tense (CEB, etc.). Here again, the meaning is a future one: it would be centuries yet before Israel would arrive at God's "holy abode," his "own mountain" (Zion), his "abode, the sanctuary," that is, the temple at Jerusalem, whose construction had to wait until the days of Solomon.[78] The mountain

---

77. See Ouweneel (2007a, 251).
78. Not the tabernacle, as Dennett (n.d., ad loc.) sees it, for Israel was not on its way to there.

that is God's inheritance is Mount Moriah (2 Chron. 3:1), often called Zion.[79]

Already during Moses' life, this place was known principally as the place that the Lord would "choose out of all your tribes to put his name and make his habitation there" (so many times between Deut. 12:5 and 31:11),[80] and that the people would have to seek (12:5). The only one who really seems to have sought and actually found it was David, who was truly concerned about the fate of the ark of the covenant. Notice the twofold appearance of the word "find" in Psalm 132:3-5: "'I will not enter my house... until I *find* a place for the LORD, a dwelling place for the Mighty One of Jacob [i.e., the temple].' Behold, we heard of it [i.e., the ark] in Ephrathah; we *found* it in the fields of Jaar." Jaar is the singular of Jearim, which we find in the name Kiriath-jearim, the place where the ark was being kept at the time, and from where David fetched it (1 Sam. 6:21; 7:1-2; 1 Chron. 13:5-6; 2 Chron. 1:4). David's diligently "finding" the ark became the prelude to the building of the temple by his son, Solomon.

## 2.7.2 Israel On Its Pilgrimage

The initiative for building the temple indeed came from king David (2 Sam. 7:1-17). As a consequence, the temple is forever closely linked with the Davidic kingship (cf. Ps. 132). Hebrew *hêkal* means both "(royal) palace"

---

79. "Zion" is a confusing concept: it is (a) the southeast hill in Jerusalem: the mountain of the "city of David" (2 Sam. 5:7; etc.), (b) the northeast hill: the temple mount (Ps. 9:11; 20:2; etc.), or (c) at present the southwest hill (with the Zion Gate).
80. Kaiser (1990, 395).

and "temple" (cf. Ps. 29:9, "temple" in ESV and many others, "palace" in the Dutch NBG-translation, the French translation of Louis Segond, and others). Within the context of Exodus 15, it is not far-fetched to conclude that Israel will "arrive" in the true spiritual sense, not in the book of Joshua, but only in the days when it will enjoy both the blessing of the Davidic kingdom and that of the temple of Solomon; in typological language: the blessing of the true Melchizedek, the King-Priest (cf. Gen. 14:18; Ps. 110; Heb. 5:6, 10; 6:20; 7:1–3).

The people were on their way to this goal as *pilgrims*, for a pilgrim is someone who undertakes a holy journey to a holy place, that is, a place where he can meet his God. Normally, when we think of Israel as a "pilgrim nation," we think of the three great festivals for which all men had to go up to Jerusalem ("at the Feast of Unleavened Bread, at the Feast of Weeks, and at the Feast of Booths," Deut. 16:16) (cf. Pss. 120–134, "songs of ascent," sometimes rendered as "pilgrim songs"; see also Isa. 30:29; Amos 8:3; Luke 2:42; Exod. 5:1; 10:9; John 12:20; Acts 8:27). However, also the history of Israel, and more broadly, of God's people on earth, bears in its totality a pilgrim character: God's people are en route to the sanctuary of the King-Priest in the Messianic kingdom.

From the passage through the Red Sea, Israel is en route until it arrives at the holy temple under the Davidic kingship. Therefore, Exodus 15:18, about God's kingship, cannot be severed from this future perspective, which at the same time has an eschatological dimension: God's people, also in the present time, are en route as pilgrims, until they arrive in the Messianic kingdom of peace and justice, where the great Davidic King will reign, and the heart of which will be the temple of Ezekiel 40–44 (this will be true, whether this temple is taken in a literal or in a figurative sense [81]). This is what the prophets speak of: "Here is the man whose name is the Branch [i.e., the Messiah], and he will branch out from his place and build the temple of the Lord. It is he who will build the temple of the Lord, and he will be clothed with majesty and will sit and rule on his throne. And he will be a priest on his throne. And there will be harmony between the two" (Zech. 6:12–13).

"And foreigners who bind themselves to the Lord to minister to him, to love the name of the Lord, and to be his servants, all who keep the Sabbath without desecrating it and who hold fast to my covenant—these I will bring to my holy mountain and give them joy in my house of prayer. Their burnt offerings and sacrifices will be accepted on my altar; for my house will be called a house of prayer for all nations" (Isa. 56:6–7).

In an analogous way, the Christian nation is on a pilgrimage to the heavenly Jerusalem. In his *Confessions*, Augustine already took up this theme. Thus he wrote at the end of Book IX: ". . . in the eternal Jerusalem, to which go out the sighs of your pilgrim people, from their exodus until their return to there" (*in aeterna Hierusalem, cui suspirat peregrinatio populi tui ab exitu usque ad reditum*).[82] In Book X.4 he uses the phrase "pilgrims with me" (*mecum peregrinorum*).

In a magnificent way, John Bunyan has taken up this theme in his *The Pilgrim's Progress*, in which he described the life of the Christian, who is on his way, not

---

81. See Ouweneel (2012a, §13.4.1).
82. www9.georgetown.edu/faculty/jod/latinconf/9.html.

to the kingdom of God, which arrives at the parousia of Christ, but to Paradise.[83]

### 2.7.3 Pilgrim Songs

This theme of the Christian as pilgrim always occupied an important place in Puritanism and Pietism, especially in the hymns. One example is a hymn by Charles Wesley:

> How happy is the pilgrim's lot,
> How free from anxious care and thought,
> From worldly hope and fear!
> Confined to neither court nor cell,
> His soul disdains on earth to dwell,
> He only sojourns here.

Or this one by Wesley:

> Ye pilgrims—partners in distress,
> Who, travelling through the wilderness,
> Are pressing onward still;
> A while forget your griefs and fear,
> And look beyond this vale of tears,
> To the celestial hill.

This one is by John N. Darby:

> 'Tis the treasure I've found in His love
> That has made me a pilgrim below;
> And 'tis there, when I reach Him above
> As I'm known, all His fullness I'll know.

John Newton's *Pilgrim's Song* begins as follows:

> From Egypt, lately freed
> By the Redeemer's grace,
> A rough and thorny path we tread,

---

83. Bunyan (2003).

> In hopes to see his face.

William J. Kirkpatrick sang:

> Weary pilgrim on life's pathway,
> Struggling on beneath thy load,
> Hear these words of consolation:
> "Cast thy burden on the Lord."

Finally we hear Frances R. Havergal:

> And often by its shady course
> To pilgrim hearts be brought
> The quiet and refreshment of
> An upward-pointing thought;
> Till, blending with the broad bright stream
> Of sanctified endeavor,
> God's glory be its ocean home,
> The end it seeketh ever.

# Chapter 3
# The Parables of the Kingdom (I)

*Then the disciples came and said to him,*
  *"Why do you speak to them in*
  *parables?"*
*And he answered them,*
*"To you it has been given to know the*
  *secrets of the kingdom of heaven,*
  *but to them it has not been given. . .*
*This is why I speak to them in parables,*
  *because seeing they do not see,*
*and hearing they do not hear,*
*nor do they understand."*

***Summary:*** *It is remarkable that, to a great extent, Jesus' instruction concerning the kingdom of God (or "of heaven," which is basically the same) was given in the form of parables: similitudes in which various aspects of the kingdom* *were compared to common things of life: a sower, a fisherman, a woman making bread, a king with servants. The parables elucidate (a) the character of the King, (b) the character of both his true and false servants, (c) the character of serving the King, (d) the differences between the kingdom in its present form and the kingdom in its future form (parables about the "end of the [present] age"). The latter feature is characteristic of Matthew; Luke places greater emphasis in the parables on the moral aspects of the kingdom. It is important to understand the typical kingdom character of the parables in Matthew, also in relation to the Messianic Torah. Finally, the false versus the true sons of the kingdom may represent the majority of Israel versus believing Gentiles, but also the false (Gentile) followers of the King versus the true (Gentile) followers of the King.*

## 3.1 Matthew's Parables

### 3.1.1 Introduction

WHEN WE CONSIDER THE four offices and personal glories of Jesus Christ, it can be well defended that Matthew is the Gospel of the King, just as Mark is the Gospel of the Servant or Prophet, Luke the Gospel of the Priest, but also of the Son of Man, and John the Gospel of the Son of God.[1] When we consider the four "living creatures" in Ezekiel 1:15-25 and Revelation 4:7, it seems to me that the lion refers to Matthew—the lion is the king among the animals (Prov. 19:12; Ezek. 32:2)—the steadily toiling (bull) calf to Mark (Jesus the obedient Servant), the man to Luke (Jesus the Son of Man), and the flying eagle to John (Jesus the Son of God descending

---

1. See Ouweneel (2007b, 476-77).

*The Parables of the Kingdom (I)*

from heaven).² Although in this study I do refer many times to Mark, Luke, and John, Matthew is our first learning material if we wish to understand God's kingdom in some more depth.

To this end, we will pay much attention to the parables in Matthew because, apart from Jesus's direct kingdom teaching, this is the most important form in which Jesus expounds the principles of the kingdom.³ I will view the parables in Matthew (the kingdom Gospel) within the framework of a moderate dispensationalist, premillennialist paradigm (see chapters 11 and 12 below).⁴ If we say that the Matthew parables often have a dispensationalist character—in contrast to the moral character of the parables in Luke—we mean that (a)

---

2. I realize that the order I give here differs from the traditional one, in which Matthew corresponds with the man, Mark with the lion, Luke with the calf, and John with the eagle; see Ouweneel (2007b, 499 n16; also 1998, 306–307).

3. Some special works on the parables include: R. C. Trench, *Notes on the Parables* (www.davidcox.com.mx /library/T/Trench%20 -%20Parables%20 (b).pdf); further (works with which I am especially sympathetic are in italic): Noordmans (1935); Baarslag (1940); Brouwer (1953); Dodd (1961); Schippers (1962); Perrin (1963); Petzoldt (1984); *Lockyer (1988)*; Scott (1989); Wenham (1989); Lambrecht (1992); K. R. Snodgrass in Green *et al.* (1992, 591–601: "Parable"); *Pentecost (1998)*; Barclay (1999); Jones (1999); Longenecker (2000); Harnisch (2001); Hultgren (2002); Jeremias (2003); Münch (2004); Schottroff (2006); Snodgrass (2008); Zimmermann (2008); Thielicke (2015). Works dealing especially with the Jewish roots of the parables include: Flusser (1981); Young (1998). Some commentaries on Matthew that correspond most with my view: Kelly (1896); Grant (1897); Gaebelein (1910); Mauro (1919); Walvoord (1974); in what follows, I will incorporate their discussions without making repeated reference to them.

4. Also see Ouweneel (2012a).

some of them describe the character of the kingdom after the rejection of the King, (b) others describe its transference from Israel to the Gentile world (the "present age"), and (c) others describe the present age in relation to the age to come.

At this point I will not be entering extensively into the history of the interpretation of the parables.[5] I will simply refer to Adolf Jülicher, who has been called the father of the modern interpretation of Jesus' parables.[6] In reaction to an unrestrained allegorizing of the parables, he fell into the other extreme by rejecting all allegorizing, even the interpretations of his parables that Jesus himself gave, and by reducing them to general moral life lessons.[7] However this may be, this has given rise to an entirely new and extensive investigation of the parables (see note 3).

From the further history of the parabolic interpretation I mention especially Eta Linnemann (1926-2009). Her work is never lacking in historiographies of parable interpretation because of her highly praised dissertation on the parables (1961), written along the lines set out by Rudolf Bultmann and Ernst Fuchs.[8] In 1978, however, she underwent a radical conversion,[9] after which she abjured the historical-critical method alto-

---

5. For this, see Jones (1999, 1-19); K. R. Snodgrass in Longenecker (2000, 3-29); see further, Erlemann (1999); Harnisch (2001); Müller *et al.* (2002).
6. Jülicher (1910).
7. On this, cf. Ridderbos (1962, 121-23).
8. Linnemann (1966); regarding her view, see a general kingdom study like that of Saucy (1997, 51-55).
9. See about this, Ouweneel (2005b, 32-37).

gether, and insisted that all her earlier books be destroyed. Not long before her death she described her new theological views.[10]

## 3.1.2 Survey

Parables are stories by Jesus in which he compares (fictional) events of daily life with the kingdom of God in order to explain to us certain principles and aspects of the kingdom. What the parable and the kingdom have in common is called the *tertium comparationis*.[11] The other part of Jesus' kingdom teaching in Matthew consists of five central sermons of Jesus that have been recorded. These sermons can easily be discerned because they always close with these words (more or less): "And when Jesus finished these sayings . . . ."[12] Because of the parallel that Matthew draws implicitly between Moses and Jesus as the "new Moses" (Lawgiver), these five sermons have been compared to the five books of Moses; they form, as it were, the "new Torah" of the "new Moses."[13] With each sermon I enumerate Jesus' parables, which in Matthew are basically *always* kingdom parables.

(a) Matthew 5–7 (the Sermon on the Mount: the "constitution" of the kingdom; closing formula: 7:28; the parallel is with the Torah as Moses had received it on another Mount: Sinai).

---

10. Linnemann (1999, 2007).
11. The tertium comparationis (Latin: "the third [part] of the comparison") is that quality shared by the two things being compared.
12. The most important sermon in Matthew (beside the five mentioned) that is *not* closed this way, and thus stands apart, is 23:1–39.
13. See extensively, Ouweneel (2016c, especially §7.4.3).

*Parable:* (1) the wise man and the foolish man (7:24–27).[14]

(b) Matthew 10 (the sending out of the apostles, warnings against persecutions, not peace but the sword; closing formula: 11:1; there is a certain parallel with the powerful testimony that Israel's exodus meant for the nations: Exod. 15:14–16; Lev. 26:45; cf. 1 Kgs. 8:53; this testimony brought fear on the nations, the gospel brings joy to the nations).

*Parables:* none.

*Interim parable:* (2) the fluting and wailing children (11:16–17).

(c) Matthew 13 (systematic kingdom teaching; closing formula: 13:53).

*Parables:*
(3) the sower (vv. 1–9, 19–23);
(4) the wheat and the weeds (vv. 24–30, 36–43);
(5) the mustard seed (vv. 31–32);
(6) the leaven (v. 33);
(7) the hidden treasure (v. 44);
(8) the pearl of great value (vv. 45–46);
(9) the net (vv. 47–50);
(10) new and old treasures (vv. 51–52).

*Interim parable:* (11) pollution (15:11).[15]

(d) Matthew 18 (a treatise on worthy subjects of the kingdom, which includes church discipline; closing for-

---

14. Notice the Greek key word *homoioō*, "compare with" or "be (made) like," in Matt. 7:24, 26, which we find also in 11:16; 13:24, 31, 33, 44–45, 47, 52; 18:23; 20:1; 22:2; and 25:1.
15. The Greek key word here is *parabolē* ("parable") in Matt. 15:15; cf. 13:36.

mula: 19:1; here again, there are several parallels with the Mosaic Torah).

*Parables:*
(12) the lost sheep (vv. 10-14);
(13) the unforgiving servant (vv. 21-35).

*Interim parables:*
(14) the laborers in the vineyard (20:1-16);
(15) the two sons (21:28-32);
(16) the unrighteous tenants (21:33-46);
(17) the wedding feast (22:1-14).

(e) Matthew 24-25 (the Olivet Discourse, or, End Time Sermon; closing formula: 26:1; here we find striking paralles—especially as far as the negative aspects are concerned—with what could be called the "end time sermons" by Moses: Lev. 26; Deut. 28 and 33).

*Parables:*
(18) the fig tree (24:32);
(19) the two servants (24:45-51);
(20) the ten virgins (25:1-13);
(21) the talents (25:14-30).

Matthew records a total of twenty-one (three times seven) kingdom parables, including seven related parables (plus one addendum) in 13:1-50 alone.

## 3.1.3 Seven Types

In my view, among the twenty-one parables listed above we may discern seven rather different *types* of parables.

I. Three short kingdom parables of a more general, moral character: (2) the fluting and wailing children, (10) new and old treasures, and (11) pollution (§3.3).

II. Two parables that shed light on the *positive* side of the kingdom only, namely, on the heart of the kingdom, the true righteous ones: (7) the hidden treasure, and (8) the pearl of great value (§3.4).

III. Five parables that in each case portray for us two contrary types of people in God's kingdom as it appeared in Jesus' day, namely, the righteous and the wicked, who, by the way, are also found in the present kingdom (in these contrasts the Messianic Torah comes to light implicitly[16]): (1) the wise man and the foolish man (wise and foolish builders in the kingdom; §3.5.1), (12) the lost sheep (the little ones versus the "religious" ones; §3.5.2), (13) the unforgiving servant (forgiveness-minded versus non-forgiveness-minded; §3.5.3), (14) the laborers in the vineyard (those living by grace and those living by "rights"; §3.5.4), and (15) the two sons (converted obstinate ones and unwilling "religious" ones; §3.5.5). In addition to these, (20) the ten virgins (§4.5.3) and (21) the talents (§4.5.4) could be mentioned, too, but I assign them to a separate category (VII).

IV. Two *transitional* parables, that is, parables of a prophetic nature concerning the transfer of the kingdom from Israel to the Gentiles, as described in the book of Acts: (16) the unrighteous tenants (§4.1), and (17) the wedding feast (§4.2).

V. Three general parables (in fact, also of a prophetic nature) concerning the evil element that would enter the kingdom after Jesus' departure, and would be mixed with the good element: (3) the sower (§4.4.1), (5) the mustard seed (§4.4.4), and (6) the leaven (§§4.4.5, 4.4.6).

---

16. See extensively, Ouweneel (2016c).

VI. Two eschatological parables, in which the intermingling of good and evil within the kingdom debouches in the "end [Greek *synteleia*] of the age" (this is the end of the history of the kingdom in its present form), which will make an end to this intermingling: (4) the wheat and the weeds (§§4.4.2, 4.4.3), and (9) the net (§4.4.7).

VII. Four eschatological parables in Jesus' Olivet Discourse: (18) the fig tree (§4.5.1), (19) the two servants (§4.5.2), (20) the ten virgins (§4.5.3), and (21) the talents (§4.5.4).

It is of essential importance to view these parables within the broader context of Matthew. As I see it, there are especially three things that the apostle wants to make clear to his (especially Jewish) readers in this Gospel.

(a) According to the many prophecies that Jesus of Nazareth has fulfilled, he is unequivocally the Messiah of Israel promised in the Old Testament. No Jew can get around this evidence.

(b) The kingdom of God has not arrived immediately in power and glory because the "sons of the kingdom" (see §4.3.2), that is Israel (8:12), have for the most part rejected their King. Therefore, the kingdom, in its form predicted by the prophets, has been postponed until the parousia of Christ. This means that Matthew's Jewish readers had to get used to the idea of a kingdom whose King is in "another country" (21:33; has gone "on a journey," 25:14; cf. Luke 19:12, "a far country").

(c) In the meantime, it is especially Gentiles who have recognized and acknowledged the identity and the glory of the Messiah. Since the fall of Israel, *these* have become the true "sons of the kingdom" (13:38; see the contrast with 8:12). Already at the outset, we see that Gentiles had an understanding of the Messiah of Israel, but the Jews themselves had almost none. The Jewish leaders did not show any interest in the birth of Jesus, but the wise from the east—Gentiles!—did (2:1-11). The greatest faith was found in certain Gentiles, not in Israel (8:10; 15:28). In 13:38, Jesus says, while interpreting the parable of the wheat and the weeds: "The field is the world," that is, from now on, the seed of the gospel of God's kingdom will be scattered all over the earth: "[T]his gospel of the kingdom will be proclaimed throughout the whole world as a testimony to all nations" (24:14; cf. 28:19, "make disciples of all nations"). It is said of the Messiah that "he will proclaim justice to the Gentiles," and "in his name the Gentiles will hope" (12:18, 21; cf. Isa. 42:1-4). (This does not mean that Matthew idealizes the Gentiles; cf. Matt. 6:7; 10:18; 20:19, 25; 24:9.)

Of course, various other classifications are possible. As an example, I mention the one by Robert Capon, who discerns three kinds of parables: (a) parables of the kingdom (in Matthew, especially those of Matt. 13), (b) parables of grace (in Matthew, e.g., those of Matt. 18), and (c) parables of judgment (in Matthew: 20:1-16; 22:1-14; 24:45-25:30).[17]

## 3.2 Why Parables?
### 3.2.1 The Secrets of the Kingdom

Much of Jesus' kingdom teaching was addressed to all his listeners, but many of them did not understand

---

17. Capon (2002).

what he was saying. There were basically two causes of this incapacity. First, if a person is not born again, he will not be able to "see" (spiritually discern) the kingdom with the enlightened eyes of his heart (cf. Eph. 1:18). By emphasizing this, Jesus cut off at the root Nicodemus' "we know" (John 3:1-5): a person does not know anything about divine things, including the kingdom of God, unless he is born again. In other words, one can know divine things—in the true sense of the word—only because of his new nature and the enlightenment by the Holy Spirit.

Second, Jesus made it even more difficult for his hearers by giving much of his kingdom teaching in the form of parables. At face value, we might think that Jesus told parables to make things more easily understandable, just like the stories many pastors tell in their sermons. However, in fact Jesus made things more difficult. This is explained as follows (Matt. 13:10-17, 34-35): "Then the disciples came and said to him, 'Why do you speak to them in parables?' And he answered them, 'To you it has been given to know the secrets of the kingdom of heaven, but to them it has not been given. For to the one who has, more will be given, and he will have an abundance, but from the one who has not, even what he has will be taken away. This is why I speak to them in parables, because seeing they do not see, and hearing they do not hear, nor do they understand. Indeed, in their case the prophecy of Isaiah is fulfilled that says: "'You will indeed hear but never understand, and you will indeed see but never perceive.' For this people's heart has grown dull, and with their ears they can barely hear, and their eyes they have closed, lest they should see with their eyes and hear with their ears and understand with their heart and turn, and I would heal them." [Isa. 6:9–10; cf. Jer. 5:21]. But blessed are your eyes, for they see, and your ears, for they hear. For truly, I say to you, many prophets and righteous people longed to see what you see, and did not see it, and to hear what you hear, and did not hear it.' . . . All these things Jesus said to the crowds in parables; indeed, he said nothing to them without a parable. This was to fulfill what was spoken by the prophet: 'I will open my mouth in parables; I will utter what has been hidden since the foundation of the world' [Ps. 78:2]."

So Jesus often gave parables to *conceal* things! Herman Ridderbos says of this, "Jesus' speaking in parables has a two-fold effect: on the one hand it is a revelation, on the other it veils something."[18] To Jesus' followers, the parables had a revealing effect because they understood a parable right away, or because it was explained to them. To his opponents and non-committed listeners, the parables had a concealing effect, not because the hearers did not understand anything of it—several times we should say: on the contrary (e.g., Matt. 21:45; John 10:36–37)—but because they did not accept the parables with their hearts in order to grasp their spiritual meaning.

Just before Matthew 13, Jesus had made a distinction between those who, both literally and figuratively, were standing "outside" (the non-disciples and the not-yet-disciples), and those who did the will of his Father, that is, the true disciples (12:46–50). Only the latter are further instructed as to the "secrets" (NKJV, NASB, etc.: "mysteries," i.e., hidden things) of the kingdom. Even in the Sermon on the Mount we already find this distinction: "Seeing

---

18. Ridderbos (1962, 125).

the *crowds*, he went up on the mountain, and when he sat down, his *disciples* came to him. And he opened his mouth and taught *them*" (Matt. 5:1-2).[19] Everybody was allowed to listen; Jesus' message was not esoteric (intended for the initiated only). Everybody could *become* a disciple of the kingdom. But first and foremost, Jesus' spiritual teaching was *addressed* to the disciples.

## 3.2.2 What Exactly Was "Hidden"?

Through the explanation of the parables and through his other teachings, Jesus revealed to his disciples various aspects of the coming kingdom of God. At the same time, he concealed these aspects through the form of the parable. The fact that Israel as a whole was not able to understand the parables was a form of judgment: they were not *allowed* to understand them (Matt. 13:13-15; Luke 19:42).[20] The faithful ones, by contrast, *were* allowed to understand, but often they were not *able* to do so (Matt. 13:17; Luke 10:23-24), either because the time had not yet arrived, or because their eyes had not yet been enlightened (cf. Eph. 1:18; Luke 24:31). Therefore, Jesus' disciples did hear the interpretation of the parables, while usually their essence still escaped even them. Some did not understand because they heard only the parable, and not its interpretation. Others did not understand in spite of the fact that they did hear both the parable and its interpretation.

---

19. Carson (1984, 128).
20. Cf. Barclay (1999, 65): the parable conceals truth to them who are either too lazy to think, or too blinded by prejudice so that they don't see.

In the meantime, Jesus' interpretations, which were explicitly given of only a few of his parables (Matt. 13:18-23, 36-43; 15:15-20; 18:21-35; implicitly, e.g., 7:24-27; 21:33-45), are very important to us because they give us an impression of the way we should explain *all* parables.

Thus, the kingdom was "hidden" in a subjective sense in that it remained spiritually closed to hearers who did not want to surrender to Jesus. However, it was also "hidden" in an objective sense in that the "secret" aspect of the kingdom referred to the kingdom's specific nature during the time that it would not yet be revealed in majesty and splendor.[21] This was a new truth, not known to the Old Testament prophets, but revealed by Jesus both in his person and in his ministry. This new truth was that the kingdom, which would arrive one day in apocalyptic power, as foreseen by the prophets, in fact had already entered into the world beforehand in a hidden form, in order to secretly work in and among people.[22]

This is of great importance because we have to say here that Jesus did indeed announce a kingdom that ultimately would satisfy the expectations of the Old Testament prophets, but he did something more, which was entirely new: he first presented the kingdom in a "hidden" form that *hardly* fulfilled Old testament expectations. The kingdom as foreseen in Daniel 7 will begin with the parousia of Christ as the lightning (vv. 13-14; Matt. 24:27), which every eye will see (Rev. 1:7). But first we have the kingdom in its hidden form, which would be

---

21. Ladd (1974, 222).
22  Ladd (1974, 225; cf. 1964, 55).

inaugurated by the Sower going out to sow the seed of the word of the kingdom (Matt. 13:3, 19; Luke 8:5, 11).[23]

What had been promised was a kingdom in power and glory, an earth full of peace and justice and of the knowledge of the Lord (Isa. 11:9). What did come was a kingdom in a hidden form, *without* outward power and glory, on an earth still full of war and injustice, far removed from being full of the knowledge of the Lord—until this kingdom, all the time working in secret, ultimately and rather unexpectedly produces that kingdom of power and majesty, namely, at the parousia of the Messiah: "The kingdom of God is as if a man should scatter seed on the ground. He sleeps and rises night and day, and the seed sprouts and grows; he knows not how. The earth produces by itself, first the blade, then the ear, then the full grain in the ear. But when the grain is ripe, at once he puts in the sickle, because the harvest has come" (Mark 4:26-29).

### 3.2.3 Five Aspects

Let us now unravel this aspect of the "hiddenness" of the kingdom in some more depth. I see five possible meanings, especially when we refer this "hiddenness" to the entire kingdom in its present form, until the return of the Messiah.

(a) The Old Testament prophets spoke almost exclusively of the Messianic kingdom of peace and justice as it will arrive —as we now know—at the parousia of Christ. The form that the kingdom presently possesses was almost entirely hidden to them (13:35, "I will utter what has been hidden since the foundation of the world"; cf.

---

23. Blackburn (1978, 40).

Luke 10:24, "many prophets and kings desired to see what you see, and did not see it, and to hear what you hear, and did not hear it"). This is the time when the King is in "a far country" (Luke 19:12; cf. Matt. 21:31; 25:14).

(b) From his ascension until his parousia, the Messiah himself is "hidden," namely, at the right hand of God, so that, parallel with this, also the spiritual life of his followers "is hidden with Christ in God" (Col. 3:3).

(c) Therefore, his dominion is also "hidden" because the King is "hidden," so that his dominion can be easily denied because the ruler is invisible and because the evil seems to prevail so often over the good (cf. Matt. 13:30; Mark 4:26–29).

(d) What constitutes the true value of the kingdom of God, and is presented in the treasure and the pearl (Matt. 13:44, 46), is hidden as well: the treasure is hidden in the field, and the pearl is hidden in the depths of the sea (if we may add the latter, since this element is not part of the parable).

(e) The true meaning of the kingdom is hidden to all who are not part of it, as well as to all who do belong to it, yet cannot grasp its true spiritual meaning (v. 36; 15:15; Mark 4:34). This may be because they do not possess the Holy Spirit (cf. John 13:7; 16:12–13), or do possess him, dwelling in them, but have a carnal mentality (cf. Gal. 5:16–18).

## 3.3  Three Parables of a General Nature
### 3.3.1  New and Old Treasures

The eighth and last parable of the kingdom of God in Matthew 13 is as follows: "Therefore every scribe who has been trained for the kingdom of heaven is like a master of a house, who brings out of his treasure what is new and what is old" (Matt. 13:52). The scribe (Greek *grammateus*) is familiar with the Scriptures (*grammata*),[24] and explains them to his pupils. He receives an enormous enrichment if he himself now becomes a pupil (disciple) of the kingdom, that is, of the King (cf. 23:34). As a scribe he is an expert, as a disciple (follower) of Jesus he is a fledgling. Those things that he already knows thoroughly (the "old things," the Tanakh) he now learns to refer to Jesus (cf. Luke 24:44) and his kingdom, and to what it means to be a subject of this kingdom ("new things"). Already in a time when the New Testament had not been (entirely) recorded, this disciple gets to know new treasures, in addition to the old treasures of which he already knew through the Old Testament. The former even come first: "new and old treasures," the newly revealed and the old familiar ones.

The scribe in the kingdom is compared to a "master of a house" (in Greek one word: *oikodespotēs*), the head of a household, which encompasses a number of members. Such a head has a number of servants under him. In Matthew, the phrase "master of the house" can have various meanings. In 10:25, it is clearly Christ himself; in 13:27 and 20:1 and 11 it is Christ or God; in 21:33 it is God; and in 24:43 it is undetermined. In our present verse the "master of the house" is the scribe who has become a disciple of Christ. As the master he has a certain responsibility with respect to the members of his-

---

24. The common word for Scriptures is *graphai* (e.g., Matt. 21:42); sometimes it is *grammata*, as in 2 Tim. 3:15. The *grammateus* is anexpert with respect to the *grammata* or *graphai*.

household: he ministers to them by sharing with them from his rich supplies.

Holy Scripture contains the law and the prophets (7:12; 22:40). What a treasure is the Mosaic Torah! But what a treasure it is, if one learns to follow the Messiah, now to know the Messianic Torah as well, as Jesus expounded it in his five sermons, especially in the Sermon on the Mount. And what a treasure it was to know the Old Testament Messianic prophecies! But what a treasure it now is to know the fulfillment of these prophecies in the person and the work of Jesus. What a treasure it was to know the Old Testament prophecies concerning the Messianic kingdom of peace and justice! But what a treasure it now is to know the kingdom in its intermediate form as well, between the first and the second coming of the Messiah.

### 3.3.2 The Fluting and Wailing Children

In my view, this parable (11:16-17; cf. Luke 7:31-32) deals with the response to the message of the kingdom of God (see Matt. 11:11-12).[25] This explanation seems to me to be more aprropriate than the one that sees in the quarreling children the behavior of the Jewish nation or of their spiritual leaders.[26] Jesus said, "But to what shall I compare this generation? It is like children sitting in the marketplaces and calling to their playmates, 'We played the flute for you, and you did not dance; we sang a dirge, and you did not mourn.'"

John the Baptist in particular had sung a dirge and fasted (v. 18). Therefore, Jesus was probably referring to him

---

25. See, e.g., France (2007, 433-34).
26. E.g., Bruce (1979, 175); Grosheide (1954, 180).

when he spoke of children singing a dirge. Jesus himself had eaten and drunk with tax collectors and sinners (v. 19). Therefore, he was probably referring to himself when he spoke of children playing the flute. Singing a dirge seeks a response of mourning, playing the flute seeks a happy response: dancing. In *both* cases, the majority of the people had not properly responded to the message, neither with a sad elegy (because of their sins and the need of repentance), nor with a happy dance (because of the joyful message of the King and his kingdom; cf. Luke 15:25). In this way, the majority of the people proved to be unwise, for true wisdom comes to light in wise works (v. 19) of wise people, the "children" of wisdom (Luke 7:35). The wise confess their sins and come to the King; the foolish stay in their sins and reject the message of the King.

The parable portrays the negative side, that is, the behavior of the foolish ones only: the majority of the people had not responded in the proper way to the message of the kingdom (cf. Matt. 11:20-24, the "woe to you," addressed to the unrepentant cities of Galilee). The fact that, thank God, some people *had* mourned about their sins, and *had* danced because of the message of the kingdom of God is sufficiently evident from other passages in Matthew (see, e.g., §3.4).

### 3.3.3 Pollution

In Matthew 15:15 (cf. Mark 7:17), Peter says, "Explain the parable to us." At first glance, one might think that he was referring to the comparison that Jesus made with blind people (Matt. 15:14). However, from Jesus' answer (vv. 16-20) it becomes clear that Peter was referring to the comparison made in verses 10-11 (cf. Mark

7:15-16): "Hear and understand: it is not what goes into the mouth that defiles a person, but what comes out of the mouth; this defiles a person."

This is called a parable because of Jesus' metaphorical speaking. When referring to what goes into the mouth he is apparently thinking of literal food (Matt. 15:17, "Do you not see that whatever goes into the mouth passes into the stomach and is expelled?"). But when he speaks of what comes out of the mouth he does not refer to breathing out or vomiting but to spoken words, which come out of the heart, and are often unclean because the heart is unclean: "[W]hat comes out of the mouth proceeds from the heart, and this defiles a person. For out of the heart come evil thoughts, murder, adultery, sexual immorality, theft, false witness, slander. These are what defile a person" (vv. 18-20; cf. Jer. 17:9, "The heart is deceitful above all things, and desperately sick").

This is a kingdom parable because Jesus implicitly deals here with the Messianic Torah, the constitution of the kingdom of God, and the contrast between this Torah and the rabbinic traditions (see the entire passage: vv. 1-20). In this indirect way, the parable is also dealing with the question about what persons are eligible for the kingdom of God. Speaking piously of the Torah, and even the life-long study of the Torah, as such do not make a person a true disciple of the kingdom as long as he has not truly repented and his heart is not yet changed. This is in line with John 3:5, where regeneration is a condition for entering the kingdom: "Truly, truly, I say to you, unless one is born of water and the Spirit, he cannot enter the kingdom of God."

## 3.4 Two Positive Parables

### 3.4.1 Two Interpretations

In contrast to the parables in Matthew 13 that, in my view, speak of an intermingling of good and evil (vv. 24–33, see §§4.4 and 4.5]), Jesus shows in other parables, especially those of the hidden treasure and the pearl of great value (vv. 44–46), the preciousness of the kingdom. These are two of the ten parables in Matthew that explicitly begin with the expression "the kingdom is like . . ." (*homoia estin*, 13:31, 33, 44–45, 47; 20:1), or "may be compared to . . ." (*homoiōthē*, 13:24; 18:23; 22:2), or "will be like . . ." (*homoiōthēsetai*, 25:1). In all these cases, we do not pay attention just to the immediately following noun but to the entire parable. That is, the kingdom is not like a treasure or a merchant, but like the entire story around this treasure or this merchant. It is the same with the man (v. 24), the mustard seed (v. 31), the leaven (v. 33), the net (v.47), the king (18:23; 22:2), the master of the house (20:1), and the ten virgins (25:1). Each time it is the complete story in which the *tertium comparationis* must be sought.

For the interpretation of these two parables it makes quite a difference whether one sees in their protagonists a reference to (a) Christ, who acquires his followers as a treasure,[27] or (b) the disciple who reaches out for the kingdom, and acquires it as a treasure.[28] In my view, both interpretations are satisfactory to a certain extent. Christ could be the man in verse 44 and the merchant

---

27. Kelly (*BT* N1:7–8, 23–24); Grant (1897, 150–54); Gaebelein (1910, 1:293–302); Walvoord (1974, ad loc.).
28. Grosheide (1954, 224–25); Carson (1984, 328); France (2007, 539–42); and many others.

in verses 45–46, who is prepared to spend everything he possesses in order to acquire the treasure (cf. 2 Cor. 8:9). This treasure would then consist of the true disciples or servants in the kingdom.

However, it is also quite satisfactory to see in the man and the merchant as the would-be disciple, who is prepared to spend everything he possesses in order to receive a share in the kingdom of God. As Jesus said to the rich young man: "If you would be perfect, go, sell what you possess and give to the poor, and you will have treasure in heaven; and come, follow me" (19:21). Please notice the corresponding expressions "sell" and "treasure," which are really a key to understanding the parable. Elsewhere, Jesus says, "Strive to enter through the narrow door. For many, I tell you, will seek to enter and will not be able" (Luke 13:24). "So therefore, any one of you who does not renounce all that he has cannot be my disciple" (14:33). In all these passages, it is the disciple who has to expend great effort in trying to enter the kingdom of God and obtain its treasures.

### 3.4.2 Arguments

I see various reasons to prefer the second interpretation, mentioned in the previous paragraph.

(a) Those who defend the first interpretation often do this as a consequence of confusing the gospel of grace and the gospel of the kingdom (see §7.5.2). For instance, they argue that the sinner has nothing to sell, nor is Christ for sale, nor is he hidden in a field, nor does the sinner hide him after having found him.[29] However, the point is that these parables do not refer to sinners seek-

---

29. Scofield (1967), ad loc.

ing redemption at all, but to (possibly already regenerated) people seeking the kingdom of God (cf. Matt. 6:33, where Jesus tells his *disciples*: "[S]eek first the kingdom of God"). This kingdom must be acquired at a costly price: self-surrender, giving up everything for Christ, pursuing the entrance into the kingdom in spite of the enemies' attempts to stop him (see §3.4.1). This is in full accord with the further teaching in Matthew, especially about "entering" into the kingdom of heaven, the efforts that are needed to this end, and the sacrifices that are demanded from the would-be disciple (see §11.1) (Matt. 5:20; 6:33; 7:13, 21; 11:12; 18:3; 19:23-24).

(b) Another error that is made in the first mentioned interpretation is that elements from one parable are used to explain elements in other parables. The fact that in the parable of the wheat and the weeds, the field is the world (13:38) does not necessarily mean that in the parable of the hidden treasure, the field is again a figure of the world. But even if we do assume this, it is quite possible to think here of the disciple who has found something hidden that escapes the attention of most people: the kingdom of God. That the man in this parable buys the field does not refer to Christ buying the world, but means nothing more than that this man must buy the field to be able to call himself the owner of the treasure. The disciple has to pay a high price in order to acquire the treasures of God's kingdom.

In any case, the parables must not be taken as allegories in which each element must have its own spiritual meaning. Thus we do not inquire about the significance of the garden plants in verse 32, the woman in verse 33, the mountains in 18:12, the woman and children in 18:25, or the jailers in 18:34, the marketplace in 20:3, the main roads in 22:9, and least of all, the bride[30] who in 22:1-14 or 25:1-13 is not even mentioned. It is difficult enough to explain the elements that *are* mentioned!

(c) The notion of "treasure" occurs more often in Matthew, and (apart from the literal treasures in 2:11) *always* refers to something that the disciple possesses or must acquire, never to something that Christ must acquire: "Do not lay up for yourselves treasures on earth, where moth and rust destroy and where thieves break in and steal, but lay up for yourselves treasures in heaven, where neither moth nor rust destroys and where thieves do not break in and steal. For where your treasure is, there your heart will be also" (Matt. 6:19-21). "If you would be perfect, go, sell what you possess and give to the poor, and you will have treasure in heaven; and come, follow me" (19:21; also cf. 12:35; 13:52).

### 3.4.3 Treasure in Heaven

At the end of the previous section, I quoted Matthew 19:21 about a "treasure in heaven." Immediately afterward we read, "And Jesus said to his disciples, 'Truly, I say to you, only with difficulty will a rich person enter the kingdom of heaven. Again I tell you, it is easier for a camel to go through the eye of a needle than for a rich person to enter the kingdom of God.' ... Then Peter said in reply, 'See, we have left everything and followed you. What then will we have?' Jesus said to them, 'Truly, I say

---

30. As does, e.g., Grant (1897, 233). By the way, some manuscripts do read "the bridegroom and the bride" in Matt. 25:1; see Metzger (1975, 62).

to you, in the new world [lit., in the regeneration[31]], when the Son of Man will sit on his glorious throne, you who have followed me will also sit on twelve thrones, judging the twelve tribes of Israel. And everyone who has left houses or brothers or sisters or father or mother or children or lands, for my name's sake, will receive a hundredfold and will inherit eternal life'" (vv. 23-29).

Here we see how the "treasure in heaven" of verse 21 is linked with the "kingdom of heaven." The same is true here with "eternal life." Too often Christians have thought that "heaven" is the same as the Paradise of the intermediate state. In this thinking, the "treasure in heaven" and "eternal life" are linked with "going to heaven."[32] However, in Matthew, "heaven" is rather what is meant by the expression "kingdom of heaven." It is heaven that rules, as we have seen. Treasures in heaven are linked with him who is enthroned at the right hand of God in heaven (26:64), and to whom all authority has been given in heaven and on earth (28:18). "Heaven" is the "other country" in 21:33 (cf. 25:14, and the "far country" in Luke 19:12), which is to be viewed from the earthly perspective.

The heart of the true disciple is located where his treasure is, that is, where the glorified Christ is, who is the heart of the kingdom of God: "If then you have been raised with

---

31. Greek palingenesia (AMP: "the renewal [that is, the Messianic restoration and regeneration of all things]"); the only other place where the term occurs, with a rather different, yet related meaning, is Titus 3:5.
32. See extensively, Ouweneel (2012a, chapters 2-3). Cf. a similar misunderstanding regarding the "inheritance that is imperishable, undefiled, and unfading, kept in heaven for you" (1 Pet. 1:4).

Christ, seek the things that are above, where Christ is, seated at the right hand of God. Set your minds on things that are above, not on things that are on earth. For you have died, and your life is hidden with Christ in God" (Col. 3:1–3). Here Christ is the One "in whom are hidden all the treasures of wisdom and knowledge" (2:3), but in connection with the kingdom: our treasure is now on the throne of the Father, and will soon be on the throne of David (cf. Rev. 3:21, "The one who conquers, I will grant him to sit with me on my throne [i.e., the throne of David, Luke 1:32], as I also conquered and sat down with my Father on his throne").

Many Christians have allowed the riches of the kingdom to be robbed from them by their own fault, that is, by being preoccupied with secondary and tertiary things. According to Romans 14, believers in Rome were quarreling about what one could eat or drink, and whether Christianity observes its own special days or whether all days are equal. As he does so often, Paul brings the discussion to a deeper level by linking it with deep underlying truths of God. In this instance, he says (vv. 17–18): " For the kingdom of God is not a matter of eating and drinking but of righteousness and peace and joy in the Holy Spirit. Whoever thus serves Christ is acceptable to God and approved by men." The more important things must always have the priority. Believers are concerned with all kinds of things,[33] but in the kingdom of God the things of the Spirit come first: righteousness, that is, acting according to what is right and fair; peace, that is, maintaining mutual rest and harmony; and joy, that is, rejoicing together in the Lord and his treasures, and in each other. In these things they must "serve"

---

33. See Ouweneel (2009b, 2012b) for important examples.

(Greek *douleuō*), this is literally "serve as slaves" (*doulos* is "slave, bondman"), as it is fitting for disciples in God's kingdom (in Matt. 10:24-25; 13:27-28; 18:23-33; 21:34-36; 22:3-10; 24:45-50; 25:14-30, "servant" is *doulos*).

What we find in Romans 14 is the anticipation of three principles, righteousness and peace and joy, which in the Messianic kingdom will be universal: "Of the increase of his government and of *peace* there will be no end, on the throne of David and over his kingdom, to establish it and to uphold it with justice and with *righteousness* from this time forth and forevermore" (Isa. 9:7). "He shall not judge by what his eyes see, or decide disputes by what his ears hear, but with *righteousness* he shall judge the poor, and decide with equity for the meek of the earth; and he shall strike the earth with the rod of his mouth, and with the breath of his lips he shall kill the wicked. *Righteousness* shall be the belt of his waist, and faithfulness the belt of his loins" (11:3-5). "And the ransomed of the LORD shall return and come to Zion with singing; everlasting *joy* shall be upon their heads; they shall obtain gladness and *joy*, and sorrow and sighing shall flee away" (35:10; 51:11).

This is the joyful hope for the Messianic future. However, in a world still full of *un*righteousness, *un*rest, *dis*harmony, and *un*happiness, the disciples of Jesus endeavor, in the power of the Holy Spirit, to display as much as they can of the kingdom of God. They do so by doing justice to others, by living peaceably with all (Rom. 12:18), and by rejoicing in the Lord always (Phil. 4:4). They live as if it is already "day" (Rom. 13:11-14; 1 Thess. 5:4-8), although spiritually it is still night. To be absorbed by matters of secondary or tertiary importance is to impede the righteousness, the mutual peace, and the joy in the Lord altogether. These matters are in contrast with the true character of the kingdom.

## 3.5 Kingdom Parables and the Messianic Torah
### 3.5.1 The Wise Man and the Foolish Man

In seven kingdom parables, Jesus discusses which moral characteristics the true disciples of God's kingdom must exhibit. We will look at two smaller parables first, and later at three larger ones.

In the Sermon on the Mount, Jesus, as the new Lawgiver (*novus Moses*) but also as the King, describes the new laws—one might say: the constitution—of the kingdom. At the end of his teaching, Jesus tells the parable of the wise man and the foolish man (7:24-27; cf. Luke 6:47-49): "Everyone then who hears these words of mine and does them will be like a wise man who built his house on the rock. And the rain fell, and the floods came, and the winds blew and beat on that house, but it did not fall, because it had been founded on the rock. And everyone who hears these words of mine and does not do them will be like a foolish man who built his house on the sand. And the rain fell, and the floods came, and the winds blew and beat against that house, and it fell, and great was the fall of it."

In this parable, Jesus describes the difference between, on the one hand, the true disciples of the kingdom, and, on the other hand, the false disciples and the outsiders. The former build on the rock, which is Jesus' Messianic teaching, or perhaps the Messiah himself (cf. Matt. 16:18).[34] The latter people do not build on this solid

---
34. But cf. Ouweneel (2010b, 62-64).

foundation but on some shaky foundation of their own or of some false religion.

The parable thus belongs to the moral type: it explains by what moral characteristics the true subjects of God's kingdom can be recognized. It is not sufficient merely to accept Jesus as Savior and Lord; no, the true disciple builds his entire life on Christ, the Rock. Those who do so will be able to withstand the tempests of life, and specifically the attacks that the evil one undertakes against Christ and his kingdom.[35] However, there are also disciples who build their life on "sand": human ideologies, philosophical or theological theories, "according to human tradition, . . . and not according to Christ" (Col. 2:8). Those who build their Christian or not-so-Christian lives on the finest and best forms of "human wisdom" (cf. 1 Cor. 2:13) will not be able to withstand any storm. The true disciple does not build on human doctrines but on Christ himself.

For the interpretation it does not matter where the storm comes from. It may come from Satan (cf. Job 1:12, 19)—be it only under God's permission—but on another occasion Scripture says: "[T[he LORD hurled a great wind upon the sea, and there was a mighty tempest on the sea" (Jonah 1:4). The storm may be an incitement from Satan, or a testing from God, but the result is the same: the house of the wise will stand, the house of the foolish will fall down.

### 3.5.2 The Lost Sheep

This is the parable of the lost sheep: "See that you do not despise one of these little ones. For I tell you that in heaven

---

35. Storms may come from the evil one; see Mark 4:39.

their angels always see the face of my Father who is in heaven. What do you think? If a man has a hundred sheep, and one of them has gone astray, does he not leave the ninety-nine on the mountains and go in search of the one that went astray? And if he finds it, truly, I say to you, he rejoices over it more than over the ninety-nine that never went astray. So it is not the will of my Father who is in heaven that one of these little ones should perish" (Matt. 18:10–14).

This passage is very similar to Luke 15:3–7, but the context is rather different. In Luke 15:1–2, we are dealing with the contrast between, on the one hand, the tax collectors and the (other) sinners, and on the other hand, the Pharisees and the scribes, and the reproach of the latter that Jesus received the tax collectors and sinners, and communed with them. In the parables of the lost sheep and the lost coin (vv. 8–10), the subject is the love of the owner, who is concerned about that one sheep and that one coin, to find them and bring them back. The addition about the "joy in heaven over one sinner who repents" (vv. 7, 10) makes clear that Jesus indeed is concerned here with the penitent tax collectors and (other) sinners. Similarly, in the subsequent parable of the prodigal son (vv. 11–32), the eldest son refers to the Pharisees and scribes, and the youngest son to the tax collectors and sinners.

In Matthew 18:10–14, the situation is a little different; here, the subject is "these little ones" (vv. 6, 10, 14; cf. 10:42; 11:25; 21:16). Here these are not so much the tax collectors and sinners but rather those who "humble themselves like a child" (vv. 4–5), that is, the weak, the vulnerable, the defenseless, who can easily fall victim to those who cause people to stumble (vv. 6–10). Jesus is the good Shepherd, who is concerned with these weak and vulnerable ones (cf. Ezek. 34:4, 16, 21), and even goes after them to save them from the grip of these deceivers. This group reminds us of those who are "poor in spirit," and in the Beatitudes are called blessed by Jesus (5:3). Jesus is concerned with the "sinners" (that is here, those living wicked lives[36]) as well as with the weak. Of course, these groups often overlap, but this is not necessarily the case.

In contrast to these, we find the "ninety-nine that never went astray" (18:13; in the words of Luke 15:7, those "who [think they] need no repentance"). These are those in Israel who are outwardly religious, of whom Jesus had said before: "I came not to call the [supposedly] righteous, but sinners" (Matt. 9:13). Jesus uses the word "righteous" here in the sense of "pseudo-righteous" (cf. 23:28, you "outwardly appear righteous to others"), people who believed they had no need of repentance because they viewed themselves as faithful observers of the law (cf. the contrast with 13:17, 43, 49; 23:29, 35; 25:37, 46; 27:19). This is what Jesus called the "righteousness of the scribes and Pharisees, as he told his followers: "[U]nless your righteousness exceeds that of the scribes and Pharisees, you will never enter the kingdom of heaven" (5:20). The good Shepherd does not

---

36. Cf. Gen. 13:13; Ps. 1:1; 26:9; 104:35; John 9:24; 1 Tim. 1:9; James 4:8; 5:20; Jude 1:15. This is in contrast with (rare) New Testament passages which teach that every human being is a sinner because of his sinful nature (Rom. 5:8, 19; Gal. 2:15, 17). In Christian practice, the latter meaning is far more common than the former one; in the Bible, the opposite is the case.

go after the self-righteous sheep but after the sheep that have gone astray, that is, those who *know* and *acknowledge* that they have gone astray: "Those who are well have no need of a physician, but those who are sick" (9:12). The kingdom of God is for the sick who want to become well, not for the sick who do not realize, or do not want to acknowledge, that they are sick, and thus do not wish to be treated by the physician.

### 3.5.3 The Unforgiving Servant

In the parable about forgiving (Matt. 18:21–35), we find another example of living, or not living, according to the Messianic Torah, which is the constitution of the kingdom of God. According to rabbinic tradition, if a person's neighbor repeatedly commits the same sin against him, that person is obliged to forgive him only three times.[37] Peter, who over time had learned to know his Master to some extent, suggested seven instead of three (v. 21), apparently thinking he was being generous. However, Jesus answered with an Eastern hyperbole: seventy times seven. (In Luke 17:4, it is seven times *in a day*; that may be 2,555 times a year, which is far more than 490 times.)

Of course, the situation presupposes that the trespasser acknowledges and confesses his sin; otherwise forgiveness would not be possible. This follows from the preceding passage (vv. 15–20): you first have to "tell" your brother "his fault" (you "expose" him; cf. the same verb in John 3:20). Only when he "listens to you," that is, admits his sin, can you give him your forgiveness. If he does not listen, he will, after several attempts, come un-

---

37. Cf. Amos 1:6; see Strack (1986, 1), ad loc.

der church discipline. There can be no forgiveness without confession of sin (cf. Prov. 28:13; 1 John 1:9; James 5:15-16). (Although, thank God, there is always the allowance of Ps. 19:12, "Who can discern his errors? Declare me innocent from hidden faults").

In the passage just referred to, the subject is the responsibility of the trespasser: he has to confess his sins in order to receive forgiveness. In the parable that follows upon it, however, the subject is the responsibility of the one who has to *grant* this forgiveness. Jesus explains that there is something more important than the strictly formal principle of the number of times one forgives (three, seven, or 490 times), namely, the disciple's moral consciousness of how much has been forgiven *him* (v. 27). From this flows the *attitude* of forgiveness that he has to show to others ("from your heart," v. 35). The issue is not only the frequency of forgiveness (quantity), but also the manner of forgiveness (quality). It ought never to become an extorted duty. Normally, the one who is forgiven much is the one who loves much (cf. Luke 7:47). However, the servant in the parable has been forgiven much, but he does not seem to realize it or accept the consequences of it; therefore he loves little.

The parable implies a partition within the kingdom of God between disciples who forgive wholeheartedly, and those who do not do so. The former resemble the Master, and therefore constitute the true disciples of the kingdom. The latter do not forgive wholeheartedly; they even trample on the soul of the Messianic Torah by not being willing to forgive. The Master himself, or God, is here the great example: in the parable he is the King who forgives his servant a debt of billions.[38] Paul says, "Be kind to one another, tenderhearted, forgiving one another, as God in Christ forgave you. Therefore be imitators of God, as beloved children. And walk in love, as Christ loved us and gave himself up for us, a fragrant offering and sacrifice to God" (Eph. 4:32–5:2); ". . . bearing with one another and, if one has a complaint against another, forgiving each other; as the Lord has forgiven you, so you also must forgive" (Col. 3:13).[39]

It is incomprehensible that the man in the parable, whom such an enormous debt had been forgiven, say, $3 billion (see note 38), is not prepared to forgive his fellow servant a debt of $5,000.00 (which is 1/600,000 of his own debt), and even has him put in prison. This is possible only if the servant has no idea how much he was forgiven, or despises it, or has forgotten about it. Any debt that a person has to another person is always immeasurably smaller than the debt any person has to God. Seeing how enormous a debt God has forgiven a disciple of the kingdom, this disciple's readiness to forgive a fellow disciple his debt should be so much the greater.

The parable is applicable in particular to the outwardly religious Israel in Jesus' day, which envied God's grace to believers from the Gentiles. We find the same jealousy in the parable of the laborers in the vineyard

---

38. If we view a denarius (the wage of a day laborer, Matt. 20:2) as the rough equivalent of $50.00, then 10,000 talents (i.e., 60 million denarii) is equivalent to $3 billion. Jesus is thus referring to a debt that is so enormous that a person would never be able to repay it, least of all with his own life (cf. vv. 25, 34).

39. Cf. Ouweneel (2010a, 334–35).

(20:11-12; see next section), and later in Acts (13:45; 14:2; 17:5). For the rest, the principle remains the same: the outwardly religious person is he who believes that he can live by rights and merits (cf. Luke 18:9-14, and the next section), and therefore becomes jealous when God shows grace to another person, who has no rights and merits to boast about.

We also see here that a disciple of the kingdom can ultimately be lost. This has nothing to do with some notion about the apostasy of genuine saints.[40] The point is rather that there are true and false disciples or servants in the kingdom. Sooner or later, those false disciples or servants will be exposed. For them, there is indeed forgiveness too, but only if they themselves are willing to forgive their brothers wholeheartedly (Matt. 18:35). Here again we encounter the distinction between the gospel of God's grace for sinners and the gospel of the kingdom (see §7.5.2). He who accepts the gospel of God's grace wholeheartedly, that is, believes in Jesus as his Redeemer, receives forgiveness unconditionally. However, within the kingdom of God it is true discipleship that counts: he who is unwilling to forgive his (repentant) neighbor from the bottom of his heart is not living according to the Messianic Torah, that is, according to the conditions of God's kingdom. Sooner or later, the falsehood of the false disciples comes to light, and they will be lost (v. 34).

In Matthew, this is the theme throughout: there are two kinds of disciples or servants in the kingdom. This was the case in Jesus' day, and it is the case in the kingdom in its intermediate form today (see below). This is

---

40. See Ouweneel (2010a, 156-62).

the same as saying that, in Matthew, the kingdom is being considered from the viewpoint of human responsibility. In Luke this is much less the case, and in John not at all. There, the kingdom of God includes only those who are genuinely regenerate (John 3:5), true followers of Jesus (John 18:36–37).

### 3.5.4 The Laborers in the Vineyard

The parable of the laborers in the vineyard (Matt. 20:1–16) tells us about a winegrower who, early in the morning, hires day laborers to work in his vineyard. At later hours, on the same day, he finds other laborers, still standing idle at the marketplace, and he hires them as well. He does the same with day laborers whom he hires even at the eleventh hour (one hour before sunset). At the end of the day, he gives all laborers the same reward—one denarius, the reward for one day of labor—in spite of the protests of those who had worked for twelve hours from sunrise.

Such a parable can be interpreted in a general-ethical sense, as so many have done. To such expositors it does not really matter whether such a parable is found in Matthew, Mark, or Luke; the moral lesson remains the same. However, within the context of Matthew, and especially of the last sentence (v. 16, "So the last will be first, and the first last"), it is inconceivable that the parable would not have a deeper sense. Grace triumphs over justice. The laborers who had worked longest were *entitled* to one denarius. However, by receiving what was their due, they did not get to know in some personal-existential way the *grace* of the "master of the house" (cf. Rom. 4:4, "Now to the one who works, his wages are not counted as a gift but as his due"). Those who had worked the least were entitled to at most one-twelfth of a denarius, but they learned about the master's goodness by receiving a whole denarius: one-twelfth justice, eleven-twelfths grace.

Here lies the essence of the parable. Grace is not for those who believe they have all the rights, such as belonging to a chosen nation, being entitled to many blessings, serving God diligently (cf. Luke 18:11–12). Rather, grace is for those, inside Israel (sinners) or even outside Israel (Gentiles), who have no rights at all. These people's sense of their own unworthiness comes to light in verse 7: "[N]o one has hired us." That means, in fact, that nobody *wants* us.

Please note the reading in verse 7b in NKJV and others: ". . . and whatever is right you will receive." Very probably, this phrase is not authentic (compare more modern translations), which is to the benefit of the interpretation: the laborers hired last can hardly claim any rights. What they received in the end was eleven times more grace than what they were entitled to.

In summary, the kingdom of God is not for religious people, who believe they have all kinds of rights with God because of their decency but who in fact live without God. Rather, the kingdom is for prostitutes, tax collectors, and other sinners, Jewish or Gentile. (When it is no longer a question of rights, there is just as much grace for Gentiles as for Jews.) The only condition is that they, Jew or Gentile, come to God with the attitude of the tax collector in Luke 18:13, "God, be merciful to me, a sinner." What the parable makes clear is this: religious people (a) do not understand grace, (b) envy grace shown to others, and (c) do not receive grace themselves; they believe that they are only being repaid according to their works. This will turn out to be disastrous: "[T]hey were judged, each one of them, according to what they had done" (Rev. 20:13; cf. 2 Cor. 11:15).

### 3.5.5 The Two Sons

What we found at the end of the previous section is well summarized in Matthew 21:31-32, "Truly, I say to you, the tax collectors and the prostitutes go into the kingdom of God before you. For John [the Baptist] came to you in the way of righteousness, and you did not believe him, but the tax collectors and the prostitutes believed him. And even when you saw it, you did not afterward change your minds and believe him." For the decent, reputable, religious people, nothing could be more irritating than the fact that prostitutes, adulterers, thieves, murderers, adulterers, sorcerers, idolaters, and that kind of scum enter the kingdom of God ahead of them. It was just as irritating to the religious hypocrites among the Jews of that day that God's grace was equally destined for abominable Gentiles (21:33-46; cf. Luke 20:16, "Surely not!").

Of course, the wicked are not allowed into the kingdom *because* they are wicked but because they repent, confess their sins, receive forgiveness, and decide to follow Jesus. Similarly, the religious are not refused *because* they are religious but because they refuse to repent, to confess their sins, to receive forgiveness, and to decide to follow Jesus. They refuse these things in spite of—or perhaps, precisely *because* of—being so religious (hypocritically pious).

## The Parables of the Kingdom (I)

The difference between these two groups is beautifully clarified by Jesus in the parable of the two sons (Matt. 21:28-32), to which the words just quoted form the ending. Jesus said, "A man had two sons. And he went to the first and said, 'Son, go and work in the vineyard today.' And he answered, 'I will not,' but afterward he changed his mind and went. And he went to the other son and said the same. And he answered, 'I go, sir,' but did not go. Which of the two did the will of his father?" Jesus' listeners answered, "The first."

The second son clearly corresponds to the workers of the first hour in the previous parable. This may seem contradictory, for the second son did not work at all, whereas the early workers in the previous parable had worked long and hard. The *tertium comparationis* is that both constitute a portrait of the religious people in Israel: the early workers lived out of (alleged) rights and did not understand or accept their master's grace, and the second son behaved as if he served his father, while in fact he did not do the will of his father. The first son corresponds to the laborers of the eleventh hour; they constitute a portrait of the tax collectors and sinners because the latter had trespassed God's commandments but later repented and began serving God (the first son), or because they learned to live by the grace of God (the late laborers).

The first group (the early workers, or the second son) has no share in the kingdom of God, in spite of their religious decency, because these people do not do the will of God after all (cf. 6:10; 7:21; 9:13; 12:7, 50). The second group (the late workers, or the first son) does receive a share in the kingdom of God, in spite of their previous sinful life, from which they turned away in order to do the will of God after all.

It is obvious that the two sons in this parable correspond precisely to the two sons in the parable of the prodigal son (Luke 15:11–32): the first son in the Matthew parable corresponds to the youngest son in the Luke parable, while the second son corresponds to the eldest son. The prodigal son turns away from the father but is restored afterward. The eldest son is seemingly always with the father, but in reality he does not know him. He does not answer to the latter's heart, and has in fact never done the will of his father, as *father*. The restored prodigal son knows the father's heart immeasurably better than the eldest son has ever known it. In other words, the youngest son gets to know the father as *father*, whereas the eldest son has never known him as father, but only as master. This comes to light clearly in verse 29, "I have served you," which is the verb *douleuō*, "to serve as a slave." This in spite of the fact that the father addresses him as "son" (v. 31, Greek *teknon*, lit. "child"). He complains, "[Y]ou never gave me a young goat, that I might celebrate with my friends" (v. 29)—not with the father. The religious have many friends, but they do not know the Father.

## 3.6 Epilogue

The parable of the two sons belongs to the so-called "temple teaching" of Jesus, which we find in Matthew 21:23–22:46 (cf. 21:12–15, 23),[41] and which consists of the following eight parts.

(a) The question concerning the authority of Jesus (21:23–27), that is, of the King, necessarily precedes the other parts. This is because with this question his entire teaching stands or falls. The spiritual leaders ask a fool-

---

41. Cf. Coates (1931, 244-47).

ish question: "By what authority are you doing these things, and who gave you this authority?" They could just as well have asked by what authority the sun shines in the sky. King Sun[42] (cf. 17:2) exercises his royal rights without accounting for this to any of his puny subjects, and in Matthew 21-22 Jesus shines his light on the entire Jewish system, and on each group separately.

(b) The parable of the two sons (21:28-32): the contrasts between two groups in Israel, namely, the religious hypocrites and the repentant sinners. (see §3.5.5).

(c) The parable of the tenants (21:33-46): the transfer of the "vineyard" from Israel to those among the Gentiles who would produce fruit for God (see §4.1).

(d) The parable of the wedding feast (22:1-14): the contrast between two groups within Israel (religious hypocrites and repentant sinners), and between two groups within the kingdom (true and false disciples) (see §4.2).

(e) The question concerning the imperial taxes (22:15-22), which ultimately amounts to the question of dedication either to God or Christ ("render to God the things that are God's," namely, people on whom God's image is imprinted, v. 21; cf. Gen. 1:26-27), or to the earthly powers (represented here by the Roman emperor).

(f) The question concerning the resurrection (22:23-33), that is, of life beyond death, which is the life of the kingdom in its future state.

---

42. "Sun" is a feminine word in the Germanic languages, but masculine in Hebrew (see Ps. 19:4-6), Greek, and Latin (and the Romance languages). Cf. Gen. 1:16, "the greater light [i.e., the sun] to rule the day."

(g) The great commandment (22:34-40), which involves the central principle of the kingdom's constitution: love for God and Christ as well as for one's neighbor (worked out especially in the Sermon on the Mount).

(h) The question concerning the son of David (22:41-46), which at its deepest level is the question how the notion of a killed Messiah on earth (whose death had already been planned by the listening Pharisees; cf. 16:21; 17:23; 21:35-39; 22:6) could be reconciled with the notion of a glorified Lord in heaven at the right hand of God (cf. Ps. 110:1).

Thus, the eight parts begin and end with matters concerning the person of the King himself: his authority and his glorification. The other six parts consist of three parables (two of which are still to be discussed) and three moral questions that are vital to the kingdom: dedication to God, resurrection life, and the kingdom Torah (love for God). In the end, this will be the kingdom: serving and loving God and his Christ beyond the powers of death, the devil, and darkness.

# Chapter 4
# The Parables of the Kingdom (II)

*And he will place the sheep on his right,*
*    but the goats on the left.*
*Then the King will say to those on*
*    his right,*
*"Come, you who are blessed by my*
*    Father,*
*inherit the kingdom prepared*
*    for you*
*        from the foundation of the world.*
*For I was hungry and you gave me*
*    food,*
*    I was thirsty and you gave me*
*        drink,*
*I was a stranger and you welcomed me,*
*    I was naked and you clothed me,*
*I was sick and you visited me,*
*    I was in prison and you came*
*        to me."*
                        Matthew 25:33–36

***Summary:*** *Both the previous chapter and its sequel of the present chapter are dealing with kingdom parables. The parable of the tenants shows how the kingdom moved largely from Israel to the Gentiles. The parable of the wedding feast shows that not only Israel became largely unworthy, but that also within the kingdom in its new form there are true and false subjects (in other parables these are described as good and bad fruits, good and bad fishes, dough and leaven, good and bad servants, good and bad bridal maids). The parables present us with both the transition of the kingdom from Israel to the Gentiles and the transition from its present from to its glorious form at the "end of the age."*

## 4.1 The Tenants

### 4.1.1 The King's Vineyard, the King's Servants

WE CAN POINT OUT all kinds of similarities in the various parables. Thus, we see the Pharisees and scribes in the laborers of the first hour (Matt. 20:1-2, 10), the second son (21:30), the tenants (21:33-41), and the invitees (22:1-7). The prostitutes, tax collectors, and sinners are seen in the laborers of the last hour (20:6-9), the first son (21:28-29), the "other" tenants (21:41-43), and the people at the street corners (22:9-10 NIV).

In Matthew 21:33-41 (cf. Mark 12:1-11; Luke 20:9-18), Jesus tells about a "master of a house who planted a vineyard" with a fence, a winepress, and a tower, that is, a place of separation and protection (cf. Prov. 18:10), and he "leased it to tenants, and went into another country." In my view, there is a striking difference between this "going to another country" (the verb *apodēmeō*, "to go abroad") and the "going on a journey" (the same verb!) in Matthew 25:14, to which the commentaries pay hardly any attention.[1] In the latter verse, "going abroad" can be identified as the ascension of Christ, at which moment he left the kingdom behind in the hands of his followers. These are the servants who must work with the talents entrusted to them until the master returns (the parousia; §4.8). However, in 21:33 the situation is very different. Here it is not the King himself who "goes abroad," but the "master of the house" (God), who afterwards sends his son (Christ), who is killed by the tenants (a wicked part of Israel) (vv. 38-39). In Matthew 25, the "going abroad" occurred almost 2,000 years ago, in chapter 21 it took place some 3,200 or 3,400 hundred years ago, at the beginning of Israel's national existence at Mount Sinai.

A similar ambiguity surrounds the term "master of the house": this refers either to God (20:11; 21:33), or to Christ (10:25), or to either one (13:27; 20:11; 24:43, 45), or to the believer (13:52).

God's "going abroad" in 21:33 refers to the time when God planted the "vineyard" Israel for the purpose of receiving good fruit from it (Isa. 5:1-2). The fruit of the vine is the wine, which cheers not only men (Ps. 104:15) but also God (Judg. 9:13; think here of the Old Testament drink offerings from Exod. 29:40 to Joel 2:14; cf. also Phil. 2:17; 2 Tim. 4:6). God "went abroad" when he withdrew from Mount Sinai, so to speak, and left the

---

[1]. On the contrary, Wright (2008, 126) assumes that, in Matt. 25:14, it is *God* going abroad (i.e., leaving at the destruction of the first temple and the beginning of the Babylonian exile); in this case, v. 19 would refer not to Christ's second but to his *first* coming. Within the context of Matt. 24-25, which deals throughout with his parousia, this seems to me inconceivable.

people to their own responsibility—although he travelled with them in the Spirit, that is, the *Shekhinah*.[2] God entrusted his "vineyard" to the spiritual leaders of the people, but they did not produce the demanded and expected fruits, that is, did not bring him the joy that he demanded and longed for (Ps. 80:9-16; Jer. 6:9; 8:13; Ezek. 15:1-8; Hos. 9:10; 10:1; Joel 1:7).

God sent to them his servants, that is, the prophets, but they killed (some of) them, as, for instance, Zechariah (2 Chron. 24:20-21; cf. Matt. 23:35). According to tradition, Isaiah was also killed (sawn in two; cf. Heb. 11:37),[3] as was Jeremiah, who was stoned[4] (also see Matt. 23:29-31, 34, 37; Acts 7:52; 1 Thess. 2:15). Finally God sent his Son to them, saying, as it were, "They will respect my Son" (which, in the fulfillment, raises the interesting question whether God did not know beforehand what was going to happen[5]). But when the "tenants" saw the Son, Israel's spiritual leaders said, "This is the heir. Come, let us kill him and have his inheritance." And they took him, threw him out, and killed him (Matt. 21:37-39).

In this way, Jesus was clearly suggesting that the leaders in Israel, who in verse 23 still asked, "By what authority are you doing these things, and who gave you this authority?", in fact knew the answer to this question very well. They knew who Jesus was: "This is the heir." He was the Son, whom God had appointed the heir of all things (Heb. 1:2). In spite of this, or rather, for

---

2. Ouweneel (2007a, 83-88).
3. See *Ascensio Iesaiae*.
4. See Pseudo-Epiphanius, *De Vitis Prophetarum*.
5. See extensively, Ouweneel (2008b, chapter 4).

this very reason, they killed him (cf. John 19:7, "We have a law, and according to that law he ought to die because he has made himself the Son of God").

### 4.1.2 New Tenants

It is striking that, in this passage, the Jewish leaders themselves declare what God must do with his vineyard: "He will put those wretches to a miserable death and let out the vineyard to other tenants who will give him the fruits in their seasons" (v. 41). Jesus then quotes Psalm 118:22-23, and confirms their words: "Therefore I tell you, the kingdom of God will be taken away from you and given to a people producing its fruits" (v. 43). Only then, the leaders understand that he had spoken of *them*. In Luke 20:16, the situation is rather different. Here it is Jesus himself who says, "He will come and destroy those tenants and give the vineyard to others." After this, the leaders, understanding very well that Jesus had spoken of them, exclaim: "Surely not!"[6] They had administered the vineyard very badly (even if they themselves might not have thought so), yet they begrudge it to others (cf. Acts 13:45; 14:2, 19; 17:5, 13; 1 Thess. 2:15-16).

However this may have been, in both cases it is obvious that Jesus understands by the "tenants" the spiritual leaders of Israel, *and* that the "vineyard," which in its New Testament form is the kingdom of God, would be taken away from Israel, and "given to a people producing its fruits" (Matt. 21:43). Whereas some parables (the weeds, the net, the two servants, the virgins, the talents) emphasize what is going to occur at the end of the age,

---

6. See Ouweneel (2007b, 212).

the parables of the tenants and the wedding feast emphasize what was happening in Jesus' own day: *the kingdom was being formally transferred to the new people of God* (the "people" of v. 43). This new people of God included (a) the faithful, penitent Israelites, who acknowledged and followed their Messiah, and (b) all those from the Gentiles who would accept the Messiah of Israel as Savior and Lord, and would begin to follow him.[7] In Matthew 16:18, Jesus describes this new community as his church (*ekklēsia*), which he was going to build (future tense!).

The most dramatic element in our parable is the expression "taken away": "the kingdom of God will be taken away [one word: Greek *arthēsetai*] from you" (v. 43). *In concreto*, this means that it is no longer possible that a person could belong to the kingdom of God merely on the basis of being born a Jew. Neither descent, nor circumcision, nor (outward) Torah-observance as such gives the Jew entrance into the kingdom of God. By the way, Ezekiel 11:19 and 36:26 had already made this clear: Israel cannot enter the kingdom in any other way than by receiving a new heart and a new spirit; this is what the New Testament calls new birth or regeneration.[8]

The kingdom is for those who will "produce its fruits," that is, bear fruit in which they gladden the heart of God (see above). For Israel, this was the fruit of gratitude, praise, worship, servitude, surrender, and dedication.

---

7. Regarding this new notion of the "people of God," see Ouweneel (2010b, 95, 103–105, 127–28). The *ekklēsia* is not "Israel" in some spiritual sense but a "different people" (the "others" of Luke 20:16).

8. Ouweneel (2010a, 71–98).

But if indeed this is the criterion of true fruit, then in God's dominion, no reason remains for limiting salvation to Israel. The "other tenants" (vv. 41, 43) include all people, Jews and especially many Gentiles, who will bear fruit before God, and thus will show themselves to be true disciples, or servants, of the kingdom of God by their surrender and dedication to the King.

## 4.2 The Wedding Feast
### 4.2.1 The Invitations

The parable of the tenants just discussed is followed immediately with that of the wedding feast (22:1-14; cf. Luke 14:16-24), which in many respects corresponds to that of the tenants. The vineyard has been replaced by a wedding, but in both cases the joy metaphor is central: the joy of the wine and the joy of the wedding, that is, the joy of the kingdom of God (cf. Rom. 14:17). The tenants of the vineyard correspond to those invited to the wedding. Literally these are the "called ones" (Greek *keklēmenoi*), which is important because this word reappears in verse 14 in the form *klētoi*. The invitees are the first who are entitled to assist at the wedding. Here again, this represents Israel, that is, those who are originally the "sons of the kingdom" (8:12; see §4.3.2). These invited ones behave in a way similar to that of the tenants in the preceding parable: they refuse to contribute to the joy of the master of the house or the king, respectively. The tenants refuse to bring in the fruit of the vineyard, and the invitees refuse to accept the invitation. Both show in this way their contempt and disinterest with respect to the master, or the king.

We must pay attention here to the double invitation: the first one is in verse 3, and the second one in verse 4. In my view, the first invitation took place during Jesus' life on earth, the second one after his ascension (Acts 2-3 and 7). Compare Matthew 23:37, where Jesus says in non-parabolic language: "O Jerusalem, Jerusalem, the city that kills the prophets and stones those who are sent to it!" This is what Israel had done in the past (cf. vv. 30-33), and what they would also do in the future (after Jesus' ascension): "I send you prophets and wise men and scribes, some of whom you will kill and crucify, and some you will flog in your synagogues and persecute from town to town" (v. 34; cf. 10:17; Acts 7:51-52, 59; 1 Thess. 2:14-15).

In Matthew 22:5-6 there is a twofold response: the first group shows indifference, the second one violence: "But they paid no attention and went off, one to his farm, another to his business, while the rest seized his servants, treated them shamefully, and killed them." The first group is neutral (insofar as that is possible), the second one consists of overt opponents. As to the latter group: just as the tenants kill the servants of the master of the house (21:35), the invitees do the same to the servants of the king. This goes beyond contempt and disinterest; it points to outright hatred. Jesus says, "If I had not done among them the works that no one else did, they would not be guilty of sin, but now they have seen and hated both me and my Father" (John 15:24). A little while later, Stephen said, "You stiff-necked people, uncircumcised in heart and ears, you always resist the Holy Spirit. As your fathers did, so do you. Which of the prophets did your fathers not persecute? And they killed those who announced beforehand the coming of the

Righteous One, whom you have now betrayed and murdered, you who received the law as delivered by angels and did not keep it" (Acts 7:51-53).

Those in the parable who eventually accept the invitation are the have-nots. Those who believe they "have" something do not come; only those who have nothing come. If the original invitees to the wedding had taken part, they would have done so because of their status, that is, their (alleged) rights. Those who actually do take part are those who do so out of pure grace; they are entitled to nothing, they receive everything for free (cf. the laborers of the eleventh hour, §3.5.4).

### 4.2.2 Judgment

In the parable of the wedding feast, we now hear a remarkable prediction, which is lacking in the parable of the tenants: "The king was angry, and he sent his troops and destroyed those murderers and burned their city" (Matt. 22:7). This prediction of Jerusalem's fall is directly ascribed to God's intervention: here, the Roman armies are even called *his* armies. How different this is from the Old Testament, where Israel's army is called God's army (Exod. 7:4; 12:41).[9] In the parable, God sends "his" army *against* Jerusalem, and this explicitly because she was the murderer of God's servants: "O Jerusalem, Jerusalem, the city that kills the prophets and stones those who are sent to it!" (23:37). Jesus also speaks specifically of the temple: "Truly, I say to you, there will not be left here one stone upon another that will not be thrown down" (24:2).

---

9. See, however, e.g., Isa. 10:5 and Hab. 1:6, where the Assyrian and the Babylonian armies are *God's* armies against *Israel*.

In the parable of the minas, we again find such severe statements: "But his citizens hated him and sent a delegation after him, saying, 'We do not want this man to reign over us'" (Luke 19:14; cf. John 19:15, "We have no king but Caesar"). This is followed by the verdict of the king: "But as for these enemies of mine, who did not want me to reign over them, bring them here and slaughter them before me" (Luke 19:27).

Now and then, we come across a philo-Semitic tendency to argue that it was not the Jews but the Romans who killed Jesus.[10] However, it is Jesus himself who spoke of "murderers" (Matt. 22:7). Peter said at the Day of Pentecost: "[T]his Jesus . . . *you* [i.e., Jews[11]] crucified and killed by the hands of lawless men [i.e., Romans]" (Acts 2:23); "you [i.e., Jews] killed the Author of life, whom God raised from the dead" (3:15). "They [i.e., Jews] put him to death by hanging him on a tree" (10:39). Stephen said, ". . . the Righteous One, whom you have now betrayed and murdered" (7:52). Paul writes, ". . . the Jews, who killed both the Lord Jesus and the prophets, and drove us out" (1 Thess. 2:14–15). Of course, the Romans are equally guilty; but it goes against the clear statements of Scripture to deny the guilt of (part of) the Jews in Jerusalem.

Jesus makes clear that for this reason the kingdom of God will be taken way from (the majority of) Israel, and will be transferred to a new people of God. The former *were not worthy of it*: "'The wedding feast is ready, but

---

10. See, e.g., pastor W. J. J. Glashouwer, www.cip.nl/nieuwsbericht_detail.asp?id=15997.

11. Please note, not *the* Jews, but only *part of* the Jews in Jerusalem (see "they" in Acts 13:28).

those invited were not worthy. Go therefore to the main roads and invite to the wedding feast as many as you find.' And those servants went out into the roads and gathered all whom they found, *both bad and good*. So the wedding hall was filled with guests" (Matt. 22:8-10). Those who *are* worthy are not worthy in themselves; in this respect there is no difference between the various groups of invitees. Rather, they have *become* worthy by accepting the invitation without claiming any rights or privileges for themselves, and learning to live out of the king's pure grace and mercy.

### 4.2.3 Bad and Good

The part of the parable of the wedding feast just quoted includes quite an important statement, which connects two types of Matthew parables. The first type describes the transfer of God's kingdom from the people of Israel to a new people of God, which is gathered from all nations of the world, including Israel itself (see §4.1.). These new people do not contain some "religious elite" but tax collectors and (others) sinners, people who have been gathered from the "street corners" and the "roads" (Matt. 22:9-10 NIV; "the streets and lanes . . . the highways and hedges," Luke 14:21, 23).

However, in themselves these new people of God are just as unworthy to be at the wedding; they can only come in by pure grace. The majority of Israel did not want to come in, whether by right or by grace. But the new people of God, who do want to come in because it is always better in the wedding hall than on the streets, do not always want to come in by grace. In the end they turn out to be no better than Israel. Just like Israel included, and includes, true godly as well as outwardly religious people, thus the new people of God, gathered from all nations, consists of "both bad and good" people. This is what the second type of parables is all about, as we will see in the next sections: parables that describe the kingdom of God in its present form as a mixture of good and bad fruit, wheat and weeds, evil and good servants, wise and foolish virgins, in short: true and false disciples.

It is essential to grasp what this involves. The kingdom parables in Matthew describe two very important and very different historical transitions.

(a) *From the kingdom in Jesus' day to the kingdom after his ascension.* The first mixture of good and bad is found in the Israel of the Gospels: at Pentecost (Acts 2), the true righteous remnant from Israel (cf. Isa. 10:19-22; Rom. 11:5) enters into the kingdom of God of the glorified King, but the wicked as well as the outwardly religious of Israel stay outside. Thus, the kingdom is transferred from the majority of Israel to a new people, consisting of Jews and Gentiles, while Jerusalem comes under judgment. In the end time, there will be a mighty revival in Israel, so that many Jews will enter the kingdom after all.

(b) *From the present to the future kingdom.* In due time, this new (Jewish and Gentile) people of God, within the kingdom of God in its present form—say, the "visible church"—turns out to be just as much a mixture of good and bad. Thus, at the end of the age a second separation will have to take place: the good ones enter the kingdom that will be founded in power and glory at Jesus' parousia, but the bad ones end up in God's judgment.

For the sake of completeness I add the following.

(c) *The Messianic kingdom.* This is not yet the new earth, where there will be no more sin. In the Messianic kingdom, too, people will be born who will submit to the King only in hypocrisy (cf. Isa. 65:20). David spoke prophetically of them in Psalm 18:45 ("foreigners came cringing to me," cf. 66:3; 81:15). This is the explanation for the tremendous success of Satan when, after the "thousand years," he is released from his "prison" to deceive the nations: he "will come out to deceive the nations that are at the four corners of the earth, Gog and Magog, to gather them for battle; their number is like the sand of the sea. And they marched up over the broad plain of the earth and surrounded the camp of the saints and the beloved city, but fire came down from heaven and consumed them" (Rev. 20:8-9).[12]

(d) *In eternity* there will be no more mixture; Jewish and Gentile righteous ones will, in all eternity, have a share in the eternal kingdom (2 Pet. 1:11), while Jewish and Gentile wicked ones will end up in the eternal fire (cf. Matt. 3:12; 5:22, 29-30; 8:12; 10:28; 13:42, 50; 18:8-9; 22:13; 23:33; 24:51; 25:30, 41). Righteousness will not only reign on earth (cf. Isa. 32:1) but *dwell* on earth (2 Pet. 3:13), that is, it will be perfectly at home in this new world.

## 4.2.4 The Man Without a Wedding Garment

In Matthew 22:11-14, we find a concrete example of one of the wicked (see the end of the previous section). This time it is not one of the evil tenants or the evil invitees (the religious hypocrites in Israel), but precisely one of

---

12. See Ouweneel (2012a, §13.5.3).

those who had been gathered from the street corners and the roads: "But when the king came in to look at the guests, he saw there a man who had no wedding garment. And he said to him, 'Friend, how did you get in here without a wedding garment?' And he was speechless. Then the king said to the attendants, 'Bind him hand and foot and cast him into the outer darkness. In that place there will be weeping and gnashing of teeth.' For many are called, but few are chosen."

Of course, the poor people from the highways did not bring their own wedding garment. It must be a garment given by the King, one that matches the glory of his Son, the bridegroom (v. 2). It is worn to honor him with it. It is the right moral equipment (practical righteousness) that is appropriate for the King's wedding (cf. Isa. 61:10, the "garments of salvation . . . the robe of righteousness").[13] Apparently, the garment was offered to all the guests, including the man who refused it. He may have thought that his own clothes, with which he came from the streets, should be good enough for the wedding. The refusal to wear this garment represents a slap in the face for the king and his son. In this way, the man showed that he was unworthy of the kingdom. None of the guests had this worthiness in themselves, but he could have received it by accepting the wedding garment. He refused it, and thus his condition turned out to be just bad as—or even worse than—that of the invitees and all the others who never received a share in the kingdom of God.

By assuming that he had enough dignity of himself, this man behaves precisely as the Pharisees and the

---

13. Carson (1984, 457); cf. Tasker (1961, 207–208).

scribes who boasted in their worthy deeds before God. In the interpretation, however, Jesus does not point here to *this* group but to the outwardly religious who eventually would be found among the new people of God as well, judged by the principle of their own responsibility. The spirit of pseudo-religion that prevailed in the Israel of Jesus' day is exactly the same as the spirit of pseudo-religion that is found worldwide in the Christian world. By pseudo-religion I mean all religiosity with which people (Orthodox, Roman Catholic, Protestant, Evangelical) still believe—consciously or unconsciously—they can stand before God because of their own merits.[14]

So we see that the parable includes a double judgment. The first sentence is pronounced against the "invited ones," that is, the natural, outwardly religious but wicked part of Israel. After this, the "sinners" may come in, both from Israel and from the Gentiles. However, there are those who believe they can be inside the kingdom without a garment that is fitting for the King, a garment of their own righteousness (cf. Isa. 64:6). Against such people, a similar sentence is pronounced as was pronounced against the religious but wicked part of Israel. In Jesus' day, Israel was a mixture of righteous (who were allowed to enter the kingdom) and wicked ones (supposedly religious or not). In its present form, the kingdom of God, consisting of Jews and Gentiles, is again a mixture of righteous

---

14. Cf. Protestant theologian Pieter Smits, who said (1959, 2): "It offends my honor that someone would have to pay for my debt. I wish to accept the consequences of my own deeds. So, as far as Paul is concerned, you can have my portion for free [*geef mijn portie maar aan Fikkie*]"; see Ouweneel (2009a, 59).

(who, at the parousia, will be allowed to enter the Messianic kingdom) and wicked ones. The judgment is precisely the same: the righteous enter the kingdom of God (in its present or in its future form, respectively), and the wicked come under God's judgment.

In my view, the final conclusion of verse 14 is valid for both cases: the called ones or invited ones are many, whether this concerns the Israelites in Jesus' day, or the children of the kingdom in the present time. But the *true* ones among them, the faithful ones, the righteous ones, the genuine disciples of the King, the good servants, the wise virgins, are far fewer in number. Both then and now—and even one day in the Messianic kingdom—the many "called ones" include good ones (the "chosen" ones of v. 14) and bad ones. In the end this is what it comes down to: not whether one is a Jew or a Gentile, Catholic or Protestant, church member or churchless, but whether one is at bottom a righteous or a wicked one, according to God's own standards as laid down in his Torah.

## 4.3  Comparable Passages
### 4.3.1  Again Matthew 13

The fact that the majority of the perhaps (outwardly) religious but ungodly Israel was going to be set aside is not only implied in parables but is also declared in explicit words by Jesus: "See, your house [i.e., the temple] is left to you desolate. For I tell you, you will not see me again, until you say, 'Blessed is he who comes in the name of the Lord'" (Matt. 23:38–39). Interestingly, though, Jesus announces here not only the putting aside of Israel, but also the future restoration of Israel. In the end time,

## The Parables of the Kingdom (II)

there will be a moment when Israel will again declare the words of Psalm 118:26 ("Blessed is he who comes in the name of the LORD! We bless you from the house of the LORD"), and will thus welcome its Messiah. This will happen at his parousia, when the restored nation will receive him as it did in Matthew 21:1-11, at Jesus' entry into Jerusalem (cf. prophetically Ps. 24:7-10). The unbelieving majority of Israel is for a while *Lo-Ammi*, "Not My People" (Hos. 1:9; 2:23):[15] the "until" of verse 39 refers to the time when Israel will again become *Ammi*, "My People."

In fact, already in Matthew 13 Jesus had indicated that, now that the religious elite in Israel had rejected him (with as its worst utterance: "It is only by Beelzebul, the prince of demons, that this man casts out demons," 12:24), from now on the entire world would be his area of activity: "the field is the world" (13:38). After two chapters in which the rejection of Jesus' proclamation reaches its climax in the rejection by the people, the leaders, and Jesus' own family, Matthew 13 marks the turning point in Jesus' presentation of the kingdom.[16] The "word of the kingdom " (v. 19) is no longer limited to Israel, but the "sower" goes out to preach this word to all people in the entire world. Thus, Matthew 13 seems to form the axis of this entire Gospel: the majority of Israel rejects its Messiah (Matt. 11-12), now the

---

15. Of course this concerns only the outward ways of God with Israel; inwardly, the bond can never be lost, and Israel has always remained God's people (cf. after the exile and before the end time: Ezra 1:3; 7:16, 25; Dan. 9:19; Hagg. 1:12; Luke 1:68; 7:16).
16. Saucy (1997, 331).

Messiah sets aside Israel as such, as a nation, for a long time (apart from the "remnant of grace," Rom. 11:5): the field is the world, the net is thrown into the sea.

In a midrashic sense, Matthew 13:1 seems to give a clue: "That same day Jesus went out of the house and sat beside the sea." The house reminds us of 12:44, 46; 15:24; 23:38 (cf. Jer. 12:7, "I have forsaken my house; I have abandoned my heritage"). The sea (cf. v. 47) seems to point to the turbulent mass of nations ("the roar of nations; they roar like the roaring of mighty waters," Isa. 17:12; cf. Rev. 17:15, "The waters that you saw . . . are peoples and multitudes and nations and languages"). It seems to point to Jesus' movement from the "house" of Israel to the "sea" of the nations, in which from now on the net will be thrown out (Matt. 13:47).

### 4.3.2 The Sons of the Kingdom

After Matthew 13, Jesus still speaks in public, but only in parables (13:11, 34–35), and even these are not for all the people: in Matthew 13 only the first four are spoken to all the people, but the last four are spoken only to the disciples (v. 36, "Then he left the crowds and went into the house"). From now on, the kingdom is a secret, a mystery, which Jesus can share only with his followers. At times, the crowd may receive a glimpse of it in the form of a parable, but sometimes not even that (see §3.2).

The initial evidence that the kingdom of God refers primarily to Israel and the subsequent transition to a kingdom that encompasses the entire world becomes strikingly manifest in the expression "sons of the kingdom." The Roman centurion in Matthew 8 proves to have great faith, which leads Jesus to say: "Truly, I tell you, with no one in Israel have I found such faith. I tell you, many will come from east and west and recline at table with Abraham, Isaac, and Jacob in the kingdom of heaven, while the *sons of the kingdom* will be thrown into the outer darkness. In that place there will be weeping and gnashing of teeth" (vv. 10-12). Here, the "sons of the kingdom" are those who were naturally entitled to the kingdom because they belonged to the chosen people of Israel. The majority of these "sons," however, ended up outside the kingdom because they did not have the faith of the centurion and of the many who, from all countries in the world, would receive a share in God's kingdom.

In Matthew 13, the expression receives a new meaning, namely, in the interpretation of the parable of the wheat and the weeds: "The one who sows the good seed is the Son of Man. The field is the world, and the good seed is the *sons of the kingdom*. The weeds are the sons of the evil one, and the enemy who sowed them is the devil. The harvest is the end of the age, and the reapers are angels" (vv. 37-39). Here, the "sons of the kingdom" are those people from all over the world—for "the field is the world"—who come to faith in the Son of Man, and become part of the kingdom of God. First, the kingdom was presented to those who belonged to the chosen people, the "invited ones" (22:3), whereas the Gentiles were left outside. However, now the kingdom is going to belong to all those who become followers of the King, and this can no longer be limited to Israel. In the version of Luke 13:29-30, "[P]eople will come from east and west, and from north and south, and recline at table in the kingdom of God. And behold, some are last [i.e., believing Gentiles] who will be first, and some are first [i.e., the unbelieving majority of Israel] who will be last" (see Matt. 19:30; 20:8, 16; Mark 10:31; Luke 13:30).

Here the "sons of the kingdom" stand in opposition to the "sons of the evil one," so that the contrast here is between the sons of God and the sons of the devil. In Matthew 5, there is a clear parallel between, first, "theirs is the kingdom of heaven" (vv. 3, 10), second, "they shall be called sons of God" (v. 9), and third, "they shall inherit the earth" (v. 5). All three promises basically amount to the same thing. Similarly, in Luke 20:36 the "sons of God" are identical to the "sons of the resurrection" (and to the "sons of light" in 16:8).

## 4.4 The Kingdom: A Mixture
### 4.4.1 The Sower

In §3.1.3 I mentioned as a fifth type of parables those in which especially the activities of "evil" and the "evil one" are described, and this usually in a historical-prophetic perspective. In some parables, the key question is who are allowed to enter the kingdom of God: either the people who are religious (the two sons), who believe they have rights before God (the laborers in the vineyard), who are invited (the wedding feast), or the people who are repentant evildoers and live by grace. In the next parables, we are dealing with two kinds of people who are already *within* the kingdom: good and evil servants (e.g., the talents), wise and foolish virgins, in short: true and false disciples (subjects) of the kingdom.

When Jesus ascended to heaven, he entrusted the kingdom to his followers: He was "like a man going on a journey, who called his servants and entrusted to them his property" (Matt. 25:14). In this way, this person—humanly speaking— takes the same risk that God took when he created the world and entrusted it to humans. In both cases it went wrong. This raises questions, such as: Did Christ, or God, know this beforehand? If so, why did he still take this risk? Or did he *want* it to happen?[17]

Unfortunately, the servants of the King were not able— and sometimes apparently were not *willing*—to prevent the evil one from attempting to seize the kingdom, so that within this kingdom a mixture arose of true and false disciples, evil and good servants. This is explained in parables that usually also point to the end of the age (see the next sections). This is the end of the history of the kingdom in its present form, when everything is put right: the good (righteous) ones enter the kingdom as it will then be established by the Son of Man in power and majesty,[18] and the evil (wicked) ones come under God's judgment.

The battle of the kingdom against the dark powers, and the partial defeat in this battle, is illustrated in a special way in the parables of Matthew 13. Already in the first parable, that of the sower (vv. 3-9; cf. Mark 4:3-9; Luke 8:4-8), we see that, as soon as the preaching of God's kingdom begins—first by Jesus, then by his apostles, then by thousands of servants—the enemy begins to work as well. It is true, the first parable is not called a kingdom parable, but the seed is explained as the "word

---

17. Cf. Ouweneel (2008b, 86-105).
18. It is striking that, on the basis of 1 Cor. 15:28, Cullmann (1941, 11) distinguishes between the "kingdom of Christ" *now* and the "kingdom of God" *then*, whereas the New Testament refers to both the present and the future kingdom as the "kingdom of God" but links the "kingdom of Christ" exclusively with the future Messianic kingdom (apart from the general statement in Matt. 28:18).

of the kingdom" (v. 19), and shortly after telling this first parable, Jesus says that the subject is the "secrets of the kingdom of heaven" (v. 11).

In the parable of the sower, Jesus speaks of the following groups with the concomitant opposing forces:

(a) Those from whom the "evil one" (i.e., Satan) snatches away the word of the kingdom sown in the hearts (v. 19; cf. v. 38). By this group Jesus was possibly referring to the Pharisees and scribes (12:28), whose *hardened* hearts were not accessible to God's Word anymore (cf. John 12:40).

(b) Those who succumb to "tribulation or persecution" (v. 21), which again presupposes the activity of evil forces (cf. 5:10-12, 44; 10:23; 23:34; 24:9, 21, 29). By this group Jesus was possible referring to people like the false disciples in John 6:60-66 (cf. 2:23-25).

(c) Those characterized by a heavy walk ("the cares of the world," cf. 6:25-33) or a sinful walk ("the deceitfulness of riches," cf. 19:23-24) (v. 22). By this group Jesus was possibly referring to his relatives (12:46-47) and similar people, who had *superficial* (cf. 13:21a) or *wordly* hearts (v. 22).

(d) Thank God there were also the true disciples of the kingdom, who had *devoted* hearts: "For whoever does the will of my Father in heaven is my brother and sister and mother" (12:50).

The opposition of the evil one is further illustrated in the next parable, that of the wheat and the weeds (vv. 24-30, 36-43), in which the evil one (the devil) sows weeds among the good wheat (v. 39). The kingdom not only obtains form in an evil world, but this evil also enters the kingdom itself, and creates there an inextricable mixture of good and evil. I repeat, as long as the King has not returned, this is the kingdom: a mixture of wheat and weeds, of good and bad fishes (vv. 47-50), of true and false disciples, of good and evil servants (24:45-51; 25:14-30), of wise and foolish virgins (25:1-13).

Apart from the parables, we find this same truth at several other places in Matthew. Thus, Jesus speaks extensively of the true disciples but also of the false ones: "Not everyone who says to me, 'Lord, Lord,' will enter the kingdom of heaven, but the one who does the will of my Father who is in heaven. On that day many will say to me, 'Lord, Lord, did we not prophesy in your name, and cast out demons in your name, and do many mighty works in your name?' And then will I declare to them, 'I never knew you; depart from me, you workers of lawlessness'" (7:21-23). The title "Lord" or "Master" is proper to disciples (followers and servants of Jesus), but this is true of both the genuine and the false disciples (cf. Matt. 25:20, 22, 24). The misleading element in Matthew 7:21-23 is that, in our thinking, the title "Lord" is much more common for the true disciple (John 13:13; cf. Rom. 10:9-10; 1 Pet. 3:15). We note that eleven disciples said "Lord," but Judas said "Rabbi" (Matt. 26:22,25). In the end, the disciple can say "Lord" only by the power of the Holy Spirit (1 Cor. 12:3). Yet, a disciple saying "Lord" (with his mouth, not with his heart) and doing great miracles can be a false disciple after all.

### 4.4.2 The Wheat and the Weeds

The opposition of the evil one and the working of evil are illustrated in a special way in the parable of the wheat and the weeds (Matt. 13:24-30, 36-43). It is the evil one (the devil) who at night, when all are asleep, sows weeds (probably darnel, a wheat-like weed) among the good wheat (v. 39). This parable has a truly prophetic character by pointing forward to the end of the age. Evil enters the kingdom itself, and brings about an inextricable mixture of good and bad elements within the kingdom. Inextricable: the master says that the two must grow together until the harvest, because only when the darnel and wheat reach full maturity, the two plants, darnel (*Lolium temulentum*) and wheat (*Triticum spp.*), can be clearly distinguished.

Interestingly, already at an early stage, the master's faithful servants begin to realize what must have happened: "Master, did you not sow good seed in your field? How then does it have weeds?" (v. 27). They do so in spite of the great similarity of the two plants. They are those who have enough spiritual discernment to recognize the work of Satan (cf. the shepherd-elders in Acts 20:28–30 and 1 Pet. 5:1–4). Satan, the great imitator, can present himself as an "angel of light" (2 Cor. 11:14), just like Jannes and Jambres imitated the signs of Moses (2 Tim. 3:8). The "beast" rising out of the earth looks like the Lamb but speaks like the dragon (Rev. 13:11), that is, Satan (12:9; 20:2). Luther called Satan *simia Dei*, "the ape of God."[19]

We must clearly distinguish here between the church and the kingdom. Whereas within the *church*, discipline has been commanded (see especially Matt. 18:15–20 and 1 Cor. 5),[20] within the *kingdom* the wheat and the darnel must grow together until the harvest, for only the Son of Man and his angels will be able to tell the good from

---

19. Luther, *WA* 24, 560–61, and other places; the expression can be traced to Caesarius of Heisterbach (†c. 1240).
20. See extensively, Ouweneel (2010b, 367–407).

*The Parables of the Kingdom (II)*

the bad fishes (Matt. 13:49), the true from the false disciples (7:21–23), the good from the evil servants. From the local *church*, the evil person must be purged (1 Cor. 5:13; the expression is adopted from Deut. 13:5; 17:7, 12; 19:19; 21:21; 22:21-22, 24; 24:7), but evil, and evil persons, *cannot* be purged from the kingdom. The domain of the kingdom of God is the entire world, and it is actually the present-day Christian world (if you like, the "visible church"), that is, the totality of all Jesus-confessors, that is, of all true as well as false disciples, all good and evil servants, all wise and foolish virgins, all good and bad fishes, all wheat as well as all darnel.

If things go well, the evil persons are purged from the local church every time one of them manifests himself or herself. However, the evil persons are purged from the kingdom only in the end: "The harvest is the end of the age, and the reapers are angels. Just as the weeds are gathered and burned with fire, so will it be at the end of the age. The Son of Man will send his angels, and they will gather out of his kingdom all causes of sin and all law-breakers, and throw them into the fiery furnace. In that place there will be weeping and gnashing of teeth. Then the righteous will shine like the sun in the kingdom of their Father" (Matt. 13:39–43).

The "servants" of the master of the house (v. 27) are human servants of Christ, working in the kingdom of God in "the [present] age" (v. 40). The "reapers" are angelic servants of Christ, working in God's kingdom at the "end of the [i.e., this] age" (v. 39; cf. 24:31). The servants let darnel and wheat grow together, the reapers separate them: the wicked (Heb. *reshaim*)—those who commit lawlessness, and also cause others to fall—are referred to the "fiery furnace," whereas the righteous (*tsaddiqim*)[21] enter the "kingdom of their Father," that is, the kingdom of God, as it will begin in its future form of power and glory at the parousia of Christ.

The reference is to the "end of the *age*" (vv. 39-40, 48). This is what is called elsewhere "this age" (Matt. 12:32; 13:40; Luke 16:8; 20:34; 1 Cor. 1:20; 2:6; 3:18; 2 Cor. 4:4; Eph. 1:21), or "the present age" (1 Tim. 6:17; 2 Tim. 4:10; Tit. 2:12), or "the present evil age" (Gal. 1:4).[22] An "age" (Greek *aiōn*) is a time period that is governed by certain moral principles (also called *aiōn*; cf. the *aiōn* of this *kosmos*, Eph. 2:2). In rabbinic tradition,[23] "this age" is the age that precedes the appearance of the Messiah and the establishment of his kingdom, and thus precedes the beginning of the "age to come" (Mark 10:30; Luke 18:30; Eph. 1:21; Hebr. 6:5). It is the same in the New Testament: the "present age" is the redemptive-historical epoch in which we live, and which will last until the parousia of Christ. Only then, the "age to come" will break in. It is therefore highly misleading, and apparently dictated by amillennialist and supersessionist

---

21. This is a well-known pair of concepts in the Old Testament; see, e.g., Gen. 18:23, 25; 1 Kgs. 8:32; Ps. 1:5-6; 7:9; 11:5; etc.; Prov. 3:33; 10:3-32 (11x); etc.; and in the New Testament: Matt. 5:45 (*ponēros* and *dikaios*); 1 Tim. 1:9 (*dikaios* and *anomos*); 1 Pet. 4:18 (*dikaios* and *asebēs*). In my view, it is the most useful pair of concepts to distinguish the good and the bad, the true and the false believers plus the unbelievers.

22. Cf. also "this world [Greek *kosmos*]" in John 8:23; 9:39; 11:9; 12:25, 31; 13:1; 16:11; 18:36, in contrast with the future world.

23. E.g., 1 Enoch 48:7; 4 Ezra 6:7-10, 20; 12:25; 14:10.

prejudices, to translate *synteleia (tou) aiōnos* in verses 39–40 and 49 as "the end of time" (CEV, ERV, etc.) or "the end of the/this world" (KJV,[24] ASV, GNV, etc.). It is *not* the end of time, or of the world: it is the end of the present age, *and the beginning of the age to come.*

### 4.4.3 "The Field Is the World"

Jesus' words, "the field is the world," require further discussion. Concerning Matthew 13:38a Richard C. Trench says:"Over these few words, simple as they may seem, there has perhaps been more contention than over any single phrase in the Scripture, if we except the consecrating words at the Holy Eucharist [i.e., This is my body]."[25] The core questions are these: Is the fact that "the field is the world" true only for the moment when the sowing occurs (the field is the entire world as the work arena of the Holy Spirit), *or* does "the world" refer to a field with half-grown wheat including the darnel? But Jesus says that the angels will gather the wicked out of "the kingdom" (v. 41); is the "kingdom" identical with the "world"? Does this parable, and do other parables, refer to believers and unbelievers in the entire world, or in the kingdom? Or are these the same thing?

Trench identifies the practical significance of these questions.[26] The Novatians and the Donatists separated themselves from the Roman Catholic Church because,

---

24. It is surprising and encouraging that NKJV changed "world" into "age" in its revision.
25. www.davidcox.com.mx/library/T/Trench%20-%20Parables%20(b).pdf, onder 'Parable of Tares'.
26. See, much more recently, Carson (1984, 325).

according to them, the church is a *holy* company, with a holiness that must be realized in a practical way by purging the evil ones from its midst (1 Cor. 5:13). Augustine responded (simply summarized): the wheat and the darnel must grow together until the harvest.[27] The Donatists answered (as implied in Augustine's argument): The "field" in which they grow together is not the church but the world; within this world, the church must occupy a holy (separated) place. Similar questions arose in the time of the Reformation: the Reformers, who advocated national churches (German: *Volkskirchen*, French: églises du peuple), chose Augustine's side. The Anabaptists, but also (originally Lutheran) Andreas Karlstadt (†1541), the Baptists (seventeenth century), and many denominations that have seceded from the Anglican, Reformed, and Presbyterian churches, as well as many Evangelical churches, advocate a church that purges the evil ones from its midst, and separates itself from the wickedness in the world as well as from churches who refuse to purge the evil ones from their midst.

A good example of this conflict is offered by John Calvin, who writes: "Let them [i.e., Donatists, Anabaptists, etc.] hear that it is like a field sown with good seed which is through the enemy's deceit scattered with tares and is not purged of them until the harvest is brought into the thressing floor. . . . But if the Lord declares that the church is to labor under this evil—to be weighed down with the mix-

---

27. See in particular his *Breviculus Collationis cum Donatistis* and *Ad Donatistas post Collationem*.

ture of the wicked—until the Day of Judgment, they are vainly seeking a church besmirched with no blemish."[28]

In my view, Calvin makes two mistakes here. First, Donatists and Anabaptists in former times, and Evangelicals today, do not seek "a church besmirched with no blemish," because they do realize that just about every church most likely includes false confessors. In *this* regard, it is indeed impossible to separate the wheat and the darnel. But churches do have the task to purge the *manifest* evil ones from their midst, and in *this* way to separate wheat and darnel. In this connection, churches must walk the narrow path between too strict a separation, inevitably leading to sectarianism,[29] and latitudinarianism, involving all too great a toleration of evil.

Calvin's second error, made already by Augustine, is to introduce the church into this parable. The parable does not refer to the church at all, neither explicitly nor implicitly. Therefore, Origen had rightly said, "The whole world, and not only the church of God, can be called 'the field.' For in the entire world the Son of Man has sown good seed."[30] This may be the correct meaning. But even if the "field" is the *Christian* world, this is a much wider circle than the church viewed as the body of Christ.

The parables deal with the kingdom of God, and nothing else, and few Christians would be willing to identify church and kingdom[31] (although one has to admit that in Matthew the two are always closely related:

---

28. Calvin, *Institutes*, 4.1.13.
29. See Ouweneel (2010b, 443–500).
30. *Contra Celsum* 144.
31. See, e.g., Ladd (1974a, 105–107); Guthrie (1981, 702–706).

16:18 *and* 19; also 18:3-4 *and* 17 *and* 23).[32] But the kingdom and the world are identical only insofar the general world dominion of God is concerned. In a more limited sense, the kingdom includes the good and evil servants *of Christ*, or the true and false disciples *of Christ*. A non-Jesus-confessor belongs to the "world" (i.e., humanity) but not to the kingdom in this narrower sense, let alone to the church. A false Jesus-confessor belongs both to humanity and to the kingdom, but not to the church (seen as the "holy congregation and gathering of true Christian believers," Belgic Confession, Art. 27). A true Jesus-confessor belongs to humanity as well as to the kingdom as well to the church. In this view, world, kingdom, and church are like three concentric circles, which never coincide.

### 4.4.4 The Mustard Seed

There are two more parables in Matthew 13 in which I discern references to a mixture of good and evil, namely, the parables of the mustard seed (vv. 31-32; cf. Mark 4:30-32; Luke 13:18-19) and the leaven (Matt. 13:33; cf. Luke 13:20-21). The mustard seed probably refers to the "black mustard" (*Brassica nigra*), an annual plant that can reach a height of some eight feet (2.4 meters). According to some expositors, we find in the parable an unnatural development of the kingdom.[33] It is not natural for a mustard seed to develop

---

32. See R. S. Rayburn (www.faithtacoma.org/sermons/Matthew/Matt13.24-33.Oct24.04.pdf).
33. See Kelly (1896, ad loc.); Grant (1897, ad loc.); Gaebelein (1910, ad loc.); Walvoord (1974, ad loc.).

into "a large tree,"[34] such as a Palestinian oak (max. 55 feet or 18 meters) or a Lebanese cedar (130 feet or 40 meters).

If this is indeed the intention of the parable, we may truly say that the Christian world is unnaturally large—today it includes one-third of humanity, the totality of all people who call themselves Christian in some way or another—compared with the true church of God on earth (the "holy congregation and gathering of true Christian believers"). Jesus foretells here that the kingdom of God would expand tremendously on earth, just as (in the previous parable) wheat and weeds together yield a much larger harvest than wheat alone. If this approach is correct, Jesus does not see this as a positive development.

The idea of a negative tendency of the parable is supported by the reference to the "birds of the air [lit., of heaven]," which often constitute a negative picture. The prophet speaks of the evil world empire of Assyria, presented as a mighty cedar: "All the birds of the heavens made their nests in its boughs" (Ezek. 31:6). In a similar way, Nebuchadnezzar, the head of the mighty Babylonian empire, is presented as a large and strong tree: "[T]he birds of the heavens lived in its branches" (Dan. 4:11-12, 21). In Revelation 18:2, the "great Babylon" is "a dwelling place for demons, a haunt for every unclean spirit, a haunt for every unclean bird" (cf. Isa. 34:11, "the hawk and the porcupine shall possess it [i.e., Edom], the owl and the raven shall dwell in it"; see also the ostriches in 13:21).

---

34. Thus important manuscripts in Luke 13:19.

This is what the kingdom of God—the Christian world—has become: an unnaturally large world power, in which "every unclean bird" can find a place. Hawks, owls, ravens, and ostriches are unclean birds (see Lev. 11; Deut. 14). Such birds are especially unclean if they are birds of prey (hawk, owl, raven, etc.); and of the ostriches it is said, "God has made her forget wisdom and given her no share in understanding" (Job 39:17).

Many expositors have doubted this approach of the parable, and have seen in it a positive development of the kingdom of God on earth. However, notice its position between the parable of the wheat and the weeds—which undoubtedly points to a mixture of good and evil—and the parable of the leaven, where again I cannot doubt that the leaven points to the unclean element in the kingdom, as we are going to consider now.

### 4.4.5 The Leaven

Let us now consider the parable of the leaven: "The kingdom of heaven is like leaven that a woman took and hid in three measures of flour, till it was all leavened" (v. 33; cf. Luke 13:20-21). Various expositors have seen in the leaven an image of evil,[35] in my view rightly so. Even in the Talmud, leaven can have a negative figurative meaning.[36] In the New Testament, we find (besides Matt. 13:33) five forms of leaven: (a) the leaven of the Phari-

---

35. E.g., Grant (1897, 146-48); Gaebelein (1910, 1:282-83, 287-93); Kelly (*BT* 20:373-74); Walvoord (1974, ad loc.).

36. E.g., Rosh haShanah 3b, where it is said of king Darius that he "fermented," which refers to his evil inclination; cf. Ouweneel (2001b, 91-92).

sees, which was hypocritical legalism and traditionalism (Matt. 16:6, 11–12); (b) the leaven of the Sadducees, who preached false doctrine (Matt. 16:6, 11–12; Acts 23:6–8); (c) the leaven of the Herodians, which was worldliness, cooperating with the worldly powers (Mark 8:15); (d) the leaven of 1 Corinthians 5:6–7, being not only moral evil but also indifference toward it; (e) the leaven of Galatians 5:9, which was legalism as a condition for salvation. All these forms of evil can be found in the kingdom of heaven as it exists today.

In my view, the counterargument of Don Carson, that this interpretation implies the introduction of anachronistic ideas such as the "confessing church,"[37] is not applicable. First, I see no need at all for the notion of the "confessing church" in the interpretation. Second, more importantly, *at many places* in Matthew, we see that Jesus predicts precisely this: in his absence (cf. 25:15), the kingdom would gradually develop into a mixture of good and evil, until the end of the age.

There are two simple and, in my view, decisive arguments for seeing the leaven as a picture of evil as a secretively working principle. First, *everywhere* in Scripture, leaven is an image of an evil principle,[38] in spite of the astonishing turn by Alexander B. Bruce,[39] who asserts that Jesus had the "courage" to turn an image of evil into a "symbol for the best in the world"! Second, viewing leaven here as an image of evil fits excellently in the totality of Mat-

---

37. Carson (1984, 319).
38. See Ouweneel (2010b, 392–93).
39. Bruce (1979, 201).

thew 13 (the sower, the weeds, the net), where we find a similar mixture of good and evil. In the present time, the kingdom of heaven looks like good flour that is thoroughly permeated with the leaven, just as the weeds have mixed inextricably with the wheat, and the good and bad fishes, too, are together in one net (§4.4.7).

Carson's argument that in the Old Testament leaven is not always an image of evil[40] is incorrect: in Leviticus 7:13 and 23:15-18, it is very well possible to connect leaven with sin in those who are bringing the offering.[41]

### 4.4.6 The Woman

If the interpretation being presented here is valid, and if "three measures" symbolizes an ephah,[42] then the "woman" in verse 33 easily reminds us of the "woman in the basket [Heb. *ephah*, a vessel of about 22 liters]." This is a woman who belongs in Shinar (Babylon, Gen. 11:1-9; cf. Josh. 7:11; Dan. 1:2), from where in Israel the "iniquity" (idolatry) was introduced (Zech. 5:5-11).

Moreover, some see a parallel between Matthew 13 and Revelation 2-3, which I will not explain here.[43] In this parallel, the fourth parable, about the woman and the leaven, corresponds to the fourth letter in Revelation, written to the church in Thyatira: "I have this against you, that you tolerate that woman Jezebel, who

---

40. Carson (1984, 319).
41. Mackintosh (2012, ad loc.); Coates (1922, 91-92, 250).
42. A "measure" is about three omers, and an omer is one-tenth of an ephah (Exod. 16:36). Sarah used the same quantity to prepare bread for her guests (Gen. 18:6); cf. Gideon (Judg. 6:19) and Hannah (1 Sam. 1:24).
43. See Pentecost (1964, 138-49, 153).

calls herself a prophetess and is teaching and seducing my servants to practice sexual immorality and to eat food sacrificed to idols" (Rev. 2:20).

In the case of the "birds of the air," we are dealing with manifest evil influences from outside, whereas in the leaven we are dealing with a secretive evil influence from within. This is what Paul says, "Do you not know that a little leaven leavens the whole lump?" (1 Cor. 5:6), and again: "A little leaven leavens the whole lump" (Gal. 5:9). In both cases, he refers to evil permeating the good in a way that can never be undone. When they heard about "leaven," Jewish hearers of Jesus would *never* have thought of a positive force, since they were unfamiliar with *Pesach*, when all leaven must be removed from the houses as a symbol of cleansing and purification from evil.[44] Jesus' Jewish hearers would also have thought of the grain offering, a quantity of fine flour, about which the LORD said, "No grain offering that you bring to the LORD shall be made with leaven, for you shall burn no leaven nor any honey as a food offering to the LORD" (Lev. 2:11). The grain offering refers to the earthly life of the Man Jesus Christ, in which all sinfulness was lacking (2 Cor. 5:21; 1 Pet. 2:22; 1 John 3:5).[45]

All in all, I cannot doubt that the parable speaks of the working of evil within the kingdom of God.

### 4.4.7 The Net

The parable of the net "that was thrown into the sea and gathered fish of every kind" (Matt. 13:47), presents to us the same mixed kingdom: an intermin-

---

44. See Ouweneel (2001b, 74–75, 89–93).
45  See Ouweneel (2009a, 102).

gling of good as well as bad fishes, just like the wheat and the weeds, the mustard tree with the birds, and the flour with the leaven (and also the good and the bad servants, the wise and the foolish virgins in Matt. 25).

Think here again of what was said about verse 1: Jesus spiritually left the house of Israel, and sat beside the sea of the nations. Just as the seed is sown into the field—and "the field is the world" (v. 38)—similarly the net is thrown into the sea of the nations. That is, from now on there can be no place on earth—or in the "sea"—where would-be disciples could not be gathered. However, just as not every place in the field yields good fruit (vv. 18-23), so too not all that is produced by the sea is useful for the kingdom of God.

The end of the parable resembles that of the parable of the wheat and the weeds: "So it will be at the end of the age. The angels will come out and separate the evil from the righteous and throw them into the fiery furnace. In that place there will be weeping and gnashing of teeth" (vv. 49-50). Notice here, however, the difference between the parable as such and its interpretation. The parable itself emphasizes what happens to the good fishes: "When it [i.e., the net] was full, men drew it ashore and sat down and sorted the good [fishes] into containers but threw away the bad [fishes]" (v. 48). The good fishes are separated from the bad fishes, the latter being simply "thrown away." Jesus' interpretation, however, emphasizes instead what happens with the bad fishes: the evil ones are separated from the righteous ones, and thrown into hell.

The good fishes are sorted into "containers." One could say: they have reached the destiny for which they had been created (cf. 2 Pet. 2:12). In the application this means that the good disciples, the "righteous" (v. 49), attain the kingdom of God in its future glorious form.

## 4.5 Parables of the Olivet Discourse[46]

### 4.5.1 The Fig Tree

We now come to the four parables in Jesus' Olivet Discourse, all of which turn out to have an eschatological character. First the parable of the fig tree: "From the fig tree learn its lesson [lit., learn a parable]: as soon as its branch becomes tender and puts out its leaves, you know that summer is near. So also, when you see all these things, you know that he is near, at the very gates" (Matt. 24:32-33; cf. Mark 13:28-29; Luke 21:29-31).

In the interpretation of this short story, which in the Greek is explicitly described as a parable, we may go deeper than to learn here something about fig trees in a very general sense. We cannot forget that, in Matthew 21:18-20, Jesus had cursed a fig tree in such a way that everyone recognizes in this tree the stiff-necked, unbelieving majority of Israel (cf. Luke 13:6-9; also see Jer. 8:13; 24:1-10; Hos. 9:10; Joel 1:7).

Parallel with this, many see in the fig tree of Matthew 24:32 similarly a picture of Israel, but now as the object

---

46. See Wenham (2003). Jeremias (2003, ad loc.) calls Matt. 25:31-46 (the judgment on the sheep and the goats) a parable but, in my view, the metaphorical language is no justification for this.

of God's indefatigable faithfulness to his covenant promise: one day the fig tree of Israel will blossom again.[47] As dramatic as the cursing of the fig tree was, just as sensational will it be when *this* fig tree will put out its leaves again. The curse in 21:19 was *eis ton aiōna*, which I take here to mean: "until the age [to come]." There is a holy "until": "See, your [i.e., Jerusalem's] house is left to you desolate. For I tell you, you will not see me again, *until* you say, 'Blessed is he who comes in the name of the Lord'" (23:38–39).

This is the "until" of Isaiah 32:14–16, "For the palace is forsaken, the populous city [i.e., Jerusalem] deserted . . . *until* the Spirit is poured upon us [i.e., Israel] from on high, and the wilderness becomes a fruitful field, and the fruitful field is deemed a forest. Then justice will dwell in the wilderness, and righteousness abide in the fruitful field." It is the "until" of Isaiah 62:1, "For Zion's sake I will not keep silent, and for Jerusalem's sake I will not be quiet, *until* her righteousness goes forth as brightness, and her salvation as a burning torch." It is the "until" of Ezekiel 21:27, "A ruin, ruin, ruin I will make it. This also shall not be, *until* he [i.e., the Messiah] comes, the one to whom judgment belongs, and I will give it to him." It is the "until" of Hosea 5:15, "I will return again to my place, *until* they [i.e., the Israelites] acknowledge their guilt and seek my face, and in their distress earnestly seek me."

Every attentive believer will be able to recognize through Israel's national and spiritual restoration that

---

47. Kelly (1896, ad loc.); Grant (1897, ad loc.); Gaebelein (1910, ad loc.); Walvoord (1974, ad loc.); *contra*, e.g., France (2007, 929).

we are getting close to the "summer" of redemptive history, that is, the Messianic kingdom in power and glory, the time of the "harvest" (Hos. 6:11). The end time—the period just preceding the parousia and the kingdom of peace—is, as it were, springtime (cf. the prophetic meaning of Song 2:11-13, ". . . the winter is past; the rain is over and gone. The flowers appear on the earth, the time of singing has come, and the voice of the turtledove is heard in our land. The *fig tree* ripens its figs, and the vines are in blossom; they give forth fragrance").

## 4.5.2 The Two Servants

We have seen several times now that, within the kingdom of God in its present form, there are true and false disciples, good and evil servants. At some places in Matthew, the disciples of the kingdom are called servants in a general sense (Matt. 10:24-25; 18:23; 20:27; 25:14), whereas at other places we find more particularly servants of the King (13:27; 21:34; 22:3; 24:45). Now the striking feature of the parable of the two servants (Matt. 24:45-51; cf. Luke 12:42-48) is that we find here the singular: first we hear of the "faithful and wise servant, whom his master has set over his household, to give them their food at the proper time," afterwards we hear of "*that* wicked servant" (Greek *ho kakos doulos ekeinos*). This is quite remarkable: it sounds as if the text speaks of one and the same servant. No wonder that several translations eliminate the difficulty: "But if that servant is wicked . . ." (CJB; cf. GNT), "But what will happen if that servant is evil . . ." (ERV; cf. ICB), "But suppose that servant is wicked . . ." (NIV; cf. NIRV). However, none of these are literal renderings of the Greek.

Before we enter more deeply into this difficulty, let us look first at the parable as a whole. The "faithful and wise servant" (v. 45) is a spiritual leader who takes care of the ones entrusted to him: "Blessed is that servant whom his master will find so doing when he comes. Truly, I say to you, he will set him over all his possessions" (vv. 46-47). The "wicked servant" is characterized as wicked especially because he no longer conducts his life and service in the expectation of the imminent return of the King. He "says to himself, 'My master is delayed'"[48] (v. 48), and as soon as he thinks this way, his whole attitude changes (v. 49). He begins to behave as if he is himself the master of the house.

As long as the servant believes that his master can return home *any moment*, he will never think such a thing but will be constantly prepared to hand the household back to the master in as excellent a condition as possible. However, as soon as he comes to the conviction that the master will stay away for some (or even, a long) time, he begins playing the boss. He "begins to beat his fellow servants and eats and drinks with drunkards" (v. 49). The beating implies a false exercise of power, which denies the authority of the King (cf. 1 Pet. 5:3). The eating and drinking implies a worldly lifestyle (vv. 48-49; cf. Rom. 13:12-14).

Regarding the good servant who is afterward called "that" wicked servant, I believe there are good rea-

---

48. Greek chronizō; NKJV: "is delaying his coming"; CJB: "My master is taking his time"; CEV: "the master won't return until late"; etc.; cf. 25:5, "As the bridegroom was delayed"; 25:19, "after a long time [meta polyn chronon] the master of those servants came."

sons to assume that Jesus is indeed speaking of one and the same servant, who manifests himself initially as a faithful and wise servant, and afterward as a wicked servant. If this is the correct approach, the servant represents the Christian world as a whole. In church history, the faithful servant has *become* the wicked servant the moment he lost sight of the imminent return of the Master.

In church history, we can identify that moment rather accurately.[49] In the first three centuries, the church lived by a vivid, premillennial expectation: Jesus would return soon, and then he would establish his Messianic kingdom of peace and justice. However, when the Roman emperor, Constantine the Great, adopted the Christian faith (AD 312), and when in 380 the church of Rome became the state religion of the Roman empire, the situation changed drastically.[50] Now that there was a Christian emperor in Rome, next to whom the bishop of Rome would more and more present himself as "pope" (*papa*, "father" of the entire Christian world), people began to believe that the Messianic kingdom had already arrived (amillennialism, or rather: "realized millennialism," the conviction that the kingdom of peace had already appeared).

It is not difficult to imagine what would now happen to the expectation of the parousia. It was pushed off to the "last day" at the very end of world history, and was therefore by definition still a long way off. This view was combined with supersessionism, the doctrine that, with respect to the promises and blessings of God, the

---

49. See Ouweneel (2010c, 207).
50. See Ouweneel (2016d, chapter 5).

church has replaced Israel, and with spiritualism, whereby the literal exegesis of the Old Testament prophecies was abandoned: land, city, and temple are spiritualized, and viewed as fulfilled in the church. Literally this became the attitude of the servant: "My master won't return in a long time."

In his story, *The Grand Inquisitor*,[51] Fyodor M. Dostoyevsky has described in a magnificent way the consequence of this development: church leaders began to believe that they themselves were the masters over church members, and behaved accordingly (see v. 49). The grand inquisitor does not want Christ to have any dealings with the church as long as Christ had not officially returned, which will occur only at the end of time, suggesting that at the moment, he is "far away." Christ's return, then, can only be an unpleasant surprise for this amillennialist church[52]: "[T]he master of that servant will come on a day when he does not expect him and at an hour he does not know and will cut him in pieces and put him with the hypocrites. In that place there will be weeping and gnashing of teeth" (Matt. 24:50–51).

In the fewest possible words, the destiny of the false church is pictured: judgment. By the false church I do *not* mean this or that denomination, but rather those Christian confessors who either no longer believe in the parousia (cf. 2 Pet. 3:3), or believe that this

---

51. In the novel *The Brothers Karamazov*; on this, see Ouweneel (2003).
52. Please note that even Luther and Calvin still clung to this amillennialism. Only later in the sixteenth century, room was created for post- and premillennial views; see Ouweneel (2012a, §§9.1.3 and 9.2).

is still far away, and in the meantime behave as if their own lives, as well as the churches entrusted to them, belong to them. This is the attitude of the "great Babylon," which says, "I sit as a queen, I am no widow, and mourning I shall never see" (Rev. 18:7; cf. Isa. 47:8), that is, I do not live as if I miss my husband. The false church behaves as if it has no "husband," that is, it does not need Jesus, and does not miss him. She may be thrilled with the example given by the *past* Jesus—the One spoken of in the Gospels—but she can very well do without the *present* and *future* Jesus. Although this description is given in different metaphorical language, it vividly portrays the attitude of the servant.

### 4.5.3 The Ten Virgins

In the parable of the ten virgins (Matt. 25:1-13), there are five who are "wise," in the sense that they possess oil and are therefore able to keep their lamps burning until the arrival of the bridegroom, and five who are "foolish," in the sense that they have lamps but cannot keep them burning because they have no oil. In the preceding parable, the "wicked servant" followed in church history upon the "faithful and wise" slave, but with the ten virgins the situation is different. First, the virgins do not just *think* that the bridegroom was delaying his coming (cf. 24:48), but we are told as a fact that he *was* indeed delayed (25:5). That is, Jesus stays away (much) longer than the disciples had thought.

Second, *all* the virgins fell asleep, the foolish as well as the wise ones. This is indeed the picture that we get from the fourth and later centuries of church history: generally speaking, the church no longer lived in terms of the expectation of the imminent return of Christ, and this was true for both the righteous and the wicked. Generally speaking, it was still true even for the early generations of Protestantism. Jesus' parousia was *confessed*—as in the Apostles' Creed: "[H]e will come to judge the living and the dead"—but was no longer *anticipated*. Moreover, just as it was not only the foolish virgins who fell asleep, but also the wise virgins, similarly, at the call of the approaching bridegroom, not only the wise but also the foolish virgins awoke (think of borderline eschatological movements like those of the Jehovah's Witnesses and the Mormons, which all sprang up in the nineteenth century).

Even more strongly than with the preceding parable, I believe that the parable of the ten virgins can be understood in a meaningful way only from a church historical perspective.[53] Thus, the question arises when in church history it was "midnight," that is, the time when the call was heard, "Here is the bridegroom! Come out to meet him" (25:6). Elsewhere I have tried to show that, in the sixteenth and seventeenth centuries, in various European countries, supersessionism and spiritualism, and thus amillennialism, began to be heavily criticized.[54] However, this did not yet mean a concrete revival of the expectation of the parousia. This happened only in the eighteenth and nineteenth centuries.

---

53  See Kelly (1896, ad loc.); Grant (1897, ad loc.); Gaebelein (1910, ad loc.); Walvoord (1974, ad loc.).

54. Cf. Ouweneel (2012a, §§9.1 and 9.2).

"Stay dressed for action and keep your lamps burning" (Luke 12:35). The lamp speaks of the believers' testimony in the world, of spiritual light that they need in spiritual darkness, of the need to keep awake while waiting for the Lord. I would suggest that the oil here is a symbol of the Holy Spirit. In the Old Testament, priests and kings were anointed with oil, in the New Testament with the Holy Spirit (Acts 10:38; 2 Cor. 1:21-22). To be sure, the parable speaks not of anointing but of light-bearing, for which the Holy Spirit is needed as well. Compare Paul's statement, "[Y]ou are light in the Lord. Walk as children of light (for the fruit of light is found in all that is good and right and true)" (Eph. 5:8-9), where other manuscripts have "the fruit of the Spirit" (NKJV, GNV, etc.), thus connecting Spirit and light.

Bearing light, being light, walking in the light, is an important mission for believers (see, e.g., Rom. 13:12; Phil. 2:15; 1 Thess. 5:4-5; 1 John 1:5-7). In the closing stage of God's kingdom in its present form, this will be one of the great questions: Which Christian confessors live by the power of the Holy Spirit, and which do not? Please note that the foolish virgins are not "weak" Christians but "false" Christians, pseudo-Christians; see verse 12, where the Lord says, "I do not know you," which implies there is no life connection between them and him (in 7:23 he adds, "Depart from me"; cf. Luke 13:25, 27). Compare this with Paul's word, "[I]f anyone loves God, he is known by God" (1 Cor. 8:3; cf. Gal. 4:9).

At the same time, in principle the parable offers hope for those who, so far, have been only outward confessors:

"[G]o rather to the dealers and buy for yourselves" (Matt. 25:9). We should not press the parable too much (cf. §3.4.2), yet we find a clear suggestion here that the oil is available to everyone. Therefore, the "dealers" we may see as God's servants through whose ministry one can receive the Holy Spirit in the end time. To be sure, the parable suggests that all the virgins who went to the dealers arrived too late for the wedding, but in the application this does not have to be the case, of course. It is never too late to be filled with the Spirit (cf. Eph. 5:18 in connection with Luke 11:13), and thus to change from a false or weak into (respectively) a true or strong disciple of the kingdom of God.[55]

This is an eschatological parable, too, because in metaphorical language we are being pointed here to the end of the present age, which will be the end of the kingdom in its present form, and the transition to the Messianic kingdom of peace. We have five such parables in Mathew: two in which the phrase "end of the age" is explicitly used (weeds and net), and three in which we are literally being pointed to the (second) coming of Christ: (a) the two servants ("the master of that servant will come on a day when he does not expect him," 24:50), (b) the ten virgins ("while they were going to buy, the bridegroom came," 25:6), and (c) the talents ("after a long time the master of those servants came," v. 19).

Please note that these last three parables make clear that Matthew is not literally suggesting that Jesus would be returning soon (see §5.3). Jesus himself shows this in three statements: "My master is delayed" (24:49), "As the bridegroom was delayed . . ." (25:5), and: "Now after a long time the master of those servants came" (v. 19).

---

55. See Ouweneel (2010d).

### 4.5.4 The Talents

The parable of the talents is the last of the kingdom parables in Matthew. It is also the last of the five eschatological kingdom parables, that is, parables in which the outcome is the "end of the age" (Matt. 13:39-40, 48). This age is called "this age," or "the present age," or "the present evil age" (§4.4.2). All three parables in Matthew 24:45-25:30 describe the "present age," and end with the appearance of the Messiah and the beginning of his kingdom of peace and justice. Matthew 25:31 then continues with this fact and the announcement of the Messianic kingdom: "When the Son of Man comes in his glory, and all the angels with him, then he will sit on his glorious throne.[56] Before him will be gathered all the nations, and he will separate people one from another as a shepherd separates the sheep from the goats. And he will place the sheep on his right, but the goats on the left. Then the King will say to those on his right, 'Come, you who are blessed by my Father, *inherit the kingdom* prepared for you from the foundation of the world'" (25:31-34).

The parable of the talents speaks about good servants, to whom "talents" have been entrusted with which they begin to trade in order to gain more talents (25:20-23). It speaks also of the "wicked and slothful" servant (v. 26), who did not really serve his master. Here, a "talent" is not what we—to be sure, because of this parable—usually call a "talent": a capacity, a skill, an ability, an aptitude. In the parable, a talent, as in 18:24, is a specific amount of money: one talent is sixty minas, and one mina is hundred denarii. If we view a denarius (the wage of a day

---

56. Lit., "throne of his glory"; cf. Jer. 17:12; Matt. 19:28 (the heavenly throne of his dominion; cf. §5.3).

laborer, Matt. 20:2) as the rough equivalent of $50.00, and a talent is 6,000 denarii, then a talent is about $300,000.[57] We read that the king's servants receive a number of talents "each according to his ability" (25:15). It is these (natural) abilities that roughly correspond to what we today call "talents." In addition to these natural abilities, each servant receives a spiritual fortune, which he may deploy for his master.

Of course, there are several similarities to the parable of the minas in Luke 19:11–27, but the differences are striking as well. I point especially to this remarkable difference: in the parable of the talents, the servants receive *different* numbers of talents but the first two make the *same* profit, namely, 100%, and thus receive the *same* reward ("Enter into the joy of your master," vv. 21, 23). In the parable of the minas, the servants each receive the *same* number of minas, namely one, but the first two servants make a *different* profit, namely, 1,000% and 500%, and thus receive a *different* reward, namely, authority over ten and five cities, respectively. The significance of this is that servants of the King are not rewarded according to their talents (gifts, ministries)—for these they have received by grace (1 Cor. 4:7)—but according to the faithfulness with which they have traded with the riches that were entrusted to them.

The entrance into the "joy of the Master"—characteristic of the kingdom (see, e.g., Song 3:11; Isa. 35:10; 51:11; 61:7; Zeph. 3:14–17; Luke 22:30; Rom. 14:17)—presupposes the servants' love for the Lord, and hence their desire to be with him and share his gladness. This is exactly what is lacking in the third servant. He calls his master a "hard man" (Matt. 25:24; cf. Luke 19:21, a "se-

---

57. See chapter 3, n38; cf. Carson (1984, 516).

vere man"), which shows that he does not know him, and therefore does not love him. We are also impressed by his stupidity, his lack of insight: he buried the talent instead of investing it with the bankers, so that at least some profit might have been gained (Matt. 25:27). The servant who does not stand in a vital relationship with the Lord is driven neither by love nor by wisdom.

It is important to point out again that the parable is not about a judgment of humanity in general, but a judgment of those who are explicitly described here as servants of the King. These do not include all human beings, but those who may be called followers of Jesus, not only the true (regenerate, good, righteous, humble) ones but also the false (unregenerate, evil, wicked, haughty) ones. This parable, too, confirms that, after Jesus' ascension, the kingdom was going to include a mixture of good and evil servants, and also that at the end of the age a separation would take place among these servants. That is, the good servants will receive a share in the Messianic kingdom of peace and justice, and will reign with Christ (cf. Luke 19:17, 19), whereas the worthless servants are cast into the outer darkness, where there is weeping and gnashing of teeth (Matt. 25:30).

### 4.5.5 Contrasts

As we conclude this chapter, it is worthwhile to reconsider what contrasts we have encountered in the parables of Matthew, that is, contrasts *within* the kingdom of God, thus corresponding to the general contrast between true and false disciples of the King.

| **Righteous ones** (*tsaddiqim*) | **Wicked ones** (*r'sha 'im*) |
|---|---|
| Wise builders (on the rock) | Foolish builders (on sand) |
| Little, weak, righteous ones | Outwardly religious ones |
| Willing to forgive | Unwilling to forgive |
| Those living by grace | Those living by (alleged) "rights" |
| Good sons (repentant stiff-necked ones) | Bad sons (dead religious ones) |
| Righteous tenants | Unrighteous tenants |
| Outcasts | Invitees |
| Fertile soil | Infertile soil |
| Good wheat | Useless weeds |
| Good fishes | Bad fishes |
| Good servants | Wicked servants |
| Wise virgins | Foolish virgins |

The righteous enter the Messianic "kingdom prepared for [them] from the foundation of the world" (cf. Matt. 25:34). The wicked go to "the eternal fire prepared for the devil and his angels" (v. 41).

# Chapter 5
# The Adversaries
# of the Kingdom

*Every kingdom divided against itself*
  *is laid waste*
  *and no city or house divided*
  *against itself will stand.*
*And if Satan casts out Satan, he is*
  *divided against himself.*
  *How then will his kingdom stand?*
*And if I cast out demons by Beelzebul,*
  *by whom do your sons cast*
  *them out?*
*Therefore they will be your judges.*
*But if it is by the Spirit of God that I*
  *cast out demons,*
  *then the kingdom of God has come*
  *upon you.*
Matthew 25:25–28

## THE ETERNAL KINGDOM: LIVING UNDER CHRIST

***Summary:*** *Ever since the Fall, the kingdom of Satan has existed in this world. Since the coming of Jesus, the kingdom of God has existed in this world. Until the "end of the age," these two kingdoms will be opposed to each other; there is a perpetual conflict between the two. By the power of the Holy Spirit, Jesus withstood Satan's kingdom, and so do his followers. With spiritual "violence" they moved out of Satan's kingdom into God's kingdom. Because of Satan's powerful hatred, the present kingdom of God for the most part experiences suffering; however, it also enjoys elements of the future triumph, already now. (Some Christians emphasize the former elements, others the latter.) In his Olivet Discourse, Jesus prepared his disciples for the future kingdom, including by pointing out that his parousia was relatively far away. (So-called "imminence passages" must be explained differently.) Jesus spoke extensively of the conditions for being a subject of the kingdom: righteousness, mercy, sincerity, simplicity, perseverance, and renunciation of evil are among them. Such moral conditions must not be played off against God's gospel of pure grace.*

### 5.1 The Powers in Jesus' day

### 5.1.1 The Battle Against Satan

IN §§1.7 AND 1.8, I gave a brief introduction to Satanology. We must now pay some more attention to Satan and his powers in direct relationship to the kingdom of God in its present form. In answer to the accusation that he drove out the demons through Beelzebul,[1] the "prince

---

1. The Greek word *Beelzeboul* comes from Heb. *Ba'al-Z'bul*, "Baal is prince," which in 2 Kgs. 1:2 in a scoffing way is turned into *Ba'al-Z'bub*, "lord of the flies" (KJV has "Beelzebub" in Matt. 12:24). The Jews gave Satan the name of this Canaanite idol; cf. Ouweneel (2016d, 44).

of demons," Jesus said, "Every kingdom divided against itself is laid waste, and no city or house divided against itself will stand. And if Satan casts out Satan, he is divided against himself. How then will his kingdom stand?" (Matt. 12:25-26; cf. Mark 3:24-26; Luke 11:17-18). In general, battle occurs *between* kingdoms—as in the case of the kingdom of God and the kingdom of Satan—not *within* a kingdom, as in a civil war; otherwise such a kingdom will ruin itself. The power with which Jesus fought against the kingdom of Satan, here especially by driving out demons, was not that of Satan but that of the Holy Spirit (v. 28). Thus, Peter records "how God anointed Jesus of Nazareth with the Holy Spirit and with power.[2] He went about doing good and healing all who were oppressed by the devil, for God was with him" (Acts 10:38).

On the cross, Jesus laid the foundation for the ultimate destruction of Satan's kingdom:[3] "The reason the Son of God appeared was to destroy the works of the devil" (1 John 3:8). "Since . . . the children share in flesh and blood, he himself likewise partook of the same things, that through death he might destroy the one who has the power of death, that is, the devil, and deliver all those who through fear of death were subject to lifelong slavery" (Heb. 2:14-15). "He [i.e., God] disarmed the rulers and authorities and put them to open shame, by triumphing over them in him [i.e., Christ; or, in it, i.e., the cross]" (Col. 2:15). Jesus himself said of this, "'Now is the judgment of this world; now will the ruler

---

2. Hendiadys: "with the power of the Holy Spirit" (cf. Phillips translation).
3. See Ouweneel (2009a, §8.4).

of this world be cast out. And I, when I am lifted up from the earth, will draw all people to myself.' He said this to show by what kind of death he was going to die" (John 12:31–33). The Holy Spirit would descend in order that he, among other things, would "convict the world concerning sin and righteousness and judgment . . . concerning judgment, because the ruler of this world is judged" (16:8–11).

The greatness of Jesus' triumph becomes evident in the enumeration of all spiritual powers above whom he has been exalted. God showed his power with regard to "Christ when he raised him from the dead and seated him at his right hand in the heavenly places, far above all rule and authority and power and dominion, and above every name that is named, not only in this age but also in the one to come" (Eph. 1:20–21). Jesus Christ is the One "who has gone into heaven and is at the right hand of God, with angels, authorities, and powers having been subjected to him" (1 Pet. 3:21–22). He was first the One in and through and for whom God had created all things, including "thrones or dominions or rulers or authorities" (Col. 1:16), and after some of these powers had fallen into the sin of rebellion, he is also the One who robs them of their power and triumphs over them.

### 5.1.2 A Kingdom Taken Violently

Jesus told his listeners: "From the days of John the Baptist until now the kingdom of heaven has suffered violence [ESV note: has been coming violently; Greek *biazetai*], and the violent [*biastai*] take it by force. For all the Prophets and the Law prophesied until John" (Matt. 11:12–13). In the version of Luke 16:16, Jesus said, "The

Law and the Prophets were until John; since then the good news of the kingdom of God is preached, and everyone forces his way into it [ESV note: everyone is forcefully urged into it; *biazetai*]."

The interpretation of Matthew 11:12 has been hotly debated.[4] First, concerning *biazetai*: does this mean "suffered violence" (as many translations have it, with variations; ESV), or "has been coming violently" (ESV note; cf. ERV, EXB, etc.)? The pivotal question is whether Jesus is speaking here of the proponents or the opponents of the kingdom. The *proponents* try, in spite of all opposition by the spiritual and human powers, to enter the kingdom with power, or, the kingdom persists with spiritual violence, in spite of all opposition. The *opponents* try to stop the kingdom violently.

The interpretation is linked with the last phrase of the verse: are "the violent" the *proponents*, who take the kingdom (i.e., get a share in it) by spiritual violence, or are they the *opponents*, who act violently against it, try "to take control of it by force" (ERV; cf. CJB, "snatch it away")? In Luke 16:16, the possibilities are more limited, but here again the last phrase is ambiguous: it is either "trying hard to get into it" (ERV; or, "everyone is forcefully urged into it," ESV note), or negatively: "would force his own way rather than God's way into it" (AMPC note).

We do not have to make a choice because for our argument the core of the matter suffices: the presence of God's kingdom in this world is linked with *violence* because it has both proponents and opponents.[5] Because

---

4. See how, e.g., Carson (1984, 265–68) and France (2007, 429–31) deal with various interpretations.
5. Flusser (2001, 52) chooses the notion of "breaking through,"

of the opponents, the proponents have to use "violence," that is, make great efforts, to get into it, and to maintain it and advance it. This explains Luke 13:24, where Jesus says, "Strive to enter through the narrow door. For many, I tell you, will seek to enter and will not be able" (cf. Matt. 7:13–14). It takes great effort to enter God's kingdom because there are opposing forces, both from within (weights that the human sinful nature would like to carry in; cf. Heb. 12:2) and from without (powers that try to stop those who desire to come in). Satan does not easily let go of his prey. A person is transferred from Satan's domain of *power* (Acts 26:18), from the realm of *darkness* (Col. 1:13; 1 Pet. 2:9), to the kingdom of God, and this always occurs with opposition on behalf of Satan's empire.

### 5.1.3 A Kingdom of Suffering

Therefore, the reverse of the thesis just mentioned is also true: because of the proponents, the opponents make great efforts to stop the kingdom of God with all possible violence. Jesus preaches his kingdom in a world in which sin and the devil seemed, and seem, to be almost omnipotent. When it is a matter of the propagation of the kingdom in an evil world, he cannot do anything else than prepare his followers for oppression: "If they persecuted me, they will also persecute you" (John 15:20). "Blessed are the poor in spirit, for theirs is the

---

and links this with Mic. 2:13 (CJB), "The one breaking through [i.e., Elijah? John the Baptist?] went up before them; they broke through, passed the gate and went out. Their king [i.e., the Messiah] passed on before them; *Adonai* was leading them." However, the Septuagint does not support such a rendering.

kingdom of heaven.... Blessed are those who are persecuted for righteousness' sake, for theirs is the kingdom of heaven" (Matt. 5:3, 10). The apostles insisted "that through many tribulations we must enter the kingdom of God" (Acts 14:22), and "[You are] considered worthy of the kingdom of God, for which you are also suffering" (2 Thess. 1:5); "all who desire to live a godly life in Christ Jesus will be persecuted" (2 Tim. 3:12).

These aspects were not part of the current Jewish expectation of God's kingdom as an empire of peace and justice, in which the righteous would have a glorious place, and from which the wicked would be removed. The notion of God's chosen people triumphantly entering the Messianic kingdom—*Oh, when the saints go marching in*—is quite different from one in which an individual has to press through a narrow door, fighting against himself and against the enemies of the kingdom.

The opposition to the kingdom of God is so strong that Jesus will have to die to make it possible that one day the kingdom will be manifested in power and glory. If we may put it this way: Jesus will have to surrender to the opposition in order to be able ultimately to prevail over it. This is one of the wonderful aspects of the cross:[6] Jesus was crucified "in weakness" (2 Cor. 13:4), and in this very manner he has destroyed the one who had the *power* of death, that is, the devil (Heb. 2:14). He had to die, so that one day death would be overcome and the kingdom of life could arrive. He had to deliver himself into the hands of the "power of darkness" (Luke 22:53), so that one day the kingdom

---

6. See Ouweneel (2009a, 194–99).

of light could dawn. To be able to say one day that *all power* in heaven and on earth had been given to him (Matt. 28:18 KJ21), the King seemingly had to succumb first. Precisely for *him* it was remarkably true what he himself, in a different context, said to Paul: "[P]ower is made perfect in weakness" (2 Cor. 12:9).

In this regard, the inscription on the cross was quite intriguing. It did not say that, for instance, he was crucified as the Redeemer of humanity or as the Reconciler of the wicked, but as the "King of the Jews." In having this inscription made, Pontius Pilate did something comparable to the inadvertent prophecy by Caiaphas (John 11:49–52). That is, it extended far beyond what Pilate himself could grasp, even though Jesus had spoken with him about his kingdom (18:33–37; cf. 1 Tim. 6:13-15). It is quite striking that one of the criminals crucified with him did grasp it to some extent (undoubtedly through the inner revelation of God's Spirit; cf. Matt. 16:17): "Jesus, remember me when you come into your kingdom" (Luke 23:42; see §1.1.3). He understood that Jesus' death was not the end, but that this dying Man would return as King one day, and would accede to the royal throne of David.

## 5.2 Suffering and Triumph
### 5.2.1 A Kingdom of Power
In the battle of God's kingdom against the power of the evil one, Jesus demonstrated his power by binding the "strong man" (Matt. 12:29; Mark 3:27; Luke 11:21). This is usually viewed as referring to Jesus' battle against Satan during the temptations in the wilderness (Matt. 4:1-11; Luke 4:1–13), where Satan proved powerless against

Jesus.⁷ After this happened, Jesus could freely "plunder his house": "when one stronger than he [i.e., Satan] attacks him and overcomes him, he takes away his armor in which he trusted and divides his spoil" (Luke 11:22). Jesus does so by delivering those possessed from demons, thereby opening for them the door to God's kingdom. Another interpretation sees "binding" and "plundering" here as one, and as fulfilled in the driving out of the demons.⁸

Especially in Mark's Gospel, this prevailing over Satan is a preponderant theme. Jesus is here the One who preaches the kingdom of God (1:14-15), and in close connection with this, drives out demons (1:27, 34, 39; 3:11; 5:13; 7:29; 16:9). In this Gospel, the demons are the first to recognize him: "[A] man with an unclean spirit . . . cried out, 'What have you to do with us, Jesus of Nazareth? Have you come to destroy us? I know who you are—the Holy One of God'" (1:23-24). "[W]henever the unclean spirits saw him, they fell down before him and cried out, 'You are the Son of God'" (3:11).

Jesus expected that the same liberating work would be done by his disciples. They were sent out to preach the kingdom of God, and strikingly had to fulfill only this condition: they had to be able to drive out the powers that resisted this kingdom: "[H]e appointed twelve (whom he also named apostles) so that they might be with him and he might send them out to preach and have authority to cast out demons" (3:14-15). To Jesus' mind, it was useless to preach the kingdom without having the *exousia* ("power, authority") to eliminate the

---

7. Geldenhuys (1983, 330); Liefeld (1984, 951).
8. Lane (1974, 143); Green (1997, 458); France (2007, 481).

opponents of the kingdom: "And he called the twelve and began to send them out two by two, and gave them authority over the unclean spirits. . . . So they went out and proclaimed that people should repent. And they cast out many demons and anointed with oil many who were sick and healed them" (6:7, 12–13). After his resurrection, Jesus said in a very general way, "And these signs will accompany those who believe: in my name they will cast out demons," etc. (16:17). Preaching the kingdom without the power to resist the demons is like drying out a flooded room without turning off the tap.

Preaching the kingdom is a demonstration of *power*; it is not a kingdom of beautiful words only but of *power* (1 Cor. 4:20; cf. 1:24; 2:4-5; 1 Thess. 1:5). Therefore, the kingdom of God may be called the Holy Spirit's sphere of operation. Without the power of this Spirit, the disciple does not get anywhere. Jesus explained that the restoration of the kingdom for Israel lay in the Father's hands, and thus suggested that—unfortunately for the disciples—it might be delayed, he said. However, he added, almost as a consolation: "*But* you will receive power when the Holy Spirit has come upon you" (Acts 1:7-8). This means: as long as the kingdom, which one day will arrive in power and majesty, is delayed, you receive something that is at least as beautiful: the power of the Holy Spirit, as a foretaste of that coming kingdom; it is the "powers of the age to come" (Heb. 6:5). In the meantime, Jesus' followers would urgently need this power, in order to witness (Acts 1:8b), to resist the enemy, and to perform the miracle signs of the kingdom.

The deacon Philip (not to be confused with the apostle of this name, Matt. 10:3; etc.), one of the men "full of the Spirit" (Acts 6:3, 5), was a striking example of this display of power: "Philip went down to the city of Samaria and proclaimed to them the Christ. And the crowds with one accord paid attention to what was being said by Philip when they heard him and saw the *signs* that he did. For *unclean spirits*, crying out with a loud voice, came out of many who had them, and many who were paralyzed or lame were healed. So there was much joy in that city. . . . [T]hey believed Philip as he preached good news about the *kingdom of God* and the name of Jesus Christ. . . . [Simon was] seeing *signs and great miracles* [lit., great powers, Greek *megalas dynameis*] . . ." (8:5–13).

## 5.2.2 First Suffering, Then Glory

The kingdom of God means a display of *power*—already now. At the same time, preaching the kingdom, and living in the kingdom now, means *suffering*. There is a continual tension between prevailing over the powers and suffering under the powers that threaten believers. It is a real battle, in which now the one party, then the other party has, or seems to have, the upper hand (cf. Joshua's battle against Amalek, Exod. 17:11). This was nowhere more evident than in Jesus' own work: he drove out a tremendous number of demons, yet seemed to succumb in the battle against the dark powers. In Gethsemane, he only had to mention his divine name, "I AM," and his opponents fell to the ground (John 18:5–6). But he also said to his disciples, "[S]hall I not drink the cup that the Father has given me?" (v. 11), and to his enemies he said, "[T]his is your hour, and the power of darkness" (Luke 22:53).

A few hours before, Jesus had told his disciples: "I assign to you, as my Father assigned to me, a kingdom, that you may eat and drink at my table in my kingdom and sit on thrones judging the twelve tribes of Israel" (Luke 22:29–30; cf. 12:32; Matt. 19:28). But just before this, he had said, "I have earnestly desired to eat this Passover with you *before I suffer*. For I tell you I will not eat it until it is fulfilled in the kingdom of God" (vv. 15–16). This is the order: first suffering, then glory. As he told the Emmaus disciples: "Was it not necessary that the Christ should suffer these things and[9] enter into his glory?" (24:26).

We find this logical and temporal order several times in the epistles: "[W]e suffer with him in order that we may also be glorified with him" (Rom. 8:17); "rejoice insofar as you share Christ's sufferings, that you may also rejoice and be glad when his glory is revealed" (1 Pet. 4:13); ". . . looking to Jesus, the founder and perfecter of our faith, who for the joy that was set before him endured the cross, despising the shame, and is seated at the right hand of the throne of God" (Heb. 12:2).

Jesus' path turns out to be the pattern for his followers as well. It is striking that, after the first announcement of his sufferings on the cross, Jesus immediately announced the road of discipleship, which would also involve a cross: "From that time Jesus began to show his disciples that he must go to Jerusalem and suffer many things from the elders and chief priests and scribes, and be killed, and on the third day be raised. . . . 'If anyone

---

9. Here, Greek *kai* has the force of "and so" (cf. DRA, WYC, etc.), or "and then" (cf. NIV, GNT, etc.) (for a similar case, cf. John 15:8 ESV).

would come after me, let him deny himself and take up his cross and follow me'" (Matt. 16:21, 24). Thus, the disciples follow the route of the Master, as we just saw in the epistles. Please note the word "(in order) that" in the quotations from Romans and 1 Peter: as long as the powers have not been eliminated, suffering is not just an inevitable evil. No, there is a goal in these sufferings: only *through* the sufferings, the disciple comes to glory: ". . . that I may know him and the power of his resurrection, and may share his sufferings, becoming like him in his death, that by any means possible I may attain the resurrection from the dead" (Phil. 3:10–11).

In some passages, there is an even more evident relationship with the kingdom of God: "If we have died with him, we will also live with him; if we endure [the powers, the opposition, the hostility], we will also *reign* with him [one word: *symbasileusomen*, be kings with him, i.e., Christ]" (2 Tim. 2:11-12). There is no other way to triumph than through suffering. The apostles taught the newly converted Christians "that through many tribulations we must enter the kingdom of God" (Acts 14:22). There is no other entrance. Notice the link between "tribulation" and "kingdom" in Revelation 1:9, "I, John, your brother and partner in the tribulation and the kingdom and the patient endurance that are in Jesus. . . ." That is, tribulation is the necessary stepping stone to the glorious kingdom, and patient endurance is needed on our side in order to go through the tribulation.

The Old Testament types speak a striking and convincing language here (cf. §2.2): only through suffering (slavery, imprisonment), Joseph ultimately became viceroy of Egypt. Only after his flight and forty years tend-ing the sheep, Moses ultimately became the deliverer and leader of Israel. Only through the barren wilderness, Moses/Joshua (a double type of Christ)[10] ultimately arrived in the promised land. Only through suffering (rejection, persecution), David ultimately became the king of Israel. Only through the most serious death threat and God's remarkable redemption, Mordecai ultimately became viceroy of the Persian empire. This is the route: through humiliation to exaltation, as the great example of Jesus illustrates in the most remarkable way (Phil. 2:6-11).

### 5.2.3 Two Types of Christians

It is very important to know the balance between these sufferings *under* the powers and the triumphs *over* the powers that believers may now and then experience, already in the present age (cf. the young men in 1 John 2:13-14, "you have overcome the evil one"). In connection with the kingdom, we meet both "Gethsemane Christians" (Christians emphasizing the sufferings aspect as exhibited by Christ in Gethsemane) and "Tabor Christians" (Christians emphasizing the triumph aspect as exhibited by Christ on the Mount of Transfiguration[11]). With a variation upon Hebrews 12:5, the former

---

10. Double types of Christ occur elsewhere in the Old Testament: Moses/Aaron (king-priest), David/Zadok (king-priest), David/Solomon (the fighting king, the peaceful king), Zerubbabel/Jeshua (king-priest).

11. Under the assumption that the Tabor was the mount of transfiguration. Note that Peter, John and James were the only three disciples who were with Jesus in his prayers, both on the mount of triumph and in the garden of suffering (Luke 9:28-36; Matt. 26:35-46).

Christians run the risk of becoming weary under the discipline of the Lord—the sufferings that the believer has to go through—whereas the latter ones run the risk of regarding this discipline lightly.

"Gethsemane Christians" argue that, as long as the kingdom has not yet arrived in power and majesty, the believer must reckon with sufferings, persecution, and oppression. In itself, this is correct, but they emphasize this aspect one-sidedly, at the expense of the aspects of power, strength, and triumph: "[T]hanks be to God, who in Christ always leads us in triumphal procession, and through us spreads the fragrance of the knowledge of him everywhere" (2 Cor. 2:14). "[T]he weapons of our warfare are not of the flesh but have divine power to destroy strongholds. We destroy arguments and every lofty opinion raised against the knowledge of God, and take every thought captive to obey Christ" (10:4-5).

In its most extreme form, such Christians have a gloomy, depressing view of life: not going "from strength to strength," until they arrive in Zion's kingdom (Ps. 84:7), but rather going from suffering to suffering. Not confident that "in all these things we are more than conquerors through him who loved us" (Rom. 8:37), but rather something like "in spite of him we are more than losers." This may be because these people either are so impressed by their own sinfulness and often even doubt their salvation, or are so impressed with the dark powers, who seem to be in charge as long as Christ has not returned. These are also the Christians who, when it comes to poverty, illness, and bondage, scarcely believe in miracles; these things supposedly belong to the sufferings that a believer must undergo for Christ's sake. This is a doctrine of resignation, sometimes based upon a misunderstanding of Lord's Day 10 of the Heidelberg Catechism.[12]

On the other side of the spectrum we find what I have called the "Tabor Christians," who strongly emphasize the power of the Holy Spirit and the resulting signs and miracles. Here, there is no passivity, and even less resignation. In its most extreme form, this attitude involves rather irreverently claiming God's miraculous power, especially in the field of health and material prosperity ("health and wealth gospel").[13] These people do know of persecutions, especially in remote countries. However, they argue that sickness, bondage, and poverty definitely do not belong to the sufferings shared by all believers but are matters against which the unlimited power of Christ can be invoked.

In both cases, at the deepest level we are dealing with the underlying kingdom view. "Gethsemane Christians" live as if Christ never said, "All authority in heaven and on earth has been given to me" (Matt. 28:18), or as if Paul never wrote: ". . . while we *were* still sinners" (Rom. 5:8)—for all they observe around them is weakness and sinfulness. In opposition to this, "Tabor Christians" live as if the parousia has already occurred and the "age to come" has already arrived in which no inhabitant will still say, "I am sick" (Isa. 33:24). "Gethsemane Christians" underestimate the power of the Holy Spirit, or limit his activity mainly to regeneration, or to the first, apostolic century. "Tabor Christians" overesti-

---

12. See Ouweneel (2005a, 71–80; 2016)
13. Ouweneel (2010c, §10.3.2).

mate the measure in which the Holy Spirit has been given to us already now, as if already today we could receive everything in a fullness that has been reserved for the Messianic kingdom of peace.

As Paul says to the Corinthian believers, "Already you have all you want! Already you have become rich! Without us you have become kings! And would that you did reign, so that we might share the rule with you!" (1 Cor. 4:8). In dispensational language Paul could have said, You err as to the age you are living in! You behave as if you live in the "age to come"—in reality you live in the "present evil age." But to the former group he might have said, You err as to the age you are living in! You speak and behave as if you are still living before Good Friday, whereas in fact you live after Easter and Pentecost!

Living in the kingdom today means striking a balance between the "Gethsemane Christians" and the "Tabor Christians," between the "not yet" and the "already,"[14] between "full salvation has not yet been realized" and "the power of the Holy Spirit is working already," between "the kingdom of power and majesty has not yet arrived" and "Jesus is already on the throne, exalted above all the powers."[15] For those who under-

---

14. See extensively, Saucy (1997); cf. Cullmann (1964, 199); Kreck (1961, 77-108); Berkouwer (1972, 74-75, 110-119, 133-39, 199, 426); Hoekema (1979, chapter 6); Heyns (1988, 399); Spykman (1992, 11, 523-26); G. K. Beale in Brower and Elliott (1997, 12-18); Hoek (2004, 34-36); Moore (2004, chapter 2); Chia (2005, 58-61); Hays *et al.* (2007, 22-23); Van Genderen (2008, 823); Pannenberg (1998, 604); McGrath (2010, 562-63); Morphew (2011, 137-46).

15. Cf. the well-known picture by Cullmann (1964, 84) concerning

stand the language of the biblical festivals: there is more of *Shavuot* (Pentecost, i.e., more of the Spirit) than "Gethsemane Christians" seem to think, and less of *Sukkot* (Feast of Booths, the great consummation) than "Tabor Christians" seem to think.[16]

## 5.3  The Announcement of Triumph

### 5.3.1  The *Palingenesia*

Jesus himself explained beyond any misunderstanding that full salvation still had to come, namely, at his parousia. He announced not only his sufferings, death, resurrection, and ascension several times (Matt. 16:21; 17:22-23; 20:17-19; John 10:11, 15, 17-18), but also his parousia. He did so explicitly in connection with the kingdom as it would be established at that time in power and majesty: "[T]he Son of Man is going to come with his angels in the glory of his Father, and then he will repay each person according to what he has done" (Matt. 16:27).

There is much comfort in this: if the kingdom in its present form entails suffering, that suffering will be brief, for Jesus "is going to come" (Greek *mellei erchesthai*), even more strongly: "is about to come" (CEB, GNT, etc.; cf. CEV, "will soon come"). Jesus emphasizes that he is coming "soon" (Rev. 22:7, 12, 20). At the same time, he indicates that it might take longer than the disciples hoped: "My master is delayed," says the servant in the parable (Matt. 24:48). "As the bridegroom was delayed, . . ." (25:5), and especially:

---

D-day (i.e., Calvary) and V-day (i.e., the parousia), which has also been criticized (Berkouwer [1972, 74-75 and references]).

16. Cf. Ouweneel (2001b).

"[A]fter a *long time* the master of those servants came and settled accounts with them" (v. 19).

The disciple of the kingdom lives in the continual expectation of his Lord's return, and that keeps him going. But at the same time, he realizes that in the meantime almost two thousand years have passed already. Nevertheless, he keeps looking forward to the coming glory—not the glory of the heavenly Paradise (in the *status intermedius*, "the intermediate state" between death and resurrection) but that of the kingdom of God on earth. Jesus speaks of this repeatedly, for instance, in this verse: "[I]n the new world, when the Son of Man will sit on his glorious throne . . ." (19:28). "New world" is here Greek *palingenesia*, "regeneration" (NKJV, etc.), "renewal of all things" (NIV), the "re-creation of the world" (MSG), that is, the "age to come" (EXB, NCV), the "Messianic age" (HCSB).[17] A striking expression indeed! All true disciples of Jesus are regenerated now already, otherwise they could not have entered into the kingdom of God (John 3:3–5, *gennaō anōthen*). But together they are on their way to the "regeneration" of the whole world, the "times of restoration of all things" (Acts 3:21, *chronōn apokatastaseōs pantōn*).

### 5.3.2 The Olivet Discourse

Especially in the Olivet Discourse, Jesus gives one prediction after another: "For as the lightning comes from the east and shines as far as the west, so will be the coming of the Son of Man. . . . Immediately after the tribulation of those days the sun will be darkened, and the moon will not give its light [cf. Isa. 13:10; 24:23; Ezek.

---

17. *Not* "ye which followed me in the regeneration" (GNV).

32:7; Joel 2:31; 3:15; Hab. 3:11], and the stars will fall from heaven, and the powers[18] of the heavens will be shaken. Then will appear in heaven the sign of[19] the Son of Man, and then all the tribes of the earth[20] will mourn, and they will see the Son of Man coming on the clouds of heaven with power and great glory. . . . For as were the days of Noah, so will be the coming of the Son of Man. For as in those days before the flood they were eating and drinking, marrying and giving in marriage, until the day when Noah entered the ark, and they were unaware until the flood came and swept them all away, so will be the coming of the Son of Man" (Matt. 24:27-30, 37-39).

"When the Son of Man comes in his glory, and all the angels with him, then he will sit on his glorious throne" (25:31). It seems to me this is not the throne of David on earth (cf. Isa. 9:7; Luke 1:32), but a throne that reminds us immediately of Daniel 7:9-10,[21] "As I looked, thrones were placed, and the Ancient of Days took his seat; his clothing was white as snow, and the hair of his head like pure wool; his throne was fiery flames; its wheels were burning fire. A stream of fire issued and came out from before him; a thousand thousands served him, and ten thousand times ten thousand stood before him; the

---

18. Greek *dynameis* (cf. 1 Cor. 15:24; Eph. 1:21; 1 Pet. 3:22), in the Septuagint often "(heavenly) hosts" (Ps. 33:6; Isa. 34:4; Dan. 8:10); YHWH *ts'baot* = *kyrios tōn dynameōn* (Ouweneel, 2016d, 27n14); that is, the celestial (evil) hosts.
19. In my view, this is an epexetical genitive: the Son of Man *is* the sign (cf. France (2007, 925-26).
20. Given the Jewish context (vv. 15-16, 20), the translation "land" seems to fit better (CJB, ISV), just as in Rev. 1:7 (same expression).
21. See France (2007, 960).

court sat in judgment, and the books were opened"—with this difference, that here it is the Ancient of Days sitting on the throne as Judge, and in Matthew 25:31 it is the Son of Man (v. 34, "the King").

This exchange, or should we say identification, occurs more often: in Daniel 7:22, it is not the Son of Man but the "Ancient of Days" who "came," as if he himself was the person of verse 13. In Revelation 1, too, it is not the Son of Man as such (v. 13) but the Lord God Almighty "who is and who was and who *is to come*" (v. 8; cf. v. 4; 4:8). Conversely, the Son of Man is here (vv. 13-14) equipped as the "Ancient of Days" in Daniel 7:9:[22] ". . . clothed with a long robe. . . . The hairs of his head were white, like white wool, like snow. His eyes were like a flame of fire." In Isaiah 6:1-3, it is *Adonai YHWH* who is sitting on the throne and is beheld by the prophet, but John 12:41 says that Isaiah saw here the glory of the (pre-incarnate) Jesus.[23] In New Testament understanding: Jesus is the Son of Man, and at the same time the Ancient of Days; more specifically, God the Son.

### 5.3.3 Two Other Events

Also before Caiaphas, Jesus testified of his coming triumph: "[F]rom now on you will see the Son of Man seated at the right hand of Power [24] and coming on the clouds of heaven." The first phrase is a reference to

---

22. Ouweneel (2007b, 173-74).
23. Cf. Ouweneel (2007b, 173-74, 238, 245, 289).
24. Greek *dynamis*, i.e., God; cf. Heb. 1:3; 8:1 (*megalosyne*). In summary, in §5.2.1, the word *dynamis* refers to the miraculous power of the Spirit, in footnote 17 it refers to a "(heavenly) host," and here it refers to God's own omnipotence.

THE ETERNAL KINGDOM: LIVING UNDER CHRIST

Psalm 110:1, "The Lord says to my Lord: 'Sit at my right hand, until I make your enemies your footstool.'" The second phrase is a reference to Daniel 7:13 (NKJV), "[A]nd behold, [One] like the Son of Man, coming with the clouds of heaven!" Jesus continually uses here his title "Son of Man," which in Daniel 7:13-14 is also connected with the everlasting kingdom that he will receive: "And to him was given dominion and glory and a kingdom, that all peoples, nations, and languages should serve him; his dominion is an everlasting dominion, which shall not pass away, and his kingdom one that shall not be destroyed." See also Matthew 13:40-41, where Jesus speaks of the Son of Man and the "end of the age," that is, the age preceding the "age to come," the "age" of the Messiah (§4.4).

Because of this promise of the parousia, the true disciple not only enjoys what the kingdom already means to him now, but he also looks forward to the full manifestation of God's kingdom under the magnificent rule of Christ, as he expresses it in the Lord's Prayer, "Your kingdom come" (Matt. 6:10; Luke 11:2). This petition, by the way, raises the question whether this means, May your kingdom arrive soon in power and majesty, or rather, May your kingdom be realized more and more today through me. Or should we, within the context of the entire prayer, make no such distinction at all? [25]

Jesus gave to three chosen disciples a foretaste of the glory of the kingdom during his transfiguration on the mountain (Matt. 17:1-8). In the scene on the mountain,

---

25. In the second case, the claim by France (2007, 246), that this is "perhaps the most clearly futuristic reference to God's kingdom in Matthew," is not correct.

it turns out that the essence of the kingdom is the very person of the glorified Christ himself. This is underscored by one of the three disciples, the later apostle Peter: "For we did not follow cleverly devised myths when we made known to you the power and coming [26] of our Lord Jesus Christ, but we were eyewitnesses of his majesty. For when he received honor and glory from God the Father, and the voice was borne to him by the Majestic Glory, 'This is my beloved Son, with whom I am well pleased,' we ourselves heard this very voice borne from heaven, for we were with him on the holy mountain" (2 Pet. 1:16-18).

In my view, the remarkable promise of Matthew 16:28 ("there are some standing here who will not taste death until they see the Son of Man coming in his kingdom") was fulfilled immediately afterward during this transfiguration on the mountain (17:1-8). This interpretation is supported by many expositors.[27] Others have applied 16:28 to the resurrection,[28] the ascension, the Day of Pentecost, the spreading of the gospel, the internal development of the gospel, or the destruction of Jerusalem.[29] However, none of these events is a coming of the Son of God in his kingdom. The scene of Matthew 17:1-8 includes a promise and an encouragement: the three disci-

---

26. Hendiadys: "the powerful coming."
27. See, e.g., Cole (1961, 140); Lane (1974, 313-14); Pesch (1977, 66-67); Wessell (1984, 697-98); Liefeld (1984, 924); Bock (2002, 572-73); Berkhof (2004, 75-76); Ratzinger (2007, 317-18).
28. E.g., Barth (2010, I/2, 688); Tasker (1961, 162); Morris (1974, 171).
29. Geldenhuys (1983, 277); Plummer (1922, ad loc.) and Carson (1984, 380-82) both mention seven possible interpretations.

ples had viewed the kingdom in its future form, and this gave them the strength to live with perseverance in the kingdom in its present form—with its preliminary triumphs, but also its persecutions and other sufferings.

## 5.4 Far Off Or Imminent?

### 5.4.1 Far Off

The fact that Jesus often seems to speak of the coming kingdom as something that was very near—in spite of the references to a time of delay (Matt. 24:48; 25:5; cf. v. 19)—has led to much debate. Expositors speak here of the *imminence passages* concerning the kingdom, that is, the (supposed) short-term expectation (German: *Naherwartung*) of the kingdom. Albert Schweitzer frankly uttered the opinion that, on this point, Jesus had simply erred (see §11.4.1).[30] However, as we have seen, Jesus has indicated in his parables in a hidden way that his coming might be delayed more than his believers had thought or hoped.

Let us look at some references. Besides Matthew 24:48 and 25:5 and 19 just mentioned, there is also 13:24–30, 36–43, a parable that clearly implies some considerable time of sowing, mixture, and ripening until the harvest. The same holds for 24:6 ("you will hear of wars and rumors of wars. See that you are not alarmed, for this must take place, but the end is not yet"). In Luke 12:38 ("If he comes in the second watch, or in the third, and finds them awake, blessed are those servants"), the suggestion is that Jesus might not come in the first watch of the night but perhaps only in the second or even third watch (i.e.,

---

30. Schweitzer (2001).

between midnight and 3:00 a.m.). If Matthew 14:25 ("in the fourth watch of the night he came to them") is typologically indicative, Jesus might even come in the fourth watch (between 3:00 p.m. and sunrise), figuratively speaking. This is the last watch of the night, just before dawn. We also think here of another symbol: Jesus as the "bright morning star" (Rev. 22:16; cf. 2:28; 2 Pet. 1:19), that is the lightbearer that appears in the sky in the early morning.

Jesus told his followers the parable of the minas "because he was near to Jerusalem, and because they supposed that the kingdom of God was to appear immediately" (Luke 19:11). The apparent intention is to indicate that this was a mistake: the kingdom of God—in its future form of glory and majesty—was *not* to appear immediately. In another parable we read, "A man planted a vineyard and let it out to tenants and went into another country *for a long while*" (20:9).

Of some interest is also John 21:22–23, "Jesus said to him [i.e., Peter], 'If it is my will that he [i.e., John] remain until I come, what is that to you? You follow me!' So the saying spread abroad among the brothers that this disciple [i.e., John] was not to die [i.e., before the parousia of Jesus]; yet Jesus did not say to him that he was not to die, but, 'If it is my will that he remain until I come, what is that to you?'" This again clearly suggests that Jesus did not expect to come back within a few decades.

## 5.4.2 Imminent?

We may safely conclude that it is simply incorrect to suggest that Jesus believed and taught that his return would happen very soon (in spite of the apparent meaning of Rev. 22:7, 12, 20), say, within some decades instead of a number of centuries.[31] This is not necessarily contradicted by Matthew 16:28, as we have seen.[32]

It is not contradicted by two other so-called "imminence passages," either.[33] First, Matthew 10:23: "[T]ruly, I say to you, you will not have gone through all the towns of Israel before the Son of Man comes." If Jesus would have meant that his disciples would preach the gospel to Israel until his parousia, either he would have erred, or the saying cannot be authentic. In our view, it is not necessary to assume either option. One may suppose that these words refer to the resurrection,[34] or to the fall of Jerusalem,[35] or that the figure of the disciples refers to all believing preachers until the end time,[36] more specifically, when the remnant of Israel will manifest itself and promulgate the gospel in its own country.[37]

Second, Matthew 24:34 is often adduced: "[T]his generation will not pass away until all these things take place."[38] The Greek word *genea* ("generation") may be

---

31. Cf. Ridderbos (1962, 444–56, 498–510); Hoekema (1979, 111–20); Brown (1994, 52–58); Erickson (1998, 1199–1200); Chia (2005, 51–55); Morphew (2011, 55). In opposition to this, see a rather conservative author such as Bockmuehl (1994, 100–102).
32. *Contra*, e.g., Gibbs (2001), who views *all* "imminence passages" mentioned in the text as fulfilled in AD 70; cf. Kimball (1984); Chilton (1987); Bray (1996).
33. See Ouweneel (2007a, §13.3.1); Berkouwer (1972, 86–89).
34. Tasker (1961, 108).
35. Carson (1984, 250–53); he adds six other interpretations.
36. Grosheide (1954, 166); Ridderbos (1965, 205–206).
37. Gaebelein (1910, 1:209); Walvoord (1974, ad loc.).
38. Cf. (besides the commentaries) Bray (1996, 196–220 [who claims

taken to mean "The people who are living then" (WE), or ("This age continues until all these things take place" (MSG), but it is also possible to take the word not in a temporal-quantitative sense (as a period of, say, forty years) but as a moral-qualitative term with the sense of "kind": this kind of people will remain until the kingdom of God arrives in glory.[39] In Mark 8:12 we twice find the expression *hē genea hautē*, which is usually rendered as "this generation." However, compare: "you people" (ERV, etc.), "the people of this day" (GNT, etc.), and "people today" (WE), with the implication: "this kind of people." This could also be the translation of Matthew 24:34, "This kind of people will not pass away . . . ." (The German *Geschlecht* and the Dutch *geslacht* emphasize not the temporal implication, but rather a moral application of the term.)

Don Carson looks in a different direction: the distress of Matthew 24:4-28, including that of the fall of Jerusalem, would be experienced by the generation living then.[40] Howard Marshall and Walter Liefeld think of the end time generation.[41]

### 5.4.3 Paul and Peter

That concludes our discussion, then, of the so-called "imminence passages" of Jesus. With Paul, too, some

---

that the "parousia" took place in AD 67-70]; Lewis and Demarest (1996, 432-33); Bryan (2002, 81-86).

39. Gaebelein (1910, 2:214-15); Grosheide (1954, 369-70); Morris (1974, 300-301).
40. Carson (1984, 507); cf. Van Leeuwen (1928, 170-71); Greijdanus (1941, 197); Cole (1961, 205-206); Tasker (1961, 227); Ridderbos (1970, 156-58); Wessell (1984, 751); Bock (2002, 573-74).
41. Marshall (1978, 780); Liefeld (1984, 1022-23).

people see a tension between a supposed short-term expectation, implying that he expected Jesus' return during his own lifetime, and his expectation that he would die before the parousia.[42] Some authors believed that, in his earlier letters (1 Thess. 4:15; 1 Cor. 15:51-52), Paul was still convinced that he would be alive at the time of the parousia, whereas in later letters (2 Cor. 5:1-10; Phil. 1:23; 2 Tim. 4:6) he implied that the parousia would take place after his death.[43]

This is pure speculation, based on far too little evidence. It is the same Paul who knows that he might die before the parousia (cf. Peter in 2 Pet. 1:14; cf. John 21:18-19), yet uses the language of faith: "*we* who are alive" (at the time Jesus comes; 1 Thess. 4:15), as each believer should do, even when lying on his death bed. Even in his earliest letters, Paul never speaks of the assurance that Jesus would come again before his (Paul's) death. He never binds himself to some prediction of time but only emphasizes that it would be "soon" (Rom. 13:11; 16:20; 1 Cor. 7:29; Phil. 4:5; cf. Heb. 10:37; James 5:8-9; Rev. 1:1).

Peter knows about this too. He says in his first letter, "The end of all things is at hand" (1 Pet. 4:7), whereas in his second letter he indicates that the delay would be so long that scoffers would get the opportunity to say, "Where is the promise of his coming? For ever

---

42. Ridderbos (1997, 489-92); Hoekema (1979, 123-26); see Witherington (1992) and B. Witherington in Brower and Elliott (1997, 171-86), who draws a comparison between Jesus and Paul with respect to the "imminence passages."
43. Dodd (1903, 109-110); Cullmann (1964, 88); Dibelius (1953, 109-110); Schoeps (1961, 103-104); Berkhof (2004; 1979, 526).

since the fathers fell asleep, all things are continuing as they were from the beginning of creation" (2 Pet. 3:3-4). He counterbalances this with the thesis that "with the Lord one day is as a thousand years, and a thousand years as one day," so that he could say, "The Lord is not slow to fulfill his promise as some count slowness" (vv. 8-9; cf. Ps. 90:4).

Peter's argument does not at all imply that he expected the Lord's imminent return.[44] At the same time, we should not diminish the spiritual force of the "at hand" and the "soon." In the New Testament, there is no real tension between such terms and the notion that the delay might yet be long. When the Lord does come—even if after two thousand years—believers will look back, and say, "The delay was for but a moment."

## 5.5 Seven Conditions for Entrance

### 5.5.1 Regeneration

In various parables (see chapters 3 and 4), we have touched on the question who are eligible to receive a share in the kingdom of God: the (so-called) "religious" ones who live by "rights," or the repentant ones who live by grace. That was a live issue in Jesus' day. For the people of his day the answer was less obvious than it may be for us, who are familiar with Jesus' teaching. Just rephrase the question as follows: For whom is the kingdom: for those who deserve it, or for those who do not deserve it? In this form, the question is much more difficult to answer directly. This is certainly the case when viewed through the eyes of the average Israelite of those days, and even from the perspective of so many

---

44. Verkuyl (1992, 447).

common Christians today. The kingdom is for poor sinners who humble themselves before God. However, we have seen that it is equally correct to say that the kingdom is for good disciples, not for bad disciples!

What is the way out of this tension? Simply stated: you come in as a humble sinner, but you have to develop into a good disciple. Also apart from the parables, Jesus repeatedly brought up this question of who was fit for the kingdom of God; his discussions of the matter supply us with the following answers. Each answer presupposes certain concomitant adversaries, who will try to keep the would-be disciples from entering the kingdom of God.

First, there is the necessity of *regeneration*, that is, a total, inner transformation and renewal of the person's heart and life: "[U]nless one is born of water and the Spirit, he cannot *enter the kingdom of God*" (John 3:5).[45] We have seen that, in practice, the kingdom of God in its present form includes a mixture of good and bad subjects, say, of disciples truly devoted to the Master and those who have no real link with him. The first and foremost underlying principle is this: in order to *inwardly* have a share in the kingdom of God, that is, to become a true disciple, a good servant, a wise virgin, etc., regeneration, the radical renewal of the heart, is indispensible. The true disciple and the good servant are not such because they—at least outwardly—are better observers of the Mosaic Torah, or even of the Messianic Torah, but because they live out of a new heart, which is governed by the Holy Spirit (cf. Ps. 51:10; Ezek. 36:26–27).

---

45. See Ouweneel (2010a, chapter 3).

The *adversaries* denied the necessity of regeneration. For instance, some Jewish leaders argued that they were the physical offspring of Abraham, implying that this sufficed to be entitled to all the blessings involved in this descent (John 8:33, 39). Jesus answered that they were indeed Abraham's offspring but not his "children"; instead, they were children of the devil (vv. 39, 44). Whether Jews or Gentiles, there are only two kinds of "children" in this world: children of God and children of the devil (1 John 3:10). Regeneration is the way for a person, whether Jew or Gentile, to become a child of God: "[T]o all who did receive him [i.e., Jesus], who believed in his name, he gave the right to become *children of God*, who were *born*, not of blood nor of the will of the flesh nor of the will of man, but *of God*" (John 1:12-13).

## 5.5.2 Righteousness

Second, there is the necessity of proper *righteousness*:[46] "[W]hoever relaxes one of the least of these commandments and teaches others to do the same will be called least in the kingdom of heaven, but whoever does them and teaches them will be called great in the kingdom of heaven. For I tell you, unless your righteousness exceeds that of the scribes and Pharisees, you will never *enter the kingdom of heaven*" (Matt. 5:19-20). To "relax" the commandments means as much as perhaps confessing them *de jure* but pushing them aside *de facto*. Jesus is speaking here of the inward righteousness of the Messianic Torah, sprouting from the disciple's heart in the power of the Spirit.

---

46. Regarding the conditions mentioned in the Sermon on the Mount, see Ridderbos (1962, 285-99).

The *adversaries* knew a very different kind of righteousness, and presented this to the people as the true one. It was the outward "righteousness" of legalism and religious hypocrisy.[47] Jesus gave this example: "Beware of practicing your righteousness before other people in order to be seen by them, for then you will have no reward from your Father who is in heaven. Thus, when you give to the needy, sound no trumpet before you, as the hypocrites do in the synagogues and in the streets, that they may be praised by others. Truly, I say to you, they have received their reward. But when you give to the needy, do not let your left hand know what your right hand is doing, so that your giving may be in secret. And your Father who sees in secret will reward you" (6:1–4).

Jesus said that the disciples' righteousness had to surpass that of the scribes and Pharisees. The examples show that this surpassing refers not to a quantitative but to a qualitative difference between the Pharisees' righteousness and the kingdom's righteousness (cf. CEV, "better than"). In order to be able to enter the kingdom of God, a *different* kind of righteousness is needed than that practiced by the legalistic-religious part of Israel thus far: one of the heart, one of the Spirit, one that really satisfies God's heart. It is the righteousness of *love*. In fact, this may seem rather self-evident. However, there is a definite snare for people to be governed by the all-dominating thought what other people may think of them (Matt. 6:1–5, 16–18; 23:5, 7, 28; John 12:43; cf. 5:41). They may still believe of themselves that they are living for the glory of God, but in fact they are living for the

---

47. See Ouweneel (2010a, chapters 8–9, especially 231–37).

appreciation of men, and thus they fall into legalism and religious hypocrisy. It is this attitude that is sharply exposed by Jesus.

### 5.5.3 Inner Sincerity

Third, there is the necessity of *inner sincerity*, in a vital connection with the Master and in genuine obedience to the Father: "Not everyone who says to me, 'Lord, Lord,' will *enter the kingdom of heaven*, but the one who does the will of my Father who is in heaven. On that day many will say to me, 'Lord, Lord, did we not prophesy in your name, and cast out demons in your name, and do many mighty works in your name?' And then will I declare to them, 'I never knew you; depart from me, you workers of lawlessness'" (Matt. 7:21-23).

The false disciple is in fact an *adversary* of the kingdom. He is a worker of "lawlessness," no matter how beautiful the works that he does may seem. "Lawlessness" (Greek *anomia*, not "iniquity," as KJV and others render the term, nor "evildoers," as NIV and others render it) is, the refusal to acknowledge God's law (*nomos*) above oneself, refusal to act out of a true recognition of the authority and the commands of the Master. It is more than "lawbreaking," as HCSB and others render the term.[48] The people involved not only break the law, they *reject* the law. They want to be autonomous (from *autos*, "self," and *nomos*, "law") that is, determine their own rules.

---

48. ESV makes the same mistake in Matt. 13:41, "law-breakers," which should be rendered as those who "practice lawlessness" (NKJV, ISV; cf. NASB, YLT).

There are basically two kinds of adversaries of the kingdom: those who openly attack the kingdom, and those who imitate the kingdom. The former act from the outside, the latter form the inside. The former behave as enemies, the latter as friends. This latter group may prophesy, as the false prophets of old did (e.g., Jer. 5:31; Ezek. 13:9); they may cast out demons, as the sons of the Pharisees did (Matt. 12:27); they may do mighty works, as Simon the Magician did (Acts 8:9), sometimes even in the name of Jesus, as the sons of Sceva tried (19:13-16). Through the former group, the devil manifests himself as the "roaring lion" (1 Pet. 5:8); through the latter group he masks himself as the "angel of light" (2 Cor. 11:14).

Here again, the attitude of the heart is pivotal; the truly sincere heart presupposes regeneration. And, one may add, it presupposes the Messianic Torah, which, apart from the core it has in common with the Mosaic Torah, differs in so many points from it (see Matt. 5, where, in what we call the Messianic Torah, Jesus exposes this true core of the Mosaic Torah).[49]

### 5.5.4 Childlike Simplicity

Fourth, there is the necessity of *childlike* simplicity, authenticity, sincerity, naïveté, without a pedestal of false pretenses: "[U]nless you turn and become like children, you will never *enter the kingdom of heaven*. Whoever humbles himself [i.e., makes himself small] like this child is the greatest in the kingdom of heaven" (Matt. 18:3-4).

---

49. See extensively, Ouweneel (2016c).

This childlikeness should not be confused with childishness, infantility, which is often found in immature disciples: "But I, brothers, could not address you as spiritual people, but as people of the flesh, as infants in Christ. . . . [Y]ou are still of the flesh. For while there is jealousy and strife among you, are you not of the flesh and behaving only in a human [or even, infantile] way?" (1 Cor. 3:1–3). "Brothers, do not be children in your thinking. Be infants in evil, but in your thinking be mature" (14:20); ". . . [we should] no longer be children, tossed to and fro by the waves and carried about by every wind of doctrine, by human cunning, by craftiness in deceitful schemes" (Eph. 4:14). "You need milk, not solid food, for everyone who lives on milk is unskilled in the word of righteousness, since he is a child" (Heb. 5:12–13).

Part of spiritual growth involves doing away with infantile behavior as well as developing the proper childlike attitude of simplicity and humility. In my view, this is related to what Jesus says in the first of the nine Beatitudes: "Blessed are the poor in spirit, for there is the kingdom of heaven" (Matt. 5:3). I read this statement in the light of, for instance, Isaiah 57:15, "I dwell . . . with him who is of a contrite and lowly spirit," and 66:2, "he who is humble and contrite in spirit and trembles at my word."[50] Again, this presupposes regeneration and the application of the Messianic Torah.

The *adversary* of the kingdom is here described as follows: "[W]hoever causes one of these little ones who believe in me to sin [lit., stumble], it would be

---

50. See France (2007, 165), who refers to the Psalms of Solomon and Qumran (1QM 14:7; 1QS 4:3; 1QH 18:14–15).

better for him to have a great millstone fastened around his neck and to be drowned in the depth of the sea" (Matt. 18:6). Jesus praises childlike simplicity in true disciples, but he points out that the little ones are also vulnerable. The enemy may take advantage of this by enticing the little ones to sin, by belittling gross sins, by mocking their godliness, etc. He deserves the severest punishment.

### 5.5.5 Renunciation

Fifth, there is the necessity of *renouncing* all, especially material, impediments: "Truly, I say to you, only with difficulty will a rich person *enter the kingdom of heaven*. Again I tell you, it is easier for a camel to go through the eye of a needle than for a rich person to enter the kingdom of God" (Matt. 19:23–24). The entrance into the kingdom of God is a "narrow door" (Luke 13:24), through which a person can enter only if he lays aside "every weight, and sin which clings so closely" (Heb. 12:1). In Luke 14:33, Jesus says it in quite strong terms: "So therefore, any one of you who does not renounce all that he has cannot be my disciple."

Paul describes such people: ". . . those who buy as though they had no goods, and those who deal with the world [i.e., earthly goods] as though they had no dealings with it" (1 Cor. 7:30–31). And elsewhere: "[G]odliness with contentment is great gain, for we brought nothing into the world, and we cannot take anything out of the world. But if we have food and clothing, with these we will be content. But those who desire to be rich fall into temptation, into a snare, into many senseless and harmful desires that plunge people into ruin and destruction. For the love of money is a root of all kinds of evils.⁵¹ It is through this craving that some have wandered away from the faith and pierced themselves with many pangs" (1 Tim. 6:6-10).

The point is not that material things as such are evil. Paul does not blame the rich (v. 17) but "those who desire to be rich" (v. 9). Worldly things, in the sense of 1 John 2:15-17, are wrong; earthly things are not wrong, because they are part of God's good creation (1 Tim. 4:4-5). However, setting your mind on earthly things is a worldly attitude (Phil. 3:19; Col. 3:2). In the kingdom, any disciple may become an *adversary* if his mind is diverted from the King to the things that are outside the sphere of the kingdom.

## 5.5.6 Spiritual Power

Sixth, there is the necessity of *spiritual power*: "Strive to enter through the narrow door. For many, I tell you, will seek to enter and will not be able" (Luke 13:24). "The Law and the Prophets were until John; since then the good news of the kingdom of God is preached, and everyone forces his way into it" (16:16).

As I have discussed earlier (§5.1.2), it seems best to understand the latter phrase as follows: every person who desires to enter the kingdom of God will have to apply spiritual "violence" in order to resist all adversaries that try to keep the would-be disciple from entering.

---

51. Lit., "[The/A] root of all evil is the love of money"; many translations read "the" (in general, the predicate has no article in Greek), many others read "a"; cf. Diogenes Laertius 6.50: "He called love of money the mother-city of all evils"; see Towner (2006, 403).

In fact, it also means that he has to resist all negative forces within himself as well. The adversaries outside us find an ally within us: this is our own "flesh," that is, our old nature. The "flesh" in the disciple is like a "fifth column": it may undermine the kingdom from within.

Again, we must carefully distinguish here between the gospel of God's grace for sinners and the gospel of the kingdom of God. In the former gospel, everything depends on God's grace; the repentant sinner only has to surrender, the Lord will do everything: "Come to me, all who labor and are heavy laden, and I will give you rest" (Matt. 11:28). However, immediately after this, the Lord says, "Take my yoke upon you, and learn from me, for I am gentle and lowly in heart, and you will find rest for your souls" (v. 29). This is discipleship, and definitely a matter of human responsibility.

We sometimes put it this way: to *become* a Christian costs you nothing (this is the gospel of God's grace for sinners), but to *be* a Christian costs you everything (this is the gospel of the kingdom of God; see §7.5.2). You come to God in utter weakness; you follow the Lord in spiritual strength. Both statements are "gospel," good news. It is good news that you may come just as you are, with all your weakness and sinfulness. It is also good news that you are not supposed to *remain* as you are: become a well-trained follower of the King. Such following brings great reward, namely, the Messianic kingdom of peace. More good news: the strength to follow him is supplied by the King himself.

### 5.5.7 Perseverance

Seventh, there is the necessity of *perseverance* in the midst of persecutions and oppression: the apostles strengthened "the souls of the disciples, encouraging them to continue in the faith, and saying that through many tribulations we must *enter the kingdom of God*" (Acts 14:22).

This passage is a little different from those quoted in the previous six sections, because in the latter we were dealing primarily with the kingdom in its present form, whereas in Acts 14 the reference seems rather to be to the kingdom in its future form. However, perhaps it is wiser in such passages not to create too a large a contrast between these two meanings, and instead emphasize the moral aspects: these are the conditions that real disciples, genuine sons of the kingdom, must satisfy.

Such an ambiguous use of the term "kingdom" is found in several places. To mention just a few: "I warn you, as I warned you before, that those who do such [wicked] things will not inherit the kingdom of God" (Gal. 5:21). "For you may be sure of this, that everyone who is sexually immoral or impure, or who is covetous (that is, an idolater), has no inheritance in the kingdom of Christ and God" (Eph. 5:5). "[W]e exhorted each one of you and encouraged you and charged you to walk in a manner worthy of God, who calls you into his own kingdom and glory[52]" (1 Thess. 2:12). "This is evidence of the righteous judgment of God, that you may be considered worthy of the kingdom of God, for which you are also suffering" (2 Thess. 1:5). There is little use in asking whether such passages refer to the kingdom in its present form, or to the kingdom in its future form. Even if the latter interpretation is preferred, the verses

---

52. Hendiadys: "his own glorious kingdom," or, "the glory of his own kingdom"; see the discussion in Morris (1959, 86).

also describe the moral features of those who are part of the kingdom in its present form.

## 5.6 Responsibility and Grace

### 5.6.1 Dimensions of the Twofold Gospel Compared

It may strike us that in none of the cases discussed in the previous sections does the Bible speak of simply believing in Jesus. In *all* seven cases, certain moral conditions were mentioned that the would-be disciple must satisfy. In this way, a typical Protestant-Evangelical threat is averted beforehand. This threat is the misleading suggestion that a person "only has to believe" to be able to go to heaven, as if that person's practical attitude and acts are of no importance.[53] A person is justified by faith, not by works (Rom. 3:28; 5:1; Gal. 2:16; 3:24)—but this faith must be a *living, fruitful* faith (see the contrast in James 2:17, 26), a faith "working through love" (Gal. 5:6). A person may enter the kingdom of God by faith, but if this faith remains fruitless, it is a dead faith, and the so-called disciple turns out to be a false disciple, even an adversary of the kingdom.

Here we see the danger of putting all the emphasis on the gospel of God's grace for poor sinners, while neglecting the gospel of the kingdom. The kingdom of God has nothing to do with the question whether, and how, one can go to heaven, but rather with the question how one can become, and be, a true follower (disciple, servant) of Jesus *on earth*. The fact that regeneration is the primary prerequisite for this has been shown above (§5.5.1). And the fact that regeneration is linked with

---

53. Cf. Ouweneel (2010a, 231–37 and chapters 12–13); also see extensively, Ouweneel (20ER).

faith in Jesus Christ is sufficiently clarified at several places in the New Testament; for instance, compare John 3:5 with verse 16, or compare 1 Peter 1:8-9, 18-19, with verses 3 and 22-23.

There is no such thing as entrance to the kingdom, and thus discipleship, without the disciple's faith surrender to the Master. However, there can be no faith surrender without true discipleship flowing from it either. The six conditions dealt with in §§5.5.2-5.5.7 make clear that this surrender of faith must *prove* itself in (a) practical righteousness, (b) inner sincerity, (c) childlike simplicity, (d) renouncing material impediments, (e) spiritual power, and (f) perseverance. These are the fruits of faith. Without these fruits, faith is dead—and a dead faith is no faith at all. Come into the kingdom by faith. If you are a true disciple, this faith will begin bearing fruit, and you will walk as a true disciple of the kingdom. If not, sooner or later you will be unmasked as an adversary.

## 5.6.2 No Responsibility Without Grace

Let me summarize what we have found so far. A true believer is a disciple in the kingdom of God. This implies, first, spiritual regeneration (renewal of the heart) by the Holy Spirit, together with a surrender of faith to the King and Master. Second, a person is not only regenerated by the Spirit, but he should also *receive* the Spirit, which is not the same (see, e.g., the distinction between Ezek. 36:26 and v. 27). Moreover, he should be *filled* with this Spirit (Eph. 5:18), learning to live by the power of the Spirit (Rom. 8:1-11; Gal. 5:16-18). The Holy Spirit as a *person* dwells in the believer (1 Cor. 6:19), and as a *power* he fills, directs, and enriches his life of faith (cf. Luke 4:14; Acts 1:8; 10:38; Rom. 15:13, 19; 1 Cor. 2:4; 1 Thess. 1:5). Third, the believer must learn the Messianic Torah through the Holy Spirit, and then must learn to live by it through this same power of the Spirit.

Just to make sure, I wish to emphasize that all this speaking of "conditions" for entering the kingdom of God and learning to live as a true disciple does not in any way compromise the grace of God.[54] Emphasizing human responsibility at the expense of divine grace is just as badly mistaken as emphasizing divine grace at the expense of human responsibility. It is God who *calls* people, namely, "into his own kingdom and glory" (1 Thess. 2:12). "[I]t is your Father's good pleasure to *give* you the kingdom" (Luke 12:32). "I *assign* to you, as my Father assigned to me, a kingdom" (22:29). It is the Father who "has delivered us from the domain of darkness and transferred us to the kingdom of his beloved Son" (Col. 1:13). These are all unmistakable tokens of grace.

The human responsibility in *entering* the kingdom and the grace of God that *brings* us into the kingdom may never be played off against each other, as has happened far too often.[55] The question whether a person receives a share in the kingdom of God is 100 percent a matter of divine sovereign grace and predestination. However, it is also 100 percent a matter of human responsibility. To be able to get into the kingdom is an act of pure divine grace; to fight in order to get in is one's own responsibility. Those who do not fulfill the condi-

---

54. See extensively, Ouweneel (2008b) on the relationship between divine sovereign grace and human responsibility.
55. Hoekema (1979, 52–53).

tions mentioned simply do not receive a share in the kingdom, and they can never blame God for that.

## 5.7 The Conditions Contained in the Beatitudes
### 5.7.1 The Principle of Righteousness

In fact, the Beatitudes in Matthew 5:3-12 indirectly supply us with conditions for entering the kingdom of God, but formulated in a different way. In these nine Beatitudes, people are called "blessed" (actually, "blissful"[56]) because of certain moral characteristics, with twice the conclusion, "for theirs is the kingdom of heaven" (vv. 3, 10), and once: "your reward is great in heaven" (v. 12). This is not the heavenly paradise of the intermediate state, but heaven as the "upper story" of the kingdom of God that one day will arrive in power and majesty (cf. Heb. 3:1; 8:1; 11:16; 12:22).[57] In fact, *all* nine Beatitudes refer to the share that the disciple will receive one day in the Messianic kingdom of peace.

The first four Beatitudes are more related to *righteousness* as a principle of the kingdom of God, and thus both with God's holiness (God is *light*, 1 John 1:5) and the disciple's conscience.

(a) Being "poor in spirit" (v. 3) is being "humble and lowly" (Zeph. 3:12), "of a contrite and lowly spirit" (Isa. 57:15; cf. 6:5; 66:2; Job 42:6; Luke 5:8; 1 Cor. 1:29). This is mourning about *yourself*. Only those who, of themselves, exhibit true lowliness and humility are eligible for the kingdom of heaven.

---

56. The Greek word *eulogētos* means "blessed" (e.g., 2 Cor. 1:3; Eph. 1:3); *makarios* means "blissful" (colloquial English: "happy," CEB, GNT, etc.).
57. See Ouweneel (2012a, chapters 2-3).

(b) "Those who mourn" (Matt. 5:4), this time not about themselves but about the outward circumstances in which the kingdom is manifest right now. They will be "comforted" (see in the same Bible chapters just mentioned: Zeph. 3:18; Isa. 57:18–19; 66:13; cf. Ps. 119:136; Isa. 40:1; Ezek. 9:4), namely, by entering the Messianic kingdom one day. The *adversaries* of the kingdom are described in the next verses: "Behold, at that time I will deal with all your oppressors" (Zeph. 3:19); "the wicked are like the tossing sea; for it cannot be quiet, and its waters toss up mire and dirt. There is no peace . . . for the wicked" (Isa. 57:20–21). In the Messianic kingdom, the mourners will find joy: "[T]he ransomed of the Lord shall return and come to Zion with singing; everlasting joy shall be upon their heads; they shall obtain gladness and joy, and sorrow and sighing shall flee away" (Isa. 35:10; cf. 51:11; Rom. 14:17).

(c) The "meek" (Matt. 5:5) are those who, in a hostile world, do not answer violence with violence: "I say to you, Do not resist the one who is evil. But if anyone slaps you on the right cheek, turn to him the other also. And if anyone would sue you and take your tunic, let him have your cloak as well. And if anyone forces you to go one mile, go with him two miles. Give to the one who begs from you, and do not refuse the one who would borrow from you" (vv. 39–42). This Beatitude is an allusion to Psalm 37:11, "[T]he meek shall inherit the land and delight themselves in abundant peace." The next verses describe the contrast with the *adversaries* of the kingdom: "The wicked plots against the righteous and gnashes his teeth at him, but the Lord laughs at the wicked, for he sees that his day is coming" (vv. 12–13).

(d) "Those who hunger and thirst for righteousness" (Matt. 5:6) are those who, in a wicked world full of injustice, are passionately longing for the Messianic kingdom (cf. Ps. 42:2; Isa. 51:1, 6–8; Amos 8:11–14). One day, they will be "satisfied," that is, they will reach the world in which everything will be peace and righteousness (cf. Isa. 9:7; Rom. 8:17). Psalm 43 describes the *adversaries* of the kingdom: "Vindicate me, O God, and defend my cause against an ungodly people, from the deceitful and unjust man deliver me!" (v. 1). The unjust man is the very opposite of all those who long for a world of justice.

## 5.7.2 Mercy and Love

The next three Beatitudes are related more to the kingdom principle of *mercy*, and thus with God's own nature (God is *love*, 1 John 4:8, 16).

(e) The "merciful" (Matt. 5:7) resemble God, just like the king says in the parable: "[S]hould not you have had mercy on your fellow servant, as I had mercy on you?" (18:33). The servant who is addressed here has been unmasked as an adversary of the kingdom. To the true disciples of the kingdom it is said, "You therefore must be perfect, as your heavenly Father is perfect" (Matt. 5:48), which in another account is this: "Be merciful, even as your Father is merciful" (Luke 18:36). "Whoever despises his neighbor is a sinner [this is again the adversary of the kingdom], but blessed is he who is generous to the poor" (Prov. 14:21). Notice the underlying coherence: if a person learns to receive God's mercy for himself, he will also be more inclined to show mercy to others. But the Beatitude says the opposite: those who are merciful will in the end receive mercy themselves, namely, by being transferred, from a wicked and cruel world, to the Messianic kingdom.

(f) The "pure in heart" (Matt. 5:8) one day shall "see" God, that is, will enjoy his presence in the Messianic kingdom (cf. Heb. 12:14; 1 John 3:2-3). Again, this is an allusion to the Old Testament: "Who shall ascend the hill of the LORD? And who shall stand in his holy place? He who has clean hands and a pure heart" (Ps. 24:3-4; cf. 15:1-5). The prophet places the true disciples in opposition to the adversaries of the kingdom: "The sinners in Zion are afraid; trembling has seized the godless: 'Who among us can dwell with the consuming fire? Who among us can dwell with everlasting burnings?' He who walks righteously and speaks uprightly, who despises the gain of oppressions, who shakes his hands, lest they hold a bribe, who stops his ears from hearing of bloodshed and shuts his eyes from looking on evil, he will dwell on the heights; his place of defense will be the fortresses of rocks; his bread will be given him; his water will be sure. *Your eyes will behold the king in his beauty*" (Isa. 33:14-17).

(g) The "peacemakers" (Matt. 5:9) are such reflections of the "God of peace" (Rom. 15:33; 16:20; Phil. 4:9; 1 Thess. 5:23; Heb. 13:20; cf. 2 Thess. 3:16) that they shall be called "sons of God," as also in verses 44-45: "But I say to you, Love your enemies and pray for those who persecute you, so that you may be sons of your Father who is in heaven." However, this is not a tame, slack peace, nor peace at all costs: "Do not think that I have come to bring peace to the earth. I have not come to

## The Adversaries of the Kingdom

bring peace, but a sword. For I have come to set a man against his father, and a daughter against her mother, and a daughter-in-law against her mother-in-law. And a person's enemies will be those of his own household" (10:34-36). Jesus' preaching brings division between those who do and those who do not accept it (the adversaries of the kingdom); but it brings peace to those who do accept it.

### 5.7.3 The Last Two Beatitudes

The last two Beatitudes stand a little apart.

(h) "Blessed are those who are persecuted for righteousness' sake" (v. 10), that is, persecuted as a consequence of their defending and upholding righteousness in a world full of *un*righteousness; as Peter puts it, "even if you should suffer for righteousness' sake, you will be blessed" (1 Pet. 3:14). Notice the connection with the fourth Beatitude: this fourth one longs for righteousness in the coming day, while this eighth one pleads for righteousness in the present day (see extensively, Matt. 6:1-18). It is the unrighteous adversaries of the kingdom who persecute those pleading the righteousness of the kingdom of God.

(i) Finally, for the first time in the Beatitudes, Jesus addresses his disciples personally (Matt. 5:11-12): "Blessed are *you* when others [i.e., the adversaries of the kingdom] revile you and persecute you and utter all kinds of evil against you falsely on my account [cf. 10:22]. Rejoice and be glad, for your reward is great in heaven, for so they persecuted the prophets who were before you [cf. 23:29-36]." Only here, a direct connection is made between being a disciple of the kingdom and being a follower of Jesus; the two descriptions are basically identical. In the present time, to the world Jesus is the rejected One, and therefore his followers are the same to the world. They now share his rejection and humiliation in order, one day, also to share his exaltation and glorification in the Messianic kingdom of peace and justice.

# Chapter 6
# The Disciples of the Kingdom

*A disciple is not above his teacher,*
*nor a servant above his master.*
*It is enough for the disciple to be like his teacher,*
*and the servant like his master.*
*Matthew 10:24–25*

*Go therefore and make disciples of all nations,*
*baptizing them in the name of the Father*
*and of the Son and of the Holy Spirit,*
*teaching them to observe all that I have*
*commanded you.*
*Matthew 28:19–20*

*If anyone comes to me*
*and does not hate his own father and mother*
*and wife and children and brothers and sisters,*
*yes, and even his own life, he cannot be my*
*disciple.*
*Whoever does not bear his own cross and come*
*after me cannot be my disciple . . . .*

THE ETERNAL KINGDOM: LIVING UNDER CHRIST

> *So therefore, any one of you who does not renounce all that he has cannot be my disciple.*
>
> Luke 14:26–27, 33

**Summary:** *Disciples (pupils, trainees) are followers of the Master, subjects of the King. Disciples love the Master, obey his instructions, and want to be like him. The Torah of the kingdom, exhibited in him, is reflected in them as well. Disciples know the friendship (intimacy) of his company. Disciples love their fellow disciples, they renounce their family members (if necessary), they daily take up their cross, denying themselves and their own possessions. Disciples follow the* halakhah *(practical kingdom principles) set forth by Jesus and his apostles. Disciples live by the power of the Holy Spirit, and by this power they are Jesus' witnesses "to the end of the earth," preaching his kingship, in spite of the ruling powers (on earth and in the heavenly places), with all persecution and tribulation. They follow him unto death, if necessary, because they know of a better "age" and a "world to come."*

## 6.1 Subjects of the Kingdom

### 6.1.1 Permeated with the Torah

Just like any other kingdom, the kingdom of God has a King and a number of subjects. In Matthew, these are sometimes referred to as "servants" (literally "slaves, bondmen" Matt. 10:24–25; 13:27, 29; 18:23–34; 21:34–36; 22:3–10; 24:45–51; 25:14–30), but the most common name is "disciples." The word is derived from Latin *discipulus*, "pupil, student" (Greek *mathētēs*), but also has the connotation of "follower," and in the New Testament also of a "confidant" (cf. John 15:15b). The most obvious meaning is indeed "pupil, student, trainee, learner" of a Master. This is never meant in the sense of a kind of theological instruction but rather the kind of teaching that we find in Matthew 28:19, where the apostles are commanded to "make disciples" (one Greek word: *mathēteusate*) of all nations. That is, to make them trainees, learners in the kingdom of God, first by administering Christian *baptism to them, second by "teaching [Greek didaskō]* them to observe all that I have commanded you" (v. 20). Teaching here does not involve (in some typically Western sense) theological instruction but (in a typically Jewish sense) Torah instruction, in this case the Messianic Torah. The "disciple" is someone who in rabbinic circles was called the *talmid* (plur. *talmidim*).[1]

Baptism is the entrance *par excellence* to the kingdom of God. In §§5.5 and 5.7 we have seen the *moral* conditions for entering the kingdom. Baptism is the *formal* admission to the kingdom. Elsewhere, I have explained why I think that baptism must not be linked primarily with the covenant (Reformed theology) or with the church (Baptist theology) but with the kingdom of God.[2] Jesus' mission for his apostles was to turn Gentiles into disciples in two steps: first, through baptism, the formal admission *to* the kingdom; second, through the Master's Torah instruction *within* the kingdom, a teaching that is just as moral-practical as the

---

1. Related English terms: *discipulus*: "discipline"; *mathētēs*: "mathematics"(originally: that which is learned); *didashō*: "didatics"; *talmid*: Talmud ("instruction").
2. Ouweneel (2016b, §4.4 and Appendix I).

moral conditions for entering. We could put it this way: Christian ministers, working among the Gentiles, baptize those in whom they encounter a *principle* of justice, sincerity, childlike simplicity, meekness, peacefulness, etc. (see §5.5), *so that* these converts may learn, in the way of the Master's commandments, to develop into real *tsaddiqim, chasidim,* meek ones, peacemakers, etc.

The primary objective is not a typically Western one—teaching what the disciple ought to *know*—but a typically Jewish one: teaching what the disciple ought to *do*. Judaism is not primarily a system of religious doctrine (theology) but of religious practice; it is not primarily about what I can *know* about God, but about how I can I *serve* God. Here, we find the connection with the kingdom of God: being a disciple of the Master is identical with being a servant of the King. The disciple must learn what the King has commanded, and subsequently learn to obey the King's commands. However, also in terms of this meaning, teaching does not involve a kind of ethical learning material, which must be learned by heart and must be reproduced for an exam. Three things coincide here: (a) learning *from* the Master is basically identical with (b) obedience *to* the Master, and this is identical with (c) becoming *like* the Master. This is because the teaching that Jesus, as the Teacher/Master, has introduced, and that can be described as the Torah[3] of Christ (1 Cor. 9:21; Gal. 6:2), coincides, as it were, with the person of the Teacher himself.[4]

---

3. Heb. *torah* is literally "teaching, instruction"; cf. Prov. 3:1; 4:2; 6:20, 23; 7:2 ("law" in KJV, etc., "teaching" in ESV, etc.).
4. See Ouweneel (2007b, §13.1.2).

Elsewhere, I have argued that, in a certain sense, Jesus *is* the Torah in his own person. This means that everything he did or said, *was* "perfect Torah," because the righteousness of the Torah was the essence of his existence.[5] Jesus *is* Torah, Jesus *lives* the Torah, as a Teacher he instructs in the Torah, as a King he commands the Torah, such that the disciple/subject himself *becomes* Torah as the Master/Teacher/King is Torah. Jesus is the goal, the essence, the sense, the meaning of the Torah; in my view, this is (part of) what Romans 10:4 is saying: Christ is *telos nomou*, "goal" (CEB, CJB), or "fulfillment" (GW, NOG), or "culmination" (ISV), or "purpose" (Voice) of the Torah (*not* the wrongly biased "Christ makes the Law no longer necessary," CEV; cf. GNT). We find his person in each iota and every dot of the Torah, just like, conversely, we find the Torah in every fiber of his person, including his "bowels" (thus literally in Ps. 40:8 JUB; or "inward parts," MEV). Similarly, the Messianic Torah permeates every thought, word, and deed of the true *tsaddiq*.

## 6.1.2 Becoming Like the Master

In this way, both the teaching of Christ and the response of the disciple (pupil, trainee, learner) become clear. If Jesus himself is the deepest essence of his own teaching, we immediately understand Matthew 10:25, "It is enough for the disciple to be like his teacher, and the servant like his master." This has sometimes been explained to mean that a disciple should not wish to be *more* than his Master (e.g., Phillips)—but it would be great if he would be at least *like* his Master (cf. CJB, "It is enough for a *talmid* that he become like his rabbi").

---

5. Ouweneel (2016c, §7.4).

Within the context, this means especially: "Students should be happy to be treated the same as their teacher" (ERV), but this is certainly a wider principle.

In Israel, Jesus was the *tsaddiq* ("the Righteous One") *par excellence,* as many have testified (Matt. 27:19, 24; Acts 3:14; 7:52; 22:14; 1 Pet. 3:18; 1 John 2:1; perhaps also James 5:6). Among many other things, this meant that he carried the Torah in his heart. Every disciple who faithfully observes the Torah of Christ becomes a *tsaddiq* himself. Elsewhere I have argued that justification by faith, especially in Romans and Galatians, does not only (or primarily) mean acquittal and rehabilitation in the sense of Roman law, but becoming a *tsaddiq* in the sense of Jewish (Old Testament) law.[6] I repeat, being Jesus' disciple does not simply mean learning his commandments by heart and trying to observe them as scrupulously as possible. No, the great longing of the true disciple is to acquire the inner mind of his Master (cf. Phil. 2:5 NIV, "have the same mindset as Christ Jesus"): "[E]veryone when he is fully trained [Greek *katērtismenos*] will be like his teacher" (Luke 6:40).

The trainee does not just obey; he *abides* in the word of the Master/Teacher (John 8:31). That is, this "word" is the atmosphere in which he lives, breathes, moves (cf. Acts 17:28). Abiding (Greek *menō*) in his word is actually abiding in the Master himself and in his love: "Abide in me, and I in you. As the branch cannot bear fruit by itself, unless it abides in the vine, neither can you, unless you abide in me. . . . If you keep my commandments, you will abide in my love, just as I have kept my Father's commandments and abide in his love"

---

6. Ouweneel (2010a, 236; 20ER, especially chapter 2).

## The Disciples of the Kingdom

(John 15:4, 10). Abiding in Jesus is abiding in his love, living out his Torah.

Various events in the New Testament illustrate in an excellent way what I am trying to say. Take the example of the rich young man, who told Jesus that he had kept all the commandments (Matt. 19:20). In a sense, he had been a good trainee, but he had never become a follower. This was not because of unwillingness but because he had never known the true Teacher/Master. Jesus showed him how he could become a perfect (i.e., fully trained) disciple: "If you would be perfect [Greek *teleios*], go, sell what you possess and give to the poor, and you will have treasure in heaven; and come, *follow me*" (Matt. 19:21). In other words, break away from everything that hinders you, become a *follower* of me, and you will become *like* me.

The rich young ruler did not manage to do this, but almost immediately after his story (Luke 18:18-30) we find that of the tax collector Zacchaeus (19:1-10). In his case, too, his riches formed an impediment, but Zacchaeus managed to overcome this by the grace of God (v. 8). This is not because he had received so much training from the Master but because he had learned to "see" the Master himself (cf. v. 3, "he was seeking to see who Jesus was"). Zacchaeus "saw" what the rich young man did not "see": who Jesus was. It is quite striking, and certainly not a coincidence, that between these two stories we find that of the blind Bartimaeus (18:35-43; for the name see Mark 10:46): as soon as he had received healing from Jesus, he "*followed him*, glorifying God" (Luke 18:43). The first thing he saw after his healing was Jesus! What is decisive is not the curriculum but the Teacher himself. It is enough for the disciple to be like his Teacher. This is accomplished not just through listening but through seeing; what the disciple has "seen" of Jesus is essential.

### 6.1.3 Teacher, Torah, Trainees

Through the parable of the good Samaritan, Jesus showed to a lawyer (an expert of the Torah) the essence (Heb. *k'lal gadol*) of the Torah: unselfish service to fellow humans purely out of love (Luke 10:25-37), even if the fellow human is an enemy of your people (9:52-56; John 4:9). Jesus himself rendered such service (cf. John 8:48, where Jesus is derogatorily called a Samaritan), and if the lawyer wanted to follow him he would have to do the same: "You go, and do likewise" (v. 37). This is a striking example, which shows how, first, the Teacher (Rabbi), second, his curriculum (the Torah, in this case the Messianic Torah), and third, the trainees (disciples, *talmidim*) form a complete system, which exhibits at least the following three characteristics:

(a) The *commandments* as such: the Teacher commands his trainees to do certain things, to avoid doing certain things, even to be certain things. Central among these commandments is the commandment of love, just mentioned. Therefore, Jesus links discipleship directly with this commandment: "A new commandment I give to you, that you love one another: just as I have loved you, you also are to love one another. By this all people will know that you are my *disciples*, if you have love for one another" (John 13:34-35). The true disciple is recognized by the true love that is in him: "God's love has been poured into our hearts through the Holy Spirit who has been given to us" (Rom. 5:5).

N.B. In this respect there is a clear similarity to the Mosaic Torah, the core of which is love as well, as Jesus himself summarized (Matt. 22:35-40).

(b) The *example* of the Teacher: there is no commandment of his that he has not fulfilled himself by being perfectly obedient to his Father: "If you keep my commandments, you will abide in my love, just as I have kept my Father's commandments and abide in his love" (John 15:10). "I always do the things that are pleasing to him" (8:29; cf. 4:34; 5:30; 6:38; 10:18; 12:49-50; 14:31). The Father's highest command was that Jesus would deliver himself up out of love for him and for his followers (Matt. 20:28; John 10:11; 13:1; 15:13; cf. Gal. 1:4; 2:20; Eph. 5:2; 1 Tim. 2:6; Tit. 2:14). Obeying Jesus commandments involves identification with Jesus himself: obedience is walking a path that he himself traveled first, through which one becomes like him. Again, it is the disciple's highest longing to follow the Master's example, thus becoming like him.

N.B. In this respect there is a great difference with Moses: he gave a good Torah, God's own Torah, but he himself was not a perfect example to the nation (cf. Num. 20:12; 27:14).

(c) The *strength* that the Teacher gives: he not only tells the trainee what he must do, and gives him not only his own example, but also the spiritual strength to put his commandments into practice. Although this does not cancel the disciple's own responsibility, we could say that, in a certain sense, it is the Teacher himself who brings about the fulfillment of the commandments within the trainee: "Whoever abides in me and I in him, he it is that bears much fruit, for apart from me you can do nothing" (John 15:5). "I have been crucified with Christ. It is no longer I who live, but Christ who lives in me" (Gal. 2:20). Elsewhere it is the Holy Spirit who is the power through which the commandments are observed (Rom. 8:2, 4; Gal. 5:16-18, 25; Eph. 3:16-19; Phil. 3:3). However, there is no essential difference between these two resources: the Holy Spirit is the Spirit of Jesus Christ, the Son of God (Acts 16:7; Rom. 8:9; 1 Pet. 1:11; Gal. 4:6).

## 6.2 King and Teacher
### 6.2.1 Subjects and Disciples

If fulfilling the Torah of Christ involves following and resembling Jesus, it is obvious that the emphasis in this fulfillment does not lie only on deeds but especially on Jesus' spiritual attitude behind the deeds. It is a matter of *being* rather than of *doing*, one of *being* like Jesus rather than imitating the *deeds* of Jesus. Of course, the deeds are an important part of being like Jesus: he who has the "mind [Greek *nous*] of Christ" (1 Cor. 2:16), considers, deliberates, feels, wants, experiences, longs, loves, believes, hopes like Christ, and from there: acts like Christ: "[W]hoever believes in me will also do the works that I do" (John 14:12). But what really matters is that behind these works the mind of Christ is also present: "Have this mind among yourselves, which is yours in Christ Jesus" (Phil. 2:5).

One of the instructive terms that Jesus used to express this is *bearing fruit*: "By this my Father is glorified, that you bear much *fruit* and so prove to be my *disciples*" (John 15:8). As James puts it: "[T]he wisdom from above is first pure, then peaceable, gentle, open to reason, full of mercy and good *fruits*, impartial and sincere. And a harvest of righteousness is sown in peace by those who make peace" (3:17-18). The term "fruit" does not refer so much to the deed but rather to the attitude behind the deed: purity, peacefulness, reasonability, mercy, impartiality, sincerity, righteousness; also holiness, goodness, thankfulness (Rom. 6:22; 2 Cor. 9:10; Eph. 5:9; Phil. 1:11; Col. 3:12-17; Heb. 12:11; 13:15). Again there is a parallel here with the Holy Spirit: in Galatians 5, over against the "works of the flesh" (v. 19) we do not find the "works [plural] of the Spirit," but the "fruit [singular] of the Spirit" (v. 22).

The connection between, on the one hand, this entire system of the Teacher with trainees and, on the other hand, the kingdom of God can now be formulated a little more precisely. In Matthew 13:52, Jesus identifies someone who has entered into the kingdom and has become part of it as someone "who has been trained for the kingdom of heaven." Many translations read here, "who has become [or, has been made] a disciple of the kingdom of heaven," the expression here being one word in Greek: *mathēteutheis* ("made a disciple," MEV, YLT). It is also explicitly as the One who has all authority in the universe, that is, the *King*, that Jesus commissions his apostles to recruit disciples for him, disciples who are to learn all that Jesus had commanded (Matt. 28:18-20). In other words, the disciple is a follower/subject of the King. There is no contrast between disciple and subject: the title of Teacher places more emphasis on instruction and training, and the title of King emphasizes more the commandments that must be obeyed, but in Jesus these positions and emphases are *completely united.* That which is taught is the Torah of Christ, that is, the whole of his commandments, that is, Christ himself.

As we saw, Jesus is the Teacher especially through his example. In this respect, one could call him a King of the old style, characteristic of antiquity and medieval times: a king who inspires his vassals and troops by his example, who goes before the others in battle, whose courage is a model for his army. Through his example, such a king shows his troops what he expects of them: David "led the troops in battle" (1 Sam. 18:13, 16 ISV; cf. CEB, EXB, etc.). "He who opens the breach goes up before them; they break through and pass the gate, going out by it. Their king passes on before them, the LORD at their head" (Mic. 2:13).

In the Sermon on the Mount, Jesus pointed out several times the direct link between the kingdom of God and discipleship. He taught his *disciples* (Matt. 5:1): "Blessed are the poor in spirit, for theirs is the kingdom of heaven. . . . Blessed are those who are persecuted for righteousness' sake, for theirs is the kingdom of heaven" (vv. 3, 10). "Therefore whoever . . . does [these commandments] and teaches them will be called great in the kingdom of heaven. For I tell you, unless your righteousness exceeds that of the scribes and Pharisees, you will never enter the kingdom of heaven" (vv. 19-20). "[S]eek first the kingdom of God and his righteousness, and all these things will be added to you" (6:33). "Not everyone who says to me, 'Lord, Lord,' will enter the kingdom of heaven, but the one who does the will of my Father who is in heaven" (7:21).

## 6.2.2 Friendship

As I mentioned before, there is a third meaning of the term "disciple": not only pupil (student, trainee) and follower, but also "confidant."[7] Jesus is a King and Teacher who is exalted far beyond his subjects and disciples, and at the same time is very intimate with them. Of Hushai we read, "Hushai the Archite was the king's friend" (1 Chron. 27:33; or, "confidant," NIV, CJB, etc.; "David's friend," 2 Sam. 16:16). Solomon says, "He who loves purity of heart, and whose speech is gracious, will have the king as his friend" (Prov. 22:11). It is a special kind of friendship because, on the one hand, it implies intimacy, and on the other hand, a great disparity in rank. No wonder Jesus says something that common friends (of the same ranking) would never say to each other: "You are my friends if you do what I command you" (John 15:14). It is the Teacher/King who commands, but at the same time shares his heart with his disciples: "No longer do I call you servants, for the servant does not know what his master is doing; but I have called you friends, for all that I have heard from my Father I have made known to you" (v. 15).

An important aspect of friendship is indeed intimacy: "[M]y companion, my familiar friend. We used to take sweet counsel together" (Ps. 55:13–14). The Old Testament speaks of the "friendship" with God (Job 29:4; NIV, "intimate friendship"; CEV, "God All-Powerful was my closest friend"). "The friendship [Heb. *sod*] of the LORD is for those who fear him" (Ps. 25:14; CJB, "*Adonai* relates intimately . . ."). "[T]he LORD used to speak to Mo-

---

7. In Dutch, these three meanings are alliterative: *leerling, volgeing, vertrouweling*.

ses face to face, as a man speaks to his friend" (Exod. 33:11). Abraham is called the "friend of God" (2 Chron. 20:7; Isa. 41:8; James 2:23).[8] Therefore God says about him, "Shall I hide from Abraham what I am about to do?" (Gen. 18:17). One keeps no secrets from a good friend; God laid his heart bare to Abraham: "For the LORD God does nothing without revealing his secret to his servants the prophets" (Amos 3:7). Jesus called his followers "friends" (Luke 12:4) and revealed his secrets to them: it was given to them "to know the secrets of the kingdom of heaven," but to others "it has not been given" (Matt. 13:11).

Abraham and Moses are the men who, in the Old Testament, are most explicitly called "friends of God," that is, related intimately with him. This is why these were the men with whom God engaged as intercessors, after he had announced to them the judgment on Sodom and Gomorrah (Gen. 18:20-21) and on Israel (Exod. 32:9-10), respectively. At Abraham's request, God promised not to destroy Sodom if at least ten righteous ones would be found there (Gen. 18:22-32). At Moses' request, God promised not to destroy Israel (Exod. 32:11-14).[9] Being intimate with God, or Christ, implies not only the confidants' joy but also their commitment to God's people and the world. Thus, David, too, the "man after God's heart" (1 Sam. 13:14; Acts 13:22), became an intercessor for his peo-

---

8. The Koran (4:125) honors him as *chalil-ul-Allah*, the intimate friend of God.
9. To be sure, at least ten (groups of) righteous ones could be found in Israel at the time: Moses, Aaron, Miriam, Joshua, Caleb, Bezalel, Oholiab, Hur, Eleazar, and the sons of Korah.

ple (2 Sam. 24:17; 1 Chron. 21:17—even though the people's distress here was David's own fault). So too, the apostle Paul, one of the most outstanding disciples and friends of Jesus in the New Testament, was a constant intercessor for God's people (Acts 20:36; Rom. 1:9-10; 10:1; 2 Cor. 13:7, 9; Eph. 1:15-17; Phil. 1:3-5, 9; Col. 1:3, 9; 1 Thess. 1:2; 3:10; 2 Thess. 1:11; 2 Tim. 1:3; Phlm. 1:4).

In this respect as well, the true disciple is a follower of Jesus because Jesus was the great intercessor on earth (cf. Luke 6:12 [in view of vv. 13-16]; 22:32; 23:34; John 11:41-42; 17:6-26), as he is now in heaven (Rom. 8:34; Heb. 2:18; 4:14-16; 7:24; cf. Rev. 8:3-4). Discipleship is actually an individual matter. But practically it can never be realized without the disciple's commitment to all of God's people, which is demonstrated concretely through intercession.

## 6.3 Conditions for Discipleship

### 6.3.1 Becoming a Disciple

In §5.5 we investigated the New Testament conditions for entering the kingdom of God. In fact, they are the same as the conditions for discipleship. However, in the latter we do find some new aspects, which we must discuss now.

At the first public appearance of John the Baptist, and subsequently of Jesus, it became immediately clear that the kingdom of God was not something in which every Jew would automatically receive his share simply because he belonged to the chosen people. The announcement of the approaching kingdom was linked with an appeal to repentance, both by John (Matt. 3:2) and by Jesus (4:17; 10:7)—an appeal directed to the Jewish nation. This appeal involved the message that one could enter the spiritual realm of the kingdom only by becoming a *disciple*. This in turn was possible only through four steps: (a) sincere confession of sins before God (3:6); (b) regeneration (3:3, 5), that is, the radical renewal of the heart by the Holy Spirit; (c) baptism, first the baptism of John (Mark 1:4; Luke 3:3), afterward Christian baptism (Matt. 28:19; Mark 16:16); (d) evidence of true repentance by means of a new lifestyle (Matt. 3:7–10, "Bear fruit in keeping with repentance").

This was the *serious* side of the announcement of the kingdom of heaven. The *joyful* side was that the announcement was linked with healing the sick and driving out demons (Matt. 4:23; 9:35; 10:7–8; 12:28).[10] Some people became disciples by first having been delivered from sicknesses or demons, such as Bartimaeus, who was healed of blindness, and afterward followed Jesus "on the way" (Mark 10:46–52). Mary Magdalene was a disciple of Jesus from whom seven demons had gone out (Luke 8:2). The possessed man in the land of the Gerasenes was first delivered, and then became a disciple of Jesus, which meant in his case that he could not stay with the Master but had to go out to announce the message himself (vv. 38–39).

The *characteristics* of true disciples of the kingdom are at the same time *conditions* for those who want to become such: true disciples of the kingdom are those who observe the Torah of Christ "in an honest and good heart" (cf. v. 15).[11] This principle is described in many

---

10. See Ouweneel (2007b, §13.4.1–2).
11. Cf. Ouweneel (2007b, §§13.1 and 13.2).

different ways, but this is the essence of it. In this context, I mention a few important themes in Jesus' teaching as recorded in Matthew: doing righteousness (5:19-20; 6:33; 21:31-32), doing the Father's will (7:21; 12:50), true humility (18:1-5; cf. 19:14), a forgiving attitude (18:23-35), the readiness to bring sacrifices (19:12, 23-24), no jealousy (i.e., begrudging others the same blessings of God; 20:1-16), producing fruit (13:1-9, 18-23; 21:42-43), no hypocrisy (23:13), looking forward to the King (25:1-13), commitment to the King (vv. 14-30), commitment to the brothers of the King (vv. 31-46). All these passages, which we need not discuss again, present to us in many different ways the moral characteristics of the kingdom's disciples.

Because of my thesis that in the Gospels disciples are in fact subjects of the kingdom of God, I point (by way of summary) to some characteristics of a disciple as described in John's Gospel:

(a) *Obedience:* "If you abide in my word, you are truly my *disciples*" (8:31).

(b) *Mutual love:* "By this all people will know that you are my *disciples*, if you have love for one another" (13:35).

(c) *Bearing fruit:* "By this my Father is glorified, that you bear much fruit and so prove to be my *disciples*" (15:8).

## 6.3.2 Denying One's Family

Luke 14 is very important because Jesus prescribes here three striking conditions of discipleship. The similarity among these three conditions is that they belong to the hardest we find in the New Testament as far as this topic is concerned. They can be realized only by a renewed heart, and in no other way than in the power of the Holy Spirit.

The first condition is denying one's family: "If anyone comes to me and does not hate his own father and mother and wife and children and brothers and sisters, yes, and even his own life, he cannot be my disciple" (v. 26). It is obvious that "hating" here is not an absolute but a relative notion. Deuteronomy 21:15 speaks of a man having two wives, the one loved and the other "hated" (KJV), which simply means "unloved," or probably, loved less (CEV, ERV, NET). Jesus cannot mean that a disciple must literally hate his parents, because this would flatly contradict the Mosaic Torah, which says, "Honor your father and your mother" (Exod. 20:12; Deut. 5:16). Jesus quotes this commandment with full agreement (Matt. 15:4; 19:19), and Paul does the same (Eph. 6:2). The New Testament also says that a husband must love his wife (Eph. 5:25; Col. 3:19; 1 Pet. 3:7), and a wife her husband (Titus 2:4). Scripture could not possibly recommend hating one's wife (or husband) and children.

In Luke 14:26, therefore, "hating" is clearly relative. Jesus is saying this: "If anyone comes to me and does not love me more than his own father and mother and wife and children and brothers and sisters, yes, and even more than his own life, he cannot be my disciple" (cf. 8:19–21; 9:57–62; 18:28–30). In John 12:25 we find a similar command: "Whoever loves his life loses it, and whoever hates his life in this world will keep it for eternal life" (cf. Matt. 10:39; 16:25). Here, too, the message is that the disciple must love his Lord more than his earthly life. In the literal sense, hating one's life would mean hating oneself, and this would flatly contract the commandment to love your neighbor *as yourself* (19:19; 22:39; Lev. 19:18; Rom. 13:9; Gal. 5:14; James 2:8).

Nevertheless, in spite of relativizing Jesus' statement, this remains a very severe and burdensome commandment for the natural person (cf. Acts 15:10; 1 Cor. 2:14): love for the Master, the King, must surpass every earthly love. The kingdom of God is dominated by love and the commandment to love. Believers have been transferred to the kingdom of the Son of his *love* (Col. 1:13 NKJV, etc.); everything in this kingdom speaks of, and is dominated by, love. Jesus is hated by his enemies (Luke 19:14; John 7:7; 15:18, 23–25), but loved by his disciples. Yes, true love for the Master/King surpasses every other love in their lives (see further §§9.5 and 9.6).

Practical examples of this first condition are found in Luke 9. Jesus told a certain person: "Follow me," that is, Become my disciple. But the man answered, "Lord, let me first go and bury my father." Jesus said to him, "Leave the dead to bury their own dead. But as for you, go and proclaim the kingdom of God" (vv. 59–60). It would seem only fair if this man could go to the funeral of his father first; some commentators therefore assume that the Lord is here adopting the hardest possible standpoint.[12] Others assume that the father was probably not yet dead at all.[13] The man could simply not separate from his father as long as the latter was still alive. This is similar to the subsequent case: "Yet another said, 'I will follow you, Lord, but let me first say farewell to those at my home.' Jesus said to him, 'No one who puts his hand to the plow and looks back is fit for

---

12. Cf. Greijdanus (1955, 258); Liefeld (1984, 935).
13. Cf. Geldenhuys (1983, 296); Green (1997, 407–408).

the kingdom of God'" (vv. 61–62). That is, do not let the people in your home be hindrances to you becoming a disciple in God's kingdom.

### 6.3.3 Denying Oneself

The second condition for discipleship is this: "Whoever does not bear his own cross and come after me cannot be my disciple" (Luke 14:27). This cross-bearing by Jesus' disciples is a subject that has led to several misunderstandings.[14]

First, the topic is not bearing *Jesus'* cross, as Simon of Cyrene had to do (Matt. 27:32), but bearing *one's own* cross.

Second, the theme is not "crucifying" one's own "flesh with its passions and desires" (Gal. 5:24), for this still involves the cross of Christ, not one's own cross. Moreover, the subject here is not sanctification (leading a holy life) but discipleship: consistently following the Lord.

Third, the subject is not a "cross" (a form of suffering, illness, adversity, distress) that God supposedly places upon people. One can hear people saying, "It is a nasty disease, but I will patiently bear my cross." However, Jesus is referring not to a cross that one passively receives (from God?), whether one likes it or not, but to a cross that a person must actively take upon himself, and do so every day anew: "If anyone would come after me, let him deny himself and *take up his cross daily* and follow me" (Luke 9:23).

Jesus' contemporaries had no difficulty with this metaphor because they were familiar with the phenomenon

---

14. See, e.g., Lane (1974, 306–308); Geldenhuys (1983, 276, 398); Green (1997, 565–66); France (2007, 410–11, 638).

of criminals that had been sentenced to death on a cross, were led out of the courtroom to the place of execution with their crosses on their backs. (The difference, though, is that the criminal was forced to bear the cross, whereas the disciple must take it upon himself voluntarily.) Such a cross-bearing implied giving up all hope for *this* world, expecting nothing but mocking and contempt from the people of this world, considering oneself of minor importance ("denying oneself"), and—as a disciple of Jesus—focusing all of one's hope upon the world to come: the kingdom of God. Paul speaks of "the cross of our Lord Jesus Christ, by which [or, through whom] the world has been crucified to me, and I to the world" (Gal. 6:14).

The disciple bears this cross daily; that is, every morning he must decide afresh whether he is prepared to share the road of humiliation and rejection with Jesus, in order also to share with him the road of exaltation and glorification in the Messianic kingdom. Jesus says, as it were, You can be my disciple only if you are prepared to follow *my* path, the lowest way, the road that I have followed to the bitter end, but a road that leads ultimately into the kingdom of glory and power.

This is a lovely paradox: taking the lowliest path is the only way to reach the top: "[W]e suffer with him in order that we may also be glorified with him" (Rom. 8:17). Paul was prepared to "share his sufferings, becoming like him in his death, that by any means possible I may attain the resurrection from the dead" (Phil. 3:10-11). "[I]f we endure, we will also reign with him" (2 Tim. 2:12). "[L]et us run with endurance the race that is set before us, looking to Jesus, the founder and perfecter of our faith, who for the joy that was set before him endured the cross, despising the shame, and is seated at the right hand of the throne of God" (Heb. 12:1-2). "[R]ejoice insofar as you share Christ's sufferings, that you may also rejoice and be glad when his glory is revealed" (1 Pet. 4:13).

### 6.3.4 Renouncing One's Possessions

The third condition for discipleship is this: "[W]hich of you, desiring to build a tower, does not first sit down and count the cost, whether he has enough to complete it? Otherwise, when he has laid a foundation and is not able to finish, all who see it begin to mock him, saying, 'This man began to build and was not able to finish.' Or what king, going out to encounter another king in war, will not sit down first and deliberate whether he is able with ten thousand to meet him who comes against him with twenty thousand? And if not, while the other is yet a great way off, he sends a delegation and asks for terms of peace. So therefore, *any one of you who does not renounce all that he has cannot be my disciple*" (Luke 14:28-33).

"Renouncing all" (other translations: forsaking, giving up all) is not the same as "giving all away." Sometimes this may be necessary. In the case of the rich young ruler, his possessions were a hindrance to his entering the kingdom of God. Therefore, Jesus advised him to sell all that he had and distribute it to the poor, in order to become a follower of Jesus (18:22). But that is not what Luke 14:33 says. Jesus' intention seems to be rather that the disciple's love and attention should no longer be focused upon his earthly blessings but entirely, undividedly, upon the Master/King. This also seems to imply making all one's possessions available for the kingdom of God.

The apostle Paul even leaves some room for the thought that the rich may enjoy their riches, but he adds immediately what, in his view, is the most beautiful mode of enjoyment: "Charge those who are rich in this world that they be not haughty, nor trust in uncertain riches, but in the living God, who giveth us richly all things to enjoy; that they do good, that they be rich in good works, ready to distribute, willing to communicate, laying up in store for themselves a good foundation against the time to come, that they may lay hold on eternal life" (1 Tim. 6:17-19 KJ21). The latter is the life of the age to come; compare verse 12: "[T]ake hold of the eternal life to which you were called." So the message is: Focus on eternal life, not on your earthly riches. You may enjoy them, but preferably by doing good with them to those who have need.

In Luke 12:21, Jesus juxtaposes the person who "lays up treasure for himself" and the person who is "rich toward God." These two do not fit together well. The true disciple of Jesus belongs to the second category. All that he is and has is placed at the disposal of the King and his kingdom.

A striking example of such a disciple is Levi (in Matthew's Gospel he is called Matthew; according to tradition, he later became the author of this Gospel): "After this he [i.e., Jesus] went out and saw a tax collector named Levi, sitting at the tax booth. And he said to him, 'Follow me.' And leaving everything, he rose and followed him. And Levi made him a great feast in his house, and there was a large company of tax collectors and others reclining at table with them" (Luke 5:27-29). The seemingly contradictory element in this passage is that Levi "left everything," began following Jesus, and was nevertheless able to organize a great meal of everything that he had "left." Indeed, he had "renounced" it, but it still belonged to him. The difference was that he had now become part of "those who deal with the world as though they had no dealings with it" (1 Cor. 7:31). Levi had assumed a very different attitude toward his possessions; from now on, he saw them as means to "do good, to be rich in good works, ready to distribute, willing to communicate."

In §6.1.2, I mentioned the example of Zacchaeus. Jesus is not reported to have commented on this tax collector's possessions, yet the man said, "Behold, Lord, the half of my goods I give to the poor. And if I have defrauded anyone of anything, I restore it fourfold" (Luke 19:8). Apparently, the mere encounter with Jesus had sufficed to bring Zacchaeus to this new attitude and lifestyle. Jesus called this "salvation" (v. 9). The man had been saved from himself and his riches in order to become a follower of Jesus, who himself had to say, "Foxes have holes, and birds of the air have nests, but the Son of Man has nowhere to lay his head" (9:58).

## 6.4 The Way (New Testament *Halakhah*)
### 6.4.1 Disciples, Christians, "Those of the Way"
The limited attention in the book of Acts to the church in terms of the meaning Paul attaches to it in his epistles (see the next chapter) is inversely proportional to the extensive attention the book gives to the kingdom of God.

The phrase occurs no fewer than eight times (1:3, 6; 8:12; 14:22; 19:8; 20:25; 28:23, 31), and in addition it speaks once of Jesus' kingship. Paul's accusers said, "These men who have turned the world upside down have come here also, and Jason has received them, and they are all acting against the decrees of Caesar, saying that there is another king, Jesus" (17:7).

The book of Acts begins with the risen Jesus, who spoke in Jerusalem for forty days about the kingdom of God: he presented himself alive to his disciples, "appearing to them during forty days and speaking about the kingdom of God" (1:3). The book ends with the imprisoned Paul, who spoke in Rome for two years of the kingdom of God: "From morning till evening he expounded to [the Jewish leaders in Rome], testifying to the kingdom of God and trying to convince them about Jesus both from the Law of Moses and from the Prophets. . . . He lived there two whole years at his own expense, and welcomed all who came to him, proclaiming the kingdom of God and teaching about the Lord Jesus Christ with all boldness and without hindrance" (28:23, 30-31). In addition to Jesus and Paul, Philip too was "preaching the gospel of the kingdom of God and the name of Jesus Christ" (8:12 JUB).

Moreover, the book of Acts often uses the typical kingdom term "disciple." This word occurs by far most frequently in the Gospels (in 223 verses), and 28 times in Acts, and—remarkably enough—not at all in the rest of the New Testament. In Acts, the word "disciple," or specifically "disciple of the Lord" (9:1), is the common word for Christian, that is, follower of Christ (6:1-2, 7; 9:10, 19, 25, 38; 11:26, 29; etc.). Only in 9:25, the trainees of Paul are called "his disciples." But this is not strange: the followers of an apostle are followers of the Lord because the apostle is a follower of the Lord: "Be imitators of me, as I am of Christ" (1 Cor. 11:1). In Acts 9:36, we find the feminine form of "disciple" ("discipless," WYC, YLT; Greek *mathētria*). In 14:21, we find the verb *mathēteuō*, "to make disciples," which we also find in Mattew 28:19.

Another characteristic term is *Christianos*, "Christian": "[I]n Antioch the disciples were first called Christians" (11:26). "Agrippa said to Paul, 'In a short time would you persuade me to be a Christian?'" (26:28). See further 1 Peter 4:16: "[I]f anyone suffers as a Christian, let him not be ashamed, but let him glorify God in that name."

Another term for "Christian" in Acts is those "belonging to the Way" (Greek *tēs hodou ontas*) (9:2). This phrase "the Way" occurs another four times: "But when some became stubborn and continued in unbelief, speaking evil of the Way before the congregation . . ." (19:9). "About that time there arose no little disturbance concerning the Way" (v. 23); "according to the Way, which they call a sect" (24:14). "Felix, having a rather accurate knowledge of the Way . . ." (v. 22).

The phrase "the Way" could be called a genuinely Jewish expression: disciples are people of a certain Way that they go, the Way of following after Jesus. Here, Christianity is not yet primarily a doctrine but, in a truly Jewish sense, a "way of life." It reminds us of the rabbinic term *halakhah*, that is, the Jewish legislation as we find it in the Torah and the rabbinic tradition, especially the Talmud. The term comes from the verb *h-l-kh*, "to go, to walk." Thus, *halakhah* is the "way [of life]" that Jews are supposed to follow. Analogously, Christianity is referred to as the Way, that is, so to speak, the Christian *halakhah*, "way [of life]," as we find it in the Messianic Torah (the law of Christ, as we find it in the Gospels; cf. 1 Cor. 9:21; Gal. 6:2) and the apostolic writings of the New Testament. As Isaiah says, "[T]hough the Lord give you the bread of adversity and the water of affliction, yet your Teacher will not hide himself anymore, but your eyes shall see your Teacher. And your ears shall hear a word behind you, saying, 'This is the way, walk in it,' when you turn to the right or when you turn to the left" (30:20-21).

Christianity is not just knowledge that must be known, but a way that must be walked. When therefore Paul speaks of "my teaching," he is not referring to a series of dogmas, but this expression is to be linked with "my conduct, my aim in life, my faith, my patience, my love, my steadfastness, my persecutions and sufferings" (2 Tim. 3:10-11). *Halakhah* is what James referred to as the "royal law" (James 2:8), that is, the legislation of God's kingdom, of the King himself. Disciples are trained by "teaching them to observe all that I have commanded you," as Jesus said in his function as King, the One who has all authority in heaven and on earth (Matt. 28:18-20). It is the sum of what he called "my commandments" (John 14:15, 21; 15:10). Or even in the singular, "the commandment of the Lord and Savior through your apostles" (2 Pet. 3:2); that is, through the apostles this commandment has come to us.

### 6.4.2 Peter and *Halakhah*

Not only did Jesus promulgate *halakhah*, but at his command, his first followers, the apostles, did the same. They not only passed on the commandments that he had issued, they also added new commandments to them. They did so on the basis of the *halakhic* authority that he gave them.[15] Phillip Sigal, who calls Jesus a "proto-rabbinical halakhist," has written extensively on this matter.[16] In Matthew 16:19, Jesus told Peter: "I will give you the keys of the kingdom of heaven, and whatever you bind on earth shall be bound in heaven, and whatever you loose on earth shall be loosed in heaven." The meaning of this "binding" and "loosing" is explained by the Jewish context of Jesus' statement. In the rabbinic tradition, "binding" and "loosing" (Heb.: *asar v'hittir*, of *asar v'sh'ra*) means "prohibiting" and "allowing" (or "imposing").[17] Jesus gave to Peter the divine authority to promulgate new *halakhah*, that is, the power to prohibit certain things and to allow certain other things.

It is of great importance that Jesus connected the *halakhic* authority granted to Peter with the "keys" of the kingdom of God, a point that comes to light in the distinguished position that Peter had among the apostles (Acts 1:15; 2:14, 38; 3:4, 12; 4:8; 5:3, 8, 15, 29; 8:20; 9:32, 38; 10:5; 11:2; 12:3; 15:7; Gal. 2:7-8), and in his two New Testament letters. Peter built on the *halakhah* of Jesus,

---

15. See Ouweneel (2007b, §13.2.2).
16. Sigal (1987, 6).
17. See, e.g., the Talmudic tracts Chagigah 3b, Ta'anit 12a and Makkot 23b (cf. Ridderbos (1962, 360-61; 1970, 13-14); Bruce (1979, 225); Bivin and Blizzard (1984, 143-49); Stern (1992, 56-58; 1997, 149-50).

and thus determined who was allowed to enter the kingdom of God, and who was not. In fact, this made him a kind of Jewish *shammash* ("manager, deacon") and *dayan* ("judge").[18] Jesus thus invested this "uneducated, common fisherman" (cf. Matt. 4:18; Acts 4:13) with the same authority possessed formerly within the Jewish community by the learned lawyers (Torah masters) and the Pharisees. In Matthew 23:4, we find some support for the view that this is indeed the meaning of "binding" and "loosing": the lawyers and the Pharisees "tie up heavy burdens, hard to bear, and lay them on people's shoulders, but they themselves are not willing to move them with their finger."

In the book of Acts, we find how Peter used this authority, and what *halakhah* he applied, when allowing entire groups to come into the kingdom of God.

1. *The Jews.* I see four *halakhic* aspects here:

(a) "Let all the house of Israel . . . know for certain that God has made [Jesus] both Lord and Christ [i.e., Messiah], this Jesus whom you crucified" (2:36), that is, confess him as God's anointed and glorified King over the kingdom of God.

(b) "Repent" (v. 38, *metanoēsate*), that is, acknowledge your former sins, and undergo a radical renewal (*meta*) of your mind (*nous*). This appeal to moral, spiritual activity finds its counterpart in what the Spirit does: regeneration (John 3:3-5).

(c) "[B]e baptized every one of you in the name of Jesus Christ for the forgiveness of your sins, and you will receive the gift of the Holy Spirit" (v. 38; cf. the case of Saul of Tarsus, 9:17 and 22:16; also see 19:5-6).

---

18. Stern (1999, 54).

(d) "Save yourselves from this crooked generation" (v. 40), that is, disassociate yourselves from Israel's sins, especially from those Jews in Jerusalem who were responsible for having killed the Messiah (v. 23).

2. *The Samaritans* (half Jewish, half Gentile; cf. 2 Kgs. 17:24–41). In their case, the advance work was done by Philip the evangelist (cf. 6:5; 21:8). He "preached good news about [or, the gospel of; one word: *euangelizomenōi*] the kingdom of God and the name of Jesus Christ," and administered water baptism to the converts (8:12). In this way, they had already actually been admitted to the kingdom of God. Subsequently, Peter, together with John, only had to formally confirm this through the laying on of hands, through which the Samaritan believers received Spirit baptism (vv. 14–17).

3. *The Gentiles*. In the preaching of Peter to Cornelius and his friends, I notice the following three *halakhic* elements:

(a) Jesus is "Lord of all" (10:36)—even over the evil powers (v. 38)—who has to be acknowledged as such. That is, submit your lives to his supreme authority, and be his disciples, his followers.

(b) Jesus is the "judge of the living and the dead" (v. 42); this is the *warning* aspect: one day he will be the Judge of all people, therefore beware.

(c) By faith in this same Jesus, a person receives "forgiveness of sins" (v. 43); this is the *encouraging* aspect: believe in him and you will be saved.

Accepting these truths immediately granted Cornelius and his friends Spirit baptism, and subsequently water baptism (vv. 44–48).

Interestingly, in none of these cases was Peter himself the one who administered water baptism. With the 3,000 in Acts 2 this was physically impossible, in Acts 8 it was Philip, and in Acts 10 certain anonymous brothers, who baptized the converts.

4. It is reported twice that Peter used the "keys" of the kingdom in a negative way. First, by excluding Ananias and Sapphira from the kingdom (by their physical death) because of their lies (5:1-11). Second, by refusing admission to the kingdom of God to Simon the Magician because of his wickedness (8:18-23).

### 6.4.3 The Other Apostles

In Matthew 18:18-20, Jesus extended the *halakhic* authority to all apostles: "Truly, I say to you [plural], whatever you bind on earth shall be bound in heaven, and whatever you loose on earth shall be loosed in heaven. Again I say to you, if two of you agree on earth about anything they ask, it will be done for them by my Father in heaven. For where two or three are gathered in my name, there am I among them."

In the first part of this statement, Jesus spoke of his apostles. But in the second part of it, he referred to any "two or three" of his followers, gathered together with (the Spirit of) Christ. Even they would have the authority to "bind" and to "loose," that is, to issue *halakhah*: to prohibit certain actions, or to impose certain actions. This does not hold for any arbitrary "two or three" disciples. The context of Matthew 18:15-20 is the church; the "two or three" are the local congregation, sitting together in judgment, led by their elders.

Jesus seems to be alluding here to a rabbinic tradition that was set forth in the Talmud much later. This tradition ties in with Malachi 3:16, "Then those who feared the LORD spoke with one another. The LORD paid attention and heard them, and a book of remembrance was written before him of those who feared the LORD and esteemed his name." "One another" here is literally "a man to his neighbor," that is, just two persons. Certain rabbis derived from this that, where two or three are sitting together to study the Torah, or more specifically, are sitting together as a tribunal to apply the Torah, the *Shekhinah* is there among them.[19] It is there as an invisible pillar of the cloud. Similarly, Jesus said that, where two or three of his followers (in a church context) would meditate upon the Messianic Torah to derive *halakhah* from it (in this case to excommunicate a trespasser), he himself would be in their midst, namely, through his Spirit.[20]

In practice, these "two or three" are especially the church leaders, first the apostles, then the teachers and elders in the local churches (Matt. 28:20; Acts 15:2, 4, 6, 22-23; 16:4; 20:28; Eph. 4:11-16; 1 Tim. 3:2; 5:17; Titus 1:9; Heb. 13:7, 17). The early Christians followed the "teaching" (Greek *didachē*) of the apostles who had just been filled with the Holy Spirit (Acts 2:42). We remember that Hebrew *torah* also means "teaching, instruction." Thus, following the apostles' teaching may be taken to mean that believers followed the *halakhah* or "oral torah" of the apostles, that is, their exegesis and practi-

---

19. Avot III.2; Berachot 6a (see Edersheim (1979, 2:124).
20. See Ouweneel (2007a, §3.4.2) on the connection between the *Shekhinah* and the Holy Spirit.

cal application of the Tanakh in the light of, and in agreement with, Jesus' own teaching. Present-day Christians, too, live not only by the words of Jesus himself, but also by the *halakhah* of the apostles, as we find it in the book of Acts, and more particularly in the divinely inspired New Testament letters. The entire New Testament is apostolic *halakhah*, given by (in alphabetical order) James, John, Jude, Luke, Mark, Matthew, Paul, and Peter (even if Jude, Luke, and Mark are never literally called "apostles").

## 6.5 Discipleship and Kingdom
### 6.5.1 The Disciples' Question

The Greek word *ekklēsia* ("church") occurs nineteen times in the book of Acts, but without any doctrinal explanation of the precise meaning of the word. At best, we understand from Acts that an *ekklēsia* is a local gathering of Christians (e.g., 8:1; 11:22, 26; 13:1; 14:23; 20:17), and the *ekklēsia* is the universal totality of Christians (20:28). The word *basileia* ("kingdom") occurs eight times, and Jesus as "King" once, but with much clearer (particularly implicit) teaching as to what precisely is meant by the kingdom of God.

We have seen earlier (§1.1.2) how striking it is that, after his resurrection, Jesus spoke with his disciples for forty days about just one topic: the kingdom of God (Acts 1:3). This makes clear what an encompassing subject this must be. We certainly may assume that Jesus spoke with his disciples about the entire Christian life, and about Christian church life as well. Apparently, he did this in such a way that this entire teaching could be summarized in the phrase "kingdom of God." Indeed, we will see clearly (§8.4) that many passages in the New Testament that do not mention this phrase are nonetheless implicitly dealing with the subject of the kingdom of God.

From the conversations during these forty days, only one question by the disciples and Jesus' response to it have been recorded, which therefore must be of singular interest: "So when they had come together, they asked him, 'Lord, will you at this time restore the kingdom to Israel?' He said to them, 'It is not for you to know times or seasons that the Father has fixed by his own authority. But you will receive power when the Holy Spirit has come upon you, and you will be my witnesses in Jerusalem and in all Judea and Samaria, and to the end of the earth'" (vv. 6–8).

It is astonishing how many expositors assume, in my view without any basis, that this was a very wrong, obsolete, mistaken question by the disciples.[21] Apparently, the disciples were convinced that, one day, the (Davidic) kingdom would be given back to Israel, that is, that one day there would again be a free and glorious kingdom of Israel with no one less that the Messiah sitting on the throne of David. It was perfectly acceptable that they expected this. Not only does Daniel 7:14 tell us that to the Son of Man "was given dominion and glory and a kingdom," and that all peoples, nations, and languages would serve him, but verse 27 also tells us: "And the kingdom and the dominion and the greatness of the kingdoms under the whole heaven shall be given to *the people* [i.e., Israel] *of the saints of the Most High*; *their* kingdom shall be an everlasting kingdom, and all domin-

---

21. See, e.g., Knowling (1979, 56); Bruce (1988, 35–36); Moerkerken (2004, 665–66).

ions shall serve and obey *them* [i.e., Israel]" (ESV note; cf. CEB, CJB, RSV, OJB, etc.).

"It shall come to pass in the latter days that the mountain of the house of the Lord shall be established as the highest of the mountains, and shall be lifted up above the hills; and all the nations shall flow to it, and many peoples shall come, and say: 'Come, let us go up to the mountain of the Lord, to the house of the God of Jacob, that he may teach us his ways and that we may walk in his paths.' For out of Zion shall go the law [the Torah], and the word of the Lord from Jerusalem" (Isa. 2:2–3).

"For to us a child is born, to us a son is given; and the government shall be upon his shoulder, and his name shall be called Wonderful Counselor, Mighty God, Everlasting Father, Prince of Peace. Of the increase of his government and of peace there will be no end, on the throne of David and over his kingdom, to establish it and to uphold it with justice and with righteousness from this time forth and forevermore" (9:6–7).

Many other passages say the same thing.[22]

### 6.5.2 Jesus' Response

We conclude that the disciples' question was appropriate and understandable: one day, the (Davidic) kingdom *will* be given back to Israel. We now have to pay careful attention to Jesus' response. In it, we do not find the slightest hint that the apostles' question was wrong, obsolete, or misplaced.[23] On the contrary, Jesus indirectly indicated that the question in itself was entirely appropriate, but that it was not for them "to know times or

---

22. See extensively, Ouweneel (2012a), especially chapters 5, 7, and 13.
23. *Contra* Reformed expositors such as Grosheide (1962, 10–11).

seasons that the Father has fixed by his own authority." I therefore understand the text as follows: Indeed, one day the kingdom *will* be restored to Israel, only you are not allowed to know *when* this will happen. In the meantime, Jesus' kingdom teaching refers not only to the future Messianic kingdom of peace and justice, but also to the kingdom in its present form. That is the kingdom between Jesus' ascension and his parousia, of which he cannot say when this will take place (cf. Mark 13:32).

Of great interest to me is the "But" (Greek *alla*) at the beginning of verse 8. What exactly is its logical force? It seems to me that Jesus wishes to say: the moment that the Father will restore the kingdom to Israel may be far away, *but* in the meantime I give you something that amply compensates for the absence of that glorious kingdom, namely, the power of the Holy Spirit. He will be, as it were, a foretaste of the coming kingdom. For the time being, the kingdom is not going to arrive in glory and majesty, but in principle the *power* of that kingdom is already here (cf. Heb. 6:5, "the powers of the age to come"). Already now, Paul's statement is true: "[T]he kingdom of God does not consist in [idle] talk [cf. vv. 18-19] but in power," namely, the power of the Spirit.

Another explanation of Jesus' response is this: In God's time, the kingdom will indeed be restored to Israel, as the prophets have foretold, *but* all God's servants have to cooperate toward that end. That is, they will have to testify of the King and his empire, at home and "to the end of the earth." For this purpose, they receive the power of the Holy Spirit, because without this, an effective testimony is not possible.

A marvelous example of such testimony was that of Philip the evangelist in Samaria: "Philip went down to the city of Samaria and proclaimed to them the Christ [Messiah]. And the crowds with one accord paid attention to what was being said by Philip when they heard him and saw the signs that he did. For unclean spirits, crying out with a loud voice, came out of many who had them, and many who were paralyzed or lame were healed. So there was much joy in that city. . . . [W]hen they believed Philip as he preached good news about [or, the gospel of] the kingdom of God and the name of Jesus Christ, they were baptized, both men and women" (Acts 8:5–8, 12).

Philip preached Christ, that is, the anointed King (v. 5), and the kingdom of God (v. 12). He preached through the power of the Spirit (cf. 6:3, 5), and this power came to light in the signs and wonders that Philip did. He not only preached the message concerning a kingdom that would arrive one day in glory and majesty, but he demonstrated this power through the healings and deliverances that occurred. Humanly speaking, it would have been inconceivable that he would only have preached. The content of his preaching was that the Samaritans had to believe in a Jew (of all people! cf. Luke 9:52–53; John 4:9) who, some years before, had been executed by crucifixion at Jerusalem. The people would simply have ridiculed him, or even have threatened him with death. But when the lame began to walk in the name of Jesus, and the possessed were delivered in the name of Jesus, the people saw the *power* of the King who was being preached to them. They began to believe, not only in his power, but in the King himself who was the source of this power.

The Spirit is the "down payment" ("guarantee," 2 Cor. 1:22; 5:5; Eph. 1:13–14) of the coming kingdom.

Therefore, Gerard den Hertog describes the Spirit strikingly as the "presence of the future."[24] This means that, to some extent, we may call the future kingdom of God a spiritual reality already today because the power of that kingdom is already present. Through this power, followers can be recruited for the King, that is, to become subjects of his kingdom. This reminds us again of the "But" of Acts 1:8: the kingdom for Israel is still postponed, but the "powers of the age to come" (Heb. 6:5; cf. 1 Cor. 4:20) are already here. The future is already operative in the present, yet remains future to a large extent.

## 6.6 The Message of the Kingdom
### 6.6.1 Thessalonica

Paul and Silas, too, preached the gospel of the kingdom that had been revealed in the power of the Spirit, namely, at Thessalonica. No doubt they also preached the gospel of God's grace for poor sinners, as Paul later told the elders of Ephesus: "I do not account my life of any value nor as precious to myself, if only I may finish my course and the ministry that I received from the Lord Jesus, to testify to the gospel of the grace of God" (Acts 20:24). But he added, "And now, behold, I know that none of you among whom I have gone about proclaiming the kingdom will see my face again" (v. 25). This is different from our present time, when many preach the gospel of God's grace for sinners, whereas the gospel of the kingdom is far less known (cf. 28:23, 31,

---

24. Den Hertog (2003, 31, chapter 3: "De Geest als 'heden van de toekomst'"), tying in with Versteeg (1969), *Het heden van de toekomst*.

where Paul debates the kingdom of God with the Jews in Rome).[25]

Paul preached what Jesus had commanded in the Great Commission. This was not only "repentance and [or, for] forgiveness of sins" (Luke 24:47), but also: *"All authority in heaven and on earth has been given to me. Go therefore* [i.e., in the light of this fact] *and make disciples of all nations, baptizing them in the name of the Father and of the Son and of the Holy Spirit, teaching them to observe all that I have commanded you"* (Matt. 28:18-20), and: "[T]hese signs will accompany those who believe: in my name they will cast out demons," etc. (Mark 16:17-18). In Thessalonica, the emphasis of Paul and his co-workers was on the gospel of the kingdom. This is evident from the accusation that was leveled against them: "These men who have turned the world upside down have come here also, . . . and they are all acting against the decrees of Caesar, saying that there is another king, Jesus" (Acts 17:6-7).

In verse 6, we find the same Greek word *oikoumenē* that we encounter in Revelation 12:9 in reference to the power domain of Satan (cf. 16:13-14). *Oikoumenē* (cf. "ecumenical," from Greek *oikeō*, "to dwell, inhabit," thus: the "inhabited world") is usually a very general term, but in Luke 2:1 it is clearly a description of the then inhabited world, namely, the Roman Empire, the power domain of the Roman emperor. On the Mount of Temptation, Satan showed to Jesus all the kingdoms of the *oikoumenē*, in order that Jesus would accept

---

25. *Contra* Schuyler English (1986, 44 note), who identifies the "gospel of the kingdom" with the "gospel of grace" (cf. in the present book §7.5.2).

them from his hand by worshiping him. Thus, in fact, Satan was offering Jesus the imperial crown over the Roman Empire (4:5-6).[26] In this way, however, namely, by kneeling down before Satan and worshiping him, Jesus did not wish to obtain his power over the Roman empire; he wished instead to obtain this through his death and resurrection, and his glorification at God's right hand. There, he is invested with all authority in heaven and on earth (Matt. 28:18), which includes the Roman Empire.

In Acts 11:28 and 24:5, and in Revelation 3:10, the *oikoumenē* is the Roman Empire as well,[27] and this is clearly in view in Acts 17:6-7, just quoted. Paul turned the *oikoumenē*, that is, the Roman Empire, upside down by preaching that there was "another [Greek *heteros*, not *allos*] King," that is, a King of a different kind than what people were used to: Jesus. One day, this King "will judge the world in righteousness" (v. 31). Whoever is baptized, is being transferred from the *oikoumenē*, the power domain of the "dragon," the demonic power behind the Roman emperor (the ruler of the eschatological Satanic empire), to the power domain of that so very "different" King (*basileus*): Jesus (cf. 18:26). We may assume that, if Paul had preached only repentance and forgiveness of sins, he would not have had too many problems. His religion would not have been very different from the many religions that were preached in the Greco-Roman world, each offering some path of moral salvation. However, Paul preached something else as well: the supreme kingship of Jesus, and in

---

26. Ouweneel (2016d, 111, 127-28).

27. Ouweneel (2016d, 43-44, 99).

this way he challenged the Roman emperor—the *basileus* of the Greek world—and even the gods of the Greek and the Romans, who were royal powers ("thrones, dominions, rulers, authorities," Col. 1:16) within their own domain.[28]

In the book of Revelation, behind the emperor we find concealed the actual ruler in the spiritual world: the "dragon." Paul in fact claimed that King Jesus was even more powerful than this dragon. Both the "great red dragon" in Rev. 12:3 and the "beast out of the sea" have ten horns and seven heads (the dragon has on the heads seven diadems, the beast has on the horns ten diadems). This is basically one and the same power in the Roman world: the beast is the earthly, human ruler, and the dragon—"the devil and Satan" (12:9; 20:2)—is the invisible angelic prince of the Roman Empire, who was worshiped by the Romans as a deity.[29] The message of Paul and Silas was that the King whom they preached was more powerful than not only the Roman emperor, but also the gods of Rome, led by Jupiter and Apollo. In the language of the book of Revelation: the tiny, weak, dying Lamb is more powerful than the raging dragon. This makes the response of the adversaries understandable: it was like that of Herod, who raged in great violence after he had heard about his rival, the newly born King of the Jews (Matt. 2).

### 6.6.2 Other Opposition

The gospel of the kingdom as the apostles preached it and for which Jesus had sent them out is this: there is

---

28. See more extensively, Ouweneel (2016d, §11.4.3).
29. See extensively, Ouweneel (2016d, 315-24) and passim.

One at the right hand of God who has all power over the world, the Roman Empire included, One who is more powerful than the emperor and the gods of Rome, who one day will appear in glory and will establish his power and majesty on earth. He is now seated, not on the throne of the emperor in Rome, but on the throne of God, and one day he will be seated on the throne of his father David in Jerusalem (cf. Rev. 3:21).

What practical significance does this message have for people? This: whoever is recruited as a subject of this King, whoever serves and follows him uprightly, will one day share the glory of the Messianic kingdom with him. Whoever rejects the King today, will later fail to enjoy the Messianic kingdom and will perish together with the King's adversaries. This is what Paul and Silas, and so many other heralds of the King, strongly pressed upon the people. They challenged them to become "defectors" as it were, that is, by renouncing the Satanic kings (human or demonic) of this world and by beginning to follow the true King. Such a challenge may sound just as unlikely as it is to "follow the Lamb" (Rev. 14:4) instead of following the dragon (cf. 6:8; 13:3).

This is what the gospel of the kingdom is all about: who is more likely to gain the final victory: the dragon or the Lamb? Yet, the wise know to make the proper choice: "It is these who have not defiled themselves with women, for they are virgins. It is these who follow the Lamb wherever he goes. These have been redeemed from mankind as firstfruits for God and the Lamb" (14:4). "The Lamb will conquer [his enemies], for he is Lord of lords and King of kings, and those with him are called and chosen and faithful" (17:14).

For the time being, such a gospel will always encounter tremendous opposition—an opposition that is basically led not by human powers but by the great angelic prince of Rome (cf. Eph. 6:12). Therefore, besides being a demonstration of the King's power, the message of the kingdom in Acts always implies suffering, rejection, persecution: the apostles strengthened "the souls of the disciples, encouraging them to continue in the faith, and saying that through many tribulations we must enter the kingdom of God" (14:22; cf. Matt. 5:10-12). In the present time, the kingdom exhibits both aspects: on the one hand, the power of the Spirit, revealing itself in signs and wonders, and on the other hand, the weakness and vulnerability that are part of the suffering (see what has been said before about "Gethsemane Christians" and "Tabor Christians," §§5.1 and 5.2). In the kingdom in its present form, healings, deliverances, even raising the dead, accomplished by Jesus' followers *in* the name of Christ, are just as real as imprisonment and the martyr's death, which Jesus' followers have to endure *for* the name of Christ.

### 6.6.3 Ephesus

All these matters were manifested in detail during another missionary visit by Paul: his stay in Ephesus. Paul "entered the synagogue and for three months spoke boldly, reasoning and persuading them about the kingdom of God. But when some became stubborn and continued in unbelief, speaking evil of the Way before the congregation, he withdrew from them and took the disciples with him, reasoning daily in the hall of Tyrannus. This continued for two years, so that all the residents of Asia heard the word of the Lord, both Jews and Greeks.

And God was doing extraordinary miracles by the hands of Paul, so that even handkerchiefs or aprons that had touched his skin were carried away to the sick, and their diseases left them and the evil spirits came out of them. . . . And this became known to all the residents of Ephesus, both Jews and Greeks. And fear fell upon them all, and the name of the Lord Jesus was extolled. Also many of those who were now believers came, confessing and divulging their practices. And a number of those who had practiced magic arts brought their books together and burned them in the sight of all. And they counted the value of them and found it came to fifty thousand pieces of silver. So the word of the Lord continued to increase and prevail mightily" (19:8–12, 17–20).

Here again, the emphasis is on the fact that Paul preached the gospel of the kingdom of God, and did so to the Jews first. When a number of them rejected his words and spoke evil of "the Way" (i.e., the Christian faith), Paul turned away from them and from now on addressed only those who were willing to hear, whether Jew or Gentile. The kingdom preaching went hand in hand with signs and wonders, as usually happened in Acts. There can be no announcement of the powerful King without some demonstration of his power. In Ephesus, the Spirit's strength became manifest in various ways: (a) healings and demonic deliverances, (b) fear upon the outsiders, (c) public confessions of the newly converted, and (d) destruction of everything linked with idolatry and magic, that is, with the powers that dominated the Roman Empire but over which Jesus Christ triumphed. At the same time, it turned out that these hostile powers could still wreak a lot of havoc.

It was, and is, not yet the time of Christ's *final* victory. It is still a battle whose front line is always shifting, and in which both parties gain their little victories, even though the ultimate victory is nevertheless certain.

The different phases in the battle, both positive and negative, are well illustrated in Acts 19. After the "success story" of verses 8-20 comes a story of opposition and defeat (vv. 23-41): "About that time there arose no little disturbance concerning the Way [i.e., the Christian faith]" (v. 23). The silversmith Demetrius launched a revolt against Paul, in which he indicated precisely where the problem lay: "Paul has persuaded and turned away a great many people [in Asia], saying that gods made with hands are not gods. And there is danger not only that this trade of ours may come into disrepute but also that the temple[30] of the great goddess Artemis[31] may be counted as nothing, and that she may even be deposed from her magnificence, she whom all Asia and the world worship" (vv. 26-27). Ephesus is "the city of the Ephesians," which "is temple keeper of the great Artemis, and of the sacred stone that fell from the sky"[32] (v. 35).

---

30. About the greatness and beauty of this temple, which was one of the seven ancient "wonders of the world," see, e.g., Knowles (1979, 412-13), and his references to ancient writers.
31. Quite a few translations have replaced the Greek names with their Roman equivalents: Diana for Artemis, Jupiter for Zeus, and Mercury for Hermes (Acts 14:12). Apparently, they did so—through the Luther Bible and KJV—in the footsteps of the Vulgate.
32. Greek *diopetēs*, in other translations: "which fell from Jupiter," or even: "of Jupiter's offspring" (DRA), "the child of Jupiter" (WYC). See below for further discussion.

Within the heavenly places, this is the spiritual battle *par excellence* (cf. Eph. 6:12): not a battle between Paul and the Ephesian silversmiths, but between, on the one hand, the King of kings and, on the other hand, the "magnificence" of the "great goddess Artemis," who was nothing but a demonic power, the angelic ruler of Asia and many other regions. Initially, the silversmiths shouted: "Great is Artemis of the Ephesians!" (v. 28), and later, all the people cried out the same slogan for two hours (v. 34). Paul, in whom the power of God's kingdom had become manifest so strongly, was then kept from going into the theater because his life was at stake (vv. 30–31), while some of his co-travellers were dragged into the theater (v. 29). God used the unbelieving town clerk to calm the masses (vv. 35–41), otherwise things would have looked very bad for Paul, humanly speaking.

Elsewhere, I have written extensively about the significance of the goddess Artemis, who in Greek mythology is the twin sister of Apollo; the two are the children of Zeus/Jupiter and Leto.[33] They represent strong demonic powers in the spiritual world, which had to be contended against by the first preachers of God's kingdom in Asia Minor and Southern Europe, just like, centuries later, Willibrord, Boniface, and others in the Germanic world had to combat Wodan/Odin and Donar/Thor as spiritual realities.[34]

---

33. See Ouweneel (1998, 24, 142, 146, 151, 183, 223).
34 According to, e.g., Collins (1976), it is the myth of Leto and her son Apollo that exhibits the greatest number of parallels with the mother and son in Rev. 21. In my view, this does not mean, however, that Rev. 12 is a "myth" going back to ancients myths

Artemis is the lady whom, as Demetrius says of her, "all Asia and the world worship" (v. 27). The "world" is here again the *oikoumenē*, the Roman Empire. This is very important: it shows that alongside the earthly god of the Roman Empire—in the book of Revelation called the dragon—there is a goddess: lady *Mystērion* (see Rev. 17-18). Artemis is one of the many names of the great virgin-mother, the queen of heaven, the feminine element in the dark world of Satan and his demons.[35] When Paul visited Asia and made so many converts there, he collided immediately with this Satanic power, which dominated Asia and was called Artemis. Paul triumphed: the uproar came to an end, and no single convert, who had been withdrawn from Artemis' power domain by the power of the Spirit, was reconquered by her. This is what baptism does: it transfers people from the domain of the dark powers to that of the blessed rule of Christ. This place is not always comfortable, but it is at least safe.

---

such as that of Leto and Apollo, but that these myths are demonic imitations in the spiritual world (see extensively.

35. Ouweneel (2016d, chapter 5).

# Chapter 7
# The Kingdom and the Church

> *I tell you, you are Peter,*
> *and on this rock I will build my*
> *church,*
> *and the gates of Hades shall n*
> *prevail against it.*
> *I will give you the keys of the*
> *kingdom of heaven,*
> *and whatever you bind on earth*
> *shall be bound in heaven,*
> *and whatever you loose on earth*
> *shall be loosed in heaven.*
> Matthew 16:18–19

**Summary:** *The beginning of the New Testament church and the kingdom of God in its present form (if we take the pouring out of the Spirit as its starting point) fell on the same Day of Pentecost. The church is the dwelling-place of the Holy Spirit, the kingdom is the Spirit's sphere of operation. The latter is usually a wider concept than the church because the church is the body of Christ, the totality of all* *true Christians, whereas the kingdom contains both true and false followers of Christ, and in a sense even the entire human race. The (local) church is just one of the many societal relationships that Christians form (beside Christian families, schools, associations, companies, etc.), whereas the kingdom is an all-encompassing notion. Roman Catholics, traditional Protestants, and free-church Evangelicals all view the relationship between the church and the kingdom in different ways, often with great practical consequences.*

## 7.1 From Matthew to Paul

### 7.1.1 Introduction

THE APOSTLE PAUL IS the only New Testament writer who has thoroughly explained to us what the church of God is.[1] Among the letter writers, he is even the only one (apart from Heb. 12:23) who uses the Greek term *ekklēsia* to refer to God's worldwide church. However, he is not the only one who has used the term; Matthew 16:18 is the first New Testament reference. Here is where we begin our investigation concerning the relationship between church and kingdom, after which we will return to Paul.

Regularly the complaint has been heard: "Jesus preached the kingdom, but what came was the church."[2] The idea, then, is that the church came about when those who waited in vain for the coming of kingdom unfortunately began organizing themselves as disciples of

---

1. See extensively, Ouweneel (2010b and 2010c).
2. Quoted in Ridderbos (1962, 337; see references there; see the entire §36, 342–56. The quote goes back to Alfred Loisy; see Berger (2004, 495–96); Ratzinger (2007, 48).

Jesus.³ If "organizing" means excessive structuring, and especially introversion, linked with a slackening attention for the kingdom of God, this indeed implied a measure of derailment. But at the same time, we realize that Jesus himself has announced his *ekklēsia*, not (only) as a product of an inevitable historical developmental process, and even less as a sign of inner degeneration, but as an organic, spiritual building, that is, distinct from human organizations and denominations. He himself would construct this building within the framework of the history of God's kingdom.

This is the first reason why it is incorrect, if not absurd, to claim that the church originated out of disappointment among the early Christians. Jesus himself announced the church, and founded her. The second reason why we have to reject the thesis, "Jesus preached the kingdom, but what came was the church," is that it falsely suggests that the church originated out of a *diminished* eschatological expectation. Herman Ridderbos has unmasked this suggestion by emphasizing the permanent eschatological perspective, which on all sides surrounds the church in its expectation and ministry.⁴ That is, the kingdom was not *replaced* by the church; on the contrary, the church is one of the glorious harbingers of the kingdom as it will one day arrive in glory and majesty, at the parousia of the King. Church and kingdom are two spiritual realities, overlapping, yet distinct, existing concomitantly, not only in the present age but also in the age to come and in the world to come.

---

3. See Ouweneel (2007b, §13.3.3).
4. Ridderbos (1962, 355); cf. Van Genderen (2008, 680).

## 7.1.2 "I Will Build My Church"

The first passage in which the church is announced is this: "I tell you, you are Peter [Greek *Petros*], and on this rock [*petra*] I will build my church, and the gates of hell [*Hades*] shall not prevail against it" (Matt. 16:18). Elsewhere, I have dealt with the interpretation of the word *petra* in this verse.[5] The relevant point is that Jesus speaks here of the (at that time) still *future* "church" that he was going to build. In the entire New Testament, there is no such thing as a "church" gathered "out of the entire human race, from the beginning of the world to its end," as stated in the Heidelberg Catechism (Q/A 54). Moreover, the Catechism is inconsistent here because, looking at the characteristics of the church as described by the Catechism, we see particularly New Testament features: "catholic" (i.e., universal or worldwide, i.e., not limited to Israel); a "community chosen for eternal life" (which implies knowing God *and* Jesus Christ, John 17:3; cf. 1 John 5:20), "united in true faith," which is the Christian faith; a community with "members"—an image reminding us of the body of Christ (Rom. 12:4-5; 1 Cor. 12:12-27; Eph. 3:6; 5:30).

We find the same tension in the Belgic Confession (Art. 27): "This church has existed from the beginning of the world and will last until the end." However, this phrase is preceded by some characteristics of the church that are typically New Testament features: ". . . a holy congregation and gathering of true Christian believers, awaiting their entire salvation in Jesus Christ, being

---

5. Ouweneel (2010b, 60-64).

washed by his blood, and sanctified and sealed by the Holy Spirit."

The New Testament church possesses its own special characteristics: in Matthew 16:18 it was still a future thing, to be born on the Day of Pentecost (Acts 2). It is the company of saints, the "body of Christ," that is viewed as unified with its glorified head in heaven at God's right hand (Eph. 1:20–2:6). She is the bride of the dead and risen Lamb (Rev. 19:6–9). As the dwelling-place of the Holy Spirit (1 Cor. 3:16; Eph. 2:20–22) it is a post-Pentecost phenomenon.[6] It is important always to emphasize the *continuity* of Old and New Testament, but also to keep in view the special features of the New Testament church.

### 7.1.3 A Future Matter

By the grace of God, there have been *believers*, or *righteous ones*, "from the beginning of the world." By the grace of God, there were always those who belonged to the "offspring of the woman" in opposition of those who were of the "offspring of the serpent" (Gen. 3:15). By the grace of God, since Abraham there are those who have been eternally blessed in him and in his offspring (12:3; 22:18; 26:4; 28:14), and others who have not. However, in the Bible this company of righteous and blessed ones is never what the Bible understands by the "church of God." *This* term is strictly reserved for those who are associated with the glorified Jesus and are the temple of God's Spirit.

Accordingly, the church is still a future thing in Matthew 16:18. The Israelite "congregation [*ekklēsia*] in the

---

6. See note 1 for extensive additional argumentation.

wilderness" (Acts 7:38) is no counter-argument against this reasoning, for *this* "congregation" of Israel was something very different from the *ekklēsia* Jesus was referring to. If the very term *ekklēsia* should prove some sort of identity between Israel's *ekklēsia* and Jesus' *ekklēsia*, then how does the reference to the (popular) "assembly" (*ekklēsia*) of Ephesus (19:32, 39, 41) fit in here? Should this use of the term *ekklēsia* prove that all Ephesian citizens were part of the Christian church? Of course not. The *term ekklēsia* may have various meanings; neither the gathering of Israelites in the wilderness nor the city assembly of Ephesus were the "holy gathering of the true believers in Christ" (Belgic Confession, Art. 27).

In the kingdom of God in its present form, the church consists of the true disciples of the glorified King, as opposed to the false confessors. The church could not have existed before the kingdom of Christ existed; and the kingdom of Christ could not have existed before the church existed. Or, to be more precise, we may argue that the kingdom was actually established from the very moment the King had taken his place at the right hand of God (aside from anticipatory statements such as Matt. 12:28; 28:18 and Luke 17:21). The church existed from the moment the Holy Spirit was poured out, by whom believers were forged together to be one body, one temple (cf. 1 Cor. 12:12-13). This latter event occurred only ten days after the former event (Acts 1-2).

Let me formulate this in a little more detail. During Jesus' time on earth, both the church and the actual rule of the kingdom were still future because as yet the Son of Man had not been glorified at the right hand of God in heaven. For at least three reasons this was important.

(a) Only at the ascension and glorification of Christ at God's right hand could the kingdom rule of Christ truly and actually be exercised. As Peter expressed it, when Jesus was exalted at God's right hand, God "made him both Lord and Christ," that is, Master of the world and anointed King (Acts 2:33, 36). The verse quoted most frequently in the New Testament declares: "The LORD says to my Lord: 'Sit at my right hand, until I make your enemies your footstool'" (Ps. 110:1). As 1 Corinthians 15:25 elucidates, Christ "must *reign* until he has put all his enemies under his feet."

(b) Only after the ascension and glorification of Jesus Christ at God's right hand could he become the head of the "body," which is the church. God "worked in Christ when he raised him from the dead and seated him at his right hand in the heavenly places, far above all rule and authority and power and dominion, and above every name that is named, not only in this age but also in the one to come. And he put all things under his feet and gave him as head over all things to the church, which is his body, the fullness of him who fills all in all" (Eph. 1:20-23; cf. 5:23; Col. 1:18; 2:19). This is the essential point: the very Lord at God's right hand is, in this very position, the head of his church. Without the glorification of Christ, neither the church nor the kingdom could exist.

(c) Only after the ascension and glorification of Christ at God's right hand could Jesus send the Holy Spirit: "[A]s yet the Spirit had not been given, because Jesus was not yet glorified" (John 7:38). "[I]t is to your advantage that I go away, for if I do not go away, the Helper will not come to you. But if I go, I will send him to you" (16:7). "Being therefore exalted at the right hand of God, and having received from the Father the promise of the Holy Spirit, he has poured out this that you yourselves are seeing and hearing" (Acts 2:33). The church is the dwelling place of the Holy Spirit: "Do you not know that you [plur.] are God's temple and that God's Spirit dwells in you?" (1 Cor. 3:16; Eph. 2:22); "in one Spirit we were all baptized into one body" (1 Cor. 12:13). This is a pivotal point: without the Holy Spirit having been sent to earth, neither the church (the dwelling place of the Spirit) nor the kingdom (the Spirit's sphere of operation) could exist.

### 7.1.4 Significance of Christ's Glorification

One reason why these things are not discerned is because some believers do not clearly see the impact of the glorification of Christ. They seem to think that Jesus came to earth from the Father, and simply returned to the Father. In a sense, this is correct, of course (see, e.g., John 16:28, "I came from the Father and have come into the world, and now I am leaving the world and going to the Father"), but there is an essential difference between his two dwellings in heaven. First, from eternity, Jesus *had been* with the Father as *God the Son*. Second, in the fullness of time he descended as Man (at the same time remaining God the Son). Third, after he had accomplished his work he returned to the Father as both God and Man—the glorified Man at God's right hand.

We need clear discernment here. From eternity, the *Son* was in the bosom of the Father (1:18); in that eternity, there was not yet a Man at the right hand of God. However, right now the *Son* is still in the *bosom* of the Father, but in addition there is a *Man* on the *throne* of the Father (Rev. 3:21). It is the same person, but these two *states of affairs* are *not* the same. If we allow these matters to be blurred—as if they all amount to the same thing—we will definitely lose sight of the proper meaning of Christ's glorification with all its consequences.

A glorified Man at the right hand of God—*this* is the first and foremost characteristic of the kingdom of God in its present sense. To this *Man* in glory all power has been given: the Father "has given him [i.e., the Son of God] authority to execute judgment, *because he is the Son of Man*" (John 5:27), that is, in that quality. God "has fixed a day on which he will judge the world in righteousness by *a man* whom he has appointed; and of this he has given assurance to all by raising him from the dead" (Acts 17:31). The *Son of Man* is "seated at the right hand of the power of God" (Luke 22:69). And as the *Son of Man* he will one day return on the clouds of heaven to accept the visible dominion over the world (Matt. 24:30; 26:64; cf. 16:28).

Just as there can be no kingdom of God in the New Testament sense without the Son of Man sitting on the throne of God, just the same there can be no church in the New Testament sense—and that is the only sense of "church" that the Bible knows—without the Son of Man sitting on the throne of God, for *as such* he is the head of the body (Eph. 1:20-23). No matter how different church and kingdom are, as we will explain later in this chapter, one thing is certain: from now through eternity, the one will never exist without the other. They began nearly simultaneously (Acts 1–2), and they will both last forever, in clear association with each other.

## 7.2 Church and Kingdom

### 7.2.1 General Relationships

In summary, there can be no kingdom without a glorified Man at God's right hand, and there can be no church without a glorified Man at God's right hand. Therefore, in Matthew 16:18 Jesus is speaking in the future tense about "*my* church,"[7] that is, the totality of all those who would be the followers and servants of Jesus, the true subjects of the kingdom of God.

Both the kingdom and the church are founded upon the very same work of Christ that he accomplished here on earth: the work of glorifying God and redeeming repentant sinners. Thus, church and kingdom are distinguished, but not separated. On the contrary, their coherence is clearly implied, especially in two respects.

First, immediately after having mentioned his (future) church, Jesus speaks of the keys of the kingdom of heaven that he would give to Peter (Matt. 16:19).

Second, in Matthew 18, Jesus' teaching about the (local) church (v. 17) stands in between his kingdom teaching about "these little ones" (vv. 1–14) and his kingdom teaching on forgiveness (vv. 21–35).

Please note that, in these chapters, we are not yet ready for Paul's teaching on the church; in Matthew, *the teaching on the church is part of Jesus' teaching on the kingdom*. In Paul's teaching, the church *extends beyond* the

---

7. The Dead Sea Scrolls speak of the Teacher of Righteousness, who would build a church/assembly/congregation (*ēda*) (4QpPs37, 3.16); see I. H. Marshall in Green *et al.* (1992, 124).

kingdom. To give an example: the kingdom is bound to time; it stands within a perspective that reaches *from* the "foundation of the world" (Matt. 13:35) until the moment that Christ delivers the kingdom to the Father (1 Cor. 15:24). However, the church is the object of God's "eternal purpose" (Eph. 3:11) and encompasses those who have been chosen "*before* the foundation of the world" (1:4), that is, since eternity, and extends into all eternity.

Jesus speaks of the church more concretely in Matthew 18:17 than in 16:18, for in the former Jesus is speaking about what the church would be concretely for the common believer: the local, structured church led by elders, in which the Word would be preached, the sacraments would be administered, and church discipline would be exercised. If the trespasser does not listen to the brothers calling him to account, "tell it to the church. And if he refuses to listen even to the church, let him be to you as a Gentile and a tax collector."

### 7.2.2 Societal Relationships

Perhaps, the local church is the most important structured "concentration point" within the kingdom of God. However, we should not overlook the fact that Christian families form such "points" as well. "Let the little children come to me and do not hinder them, for *to such belongs the kingdom of heaven*" (Matt. 19:14). A child is "holy" (on holy ground) if at least one of the parents is a believer (1 Cor. 7:14). Notice the reference to the "Lord" (implying royal authority) in Eph. 6:4 ("Fathers, do not provoke your children to anger, but bring them up in the discipline and instruction of the Lord") and in

Col. 3:20 ("Children, obey your parents in everything, for this pleases the Lord"). Children in Christian families are explicitly linked to the kingdom of God. As has been said, the church consists of individual believers, but the kingdom consists of families.

We could go one step further, though, for in principle the same holds for Christian schools, companies, associations, political parties, and nation states.[8] The kingdom of God consists of many Christian societal relationships, including the ones just mentioned. The only difference is this: marriages and families are based upon God's creational order; they date from before the Fall (Gen. 1:28; 2:18-25). Christian schools, companies, associations, political parties, and nation states are the products of humanity's cultural-historical activities. But even these cannot be severed from God's creational order, for, as Kuyperian theology and philosophy would emphasize,[9] they are the fruits of God's cultural mandate, both before the Fall ("The LORD God took the man and put him in the garden of Eden to work it and keep it," 2:15) and after ("the LORD God sent him out from the garden of Eden to work the ground from which he was taken," 3:23).

However this may be viewed, the kingdom of God does not consist of individual people only but also of the societal relationships in which they function, insofar as these relationships are submitted to the commandments of Christ. I repeat, the *church* consists of in-

---

8. See extensively, Ouweneel (2014); cf. Noordegraaf (1980, chapter 7).
9. As a standard work, see the "Stone Lectures" of Abraham Kuyper: Kuyper (2009).

dividual believers—members of the body of Christ—but the *kingdom* consists of marriages and families, schools and companies, etc., insofar as they are "in the Lord" (cf. 1 Cor. 7:39; Col. 3:18-20), that is, submitted to his "Lord"-ship (see §8.4). When, at some future time, the Sun of righteousness will rise (Mal. 4:2; cf. Matt. 17:2; Acts 26:13; Rev. 1:16), the "day" of God's kingdom will rise over the earth in splendor and glory (Rom. 13:12; 1 Thess. 5:1-8; 2 Pet. 1:19). At present, it is still "night," during which, however, Christian marriages and families, Christian schools and companies, etc., that is, societal relationships that are "in the Lord," will shine as bright lights (cf. Matt. 5:14-16; Phil. 2:16), harbingers of the coming glorious kingdom.

In the enumeration just given, the (local) church has been mentioned as one of many societal relationships in which Christians function. In this respect, there is a clear difference with the kingdom of God: the (local) church is only one of these relationships—the kingdom of God encompasses them all. In my view, every theology concerning the relationship between church and kingdom will fail if this distinction is not made. The (local) church is merely one of an entire series of societal relationships that Christians form within the framework of God's kingdom as a result of God's creational command.

### 7.2.3 The Church Over Against the Kingdom?

The kingdom exists and functions wherever the Lordship of Christ is acknowledged and obeyed: in individual lives and in many societal relationships, of which the local church is only one. However, it cannot be denied that the church does play a pivotal role in the kingdom: it is *here* that the preaching of the Word takes place that radiates in all the other societal relationships in which Christians function. Therefore, John Calvin saw the church as the center from which God's dominion takes form in the various relationships of our earthly lives.[10] To say it with Augustine: here, something of the *civitas Dei*, the "city" or "state of God," is already becoming visible.

The view of the Montanists (second/third century), for instance, and of the Anabaptists (sixteenth century), that there is a *contrast* between the (established) church and the kingdom of God, has become a minority view, and rightly so. Of course, it is acceptable to protest the secularization that has occurred in the established churches (Roman Catholic, Eastern Orthodox, Lutheran, Calvinist, Anglican) as well as in evangelical congregations. However, this does not constitute a contrast with the kingdom of God because, in the present age, this kingdom, just like the visible church, has become an intermingling of good and evil as well. Protests against the established church(es) do not bring Christians any closer to the kingdom of God,[11] because by definition such Christians are, and remain, part of the Christian world: as part of the visible church. Christians cannot leave the Christian world without ceasing to be Christians. They may try to form congregations of true born-again and devoted believers, but they will not succeed; after a decade or so they will be like all the rest, as church history has proven time and again. The body of

---

10. Graafland (1973, 52).
11. Küng (2001, 88–96).

Christ is holy; but there are no holy (unmixed) congregations and denominations.

Both the church and the kingdom can be defined in a wider and in a narrower sense. In the wider sense, the (visible) church is the Christian world, which coincides with the kingdom of God in its wider sense. This is the church as represented by the seven churches of Asia (Rev. 2 and 3), at least five of which were such unhappy mixtures of good and evil. In the narrower sense, the kingdom of God comprises only the born again (John 3:3, 5), and the church is the "holy gathering of the true believers in Christ" (see above). In this sense, the church stands in opposition to all false Christians ("false brothers," 2 Cor. 11:26; Gal. 2:4; cf. 1 Cor. 5:11), and all non-Christians. However, the kingdom's "field" is emphatically "the world" (Matt. 13:38; see §3.1.3 and following). We need think here only of the Holy Spirit to illustrate the point I am trying to make: the Spirit's present dwelling place on earth is the church of God (1 Cor. 3:16; Eph. 2:20–22), but his field of operation is the entire world. Where we find the kingdom of God, we find the Spirit working, and where the Spirit is working, we find the kingdom of God (see §8.1).

In its actual sense, the church comprises only true believers in Christ; the kingdom comprises all people who (truly or falsely) have accepted the rule of Christ in their lives. One could call the church a *sign* of the kingdom:[12] what has become reality in her will one day become reality in the entire world. Today, every knee in the church bows before Jesus, while soon *all* inhabitants of the earth will bow their knees before him (cf. Phil. 2:10; cf. Isa. 45:23; Matt. 27:29; Rom. 14:11). Because of

---

12. Heyns (1988, 353–54).

her sign character, the church is continually oriented toward the world: the disciples of Christ are the "salt of the earth" and the "light of the world" (Matt. 5:13-14).

One could also say the same thing in the following way. Today, the kingdom is on a small scale what one day it will be on a worldwide scale. Through the Holy Spirit, it is today a sphere of true divine *righteousness* in the midst of a world full of unrighteousness. It is a sphere of true divine *peace* in the midst of a world full of war and violence. It is a sphere of true divine *joy* in the midst of a world full of sadness and mourning (Rom. 14:17). One day, the entire world will be filled with true divine righteousness, peace, and joy (cf. Isa. 9:7; 32:17; 55:12).

## 7.3 The Church and the Coming Kingdom
### 7.3.1 "*In* the World"

If we say that Jesus' disciples are the "salt of the earth" and the "light of the world" (see previous section), we do well to consider that, in practice, the church is rarely this salt and light *as church*. It is not the church (in its function as church) that establishes Christian schools, companies, associations, and political parties; the church does not engage in the arts, or science, or politics; the church does not establish a judicial or economical order. It is always individual believers who do this kind of work. They do so either individually, or they organize themselves in Christian cooperative relationships (school boards, labor councils, boards of directors, etc.) to do Christian work. It is not the church (in its function as church) that extends the kingdom of God in this world, but individual believers do so, personally or (usually) collectively through gospel societies, missionary organizations, etc. (even if church *denominations* may found schools, gospel societies, etc.). More concretely, strictly speaking, individual Christians do not do such missionary work as members of Christ's body but as disciples in God's kingdom. Not every group of Christians can be called "church."

Reformed theologian Johan Heyns has well formulated this state of affairs by saying that the Christian family, the Christian school, the Christian committee, the Christian cultural association, the Christian state, Christian science and art, are all manifestations of the kingdom. As such they are not the church, neither the church as "organism" nor the church as "organization." There is an ecclesiastical manifestation of God's kingdom in the form of church denominations, and there are thousands of non-ecclesiastical manifestations of God's kingdom.[13]

Jesus' disciples always perform their tasks under the tension mentioned earlier: being *in* the world but not being *of* the world (John 17:11, 14, 16, 18). The kingdom is "not of this world," as Jesus himself emphasized to Pilate (18:36); it is not from "below" but from "above." However, at the same time the world is a domain that is seasoned with the salt of this kingdom. Being "in the world" implies that believers take part in Christian—and even "neutral"—schools, companies, associations, political parties, and in (strongly secularized) politics, arts, and sciences. It seems to me that, in principle, there is no function within ordered society that could not be fulfilled by a Christian. (I am not

---

13. Heyns (1988, 354).

speaking about the "under[!]world" of prostitution and crime.) But this is not the same as saying that the church fulfills these functions!

Please note, church consistories or sessions (councils of elders, etc.) do not raise children, do not teach school subjects, do not run a business, and are not active as church leaders in politics, the arts, or the sciences. They are not even *called* to do such things. Individual Christians, or Christian organizations, are called to do these things. It is not the church (or whatever church denomination) that extends God's kingdom in this world—individual Christians, or Christian organizations, do so. Christians do so not in their function as members of Christ's body, but in their function as disciples of Jesus. Of course we may not separate these, but we should certainly distinguish them.

### 7.3.2 The Scope of the Kingdom

In this context, it is interesting that Herman Ridderbos has defined the kingdom as "not narrow but wide," as wide as the entire creation. Believers are free in Christ to take part in the entire life of eating and drinking, marrying, learning and teaching, buying and selling, painting and being painted, reigning and being reigned, etc. But, he argues, in this Christian freedom there lies a Christian mission, for believers must be in service to God, and thus to God's creation, humanity in particular.[14]

Earlier Herman Bavinck had emphasized that the kingdom is not organized, at least not here on earth. In principle, the kingdom exists wherever the spiritual

---

14. Ridderbos (1995); cf. Spykman (1992, 479-80).

benefits of Christ have been granted, and nowhere on earth is the kingdom perfected and completed. But the church is—Bavinck should have said: (individual) believers are—the means through which Christ distributes the benefits of the kingdom in the world, and prepares the completion of the kingdom.[15]

At any specific moment, the church is an entity consisting of the total number of all true believers as known to God who are at that moment alive on earth. In this sense, the kingdom is never a static entity, but a far more fluid phenomenon. The kingdom is like "the Spirit of God hovering over the face of the waters" (Gen. 1:3), touching and driving people, constantly changing people and societal relationships of all kinds, "turning" the hearts of kings (presidents, prime-ministers) as a "stream of water" (cf. Prov. 21:1), driving the "chariots" between "mountains of bronze" (Zech. 6:1), reviving backsliding followers of Jesus, admonishing and encouraging them, constantly fighting the good fight against the powers of darkness.

Geerardus Vos emphasized that Jesus considered every normal and legitimate domain of human life as intended to form a part of God's kingdom.[16] This is like Kuyper's earlier statement: "There is not a square inch in the whole domain of our human existence over which Christ, who is Sovereign over all, does not cry, Mine!"[17] Therefore, the scope of God's kingdom must not be restricted in any way, says Al Wolters, which we would do if we were to divide the world into a sacred part and a

---

15. Bavinck (2008, 4:298).

16. Vos (1903, 88).

17. Kuyper (1880), quoted in Bratt (1998, 488).

profane part, or if we were to limit the kingdom to personal godliness, to the institutional church, to the eschatological future, or to humanitarian aspirations.[18]

There are indeed limitations to the church in its actual New Testament sense: only true believers are part of it. However, there are no limitations to the kingdom: it may be defined as the totality of Christian confessors, but it may also be defined as encompassing God's entire creation. Jesus himself said, "The field is the world" (Matt. 13:18). "The earth is the LORD's and the fullness thereof, the world and those who dwell therein" (Ps. 24:1; cf. 1 Cor. 10:26). "[T]he earth shall be full of the knowledge of the LORD as the waters cover the sea" (Isa. 11:9; cf. Hab. 2:14). This will be completely true in the age to come, but the present age is the prelude to it.

### 7.3.3 "Not *of* the World"

The kingdom of God is not only "in the world," it is *everywhere* in the world. At the same time, being "not *of* the world" means that the disciple of Jesus is always confronted with the activity of sin and Satan in various societal relationships, and this can lead to tensions. As Paul puts it, believers are "children of God without blemish in the midst of a crooked and twisted generation, among whom you shine as lights in the world" (Phil. 2:15). Not *of* the world: that is, without blemish *in opposition to* the crooked and the twisted—but certainly *in* the world: without blemish *in the midst of* the crooked and the twisted, sometimes intermingled with them in an outwardly inextricable way, as iron particles may be mixed with grains of sand (cf. the metaphor of Dan.

---

18. Wolters (1985, 60–61, 65).

2:43, though it is being used here with a different meaning). Yet, the great difference comes to light when a strong magnet is held above the mixture to attract the iron but not the sand.

It is quite helpful to keep in mind here the distinction between the two dimensions of *structure* and *direction*, which I have discussed elsewhere.[19] The term *structure* has to do with the creational structures, the structural laws that God has instituted for the various creatures and cosmic modalities, and also for the societal relationships within creation. *Direction* is a dimension that is, so to speak, perpendicular to that of structure; it involves the directedness of any entity, event, or state of affairs. There are numerous structures, but there are only two directions: either the positive direction toward the Creator and his honor, or the apostate direction away from the Creator, to his dishonor.

This neatly describes the position of Christians in the present world. They participate in *all* the structures of creation, without any exception. However, they do so in a dimension that is opposite to that of unbelievers. Believers are active *in* society, and also *for* society, but not for their, or its, own glory. They are active in view of that toward which society is moving: the kingdom of God in power and glory. There are secular (and falsely religious, etc.) families, secular (and falsely religious, etc.) schools, secular (and falsely religious, etc.) companies, secular (and falsely religious, etc.) associations, etc., and there are Christian families, Christian schools, Christian companies, Christian associations, etc. The former serve their own interests only; the latter—if they truly fulfill their

---

19. See Ouweneel (2014b, chapter 4)

duty—serve the interests of God and of Christ and his kingdom. All families, schools, companies, associations, etc., involve *structure*; their character as secular (and falsely religious) versus Christian involves *direction*.

In the church, society sees its own religious destination reflected, as it were (at least if it has enlightened eyes to perceive this).[20] That is, if unbelievers would only wish to see it—or would be able to see it—they would behold in (the bright side of) the church what the entire world will look like one day. The Christian never just accepts the world as it is but only as it must become, and one day *will* become. He stands in the midst of the world, but with his heart he is already in the "world to come" (Heb. 2:5) and in the "age to come" (Mark 10:30; Luke 18:30; Eph. 1:21; Heb. 6:5). He knows that, even in the power of the Spirit, he himself will never bring about this new world, not even with the help of millions of other Christians. But he also knows that, in the power of the Spirit, he may endeavor to bring this world as close to its goal as he can. He knows that the end result will be 100 percent the Lord's work. But he works as if the end result would be 100 percent his responsibility.

## 7.4 Various Views

### 7.4.1 Roman Catholic

The relationship between the church and the kingdom of God has been explained in various ways, partly because of different standpoints regarding the eschatological meaning of the kingdom.[21] Here I can only mention several (rather representative) views.

---

20. Cf. Heyns (1988, 373).
21. See extensively, Ouweneel (2012a).

*The Kingdom and the Church*

(a) In the *Roman Catholic* view, the kingdom of God coincides with the visible—that is, the Roman Catholic—church, or at least the latter is the core of the kingdom.[22] Here, to a great extent, the kingdom is linked with one given denomination. Not the church as the holy gathering of *all* believers in Christ (Catholic, Orthodox, Protestant), but one single denomination out of the thousands of denominations in the Christian world. It is not even the oldest denomination for, as the specifically *Roman* church, it is younger than the Armenian, Coptic, Syrian, or Ethiopian church. It is not even a truly catholic church because the terms "Roman" and "Catholic" are contradictory: "Roman" excludes Orthodox and Protestant, and all the others. Seen from this viewpoint, the term "Catholic" in the name "Roman Catholic" is a sectarian term.

By the way, the same (sectarian) tendency is found where certain *Protestant* denominations establish schools, associations, and political parties that are intended only for their own church members and their children, and in which church leaders, in their function as church leaders, govern such entities.[23] Especially Kuyperian Reformed denominations (in different varieties, in the Netherlands, in North America, in South Africa, and elsewhere) have succumbed to this tendency. Already John Calvin wrongly stated: ". . . the church is Christ's Kingdom . . ."—meaning by "the church" his own brand of church.[24]

---

22. Cf. how Hans Küng follows another course in this: Eggenberg (2010, chapter 2).
23. L. Berkhof (1996, 569).
24. Calvin, *Institutes*, 4.2.4.

## 7.4.2 Reformed

(b) *Herman Bavinck* emphasized that the church is a notion with present-day (German *diesseitige*, "this-worldly") significance, and the kingdom is especially an eschatological ("other-worldly") notion. Therefore, the church is organized, and the kingdom is not.[25] The church consists of a well-defined number of people, but the kingdom exists wherever Christ is working through his Spirit.

There is a lot of truth in these descriptions, yet, in my view, they are not sufficiently accurate. First, the former holds only for *organized* churches (denominations), not for the body of Christ, the "holy gathering of true believers in Christ." Any organized church and this "holy gathering" at best overlap (there are many denominations but there is only one body of Christ). To make it even more complicated, I fear most local churches do not contain only believers, whereas in most cases the true believers in a certain locale are distributed among several organized churches. And as far as the kingdom is concerned, to a certain extent it too is well-defined as either consisting of all Christian confessors, or as covering the entire world. As such, the kingdom is even more easily identifiable than the church as the "holy gathering of all true believers."

Second, I do not think the contrast between present-day (this-worldly) and eschatological (other-worldly) notions is a correct one. Both church and kingdom belong to both the present world and to the world to come, that is, they are both this-worldly and eschatological. Be-

---

25. Bavinck (2008, 4:297–98); also see §55 on the power of the church in relation to the kingdom.

sides, the church should not be viewed too much as a static entity, in contrast with a dynamic (continually developing) kingdom.[26]

(c) *Louis Berkhof* believed that the operative sphere of God's kingdom is wider than that of the church because the kingdom seeks expression throughout life in all its manifestations.[27] He called the visible church the most important external organization of the kingdom, and the only one instituted by God.

We have seen that the latter claim cannot be right: marriage, the family, and the state have been instituted by God as well, the former two before the fall into sin, and the latter one in historical development since the Fall.[28] Where marriage, the family, and the state manifest themselves in their Christian character, they are all organized forms of God's kingdom just as much as the church. I do not have in view here Christian schools, Christian companies, Christian political parties, Christian associations, etc., which do not go back to explicit institutions by God but are definitely fruits of God's "cultural mandate" (see above).

Moreover, Berkhof identified the (invisible) church and the kingdom of God so closely that it seems as if "kingdom" is one of the special names of the church, just like body, house, and bride.[29] In this way, the relationship between the two is not properly presented, though. The kingdom of God is wider than the

---

26. Cf. H. Berkhof (1990, 402–404).
27. Berkhof (1996, 569–70).
28. See Ouweneel (2014a).
29. Berkhof (1996, 569).

church, which is the core of the kingdom, as he himself said earlier.

(d) *Johan Heyns* called the church (a) a *sign* of the kingdom, (b) a *part* of the kingdom ("the fighting vanguard and a triumphant fragment of God's kingdom"), and (c) a hint (harbinger) of the *fullness* of the kingdom.[30] This seems to me a succinct but appropriate approach to the matter.

### 7.4.3 Others

(d) *George Ladd* compared the two such that the kingdom is the rule of God, and the church is the group of people standing under this rule.[31]

This description does not strike me as very accurate either. It seems to me the notion of kingdom involves more than a rule; it also involves a King, a territory, and a number of subjects. The laws of a kingdom never constitute that kingdom as such. As we have seen, the territory of God's kingdom is either (1) the totality of all the regenerate (John 3:5), or (2) the totality of all Christian confessors (wheat and weeds, wise and foolish virgins, etc.), or (3) the entire world: the "field" of the kingdom is the "world" (Matt. 13:38).

(f) *Wolfhart Pannenberg* pointed out that the church is not simply identical with the imperfect original form of the kingdom of God, because this would mean that church and kingdom would coincide in the end.[32] The church is a company of people who rejoice in the com-

---

30. Heyns (1988, 353–55).
31. Ladd (1964, 259–60); cf. Erickson (1998, 1051–52).
32. Pannenberg (1998, 30–32).

ing kingdom, and to whom the preaching of the kingdom has been entrusted.

Here, too, the emphasis is on the eschatological character of the kingdom. In this way, it remains unclear how the church relates to the kingdom of God in its *present* form. The same holds for Hans Küng, who sees the church as a "fore-sign" of the (coming) kingdom of God, and Jürgen Moltmann, who sees her as the "anticipation" of the (coming) kingdom.[33]

## 7.5 Final Remarks

### 7.5.1 Summary of Kingdom Teaching

The kingdom of God in its present form is the rule of Christ over the entire creation, concealed behind, but also manifesting itself in, all authorities in this world, who therefore are servants of God (Rom. 13:4; cf. Prov. 21:1).

More specifically, the kingdom involves the rule of Christ over the hearts and lives of all those who profess to follow and serve him, whether or not they truly serve him: there are true and false disciples, good and evil servants, good and bad fishes, wheat and weeds, obedient sons and disobedient sons.

This rule involves individual believers, but also the societal relationships that they form: marriages, families, church denominations, and local congregations, nation states, associations, schools, companies, political parties, etc.

In the widest sense, the kingdom of God comprises the entire creation, or all of humanity. In a somewhat

---

33. See Küng (2001); Moltmann (1975); see also Zorn (1962); Pannenberg (1998, chapter 12); Saucy (1997, 239–47); Lohfink (1998); Eggenberg (2010).

narrower sense it comprises all those who maintain a Christian confession; the Christian world. In the narrowest sense, the kingdom of God is the totality of all disciples of Christ who are truly born again (John. 3:5). Similarly, the church in its widest sense comprises the entire Christian world, or at least the totality of all professing Christians who are members of local congregations (what is sometimes called the "visible church"). In the narrower sense, it is the body of Christ, which includes only true believers, sealed with the Holy Spirit (sometimes called the "invisible church").

Whatever description of God's kingdom we choose, we must employ categories that are very different from the church as the holy gathering of all true believers of Christ, the body of Christ, the house or temple of God on earth, the bride of the Lamb. Not everyone in *Christian* families, schools, companies, political parties, associations, etc., is a born-again believer; in the body of Christ, by definition everyone is. Moreover, the Christian's *character* is different: in the kingdom of God, Christians are followers (disciples) and servants of Christ, while in the church they are members of the body.

The kingdom of God in its present form consists of disciples of Christ, good and evil ones, whereas the body of Christ consists of Spirit-sealed believers. The latter may be spiritual but can also be carnal. However, this is something essentially different from the wicked servant of the King, who in the end is cast into the "outer darkness," where there will be "weeping and gnashing of teeth" (Matt. 8:12; 22:13; 25:30), or the foolish virgins, to whom in the end the door to the marriage feast is shut (25:10-12).

### 7.5.2 The Twofold Gospel

In previous chapters, I referred several times to the twofold gospel: on the one hand, the gospel of God's grace for poor sinners—"the gospel of the grace of God" (Acts 20:24)—and on the other hand, the "gospel of the kingdom," preached by Jesus (Matt. 4:23; 9:35) and by his followers (24:14). It is obvious that they overlap to a great extent. One might even say that there is only one gospel, but with some very different aspects.

Let me offer a brief summary of the main differences between these dimensions of the twofold gospel.

### (a) *The gospel of God's grace*

*Negative news:* you are a sinner, and because of your sins you are on the way to eternal perdition.

*Positive news:* by God's grace, Jesus Christ bore on the cross of Calvary the sins of all those who believe in him; he underwent God's judgment upon these sins; he died for all who believe in him, and rose again from the dead.

*Appeal:* repent from your former life, sincerely confess your sins before God and throw yourself into his arms, believe in Jesus Christ and accept him as your Savior, and you will be saved forever by the grace of God!

*Promise for today:* although you still have your sinful nature ("the flesh"), by the power of the Holy Spirit you may lead a life of holiness, so that the power of sin will never rule over you again.

*Promise for the future:* when the Lord returns, you will be delivered from the "flesh" and from all the frailties of the present body, and receive your glorified body, which will be like Christ's own body, and you be with him in the Father's house in eternity.

## (b) *The gospel of the kingdom*

*Negative news:* you are part of the kingdom of Satan and, if you do not change your position, one day you will perish together with Satan and his kingdom.

*Positive news:* Jesus Christ is the great Victor, the Conqueror, the risen, ascended, and glorified King of kings sitting at God's right hand in heaven; he is much more powerful than Satan, so that in the end his kingdom will prevail over that of Satan.

*Appeal:* believe in the King of kings, so that you will be transferred form Satan's kingdom to Christ's kingdom; become a follower, a disciple, a subject of the King of kings, accept him as your Lord, so that one day you will reign as king together with him.

*Promise for today:* although Satan and his agents may still deploy a lot of resistance, by the power of the Holy Spirit you may engage in the spiritual battle against the powers of darkness, and gain spiritual victories.

*Promise for the future:* when the Lord comes again, Satan's power will be finally and definitively broken, you will prevail with Christ, and begin to rule together with him in his Messianic kingdom of peace and justice, and continue doing so forever afterward.

# Chapter 8
# The Spreading
# of the Kingdom

*... you among whom I [i.e., Paul]
 have gone about
proclaiming the kingdom....*
Acts 20:25

*From morning till evening he [i.e.,
 Paul] expounded to them [i.e., the
 Roman Jews],
testifying to the kingdom of God
and trying to convince them about Jesus
both from the Law of Moses and from
 the Prophets....*
Acts 28:23, 30-31

*[The Father] has delivered us from
 the domain of darkness
and transferred us to the kingdom
 of his beloved Son.*
Colossians 1:13

***Summary:*** *The presence and activity of the Holy Spirit is very important in the kingdom. By the Spirit, new subjects are added, and the Spirit gives power and guidance. By the Spirit the kingdom is spreading in the world, preached by the apostles and their millions of successors. What is preached is both the kingdom in its present form (a hidden kingdom with a hidden King) and the kingdom in its future form, as it one day will break through in glory and majesty at the parousia of the King. In the New Testament letters, both forms are amply elucidated. Paul underscores the present significance of the kingdom in several passages; one could even say that Paul implicitly refers to the kingdom every time he speaks of the Lordship of Christ, and our submission to it. In spite of protests, we maintain the vital importance of serving Christ as Lord as a sign of true regeneration. The same topic is also dealt with in the rest of the New Testament.*

## 8.1 Church, Kingdom, and Spirit in Paul's Ministry
### 8.1.1 *Trait d'Union*

IN THE WIDEST SENSE, the kingdom of God exists and functions wherever the activity of the Holy Spirit is visible in the world. More concretely, not only where new churches originate, but where the gospel of the kingdom also has an effect on families, schools, companies, associations, and even in art and science, politics, and the judicial and economic order. In the beautiful words of the Heidelberg Catechism (Q/A 123): "'Your kingdom come' means: Rule us by your Word and Spirit in such a way that more and more we submit to you. Preserve your church and make it grow. Destroy the devil's work; destroy every force that revolts against you and every conspiracy against your holy Word. Do this until your kingdom fully comes, when you will be all in all."

The Holy Spirit is a kind of "hyphen" between the church and the kingdom: the church is the dwelling place of the Spirit (1 Cor. 3:16; Eph. 2:22), the kingdom is the Spirit's sphere of operation (Rom. 14:17). The church is en route to the kingdom, as it were: to the Messianic empire of power and glory, and the Holy Spirit is on his way to this as well (cf. §2.4). During the twentieth century, special attention has been given to the relationship between the Holy Spirit and the eschatological aspects of God's kingdom.[34] This relationship is evident already from the way the Old Testament prophecies connect the Holy Spirit with the coming Messianic kingdom (e.g., Isa. 11:1-2; 42:1; 61:1-2 [Luke 4:17-19]; Ezek. 36:25-27; 37:14). The Spirit will be poured out on the "sons" of that kingdom (cf. Matt. 13:38). In fact, this apparently implies a *double* pouring out: one at the beginning of God's kingdom in its present form (Acts 2), and one at the beginning of the kingdom in its future form (Isa. 32:15-17; 44:2-4; Ezek. 39:29; Joel 2:28-32 [Acts 2:17-21]; Zech. 12:10). In other words, one at that beginning of the present age, one at the beginning of the age to come.

Jesus emphatically linked the breakthrough of God's kingdom in his day with the activity of the Holy Spirit: "[I]f it is by the Spirit of God that I cast out demons, then the kingdom of God has come upon you" (Matt. 12:28). That is, the Spirit's activity was the *proof* that God's kingdom had arrived. At the start of his ministry, Jesus announced: "'The Spirit of the Lord is upon me, because

---

34. See, e.g., Vos (1912); Hamilton (1957); Hoekema (1979, chapter 5).

he has anointed me to proclaim good news to the poor. He has sent me to proclaim liberty to the captives and recovering of sight to the blind, to set at liberty those who are oppressed, to proclaim the year of the Lord's favor' [Isa. 61:1–2]. . . . Today this Scripture has been fulfilled in your hearing" (Luke 4:18–21). Besides preaching the kingdom and performing the signs of the kingdom by the Holy Spirit (cf. Acts 8:6, 12), Jesus was also going to be the One *baptizing* with the Holy Spirit (Matt. 3:11; Mark 1:8; Luke 3:16; John 1:33; Acts 1:6).

## 8.1.2 The Spirit and Sonship

The apostle Paul, too, speaks of the Holy Spirit's work in an eschatological sense: "[N]ot only the creation, but we ourselves, who have the firstfruits of the Spirit, groan inwardly as we wait eagerly for adoption as sons, the redemption of our bodies" (Rom. 8:23). With this word "firstfruits" (Greek *aparchē*), Paul is referring to a ministry of the Spirit that is quite characteristic for his teaching. *Aparchē* points to both the *beginning* of a process and to the absolutely certain *outcome* of that process. With respect to the Spirit, this means that the realization of the kingdom of God has begun, and that this process will certainly be moved to its intended culmination. In this sense, the Spirit is the *arrabōn*, that is, both the "down payment" of the reality of God's kingdom and the "guarantee" for the full realization of it (see §8.1.3).[35]

Because believers possess the Spirit as a "down payment," this means that already today they experience, to a certain extent, the "powers of the age to come"

---

35. Moo (1996, 519–20).

(Heb. 6:5). There will be no blessing in the glorious Messianic kingdom to come of which believers do not possess an advance deposit already in the present age. "In the Holy Spirit," they know within the kingdom a certain measure of righteousness, peace, and joy (Rom. 14:17), in spite of still being surrounded by injustice, disharmony, and sadness (and receiving their share of *this* as well).

This eschatological aspect also comes to light in the concept of "sonship" (Greek *huiothesia*, "adoption as sons").[36] Every believer is a *child* of God, for he is reborn of the Spirit (John 3:5), and has received the Spirit dwelling within him (Rom. 8:9; 1 Cor. 6:19; 2 Cor. 1:21-22; Eph. 1:13-14; 4:30). However, to be called a *son* of God more is needed; let me identify seven New Testament characteristics of God's sons.

(a) "Love your enemies, and do good, and lend, expecting nothing in return, and your reward will be great, and you will be sons of the Most High" (Luke 6:35).

(b) They walk in the light: they are "sons of light," as opposed to the "sons of this world" (16:8).

(c) Sons of God live by the power of the Spirit: "[A]ll who are led by the Spirit of God are sons of God" (Rom. 8:14).

(d) They live through the "Spirit of adoption [i.e., adoption as *sons*, *huiothesia*]," by whom they cry, "Abba, Father!" (v. 15; cf. Gal. 4:5-6).

(e) They turn away from evil: "Therefore go out from their midst, and be separate from them, . . . and touch no unclean thing; then I will welcome you, and I will be

---

36. Cf. Ouweneel (2010a, 114-16).

a father to you, and you shall be *sons and daughters* to me" (2 Cor. 6:17-18).

(f) They bravely, patiently, and joyfully endure the discipline (Greek *paideia*, education, training) of God (Heb. 12:7).

(g) They gain spiritual victories over evil: "The one who conquers will have this heritage, and I will be his God and he will be my *son*" (Rev. 21:7).

In the spiritual development of the sons of God, in their dealing with evil, in their growing in the power of the Spirit, there is again an eschatological dimension becoming visible: "[T]he creation waits with eager longing for the revealing of the sons of God" (Rom. 8:19). That is, the true nature of the sons of God will be brought to light one day, namely, in the day of the glorious appearance of God's kingdom. The development of this sonship is completed only when the believer's physical body will be "redeemed" (v. 23), that is, will share in complete salvation, on the day when no longer this mortal body (v. 11) but the resurrection body will be the dwelling place of the Spirit (cf. 1 Cor. 6:19). It is the day that our "lowly" body will be transformed to be like Christ's "glorious" body (Phil. 3:21).

## 8.1.3 Sons and Heirs

In this context, Paul speaks of the sons being "heirs" (Gal. 4:6-7; cf. Rom. 8:17). The inheritance that is involved here is never heaven as such, although the inheritance is reserved *in* heaven for believers (1 Pet. 1:4). Even less is it heaven as the intermediate state between death and resurrection. The inheritance is always related to the world to come: Abraham is "heir of the world"

(Rom. 4:13), namely, the world of the Messianic kingdom. Christ is the primary "heir" of the world, and believers are "fellow heirs" with him (Rom. 8:17), that is, "in him" they have obtained the inheritance as well (Eph. 1:9-11, not "*made* an inheritance," ASV, AMPC).

Here again, the Holy Spirit is clearly involved: God has made "a plan for the fullness of time, to unite all things in [Christ], things in heaven and things on earth [i.e., the totality of visible creation]. In him we have obtained an inheritance [or, have been made heirs (viz. of this same creation)]. . . . In him you also, when you . . . believed in him, were sealed with the promised Holy Spirit, who is the guarantee [or, down payment] of our inheritance [i.e., the visible world] until we acquire possession of it, to the praise of his glory" (Eph. 1:10-14).

Paul uses here the Greek word *arrabōn* (older translations: "earnest"), which is a Hebrew loanword: '*ērabon* (cf. Gen. 38:17-20). It is both a "down payment" (cf. Rom. 8:23, "firstfruits [*aparchē*] of the Spirit"), and a "guarantee" that one day the entire debt will be paid off. The Holy Spirit whom believers have received already today forms the guarantee for their share in the coming Messianic kingdom, and even for the realization of *all* God's promises: "[A]ll the promises of God find their Yes in him. That is why it is through him that we utter our Amen to God for his glory. And it is God who establishes us with you in Christ, and has anointed us, and who has also put his seal on us and given us his Spirit in our hearts as a *guarantee*" (2 Cor. 1:20-22; cf. 5:5). The believer who wants to make sure that he will reign with Christ in the Messianic kingdom need only ask himself whether he has received the Holy Spirit (cf. Acts 19:2).

This is an important point. It is not only *through* the Spirit that people receive a share in the kingdom of God (John 3:5)—this is the work of regeneration—but they also *receive* the Spirit. He comes to dwell in them and as such is the guarantee that they will be fellow heirs of the Messianic kingdom. Regeneration by the Spirit and the indwelling of the Spirit are two different things. All Old Testament believers were regenerated; they lived "by the Spirit" (1 Pet. 4:6 CEB, CJB). But only very few of them *received* the Holy Spirit, and this only in view of a certain ministry (judges, prophets). To make this possible, a pouring out of the Spirit was needed, as happened in Acts 2, and as will occur at the beginning of the Messianic kingdom: ". . . the Spirit is poured upon us from on high, and the wilderness becomes a fruitful field, and the fruitful field is deemed a forest" (Isa. 32:15). "I will pour water on the thirsty land, and streams on the dry ground; I will pour my Spirit upon your offspring, and my blessing on your descendants" (44:3).

When in Ezekiel 36 the question is discussed which Israelites will share in the Messianic kingdom, the Spirit is identified in terms of his twofold activity: the cleansing Spirit and the indwelling Spirit. First, God says (vv. 25–26), "I will sprinkle clean water on you, and you shall be clean. . . . And I will give you a new heart, and a new spirit I will put within you." This is God's work *through* the Spirit (although the latter is not mentioned here). But then it is added (v. 27), "And I will put my Spirit within you." It is like a man who first builds, or restores, a house for himself, and then comes and dwells in this house. First, the Spirit renews a person, and then he comes and dwells in this renewed person. And while dwelling in the believer, he is a constant reminder of the coming inheritance; he is both a down payment of the Messianic kingdom glory—a first portion—and the guarantee that the rest of this glory is going to follow.

## 8.2 The Coming Kingdom

### 8.2.1 Eternal Life and the Inheritance

Just as in the teaching of Jesus, in Paul's ministry we encounter the kingdom of God both in its present and in its future forms. As far as the latter form is concerned, let me tie in first with what was said in §8.1.3. Paul uses a term that occurs in the Gospels as well: "inherit." The Son of Man says to the "sheep": "Come, you who are blessed by my Father, inherit the kingdom prepared for you from the foundation of the world" (Matt. 25:34). On an earlier occasion, he had said, "Blessed are the meek, for they shall inherit the earth [or, land; see CJB, ERV, etc.]" (5:5), that is, the earth of the Messianic kingdom, or more specifically, the promised land of Israel. The quotation is from Psalm 37:11, "[T]he meek shall inherit the land [cf. v. 3] and delight themselves in abundant peace."

In Matthew 19:29, Jesus speaks of "inheriting eternal life" (cf. Mark 10:17; Luke 10:25), which amounts to the same as inheriting the Messianic kingdom because, in the Old Testament, "eternal life" is the life of the Messianic kingdom: "At that time . . . there shall be a time of trouble, such as never has been since there was a nation till that time. But at that time your people shall be delivered, everyone whose name shall be found written in the book. And many of those who sleep in the dust of the earth shall awake, some to *everlasting life,* and some to shame and everlasting contempt. And those who are wise shall shine like the brightness of the sky above; and those who turn many to righteousness, like the stars forever and ever" (Dan. 12:1-3). In my view,[37] this is also the prophetic message of Psalm 133:3, ". . . the mountains of Zion! For there the LORD has commanded the blessing, *life forevermore*." It is the same with "inheriting salvation" (Heb. 1:14), "inheriting the promises" (6:12), and "inheriting all this" (Rev. 21:7 NIV). In all these cases, the Messianic kingdom is involved; in Hebrews this is called the "world to come" (2:5), the "age to come" (6:5), the "good things to come" (10:1), and the "city to come" (13:14).

In an analogous way Paul says, "[D]o you not know that the unrighteous will not *inherit* the kingdom of God? Do not be deceived: neither the sexually immoral, nor idolaters, nor adulterers, nor men who practice homosexuality, nor thieves, nor the greedy, nor drunkards, nor revilers, nor swindlers will *inherit* the kingdom of God" (1 Cor. 6:9-10). "I tell you this, brothers: flesh and blood cannot *inherit* the kingdom of God, nor does the perishable inherit the imperishable" (15:50). "Now the works of the flesh are evident: sexual immorality, impurity, sensuality, idolatry, sorcery, enmity, strife, jealousy, fits of anger, rivalries, dissensions, divisions, envy, drunkenness, orgies, and things like these. I warn you, as I warned you before, that those who do such things will not *inherit* the kingdom of God" (Gal. 5:19-21).

In each of these cases, "to inherit" (Greek *klēronomeō*) means to receive something as an inheritance, sharing

---

37. Cf. Ouweneel (2010a, 102-105).

in an inheritance *(klēros* or *klēronomia*, literally something that has been allotted to a person). Just as the Israelites received the land of Canaan "as an inheritance" (Acts 13:19; cf. 7:5; Heb. 11:8), similarly New Testament believers receive "the inheritance among all those who are sanctified" (Acts 20:32 *klēronomia*; cf. 26:18 *klēros*), that is, an "inheritance in the kingdom of Christ and God" (Eph. 5:5 *klēronomia*). Paul speaks of the "inheritance of the saints in light," which is connected with the "kingdom of his beloved Son" (Col. 1:12-13).

## 8.2.2 Moral Characteristics

It is striking that Paul emphasizes moral criteria for inheriting the kingdom of God, and this in letters to Christians. I just quoted 1 Corinthians 6:9-10 and Galatians 5:19-21. Ephesians 5:5 is even more explicitly addressing Christians: "For you may be sure of this, that everyone who is sexually immoral or impure, or who is covetous (that is, an idolater), has no inheritance in the kingdom of Christ and God." In a typically Protestant or Evangelical way, one might think that *the* criterion for entering the kingdom is whether one has believed in Jesus Christ. Of course this is implied here; one cannot have done any good works apart from faith in Jesus and the power of the Holy Spirit. However, the person who *claims* to believe in Jesus, but continues in sexual immorality, idolatry, thefts, greed, drunkenness, slander, sorcery, enmity, strife, jealousy, fits of anger, rivalries, dissensions, divisions, envy, drunkenness, orgies, etc., deceives himself.

In this sense, one could definitely say, no matter how un-Protestant it may sound, that no person will receive a share in the kingdom of God who has not done good works.[38] Faith is only genuine faith if it "works through love" (Gal. 5:6). "[F]aith by itself, if it does not have works, is dead" (James 2:17). "In the same way, let your light shine before others, so that they may see your good works and give glory to your Father who is in heaven" (Matt. 5:16). Even the criminal on the cross did good works (by the power of the Spirit): he recognized his sins and the judgment that had come upon them, he spoke well of Jesus to others, and he entrusted himself to Jesus for his future (Luke 23:39–43).

In Matthew 25, too, inheriting the kingdom of God depends on moral conditions: feeding the hungry, giving to drink to the thirsty, housing the strangers, clothing the naked, visiting the sick and the prisoners (vv. 35–40).[39] The kingdom of God is for the poor in spirit, for those who mourn about this world, for the meek, for those who hunger and thirst for righteousness, for the merciful, for the pure in heart, for the peacemakers (Matt. 5:3–9). In short: the kingdom of God is for the *tsaddiqim* (the "righteous"; cf. the "unrighteous" in 1 Cor. 6:9), not for the *reshaim* (the "wicked"). Paul is in full agreement with the kingdom teaching of Jesus. It is true that one cannot be a *tsaddiq* apart from the atoning work of Christ and the power of the Holy Spirit,[40] but that is not the point right now.

This moral aspect of the kingdom returns repeatedly in Paul's letters: Christians must "walk in a manner worthy of God, who calls you into his own kingdom and glory" (1 Thess. 2:12). Paul boasts "for your steadfast-

---

38. See Ouweneel (2010a, 231–37).
39. Cf. Ouweneel (2010c, 340–45).
40. Cf. Ouweneel (2010c, chapter 9).

ness and faith in all your persecutions and in the afflictions that you are enduring. This is evidence of the righteous judgment of God, that you may be considered worthy of the kingdom of God, for which you are also suffering" (2 Thess. 1:4-5). This being "considered worthy," too, seems to contravene notions such as "justified by faith" and "by grace." But of course, Paul does not ascribe any worthiness before God to humans as such. Nor does he refer to the *positional* worthiness of the reborn person in Christ, such as in Colossians 1:12 (JUB), "... the Father, who has made us worthy to participate in the inheritance of the saints in light" (cf. 1 Cor. 6:2 NKJV). No, Paul is speaking here of a *practical* worthiness, based on the Christian's walk, like in the following expressions: "in a way worthy of the saints" (Rom. 16:2), "to walk in a manner worthy of the calling to which you have been called" (Eph. 4:1), "let your manner of life be worthy of the gospel of Christ" (Phil. 1:27), "to walk in a manner worthy of the Lord" (Col. 4:1; cf. Acts 5:41; 1 Cor. 11:27; 3 John 1:6). Continually we find the same notion: only those who have a worthy walk—say, a walk according to the Messianic Torah—will have a share in the kingdom of God.

## 8.2.3 The Present and the Future

It is not always easy to determine whether, when speaking of the kingdom of God, Paul is referring to the kingdom in its present form or to the kingdom in its future form, or both. In most of the passages quoted so far, the reference seems to be especially to the kingdom in its future, glorious form. This is also the case in 2 Timothy 4:1-2, "I charge you in the presence of God and of Christ

Jesus, who is to judge the living and the dead, and by his appearing and his kingdom: preach the word; be ready in season and out of season; reprove, rebuke, and exhort, with complete patience and teaching."

What Paul means to say here is to preach the gospel *in view of* and *in the light of* the coming judgment of God and the coming appearance of Jesus Christ on the clouds of heaven and his subsequent establishment of the Messianic kingdom.[41] The listeners should know about the threat of the coming judgment but also of the glorious kingdom that is in the offing. The gospel of Christ warns against the former, and prepares for the latter. The gospel of God's grace for sinners places little emphasis on this eschatological dimension, or at best on heaven (the intermediate state) where believers go when they pass away. However, in the gospel of the kingdom, this reference to the *eschaton* is of eminent importance (cf. §7.5.2).

All gospel preaching is, or ought to be, a preparation for the coming of the King: "The times of ignorance God overlooked, but now he commands all people everywhere to repent, because he has fixed a day on which he will judge the world in righteousness by a man whom he has appointed; and of this he has given assurance to all by raising him from the dead" (Acts 17:30–31). This is Paul speaking to pagans; compare Peter speaking to Jews: "Repent therefore, and turn back, that your sins may be blotted out, that times of refreshing may come from the presence of the Lord, and that he may send the Christ appointed for you, Jesus, whom heaven must receive until the time for restoring all the things about which God spoke by the mouth of his holy prophets

---

41. Cf. Towner (2006, 598).

## The Spreading of the Kingdom

long ago" (3:19–21). Believers live in Christ's invisible but real kingdom *today*, and prepare themselves for the visible, glorious kingdom arriving on the *coming day*.

Paul speaks of the future kingdom most clearly in 1 Corinthians 15:23–28, "But each [rises from death] in his own order: Christ the firstfruits, then at his coming those who belong to Christ. Then comes the end, when he delivers the kingdom to God the Father after destroying every rule and every authority and power. For he must reign until he has put all his enemies under his feet. The last enemy to be destroyed is death. For 'God has put all things in subjection under his feet.' [Ps. 8:6] But when it says, 'all things are put in subjection,' it is plain that he is excepted who put all things in subjection under him. When all things are subjected to him, then the Son himself will also be subjected to him who put all things in subjection under him, that God may be all in all."

The following main elements can be distinguished here.[42]

(a) Jesus will return, and on that day "those who belong to Christ" will rise from the dead (cf. 1 Cor. 15:50–55; 1 Thess. 4:13–18; also see Rev. 20:5, "The rest of the dead did not come to life until the thousand years were ended").

(b) Christ will "reign" (exercise his kingship) "until he has put all his enemies [the last of which is death] under his feet" (cf. Rev. 20:7, 14: when the thousand years are ended, Death and Hades are thrown into the "lake of fire").

---

42. See more extensively, Ouweneel (2012a, 566–68 and passim).

(c) At the end of his reign (Rev. 20:1-7, the thousand years, whether literal or figurative, but at least a certain period *after* Christ's parousia [19:11-21] and *before* the new heavens and the new earth [21:1-8]), Christ gives the kingdom back "to God the Father after destroying every rule and every authority and power."

(d) In all eternity, God—this is the Triune God!— will be "all in all" (cf. Rev. 21:1-5, "Then I saw a new heaven and a new earth, for the first heaven and the first earth had passed away, and the sea was no more. . . . And I heard a loud voice from the throne saying, 'Behold, the dwelling place of God is with man. He will dwell with them, and they will be his people, and God himself will be with them as their God. He will wipe away every tear from their eyes, and death shall be no more, neither shall there be mourning, nor crying, nor pain anymore, for the former things have passed away.' And he who was seated on the throne said, 'Behold, I am making all things new'").

## 8.3  The Present Kingdom
### 8.3.1  Colossians 1:12-13

There are not many passages where Paul speaks unequivocally of God's kingdom in its present form. However, in some passages mentioned earlier (1 Thess. 2:12 and 2 Thess. 1:4-5), the present dimension of the kingdom cannot be excluded. Colossians 4:11 speaks of "fellow workers for the kingdom of God," in which there is no unequivocal reference to the present or the future meaning of the kingdom, either. This is different in 1:12-14, ". . . the Father, who has qualified you to share in the inheritance of the saints in light. He has delivered us from the domain of darkness and transferred us to the kingdom of his beloved Son, in whom we have redemption, the forgiveness of sins." Nowhere does Paul seem to express more clearly the thought that we *have been* transferred to the kingdom of God, which is thus presented here in its present meaning (without excluding the future meaning, of course).

Of special interest here is the contrast between the power of darkness and the kingdom of love. Darkness and love as such are not really contrary, but as a spiritual notion darkness is always linked with hatred and death, just as love is always linked with light and love.[43] Similarly, in Acts 26:18 darkness and Satan stand in opposition to light and God, respectively (cf. 1 Pet. 2:9; Isa. 42:16). In Colossians 1:13, the kingdom is a sphere of love, namely, primarily the Father's love for the Son. In Hebrews 1:2, the Son is "the heir of all things" *before* he is said to be the One through whom the world was created. In other words, the world was not only created *through* the Son but also *for* (unto, because of) the Son: "For by [lit., *in*] him all things were created ... all things were created *through* him and *for* him" (Col. 1:16). The world is the Father's gift of love to the Son—world rule is for the Son of his love—just as the Son is the Father's gift of love to the church (Eph. 1:22).

Apparently, the implication of Colossians 1:13 is that this love is also transferred to believers: the Father loves the followers (or subjects) of his Son, who are his children, just as, conversely, God's children love the Father

---

43. It has been said that the kingdom of the three D's (the devil, death, and darkness) stands in opposition to the kingdom of the three L's (love, life, and light).

and the Son. Indeed, it is striking that Paul describes believers several times as those who not only believe in God and Christ but also *love* him: "[W]e know that for those who love God all things work together for good" (Rom. 8:28); "... what God has prepared for those who love him" (1 Cor. 2:9). "Grace be with all who love our Lord Jesus Christ with love incorruptible" (Eph. 6:24). We find the same with James (1:12; 2:5) and John (1 John 4:20-21; 5:2).

In this we find the secret of following Christ (see §9.5). Why would a person give up everything and bring so many sacrifices to serve him if these did not proceed from love? The disciple has come to know the Master as the Son who is loved by his Father (cf. Matt. 3:17; 17:5), and has come to love him as well. God has "chosen those who are poor in the world to be rich in faith and heirs of the kingdom, which he has promised to those who love him" (James 2:5). In 1 Corinthians 16:22 Paul says, "If anyone has no love for the Lord, let him be accursed. Our Lord, come [Greek text: *Maranatha*]!" It is life or death; there is nothing in between. The person who loves the Lord will share in the kingdom of God, and thus in the highest bliss. The person who does not love the Lord will share in the greatest disaster, without having to do anything further to reach this than to remain in his unbelief. Reference to the coming kingdom lies hidden in the Aramaic *Maranatha* ("Our Lord comes" *or* "Our Lord, come!").[44]

## 8.3.2 1 Corinthians 4:19-20

Paul refers to the present form of God's kingdom in 1 Corinthians 4:19-20. Even though, with Paul, the king-

---

44. Cf. Fee (1987, ad loc.); Thiselton (2000, ad loc.).

dom of God is basically always an eschatological concept, yet he sometimes clearly draws the reality of it into the present, as he seems to do here: "I will come to you soon, if the Lord wills, and I will find out not the talk of these arrogant people but their power. For the kingdom of God does not consist in talk [Greek *logos*] but in power (*dynamis*)."[45] The *logos* ("word") here is not referring to the Word of God but to the "idle talk" (NET) of the "puffed up" (according to many translations), to Paul's critics and opponents. Idle talk does not help the kingdom to advance; what matters is the power of the Holy Spirit. It is improper for people to criticize the apostle without even having the appearance of the power that was at his disposal, the power of miracles "to bring the Gentiles to obedience—by word and deed, by the power of signs and wonders, by the power of the Spirit of God" (Rom. 15:18–19).

Surely there is in this power a future dimension; the power involved is elsewhere referred to as the "powers [*dynameis*] of the age to come" (Heb. 6:5). But the latter verse also says that these powers can be tasted already today. Acts 1:6–8 says implicitly that the apostles would receive the power of the Holy Spirit—as was fulfilled in 2:43 on the Day of Pentecost—as a down payment of the coming kingdom. Already today, God's kingdom and God's power belong together: Philip preached the gospel of the kingdom and performed "great miracles" (Greek *dynameis*, lit., "powers") (Acts 8:12–13). Paul preached the gospel of the kingdom and "God was doing extraordinary miracles [*dynameis*, lit., powers] by the hands of Paul" (19:8–11).

---

45. Barrett (1968, 118); cf. Saucy (1997, 340 n92).

Such servants of the Lord simply did nothing but what Jesus had commanded his apostles, and later the seventy(-two), to do: "And proclaim as you go, saying, 'The kingdom of heaven is at hand.' Heal the sick, raise the dead, cleanse lepers, cast out demons" (Matt. 10:7-8). "[H]e sent them out to proclaim the kingdom of God and to heal" (Luke 9:2). "Heal the sick in it [i.e., in the city they visited] and say to them, 'The kingdom of God has come near to you'" (10:9). In this way, Jesus' followers did what he himself had done, and what they had to continue: "[W]hoever believes in me will also do the works that I do; and greater works than these will he do, because I am going to the Father" (John 14:12).

Jesus spoke to the people "of the kingdom of God and cured those who had need of healing" (Luke 9:11). "[H]e went throughout all Galilee, teaching in their synagogues and proclaiming the gospel of the kingdom and healing every disease and every affliction among the people" (Matt. 4:23). "Jesus went throughout all the cities and villages, teaching in their synagogues and proclaiming the gospel of the kingdom and healing every disease and every affliction" (9:35). During all this time, the kingdom and the power of God went hand in hand. If the present kingdom of God is anything, it is a kingdom of love, but just as much a kingdom of power: the power of the mighty King, power to convert, to renew, to heal, to deliver.

### 8.3.3 Romans 14:17-18

Finally Romans 14:17-18 must be mentioned: "For the kingdom of God is not a matter of eating and drinking but of righteousness and peace and joy in the Holy Spirit. Whoever thus serves Christ is acceptable to God and approved by men." First, we hear what the kingdom is *not*: its power and reality do not become visible in the endless disputes of believers among themselves about many matters of merely secondary and tertiary importance. Many Christians put a lot of energy in such matters as if the entire existence and the full meaning of God's kingdom depend on it. According to them, we can speak of a "complete" Christianity only if we have the right view of the one (denominational) church, the pope and the Virgin Mary (Roman Catholics), or of the covenant of grace (some objectivistic Calvinists), or of predestination (some subjectivistic Calvinists), or of the right doctrine of baptism (read: adult baptism through immersion) (Baptists), or of the second blessing of Spirit baptism and glossolalia (Pentecostals), or of separation from evil as God's principle of unity (Exclusive Brethren), etc.

In all such cases, if matters are pursued to their extremes (which is often not the case at all, thank God), the view of God's kingdom in all its width and depth is replaced by *shibboleths* (cf. Judg. 12:5-6). These are key ideas with which Christians measure one another, and often even condemn other Christians.[46] Paul says, "Let not the one who eats despise the one who abstains, and let not the one who abstains pass judgment on the one who eats, for God has welcomed him. Who are you to pass judgment on the servant of another? It is before his own master that he stands or falls. And he will be upheld, for the Lord is able to make him stand. One person

---

46. This is the basis of sectarianism; see Ouweneel (2010b, chapters 13-14).

esteems one day as better than another, while another esteems all days alike. Each one should be fully convinced in his own mind. The one who observes the day, observes it in honor of the Lord. The one who eats, eats in honor of the Lord, since he gives thanks to God, while the one who abstains, abstains in honor of the Lord and gives thanks to God" (vv. 3–6). By way of summary, Paul says, "Accept one another, then, just as Christ accepted you, in order to bring praise to God" (15:7 NIV).

By condemning contrary views on secondary or even tertiary matters, the accusers are not rendering *justice* to the others, and this is the very first principle of God's kingdom that Paul mentions here: "righteousness." Do justice to other opinions, as long as those adhering to them earnestly try to the best of their ability to base these opinions on Scripture. Moreover, in this way the critics do not advance mutual *peace*, whereas this is a second vital principle of the kingdom: "So then let us pursue what makes for peace and for mutual upbuilding" (14:19). "If possible, so far as it depends on you, live peaceably with all" (Rom. 12:18). "Strive for peace with everyone, and for the holiness without which no one will see the Lord" (Heb. 12:14). Those who present secondary and tertiary matters as primary matters (even deriving their names from them: *Roman* Catholics, Baptists, Pentecostals, Federalists [covenant theologians]), will become so focused upon them that they will lose sight of the kingdom of God, and thus of the Lord. Such people also fail to practice the third principle: the *joy in the Holy Spirit*. People who pursue "rivalries, dissensions, sects" (Gal. 5:20 YLT) will fail in the fruit of the Spirit: "love, peace, joy" (v. 22).

This legalistic spirit of (external) religiosity, which emphasizes the details but overlooks the essence, is perduring. Jesus blamed the Pharisees and scribes for being hypocrites: "For you tithe mint and dill and cumin, and have neglected the weightier matters of the law: justice and mercy and faithfulness. These you ought to have done, without neglecting the others. You blind guides, straining out a gnat and swallowing a camel" (Matt. 23:23-24). That is, you are upset with one tiny unclean bug but you thoughtlessly swallow the large unclean animal in your wine cup. Quite a witty way to unmask this kind of people!

Believers must serve Christ, says Rom. 14:18, that is, "serve as slaves" (Greek *douleuō*), namely, "in this" (*en toutōi*), that is, by focusing upon the things that really matter in God's kingdom: "righteousness and peace and joy" (v. 17).[47] Such Christians are a joy to God's heart, and approved (accepted) by other people. The Christian world includes too many people who are focusing on "gnats," and in some cases they are even prepared to create church divisions because of them. Thus, they lose sight of the essence of God's kingdom. Generally speaking, non-Christians do not like nitpickers; Christians should not appreciate them either.

## 8.4 Jesus' Lordship
### 8.4.1 The Lordship of the King

Actually, the number of times that Paul explicitly mentions the kingdom is limited. The number of times that he implicitly hints at the truth of the kingdom is much larger. It is obvious that, wherever Paul emphasizes the

---
47. Moo (1996, 858).

Lordship of Jesus, whether his Lordship over the world or over believers, the truth of the kingdom is implied or included. Karl L. Schmidt rightly says, "We can thus see why the apostolic and post-apostolic church of the NT did not speak much of the *basileia tou theou* [kingdom of God] explicitly, but always emphasized it implicitly by its reference to the *kyrios Iēsous Christos* [the Lord Jesus Christ]."[48] Let me simply refer to the Day of Pentecost, where Peter said that God had "made him both Lord and Christ [i.e., Messiah, the Anointed One]" (Acts 2:36).

In some cases, it is immediately evident that Jesus' Lordship refers to God's kingdom: ". . . Therefore God has highly exalted him and bestowed on him the name that is above every name, so that at the name of Jesus every knee should bow, in heaven and on earth and under the earth, and every tongue confess that Jesus Christ is Lord, to the glory of God the Father" (Phil. 2:9-11). Similarly in 2 Timothy 4:18, "The *Lord* will rescue me from every evil deed and bring me safely into his heavenly *kingdom*." In my view, the latter means here, as at other places: a heavenly kingdom *on earth*. As Philip Towner puts it: the reference is to "the kingdom of Christ as presently real but yet future in its culmination, awaiting 'that day' when heavenly realities enter fully the earthly sphere (4:8)."[49]

Of special interest in this context is the expression "day of the Lord" in Paul's letters, or in the New Testament in general. Sometimes we are dealing here with an Old Testament expression, Hebrew *yom YHWH*, Greek *hēmera [tou] kyriou*. This may be a direct quotation, such

---

48. Schmidt (1964, 1:589).
49. Towner (2006, 647).

as in Acts 2:20 ("the day of the Lord comes, the great and magnificent day," cf. Joel 2:31), or an indirect reference (e.g., 1 Thess. 5:2; 2 Thess. 2:2; cf. 2 Pet. 3:10). An underlying problem is that the Greek word *kyrios* can have two very different meanings in the New Testament.[50] First, following the Septuagint, writers use it as a rendering of God's name, YHWH, especially in Old Testament quotations. But second, it refers to the Man Jesus Christ, sometimes before his death and resurrection (e.g., Matt. 21:3; Luke 7:13, 19), sometimes after his resurrection and before his ascension (Mark 16:19; Luke 24:3; Acts 1:21), but most often after his ascension and glorification (many times in the Acts and the letters). In the latter case, the "day of the Lord" may be the day of his appearance and the establishment of his kingdom (1 Cor. 1:8; 5:5; 2 Cor. 1:14; cf. "that day," Matt. 7:22; 24:36; 26:29; Luke 10:12; 21:34; Rom. 2:16; 1 Thess. 5:4; 2 Thess. 1:10; 2:3; 2 Tim. 1:12, 18; 2 Tim. 4:8; "day of (Jesus) Christ," Phil. 1:6, 10; 2:16).[51]

## 8.4.2 Confessing the Lord

In Romans 10:9–10, Paul emphasizes confessing Jesus as *Lord* as an essential condition for salvation: "[I]f you confess with your mouth that *Jesus is Lord* and believe in your heart that God raised him from the dead, you will be saved. For with the heart one believes and is justified, and with the mouth one confesses and is saved."

---

50. Aside from secular meanings, such as in Acts 25:26, where *kyrios* refers to the Roman emperor.
51. *Hē kyriakē hēmera* ("the Lord's day," Rev. 1:10) is a different expression; it has often been explained as referring to the first day of the week.

One cannot be saved if one accepts Jesus only as Savior. In other words, one should accept both dimensions of the twofold gospel, both by receiving God's grace for sinners and—explicitly or implicitly—by submitting to God's kingly rule (cf. §7.5.2). The former brings a person to *heaven*, the latter makes him a follower of Jesus on *earth*. Without the latter, the former cannot become a reality (and, of course, the reverse is true as well). Surrendering in faith to Christ is necessarily surrendering to him as Savior but also to him as Lord; the two cannot be separated.[52]

Naturally, the reference is not to some confession with the lips only. "[N]o one can say 'Jesus is Lord' except in the Holy Spirit" (1 Cor. 12:3), but of course Paul speaks here of a sincere declaration, spoken from the heart. In other words, truly acknowledging Jesus as Lord is expressed in concrete acts of obedience, surrender, devotion, dedication, and discipleship.[53]

N. T. Wright emphasizes that the calling to faith is simultaneously a calling to obedience.[54] This is because, says he, the One in whom we believe is the legitimate Lord and Master of the world. (The language that Paul used concerning Jesus would have reminded his hearers immediately of the language they were accustomed to hearing in reference to the Roman emperor.) This is why Paul could speak of "the obedience of faith" (Rom. 1:5; 16:26; cf. 6:17; 10:16; 15:18; 16:19).[55] Wright points

---

52. Cf. Stott (1959, 37); Boice (1986, 10, 21).
53. See Ouweneel (2010a, 126–29).
54. Wright (2007, 180).
55. Wright understands this "obedience of faith" as the obedience that comes from faith; on this, see Ouweneel (2010a, 141 n6).

out that the Greek word used by the early Christians for "faith," *pistis*, can also mean "loyalty" or "faithfulness." The message of the gospel is the good news that Jesus is the one, true "emperor," who rules the world according to his own standard of self-sacrificing love.

Indeed, the emperor of Rome was venerated as "Lord and God" (Latin, *dominus et deus*; Greek, *kyrios kai theos*; cf. Acts 12:22; 25:26). In opposition to this, Peter testified of Jesus that God had made *Jesus* "both Lord and Christ [Messiah]" (2:36), and "he is Lord of all" (10:36). Thomas made the tremendous confession that this very Jesus, newly risen from the dead, and no one else, was "Lord and God" (*kyrios kai theos*) or more correctly, "*my* Lord and *my* God" (*ho kyrios mou kai ho theos mou*, John 20:28). There can be no true faith without this very personal recognition of Jesus as "my" Lord (cf. Luke 1:43; John 20:13, 28; Phil. 3:8) and "my" God (Rom. 1:8; 1 Cor. 1:4; 2 Cor. 12:21; Phil. 1:3; 4:19; Phlm. 1:4).

In Romans 14:4–9, Paul emphasizes the same fact, now from the viewpoint that every believer is personally responsible to his Lord: "Who are you to pass judgment on the servant of another? It is before his own master that he stands or falls. . . . For none of us lives to himself, and none of us dies to himself. For if we live, we live to the Lord, and if we die, we die to the Lord. So then, whether we live or whether we die, we are the Lord's. For to this end Christ died and lived again, that he might be Lord both of the dead and of the living." The same Jesus who one day will be Lord of the dead and the living is now the Lord of every individual follower of his. This same thought is found elsewhere: "[H]e died for all, that those who live might no longer live for themselves but for him who for their sake died and was raised" (2 Cor. 5:15); and: "You are serving the Lord Christ" (Col. 3:24; cf. 4:1, "you have a Lord [*kyrios*] in heaven," WYC).

One could hardly imagine a person willing to *receive* everything from Jesus who would be unwilling to *give* everything to Jesus: his heart, his life, his possessions. The conversion of Saul of Tarsus began with the question, "Who are you, Lord?," immediately followed by the question, "What shall I do, Lord?" (Acts 22:8, 10). He became an imitator of Christ the Lord: "Be imitators of me, as I am of Christ" (1 Cor. 11:1; cf. 1 Thess. 1:6, "[Y]ou became imitators of us and of the Lord"; cf. 1 Pet. 2:21; Rev. 14:4). This is why it has been said: *becoming* a Christian costs you nothing (the gospel is free), but *being* a Christian costs you everything (with the addition that you receive everything back). This is expressed in the concept of discipleship (Luke 14:26-27, 33; see chapter 6 above),[56] and also in James 2, where genuine faith is manifested only through works of obedience (vv. 20-24).

### 8.4.3 Other Examples of Lordship

It is quite remarkable how often the title "Lord" is used in connection with the Lord's Supper. Paul speaks of the cup of the Lord, the table of the Lord, the Lord's death, and the body and blood of the Lord (1 Cor. 10:21-22; 11:26-27; in 11:20 ["the Lord's supper"] the word is not the noun *kyriou* but the adjective *kyriakon*; only in 11:29 is the addition "of the Lord" uncertain[57]). In this way, the Lord's Supper is conspicuously linked with the kingdom of God; see especially 11:26, "you proclaim the Lord's

---

56. MacArthur (1988, 21, 30).
57. See Metzger (1975, 562-63).

death *until he comes.*" It reminds us of Jesus' own words: "Truly, I say to you, I will not drink again of the fruit of the vine until that day when I drink it new in the kingdom of God" (Mark 14:25). The Lord's Supper commemorates the triumph of Christ. It testifies that Jesus is Lord, a testimony proclaimed in the presence of all the defeated powers; as David said, "You prepare a table before me in the presence of my enemies" (Ps. 23:5). In this way, it is also an expression of (renewed) dedication to him. As Psalm 116 says, "What shall I *render* to the LORD for all his benefits to me? I will lift up the *cup of salvation* and call on the name of the LORD, I will pay my *vows* to the LORD in the presence of all his people" (vv. 12–14).

Equally remarkable is that Paul uses the word "Lord" five times in 1 Thessalonians 4:15–17, "For this we declare to you by a word from the *Lord*, that we who are alive, who are left until the coming of the *Lord*, will not precede those who have fallen asleep. For the *Lord* himself will descend from heaven with a cry of command, with the voice of an archangel, and with the sound of the trumpet of God. And the dead in Christ will rise first. Then we who are alive, who are left, will be caught up together with them in the clouds to meet the *Lord* in the air, and so we will always be with the *Lord*." The reference is not to some "rapture" of the "bride of Christ," that is, the church in this quality,[58] but to the warriors of the Lord who, with a military command (Greek *keleusma*) and a trumpet (probably derived from Jewish apocalyptic),[59] are released from their duties

---

58. So, e.g., Schuyler English (1986, 60); cf. Hoek (2004, 209).
59. See the link with the "archangel," i.e., Michael, who blows the trumpet to announce God's approach for judgment (*Apoc. Mosis* 22); Moffatt (1979, 38).

and enter their rest (*Oh, when the saints go marching in* . . .; a bride does not march and is not commanded). The battles and sufferings of Jesus' followers are over; the kingdom of God arrives in power and majesty.

In 1 Corinthians 12:3 Paul says, "[N]o one can say 'Jesus is Lord' except in the Holy Spirit." As I mentioned, the confession of Jesus' Lordship counts only if it comes from the heart, and this is possible only in the power of the Spirit. A confession just of the lips does not suffice; a real surrender is demanded. As Jesus said, "Not everyone who says to me, '*Lord, Lord,*' will enter the kingdom of heaven, but the one who does the will of my Father who is in heaven. On that day many will say to me, '*Lord, Lord,* did we not prophesy in your name, and cast out demons in your name, and do many mighty works in your name?' And then will I declare to them, 'I never knew you; depart from me, you workers of lawlessness'" (Matt. 7:21–23). "Afterward the other virgins came also, saying, '*Lord, lord,* open to us.' But he answered, 'Truly, I say to you, I do not know you'" (25:11–12). "Why do you call me '*Lord, Lord,*' and not do what I tell you?" (Luke 6:46). In the New Testament, this double "Lord, Lord" is used only in a negative sense; it is an equally urgent appeal, though, similar to the double "Abraham" (Gen. 22:11), "Jacob" (46:2), "Moses" (Exod. 3:4), "Samuel" (1 Sam. 3:10), "Martha" (Luke 10:41), "Simon" (Luke 22:31), and "Saul" (Acts 9:4; 22:7; 26:14).

Finally, I refer to Ephesians 4:4–6, "There is one body and one Spirit—just as you were called to the one hope that belongs to your call—one Lord, one faith, one baptism, one God and Father of all, who is over all and through all and in all." There are seven "units" here, of which, in my view, the first three belong together, as well as the second group of three.⁶⁰ The first three, the one body, the one Spirit, and the one hope, may refer to the *inner* side of Christian unity, linked with the church as the body of Christ and the inner working of the Spirit. Then follows the *outward* side of Christian unity, the *external* testimony in this world, linked with the kingdom of God: one Lord (as the King in this kingdom), one faith (here not the heart's believing, but the believed truth: "Christian faith," as the foundation of the kingdom), one baptism (as the introduction to the kingdom). After the *body* and the *kingdom* we have, thirdly, the *family* of God: "[O]ne God and Father of all, who is over all and through all and in all" (v. 6). In my view, this refers to God's Fatherhood with respect to believers.⁶¹

## 8.5 Disavowing Jesus' Lordship

### 8.5.1 Ryrie and Hodges

It is a striking denial of the gospel of God's kingdom when some authors emphatically reject the Scriptural proofs of §8.4 as conditions of salvation.⁶² Thus, Charles Ryrie says that the message of faith alone and the message of faith plus "commitment of life" cannot both be the gospel. In a rather naïve way, he concludes that one of the two must be a false gospel and must come under the curse of distorting the gospel or preaching another

---

60. So, e.g., Grant (1901, 340-41).
61. Cf. the Annotations of the Dutch States Translation (Statenvertaling); Wood (1978, ad loc.) (*contra* many expositors).
62. See the review by Demarest (1997, 265-70); see Ouweneel (2010a, 128-30).

gospel (Gal. 1:6–9).[63] This is an ultra-Protestant response, born from what I call the "Roman trauma," in which every reference to good works, and thus commitment, surrender, and dedication, is *a priori* suspected. Apparently, Ryrie takes the *sola fide* ("by faith alone") so literally that he does *not* allow us to say that faith is not genuine faith without surrender to Christ as Lord.

Now, to begin with, Scripture does not know the expression "justification by faith *alone*." Jesus says, "[O]nly believe" (Mark 5:36; Luke 8:50), but this stood in contrast to the fears and doubts of Jairus. In itself I do not object to the expression "by faith alone," as long as "faith" is taken here in its proper biblical sense. In opposition to all self-willed Torah-observing, "faith alone" is the way of salvation. But what is this faith? Zane Hodges describes faith as the inner conviction that what God tells us in the gospel is true. In his view, this is saving faith, and this alone.[64] However, first, I am certain that the devil also believes all that God tells us in the gospel. He knows far too well that God forgives repentant sinners because of the blood of Christ. Second, Hodges' approach is far too Western-intellectualist. I am afraid that there might be quite a number of young people in many churches who thoughtlessly and passively believe everything that comes to them through the gospel, without ever having truly repented and without ever having been regenerated. Faith involves not just accepting certain statements as true, but *surrendering* to the One who makes these statements.[65] As the Heidelberg Cate-

---

63. Ryrie (1969, 170).
64. Hodges (1989, 31).
65. Ouweneel (2010a, §5.2).

chism (Q/A 21) says: "True faith is not only a sure knowledge by which I hold as true all that God has revealed to us in Scripture; *it is also a wholehearted trust*, which the Holy Spirit creates in me by the gospel" (italics added).

This entrusting oneself to God, this genuine surrender to him, is the very thing Hodges denies. To this end, he uses the story of the Samaritan woman (John 4:1-30): she only had to receive the living water, and did not have to surrender. Hodges even argues that repentance as a condition for salvation is a corruption of justification by faith alone, and that to demand that one must receive Jesus as Lord would be to return to the principle of the law.[66] But first, if repentance is not a condition, then why did Jesus and the apostles constantly urge the people to repent (Greek *metanoia*; Matt. 4:17; Luke 5:32; 13:3, 5; Acts 2:38; 3:19; 17:30; 26:20), often in a direct relationship with faith (Matt. 21:32; Mark 1:15; Acts 20:21; Heb. 6:1)? Second, Jesus' very pointing out to the Samaritan woman the misery of her sins became the turning point for her, as we see from her remarkable words: "He told me all that I ever did" (John 4:39). Third, what is wrong with the principle of the law? No one can be saved by works of the law as such—yet believers are under the "law of Christ" (1 Cor. 9:21; Gal. 6:2), under the commandments of Jesus or God (John 14:15, 21; 15:10; 1 John 2:3-4; 3:2, 24; 5:2-3).

## 8.5.2 Refutation

The view of Ryrie and Hodges is an emphatic denial of the gospel of the kingdom (cf. §7.5.2). It is a one-sided concentration on the gospel of God's grace for sinners,

---

66 Hodges (1989, 18).

and this moreover in its thinnest form. The authors have heard Jesus' Great Commission in Luke 24:47 ("that repentance and forgiveness of sins should be proclaimed in his name to all nations"), but they have never heard Jesus' Great Commission in Matthew 28:19, "make *disciples* of all nations." That is, do not preach salvation only but turn converts into *followers* of me. The authors claim that we are saved "by faith *alone*," but to Paul this is apparently insufficient: "[I]f you confess with your mouth that *Jesus is Lord* and believe in your heart that God raised him from the dead, you will be saved. For with the heart one believes and is justified, and with the mouth one confesses and is saved." Do not only believe in Jesus as Savior but also confess him as Lord. This is not just a confession of lips: "Sanctify *in your hearts* Christ as Lord" (1 Pet. 3:15 ASV).

Ryrie and Hodges claim that we are saved "by faith *alone*," and in their view this "alone" excludes, for instance, repentance and surrender. If these things are also present, that is to be appreciated, but, according to them, these are not a *condition* for salvation. However, why would God forgive us our sins if we did not mourn over them? And why would he forgive us our sins if he did not see in our hearts a purpose to surrender to his will from now on? "[H]e who confesses *and forsakes* [his transgressions] will obtain mercy" (Prov. 28:13).

The core of the matter is this. If we are saved "by faith alone," repentance and surrender are not something additional (so that it would not be "faith *alone*" anymore) but they are *included* in genuine biblical faith. Faith is not biblical faith if it does not entail, on the one hand, repentance and confession of sins and, on the other hand, a faithful surrender to Christ and submission to his Lordship. Jesus says, "My sheep *hear my voice, and I know them, and they follow me. I give them eternal life*" (John 10:27-28). Notice the order of things here! There is no true *fides qua creditur* ("faith by which one believes") without the concomitant: "Follow me!" "I am the light of the world. Whoever follows me will not walk in darkness, but will have the light of life" (8:12). There is no spiritual light for those who believe in the Savior but do not follow the Lord.

As we live in the end times, we should give heed to Matthew 24:14 more than ever: "[T]his *gospel of the kingdom* will be proclaimed throughout the whole world as a testimony to all nations, and then the end will come." The gospel of the kingdom is *not*: "Christ Jesus came into the world to save sinners" (1 Tim. 1:15)—this is the gospel of the grace of God (cf. Acts 20:24). It is a good and important gospel, and we keep preaching it. But the gospel of the kingdom is this: "[W]hat we proclaim is . . . *Jesus Christ as Lord*" (2 Cor. 4:5). It is about "*obeying* the gospel of our *Lord* Jesus" (2 Thess. 1:8). No person will ever be saved who (supposedly) accepts Jesus as the One who bore his sins but refuses in effect to accept him as the Master of his life: "For if we live, we live to the *Lord*, and if we die, we die to the *Lord*. So then, whether we live or whether we die, *we are the Lord's*. For to this end Christ died and lived again, *that he might be Lord* both of the dead and of the living" (Rom. 14:8-9).

### 8.5.3 The Opponents

The debate is rather intense because others have used equally strong language to defend the opposite of what

Ryrie and Hodges have asserted. Just as Ryrie called the message of faith plus surrender a false gospel, Aiden W. Tozer called the view that repentance and surrender are not needed pure heresy, even in the title of his book.[67] Several authors have called Ryrie and Hodges "modern antinomian extremists" and teachers of a "lawless grace."[68] Thus, the one party accuses the other one of legalism, and the other accuses the first one of antinomianism. James I. Packer spoke of the *faith-only-ism*, and pointed to the illogical nature of it: how can one think that a person has to believe only in Jesus as the One who has borne our sins if that person is not sincerely willing to break with sin, and to this end willing to submit his life to the rule of King Jesus?[69]

To me Packer's position is perfectly correct. He who shouts, "Faith is enough!," may recall James 2:19, "Even the demons believe—and shudder!" Faith is "completed" (Greek *eteleiōthē*) in the works of obedience and service that flow from it (v. 22). One is saved by faith alone—but this faith is not "complete" without its fruits, such as surrender to Christ, discipleship, and obedience to his commandments. Without this, it is even "dead" (v. 26). One is saved by faith alone—but this must be a living, fruitful faith, otherwise it *is* not genuine faith. Faith is not faith if it is not "working through love" (Gal. 5:6). In order to function, an electric torch needs a "battery only"—but the whole thing will function only if this battery produces power; otherwise it is a "dead battery." As Paul says, "Examine yourselves, to see whether you are

---

67. Tozer (1991, *I Call It Heresy*).
68. Various authors in Horton (1992).
69. Packer (1970, 89).

## The Spreading of the Kingdom

in the faith. Test yourselves. Or do you not realize this about yourselves, that Jesus Christ is in you?—unless indeed you fail to meet the test!" (2 Cor. 13:5).

Bruce Demarest rightly emphasizes that faith itself is already an act of obedience (Acts 5:32; 6:7; Rom. 1:5; 10:16; 15:18; 16:26; 2 Thess. 1:8; 1 Pet. 1:2; 4:17), and that, conversely, disobedience is identified with unbelief (John 3:36; Eph. 2:2; Titus 3:3; Heb. 4:6). Obedience is inherent to the nature of faith. A would-be Christian who accepts Jesus without wishing to commit and submit himself to him entertains a faith in Jesus as Savior but not in Jesus as Lord. Such a faith *is* not faith in the biblical sense. Faith is confidence not only in the Jesus who died for us, but also in the Lord who was placed "above all rule and authority and power and dominion, and above every name that is named" (Eph. 1:21). "So then, just as you received *Christ Jesus as Lord*, continue to live your lives in him . . . in Christ you have been brought to fullness. He is the head over every power and authority" (Col. 2:6, 10 NIV).

Even the readers in Paul's own day did not understand him on this point, wrongly assuming that his doctrine of justification by faith involved a license to keep sinning:[70] "'[W]hy not do evil that good may come?'—as some people slanderously charge us with saying. Their condemnation is just" (Rom. 3:8). "What shall we say then? 'Are we to continue in sin that grace may abound?' By no means! How can we who died to sin still live in it? . . . What then? 'Are we to sin because we are not under law but under grace?' By no means!" (6:1-2, 15). The apostle Peter seems to have been aware of this apparent

---

70. Berkhof (1979, 435).

difficulty in Paul's teaching: "[C]ount the patience of our Lord as salvation, just as our beloved brother Paul also wrote to you according to the wisdom given him, as he does in all his letters when he speaks in them of these matters. There are some things in them that are hard to understand, which the ignorant and unstable twist to their own destruction, as they do the other Scriptures" (2 Pet. 3:15-16).

The teaching of Ryrie and Hodges is so dangerous because it risks leading to similar misunderstandings as those addressed by Paul. Nowhere in the New Testament do we ever encounter such a thing as a faith *by itself*, but only a faith that becomes *active* in producing the fruit of the Spirit (Gal. 5:22) and in fulfilling the law of Christ (6:2). Paul says, "[B]y grace you have been saved through faith . . . not a result of *works*." But this is immediately followed by: "For we are his workmanship, created in Christ Jesus for *good works*" (Eph. 2:8-10). *The very same letter that tells us that w*e not saved by "works of the law" (Rom. 3:20, 27-28) tells us this self-evident truth: "Owe no one anything, except to love each other, for the one who loves another has fulfilled the law. . . . 'You shall love your neighbor as yourself.' Love does no wrong to a neighbor; therefore love is the fulfilling of the law" (13:8-10).

In brief, without the addition of the gospel of the kingdom, the gospel of God's grace for sinners could easily lead to antinomianism (the rejection of the "principle of the law" as such), or what Dietrich Bonhoeffer called "cheap grace" (*billige Gnade*).[71] It may sound harsh, but this is precisely what Ryrie and Hodges have

---

71. See especially Bonhoeffer (1995); cf. Landgrebe (1986).

done: preach a gospel of cheap grace. Grace is *free* but not cheap. It cost God what was dearest to him: his Son. Accepting the gospel of grace is free, but living by it will also cost the believer what is dearest to him: his heart.

## 8.6 The Kingdom in Other Letters
### 8.6.1 The Kingdom in Hebrews 12:28-29

"Therefore let us be grateful for receiving a kingdom that cannot be shaken, and thus let us offer to God acceptable worship, with reverence and awe, for our God is a consuming fire."

As far as I can see, the book of Hebrews contains three explicit references to Jesus' kingship. The first is 1:8, where the writer quotes Psalm 45:6, applying it to Jesus: "Your throne, O God, is forever and ever, the scepter of uprightness is the scepter of your kingdom." That is, your royal scepter is a righteous scepter; in the Messianic kingdom you will rule in righteousness. The second reference is in 7:1-3, where Melchizedek is described as "resembling the Son of God" (v. 3): he is "first, by translation of his name, king of righteousness, and then he is also king of Salem, that is, king of peace" (v. 2). He is a type (image, foreshadowing) of the Messianic King, who one day will rule in righteousness and peace.

The third and last reference is in the verse just quoted, in which the "kingdom that cannot be shaken" refers again to the future Messianic kingdom. This kingdom is received by believers, which means primarily that they are admitted into it, and probably also that they will share Jesus' rule in it. Jesus receives the kingdom from God's hands (Dan. 7:13-14), and believers receive it from the hands of the Father and of Jesus: "Fear not, little flock, for it is your Father's good pleasure to give you the kingdom" (Luke 12:32); "I assign to you, as my Father assigned to me, a kingdom" (22:29). Today, believers are *subjects* in God's kingdom, but in the coming day they will be *co-rulers*. Today, they are under Jesus' reign, but in the coming day they will reign with him.

It will be a "kingdom that cannot be shaken" (others: an "unshakable kingdom"), that is, it cannot be put out of balance, let alone that it could perish. Even the kingship of David's house under the old covenant turned out to be shakable (think of Absalom's rebellion, which occurred already during David's rule: 2 Sam. 15-18). Yet, in the time of David's kingship God had made him this promise: "When he [Solomon, or any royal descendent of David] commits iniquity, I will discipline him with the rod of men, with the stripes of the sons of men, but my steadfast love will not depart from him, as I took it from Saul, whom I put away from before you. And your house and your kingdom shall be made sure forever before me. Your throne shall be established forever" (2 Sam. 7:14-16). Eventually, this promise will be fulfilled in and through the Messianic kingdom, in which *the* Son of David will sit on the throne of David (Isa. 9:7; Luke 1:32; cf. Jer. 33:17).

All human kingdoms will come to an end in due time. What remains is a kingdom that, beyond the "thousand years" of Revelation 20:1-7, will be an everlasting kingdom, in which believers will reign with Christ "forever and ever" (22:5).

Although it is only in this passage that the writer of Hebrews speaks explicitly of the Messianic kingdom, he refers to it implicitly in several different ways, in particular through the participle of the Greek verb *mellō*:

(a) the "world to come" (*hē oikoumenē hē mellousa*), that is, the inhabited earth during the Messianic kingdom (2:5);

(b) the "age to come" (*mellōn aiōn*), that is, the age of the Messianic kingdom (6:5; in Rev. 20:1–7 "thousand years");

(c) the "good things to come" (Greek *ta mellonta agatha*), that is, the divine blessings of the Messianic kingdom (10:1);

(d) the "things to come" (*mellonta*) that is, ultimately again the blessings of the Messianic kingdom (11:20 NKJV, etc.);

(e) the "city to come" (*hē polis mellousa*) that is, so to speak, the heavenly capital of the Messianic kingdom (13:14).

Another keyword in Hebrews is "heavenly." It never refers to the intermediate state (Paradise). Sometimes it refers to heaven in a general sense (3:1; 6:4; 8:5; 9:23), sometimes specifically to the "kingdom of heaven": the "heavenly country" (*patris epourania*), that is, so to speak, the heavenly "upper story" of the Messianic kingdom (11:14–16), and the "city of the living God, the heavenly Jerusalem," that is, the heavenly capital of the Messianic kingdom (12:22; cf. 13:14).

## 8.6.2 The Kingdom in James 2:5

"Listen, my beloved brothers, has not God chosen those who are poor in the world to be rich in faith and heirs of the kingdom, which he has promised to those who love him?"

Here again it is particularly the future form of God's kingdom that is in view; faith sees everything as being within the framework of the coming kingdom.[72] Being an heir of the kingdom (cf. Rom. 8:17; Gal. 4:7; Titus 3:7) is the same as having an inheritance in God's kingdom (Eph. 1:11, 14, 18; 5:5), or inheriting the kingdom (1 Cor. 6:9–10; 15:50; Gal. 5:21; Heb. 1:14). I see a link here with the description of Christ in James 2:1, "our Lord Jesus Christ, the Lord of glory," which reminds us of 1 Corinthians 2:7-8, "[W]e impart a secret and hidden wisdom of God, which God decreed before the ages for our glory. None of the rulers of this age understood this, for if they had, they would not have crucified the Lord of glory." Apparently we have a Hebraism here; the writer's intention is "the glorious (magnificent, resplendent) Lord" of the coming kingdom.[73]

To the Lord of glory, the present world meant humiliation, rejection, and crucifixion. He had no riches in this world; he did not even have anywhere to lay his head (Matt. 8:20). As the Lord of glory he has no inner connection with the present world, only with those whom he has drawn from this world (Gal. 1:4). These are followers who, just like him, look forward to the future glory of the Messianic kingdom. No one can imagine this better than "those who are poor in the world," that is, those who in the present world possess virtually nothing, and who in the future world will possess virtually everything, together with the Lord of glory. The less

---

72. See Ouweneel (1981, 37–39).
73. Cf. "crown of holiness" (Exod. 29:6 JUB) = holy crown; "King of glory" (Ps. 24:7–10) = glorious King; "king of righteousness" (Heb. 7:2) = righteous King, etc.

one has in the present world, the more one looks forward to that other world (cf. §4.2).

I see a second link with James 2:8, where the writer speaks of the "royal (kingly) law"; freely rendered: the "law of the kingdom of God," the central commandment of love: "You shall love your neighbor as yourself" (Lev. 19:18). This love for the neighbor cannot be separated from love for God; therefore, James 2:5 mentions this as a necessary condition: God has promised the kingdom to "those who love him" (cf. 1:12; Rom. 8:28; 1 Cor. 2:9; Eph. 6:24; 1 John 4:20-21; 5:2). Love is both the condition for *entering* the kingdom and the law for those who *are in* the kingdom (see further §§9.5 and 9.6). The kingdom is the place where believers contemplate the Father's love for his Son (cf. Col. 1:13), as well as the place where they themselves will love God and Christ and their neighbors. In James 1:17, God is the "Father of *lights*," here he is the God of *love* (cf. 1 John 1:5; 4:8, 16).

### 8.6.3 The Kingdom in 2 Peter 1:10-11

"Therefore, brothers, be all the more diligent to confirm your calling and election, for if you practice these qualities you will never fall. For in this way there will be richly provided for you an entrance into the eternal kingdom of our Lord and Savior Jesus Christ."

This is again a wonderful example of the fact that the New Testament never suggests that, if a person simply believes or knows that he is elect, everything will be all right with him. Salvation can never be separated from good works as the necessary result of faith—necessary in the sense that, if the fruit is lacking, this faith turns out not to have been a genuine, saving faith at all (2 Cor.

13:5). The believing person must "confirm" his "calling and election," that is, deliver the practical proofs that he indeed *has* been called and elected.[74] Only in this way, will an entrance into the "eternal kingdom" of Christ be richly provided for him.

This is something essentially different from the "signs of conversion" that certain hyper-Calvinist, but also certain Evangelical, circles are looking for. Here, the authenticity of someone's conversion is measured by the impressive story he can tell about the way he was saved. In no way is this the biblical criterion. Timothy would certainly have failed this test, for he had believed from early childhood, and apparently could not tell an exciting conversion story like, for instance, Paul could (2 Tim. 1:5; 3:14–15). This is the wrong approach. We ought to look not for signs of one's conversion—as an event—but for evidence of having been converted, that is, for "fruit in keeping with repentance" (Matt. 3:8). We think here again of the many practical conditions that, in the Gospels and Acts, are linked with entering the kingdom of God (§5.5). A person is shown to be elect or a believer not because he has a good story about his conversion, but because others see the fruits of this election, that is, the fruits of his faith. In hyper-Calvinist circles, many persons exhibit the fruits intended here, which demonstrate their salvation, but because of the doctrine preached they do not dare to call themselves children of God.[75]

The expression "eternal kingdom" does not refer simply to heaven as the place where believers dwell be-

---

74. See Ouweneel (2008b, 251–52; 2010a, 315).

75. See extensively, Ouweneel (2008c; 2010a, §5.6).

tween their death and resurrection (the intermediate state). Thus, Greijdanus writes: *"in the eternal kingdom of our Lord*, when you die. . . . A godly life provides a wide[76] deathbed."[77] Strachan draws a parallel with John Bunyan's *Pilgrim's Progress* (Part I) in which upon death, pilgrims enter the "celestial city."[78] But this is not what the expression "eternal kingdom" means. Nor does it refer to heaven in the sense of the believers' dwelling place after their resurrection. The actual sense of the term "kingdom" must always be honored. Even if Scripture speaks of "thousand years" (Rev. 20:1–7), the kingdom is essentially an everlasting one. To the Son of Man "was given dominion and glory and a kingdom, that all peoples, nations, and languages should serve him; his dominion is an everlasting dominion, which shall not pass away, and his kingdom one that shall not be destroyed" (Dan. 7:14). "[T]he saints of the Most High shall receive the kingdom and possess the kingdom forever, forever and ever" (v. 18). "And the kingdom and the dominion and the greatness of the kingdoms under the whole heaven shall be given to the people of the saints of the Most High; his [or, their] kingdom shall be an everlasting kingdom, and all dominions shall serve and obey him [or, them]" (v. 27; see further 4:3; Ps. 145:13; 2 Pet. 1:11).

"[H]is servants will worship him. They will see his face, and his name will be on their foreheads . . . and

---

76. This is a Dutch devotional term (*ruim*): a deathbed with a "richly provided entrance."
77. Greijdanus (1931, 112).
78. Strachan (1979, 128).

they will reign forever and ever" (Rev. 22:3-5), that is, "reign as kings" (Greek *basileusousin*).

## 8.7 The King in Revelation
### 8.7.1 God and Christ as King

God is described as the "King of the nations" (Rev. 15:3; cf. 2 Chron. 20:6; Ps. 10:16; 22:28; Jer. 10:7), which means that the entire world constitutes his kingdom. Other manuscripts read "King of the ages," which amounts to "King of all eternities," or simply "eternal King"; as Paul says, "Now to the eternal king, immortal, invisible, the only God, be honor and glory forever and ever!" (1 Tim. 1:17). Tobit 13:6 says, "[E]xalt the king of the ages" (trans. A. Di Lella). And 1 Enoch 9:4, "And they said to the Lord of the ages: 'Lord of lords, God of gods, King of kings, and God of the ages . . .'" (trans. R. H. Charles).

The Textus Receptus has "King of the saints," unfortunately adopted by several translations, although it hardly finds any support in the original manuscripts.

For the expression "King of the nations," one may compare Christ's description as "the faithful witness, the firstborn of the dead, and the ruler [Greek *archōn*] of the kings of the earth" (1:5 NASB).[79] The first "of" in the last phrase is "over": Christ is not only King over the nations but even King over the kings of the nations. He will have the supreme authority over all the kings of the world.

"[T]he Lamb . . . is Lord of lords [*kyrios kyriōn*] and King of kings [*basileus basileōn*]" (17:14). "On his robe and on his thigh he has a name written, King of kings

---

79. See Johnson (1981, 421-22) regarding who these "kings of the earth" might be.

(*basileus basileōn*) and Lord of lords [*kyrios kyriōn*]" (19:16). In 1 Tim. 6:15, it is God who is referred to with almost the same title: "King of kings [*basileus tōn basileuontōn*] and Lord of lords [*kyrios tōn kyriontōn*]," literally: "King of those reigning as kings and Lord of those ruling as lords." In Revelation, three titles express Jesus' royal glory: *archōn* ("Ruler," 1:5), *kyrios* ("Lord," 11:8; 17:14; 19:16; 22:20-21), and *basileus* ("King," 17:14; 19:16).

These genitives ("of lords," "of kings") do not point to possession or something similar, but they are Hebraisms: highest Lord/King, Lord/King *par excellence* (cf. "holy of holiest" = most holy place; "Song of songs" = highest song [German *Hohelied*, Dutch *Hooglied*]; "heaven of heavens" = highest heaven). The meaning is not so much "King *over* the kings" (unlike 1:5, "Ruler *over* the kings") but rather "the highest *among* the kings," the "Supreme King."

In the Old Testament, the expression "king of kings" (supreme king) is used for great and mighty, though earthly, kings: Artaxerxes (Ezra 7:12; CEV: "great king"; NIRV: "greatest king of all") and Nebuchadnezzar (Ezek. 26:7; Dan. 2:37; several translations: "greatest king").

### 8.7.2 Revelation 1:5-6 and 5:9-10

It is obvious that Revelation, *the* eschatological book of the New Testament, is full of teaching about the kingdom of God, although the term as such occurs only five times. In 1:5-6, the emphasis seems to be on the present form of the kingdom, although the eschatological dimension might be preponderant: "To him who loves us and has freed us from our sins by his blood and made us a *kingdom*, priests to his God and

Father, to him be glory and dominion forever and ever. Amen." Similarly in 5:9–10, "Worthy are you to take the scroll and to open its seals, for you were slain, and by your blood you ransomed people for God from every tribe and language and people and nation, and you have made them a *kingdom* and priests to our God, and they shall reign on the earth."

What strikes us here is the expression "*made us a kingdom.*" This can amount to "made us kings" (so KJV, etc.; cf. CEV: "lets us rule as kings"; NIRV: "made us members of his royal family"), but also: "made us subjects of a kingdom"; thus, e.g., AMP: "formed us into a kingdom [as His subjects]." I have some preference for the first interpretation because of the parallel with the following term: "made us priests." That is, he made us both kings and priests.

Some connect the two descriptions, "kings" and "priests," in the following way: "made us a kingdom of priests," or "a kingdom, that is, priests" (EXB; cf. GNT, etc.). This is because of Exodus 19:6. Indeed, the reference is clearly to this Old Testament passage, where the Lord God promises the Israelites that, if they would keep the covenant, they would be a "kingdom of priests." Walter Kaiser pointed out that this expression (Hebrew *mamlēket kohanim*) could mean four different things: (a) "kings, that is, priests," (b) "kingly [royal] priesthood" [cf. 1 Pet. 2:9, "you are a royal priesthood"], (c) "priestly kingdom," or (d) "kings [and] priests."[80] In my view, the idea is not so much that Israel would be part of, or would constitute, *God's* priestly kingdom, but that they *themselves* would be kings and priests. God is a

---

80. Kaiser (1990, 417).

King, but it does not make sense to call him a Priest. It is God's people, both in the Old and the New Testament, who are called kings and priests. In this way, they resemble Jesus himself, who is both King and Priest. The difference is that we are merely kings, but he is the King of kings (Rev. 19:16); we are priests, but he is the High Priest (the Priest of priests, so to speak[81]) (Heb. 2:17; etc.).

Indeed, in the kingdom in its present form, believers are "merely" subjects. But in the Messianic kingdom they will be kings together with Christ (Rev. 20:4, 6), though in such a way that he will be head and shoulders above them (cf. the striking physical parallel with king Saul: "From his shoulders upward he was taller than any of the people," 1 Sam. 9:2). Together with Christ, his believing co-regents will be exalted above the "kings of the earth," just as he is (Rev. 1:5).

### 8.7.3 Revelation 1:9 and 20:4–6

"I, John, your brother and partner in the tribulation and the kingdom and the patient endurance that are in Jesus, was on the island called Patmos on account of the word of God and the testimony of Jesus."

In a free rendering, John says, "We are together in Jesus, and we share these things: suffering, the kingdom, and patient endurance" (ERV). Here again, this sharing can mean: having a share or inheritance in the kingdom in its present form, being a subject of this kingdom, but also being a co-ruler with Christ in the future

---

81. This expression does not occur in the Old Testament, though; "the high priest" is *hakkohen haggadol*, lit., "the great priest." In Hebrews, "high priest" is generally *archiereus*, but in 10:21 it is *hiereus megas*, "great priest."

Messianic kingdom. Because of the terms "suffering" and "patient endurance," I prefer to think here of the kingdom in its present form. We are now suffering in the present kingdom, and this is the path of entering the future kingdom (cf. Acts 14:22; 2 Thess. 1:5–7). Patient endurance in the midst of the sufferings is a necessary condition for such entrance (cf. Rom. 5:3–4; 8:17; 2 Tim. 2:12). Through sufferings (which the wicked inflict upon believers) and patient endurance (which believers manifest during the sufferings), the faithful enter the Messianic kingdom as it will arrive at the parousia.

The book of Revelation contains quite a few references to the believer's reigning with Christ in the future kingdom: "The one who conquers and who keeps my works until the end, to him I will give authority over the nations, and he will rule them with a rod of iron, as when earthen pots are broken in pieces, even as I myself have received authority from my Father" (2:26–27). Notice the "he" here: he who conquers will "rule the nations with a rod of iron"—something that elsewhere is said of the Messiah: "You shall break them with a rod of iron and dash them in pieces like a potter's vessel" (Ps. 2:9); ". . . a male child, one who is to rule all the nations with a rod of iron" (Rev. 12:5; cf. 19:15). The conquering believer is here co-ruler with Christ: "The one who conquers, I will grant him to sit with me on my throne, as I also conquered and sat down with my Father on his throne" (3:21). Notice the difference: *today* Jesus sits on the heavenly throne with his Father, at the *coming day* he will sit with the conquering believers on *his own* throne, the earthly throne of

David (Isa. 9:7; Luke 1:32; cf. his "glorious throne" [Matt. 25:31], literally the "throne of his glory" [NKJV, etc.], that is, his "royal throne" [CEV, GNT]).

"Then I saw . . . the souls of those who had been beheaded for the testimony of Jesus and for the word of God. . . . They came to life and reigned with Christ for a thousand years. . . . [T]hey will be priests of God and of Christ, and they will reign with him for a thousand years" (20:4–6). Please note that the English verb "to reign" (Greek *basileuō*, from *basileus*, "king") comes (through the French *régner*) from the Latin *rex* (root *reg-*), "king"; it thus means "to reign as kings." Believers will be kings with Christ in the period (literally or figuratively "thousand years") between his parousia (19:11–21) and the new heavens and earth (21:1–8).

## 8.8 The Messianic Kingdom in Revelation
### 8.8.1 Revelation 11:15–18

"Then the seventh angel blew his trumpet, and there were loud voices in heaven, saying, 'The kingdom of the world has become the kingdom of our Lord and of his Christ, and he shall reign forever and ever.' And the twenty-four elders who sit on their thrones before God fell on their faces and worshiped God, saying, 'We give thanks to you, Lord God Almighty, who is and who was, for you have taken your great power and begun to reign [one word: *ebasileusas*: commenced your rule over the kingdom; see further in §8.8.3]. The nations raged, but your wrath came, and the time for the dead to be judged, and for rewarding your servants, the prophets and saints, and those who fear your name, both small and great, and for destroying the destroyers of the earth.'"

Remarkably, God and Christ are linked together in their royal rule. It is the kingdom of our Lord and of his Christ. The name "Lord" refers here unequivocally to the divine name YHWH, already in the Septuagint rendered as *kyrios*. It is God who lays the world at the feet of his Anointed. Psalm 8 says, "... the son of man ... you have made him a little lower than the heavenly beings and crowned him with glory and honor. You have given him dominion over the works of your hands; you have put all things under his feet" (vv. 4-6). These words, which refer here primarily to the first man, the first Adam, are applied in Hebrews 2:5-9 to the Second Man, the Last Adam, the anointed Son of Man.

A second remarkable point is the phrase "he shall reign" (*basileusei*, sing.): the "he" who will reign refers back to both "our Lord" and "his Christ." That is, the "he" who reigns is God reigning through the Son of Man (cf. "may our God and Father ... and our Lord Jesus direct our way to you" [1 Thess. 3:11] and "may our Lord Jesus Christ himself and God our Father ... comfort your hearts" [2 Thess. 2:16], where the verbs are singular, as if speaking of just one person.)[82]

A similar apparent confusion of God and Christ is implied in Revelation 11:17 in the expression "Lord God Almighty" (*kyrie ho theos ho pantokratōr*; cf. Heb. *Adonai El Shaddai*). He is described as the One "who is and who was." The "who is" is a reference to his eternal existence (cf. YHWH, "I am," Exod. 3:14-15), and the "who was" is a reference to

---

82. The epistle of 1 John contains several examples where a singular form of a verb might refer to either God or Christ, either to the Father or the Son, or to both in one passage; see, e.g., 2:24-25; 2:28-29; 3:1-2. See Ouweneel (2007b, 200, 273).

his relationship with the Old Testament believers on earth. Now the remarkable thing is that Revelation 1:8 says, "who is and who was and *who is to come*, the Almighty," and 4:8, "the Lord God Almighty, who was and is and *is to come*." The One who "is to come" is in Revelation unequivocally Christ—but he is here identified with the Lord God Almighty (cf. §5.3.1). The Man Christ Jesus *is* God the Son, *Adonai El Shaddai*. It reminds us of Daniel 7, where in verse 13 it is the Son of Man who "came," but in verse 22 it is the Ancient of Days who "came." The Son of Man *is* at the same time the Ancient of Days, more specifically God the Son. According to his divine nature, the "Lord" who, as a *Man*, was crucified at Jerusalem (Rev. 11:8) is the same as the One mentioned in verse 15 "our Lord" (though here distinguished from the *Man* "Christ"), and in verse 17 "Lord God Almighty."

In Revelation 11, the addition "who is to come" would have been superfluous because the Lord is viewed here as having come already: he *has* received his great power and *has* begun to reign. And this "he" is the Almighty God, and at the same time the Son of Man, who *is* God the Son.

### 8.8.2 Revelation 12:10

"And I heard a loud voice in heaven, saying, 'Now the salvation and the power and the kingdom of our God and the authority of his Christ have come.'"

The "power and the kingdom" might be taken here as a hendiadys: the "powerful kingdom." We have clear-cut examples of this grammatical phenomenon in New Testament Greek: "the Holy Spirit and power" (Acts 10:38), that is, "the power of the Holy Spirit"; "power and coming" (2 Pet. 1:16), that is, "powerful coming." It is also possible to take the *kai* here to be explicative: "the power, viz., the kingdom" (cf. 2 Cor. 1:22 and 5:5 [KJV], the "earnest of the Spirit," that is, the "earnest, viz., the Spirit"; NKJV: "the Spirit as a guarantee"). Whatever the case may be, the Messianic kingdom of God, as it will begin at Christ's parousia, will be the greatest possible revelation of divine power, glory, and majesty. Compare similar passages: "For Yours is the kingdom and the power and the glory forever" (Matt. 6:13b NKJV). "[T]here are some standing here who will not taste death until they see the kingdom of God after it has come with power" (Mark 9:1). "[T]he kingdom of God does not consist in talk [idle words] but in power" (1 Cor. 4:20).

We hear in Revelation 12:10, on the one hand, about "the kingdom of our God," and on the other hand, about "the authority of his Christ [Messiah, Anointed One]," but there can hardly be much difference between the two expressions. Just as in Revelation 11:15-18, it is the kingdom of *God*, in which his Messiah (Anointed One) exercises the actual royal power, on behalf of God and for his glory. It remains *God's* kingdom, but he has entrusted the authority (power) over it to his Anointed One. (Cf. Matt. 13: the kingdom of the Son of Man [v. 41] is identical with the kingdom of the Father [v. 43].) God had anointed Jesus with the power of the Holy Spirit (Acts 10:38), and now he entrusts to this anointed King the power over his kingdom.

## 8.8.3 Revelation 19:6

"Then I heard what seemed to be the voice of a great multitude, like the roar of many waters and like the sound of mighty peals of thunder, crying out, 'Hallelujah! For the Lord our God the Almighty reigns [or, has begun to reign; Greek *ebasileusen*; cf. 11:17].'"

## The Spreading of the Kingdom

We find here the same name of God (*kyrios ho theos ho pantokratōr* [cf. Heb. *Adonai El Shaddai*]) that we found earlier. This is a common name for God: "God Almighty" (first used in Gen. 17:1), but we saw that in Revelation 1:8 and 4:8 it is God Almighty who "is to come," and this refers to God's Anointed One, the Messiah. Therefore, immediately after 19:6 we have the description of the wedding of the Lamb (vv. 7-9), and this same Lamb is called a bit later: "King of kings and Lord of lords" (v. 16; cf. 17:14). In the end, saying that the kingdom is God's is the same as saying that the kingdom is the Son of Man's. It is *God* (the Triune God!) who will come to establish the Messianic kingdom, and the One who does come is the Messiah, the Son of Man, who in his person is God the Son.

As far as the form *ebasileusen* is concerned (cf. *ebasileusas* in 11:17): it would normally be rendered as "*has* reigned," but in 11:17 and 19:6 it must be rendered as "has begun to reign" (an ingressive aorist). Thus, here it does not mean "reigns (since the remote past, always, uninterruptedly, forever)" (a gnomic aorist). Of course, in itself it is true that God reigns from eternity to eternity (cf. Exod. 15:18); one might even assume this meaning in Revelation 19:6 because the verse speaks of God's kingship, not Christ's. As long as Christ has not appeared in person, his kingship is not referred to in Revelation 19 (see vv. 15-16; 20:4). However, we have to consider the fact that Christ himself is included in the title "Lord God Almighty" (*kyrios ho theos ho pantokratōr*) referring to the Triune God (cf. for this combination also Rev. 4:8; 11:17; 15:3; 16:7; 21:22). Moreover, we saw that in 1:8 and 4:8 the Almighty God is the One "who is to come," namely, in the person of the Christ. Therefore, the aorist in 19:6 seems to refer to this very fact that God is on the verge of establishing his kingship in "his Christ" (cf. 11:15).

This prophecy is all the more striking when we consider the fact that, according to many expositors, it was written during the time of the very powerful emperor Domitian, who had called himself "Lord and God" (Latin, *dominus et deus*; Greek, *kyrios kai theos*).[83]

### 8.8.4 Revelation 22:3-5

"No longer will there be anything accursed [in the new Jerusalem], but the throne of God and of the Lamb will be in it, and his servants will worship him. They will see his face, and his name will be on their foreheads. And night will be no more. They will need no light of lamp or sun, for the Lord God will be their light, and they will reign forever and ever."

Near the end of Revelation, we hear once more of the kingdom of God, now with the emphasis on the role of God's servants in it. In my view, it follows from Revelation 21:9 that the New Jerusalem is the bride of the Lamb, that is, the church of the living God. At the same time, it appears to be the heavenly capital of the Lamb's kingdom (cf. Heb. 11:10, 16. 12:22; 13:14; also cf. Gal. 4:25-26).[84] The servants are here called *douloi*, literally, "slaves, bondmen." Since the KJV, the cognate verb, *douleuō*, has often been

---

83. Suetonius, *Domitian*, 13.
84. See more extensively, Ouweneel (2012a, §§11.4.2, 11.6).

rendered "to serve (as a slave)," but in the present verse the verb is not *douleuō*, but *latreuō*, "to render priestly service" (cf. Matt. 4:10; Luke 2:37; 4:8; Acts 24:14; 26:7; 27:23; Phil. 3:3; 2 Tim. 1:3; Heb. 9:9, 14; 10:2; 12:28; for the cognate noun *latreia*, "priestly service," see Rom. 9:4; 12:1; Heb. 9:1, 6). It is a holy service of praise and worship, rendered by God's servants forever and ever.

Perhaps the name on the servants' foreheads (v. 4) is the same associated with the high priest: "Holy to the LORD" (Exod. 28:36-38), signifying complete devotion in one's priestly service.[85] The servants are king-priests (cf. 1:5-6; 5:9-10), who render a service of worship to the King of kings and Lord of lords: kings worshiping the King, lords worshiping the Lord. Notice again the singular "him," which refers back to both "God" and "the Lamb."

The expression, "They will see his face," is fitting for servants of the King. In Esther 1:14 the vassals—who are princes themselves—of king Ahasuerus "saw the king's face," that is, were very close to him (ERV); "the inner circle with access to the king's ear" (MSG) (cf. 2 Sam. 14:24, 32 NKJV). In Matthew 18:10 it is said of certain angels that they "always see the face of my [i.e., Jesus'] Father who is in heaven." "Seeing someone's face" thus means: "being in the service of," or perhaps rather: "belonging to the intimate company of." Revelation 22:3-5 refers to servants who will remain servants (slaves, bondmen) of God, but who at the same time are kings, and will remain kings: *kings* over God's world, and *slaves* of the King

---

85. Swete (1951, 301).

of kings. As everlasting as is the kingdom of God (Dan. 7:13-14; 2 Pet. 1:11), so everlasting is the rule by God's servants.

# Chapter 9
# Faith, Hope, and Love in the Kingdom

> *[The apostles were] strengthening the souls of the disciples, encouraging them to continue in the faith,*
> *and saying that through many tribulations we must enter the kingdom of God.*
> Acts 14:22

> *[H]as not God chosen those who are poor in the world to be rich in faith and heirs of the kingdom, which he has promised to those who love him? . . .*
> *If you really fulfill the royal law according to the Scripture, "You shall love your neighbor as yourself," you are doing well.*
> James 2:5, 8

***Summary:*** *The apostle Paul speaks of three vital elements of the Christian life, which are also characteristic of the kingdom of God: faith, hope, and love. Faith (confidence) is needed to enter the kingdom, to endure the hardships of the kingdom, to experience and apply the power of the kingdom. Some disciples have little faith, some have a growing faith, some have a great faith. Hope keeps the disciple going: through the persecutions and tribulations, he remains focused upon the forthcoming parousia of the King, and the establishment of his kingdom in power and glory. The Christian hope is always oriented to the coming kingdom, not to the intermediate state (between death and resurrection). Love is the most characteristic principle: love between the Father and the Son, between God and his subjects (who are his children), between Christ and his church, and the love of the disciples to God, to their King, and last but not least, to each other. This mutual love is the main attribute of the true disciples.*

## 9.1 The Kingdom and Practical Faith
### 9.1.1 Sight and Faith

A NUMBER OF ASPECTS of the kingdom of God can be conveniently illustrated by means of the well-known triad of 1 Corinthians 13:13, faith, hope, and love. The term "faith" in chapter 13 points back to verse 2: "[I]f I have all faith, so as to remove mountains, but have not love, I am nothing." This statement goes back to words by Jesus himself: "[I]f you have faith like a grain of mustard seed, you will say to this mountain, 'Move from here to there,' and it will move, and nothing will be impossible for you" (Matt. 17:20; cf. 21:21). One chapter before, 1 Corinthians 12:9, faith is one of the *charismata* (portions of *charis*, "grace") of the Holy Spirit.

The second element in 1 Corinthians 13:13, hope, points back to verses 10 and 12: "[W]hen the perfect comes, the partial will pass away. . . . For now we see in a mirror dimly, but then face to face. Now I know in part; then I shall know fully, even as I have been fully known." The third element, love, is the actual subject of the entire chapter; I quote only verses 4-7: "Love is patient and kind; love does not envy or boast; it is not arrogant or rude. It does not insist on its own way; it is not irritable or resentful; it does not rejoice at wrongdoing, but rejoices with the truth. Love bears all things, believes all things, hopes all things, endures all things."

If we speak of faith here, this does not refer to what is called "saving faith." Rather, it is the practical confidence with which a follower of Jesus endures all the troubles and tribulations of the kingdom of God in its present form. Peter speaks of "you, who by God's power are being guarded *through faith* for a salvation ready to be revealed in the last time. In this you rejoice, though now for a little while, if necessary, you have been grieved by various trials, so that the *tested genuineness of your faith*—more precious than gold that perishes though it is tested by fire—may be found to result in praise and glory and honor at the *revelation of Jesus Christ*. Though you have not seen him, you love him. Though you do not now see him, you believe in him and rejoice with joy that is inexpressible and filled with glory, obtaining the outcome of your faith, the salvation of your souls" (1 Pet. 1:5-9).

Peter speaks of a salvation that will be "revealed in the last time" (v. 5), that is, the end time that issues in the Messianic kingdom, namely, at the "revelation" of

Christ (v. 7), that is, his parousia (cf. 1:13; 4:14; Rom. 2:5; 1 Cor. 1:7; 2 Thess. 1:7), or his "appearance" or "appearing" (2 Thess. 2:8; 1 Tim. 6:14; 2 Tim. 4:1; Titus 2:13). As long as this has not yet taken place, Jesus' followers will have to walk by faith. In my view, Peter has written his first letter particularly to Jewish believers.[1] For them it was very hard to accept the idea of a kingdom with an invisible, absent King. They had grown up with the thought that the kingdom would arrive at the moment the Messiah would come. He would sit on the throne of David, and then peace and righteousness would enter the world. He would reign in power and majesty, and all would see him.

This is exactly what will happen one day (Rev. 1:7). However, in the meantime it is inevitable that there are those who still wonder whether Jesus is the Messiah sent by God and bringing in the kingdom of God. There is not yet enough to *see* (in spite of all signs and wonders even today). In 2 Corinthians 5:7 it is said, "we walk by faith, not by sight." To grasp what is seen, one does not need faith. Conversely, what is *not* seen can at most be believed. "[F]aith is ... the conviction of things not seen" (Heb. 11:1). The less that one can perceive of the kingdom of God—as long as it has not yet been established in power and majesty—the greater is the need for faith on the part of Jesus' followers, and the more precious is this faith to God (1 Pet. 1:7).

### 9.1.2 Believing in Jesus

In John 14:1, Jesus says to his disciples, "You believe in God; believe also in me" (NIV). This does not mean that from now on they had to come to the faith that Jesus

---

1. See, e.g., Guthrie (1981, 794-95); cf. Gal. 2:9; 1 Pet. 1:1.

was the Messiah and the Son of God, for this they had believed for several years (cf., e.g., Matt. 16:16). Apparently, Jesus wanted to say that he was going to leave them, and thus a new situation was going to begin for them.[2] Immediately he adds that he would go the house of his Father (v. 2). Jesus prepares his disciples for this because his return to the Father would also change the relationship between him and his followers. From now on, they would have to believe in him, the invisible One, about whom they would have to accept all kinds of things that they would not be able to see for themselves. After his death, resurrection and ascension—of which they had been witnesses—they would have to believe that he had returned to his Father, that he sat at God's right hand, that he was there as their Advocate, and that one day he would return to establish his kingdom in power and glory. They would not be able to see these realities, and thus had to accept them in faith.

To be sure, some people have seen *something*: Stephen (Acts 7:56), Paul (18:9; 22:17-18; 1 Cor. 9:2), Ananias (Acts 9:10), and John (Rev. 1:12-17) saw the glorified Christ in visions, or at least they heard his voice (Acts 9:4-7; 23:11). Moreover, Peter, John, and James had received glimpses of the future Messianic kingdom during the transfiguration on the mountain (Luke 9:27-36; cf. Peter's own comment in 2 Pet. 1:16-19). Yet, on the whole, when it comes to the present position of Christ, believers must live by faith.

Faith is characteristic of the kingdom of God in its present form. It is a kingdom not with a Messiah sitting on the throne of David here on earth, in Jerusalem, but

---

2. Kelly (1966, 282-83).

THE ETERNAL KINGDOM: LIVING UNDER CHRIST

with a Messiah sitting on the throne of his Father in heaven. Jesus clearly distinguishes between the two: "The one who conquers, I *will* grant him to sit with me on *my* throne, as I also conquered and *sat* down with my Father on *his* throne" (Rev. 3:21). The text speaks of two different thrones, at two different times. In the *coming day*, during the Messianic kingdom, Jesus will sit on his own throne; this is the throne of David at Jerusalem (Isa. 9:7; Luke 1:32; typologically, 1 Kgs. 2:12, 24, 33, 45). This throne is also called the "throne of Israel" (1 Kgs. 8:20, 25; 9:5; 2 Chron. 6:10, 16), and also the "throne of the LORD" (1 Chron. 29:23). However, *today* Jesus does not yet sit on his own throne, the throne of David (cf. the "glorious throne" of Matt. 25:31), but in heaven, on the throne of his Father, at his right hand. This heavenly throne is never called the throne of Jesus Christ, or of the Son of Man, or of the Son of David, or of the Son of God. They are two different thrones. All people will be able to see his future session; his present session no one on earth can see (apart from the glimpses mentioned that a few have received).[3]

Throughout the centuries, orthodox Jews have used the same arguments to claim that Jesus could not be the Messiah.[4] If he had been the Messiah, he would have fulfilled the prophecies, he would sit on the throne of David at Jerusalem, and there would be peace and justice

---

3. Also notice the prophetic glimpses of Isa. (6:1, "I saw the Lord sitting upon a throne, high and lifted up"; cf. John 12:41, "Isaiah ... saw his [i.e., Christ's] glory and spoke of him") and Ezekiel (1:26, "above the expanse ... there was the likeness of a throne ...; and seated above the likeness of a throne was a likeness with a human appearance").
4. See, e.g., www.simpletoremember.com/articles/a/jewsandjesus#1.

in the world. In principle, this is perfectly correct, of course—except in one respect. Jesus himself has explained that the kingdom of power and glory would arrive only at his parousia. To him had been given all authority in heaven and on earth (Matt. 28:18), but this authority, and the effects thereof, will become visible only when he returns. In the meantime, we are to live by our faith. "The righteous shall live by his faith" (Hab. 2:4b). Jesus' followers must believe Jesus' own words, or the testimony of those who have recorded his words, that he is now in heaven, and that one day he will return. Jesus has already fulfilled many prophecies; faith knows that at his parousia he will fulfill all the rest.

### 9.1.3 Powerful Believing

Such a faith is inconceivable without the power of the Holy Spirit. Therefore, Jesus spoke of the Spirit during his teaching on the kingdom of God: "So when they had come together, they asked him, 'Lord, will you at this time restore the kingdom to Israel?' He said to them, 'It is not for you to know times or seasons that the Father has fixed by his own authority. But you will receive power when the Holy Spirit has come upon you, and you will be my witnesses in Jerusalem and in all Judea and Samaria, and to the end of the earth'" (Acts 1:6-8). The kingdom is an empire full of power (1 Cor. 4:20); Hebrews 6:5 speaks of the "powers of the [Messianic] age to come." The Messiah is not there yet, the kingdom has not yet been established in glory and majesty, but the *powers* of this future kingdom are there already. This is the power of the Holy Spirit.

This power is not yet present in the same measure as in the Messianic kingdom. For instance, in this glorious kingdom no inhabitant will say, "I am sick" (Isa. 33:24). This wonderful time has not yet arrived—but already there is so much power that those who *wish* to believe can receive much help (see, e.g., Matt. 8:10; 9:22, 29; 15:28; Mark 5:36; 9:24; Acts 3:16; James 5:15). No one can see Jesus at the right hand of God. But every miracle in the power of the Holy Spirit is a sign of his real presence in heaven.

This evidence of the presence of the Spirit's power was present when Jesus himself was still on earth—both in his own ministry and in that of his followers—and it was present after he had ascended to heaven.

(a) He proclaimed "the gospel of the kingdom and healing every disease and every affliction among the people" (Matt. 4:23; cf. 9:35). "[I]f it is by the Spirit of God that I cast out demons, then the kingdom of God has come upon you" (Matt. 12:28).

(b) Jesus sent out the apostles, and commanded them to proclaim: "'The kingdom of heaven is at hand.' Heal the sick, raise the dead, cleanse lepers, cast out demons" (10:7-8). Similarly to the seventy-two, he said: "Heal the sick in [any town] and say to them, 'The kingdom of God has come near to you'" (Luke 10:9-10).

(c) "So then the *Lord* Jesus, after he had spoken to them, was taken up into heaven and sat down at the right hand of God. And they went out and preached everywhere, while the *Lord* worked with them and confirmed the message by accompanying signs" (Mark 16:19-20).

## 9.2 A Threefold Cord
### 9.2.1 Seeking the Kingdom

Kingdom, faith, and the Holy Spirit form an important triad, like the "threefold cord" of Ecclesiastes 4:12. Without the Spirit, people will not come to faith in the glorified Lord. The Spirit convicts "the world concerning sin and righteousness and judgment: concerning sin, because they do not believe in me; concerning righteousness, because I go to the Father, and you will see me no longer; concerning judgment, because the ruler of this world is judged" (John 16:8–11).

These three things can be accepted by faith only, and the Holy Spirit works this faith in the hearts of Jesus' disciples. He is even called the "Spirit of faith" (2 Cor. 4:13 BRG, JUB—unless a human "spirit of faith" is intended here). Being "full of faith" and being "full of the Holy Spirit" (cf. Acts 6:5; 11:24) therefore go hand in hand. But the reverse is true as well: there can be no genuine life in the power of the Spirit without sufficient faith. When someone is "of little faith" (Matt. 6:30; 8:26; 14:31; 16:8; 17:20), that is, has little practical confidence in God, there is also little power to perform any good work. Jesus' response to "little faith" is this, among other things: "*[S]eek first the kingdom of God* and his righteousness, and all these things will be added to you" (Matt. 6:33). Be focused upon God's kingdom, and God will do all the rest.

Of course, when Jesus spoke these words in the Sermon on the Mount, there was not yet a glorified Messiah at God's right hand in heaven. In those days, Jesus' words in Matthew 6:33 could not mean much more than this: submit to God's rule in your life, pursue his righteousness, that is, either the righteousness that is proper to him, or that he demands of you. Earlier in this Sermon, Jesus had spoken of those who "hunger and thirst for righteousness" (5:10). In their thinking, not physical hunger and thirst must come first, but their ardent aching for the righteousness of the kingdom of God. This is the message that Jesus utters in 6:33: Do become a real *tsaddiq* ("righteous one") in the kingdom of God, according to the Torah of the kingdom (cf. James 2:8), and God will do the rest. He will not fail the righteous: "I have not seen the righteous forsaken" (Ps. 37:25). If the *tsaddiq* "walks righteously and speaks uprightly . . . his bread will be given him; his water will be sure" (Isa. 33:15–16). If a person is of little faith, the world might prevail over him. If he has a great faith, he will overcome the world (cf. 1 John 5:4), just as Jesus has overcome the world (John 16:33).

After Jesus' ascension, his "Seek first the kingdom of God" has acquired an even much deeper meaning. As a Man, Jesus accomplished the work of redemption, and as a Man God gave him the glory that he, as the Son, had possessed with the Father from all eternity (John 17:5).[5] The Man Jesus Christ, glorified at God's right hand, has control over all things. Jesus wants his followers to preach everywhere that he has all authority in heaven and on earth (Matt. 28:18–19)—but then they themselves must begin believing this in everyday circumstances.

This is what the apostles did. The first time "faith" or "believing" occurs in Acts, it refers to what is called "saving faith" (2:44). But the second time the term refers to practical confidence in God (3:16): Jesus' "name—by

---

5. See Ouweneel (2007b, 430–33).

*faith* in his name—has made this man strong whom you see and know, and the *faith* that is through Jesus has given the man this perfect health in the presence of you all." Here we see, for the first time since the Holy Spirit was poured out, that faith has practical, concrete power. On the one hand, Jesus' name worked the miracle, but on the other hand, Peter and John's faith in this name did it. A wonderful example of God's sovereign grace and human responsibility working together!

The kingdom of God had truly arrived, though only in preliminary form. Even in *this* form of the kingdom the power of the Holy Spirit is present. However, in the description of the lame man's healing, the Spirit is not mentioned at all: *faith* is at work (albeit in the power of the Spirit). The "name" of Jesus has healed the man, but this worked through Peter and John's *faith* in this name; it worked as a kind of "antenna" through which the power of the Lord could flow to the paralyzed man (see §9.2.3). The name as such was not enough; Jesus' followers had to attach their faith to it, so to speak. The power of the kingdom works through its subjects.

### 9.2.2 Great Faith

Peter had said to the lame man, "What *I* do have I give to you" (v. 6), not "What *God* has." Of course, in itself this latter would have been correct, but the emphasis here is not on what God could do for this lame man but what the apostles in faith could do for him now that they had received the Holy Spirit and faith. Peter and John had received something in order to pass it on, namely, the power of the age to come (Heb. 6:5), the power of the kingdom of God (1 Cor. 4:20), the power of the Holy

Spirit (cf. Mic. 3:8; Acts 1:8; 10:38; 1 Cor. 2:4; 1 Thess. 1:5). When, after the healing, Peter addressed the people, he did indeed refer to this kingdom of God, which would arrive as soon as the people would repent: "Repent therefore, and turn back, that your sins may be blotted out, that times of refreshing may come from the presence of the Lord, and that he may send the Christ appointed for you, Jesus, whom heaven must receive until the time for restoring all the things about which God spoke by the mouth of his holy prophets long ago" (vv. 19–21).

Peter and John had a "great faith." Earlier, Jesus had explained what this means. In Matthew we find two persons who are said to have had a "great faith," and both of them were non-Jews, who because of their great faith were admitted to the kingdom of God. A Roman centurion had a sick servant, for whom he requested Jesus' help (Matt. 8:5-13). But when Jesus offered to come to him the centurion thought this to be unnecessary. A simple command would be sufficient; whether this was given nearby or from afar did not matter (cf. the contrast with Luke 8:41; John 4:47–49). Now this was typical of a great faith, which feature Jesus said was found nowhere in Israel (v. 10). The "great" thing in it was this: a great faith has such a clear view of Jesus' own greatness that it expects great things of him through just one word. Jesus is so great that he merely had to do something "little" to cause great things to happen. A faith that has a deep awareness of Jesus' greatness is a great faith.

Jesus made clear that this is the kind of faith that a person needs for the kingdom of heaven. People like this centurion "will come from east and west and recline at table with Abraham, Isaac, and Jacob" during the great banquet in the kingdom of heaven, when this will have arrived in power and majesty (v. 11; cf. Isa. 25:6). And many people for whom the kingdom was originally intended, the "sons of the kingdom," will stay outside through their own fault (v. 12). They will even lose this title, since it will be transferred to the true subjects of the kingdom, who will be brought in from the entire world: "The field is the world, and the good seed is the sons of the kingdom" (13:38). Thus, Matthew shows his Jewish readers why so many Jews have remained outside the kingdom, whereas so many Gentiles have found a place in it.

The second example is in Matthew 15:22-28. This story is about a Canaanite woman, whose daughter was severely oppressed by a demon. She came to Jesus, who first pretended not to hear her. Finally he said that he "was sent only to the lost sheep of the house of Israel" (v. 24; think again of Matthew's Jewish readers!). But the woman knelt before him, and argued that, when the children (i.e., the Israelites) are eating bread at the table, the crumbs that fall from the table are eaten by the dogs (i.e., the Gentiles). Her point was: one crumb will be enough to heal my daughter. Here we find the same principle as with the centurion. To him one word sufficed, to the woman one crumb sufficed, to bring about the miracle. The greater that Jesus is in someone's sight, the less that person needs from him in order to experience great wonders. Jesus said, "O woman, great is your faith! Be it done for you as you desire" (v. 28). Please note: he does not say, Be it done according to God's sovereign will (although this is not excluded, of course), but according to *her* believing will.

### 9.2.3 Miracle-Working Faith

On other occasions as well, Matthew shows us that a miracle depends not only on God's sovereign power or will, but also on a person's faith. Jesus told the centurion, "[L]et it be done for you *as you have believed*" (Matt. 8:13; CEV: "Your faith has made it happen"). When Jesus saw the faith of the four friends who brought a paralytic friend to him, he granted the man forgiveness as well as healing (9:2). He said to a sick woman and to two sick men who had received healing, as well as to a sinful woman who had received forgiveness: "Your *faith* has made you well" (Matt. 9:22; Luke 17:19; Mark 10:52; Luke 7:50). Here, "making well" (Greek *sōzō*) has the sense of both "saving" and "healing."

In all such situations, faith—whether that of the minister, or the friends, or the parents, or the sick, or the sinful—is the "antenna" through which the power of God can flow to the person who needs it. If there is no antenna, a radio cannot work. If there is no faith within a given situation, God's power does not become active: Jesus "did not do many mighty works [at Nazareth], because of their unbelief" (Matt. 13:58; Mark 6:5 even says, "he *could* do no mighty work there").

When Jesus met two blind men, he said to them, "Do you believe that I am able to do this?" They said to him, "Yes, Lord." Then he touched their eyes, saying, "*According to your faith* be it done to you" (Matt. 9:28–29). That is, *because* you have believed (CEV, etc.), or, after the *measure* of your faith. Of the crippled man at Lystra we read, "He listened to Paul speaking. And Paul, looking intently at him and seeing that *he had faith to be made well* [*sōzō*], said in a loud voice, 'Stand upright on your feet.' And he sprang up and began walking" (Acts 14:9-10). Paul's "seeing" here may be an example of what in 1 Corinthians 12 is called a "word of knowledge" (v. 8) or the "discerning of spirits" (v.10 NKJV).

Jesus taught Jairus, "Do not fear, only *believe*" (Mark 5:36). The father of the boy with the unclean spirit said to Jesus, "If you can do anything, have compassion on us and help us." But Jesus answered, "'If you can'! All things are possible for one who *believes*" (9:22-23). The father made the miracle dependent of Jesus' ability. But Jesus shifted the responsibility back to the father himself: the miracle would depend on the man's faith. Not only is Jesus' ability or God's sovereign grace the measure for kingdom miracles, but so too is the faith that the recipient needs to have according to his own responsibility. A person receives in proportion to his faith, and gives in proportion to his faith (Acts 3:6; cf. v. 16; cf. Rom. 12:6). The greater the faith, the greater the miracles he may expect in God's kingdom. In all the cases mentioned, objectively the power of the Holy Spirit, but subjectively the faith of the people concerned, are both the key to the kingdom miracle. Faith is the "channel" through which the Spirit's power can "flow."

The examples that we find in the Gospels usually involve healings and deliverances. But of course, the kingdom of God involves many more miraculous works of God than these. Disciples of the King need faith for *all* breakthroughs in God's kingdom. Thus, in Luke 8:22–25 Jesus quieted a storm, and said to his disciples, "Where is your faith?" It is therefore understandable that, on another occasion, the disciples asked, "Increase our faith" (Greek *Prosthes hēmin pistin*, lit., "Increase to us faith"; cf. DLNT, WYC). Jesus' response seems to be rather discouraging: "If you had faith like a grain of mustard seed, you could say to this mulberry tree, 'Be uprooted and planted in the sea,' and it would obey you" (v. 6). This may sound as if Jesus wanted to say, Faith as *small* as a mustard seed (cf. Matt. 13:32).[6] But it does not say this, and it is not necessarily Jesus' intention. If someone has faith like a mustard seed, this will profit him only if he puts that seed into the ground. Faith like a mustard seed is faith that he may invest in God, so that it will bud and grow, and perhaps will become a tree (cf. the same in Matt. 13:32). Faith must never be pictured as a kind of independent power in itself; faith is always *in* someone or something. If the disciple invests his faith in King Jesus, it is Jesus who will produce miracles from that faith for the furtherance and expansion of the kingdom.

In 1 Corinthians 12:9, faith is one of the five *charismata* (literally as much as "portions of grace"). These allotments of grace are not permanent talents, abilities, and capacities, but gifts of grace that God grants at a given time, when a person needs them, depending on the circumstances in which he finds himself.[7] This is the tremendous faith that Elijah had, who challenged the

---

6. Thus, e.g., Geldenhuys (1983, 432); Green (1997, 613); more nuanced: France (2007, 662–63 (on Matt. 17:20).
7. See Ouweneel (2007a, 314–15).

priests of Baal to bring fire come down from heaven, and finally Elijah himself had the courage, in the presence of all the people, to ask God for this fire (1 Kgs. 18). This is the "shield of faith" that the follower of Jesus needs in order to achieve spiritual breakthroughs during the advance of God's kingdom, in direct opposition to every show of strength and all artifices of the evil powers (Eph. 6:11, 16).

## 9.3 Kingdom Hope[8] in the Old Testament
### 9.3.1 Genesis

Several times we have considered the fact that many Christians have been brought up with their eye of faith directed toward heaven as the blissful place where believers go when they fall asleep in death. Before the Reformation, Dante Alighieri (1265-1321) and Thomas à Kempis (c. 1380-1471) were among those who contributed to this picture. After the Reformation perhaps no writer did so more than John Bunyan (1628-1688). His *The Pilgrims' Progress* describes the Christian's pilgrimage on his way to the "celestial city," which the believer reaches when he passes away.[9] To Christians who have been formed by this presentation of things, it may come as a surprise that Scripture virtually *never* speaks in this vein. First, the Old Testament *nowhere* speaks of a blessed state of believers between their death and resurrection, as I have tried to show elsewhere.[10] The hope of the Old Testament believer is *al-*

---

8. Cf. Chia (2005, chapter 8); Wright (2008); this is the more popular version of the extensive Wright (2003).
9. For a modern edition, see Bunyan (2003).
10. Ouweneel (2012a, chapters 1-2).

*ways* focused upon the Messianic kingdom. Here I mention some striking examples.

(a) *Genesis 5:24.* "Enoch walked with God, and he was not, for God took him." Notice the unfounded addition in AMP: ". . . [away to be home with Him]." There is nothing in the Old Testament to warrant such an addition (cf. Heb. 11:5). Nor is it an "ascension to heaven," as we read about in 2 Kings 2:11, "Elijah went up by a whirlwind into heaven." These passages do not tell us anything about where believers go when they die, because both Enoch and Elijah passed away *without* dying. Aart Moerkerken is therefore totally mistaken in claiming that when believers die, they are taken up to heaven "like an Enoch and an Elijah."[11]

(b) *Genesis 49:18.* In the midst of blessing his sons, Jacob exclaims, "I wait for your salvation, O LORD." Although the confusion arises more easily in the older Dutch translations (which read *zaligheid* ["blissfulness"] instead of "salvation"), even English writers have thought of heaven. Thus Matthew Henry writes: "Jacob, almost spent, and ready to faint, relieves himself with those words, I have waited for thy salvation, O Lord! The salvation he waited for was Christ, the promised Seed; now that he was going to be gathered to his people, he breathes after Him to whom the gathering of the people shall be. He declared plainly that he sought heaven, the better country, Heb 11:13,14. Now he is going to enjoy the salvation, he comforts himself that he had waited for the salvation. Christ, as our way to heaven, is to be waited on; and heaven, as our rest in Christ, is to be waited for. It is the comfort of a dying saint thus to have

---

11. Moerkerken (2004, 228).

waited for the salvation of the Lord; for then he shall have what he has been waiting for."[12] Much more recently, Victor P. Hamilton sees in the verse "a ringing testimony by the elderly patriarch to his renewed faith in God that he shall one day be delivered by his God and experience eternal salvation."[13]

Others have rightly grasped that the verse has nothing to do with going to heaven but everything with the future salvation of Israel in the Messianic kingdom. In a general sense, the *Geneva Study Bible* says, "Seeing the miseries that his posterity would fall into, he bursts out in prayer to God to remedy it." According to John H. Sailhamer, Jacob's words point to the fact that in "the individual and future destiny of the sons [of Jacob] is embodied the hope of all Israel. That hope is of a future prosperity for the nation and a future victory over their enemies. At the center of that hope is the king from the tribe of Judah."[14] Jacob's words contain his expectation of the Messianic kingdom, which would involve the complete salvation of his descendants, the people of God.

Two keys to this interpretation are, first, verse 1, "Gather yourselves together, that I may tell you what shall happen *to you* [i.e., Jacob's sons, and hence: Israel's twelve tribes] *in days to come*"; Genesis 49 is prophecy about Israel! Second, there is the direct reference to the Messiah in verse 10 ("The scepter shall not depart from Judah, nor a lawgiver from between his feet until Shiloh come; and unto Him shall the gathering of the people

---

12. http://biblehub.com/genesis/49-18.htm; on the same page, see also the similar explanation by John Gill.
13. Hamilton (1995, 671).
14. Sailhamer (1990, 278).

be," KJ21), which confirms the prophetic interpretation. We might say that, in verse 18, Jacob represents the faithful part of Israel, which, throughout the ages, looks forward to the ultimate salvation under the Messiah in his kingdom.

### 9.3.2 Asaph and Solomon

(c) *Psalm 73:24*, "You guide me with your counsel, and afterward you will receive me to glory," says Asaph. Of course, Matthew Henry and others think again of the intermediate state (heaven). Even Gerhard von Rad says of this verse, "One may say that here the OT belief in the hereafter finds its purest formulation." Better is John Gill, who mentions the kingdom (although, to him, the kingdom seems to coincide with heaven): "[A]nd afterward receive me to glory; into a glorious place, an house not made with hands, a city whose builder and maker is God, into a kingdom and glory, or a glorious kingdom; and into glorious company, the company of Father, Son, and Spirit, angels and glorified saints, where glorious things will be seen, and a glory enjoyed both in soul and body to all eternity; for this glory is eternal glory, a glory that passes not away."[15]

Hebrew *l-q-ch* does not mean "take *up*" (so HCSB, WYC), which supposedly would refer to heaven, but either "take *away*" (by death; cf. Isa. 53:8), or "receive," namely, in the glory of the coming Messianic kingdom. This again can be taken in two ways: either "*(in)to* glory" (KJV, ESV, NIV, etc.) or "*with* glory" (Vulgate, CEB, WYC). Compare 1 Thessalonians 2:12, "God, who calls you into his own kingdom and glory." Jan Ridderbos

---

15. http://biblehub.com/psalms/73-24.htm.

rightly wonders whether *kavod* "can be by itself a reference to the heavenly glory."[16]

John Gill still points to another, more literal translation of Psalm 73:24b, "[S]ome render it, 'after glory [Hebrew *achar kavod*[17]] thou wilt receive me' [so Henry Hammond]; that is, after all the glory and honour thou hast bestowed upon me here, thou wilt take me to thyself in heaven; so the Targum, 'after the glory is completed, which thou saidst thou wouldst bring upon me, thou wilt receive me,'" namely, (as I take it) in the Messianic kingdom. The glory is then either the glory that God grants the believer during his life, or the glory of the appearing Messiah and the establishment of his kingdom.

(d) *Proverbs 14:32.* "The wicked is overthrown through his evildoing, but the righteous finds refuge in his death." Allen P. Ross believes "this verse may be a shadowy forerunner of that truth" (viz., the hope for immortality).[18] Arndt Meinhold cannot avoid the conclusion that here we see a refuge for the righteous that lies beyond the limits of death.[19] Rashi comments, "When he will die, he is confident that he will come to the Garden of Eden," that is, Paradise.[20] But Ibn Ezra and other Jewish expositors have a simpler explanation: "[T]he righteous man, imbued with trust in God, does not abandon hope though he be in so

---

16. Ridderbos (1958, 247).
17. The very same expression is found in Zech. 2:8, where most translate it "after [the] glory."
18. Ross (1991, 991).
19. Meinhold (1991, I.245).
20. Quoted by Waltke (2004, 608).

desperate a plight that he imagines himself to be at the point of death."[21] Others read (in line with the Septuagint[22]), "[T]hose who do what is right are protected by their honesty" (ICB), or "find a refuge in their integrity" (GNT, MSG, [N]RSV).

(e) *Ecclesiastes 12:5-7*. "[M]an is going to his eternal home ... and the dust returns to the earth as it was, and the spirit returns to God who gave it." For every reader steeped in the Greek dualism of body and soul/spirit—so foreign to Scripture—it is "evident" that the "dust" is the body that descends into the grave, and the soul/spirit goes to the hereafter.[23] However, precisely what is being said in verse 7, what else is this saying than that "the breath [*ruach*] returns to God" (CEV, GNT, LEB, etc.), who gave it in the first place (cf. Gen. 2:7)? And what is someone's "eternal home" in *this* context other than the grave (so ERV, EXB, NIRV, NLT)? Compare 3:19-21, "[W]hat happens to the children of man and what happens to the beasts is the same; as one dies, so dies the other. They all have the same *ruach*, and man has no advantage over the beasts, for all is vanity. All go to one place [!]. All are from the dust, and to dust all return. Who knows whether the *ruach* [breath, CEB, NASB] of man goes upward and the *ruach* of the beast goes down into the earth?"

As to the "eternal home," John Stafford Wright says it speaks of "the inevitable end, the long home of Sheol,[24]

---

21. See Cohen and Rosenberg (1985, 93).
22. It seems to read *betomo* instead of *bemoto*.
23. So, e.g., Aalders (1948, 250-51).
24. Usually, sheol does not mean anything more than the grave; only very rarely is there a glimpse of some hereafter, as in Isa.

inaugurated with the wailing of the professional mourners."[25] So also Tremper Longman: "If 12:1–5b describes old age, then v. 5c climaxes the section by talking about death. Eventually, everyone goes to their *eternal home*, the grave."[26] "Eternal" because in Ecclesiastes the resurrection remains entirely outside the picture; or "eternal" simply means here: "as long as the present age lasts," or even more simply: "for a very long time."

### 9.3.3 Old Testament Hope

A person's view of this earth's future is directly correlated with the hope he has, and the latter depends on that person's view of humanity, of the world, of life.[27] A Marxist or a hedonist has a different hope than a Christian because he has a different view of humanity and the world. But also the Christian who is entirely focused on the heavenly Paradise, in the sense of the intermediate state (between death and resurrection), has a different view than the Christian who is focused on the establishment of God's kingdom in this world. The latter is the hope that was cherished already by Old Testament believers. The former hope is individual—not to say individualistic—and in essence is selfish: it is "my" eternal happiness that matters. The latter hope, that of Jacob and Asaph if I interpret Genesis 49 and Psalm 73 correctly, is collective, and oriented toward the bliss of all

---

14:9, "Sheol beneath is stirred up to meet you [i.e., the king of Babylon] when you come; it rouses the shades to greet you, all who were leaders of the earth."

25. J. S. Wright (1991, 1194).
26. Longman (1998, 272).
27. Doyle (1999, 34).

the people of God in the Messianic kingdom. As Otto Weber put it, "Whenever we speak of the Kingdom of God, the subtlest form of self-centeredness is dismissed from the Christian expectation. The point is not that we are to 'become blessed,' [*selig werden*] that we attain 'immortality,' that we shall participate in 'eternal life,' or that the burdens of our world and our history will be removed from us."[28]

In the hope of the kingdom of God, as depicted in Old and New Testament, the issue is ultimately the highest satisfaction for God *himself*—a joy that he shares with his people. It is the fulfillment of the highest divine wisdom: "I [i.e., the wisdom of God] was beside him, like a master workman, and I was daily his delight, rejoicing before him always, rejoicing in his inhabited world and delighting in the children of man" (Prov. 8:30–31). This is about the *beginning* of the world, but it is all the more true for the *ultimate goal* of the world: "[T]he ransomed of the Lord shall return and come to Zion with singing; everlasting joy shall be upon their heads; they shall obtain gladness and joy, and sorrow and sighing shall flee away" (Isa. 35:10; 51:11). On the one hand, it involves God who "will rejoice [Hebrew *s-i-s*] over you with gladness; he will quiet you by his love; he will exult over you with loud singing" (Zeph. 3:17); on the other hand, it involves his people: "Sing aloud, O daughter of Zion; shout, O Israel! Rejoice [*c-l-z*] and exult with all your heart, O daughter of Jerusalem!" (v. 14).

I just mentioned Marxism; the Old Testament hope has been secularized in a peculiar way by the atheist Jew, Karl Marx (1818–1883), who replaced the hope of

---

28. Weber (1981, 2:676).

the earthly Paradise of God's kingdom with the hope of a communist "paradise." This subject has been taken up by another atheist Jewish philosopher, Ernst Bloch (1885-1977), who even made it the cornerstone of his entire thinking. This is apparent from the title of his three-volume main work, *The Principle of Hope* (1954-1959).[29] Bloch in turn influenced the German theologian Jürgen Moltmann (b. 1926),[30] who connects the concept of hope with the expectation of God's kingdom (see §11.6.1).[31]

The Messianic kingdom, *not* the intermediate state, is our hope (see §9.4): "The Kingdom of God stands at the center of all Christian expectation and it comprehends everything which must be said about it in detail."[32] As Wolfhart Pannenberg put it: "In Israel expectation of God's rule developed as the hope of a future in which God's just will would be done without break or limit, both in Israel itself and also among the nations."[33]

## 9.4 Kingdom Hope in the New Testament
### 9.4.1 The Intermediate State

In contrast with the Old Testament, there are a few references in the New Testament to the blissful state of believers between death and resurrection (see especially Luke 16:19-31; 23:43; 2 Cor. 4:18-5:8; Phil. 1:23; Rev. 6:9-

---

29. See Bloch (1995); cf. how Bauckham and Hart (1999) take up this theme of hope.
30. Moltmann (1993; see also 1976).
31. Regarding Moltmann's eschatology and kingdom theology, see Bauckham (2005) and Bauckham and Guttesen (2009).
32. Weber (1981, 2:675).
33. Pannenberg (1998, 30).

11).³⁴ Several times, however, the Bible passages point beyond the intermediate state to the kingdom of God. Thus, apart from Philippians 1:23 ("be with Christ" in the intermediate state) there is the longing for the resurrection of believers (3:10-11) and the parousia of Christ (3:20-21; 4:5).

Especially in Luke 23:42-43 the connection is striking. The crucified criminal asked, "Jesus, remember me when you come into your kingdom." Jesus responded, "Truly, I say to you, today you will be with me in Paradise." The question by the converted criminal on the cross was entirely in accordance with the Old Testament redemptive hope. He had understood that Jesus was the anointed King (Messiah). Therefore, he concluded that Jesus would necessarily rise from the dead, that he would receive the kingdom from God's hands, and would return in glory and power.³⁵ The man asked if, when that moment arrived, Jesus would remember him, so that he, too, would rise from the dead, and would receive a share in the Messianic kingdom. His eye was focused on the resurrection and the kingdom, not on the intermediate state. All the more striking is Jesus' response, given with emphasis ("Truly, I say to you"): "I promise you that *this very day* you will be with Me in paradise" (VOICE), not only at Jesus' parousia.

Here, the attention is shifted from the parousia to the intermediate state as a comfort for the crucified man. However, we should not generalize this, as if it is better to focus on the intermediate state than on the parousia. Usually it is rather the opposite: on the whole

---

34. See extensively, Ouweneel (2012a, chapters 1-2).
35. Luce (1933, ad loc.).

the New Testament is far more focused on the parousia and the subsequent Messianic kingdom than on the intermediate state. To put it in poignant terms: the intermediate state, no matter how blessed, is destined for those believers who do not have the privilege of living until the parousia and the establishment of the Messianic kingdom. It is the latter that matters; in the Bible, the intermediate state is never an aim in itself. In Philippians 1:23 Paul does not say that Paradise is "far better," but the being "with Christ" is the best thing we can anticipate, and this is what believers will enjoy when they pass away, but also when, at Jesus' parousia, they will be brought into his presence: "I will come again and will take you to myself, that *where I am* you may be also" (John 14:3). "Father, I desire that they also, whom you have given me, may be with me *where I am*" (17:24). "Then we who are alive, who are left, will be caught up together with them in the clouds to meet the Lord in the air, and so we will always be *with the Lord*" (1 Thess. 4:17).

### 9.4.2 Waiting and Longing

The intermediate state is an inevitable reality for those who pass away. It is wonderful for believers but not the goal for which they lived. In the New Testament, the Christian never lives in the joyful expectation of bliss after *his* departure, as so many medieval Christians did and so many present-day Christians still do, but of the bliss after *Jesus'* return. We may even say that the deceased in Paradise, in their disembodied state, do exactly the same as we do: they are *waiting* for this same return of Jesus and his glorious kingdom: "When [the Lamb] opened the fifth seal, I saw under the altar the souls of those who had been slain for the word of God and for the witness they had borne. They cried out with a loud voice, 'O Sovereign Lord, holy and true, how long before you will judge and avenge our blood on those who dwell on the earth?' Then they were each given a white robe and told to rest a little longer, until the number of their fellow servants and their brothers should be complete, who were to be killed as they themselves had been" (Rev. 6:9–11).

It is not only they who, in the hereafter, wait for the Messianic kingdom, but even Jesus, though glorified at God's right hand, is still waiting: "[W]hen Christ had offered for all time a single sacrifice for sins, he sat down at the right hand of God, *waiting* from that time until his enemies should be made a footstool for his feet" (Heb. 10:12–13). Jesus has finished his work on earth, and is now waiting until its full results will become visible in the kingdom of God.

In the New Testament, *phrases* like "waiting for" or "looking for," insofar as they have an eschatological meaning, are exclusively focused on Jesus' parousia and the establishment of his kingdom. Joseph of Arimathea was *looking for* the kingdom of God (Mark 15:43); Simeon was righteous and devout, *waiting for* the consolation of Israel (Luke 2:25); the prophetess Anna and many others were *waiting for* the redemption of Jerusalem (v. 38; cf. 24:21); Paul and all the faithful in Israel had a *hope* in God that there would be a resurrection of both the just and the unjust (Acts 24:15). The creation *waits with eager longing for* the revealing of the sons of God (Rom.

8:19; cf. v. 21), that is, at Christ's parousia: "[H]e comes on that day to be glorified in his saints, and to be marveled at among all who have believed" (2 Thess. 1:10).

Believers groan inwardly as they *wait eagerly for* adoption as sons, that is, the redemption of their bodies (v. 23), *waiting for* the revealing of our Lord Jesus Christ (1 Cor. 1:7; 1 Pet. 1:13), *eagerly waiting for* the hope of righteousness (Gal. 5:5). They *await* the Savior, the Lord Jesus Christ, from heaven who will transform their lowly body to be like his glorious body, "by the power that enables him even to subject all things to himself" (Phil. 3:20-21). They *wait for* God's Son from heaven, whom he raised from the dead, Jesus, who delivers us from the wrath to come (1 Thess. 1:10). They are *waiting for* "our blessed hope, the appearing of the glory of our great God and Savior Jesus Christ" (Titus 2:13). They are *waiting for* and *hastening* the coming of the day of God (2 Pet. 3:12); according to his promise they are waiting for new heavens and a new earth in which righteousness dwells (v. 13).

The believer's hope is oriented toward the coming kingdom, which will be a mighty revelation of God's glory: "[W]e rejoice in the hope of the glory of God" (Rom. 5:2; cf. Col. 1:27, "Christ, the hope of glory"). Sometimes, the term "heaven" is mentioned—"the hope laid up for you in heaven" (Col. 1:5)—but nowhere does this refer explicitly to the intermediate state. On the contrary, 1 Peter 1:3-5 says, "According to his great mercy, [God] has caused us to be born again to a living hope through the resurrection of Jesus Christ from the dead, to an inheritance that is imperishable, undefiled, and unfading, kept in heaven for you, who by God's power are being guarded through faith for a salvation ready to be revealed in the last time." Here, "heaven" is in no way related to the intermediate state[36] but to the "last time"—the time of the Messianic kingdom—and the salvation that will be revealed in it. Similarly, the "hope of eternal life" (Titus 1:2; 3:7) does not refer to Paradise but to the kingdom (cf. Dan. 12:2; Matt. 19:16, 29; 25:34, 46; Luke 18:30).

### 9.4.3 Living in Hope

The early church had this motto: *Illicitum non sperandum*, that is, "It is not allowed not to hope."[37] Paul gives us Abraham as an example of one who "in hope believed against hope" (Rom. 4:18). To the Sanhedrin he said, "It is with respect to the hope and the resurrection of the dead that I am on trial" (Acts 23:6). To governor Felix he said that he had "a hope in God, which these men themselves accept, that there will be a resurrection of both the just and the unjust" (24:15). And to king Agrippa he said, "And now I stand here on trial because of my hope in the promise made by God to our fathers, to which our twelve tribes hope to attain, as they earnestly worship night and day. And for this hope I am accused by Jews, O king!" (26:6–7). To the Jewish leaders in Rome he said, "[I]t is because of the hope of Israel that I am wearing this chain" (28:20). And to believers in Rome he wrote: "[W]e rejoice in hope of the glory of God" (Rom. 5:2); ". . . in hope that the creation itself will be set free from its

---

36. Totally mistaken is MSG here: "Because Jesus was raised from the dead, we've been given a brand-new life and have everything to live for, including a future in heaven." Cf. John Gill: ". . . an house eternal in the heavens" (http://biblehub.com/1_peter/1-4.htm).

37. Verkuyl (1992, 447).

bondage to corruption and obtain the freedom of the glory of the children of God" (8:20–21). Hebrews 11:1 says, "[F]aith is the assurance of things hoped for, the conviction of things not seen." And so we could go on.

Several times, Jesus himself stirred up the hope of people (his followers, or the sick), by the well-known expression: "Take heart" ("Be of good cheer," "Take courage," etc.; in Greek one word: *tharsei*, Matt. 9:2, 22; Acts 23:11; plural: *tharseite*, Matt. 14:27; John 16:33). Especially John 16:33 has great kingdom significance: "In the world you will have tribulation. But take heart; I have overcome the world." Through his first coming, on the cross Jesus overcame the world by,defeating in principle the powers of evil and reclaiming creation for God. As a consequence, his followers may take heart and may gladly look forward to the future of God's kingdom, which will involve the definitive end of the present world.

In 1965, the Second Vatican Council published the document "Joy and Hope" (*Gaudium et spes*), which in several places expresses the hope for the kingdom of God in remarkable words: "The joys and the hopes, the griefs and the anxieties of the men of this age, especially those who are poor or in any way afflicted, these are the joys and hopes, the griefs and anxieties of the followers of Christ. Indeed, nothing genuinely human fails to raise an echo in their hearts. For theirs is a community composed of men. United in Christ, they are led by the Holy Spirit in their journey to the Kingdom of their Father [Matt. 13:43] and they have welcomed the news of salvation which is meant for every man."[38]

---

38. Gaudium et spes, §1 (http://www.vatican.va/archive/hist_

"On this earth that Kingdom is already present in mystery [Matt. 13:11 KJ21]. When the Lord returns it will be brought into full flower."[39]

"Whoever in obedience to Christ seeks first the Kingdom of God [Matt. 6:33], takes therefrom a stronger and purer love for helping all his brethren and for perfecting the work of justice under the inspiration of charity."[40]

"Not everyone who cries, 'Lord, Lord,' will enter into the kingdom of heaven, but those who do the Father's will by taking a strong grip on the work at hand [Matt. 7:21]. Now, the Father wills that in all men we recognize Christ our brother [cf. 25:40] and love Him effectively, in word and in deed. By thus giving witness to the truth, we will share with others the mystery of the heavenly Father's love. As a consequence, men throughout the world will be aroused to a lively hope—the gift of the Holy Spirit—that some day at last they will be caught up in peace and utter happiness in that fatherland radiant with the glory of the Lord."[41]

## 9.5  The Beloved King[42]//
### 9.5.1  Colossians 1:13

After having briefly considered faith and hope in connection with the kingdom, let us now consider the principle of love. Some of the points I will cover have

---

councils/ii_vatican_council/documents/vat-ii_const_19651207_gaudium-et-spes_en.html).

39. *Gaudium et spes*, §39.
40. *Gaudium et spes*, §72.
41. *Gaudium et spes*, §93.
42. Regarding the kingdom and love, see Ridderbos (1962, 321–29).

been mentioned before, but will now be discussed in their context. Two Bible passages come to the fore immediately: the Father "has delivered us from the domain of darkness and transferred us to the kingdom of his beloved Son [lit., the Son of his love]" (Col. 1:13). "If you really fulfill the royal law [i.e., law of the kingdom] according to the Scripture, 'You shall love your neighbor as yourself,' you are doing well. . . . So speak and so act as those who are to be judged under the law of liberty. For judgment is without mercy to one who has shown no mercy. Mercy triumphs over judgment" (James 2:8–13).

Colossians 1:13 is really a key verse that shows, among other things, the contrast between the kingdom of darkness and that of light, the kingdom of hatred and that of love, the kingdom of death and that of life, in short: the kingdom of Satan and that of Christ. These two powerful kingdoms stand in opposition to each other. A continual spiritual battle rages between them in the invisible realm. What matters right now is this special formulation: transferred to the kingdom of the Son of his Father's love. This is a kingdom of which the Son is the center, namely, as the One who is loved by his Father, as the Father himself had said on two occasions: "This is my beloved Son, with whom I am well pleased" (Matt. 3:17; 17:5).

Jesus himself spoke of this love several times: "The Father loves the Son and has given all things into his hand" (John 3:35). "[T]he Father loves the Son and shows him all that he himself is doing" (5:20). "For this reason the Father loves me, because I lay down my life that I may take it up again" (10:17). "As the Father has loved me, so have

I loved you. If you keep my commandments, you will abide in my love, just as I have kept my Father's commandments and abide in his love" (15:9–10). "Father, . . . you loved me before the foundation of the world. . . . I made known to them your name, and I will continue to make it known, that the love with which you have loved me may be in them, and I in them" (17:24–26).

Jesus was deeply conscious of the Father's love, which was a driving force in his life as Man on earth. At the same time he also spoke of his own love toward the Father during the last hours in the upper room, before he began walking his path to imprisonment and the cross: "I do as the Father has commanded me, so that the world may know that I love the Father" (John 14:31). This connection between his love and the Father's commandments is quite special: I love the Father, therefore I obey him, he says. A child who loves his parents tries to obey his parents, not out of coercion but out of love: "My son, do not forget my teaching [Hebrew *torah*], but let your heart keep my commandments [*mitswot*], for length of days and years of life and peace they will add to you. Let not steadfast love and faithfulness forsake you; bind them around your neck; write them on the tablet of your heart. So you will find favor and good success in the sight of God and man" (Prov. 3:1–4; cf. Rom. 14:17–18).

In Colossians 1:13 Paul shows us *who* the king is, the ruler in the kingdom of God. Indeed he is the King of kings and the Lord of lords (cf. Rev. 19:16), but at the same time Paul makes clear to us that this person is not only important because of his offices, but primarily because of who he *is*. He is the focal point of all the Father's love. Here the message is that, if a person wishes to follow Jesus, he should know him not only as a historical figure, or even as the One who accomplished the work of atonement. He should know him *as the Father knows him*, should love him *as the Father loves him*. Believers have the highest *respect* for Jesus because of his offices; they have *love* for Jesus because of his person. The former refers to *what* Jesus is, the latter refers to *who* Jesus is.[43]

## 9.5.2 Vertical Love

Love is a key word in the kingdom, because people will never become followers of Jesus—with real surrender, dedication, and commitment—if they have not learned to love Jesus: "If you love me, you will keep my commandments. . . . Whoever has my commandments and keeps them, he it is who loves me. And he who loves me will be loved by my Father, and I will love him and manifest myself to him. . . . If anyone loves me, he will keep my word, and my Father will love him, and we will come to him and make our home with him. Whoever does not love me does not keep my words" (John 14:15, 21–24). "If you keep my commandments, you will abide in my love, just as I have kept my Father's commandments and abide in his love" (15:10; cf. 1 John 5:3; 2 John 1:6).

We thus see that the kingdom is not only about the love of the Father for his Son, and about the love of the Father and the Son for Jesus' followers, but also about the way these followers *return* this love in their affec-

---

43. Cf. Berkouwer (1972, 443–44) on the relationship in the kingdom of God between, on the one hand, power, and on the other hand, love, beauty, and glory.

tion for the King: "We love because he first loved us" (1 John 4:19). According to our best knowledge of the Bible manuscripts, the remarkable absence of an object in the main clause is correct here (the object, "him," was inserted in later manuscripts; see KJV, etc.[44]). In this way, Greek *agapōmen* ("we love" *or* "let us love") describes the general character of God's children: they are "lovers," both of God and Christ, and of God's children.[45]

As long as people do not grasp the secret of love, they will be able to see the kingdom only as a system of coercion. The laws of the kingdom will then turn into a system of legalism. In reality, the kingdom is permeated with love: the Father's love for the Son, the Son's love for the Father, the Father's love for his children, the Son's love for his followers, our love for the Father, our love for the King, our love for our fellow believers, and all this in the love of the Holy Spirit (Rom. 15:30). Love and legalism are like water and fire: "[W]oe to you Pharisees! For you tithe mint and rue and every herb, and neglect justice and the love of God. These you ought to have done, without neglecting the others" (Luke 11:42).

The moment a person grasps this, there is no (legalistic) "ought to" anymore. Love, which is the key term in Colossians 1:13, is by definition voluntary. The Father transfers us to a kingdom where not only he but *everyone* loves his Son. The Father loves the Son for many reasons, but also because he gave himself up for us into death. We "walk in love, as"—and also *because*—"Christ loved us and gave himself up for us, a fragrant offering and sacrifice to God" (Eph. 5:2; cf. Gal. 2:20b). Not only is there no room for coer-

---

44. See Metzger (1975, 713).
45. Barker (1981, 347).

cion here, neither is there room for the idea that we might derive rights from this love for the neighbor ("one good turn deserves another"). Both ideas are fundamentally alien to the notion of love. One shows love, not because one "has to," nor in order to receive something back, but because one loves. The true disciple cannot help but love.

### 9.5.3 Horizontal Love

In addition to vertical love, there is horizontal love in the kingdom of God. The former is between the Father and the Son, between the Father and believers, between the Son and believers, in the power of the Holy Spirit. However, it is absolutely inconceivable that this vertical love could ever exist without the horizontal love between believers. This is one of the great subjects of John's first letter: if a person does not love God's children, he does not love God either (3:10-18; 4:7, 11, 12, 20-5:2). If the love of God has been poured out into a person's heart (Rom. 5:5), this love will bubble up and flow out on all sides: "'Whoever believes in me, as the Scripture has said, "Out of his heart will flow rivers of living water."' Now this he said about the Spirit, whom those who believed in him were to receive" (John 7:38-39).

James 2 deals with the matter in a very direct, practical way.[46] If an unknown person with gold jewels and fine clothing comes into a church, people are strongly tempted to give him a nice seat. And if a poor man comes in, one carelessly points him to an inconspicuous place. However, verse 5 says that God "has chosen those who are poor in the world to be rich in faith and heirs of the kingdom, which he has promised to those who love

---

46. See Ouweneel (1981, ad loc.).

him." James does not say that, as humans, the rich and the poor are all equal—although in itself this is true, of course—but that God has a higher regard for the poor. This is an important message of Luke, who repeatedly refers to the poor (4:18; 6:20; 7:22; 12:33; 14:12-13, 21; 16:20-22; 18:22; 19:8; widows: 2:37; 4:25-26; 7:11-12; 18:3-5; 20:47; 212:2-3), and to the dangers of riches (1:53; 6:24; 8:14; 12:16-21; 16:11, 19-22; 18:23-25; 19:2; 21:1).

Of course, the poor are not automatically members of God's kingdom just because they are poor.[47] We all know that there are wicked ones among the poor, and righteous ones among the rich. A good example is Joseph of Arimathea, who was rich and yet a disciple of Jesus, "looking for the kingdom of God" (Matt. 27:57; Mark 15:43; Luke 23:50; John 19:38). But it is certainly true that the percentage of the wicked is higher among the rich than among the poor, and the percentage of the righteous is higher among the poor than among the rich: "How difficult it is for those who have wealth to enter the kingdom of God! For it is easier for a camel to go through the eye of a needle than for a rich person to enter the kingdom of God" (Luke 18:24-25). James 2 tells us that those who are "poor in the world" (i.e., have few earthly possessions) have been chosen "to be rich in faith and heirs of the kingdom, which he [i.e., God] has promised to *those who love him.*" This clearly shows that a person is not chosen for the kingdom because he is poor but because he loves God. It is true, however, that poor people love and trust God more easily than rich

---

47. This must also be true of Lazarus (Luke 16:19-31). The important key to his faith is his name, coming from Hebrew *Eleazar*, "God helps" (Eleazar in Exod. 6:23, etc.).

people, who easily trust in their riches and capacities. Compare the prayer by Agur: "[G]ive me neither poverty nor riches; feed me with the food that is needful for me, lest I be full and deny you and say, 'Who is the LORD?' or lest I be poor and steal and profane the name of my God" (Prov. 30:8-9). Agur is afraid that riches will diminish his love for God.

The kingdom is for those who love God. The kingdom of God is a place of love; to enter, love must be worked in a person's heart by the Holy Spirit. There must be love to be able to keep the laws of the kingdom. But more than that: the commandment of love is itself one of the laws of the kingdom. Or rather, it is actually *the* law of the kingdom. In James 2:8 we hear about the "royal law" (Greek *nomos basilikos*), that is, the "law of the kingdom" (*nomos basileias*), that is, the "law of Christ" (*nomos tou Christou*, Gal. 6:2; cf. *ennomos Christou*, 1 Cor. 9:21). This is the whole of Christ's commandments, which all turn around the one, central commandment of love: "A new commandment I give to you, that you love one another: just as I have loved you, you also are to love one another. By this all people will know that you are my disciples [i.e. subjects of the kingdom], if you have love for one another" (John 13:34-35). This ties in with the Golden Rule of Jesus: "[W]hatever you wish that others would do to you, do also to them, for this is [the entire content of] the Law and the Prophets" (Matt. 7:12).

This is the central law of the kingdom: "Love!" (Greek *agapōmen* in 1 John 4:19, taken as an imperative: "Let us love!"). In the kingdom of God, people love God so much and are so deeply conscious of the love that God has for them that they also love others, especially if these others are also followers of Jesus: "So then, as we have opportunity, let us do good to everyone, and especially to those who are of the household of faith" (Gal. 6:10). As Jesus said in the parable of the unforgiving servant: "You wicked servant! I forgave you all that debt because you pleaded with me. And should not you have had mercy on your fellow servant, as I had mercy on you?" (Matt. 18:32–33). "Be kind to one another, tenderhearted, forgiving one another, as God in Christ forgave you" (Eph. 4:32). "If anyone says, 'I love God,' and hates his brother, he is a liar; for he who does not love his brother whom he has seen cannot love God whom he has not seen. And this commandment we have from him: whoever loves God must also love his brother" (1 John 4:20–21). This is a law without any exceptions.

## 9.6 Characteristics of Love

### 9.6.1 Tolerance

As we just saw, vertical love leads to horizontal love. This is a central law in the kingdom. Paul works this out in Romans 12, which begins with the total self-surrender of the Christian (v. 1), and the concomitant transformation (Greek *metamorphōsis*) of his entire mind (*nous*, v. 2). Subsequently, Romans 14 gives us a very concrete example (cf. §8.3.3): how do church members deal with differences of opinion in the church? How do the two parties relate to each other in a way that is appropriate in the kingdom?[48] A serious dispute is an ideal test for the love within a congregation. Surely in a small community, closely knit together, people have to tolerate

---

48. See extensively, Ouweneel (2009b, 2011).

much in each other. For instance, people have to accept that the one person allows himself greater liberties than another person does when it comes to what one may eat, or what days have to be honored above other days.

Such a situation of various liberties does not even have to be wrong. Both parties might be right because what the one person may do with liberty the Lord might not allow to the other ("Each one should be fully convinced in his own mind," i.e., as to the will of the Lord; v. 5b). In his relationship with the Lord it might be better for a Christian to do, or precisely not to do, certain things. Every believer has his own understanding of things, his own spiritual development, and especially his own motives. He who does, or omits doing, certain things because of a legalistic attitude is always wrong. He who does, or omits doing, certain things because he wishes to demonstrate that he is his own master is always wrong as well. He who does, or omits doing, certain things because he loves *the* Master is always right, even though his understanding might have been wrongly educated (vv. 6–8).

In practice such a situation turns out to be cumbersome: how far may tolerance extend? This is the point where Paul says in verse 17: in the kingdom of God it is not that kind of differences that matter. They are not important enough to quarrel about to such an extent that someone might even enforces a division in the congregation. He who does this, whether he is "weak" or "strong" (or believes himself to be strong), does not act *out of love* (v. 15). Subsequently, after having said what the kingdom of God is not—fighting over matters of secondary or even tertiary importance—Paul says, "[T]he kingdom of God is . . . righteousness and peace and joy in the Holy Spirit." Not righteousness and peace and joy *per se*, for these might be false imitations, originating from our sinful flesh. The Bible shows that there is false "righteousness" (Isa. 64:6), false "peace" (Luke 11:21 NKJV), and false "joy" (Eccl. 7:6). No, Paul is speaking of righteousness and peace and joy worked by the Holy Spirit. He who shows himself in this way to be a servant of Christ "is acceptable to God and approved by men" (Rom. 14:18). This is the person who addresses others in love, respects the views of others (see Rom. 15:7 NIV, "Accept one another"), and knows how to deal with differences in a loving way, out of the love that has been poured into his own heart (5:5).

The law of love demands the greatest sacrificial attitude toward our fellow believers. For his followers, Jesus was the example of this by bringing the greatest sacrifice: his own life. Therefore, Jesus says not only that believers should love each other, but also that the greatest way to show this love is the willingness to put their lives at risk for the other: "This is my commandment, that you love one another as I have loved you. Greater love has no one than this, that someone lay down his life for his friends" (John 15:12–13). "This is how we know what real love is: Jesus gave his life for us. So we should give our lives for each other as brothers and sisters" (1 John 3:16 ERV). This is superhuman; it can be accomplished only through a superhuman power: that of the Holy Spirit.

### 9.6.2 Mercy

Here we must mention a particular form of love, namely, mercy, compassion; as James says, "Yes, you must show mercy to others. If you do not show mercy, then God will not show mercy to you when he judges you. But the one who shows mercy can stand without fear before the Judge" (2:13 ERV). "Blessed are the merciful, for they shall receive mercy" (Matt. 5:7). "Be merciful, even as your Father is merciful" (Luke 6:36). Again, Jesus was the great example. Why did he heal the sick (Matt. 14:14; 20:34; Mark 1:41; 9:22; cf. Luke 10:33), raise the dead (Luke 7:13), hand out bread to the crowd (Matt. 15:32), give guidance to those roving around (9:36), and grant forgiveness to the guilty (cf. 18:27; cf. Luke 15:20)? Sure, he did this to show that he was the anointed King, and that the kingdom of God was breaking through (cf. Matt. 9:35, ". . . proclaiming the gospel of the kingdom and healing every disease and every affliction"). But he also did it simply because he was "moved with compassion" (KJV).

Mercy flows forth from love. It is the kind of love that goes out to those who are in misery (cf. Latin *miseria*, "misery," and *misericordia*, "mercy"). Of the fruit of the Spirit (Gal. 5:22-23), love is the first feature that is mentioned. Perhaps it could be said that all the other eight features depend on this first one; that is, kindness, goodness, gentleness, etc. flow forth from love.[49] As Paul says elsewhere, "Put on then, as God's chosen ones, holy and beloved, compassionate hearts, kindness, humility, meekness, and patience, bearing with one another and, if one has a complaint against another, forgiving each other; as the Lord has forgiven you, so you also must forgive. And above all these put on love, which binds everything together in perfect harmony" (Col. 3:12-14).

---

49. Cf. Greijdanus (1922, 127).

We may notice here that "to be moved with compassion" is Greek *splanchnizomai*, from *splanchna*, "bowels." It reminds us of the word "belly" (*koilia*) in John 7:38 (KJ21): "He that believeth in Me, as the Scripture hath said, out of his belly shall flow rivers of living water." Verse 39 shows that this refers to the Holy Spirit. The "water" flowing here from the "belly" (or "bowels") may be an indication that the primary meaning here is that the work of the Holy Spirit in the believer is one of compassion toward others, just as this was a primary feature of Jesus' own ministry. When it comes to the works of the Spirit, many like to think immediately of glossolalia, healings, deliverances, and other miracles. But these are the P, Q, and R, or even the X, Y, and Z of the Spirit's work. Among the A, B, and C of the Spirit's activity within believers, we instead find things like plain obedience (Rom. 8:14), compassion (John 7:38-39), worship (Eph. 5:18-20), prayer (Eph. 6:18; Jude 1:20), witnessing (Acts 1:8), inner transformation (2 Cor. 3:17-18), etc.

### 9.6.3 The Law of Love

In the kingdom of God, we find a community of disciples of Jesus who have great love for the King, and therefore also for each other. I refer again to John 13:34-35, "A new commandment I give to you, that you love one another: just as I have loved you, you also are to love one another. By this all people will know that you are my disciples, if you have love for one another." By their love for each other, Christians are recognized as followers of Jesus, just as Jesus himself was known by his love for his friends (cf. 11:5, 36; 15:13-15). Christians are not primarily recognized by their orthodox confession of faith, their wonderful church services, their well-founded theology, etc., no matter how important and beautiful these things are in themselves.

The spiritual leaders of Israel recognized that the apostles had been with Jesus (Acts 4:13). Of course this is meant in the literal sense but it may be applied spiritually. Those who are "with Jesus" will more and more shine like Jesus, just as Moses had been with God, and as a consequence his face shone (Exod. 34:29–30). People should recognize Jesus' followers by a love that no longer fits into common, ordinary categories of human affection and of "being nice" to each other. It is a love that surpasses this, a love that in fact is supernatural: a love flowing from the Holy Spirit (cf. Rom. 5:5), and characterized above all by sacrifices brought for others: "[W]alk in love, as Christ loved us and gave himself up for us, a fragrant offering and sacrifice to God" (Eph. 5:2).

In Luke 11 Jesus fiercely rebukes the Pharisees and the Torah-scholars, people for whom religion was mainly an external matter: "[W]oe to you Pharisees! For you tithe mint and rue and every herb, and neglect justice and the love of God" (see §8.3.3). When it was a matter of the Torah, these spiritual leaders were so meticulous that, when they returned from their vegetable garden, they took precisely 10 percent from every herb, for these tithes had to be set apart for the temple. But they neglected the things that really mattered: justice, love, mercy, faithfulness (Matt. 23:23). They were good at tertiary things, but complete dummies as far as the primary things were concerned. "You blind guides, straining out a gnat and swallowing a camel!" (v. 24).

Whether it is a matter of the Mosaic Torah or the Messianic Torah, in all cases what is central are not certain good works but the true motivation behind these works: love for God and for the neighbor. If a person fulfills the laws of God's kingdom without love, this is completely worthless, no matter how pious and godly such a person may be in his own eyes and in those of his friends. To God, he is no better than the average wicked person. As the prophet said, "There is no faithfulness or steadfast love, and no knowledge of God in the land" (Hos. 4:1). "Your love is like a morning cloud, like the dew that goes early away. . . . For I desire steadfast love and not sacrifice, the knowledge of [i.e., intimacy with] God rather than burnt offerings" (6:4–6). "So you, by the help of your God, return, hold fast to love and justice, and wait continually for your God" (12:6). "He has told you, O man, what is good; and what does the LORD require of you but to do justice, and to love kindness, and to walk humbly with your God?" (Mic. 6:8). "Render true judgments, show kindness and mercy to one another, do not oppress the widow, the fatherless, the sojourner, or the poor, and let none of you devise evil against another in your heart" (Zech. 7:9–10).

The kingdom of God is not for the selfish (cf. Gal. 5:20–21) and not for the greedy (Luke 16:14–18; Eph. 5:5). It is for those who are driven by true, sincere, ardent love, and this is the same as saying that it is for those who have been filled with the Holy Spirit (Eph. 5:18). The laws of the kingdom can be fulfilled only in a spirit of love—a love that no one has of himself, a love that cannot be measured in normal categories, a supernatural love: "God's love has been poured into our hearts through the Holy Spirit who has been given to us" (Rom. 5:5). Where the Spirit is working, there the kingdom of God becomes manifest. And what more important thing could the Holy Spirit do than to work divine love in the hearts of Jesus' followers? This means, at the deepest level, to have Christ formed in their hearts (cf. 2 Cor. 3:17–18; Gal. 4:19).

Where this love unfolds, where it flows, bubbles, and bursts forth in every direction, there the kingdom of God becomes manifest in its most magnificent way. This is the love with all its blessed effects that believers wish for their fellow believers, for all humanity, and for themselves. We might say that, in the present age, the kingdom of God becomes manifest no more beautifully and impressively than in the true love between the Lord and his disciples, and between these disciples themselves, a love flowing from the power of the Holy Spirit.

# Chapter 10
# Early History of Kingdom Theology

> *I saw in the night visions,*
>   *and behold, with the clouds of heaven*
> *there came one like a son of man,*
>   *and he came to the Ancient of Days*
>   *and was presented before him.*
> *And to him was given dominion and*
>   *glory and a kingdom,*
> *that all peoples, nations, and languages should serve him;*
> *his dominion is an everlasting dominion,*
>   *which shall not pass away,*
> *and his kingdom one*
>   *that shall not be destroyed.*
>                               Daniel 7:13–14

**Summary:** *A survey of the history of kingdom theology begins with Israel: how did (and do) the rabbis view the Messianic kingdom? What has supersessionism ("Israel has been* *replaced by the church"), in which ethnic Israel no longer plays the central role, done to kingdom theology? How could supersessionism originate at all—under what historical circumstances? How did (and does) it relate to anti-millennialism? What was the role of Augustine and the Reformers in this? Why and how did the new interest in Israel and the Messianic kingdom arise in the sixteenth, and especially the seventeenth, centuries? In this regard, what was the contribution of Reformed theologians? What are the different strands of millennialism (a-, post-, and pre-millennialism), how did they originate, and how do they relate? Where are the origins of these strands among the church fathers?*

## 10.1 Jewish Basileology

### 10.1.1 A Future Jewish Kingdom?

EARLY CHRISTIAN BASILEOLOGY AND eschatology were based not only upon the Old and the New Testament, but also upon Jewish apocalyptic writings that were produced during the intertestamental period. The term "apocalyptic" indicates that these writings, to a certain extent, resemble the New Testament book of Revelation (Greek *Apokalypsis*). They are characterized by dreams and visions, as we find them in the Old Testament particularly in Isaiah 24–27, Ezekiel, Daniel, Amos, and Zechariah. They are further characterized by the extensive occurrence of complicated metaphors and numerical symbolism (cf. Dan. 7–12), the emphasis on cosmic phenomena (cf. Matt. 24; Rev. 6, 8 and 16), the appearance of angels as revealers of mysteries (cf. Dan. 10; Zech. 1–6; Rev. 1:1; 17:7; 22:8), and a special emphasis on the end time, the period just before the appearance of the Messiah (cf. Dan. 8:17, 19; 9:26; 11:27, 35, 40, 45; 12:4, 6, 9, 13). These

## Early History of Kingdom Theology

books are often pseudepigraphic, which means that they present themselves as written by well-known Old Testament figures such as Enoch, Baruch, and Ezra.

Apocalyptic writings are strongly focused on the future: the forthcoming destruction of the Satanic world powers and the breakthrough of the Messianic kingdom. Very concretely the notion of a Messianic kingdom is dealt with in 1 Enoch 93:3-17 (c. 167 BC); 4 Ezra (or Esdras) 7:26-44 and 12:31-34 (c. AD 90); 2 Baruch 29:3-30:1; 40:1-4; 72:2-74:3 (c. AD 100).[1] Note that some of these writings have been written *after* the arrival of Christianity, and may have been partly influenced by it. In all these writings we find the following general eschatological program: the present age, then the age to come with the temporary Messianic kingdom, and finally the everlasting kingdom of God. Some rabbis held similar views, such as Eliezer ben Hyrcanus (c. AD 90), Jehoshua (c. AD 90), and Akiva (c. AD 135).

In general, the eschatology of the rabbis understood the Old Testament prophecies in their literal sense:[2] according to the rabbis, these prophecies deal with a literal restoration of the literal people of Israel in the literal land of Israel, on the literal Mount Zion, in a literal kingdom of peace and justice, under the literal Messiah on the literal throne of David. Often we come across a certain literal*ism*, though, understanding things too literally, with too much emphasis on details while neglecting

---

1. See Hays *et al.* (2007, 287).
2. See especially the many eschatological references in the Talmud, e.g., Sanhedrin 98a, and the commentary on them by Maimonides (*Mishneh Torah*).

the main lines. In contrast with this, the Hellenized Alexandrian Jew Philo (20 BC–AD 40) followed the opposite approach: that of allegorizing, spiritualizing the Old Testament, including the prophecies.

Intertestamental Judaism expected a national Jewish kingdom under the Messiah.[3] It is of great interest that post-New Testament rabbinic Judaism also dealt with Israel's opponents of the time, namely, the Roman Empire. In its treatment of the matter, "Edom" was often the code name for the pagan Roman, and from the fourth century, for the "Christian" Roman Empire. I have discussed this view extensively elsewhere, and explained my comprehensive agreement with it.[4] It is fascinating to see how this rabbinic approach collided with early Christian "spiritualism" (spiritualizing the prophecies) and supersessionism ("the church is the true Israel"). For instance, Jerome pointed to the Jewish view of the Messianic kingdom.[5] Malachi 1:4–5 speaks of Edom's destruction and the glorification of YHWH beyond the borders of Israel. With a certain disdain, Jerome related that the Jews believed that Edom represents the Romans, and tell themselves that, when the Roman Empire would be destroyed, world government would come to *them*.[6] And in his *Commentary on Daniel*, in his comments on Daniel 2:34–35, 45, Jerome scorns the idea

---

3. Saucy (1997, 314–15).
4. Ouweneel (2012a; 2016d, especially Excursus 7).
5. Jerome (*Comm. Mal.* ad loc.).
6. *Judaei falso sibi blandiuntur, Edom Romanos et Israel in consummatione mundi se prophetari: quod destructo Romano imperio, hoc est Idumaeo, regnum orbis veniat ad Judaeos*; quoted by Kocken (1935, 7).

that, according to the Jewish expositors, the Messianic kingdom would be a *Jewish* kingdom.[7]

In some early Protestant confessions, the entire idea of a future Messianic kingdom was called "Jewish." Thus, the Augsburg Confession (1530) condemned those "who now scatter Jewish opinions, that, before the resurrection of the dead [cf. Rev. 20:11-15], the godly shall occupy the kingdom of the world, the wicked being every where suppressed."[8] The Edwardine Articles (Art. 41) of the Anglicans (1553) spoke of *iudaica deliramenta* ("Jewish follies") into which the millenarians supposedly have fallen.

Similar words are found in the Second Helvetic Confession (1562/4): "We further condemn Jewish dreams that there will be a golden age on earth before the Day of Judgment, and that the pious, having subdued all their godless enemies, will possess all the kingdoms of the earth. For evangelical truth in Matt., chs. 24 and 25, and Luke, ch. 18, and apostolic teaching in II Thess., ch. 2, and II Tim., chs. 3 and 4, present something quite different."[9] As if a certain doctrine can be refuted by simply pointing to some Bible passages (which are known also to one's opponents) without giving one's own interpretation of them!

### 10.1.2 Restoring the Kingdom to Israel

In this context, the question of the disciples as well as the response by the risen Lord are relevant again (see

---

7. ... *quod Judaei ... male ad populum referunt Israel, quem in fine saeculorum* [viz., after the destruction of the Roman Empire] *volunt esse fortissimum, et omnia regna conterere, et regnare in aeternum*; Kocken (1935, 7).
8. http://www.ccel.org/ccel/schaff/creeds3.iii.ii.html, Article 17.
9. https://www.ccel.org/creeds/helvetic.htm, chapter XI.

§§1.1.2, 5.2.1, 6.5.1, 8.3.2 above): "Lord, will you at this time restore the kingdom to Israel?" Jesus answered, "It is not for you to know times or seasons that the Father has fixed by his own authority." In no way, Jesus suggested that the disciples' question was inappropriate, erroneous, irrelevant, or outdated. This in contrast, for instance, to the Annotations to the Dutch States Translation (*Statenvertaling*, 1637): the disciples "believed, according to the common error, that the [Messianic kingdom] was going to be a worldly kingdom." Indeed, the kingdom will not be "worldly" in the sense of sinful, carnal, devilish (cf. John 18:36), but certainly "worldly" in the sense of earthly: a kingdom in this world (cf. "*in* the world" and "*not of* the world," 17:11-16). In my view, Jesus implicitly indicated that the kingdom would indeed be restored *to Israel*, but only at a time that the Father had determined, which Jesus could or would not reveal. If you ask, "When will it happen?," and I answer: "That is hidden," this implies that it *will* happen, but at an unknown time. It does *not* suggest that asking "When?" as such is foolish—on the contrary.

The Jewish view that, when the "Edomite" (i.e., Roman) Empire collapses, an Israelite empire will arrive, is also found in Flavius Josephus (*Jewish Antiquities*), and in 4 Ezra and 2 Baruch.[10] Edmund Kocken ventures to write that this Jewish view is "totally different from the Christian view in this context."[11] What he means, of course, is: totally different from spiritualist supersessionism. In my view, the rabbis were perfectly right, and Jerome and his many successors were completely wrong. The "people of

---

10. See references in Kocken (1935, 6-7); Adamek (1938, 27-28).
11. Kocken (1935, 6).

the saints of the Most High" (Dan. 7:27), who in the Messianic kingdom will form the center of the world (see, e.g., Isa. 2:2-3 [= Mic. 4:1-2]; 56:1-8; 60:8-16; Zech. 8:23), can be nothing other than what Daniel and his readers necessarily understood by it: Israel. In this sense, one can definitely say that the Messianic kingdom will be a Jewish kingdom: in Daniel 7, the kingdom/kingship is given to the Son of Man (vv. 13-14), but also to "(the people of) the saints of the Most High" (vv. 18, 22); "*their* [i.e., Israel's] kingdom shall be an everlasting kingdom, and all dominions shall serve and obey *them*" (v. 27 ESVUK).[12,13]

Unfortunately, because of supersessionism, the idea of a "spiritual," and "therefore" non-Jewish kingdom has become deeply rooted. Thus, Herman Bavinck says that Jesus introduced a "big change" with respect to Jewish tradition: Jesus "interpreted that kingdom, not first of all as a political but as a religious-ethical dominion."[14] It is undoubtedly true that, with Jesus, the kingdom receives a far more religious-ethical significance than was ever the case in Jewish eschatology. But why must these be mutually exclusive? In other words, why could a political kingdom not simultaneously be religious-ethical, and *vice versa*?

### 10.1.3 Küng on the Kingdom

Reformed and Roman Catholic theologians find each other here. Thus, Hans Küng says, "The 'reign of God'

---

12. Within the context, it is far more obvious that the suffix -*h* ("his, its") refers back to '*am* ("people") than to "Most High," since '*am* is the subject of the argument (cf. CEB, EXB, GW, GNT, etc.).
13. For an extensive discussion of this, see Ouweneel (2012a).
14. Bavinck (2006, 3:246; cf. 497: "It [the kingdom] is spiritual, not political, in nature. . . .")

is not for Jesus . . . an earthly, national and religio-political theocracy. It is rather a *purely religious kingdom*. Jesus is always at pains to refute the misapprehensions of his people, but also and especially of his disciples, that he had come to free them from misery and foreign domination and to set up once mare the earthly kingdom of Israel."[15]

As examples of such erroneous (Jewish) expectations among the disciples, Küng mentions Luke 23:42 ("Jesus, remember me when you come into your kingdom"), 24:21 ("But we had hoped that he was the one to redeem Israel"), and Acts 1:6 ("Lord, will you at this time restore the kingdom to Israel?"; see above). To be sure, in all these cases, Jesus responded in a way different from what the speakers apparently expected. However, *in none of these cases* did he reject his followers' view as such. This is where Küng is mistaken. In Luke 23:42–43, Jesus did not at all contradict the expectation of the converted criminal, but rather comforted him by telling him that he would not have to wait until the arrival of the kingdom but would be with Jesus in Paradise that very same day. This did not at all change the fact that, one day, Jesus will indeed "come into his kingdom." Similarly, in Luke 24:25–26 Jesus *confirms* the kingdom view of the Emmaus disciples—he will redeem Israel one day—but adds the element that they had overlooked: it is only through sufferings that the Messiah enters his Messianic kingdom glory.

We must observe here that theologians such as Bavinck and Küng speak critically of the disciples' kingdom views, whereas Jesus himself did not do so at all—

---

15. Küng (2001, 49; cf. 72–73).

quite the contrary. That these theologians criticize such views must be explained from their own basileological paradigms, which have room only for an entirely spiritualized kingdom of God.

Another mistaken example given by Küng concerns the question of James and John: "Grant us to sit, one at your right hand and one at your left, in your glory." Jesus did *not* respond by saying that this question was based on a mistaken kingdom view, but: "[T]o sit at my right hand or at my left is not mine to grant, but it is for those for whom it has been prepared" (Mark 10:37-40). In this way, Jesus implicitly *acknowledged* their kingdom view, exactly as in Acts 1:6-7. The disciples were imbued with the Jewish Messianic expectation of those days. In contrast with the allegations of Küng and many others, Jesus' expectation was not at odds with the Jewish one but closely corresponded with it (cf. also Matt. 19:28). The reason is simple: Jewish basileology itself agreed thoroughly with the Old Testament, and Jesus agreed with both. To say it in Küng's terminology: the kingdom of God is definitely a "religious dominion," but this does not exclude the fact that *at the same time* it definitely is "an earthly-national and religious-political theocracy."

### 10.1.4 All Too Earthly

Of course, people can exaggerate things in this respect. During the British Interregnum (1649-1661), under the dictatorship of Oliver Cromwell, a group of his supporters was active in England: the so-called *Fifth Monarchists* (or *Quintomonarchists*, or *Fifth Monarchy Men*). These were ultra-radical revolutionaries. They believed in the "fifth monarchy (kingdom, empire)" that would arrive after the fall of the Roman Empire, but believed also that this would take place in 1666, among other things because the number of this year ended with the ominous number 666 of Revelation 13:18. By the way, in the same period (1650), Cromwell, who himself was a Puritan, allowed the Jews to return to England, from which they had been expelled in 1290. However, he refused to help them return to Palestine. All this had more to do with political and economical interests than with religious ideals.

In 1660, the British monarchy was restored, so that the plans of the Quintomonarchists crumbled. Most of them were executed or imprisoned for high treason.[16] Since their movement, belief in a "fifth empire," after the fall of the Roman Empire, unfortunately has acquired an ill reputation, as if it were automatically linked with radicalism. It was the same as with the repulsive escapades of John Bockelson ("John of [the Dutch city of] Leiden") in the German city of Münster (1533–1535), where the kingdom of God (the "Anabaptist Kingdom") was supposedly founded.[17] Such adventures (and failures) have regrettably yielded tremendous resistance against all sorts of millennialist views. It is understandable, but also quite unfair, that amillennialists lump together all millennialist views.

In the Netherlands, some Reformed theologians believed in a spiritual restoration of Israel, such as Gisbertus Voetius (†1676), while others believed in an earthly Messianic kingdom, such as Jacobus Koelman (†1695). However, they strongly emphasized that they were not

---

16. See Rogers (1966); Capp (1972).
17. See Arthur (1999).

Quintomonarchists, or they fiercely opposed these people.[18] Thus, Koelman rejected the view of the Huguenot Pierre Jurieu (†1713) that a restored Israel would one day rule over the other nations, as if they were "the most excellent part of the fifth Monarchy."[19] After 1660, theologians who were explicit Quintomonarchists opposed these positions, and thus ran into problems, such as Joannes Ernestus Jungius (†1775).[20] Unfortunately, it seems as if the debate around a millennialist basileology can no longer be separated from past radicalist adventures.

When Paul claimed in response to the Jewish leaders in Rome that he was wearing a chain "because of the *hope of Israel*" (Acts 28:20), this hope could be nothing other than what these Jewish leaders necessarily understood by it: the coming of the Messiah and the establishment of the kingdom as described, for instance, in Isaiah 32, Micah 4:1–5, and Zechariah 14: a kingdom whose center would be the earthly Jerusalem. After his conversion, Paul also shared along with Israel the "hope in the promise made by God to our fathers, to which our twelve tribes hope to attain" (Acts 26:6–7). Paul would have been a liar if he had told the Jews that he shared *their* Messianic hopes if in fact in his heart he had spiritualized this hope. No doubt, Paul knew of a "Jerusalem above" (Gal. 4:26)—

---

18. Van Campen (2007, 52, 177–80; cf. 440; 333: Samuel Maresius spoke derogatorily of the "fifth monarchy of the Anabaptists, Fanatics, and Quakers").
19. Van Campen (2007, 179).
20. Van Campen (2007, 541).

but that did not necessarily change his hope for the "Jerusalem below."

## 10.2 The Constantinian Turn
### 10.2.1 Consequences

In my work, *The Ninth King*, I have reviewed the rise of Augustinian supersessionism against the background of the great "Constantinian turn."[21] After the conversion of emperor Constantine the Great (AD 312) and the Edict of Milan (AD 313), Christianity, no longer persecuted, began to permeate the Roman Empire. In AD 380, one of Constantine's successors, emperor Theodosius, together with his co-emperors Gratian and Valentinian II, gave orthodox Christianity the status of state religion of the Roman Empire (edict *Cunctos populos*). Here the term "orthodox" means: Nicean (i.e., based on the Council of Nicea, 325), in opposition to Arianism, to which several predecessors had adhered. In AD 392, Theodosius forbade pagan religions.

Thus, the centuries-long pagan Roman Empire became a Christian ("catholic") empire, at least in name. The arrival as well as the theological idealizing of this Christian empire darkened the picture of the Messianic kingdom in its biblical sense. The reason was that people saw this kingdom concretely realized in the Christian Roman Empire of those days. The Messianic kingdom had supposedly shifted from being a future kingdom to becoming a present reality. Therefore, they were also convinced that this empire would continue until Christ's parousia; after this, the new heavens and the new earth would arrive. From now on, the church

---
21. Ouweneel (2016d, 153–58).

took the lead in politics and in the wars of this world, and recognized the emperor as its head and as the leader of its assemblies—not because he was necessarily a Christian (Constantine had himself been baptized only on his deathbed—by an Arian), but because he was the Roman emperor.

Such a church necessarily develops an entirely new theology, some important points of which I summarize here.[22]

(a) The rise of *caesaropapism:* the church submitted to the state, and church leaders became subservient to the emperor (later: to other heads of state). Subsequently, especially in the eleventh and twelfth centuries, the so-called investiture struggle emerged, the power struggle between the emperor of the Holy Roman Empire of the German Nation and the pope concerning the appointment of higher clergymen. This battle was based on the notion of a "Christian" empire as such. The question was simply who in this empire was the true ruler in the spiritual sense, that is, the true representative of Christ: the pope or the emperor?

(b) The rise of the *persecution of the Jews:* beginning with the Council of Nicea (325), the end of Christian persecution meant the beginning of Jewish persecution. This was because the Jews did not want to comply with the Christian church, and because of rising supersessionism ("we are the true Israel"; see [e] below). Consciously or unconsciously, the "Christian" empire became the rival of the Jews, who assiduously kept expecting their "Jewish" Messianic empire. The new Christian rulers seemed to cherish the desire to bring

---

22. See Ouweneel (2016d, 151–58).

this rivalry to a head by means of violence. Later Christian leaders scarcely considered the fact that the "Christian" empire had gradually reached its end—and at the parousia of Christ will definitively come to its end—and that the expectation of the "Jewish" empire stills holds, without having been in the least disturbed.

(c) The decrease of *healing miracles:* after several centuries when the New Testament healing ministry had flourished mightily, it strongly diminished after the Constantinian turn. This was due, on the one hand, to the weakening of the church and, on the other hand, to the mingling of the healing ministry with pagan elements.[23] The more the "Christian" empire was spiritualized—due also to the Hellenist idea of the superiority of the soul/spirit over the body[24]—the less attention was devoted to people's physical needs.

## 10.2.2 Militarism

(d) The rise of *militarism:* when Constantine had gained the victory over his opponents, this supposedly proved not only that Christ was stronger than the ancient Roman gods, but also that he by nature was a war god, a god of military victory. The Christian conscientious objector to military service, who formerly had been a "soldier" of peace, now turned around one hundred and eighty degrees. He became a warrior in Constantine's armies to help him spread the Christian faith across Europe with the help of the sword. Already two years after Constantine's victory, in 314, the Council of Arles decided that objectors to military service had to be banned from the church. Godly church fathers

---

23. See Ouweneel (2016d, chapter 2).
24. See Ouweneel (2008a, chapters 6-8).

such as Athanasius, Ambrose, and Augustine, all approved of military service as such—whereas, for instance, pre-Nicene theologians Tertullian and Origen had strongly spoken *against* it. Dutch theologian Gerrit Jan Heering (†1955) called this turn from anti-militarism to militarism "Christianity's fall into sin."[25]

One of the elements in this changed attitude was the fact that some of the outstanding Christian soldiers from the preceding period were given the status of saint, such as St. George (Geourgios), who in 303 had been decapitated as a martyr.[26] He was surrounded with all kinds of legends, especially his victory over the "dragon." Ancient, but still semi-pagan England even turned him into their *genius* (patron saint), entirely in line with the *genius* in ancient Roman mythology. In the United States, no fewer than six towns and cities are named after St. George. (The U.S. state of Georgia was named after king George II of Great Britain but, of course, his name goes back to St. George as well. St. George is also the national saint of the country of Georgia.)

Another example of such a venerated Roman soldier is St. Theodore of Amasea, a Roman general who died for his faith in 306. Later, a Byzantine emperor made him the *genius* (patron saint) of Venice; "San Teodoro" still stands on a high column near Doge's Palace. (After the theft of the relics of the Gospel writer, Mark, from Alexandria, the latter took the place of Theodore as Venice's patron saint.) During the time of the Crusades, St. Theodore was adopted by crusaders as their patron saint.

---

25. See Heering (1972, book title).
26. Ouweneel (2016d, 149, 157–58).

### 10.2.3 Supersessionism

(e) The rise of *supersessionism:* formerly, the *pagan* empire had been viewed as the great opponent of the church, and thus as *the* instrument of Satan. Since the Constantinian turn, the empire had changed its character one hundred and eighty degrees. It was now the ally of the church, and thus God's instrument in the development of a true "Christian" world: the *corpus Christianum*. Earlier church fathers had seen in the image of Nebuchadnezzar in Daniel 2 the four *pagan* empires, of which the Roman Empire was the last one.[27] However, from AD 324, the year in which Constantine survived as the sole emperor of the empire, and in which the first St. Peter's Church was founded in Rome, there *was* no longer a pagan empire. It had been succeeded by a "Christian" empire. In Daniel 2 and 7, the last pagan empire, the Roman one, is succeeded by the empire of Christ. So what was more obvious than to suppose that the Christian empire that became manifest in the fourth century was the promised Messianic kingdom, which had destroyed all preceding pagan empires?

The area of the Roman Empire, which was ever further Christianized, was the domain in which the kingdom of Christ was developing. The establishment of the earthly church through human activity would be the means to realize this kingdom of Christ, and thus to fulfill the prophecies. The man who has expounded this great vision in a magnificent way was Augustine in his work *The City of God (De Civitate Dei,* "On the city [or state, or actually: the empire] of God," c. 420).[28] The opposite of what many

---

27. Ouweneel (2012a, chapter 6).
28. See, e.g., the modern translation by Dyson (1998).

Christian optimists expected did in fact occur: it was not so much the church that Christianized the empire, but the empire secularized and paganized the church. It was not Christ prevailing over the pagan gods, but these gods prevailed to a large extent over the Christian world.[29]

The theology after the Constantinian turn is characterized by supersessionism (or substitutionalism, or replacement theology). This is the theology that assigns to Israel the curses once pronounced upon the nation (e.g., Deut. 27:15-26), and claims for the church the blessings once pronounced upon Israel (e.g., Lev. 26; Deut. 28). To be sure, theologians often formulate this in a more subtle way: the (few) true Jesus-believers in Israel have not been replaced but augmented with the Jesus-believers from the Gentiles, and together they supposedly form the "Israel of God," that is, the church.

First, however, there is no single place in Scripture where the *ekklesia* of God is referred to as some "(spiritual) Israel," not even Romans 2:28-29, 9:6, 11:17, or Galatians 6:16.[30]

Second, what a strange "Israel" this is, which has abjured all that is typically Israelite (circumcision, Sabbath, festivals, food laws, etc.), in spite of, for instance, Matthew 5:17, where Jesus says that he had not come to abolish the Law. To be sure, Gentile believers were never placed under the Mosaic Torah (Acts 15:28-29). However, for Jewish believers the Torah was never set aside (cf., e.g., Acts 21:23-26, where Paul even provided for animal sacrifices; 28:17, where Paul says he always submit-

---

29. See Ouweneel (2016d, chapter 5).
30. See extensively, Ouweneel (2010b, chapter 3).

ted to what was later called the Oral Torah). *Nothing can ever be called Israel that is not under the Mosaic Torah.*

Third, actually the two descriptions ("Israel is replaced by the church," *or* "Israel is augmented with Gentile believers") amount to the same thing, for this church does replace more than 99% of ancient ethnic Israel. However, it is *this* ethnic Israel that is "the" Israel in the Bible. There is no other Israel. This is the Israel that still exists under the preserving hand of God, and upon which the irrevocable promises of God still rest (Rom. 11:29).[31] If there is such a thing as a "spiritual Israel," these are God's faithful ones—the *tsaddiqim*—in the midst of ethnic Israel, and nowhere else.

## 10.3 Anti-Millennialism

### 10.3.1 Church Buildings

Anti-millennialism and supersessionism usually go hand in hand. Post-Constantinian theology viewed the kingdom of Christ as coming no longer after his parousia, but in its own day, that is, the time that had begun with the Constantinian turn, which will end with the parousia. Before this turn, most leading church fathers were (pre-)millennialists, which entailed their belief in a kingdom of God on earth after the parousia. This was the view of especially Papias, Justin Martyr, Irenaeus, Tertullian, Commodian, Victorinus, Methodius, and Lactantius.[32] Others also mention the Pastor of Hermans and Pseudo-Barnabas.[33]

---

31. Cf. Ouweneel (2011a, §§1.3.4 and 2.3.2).
32. See Lewis and Demarest (1996, 378–80); extensively, Hill (2001, 11–44).
33. Saucy (1997, 316).

To be sure, there were also non-millennialists, who instead viewed the kingdom of God as heavenly, or at least did not give any sign of expecting a kingdom of God on earth.[34] Sometimes this was because of an allegorizing hermeneutic, such as that practiced by the Alexandrian school.[35]

After the Constantinian turn, the picture changed radically, because, as I said, with the Christianization of the Roman Empire the Messianic kingdom of peace and justice seemed to have arrived. In his eulogy to Constantine, Eusebius called him the new Moses.[36] Indeed, a new, Mosaic theocracy had arisen, an imitation of ancient Israel, which supposedly had been done away with. For the first time, real church buildings were built as reminiscences of Solomon's temple. The main churches were the first St. Peter at Rome (AD 324) and the Hagia Sophia at the "new Rome," Constantinople (AD 536). They were consecrated to the two great figures in the rising Western church: the apostle Peter, whose tomb was in Rome, and the Virgin Mary, who was viewed as the incarnation of "Sophia," the wisdom of God (Prov. 8:22-31), hence the name Hagia Sophia.[37]

These were magnificent buildings, which equalled the ancient temple(s) of Israel. To some extent, they were even designed as imitations of the Old Testament tabernacle or temple, with an outer court for the non-initiated, the actual temple for the laymen, and the shielded sanctuary with the altar, designated only for the

---

34. Lewis and Demarest (1996, 75-77).
35. Saucy (1997, 316-17, n23).
36. *De Vita Constantini*, I.12.
37. Ouweneel (1998, chapters 2 and 6; 2007a, 83-88).

priests. The apostles (see especially Galatians) had strongly warned against any Judaizing because it creates again a distance between God and his people. However, in these churches and in other ways, Judaizing prevailed again. A new priesthood was introduced that, like the Old Testament priesthood, again had to mediate between God and the people in these "temples."

## 10.3.2 The "Last Day"

Before the Constantinian turn, Eusebius of Caesaria, the writer of the well-known *Church History* (*Ekklēsiastikē Historia*), taught that Isaiah 35 and Psalm 46 referred to the future Messianic kingdom. After the turn, however, he applied these chapters to the new church buildings of his time, like the church at Tyre (consecrated AD 336), which he described as a "new and much better Jerusalem."[38] Now he also asserted that the magnificent church that Constantine wanted to build in ancient Jerusalem, the Church of the Holy Sepulchre (begun in AD 326), might be the fulfillment of the prophecy concerning the New Jerusalem (Rev. 21).[39] The dragon being thrown down from heaven, described in Revelation 12, he explained as Constantine's victory over the pagan empire.[40] When Constantine gave his sons and a nephew a share in his imperial rule, Eusebius saw this as the fulfillment of Daniel 7:18, "the saints of the Most High

---

38. On Eusebius, see Froom (1950, 361–72); Eusebius' *Demonstratio Evangelica* (in which he explains his eschatology) is available at www.ccel.org/ccel/pearse/morefathers/files/index.htm.
39. Eusebius, *Vita Constantini* 33 (www.fordham.edu/halsall/basis/vita-constantine.html).
40. Eusebius, *Vita Constantini*, 3.

shall receive the kingdom."[41] Thus, the great revolution in prophetic insights was beautifully illustrated in Eusebius' changed thinking. The same was true for other teachers of the church.[42]

Because of all the successes and new possessions of the church, her rising glory and power, the expectation of Christ's parousia faded entirely into the background. Why look forward to a future kingdom of Christ if this kingdom was already manifesting itself in such a magnificent way? For three centuries, church teachers such as Justin Martyr, Irenaeus, Tertullian, Hippolytus, and Lactantius had unanimously expected a millennial kingdom *after* the parousia (see §10.6.2). However, after the great turn, the situation changed drastically within a short time. Already Eusebius, and also Ambrose, Prudentius, and Jerome rejected (pre-)millennialism. Further we must mention the Donatist Tychonius, who is little known but apparently formed the source for the eschatological views of Augustine.[43] Tichonius replaced the idea of a future millennial kingdom (pre-millennialism) with the idea of a millennial kingdom *now* (a-millennialism or realized millennialism[44]). This kingdom supposedly had begun at the resurrection of Christ, while Tichonius pushed the parousia to the last day of world history.

The phrase "last day" is quite common in John's Gospel: the resurrection of believers occurs on this day (6:39–40, 44, 54; 11:24), and God's judgment is on the

---

41. Eusebius, *Vita Constantini*, 9.
42. See Froom (1950, 349–99).
43. Froom (1950, 465–73, 475, 481).
44. Linguistically this phrase is an oddity; see §11.5.

last day (12:48). The Vulgate has here *novissimus dies*, the "newest day," often referred to in German and Dutch as the "youngest day." If it is the last day of world history, then no day will ever be "newer" or "younger" than this one. Of course, quite another explanation of this day is possible, and in my view far more obvious. In Matthew 24:3, the disciples ask Jesus about the "end of the age" (Greek *synteleia tou aiōnos*). Because of supersessionist prejudices, this has often been translated as "end of the world" (KJV, etc.; see §4.4.2). But in Matthew, there is never any specific reason (apart from supersessionist prejudices) why the Greek word *aiōn* should be translated "world" instead of "age."[45] Thus, Jesus is distinguishing between "this age" (the "present age") and the "age to come" (the "Messianic age") (12:32; cf. Mark 10:30; Luke 20:34–35). Therefore, in Matthew 13:39–40, 49; 24:3, 13–14; 28:20, the "end" is not the end of the world (which is *after* the Messianic age), but the end of the present age, which precedes the Messianic age.

### 10.3.3 Augustine

Augustine was the most important church father who developed the new view of the Messianic kingdom further. He did so within a century after the Constantinian turn.[46] The Messianic rule is supposedly not in the future, but in the present. It takes shape within the Roman Empire under the leadership of the emperor, namely, by means of the church under the leadership of the bishop of Rome.

---

45. This seems to be true throughout the New Testament, except perhaps in Heb. 1:2 and 11:3 ("worlds").

46. See especially his *The City of God Against the Pagans* (1998).

Revelation 20:1–6 was viewed as entirely fulfilled, except for the "second resurrection," that is, the bodily resurrection at the parousia. Augustine, and many after him, spiritualized the "first resurrection" and applied it to regeneration. The "bottomless pit" into which Satan is bound and thrown was explained as the totality of the not yet converted nations. At the end of world history, the devil would be released for three and a half years. The "thrones" in verse 4 are supposedly the present-day ecclesiastical seats, and the "camp of the saints" is the worldwide ("catholic") church. The Jews had to be converted to this church, and thus were forced to abjure their Jewish background. The Roman Catholic Church was the stone of Daniel 2:34–35, 45, which destroyed the statue, and expanded into a "mountain," a world power. It would be the "New Jerusalem" (Rev. 21).

History has shown to what dramatic consequences this doctrine has led. Less than a century later, around AD 500, Rome's bishop had definitively emerged as the sole ruler within the Roman Catholic Church. The seat of the emperor, Rome, necessarily was the seat of the church ruler, the pope, as well. Both were in the city of Peter's tomb; Peter, pope, and emperor belong together forever. More than anything, supersessionism and anti-millennialism have turned the catholic (i.e., worldwide) church into a *Roman* Catholic Church.

It is all the more saddening that the Reformers, Martin Luther, Ulrich Zwingli, and John Calvin, adopted supersessionism and anti-millennialism without any criticism. Luther had been an Augustinian monk, and Calvin, too, was thoroughly Augustinian in his thinking. It is all the more gratifying that already in the sixteenth, and especially in the seventeenth centuries, better insights began to break through, as we will see in the next sections.

## 10.4 The Way of Augustine
### 10.4.1 Israel and the Church

The Reformers paid too little attention to basileology; they added few new elements to what Augustine had already written. John Calvin wrote commentaries on all the Bible books, except Song of Solomon (a book that, in my view, could be described as an eschatological midrash) and Revelation. Luther and Calvin simply adopted Augustinian spiritualism and supersessionism. These views also found their way into the chapter superscriptions of the King James Version (1611), for instance, above Isaiah 60: "The glory of the Church, in the abundant access of the Gentiles . . . ." Or above Joel 3: ". . . His blessing upon the Church." Or above Micah 4: "The glory, peace, kingdom, and victory of the Church."

One could argue that this kind of terminology does not necessarily imply supersessionism, but only the idea of "the church from Adam"; compare the Belgic Confession Art. 27 ("This church has existed from the beginning of the world") and the Heidelberg Catechism Q/A 54 ("the Son of God . . . from the beginning of the world to its end, gathers [the church]").[47] However, it is quite difficult to separate the "church-from-Adam" idea from supersessionism. Old Testament Israel is called "the church," or if one so wishes, the "visible church." Regenerate Israel would then be the "invisible church." In such a view it is hardly avoidable that theologians

---

47. See extensively, Ouweneel (2010b, 88–89).

call the New Testament church "Israel," or understand the term "Israel" in Romans 11 and Revelation 7 as referring to the church. However, this is not done unanimously. In the superscriptions above the latter chapters in the King James Version, reference is made to Israel but not to the church.

The Annotation to the States Translation (*Statenvertaling*, the Dutch equivalent of the King James Version) comments on Revelation 7:4, "Some take this in the literal sense of the elect from the Jews. ... Others take it as the Israel of God [Gal. 6:16] gathered together from Jews and Gentiles [read, the church], ... ." Perhaps we may encounter among the former group (the "some") those theologians who developed a different view on Israel and the church, and were open regarding the "land promise" (the biblical promise of Israel's return to the literal land of Israel in the end time).[48] From the sixteenth to the eighteenth centuries, this group emerged into greater prominence. It is worth paying attention to these theologians.

### 10.4.2 The First Group

The *first* group of theologians who departed from the course set out by Luther and Calvin included those theologians in the Calvinist tradition who believed that Romans 11:26-27 definitely speaks of ethnic Israel, and not of some spiritual Israel. They were deeply conscious of the fact that in so doing, they were diverg-

---

48. See Van Campen (2007), in the chapters concerning the various theologians dealt with. For the Puritans, see, e.g., M. Musser, *The Puritans and Israel*, http://1024project.com/2014/01/14/the-puritans-and-israel/.

ing from the Augustine–Jerome–Melanchthon–Calvin line. At the same time, however, like these earlier theologians, they spiritualized the Old Testament prophecies, and rejected the idea of a literal return to Palestine, and a restoration of Israel in this land. The church is still the "church from Adam," and no other company of believers exists.

In holding this view, Theodore Beza (†1564) differed from his teacher and predecessor, Calvin. In Germany, Johann Benjamin Koppe (†1791) may be mentioned. In the Netherlands, I mention Gisbertus Voetius (†1676), and Voetians (followers of Voetius) such as Johannes Hoornbeeck (†1666), Franciscus Ridderus (†1683), and Abraham Hellenbroek (†1731). They all believed in a spiritual restoration of Israel, but they rejected the idea of a Jewish return to Palestine as fulfillment of any Old Testament prophecy. They were all real Augustinians: the church is the "church from Adam" as well as the "spiritual Israel," and the Old Testament prophecies were spiritualized. Israel is going to be restored only spiritually; that is, in the end time there will be a massive conversion among the Jews, and they are then added to God's one covenantal people of all time, whether you call this "the church of all ages," or "spiritual Israel," or whatever. There is no place for a physical-national restoration of Israel, including the fulfillment of the land promise. Actually, there is no basic difference between individual Jewish conversions throughout church history and a massive Jewish conversion in the end time. Here, Augustinianism still fully prevails.

The newer interpretation of Romans 11 that diverged from the Augustinian tradition, was probably inspired by reformers such as Martin Bucer (the reformer of Strasbourg; †1551), Andreas Osiander (Germany, †1552), Peter Martyr Vermigli (Italy, †1562), Theodore Beza (Geneva), David Paraeus (Germany, †1622), and Franciscus Junius (a Dutchman in England; †1677), and British Puritans such as William Perkins (†1602), Thomas Brightman (†1607), Sir Henry Finch (†1625), James Durham (†1658), and George Hutcheson (1674). But with some of these we have already touched upon the second group: those who believed in both a spiritual and national restoration of Israel; Brightman is considered to be the father of this movement.

## 10.5 The Battle Against Spiritualism
### 10.5.1 The Second Group

The *second* group of Calvinist theologians who thought about the position and future of Israel included theologians who applied Romans 11:26-27 to ethnic Israel, just like the first group. The great difference is that they additionally believed in the fulfillment of the land promise, that is, the literal return to, and Israel's restoration in, the Holy Land at some future time. However, they did not believe in the rebuilding of the temple as described in Ezekiel 40-44. This group occupies a position between those who believe in an ultimate massive conversion of Israel but entirely spiritualize the Old Testament prophecies (see previous section), and those also believe in such a conversion of Israel but additionally adhere to a largely literal interpretation of the Old Testament prophecies (see §10.6).

The theologians of the second and the third group were those who believed in a national restoration of Israel in its own land. It is quite remarkable that they did so at a time when, given the political circumstances, such a national restoration seemed highly unlikely. Around the time of the Reformation, the Ottoman Empire had conquered the Middle East (1516–1517), including Palestine. In 1529 and 1683, the seemingly invincible Ottoman Muslims were threatening even Vienna, and thereby the whole of Western Europe. In the Holy Land, their power would last for exactly four centuries, that is, until 1917, near the end of the First World War, when Palestine fell into British hands.

Who in the seventeenth, eighteenth, and nineteenth centuries ventured to dream of a national restoration of Israel in its own land? Without distinguishing between the second and the third groups for the moment, I mention here the Puritans Thomas Draxe (†1618, see his *The Worldes Resurrection, or the General Calling of the Jewes*, 1608), Edmund Bunny (†1619, see his *The Scepter of Judah*, 1584), Sir Henry Finch (†1625, see his *The World's Great Restauration, or Calling of the Jews*, 1625; dispensationalist *avant la lettre*), William Gouge (†1653; another dispensationalist), Robert Maton (†1653? see his *Israel's Redemption*, 1642), Peter Bulkley (†1659; American; see his *The Gospel Covenant*, 1646), Thomas Goodwin (†1680; see his premillennialist commentary on the Apocalypse), and Increase Mather (†1723; see his *The Mystery of Israel's Salvation*, 1669). All these authors and their works clearly show that premillennialism and dispensationalism are much older than the nineteenth century.

### 10.5.2 Jacobus Koelman

In the Netherlands, we must first mention the Voetians Jacobus Koelman (†1695) and William à Brakel (†1711), who also emphatically believed in a national restoration of Israel, including a return to the Holy Land, and a restoration of the holy city of Jerusalem. According to Koelman, Scripture is so clear about Israel's future restoration "that it may be called a great miracle that many Reformed are still so blind to it, and beset with prejudices."[49] He understands the Israel mentioned in Ezekiel 40-48 to be literal, although he does not believe in a literal rebuilding of the temple and the restoration of the sacrificial ministry.[50]

Koelman saw the fulfillment of these prophecies within the context of the (supposed) heyday of the church in the end time. In his view, these are the "thousand years" of Christ's dominion (Rev. 20:1-7). He described the restoration of Israel as the conversion of Israel to the Christian religion, and this would "be a large part, even the most peculiar part of that glorious state of the church."[51] In a basileological respect, this must be understood such that the "thousand years" of Revelation 20:1-7 are not future, but that "the heyday of the church in principle had already begun [in Koelman's day], and would gradually increase in glory and extent."[52] Especially through this flourishing of the church, the Jews would be brought to jealousy, and would convert to Christ. This would go hand in hand with the return to their land. "To me it is beyond doubt that they, as an entire nation, will return to their own land, that

---

49. Quoted by Van Campen (2007, 166).
50. Quoted by Van Campen (2007, 167).
51. Quoted by Van Campen (2007, 167).
52. Van Campen (2007, 170).

[at present] lies devastated."[53] When they will have taken their land again, they will "rebuild Jerusalem, and renovate the other devastated places."[54]

Today, we would call Koelman a postmillennialist,[55] the view that the parousia will take place *after* the "thousand years," that is, *after* the heyday of the church and the spiritual *and* national restoration of Israel. In other words, already before the parousia, the kingdom of God will manifest itself in power and glory. In this respect, the seventeenth- and eighteenth-century postmillennialists diverged fundamentally from the premillennialists of the first to the third centuries. The latter believed that the parousia would *precede* the "thousand years," so that in the present age until its very end nothing would become visible of God's kingdom of power and glory. No wonder Koelman turned sharply against the premillennialists.[56] In this respect, he and others still thought in a fully Augustinian way. In a basileological respect, the central question is this: Will the church experience the kingdom in power and glory *before* the parousia, or will this occur only *after* the parousia?

### 10.5.3 William à Brakel

William (Dutch: Wilhelmus) à Brakel (1635–1711) was a theologian in the tradition of the Dutch Second Reformation (*Nadere Reformatie*). He has told us how his father, Rev. Theodore à Brakel (†1669), spoke on his

---

53. Quoted by Van Campen (2007, 171).
54. Van Campen (2007, 171).
55. Van Campen (2007, 180).
56. Quoted by Van Campen (2007, 177–178).

deathbed "of the conversion of the Jews and their restoration, as well as of a more glorious state of the church of Jesus Christ on earth."[57] William à Brakel has described this view extensively in his work, *The Christian's Reasonable Service* (*Logikē Latreia*[58]). In the Netherlands, this has become one of the best known religious publications of all time. Here, Brakel claims emphatically that the church has *not* taken the place of Israel, that the term "Israel" may be spiritualized nowhere in the Bible, and that, conversely, New Testament believers from the Gentiles are never referred to with the term "Israel."[59]

"Father Brakel," as he was affectionately called, has seen a great light. If the Reformed world in its entirety had only listened better to him and his fellow thinkers, Reformed eschatology and basileology would have looked much better today. Brakel even specified that the Jews would first return to their land, and only then

---

57. In an appendix of Th. à Brakel, *De trappen des geestelijken levens*, 435 (Van Campen (2007, 192-93 n6).
58. This Greek phrase comes from Rom. 12:1, "spiritual worship" (ESV note: "rational service"; [N]KJV: "reasonable service"). This work was first published in 1700; the rest of the title reads: "In which Divine Truths concerning the Covenant of Grace are Expounded, Defended against Opposing Parties, and their Practice Advocated as well as The Administration of this Covenant in the Old and New Testaments, exhibited in an explanation of the Revelation of John" (*In welke de Goddelijke waarheden van het genadeverbond worden verklaard, tegen partijen beschermd en tot beoefening aangedrongen, alsmede de bedeling des verbonds in het Oude en Nieuwe Testament en de ontmoeting der kerk in het Nieuwe Testament, vertoond in een verklaring van de Openbaring van Johannes*). The English translation was published in 1992-1995.
59. Quoted by Van Campen (2007, 196).

would the conversion of Israel occur.[60] By the way, to Brakel this conversion means that *all* Israel will "acknowledge and confess that Jesus is the Christ, the promised Messiah, the Savior,"[61] but that only part of them would be born again. If that were true, one wonders what is the exact meaning of the word "saved" in Rom. 11:26. The problem is a real one, though, because very few expositors would defend the position that, at the parousia of Christ, every single Jew then living on earth will be saved for eternity.

Just like Koelman, Brakel must be called a postmillennialist.[62] Israel will be restored in its land, where they will take part in the glorious "state of the church of the thousand years that has been predicted in Revelation 20."[63] He likewise assumed that the kingdom of God would arrive in the *present* age in power and glory. Together with Christ, believers would reign as kings and priests, and there would be an "extraordinary extension of the church" among the Gentiles.[64] And all of this would occur before the parousia, on the basis of the unshakable Augustinian belief that the parousia will involve the end of all world history and the beginning of the new heavens and the new earth. Brakel does see room for some spiritual intervention of Christ at the beginning of the "thousand years," but supposedly this will not be the actual parousia.[65]

---

60. Van Campen (2007, 200).
61. Brakel (1995, 4:518); Van Campen (2007, 197).
62. Tukker (1981, 25–27); Van Campen (2007, 201).
63. Quoted by Van Campen (2007, 198).
64. Quoted by Van Campen (2007, 202).
65. Quoted by Van Campen (2007, 203).

Brakel also remained an Augustinian in the sense that Israel would not occupy a separate position alongside the New Testament church of the Gentiles; together they will form one church. Nevertheless, the Jews will live in their own land under the "most wise, gentle and glorious dominion" of Christ.[66] But not outside the land; Brakel rejected the idea of a Jewish rule over other countries, or even over the entire earth (cf. §10.1). He also rejected the idea of a rebuilding of the temple, as well as a restoration of the sacrificial ministry.[67] In this way, in spite of his ardent desire to take the Old Testament prophecies literally, this was the extent of what his strongly Augustinian prejudices allowed him to believe.

Most Cocceian theologians in the Netherlands, that is, followers of Johannes Cocceius (†1669)—in certain respects opponents of the Voetian theologians, followers of Gisbertus Voetius (†1676)—firmly believed in a return of Israel to the promised land, and in a restoration of Jerusalem and the other cities. Often, the Cocceians referred to Deuteronomy 32:43 ("He repays those who hate him and atones his people's land"), where God promises the atonement not only of the people, but also of the land. However, several theologians in this group (Hero Sibersma, Henricus Groenewegen, David Flud van Giffen, Friedrich Adolph Lampe, Joannes Ernestus Jungius) firmly rejected the idea of a restoration of the temple and of the sacrificial ministry at Jerusalem. Moreover, the Cocceians were sometimes torn

---

66. Quoted by Van Campen (2007, 204).
67. See J. van Genderen in Brienen et al. (1986, 177); Van Campen (2007, 206).

between the ancient, deeply rooted spiritualism and belief in a literal fulfillment of the prophecies. Cocceius himself, and his pupil Hero Sibersma, were remarkable examples of this.[68]

## 10.6 Further Openness to Israel
### 10.6.1 Van der Groe and Cocceius

A *third* group included those who interpreted both Romans 11:26–36 and the Old Testament prophecies literally, especially the "land promise" (return of ethnic Israel to the land of their fathers), and who also believed in a literal rebuilding of the temple in the sense of Ezekiel 40–44. Among the Voetians, Theodore van der Groe (†1784) is a good example of this view. He believed in both a spiritual and a national restoration of Israel in the Holy Land: "Oh, what a joyful and blessed time will this be on earth, when the almighty God, after its long-time rejection, with his own hand will graft ancient Israel into his covenant again."[69] Van der Groe remained fully Augustinian, though, since in his view, believing Jews and believing Gentiles will dwell "in one house and church"; he had no room for a separate position of Israel.

Van der Groe, too, turned out to be a postmillennialist: he expected a glorious state of the church, in which believers together with Christ as King will reign during the "thousand years."[70] Apparently, he too expected that the kingdom of God in power and glory will arrive before the end of the present age. At the same time, he was

---

68. See Van Campen (2007) on the authors mentioned.
69. Quoted by Van Campen (2007, 241).
70. Van Campen (2007, 245).

the only Voetian who believed in a restoration of the Jewish religious ministry in Jerusalem, although he did not make clear in what exact sense he imagined this to happen. His literal view of the fulfillment of all the Old and New Testament prophecies concerning Israel strongly reminds us of premillennialists, although he did maintain that the parousia would take place after the "thousand years." He thus rejected the idea of a physical, visible rule of Christ from Jerusalem.[71]

Johannes Cocceius and some of his followers also believed in both a spiritual and national restoration of Israel, as well as in a literal fulfillment of the prophecies, including the restoration of the temple at Jerusalem and the worship there. They were of the opinion that the Gentiles would take part in this worship, namely, in the sense of Zechariah 14:6: each year, all the nations would go to Jerusalem to celebrate the Feast of Booths. Cocceians such as Jacobus Alting (†1679) and Joachim Mobachius (†1790) cautiously left open the possibility of the rebuilding of the temple. However, the idea of a restoration of the sacrificial ministry was (and is) very hard to accept for almost all Reformed theologians, and of course also for Roman Catholics, Lutherans, Anglicans, and many non-dispensationalist Evangelicals.

## 10.6.2 Other Voices

Generally speaking, the Dutch theologians who had the most outspoken views concerning the future of Israel exhibited the greatest affinity with Puritans such as Thomas Brightman (†1607), Joseph Mede (1639), Thomas Shepard (†1649), James Durham (†1658),

---

71. Van Campen (2007, 246).

Samuel Rutherford (†1661), William Greenhill (†1671), George Hutcheson (†1674), Thomas Goodwin (†1680), John Owen (†1683), and Thomas Boston (†1732), but also with Huguenots such as Jean de Labadie (†1674) and Pierre Jurieu (†1713), and German theologians such as Johannes Piscator (†1625), and Johann Heinrich Alsted (†1638).

It is quite remarkable that so many American, British, Dutch, French, and German Calvinist theologians emphasized the future restoration of Israel. They firmly believed in the literal fulfillment of Romans 11:26–27, and in many cases in a literal return of ethnic Israel to the Holy Land, and in the restoration of Jerusalem, sometimes including the temple. Augustinian supersessionism and spiritualism had held a firm grip on Martin Luther and John Calvin, but the theological scene soon changed. This return to a more literal approach to Old Testament prophecies was a relief. It did not happen for the first time in the nineteenth century, as some Evangelicals might think, but already in the seventeenth century, and here and there in the sixteenth century. In those days, a national restoration of Israel in the Holy Land was politically impossible. All the greater, therefore, is the miracle that these theologians believingly accepted the prophetic Word as it came to them, without spiritualizing it away.

Of course, there were others. Some Reformed theologians kept blatantly defending a full-fledged supersessionism and spiritualism, such as Samuel Maresius (†1673) and Jacobus Fruytier (†1731). It can hardly be a coincidence that these were the very theologians who exhibited an insolent anti-Semitism. Fruytier wrote bitterly and harshly about the Jews of his day, and about the history of Judaism since their rejection of Jesus, doing so even in a widely distributed booklet for youngsters.[72] One wonders whether the founders of the Jacobus Fruytier Comprehensive School at Apeldoorn (the Netherlands) were aware of this.

Johannes Cocceius and the Cocceians, sounded other notes that were equally important. One of their most typical starting points was the assumption of a certain harmony in the prophetic promises: they refer to each other, and form a coherent whole.[73] Campegius Vitringa formulated nineteen hermeneutical principles for interpreting the prophecies, one of the most important ones being that prophecies have to be read literally, unless the contrary is absolutely evident.[74]

### 10.6.3 An Important Hermeneutical Rule

A good example of the approach that I have chosen in the present book and in my eschatology,[75] is the aforementioned William à Brakel, who in *The Christian's Reasonable Service* pleaded for understanding the prophecies literally as much as possible. To be sure, many prophecies to Israel have had a primary fulfillment, especially in the return from the Babylonian captivity and in the first coming of Jesus. However, I follow what I see as an essential hermeneutical rule: there is not a single Old Testament prophecy that has already been completely fulfilled. The prophecies concerning

---

72. Van Campen (2007, 258–59).
73. Van Campen (2007, 282, 293; cf. 431).
74. Van Campen (2007, 462).
75. Ouweneel (2012a).

the return from the Babylonian captivity or the first coming of Jesus *always* stand in an eschatological context. That is, their ultimate fulfillment is *always* linked with the parousia of Jesus and the establishment of the Messianic kingdom.

Let me briefly provide a few examples. In Jeremiah, the "return" prophecies have all been viewed as fulfilled in the return from Babylon, not to mention the supersessionist application of these prophecies to the church's "return" from Babylon (cf. Rev. 17-18). However, in Jeremiah 30-33 these prophecies are placed in the context of the coming of Messiah and the establishment of his kingdom. Clear examples are the reference to "David their king" (30:9), the "prince" and "ruler" (v. 21), and the "Branch" (33:15; cf. v. 17), as far as the Messiah is concerned. Moreover, the return from exile is not from Babylon only, but from all the nations in the world (30:11; 31:8), involves all the twelve tribes (30:3; 31:27, 31; 33:7), occurs in the "latter days" (30:24), etc.

Similarly, virtually all prophecies concerning the first coming of Jesus stand in an eschatological context; that is, they imply his parousia and the establishment of his kingdom of peace and justice. I refer only to Psalm 2:7 (see vv. 4-12); 22:1 (see vv. 23-31); 69:4-5, 9 (see vv. 34-36); Isaiah 9:6 (see v. 7); 11:1 (see vv. 1-16); 53:2 (see vv. 10-12); Micah 5:2 (see vv. 1-15); Zechariah 9:9 (see vv. 10-17); and 12:10 (see vv. 4-14). If the prophecies concerning the first coming of Jesus (his birth and his life on earth) must be taken literally—and who would deny that?—then the prophecies concerning his parousia and the Messianic kingdom must be taken literally as well. You cannot, so to speak, have a literal birth of the Messiah in Isaiah 9:6, and a non-literal "throne of David" in verse 7. You cannot have a literal town of Bethlehem in Micah 5:2, and a non-literal "our land" in verses 5–6, nor the "remnant" of a literal "Jacob in the midst of many peoples" in verses 7–8. You cannot have a Messiah sitting on a literal donkey in Zechariah 9:9, and a non-literal "Ephraim" and "Jerusalem," and non-literal "seas" and a non-literal river Euphrates in verse 10.

## 10.7 Millennialism: Historical-Theological

### 10.7.1 Terminology

The debate concerning millennialism (also called chiliasm) constitutes not only an eschatological, but also a basileological problem: (a) Do we experience already in the present age the breakthrough of God's kingdom in power and glory, or (b) are we going to experience this during a later part of the present age, or (c) may we expect this only after Jesus' parousia? In other words, will the age to come arrive (b) before, or (c) after the parousia? With these three possibilities, three movements are identified.

(a) *Amillennialism* (or *achiliasm*, or *realized millennialism*): here, God's kingdom in power and glory is described as the new heavens and the new earth. There is no expectation of a future kingdom of a "thousand years." If we are now living in the kingdom of the "thousand years," then it is not a kingdom of power and glory, unless one would like to limit the glory of this kingdom to heaven.

(b) *Postmillennialism* (or *postchiliasm*): that is, the parousia of Christ is expected only *after* the kingdom of the "thousand years" (taken literally or figuratively), a kingdom that today is still future (*post* = after).

(c) *Premillennialism* (or *prechiliasm*): that is, the parousia of Christ is expected *before* the kingdom of the "thousand years" (taken literally or figuratively) (*pre* = before).[76]

This entire debate centers around the "thousand years" of Revelation 20:1-7. "Thousand" is *mille* in Latin, and *chilia* in Greek, which explains the terms used (*millennium*, including the word *annum* ["year"] = "thousand year period"). In eschatological literature, *millennium* has become a common word for the Messianic kingdom of peace. The reason why we speak of a "kingdom" is that Revelation 20:4 and 6 speak of "reigning" (Greek *basileuō*), that is, "reigning as kings." The reason we speak of a "kingdom of *peace*" (German *Friedensreich*, Dutch *vrederijk*) is that many expositors equate this kingdom with the kingdom that is described extensively and enthusiastically in the Old Testament prophecies: "Of the increase of his government and of peace there will be no end, on the throne of David and over his kingdom, to establish it and to uphold it with justice and with righteousness from this time forth and forevermore" (Isa. 9:7).

If only the term "millennialism" or "chiliasm" is used—without a prefix—usually premillennialism ("premil" for short) is meant: the idea that Jesus will re-

---

76. For comparative discussions, see, e.g., Feinberg (1961); Clouse (1977); Boettner (1990); Grenz (1992); Spykman (1992, 534-43); Lewis and Demarest (1996, 373-86, 426-29); Erickson (1998, 1212-24; 1999); Schwarz (2000, chapter 6); Bloesch (2004, chapter 5); Hoek (2004, 178-98); Duffield and Van Cleave (2008, 583-84); Van Genderen (2008, 847-53).

turn *before* the "thousand years." Premil and postmil groups agree that the "thousand years" are still future, whereas the amil position believes that the "thousand years" are now. Premil and amil groups agree that nothing stands in the way of Jesus' immediate return, whereas postmil believe that first the "thousand years" must occur. Postmil and amil groups agree that Jesus' parousia will be immediately followed by the new heavens and the new earth, whereas premil believe that first the "thousand years" must occur.

The main differences with respect to the interpretation of Revelation 20:1-6 are the following ones (leaving aside for a moment all the varieties *within* a-, pre-, and postmil).

(a) *When is the millennium?* Amil: the "thousand years" are in the past and/or in the present (Rev. 20:4-6 is a recapitulation of the preceding chapters). Premil/postmil: the "thousand years" are in the future, either before (postmil) or after (premil) the parousia.

(b) *What is the heart of the millennium?* Amil/postmil: the heart is the church, that is, "spiritual Israel." Premil: the heart is converted ethnic Israel, whereas the church, consisting of all Jesus-believing Jews and Gentiles from before the parousia, will be glorified in heaven during the millennium.

(c) *When is Satan bound?* Amil: Satan was bound during the first coming of Christ (cf. Luke 10:18). Postmil: same view, *or* Satan is bound more and more as the church reaches its heyday. Premil: Satan is bound directly following the parousia (Rev. 20:1-3, which is after 19:11-21).

(d) *What are the first and the second resurrections?* Amil/postmil: the first resurrection (Rev. 20:4-6) is the regeneration of believers (cf. John 5:25; Eph. 2:5-6; Col. 2:12; 3:1), while the second resurrection is the bodily resurrection of all people. Premil: the first resurrection is the bodily resurrection of believers, before the millennium, while the second resurrection is the bodily resurrection of the unbelievers, after the millennium (Rev. 20:5, 12).

## 10.7.2 Church Fathers

Basically, premillennialism is the dominant eschatological view of the orthodox rabbis in the sense that they believe in a very near, earthly kingdom of peace and justice, which will arrive with the coming of the Messiah (even if we find with them a less clear insight in the transition of this Messianic kingdom to the eternal state). Moreover, premillennialism was the dominating view among the church fathers until the Constantinian turn.[77] Papias,[78] Pseudo-Barnabas, Justin Martyr, Melito of Sardis, Hippolytus of Rome,[79] Tertullian, Commodi-

---

77. See D. Fairbairn in Blomberg and Chung (2009, 105-117) on the claim that before AD 300, forms of a- and postmillennialism existed as well.

78. https://en.wikipedia.org/wiki/Papias_of_Hierapolis: "Eusebius [*Hist. Eccl.* 3.39] concludes from the writings of Papias that he was a chiliast, understanding the Millennium as a literal period in which Christ will reign on Earth, and chastises Papias for his literal interpretation of figurative passages, writing that Papias 'appears to have been of very limited understanding', and felt that his misunderstanding misled Irenaeus and others." nl.wikipedia.org/wiki/Papias: "The work of Papias was forgotten, especially because he was blamed for believing that, at the parousia of Jesus, a millennial kingdom of peace would arrive as described by John in the Bible book Revelation."

79. Hill (2001, 160-69) counts him among the non-millennialists.

an, Theophilus, the Egyptian bishop Nepos, Victorinus of Pettau, Lactantius,[80] Methodius, and Apollinaris van Laodicea (second/third century) all held to some form of premillennialism.[81] The Montanists, the Donatists, and some Gnostic movements were premillennialist as well.[82] Even in the fourth century, we still find premillennialist notions with Ambrose of Milan. Ernest Lee Tuveson concludes that the doctrine of the millennial kingdom appears to have been very strong until late in the rule of Constantine.[83] I limit myself to a few quotations.

Justin is often quoted as a star witness: "I and others, who are right-minded Christians on all points, are assured that there will be a resurrection of the dead, and a thousand years in Jerusalem, which will then be built, adorned, and enlarged, [as] the prophets Ezekiel and Isaiah and others declare."[84] In his next chapter, Justin supports this view with passages from Isaiah and Revelation.

Early in the third century, Hippolytus of Rome wrote: "And 6,000 years must needs be accomplished, in order that the Sabbath may come, the rest, the holy day 'on which God rested from all His works.' [Gen. 2:2] For the Sabbath is the type and emblem of the future kingdom

---

80. Lactantius in the *Divinae Institutiones* forms the culmination point of millennialism in the West, so G. G. Blum (1981, 731).
81. M. van Duijn in Van 't Spijker *et al.* (1999, 156–58).
82. Doyle (1999, 58–62) therefore counts this premillennialism among the deviations from New Testament themes, together with Gnosticism and moralism—as if *every* doctrine of a heretic is automatically a heresy.
83. Tuveson (1964, 14).
84. *Dial. Tryph.* 80 (www.ccel.org/ccel/schaff/anf01.viii.iv.lxxx.html).

of the saints, when they 'shall reign with Christ,' [Rev. 20:4, 6] when He comes from heaven, as John says in his Apocalypse: for 'a day with the Lord is as a thousand years.' [2 Pet. 3:8]."[85]

Irenaeus was clearly a premillenialist. He wrote: the blessing for Israel "belongs unquestionably to the times of the kingdom, when the righteous shall bear rule upon their rising from the dead; when also the creation, having been renovated and set free, shall fructify with an abundance of all kinds of food . . . and that all animals feeding [only] on the productions of the earth, should [in those days] become peaceful and harmonious among each other, and be in perfect subjection to man. . . . And these things are borne witness to in writing by Papias, the hearer of John, and a companion of Polycarp."[86]

Church historian Philip Schaff claimed that the most conspicuous point in the eschatology of the ante-Nicene period was prominent millennialism, the belief in a visible rule of Christ in glory on earth with the risen saints during a thousand years before the general resurrection and the accompanying judgment. He says it was not the doctrine of the church embodied in some confession of faith, or form of devotion, but a wide-spread view of famous teachers such as Barnabas, Papias, Justin Martyr, Irenaeus, Tertullian, Methodius, and Lactantius, while Caius, Origen, Dionysius the Great, Eusebius (just as Jerome and Augustine subsequently) combated it.

---

85. *On the Hexæmeron* (www.newadvent.org/fathers/0502.htm).
86. *Adv. Haer.* V.33.3–4 (http://www.newadvent.org/fathers/0103533.htm).

Daniel Whitby (†1725), the founder of postmillennialism—thus, relatively speaking, a rather recent doctrine—had to acknowledge that, for two hundred fifty years, premillennialism had been considered to be an apostolic tradition by the best Christians. This is quoted by George Peters,[87] who gives an extensive enumeration of all prominent premillennialists of the first three centuries.[88] He also claims that, from the first two centuries, *no single* author is known who has combated premillennialism.[89]

A convinced amillennialist such as Oswald Allis had to acknowledge, too, that premillennialism was widespread in the early church, and that it was only Augustine who, to a large extent, replaced it with spiritualist supersessionism.[90] And Nathanael West wrote that history has witnessed no doctrinal consensus more unanimous than the consensus of the Apostolic Fathers concerning the parousia *before* the millennium.[91] Only in the third century did the first opposition arise, especially by raising doubts as to the authorship of Revelation and of certain Old Testament passages.

### 10.7.3 Other Views

Perhaps the idea of such an absolute supremacy of premillennialism is a little exaggerated. Some authors believe that Pseudo-Barnabas was an amillennialist, just like the *Alogi* (heretics in Asia Minor, around AD 170,

---

87. Peters (1952, 1:482–83).
88. Peters (1952, 1:494–96).
89. Also see Feinberg (1961, 243–48).
90. Allis (1945, 7).
91. West (1981, 332); see for asserting the opposite Lee (2006).

who rejected John, 1–3 John, and Rev.). Under the influence of spiritualizing neo-Platonism, Clement of Alexandria and Origen rejected premillennialism. We see this more often: premillennialism is rejected not on strictly exegetical grounds but because of the rise of spiritualism. I am not aware of a theologian during the first three centuries who tried to refute premillennialism on purely exegetical grounds.

With Eusebius, Jerome, and Augustine, we have entered the time of the Constantinian turn and afterward. We have seen that, during this turn, many felt that the Messianic kingdom had arrived, a feeling that totally changed the eschatological picture. In the fourth century, millennialism was not only combated but viewed as a heresy. Today, many are not aware of this, but the phrase "whose kingdom shall have no end" (*hou tēs basileias ouk estai telos*) in the Nicene Creed was intended as a direct attack upon the premillennialists.[92] The conviction was that there would be no kingdom of a thousand years but only an everlasting kingdom. This shows immediately on what weak exegetical grounds premillennialism was combated. To be sure, premillennialists, too, have in their Bibles Daniel 7:14 ("his dominion is an everlasting dominion, which shall not pass away, and his kingdom one that shall not be destroyed"), Luke 1:33 ("he will reign over the house of Jacob forever, and of his kingdom there will be no end"), and Revelation 22:5 ("and they [i.e., the glorified saints] will reign forever and ever"). One can easily believe in an eternal kingdom of Christ, and yet be a millennialist.

---

92. Hall (1992, 171).

The implication of premillennialism is that the power and glory of God's kingdom will come to light only at the parousia of Christ. However, after the Constantinian turn, (earthly, worldly) power and glory were precisely what the Christian emperor as well as the bishop of Rome needed. Pushing aside premillennialism, together with spreading amillennialism, was thus a necessary theological tool in the rise of the papacy. During the present "millennial kingdom," the pope ruled as Christ's substitute on earth. Therefore people owed him their absolute obedience (some speak here of the Thyatira stage of the church[93]). People saw the prophetic predictions of the glory of the Messianic kingdom fulfilled in the domination, riches, and splendor of the Roman Catholic Church. The reward and exaltation of believers no longer depended on the parousia but on the power of papacy. Premillennialism was a concrete threat to this doctrine, and had to be combated with every available strength.[94] Premillennialists look forward to the glory of the kingdom, and thus to the parousia—amillennialists seek this glory *now*.

In this respect, I see no fundamental difference between the rising papacy from the fourth century onward, and the Reformed activism of Abraham Kuyper around 1900, which acquired its most extreme form in so-called Dominion theology. The latter is often confused with Evangelical kingdom theology, for instance, by referring to both of them as forms of "Kingdom Now" theology. Evangelical kingdom theology does often emphasize the significance of signs and wonders today, but

---

93. See Ouweneel (2010c, chapter 2).
94. Peters (1952, 1:516–17).

is *not* political: it does not strive for a theocratic world government, that is, a political establishment of the millennial kingdom. Charismatic kingdom theology can very well be premillennialist; Dominion theology, or Christian Reconstructionism, in its strict sense, is postmillennialist. To enhance the confusion: if I understand C. Peter Wagner's "New Apostolic Reformation" correctly, it is a peculiar variety of Charismatic kingdom theology with traces of Calvinist Dominion theology.[95]

One of the greatest objections that anti-premillennialists in the early church raised against premillennialists was the latter's earthly view regarding the millennial kingdom, with all the pleasures that were thought to belong to it. Thus, Augustine opposed the lavish feasts of the premillennialist Donatists in such a way as to suggest a direct connection between their sensuous behavior and their earthly expectations concerning the end time.[96] Manlio Simonetti ascribed the spiritualization of the prophecies partly to the rise and influence of (neo-)Platonic spiritualism, with its stronger emphasis on the soul than on the body. The argumentation is not quite convincing given the fact that precisely the pope and the emperor, who saw themselves as the spiritual and secular representatives of Christ on earth, respectively, often led opulent lives on earth.

Another important factor was the ever growing anti-Semitism, that had already begun with the Council of Nicea (AD 325) (see §10.2.1). People found premillennialism too "Jewish." Everything that reminded them of the Jewish expectation of the Messianic kingdom was

---

95. See, e.g., Wagner (2008).
96. *De civ. Dei* XX.7.

rejected by more and more Christians. The post-Constantinian battle against premillennialism cannot be separated from this theological anti-Semitism and (neo-Platonic) spiritualism—nor from a purely horizontal imperial and ecclesiastical political ambition for power. Theological disputes are seldom about purely exegetical questions; all too often a major role is played by various ideological "-isms."

In the wake of Augustine, the Middle Ages included hardly any premillennialism. To put it more strongly, millennialism had become a heresy, as it is still to the Roman Catholic Church, and I assume also to some Reformed theologians.[97] The Protestant Reformers, too, saw millennialism as nothing but a "Jewish dream."[98] The thoroughly eschatological notion of the kingdom of God increasingly acquired a present meaning: the Christian church and state *are* in principle (in bud form) the kingdom of God. As Julian of Toledo (seventh century) formulated the amillennialism of his day: the millennial kingdom is the church of God, which by spreading its faith and works is extended as a kingdom of faith from the time of the incarnation until the time of the coming judgment.[99]

---

97. See, e.g., in the Netherlands, J. Douma (2008, especially chapters 4–6).

98. Schaff (1910, 619).

99. *Antitheses* II.69 (*PL* 96, 697).

# Chapter 11
# Later History of Kingdom Theology

*So do not let what you regard as good*
   *be spoken of as evil.*
*For the kingdom of God is not a*
   *matter of eating and drinking*
   *but of righteousness and*
   *peace and joy in the Holy Spirit.*
*Whoever thus serves Christ*
   *is acceptable to God and approved*
   *by men.*
*So then let us pursue*
   *what makes for peace and for*
   *mutual upbuilding.*
                    Romans 14:16–19

*[T]he kingdom of God does not con-*
   *sist in talk*
*but in power.*
                    1 Corinthians 4:20

**Summary:** *This chapter offers a further analysis of pre- and post-millennialism, and of various strands of more lib-*

*eral schools: "old-liberal," "consistent," "realized," "transcendent/existential," and "liberation" kingdom theology. Some modern strands in more conservative circles are "dominion" and "prosperity" theology, both of which have great consequences for one's view of the kingdom. Basic misunderstandings in kingdom theology include the idea of the "delayed" parousia, the trend of spiritualizing the kingdom, a false view of the relationship between kingdom and church, the idea of the "already fulfilled" parousia, and several forms of materialism and secularism. The chapter concludes with surveys of the pre-millennial view and of all the underlying issues.*

## 11.1 Protestant Premillennialism

### 11.1.1 The Reformers

WE WILL OMIT DISCUSSION of the millennialist pretenses that emerged time and again during the Middle Ages,[1] and mention only that premillennialism never entirely disappeared during the time before the Reformation (fourth to fifteenth centuries). Charles Ryrie quotes the Waldenses and the Cathars, who preserved the faith of the earliest church fathers.[2] George Peters quotes the Albigenses, the Wycliffites, and the Bohemian Brethren as well.[3] Unfortunately, the Reformers did not adopt the faith of the earliest church fathers and of these pre-Reformational fellow believers, but instead adopted Augustinian amillennialism entirely. Of course, this was due not to bad intentions, but it seems to me that the Reformers were simply too busy with soteriology and the

---

1. See extensively, Cohn (1970).
2. Ryrie (1953, 27–28).
3. Peters (1952, 1:521).

reformation of church structure to take time to study eschatology thoroughly. This is an example of the "incompletenesses" of the works of the church in its new Sardis stage (Rev. 3:2), as some have called this phase in church history.[4]

Martin Luther and John Calvin utterly rejected millennialism in any conceivable form. The Lutherans formally condemned millennialism in their Augsburg Confession (Art. XVII): "They [i.e., the Lutherans] condemn also others who are now spreading certain Jewish opinions, that before the resurrection of the dead the godly shall take possession of the kingdom of the world, the ungodly being everywhere suppressed."[5]

Calvin wrote: "[I]n Paul's day he began to overthrow it [1 Cor. 15:12ff.]. But a little later there followed the chiliasts, who limited the reign of Christ to a thousand years. Now their fiction is too childish either to need or to be worth a refutation. And the Apocalypse, from which they undoubtedly drew a pretext for their error, does not support them. For the number 'one thousand' [Rev. 20:4] does not apply to the eternal blessedness of the church but only to the various disturbances that awaited the church, while still toiling on earth. On the contrary, all Scripture proclaims that there will be no end to the blessedness of the elect or the punishment of the wicked [Matt. 25:41, 46]. . . . Those who assign the children of God a thousand years in which to enjoy the inheritance of the life to come do not realize how much reproach they are casting upon Christ and his Kingdom. For if they do not put on immortality, then Christ him-

---

4. See Ouweneel (2010c, chapter 2).
5. http://bookofconcord.org/augsburgconfession.php.

self, to whose glory they shall be transformed, has not been received into undying glory [1 Cor. 15:13ff.]. If their blessedness is to have an end, then Christ's Kingdom, on whose firmness it depends, is but temporary.... [L]et us pass over these triflers, lest, contrary to what we have previously said, we seem to judge their ravings worth refuting."[6]

The reader is struck by several aspects here: (a) The harsh and unfair language toward fellow believers ("fiction," "puerile, "triflers," their "dreams" do not deserve refutation). (b) An incomprehensible misunderstanding about millennialism (as if the thousand years would imply a limit to the everlasting blessedness of believers). (c) Claims about the interpretation of Revelation 20 without any support or argumentation. One might say that such a harsh attitude was common in those days, but that is too cheap. In *all* stages of church history, theologians ought to be fair toward their opponents, ought to try to understand their views instead of tilting at windmills, and ought to adduce arguments for their own views.

Heinrich Bullinger says in the Second Helvetic Confession (chapter XI): "We further condemn Jewish dreams that there will be a golden age on earth before the Day of Judgment, and that the pious, having subdued all their godless enemies, will possess all the kingdoms of the earth. For evangelical truth in Matt., chs. 24 and 25, and Luke, ch. 18, and apostolic teaching in II Thess., ch. 2, and II Tim., chs. 3 and 4, present something quite different."[7] Again, this attitude is to

---

6. Calvin, *Institutes*, 3.25.5.
7. https://www.ccel.org/creeds/helvetic.htm.

be rejected, even though it appears in an official confession! It is naïve and unfair to simply refer to Bible passages to prove your opponent wrong. The opponent knows these passages as well as you do, but believes that they agree with his own views. Theologians ought to *expound* Bible passages in their reasonings, not just refer to them.

Thomas Cranmer described the millennial kingdom as a "fable of Jewish origin." This was in the 1553 version of the Anglican Articles (Art. 41). Interestingly, in the revision of 1563, this phrase was left out.

## 11.1.2 The Revival of Premillennialism

In spite of all their criticisms, the Reformers unintentionally contributed to the revival of millennialism through their fundamental return to the "literal" (grammatical-historical, anti-allegorizing) method of Bible exegesis. The expositor who consistently follows this path will, sooner or later, have to form his judgment about the spiritualist approach of the biblical prophecies. However, this literal interpretation of prophecy was new, and using it resembles learning to drive a car: one must learn to properly estimate the curves in the road. Thus, various early-Protestant theologians in their new approach fell over the edge right away. Already in the sixteenth century, we encounter millennialists with an often rather sensual-earthly mentality. I already mentioned the examples of the Quintomonarchists and of John Bockelson in Münster (§10.1.4). There were more such premillennialists who linked their views with a revolutionary-political agenda, intending to see their eschatological views realized in their own day.

Genuine premillennialists in sixteenth- and seventeenth-century Western Europe, who were not all of such a revolutionary mind, included theologians such as Joseph Mede (especially in his famous *Clavis Apocalyptica*), Jean de Labadie, Alhard de Raedt, and perhaps also Johannes Piscator, Johann Heinrich Alsted, Hugh Latimer, Thomas Brightman, Jan Amos Comenius, Petrus Serrarius, Hendrik Alting and his son Jacobus Alting, and Pierre Jurieu. In addition to these theologians, also mentioned by Theo van Campen, I mention with honor Robert Maton Nathanael Homes, Ralph Farmer, William Sherwin, Thomas Goodwin, Robert Cressener, Johann W. Petersen, Robert Fleming, Charles Daubuz, Thomas Hartley, Magnus F. Roos, Johann J. Hess.[8] All these authors have been heavily attacked by others.[9] Even moderate postmillennialists such as Theodore van der Groe (§10.6.1) sometimes had to endure severe criticism.[10]

Insofar as theologians in those days adhered to some form of millennialism, that is, belief in a future millennial kingdom, they emphasized that they meant a spiritual kingdom, without any earthly pleasures and lusts; so, for instance, Franciscus Ridderus, Henricus Groenewegen, and David Flud van Giffen.[11] Obvious postmillennialists such as William à Brakel, David Flud van Giffen, and Campegius Vitringa categorically denied that their views had anything to do with millennialism because they were

---

8. See Peters (1952, 1:538).
9. Van Campen (2007, 150–51, 176, 180, 204, 295–96, 332, 336–37).
10. Van Campen (2007, 245–46).
11. Van Campen (2007, 148–49, 408, 446–47).

afraid that they would be associated with all too carnally minded millennialists.[12] Especially millennialists who also believed in a future restoration of Israel in the Holy Land, and the restoration of Jerusalem and the other Jewish cities, perhaps even the building of the Third Temple, were condemned for their earthly expectations.

Conversely, theologians who did believe in a national and spiritual restoration of Israel distanced themselves from what *they* understood by millennialism. Every author could imagine another millennialism that was more earthly than his own variety, and thus distance himself from (this kind of) millennialism. At any rate, it is certainly true that millennialism—here especially the postmillennialist belief in a future heyday of the church, *before* the parousia of Christ—and the belief in a national and spiritual restoration of Israel are not automatically linked.[13]

## 11.2 Protestant Postmillennialism

### 11.2.1 A Confused Picture

In addition to the obvious and not-so-obvious premillennialists already mentioned, there are at least as many obvious postmillennialists to be found in the seventeenth and eighteenth centuries. The strongly anti-Reformed Anglican Daniel Whitby (1638-1726), who later developed Arian and Unitarian tendencies, is often viewed as the father of postmillennialism. See especially the appendix "A Treatise of the Millennium" in his *Paraphrase and Commentary of the New Testament* (1703).[14] As far as

---

12. Van Campen (2007, 202, 204, 440, 478-80).

13. Van Campen (2007, 578).

14. See www.preteristarchive.com/StudyArchive/w/whitby-daniel.

the Netherlands is concerned, I mention among others (in the order of birth): Johannes Coccejus, Theodore à Brakel, Andreas Essenius, Jacobus Koelman, William à Brakel, David Flud van Giffen, Campegius Vitringa, Friedrich Adolph Lampe, Joachim Mobachius, Theodore van der Groe, and Joannes Ernestus Jungius (cf. §10.5.3).[15]

Such a simple enumeration should not conceal the fact that the mutual differences and uncertainties are large. No wonder: someone like Johannes Cocceius believed that the millennial kingdom is already behind us, but at the same time believed in a future heyday of the church before the parousia. Because of this last point, his views fit the definition of postmillennialism. In other cases it is unclear whether an author is a pre- or a postmillennialist. This point depends on the question whether "the" parousia (and not some invisible intervention) of Christ precedes the Messianic kingdom, or follows upon it. Thus, Willem J. van Asselt was of the opinion that Jacobus Koelman had premillennialist ideas, whereas Theo van Campen ascribed to him especially postmillennialist views.[16] And as to William à Brakel: one author called him definitely not a millennialist, another one called him a partial or apparent millennialist, a third one called him an obvious postmillennialist.[17]

---

html; regarding him and other early Anglican millennialists, see De Jong (1970).

15. Van Campen (2007, 294-96, 192, 139, 167, 174, 198, 201-204, 427, 439, 475-76, 489, 498, 501-502, 504-505, 535, 543).
16. Van Campen (2007, 180).
17. Van Campen (2007, 200-201).

I repeat: we identify as a postmillennialist everyone who (a) believes in a *future* heyday of the church on earth (linked or not linked with a national and spiritual restoration of Israel) before the parousia of Christ, and (b) believes that with this parousia the eternal state will arrive (the new heavens and the new earth). In this description, it hardly matters whether the theologian concerned associates this future heyday of the church with Revelation 20:1-6, takes the "thousand years" literally, or calls himself a (post)millennialist.

## 11.2.2 Critical Questions

It is certainly no coincidence that millennialism appealed so strongly especially to leaders of Puritanism in Great Britain, of the Second Reformation in the Netherlands, and of Pietism in Germany. During the eighteenth century, the Englishman Daniel Whitby, the German Johann Albrecht Bengel, and the American Jonathan Edwards, did not view themselves as premillennialists, but did stoke the fires of millennialist ideas, which continued burning in the nineteenth century.[18] And unavoidably, good views were mixed with false ideas. I already mentioned the Arian and Unitarian tendencies of Whitby. Bengel believed that the millennial kingdom would begin in 1836; in that year Satan would be bound, and a massive conversion of Jews and Gentiles would occur. And a thousand years later (in 2836), a second millennial kingdom would arrive, when the risen saints would reign.[19] Edwards taught that a kind of millennial kingdom would begin in 1866, that is, 1,260

---

18. Schwarz (2000, 330).
19. Van Campen (2007, 490).

years after AD 606, when Rome was acknowledged as having universal authority.[20]

Such erroneous views did not help make millennialism any more credible. But apart from them, theologians such as Bengel and Edwards, and many others, helped others to clearly recognize the fact *that* some millennial kingdom would arrive one day, *and* that its establishment would be linked with the national and spiritual restoration of Israel. Perhaps no man has summarized and reformulated these views more ably, and with more worldwide influence, than the Anglo-Irish John N. Darby (1800–1882).[21]

In the next chapters, we will review modern millennialism, including the theological arguments *pro* and *contra* the notion of a future millennial kingdom. However, at this point we may draw the following basileological conclusion: it makes an enormous difference whether one believes that we are living today under the rule of Christ, that is, in the Messianic kingdom, *or* whether one believes that the rule of Christ, that is, in the Messianic kingdom, will be brought about in the future only, either before or after the parousia. Among other things, these are the underlying problems.

(a) Where does it follow from Scripture that Christ rules today as the Son of Man, that is, as distinct from the general dominion of (the Triune) God? To be sure, all authority in heaven and on earth *has* already been given to him (Matt. 28:18), but that is not necessarily the same as actually reigning. Luke 19:12 describes in

---

20. Quoted in Stilley (1996, 100).
21. See especially the prophetic volumes in his *Collected Writings*: Darby (n.d.).

parabolic language that Jesus has gone into a "far country" (heaven) "to receive for himself a kingdom and then return." The Messianic kingdom begins at the parousia, not before.

(b) What is the amillennialist response to the claim that, if Christ were exercising world dominion today, this would contrast blatantly with the picture that the prophecies give us of the Messianic kingdom? Basically, the rabbis were always right when they asserted that Jesus did *not* bring in the Messianic kingdom as it has been described by the Old Testament prophets. Today, Jesus does reign in the hearts and lives of believers—but this is something essentially different from the world dominion that he will exercise in the age to come.

(c) Paul tells the Corinthians that "the saints will judge the world" (1 Cor. 6:2), and that the righteous will inherit the kingdom of God (cf. v. 9), but gives them this reproach: "Already you [supposedly] have all you want! Already you have become rich! Without us you have become kings! And would that you did reign, so that we might share the rule with you!" (4:8; cf. v. 20; Rev. 2:26-27; 3:21; 20:4, 6). We are dealing here with what sometimes has been called an *overrealized eschatology*: too much emphasis on the "already now," and too little on the "not yet" (cf. §5.2).[22] Believers *have* been made a kingdom (Greek *basileia*, Rev. 1:6; 5:10; cf. 1 Pet. 2:9), but they do not yet reign (*basileuō*, Rev. 20:4, 6). *De jure* they are kings, but not yet *de facto*; they are, so to speak, crown princes.

---

22. Fee (1987, ad loc.); Thiselton (2000, ad loc.).

## 11.3 Old-Liberal Basileology
### 11.3.1 What Is Liberal?

Of course, *the* Christian, or even *the* Evangelical basileology does not exist. If some apparent consensus ever existed, then certainly it has not existed since the time of the Enlightenment, which did away with the belief in a literal, physical parousia. This belief and its denial constitute the essential difference between a conservative and a liberal basileology. A literal parousia involves a coming of the bodily, visible Christ (Rev. 1:7, "with the clouds, and every eye will see him"), which will be "as the lightning comes from the east and shines as far as the west" (Matt. 24:27), and takes place "with power and great glory" (v. 30). It will be a coming to judge the wicked, to save the faithful, to raise deceased believers, and to establish the Messianic kingdom (no matter how this is understood).

There are several kinds of liberal basileologies, as we will see, but on this point they all agree: we are not to expect such a physical, visible parousia. First, the enlightened mind supposedly can no longer rationally account for such a hope; it is viewed as part of New Testament mythology. Second, statements concerning such a parousia tell us more about the eschatological visions of the apostles and the early church than that they ought to be accepted as divinely authoritative statements.

Liberal basileology is a product of Enlightenment thinking, which did away with notions such as those of revelation, Scriptural inspiration, virgin birth, and resurrection, and thus also the physical, visible parousia occurring in space and time. In short, the Enlightenment rejected anything supernatural, that is, anything that could not be described in terms of the natural laws known to us. Liberal theology does not rest primarily on biblical exegesis, but on the philosophical prejudices of anti-supernaturalism.

In the description of liberal basileology, I follow Theissen and Metz to a large extent.[23] Beginning with Albrecht Ritschl (see below), they distinguish six phases in the theological research concerning the kingdom of God. In his book on Jesus, Joseph Ratzinger (pope Benedict XVI) distinguishes three different views, namely, an ecclesiocentric, a Christocentric, and a regnocentric view. These are the views that place the church, Christ, and the kingdom itself (taken as totally secular), respectively, in the center.[24] In this latter development, Ratzinger sees a disquieting similarity to the third temptation of Christ: "Again, the devil took him to a very high mountain and showed him all the kingdoms of the world and their glory. And he said to him, 'All these I will give you, if you will fall down and worship me'" (Matt. 4:8-9). Apparently this means that a kingdom of "God" in which human achievement is more central than God and Christ is instead a kingdom of the devil than of God. It is a kingdom that is reverently ascribed to God but in fact is brought about by genuflecting to the devil.

---

23. Theissen and Merz (1998, 242-245); also see Ridderbos (1962, xi-xxxiv); Berkouwer (1972, 25-27, 68-69, 87-89); Ladd (1964, 3-44); Hoekema (1979, 288-316); Willis (1987); Saucy (1997); Erickson (1998, 1156-1168); Schwarz (2000, 107-120); Van Genderen (2008, 824-26).
24. Ratzinger (2007, 49-54).

## 11.3.2 Ritsch and Harnack

Through the inspiration of Enlightenment ethics, liberal basileology began with the *old-liberal*, or as I like to call it, the *ethicistic* basileology of Albrecht Ritschl (1822–1889), followed by Adolf von Harnack (1851–1930). These theologians taught that we must view the kingdom of God in a strictly horizontalist sense. It is brought about here and now through human efforts. This liberal-ethical view has continued to the present time. At its fringes it intermingles with secular ideologies such as those of socialism and Marxism, which each in their own way preach a secularized Utopia.[25] Whether the kingdom of God will arrive or not depends on passionate idealists, who push for a better society, with or without the "help of God" (whatever this may mean).

In itself, striving for a better world is of course a praiseworthy commitment. With some goodwill, one could even call the improvements that have thus far been achieved in this way precursors of the Messianic kingdom. But as such they do not lead to the Messianic kingdom because this is not the way in which it is brought about. Christians should be the very first to pursue a better society. But this is not the way in which the Messianic kingdom is realized; this happens through the personal, majestic intervention of Christ.

The similarity between the ethicistic view and conservative basileology is that both believe in a future kingdom of God. The difference is that this kingdom is brought about, according to the former view, by human achievement, and according to the latter view, through

---

25. Cf. Gerlach (1920 book title: *Communism As Doctrine of the Millennial Kingdom*).

the work of God, "as the mighty sovereign act of God himself."[26] Of course, this is not an absolute but only a gradual difference: the former view does not necessarily exclude God's help, and the latter view does not necessarily exclude human effort (cf. 2 Pet. 3:12, "*hastening the coming of the day of God*"). Yet, the difference is essential. The core of this liberal view is emancipated, autonomous humanity, on whose labors the ultimate result ultimately depends. Perhaps, the conservative view has sometimes left the result too passively in God's hands ("Hush, wait, everything will become new," as Hanna Lam poetized). However, the old-liberal view has gone to the other extreme in leaving room for at most God's providence in bringing about the kingdom.

## 11.4 "Consistent" Basileology

### 11.4.1 An Illusion?

The old-liberal view discussed above in §11.3 was attacked by no one less than Ritschl's own son-in-law, Johannes Weiss (1863–1914).[27] Just like Albert Schweitzer (1875–1965) after him,[28] and later also Fritz Buri and Martin Werner, Weiss propounded a *consistent* basileology, as Schweitzer called it. They claimed that the kingdom of which Jesus spoke was definitely intended as a future, apocalyptic kingdom of peace and justice, in agreement with the Jewish apocalyptic of those days. This kingdom was not the result of human effort but of divine intervention. On this point, Weiss and Schweitzer agreed with conservative basileology: Jesus and

---

26. Küng (2001, 58).
27. Weiss (1892).
28. Schweitzer (1985, 2001).

the apostles expected the physical, visible parousia of Jesus and the arrival of the Messianic kingdom. The old-liberal basileology explained the kingdom in a figurative, secularized way; consistent basileology explained it in a literal way.

The enormous difference with conservative basileology is this: according to Weiss and Schweitzer, Jesus and the apostles unfortunately fell prey to an illusion. A concrete example: Werner G. Kümmel said that it is impossible to maintain that Jesus had *not* erred.[29] The idealistic kingdom that Jesus and his apostles expected has turned out to be a mistake, a dream. It never arrived, and thus it makes no sense to us today. Instead, we should endeavor to live in the present time as followers of Jesus, and try to forget the beautiful dream of the Messianic kingdom.

Although Oscar Cullmann did not go nearly as far, he too ventured to say that in 1 Thessalonians 4:15 Paul still expressed the opinion that he would be alive at the time of the parousia, but he changed this opinion in his later letters.[30] This is a peculiar example of misunderstanding with respect to the existential strength of the true Christian hope, which talks about "*we* who are alive [at the parousia]," even if one presumes that one will die before this. It is the same Jesus who said that he would stay away a "long time" (Matt. 25:19) but who also said five times that he would come "soon" (Rev. 2:16; 3:11; 22:7, 12, 20; cf. 1:1; 22:6).

Schweitzer spoke of the "delay (postponement) of the parousia" (*Parusieverzögerung*), which is a mistaken

---

29. Kümmel (1957, 87).

30. Cullmann (1964, 88), referring to 2 Cor. 5:1–2; Phil. 1:23.

phrase:[31] neither within nor outside the New Testament is there ever a question of a postponement of the parousia, let alone its cancellation.[32] In my view, the error in "consistent" eschatology is this: the fact that believers have been waiting for the Messianic kingdom already for two thousand years does not prove that it will never come, or even that it has been postponed (deferred, suspended). In his parables, Jesus himself had already indicated in a concealed way that his coming might take place later than his disciples thought or hoped (Matt. 13:24-30, 36-43; 24:6, 48-49; 25:5,19; Luke 12:38, 45; 19:11; 20:9; cf. also John 21:22-23). It is therefore a mistake to claim that Jesus himself expected his parousia very soon (see §5.4).[33]

It is totally arbitrary to set aside as non-authentic or as "church theology" (*Gemeindetheologie*) all those passages that seem to contradict the imminent expectation (*Naherwartung*).[34] Jesus does both: he pleads for "staying awake" *and* argues that the "hour" of his parousia is unknown; he even does it in one and the same sentence: "Therefore, stay awake, *for* you do not know on what day your Lord is coming" (Matt. 24:42). This may occur

---

31. Berkouwer (1972, 65-66, 79-81, 91-92). In Matt. 24:48, I prefer translations such as "will not come back soon" (ERV; cf. NIV, etc.) to the common "is delayed" (ESV, etc.), or "is delaying his coming" (NKJV) (similarly in 25:5).

32. Werner (1941, 98) claimed that Christian dogma arose to fill the gap that had arisen between the imminent expectation (*Naherwartung*; see §5.4) and the supposed delay of the parousia.

33. Cf. Ridderbos (1962, 444-56, 498-510); Brown (1994, 52-58); Morphew (2011, 55). For another opinion, see Bockmuehl (1994, 100-102).

34. Berkouwer (1972, 85-86, 105-106).

during the first watch, but it could just as easily occur in the second, the third, or even the fourth watch (v. 43; cf. 14:25; Luke 12:38). Jesus does not say: stay awake, for I am coming very soon, but: stay awake *because* you do not know when I will come. The need to stay awake implies that the parousia will be later rather than sooner.

## 11.4.2 A Delayed Parousia

The idea that Jesus' eschatology does not necessarily imply a parousia that is literally "near" is not contradicted by passages such as Matthew 10:23; 16:28; 24:34 (see §5.4).[35] Therefore, these passages cannot be used as evidence that Jesus erred with regard to his return.

The error ("it takes so long, so it will not come") belongs to the category of 2 Peter 3:3-4, "[K]nowing this first of all, that scoffers will come in the last days with scoffing, following their own sinful desires. They will say, 'Where is the promise of his coming? For ever since the fathers fell asleep, all things are continuing as they were from the beginning of creation.'" Without suggesting that Weiss, Schweitzer, Buri, and Werner are scoffers, the ultimate effect of their views is the same: the parousia as well as the post-parousia Messianic kingdom have turned out to be mistakes.

Gerrit C. Berkouwer refers to Gerhard Sevenster, who in 1951 convincingly showed that there is no contrast between New Testament passages suggesting an imminent expectation (see, e.g., Phil. 4:5; Heb. 10:37; James 5:8-9; 1 Pet. 4:7; Rev. 1:3; cf. 1 Cor. 7:29, 31 ["is passing away"][36]) and the delayed parousia. I maintain

---

35. See also Ouweneel (2007b, 461).
36. Berkouwer (1972, 82-83).

this in opposition to, for instance, Erich Grässer, Philipp Vielhauer, Götz Harbsmeier, and Hanz Conzelmann, who all speak of a "crisis" in New Testament hope.[37] Berkouwer rightly argues that one could speak of a crisis only if, through Jesus' staying away, belief in the promised parousia would have begun to dwindle among Christians. However, this is not the case at all. To be sure, the "end tarries" (cf. Hab. 2:3 KJV), but the hope has not decreased. Take, for instance, 2 Peter 3:3–4 mentioned above: the passage does not speak at all of disappointment among the faithful but of scoffing among the unfaithful. As Berkouwer puts it, Jesus does come "unexpectedly" (*onverwachts*), that is, as a surprise, but not "unexpected" (*on-verwacht*), or as a thief surprises you (cf. 1 Thess. 5:4).[38] He calls it folly to speak of a crisis, and describes the entire "consistent eschatology" as "a construct" (read, "speculation").

Hendrikus Berkhof, too, argues that, in the wake of Schweitzer, the problem of the non-occurring parousia has been exaggerated far too much, as if it had caused the church a deep and lasting trauma.[39] He then quotes Karl Barth,[40] Wolfhart Pannenberg,[41] and himself,[42] who have adduced Christological, anthropological, and Christological-pneumatological explanations, respec-

---

37. Berkouwer (1972, 70–72).
38. Berkouwer (1972, 73–74, 77, 85); he points to Old Testament examples (77): Ps. 74:9–11, 22–23; 89:47, 50; Isa. 21:11–12; Ezek. 12:21–28; Hab. 1:2.
39. Berkhof (1979, 314).
40. Barth (2010, IV/3, 365–85).
41. Pannenberg (1977, 106–108).
42. Berkhof (2004, 81, 101).

tively, for the fact that the parousia has taken more time than many early Christians had presumed. These explanations amount to this: Jesus involves people and human history in the realization of his great end goal: the establishment of the Messianic kingdom. This is an important view: believers do not passively wait for the coming of the kingdom but actively prepare it. They work as if the breakthrough of the kingdom depends entirely on them ("waiting for and *hastening* the coming of the day of God," 2 Pet. 3:12), and they expect this breakthrough as if it depends entirely on God. However this may be, they look forward to the literal parousia at the end of this (present) age (cf. §§4.4.2–4.4.3 above).

### 11.4.3 The Necessity of a Delayed Parousia

In line with what I just said—a certain *world history* is needed before the parousia can occur—let me make a few additional remarks.

(a) "[The] gospel of the kingdom will be proclaimed throughout the whole world as a testimony to all nations, and then the end will come" (Matt. 24:14), that is, the end of the present age (v. 3). In other words, Jesus cannot come again as long as not all nations have been reached with the gospel of the kingdom, and I would add: as long as there are not yet devoted Christians among every tribe and language and people and nation (Rev. 5:9; 7:9). It is the expectation of many, for that matter, that this goal will be reached before the middle of the present century.[43] Until the eighteenth century, the gospel had scarcely spread beyond Europe and the colonies in the New World (apart from the Middle East and

---

43. Cf. www.finishingthetask.com.

North Africa, which later had been conquered by the Islam, however).

(b) There could be no parousia as long as Israel is not back in its own country. All the Old Testament prophecies about the parousia and the establishment of the Messianic kingdom presuppose a nation of Israel in the Holy Land. Even after the return from the Babylonian exile, it is said (in a literal translation): "I will sow them among the peoples; and they shall remember me in far countries; and they shall live with their children, and shall return" (Zech. 10:9 ASV; cf. [N]KJV, NASB). The eschatological context of Matthew 24:15-21 presupposes Israel in its own land, just before the parousia. During the 1,260 days of the end time (i.e., the last half "week" of Dan. 9:24-27; cf. Rev. 12:6; 13:5, "forty-two months"), there will be a temple and an altar in the holy city (Rev. 11:1-3). The state of Israel has existed only since 1948, and ancient Jerusalem has returned to Jewish hands only since 1967: "Jerusalem will be trampled underfoot by the Gentiles, until the times of the Gentiles are fulfilled" (Luke 21:24), that is, by the end of the "times of the Gentiles" Jerusalem will *not* be trampled underfoot by the Gentiles anymore.

(c) Elsewhere I have extensively explained the prophetic view of the four world empires.[44] The fourth is the Roman Empire, whose history consists of two phases: the first one represented by the two legs (the Western and Eastern parts of the empire), the second one by the ten toes of the image in Daniel 2 and the ten horns of the fourth beast in Daniel 7. This theme is picked up again in Revelation 13:1 (cf. 17:3), "I saw a

---

44. Ouweneel (2012a, chapter 6; 2016d, chapter 4 and following).

beast rising out of the sea, with ten horns and seven heads, with ten diadems on its horns and blasphemous names on its heads." The explanation is given in 17:7-8, 12-14: "I will tell you the mystery of . . . the beast with seven heads and ten horns. . . . . The beast that you saw *was, and is not, and is about to rise* from the bottomless pit and go to destruction. . . . And the ten horns that you saw are ten kings who have not yet received royal power, but they are to receive authority as kings for one hour, together with the beast. These are of one mind, and they hand over their power and authority to the beast. They will make war on the Lamb, and the Lamb will conquer them, for he is Lord of lords and King of kings, and those with him are called and chosen and faithful."

Notice the words in italics: there would be a time when the Roman Empire would have lost its power (Rome fell in AD 476, Constantinople in 1453, but the Holy Roman Empire of the German Nation only in 1806, and its two "successors," the empires of Napoleon and Hitler, in 1815 and 1945, respectively), and would seemingly have disappeared from the scene. However, in the end time the Empire is revived, now as an alliance of "ten kings" (ten heads of state, or ten parts of the [Western?] world). I cannot possibly enter into all the details here; suffice to say that the parousia cannot occur as long as this eschatological world power (some say, re-united Europe; others, the reunited Western world; still others, the entire world) has not yet reappeared.

In retrospect, we can confidently say that Jesus could not possibly have returned after one generation. It would take many centuries before all the nations of the world would have been evangelized, and before dispersed Israel would return to its land to build a new society there, and before the destroyed Roman Empire would revive again, now as a voluntary alliance ("they are to receive authority as kings for one hour, together with the beast. *These are of one mind*, and they hand over their power and authority to the beast").

## 11.5 Realized Basileology
### 11.5.1 Focusing on the Present

The views of Weiss and Schweitzer were followed by the *realized basileology/eschatology* of Charles H. Dodd (1884–1973).[45] The name of this position is linguistically inaccurate for, of course, it is not the basileology/eschatology that is realized but (supposedly) the kingdom of God.[46] According to Dodd, the new world announced by Jesus arrived many centuries ago already, namely, through his Spirit in God's church. It is not a kind of fancy kingdom we have to look forward to, but a real and realistic kingdom in the present. It is not a matter of expectation but of fulfillment. For instance, Dodd believes that expressions like "day of the LORD" (e.g., Zeph. 1:7–16) and "eternal life" (Ps. 133:3; Dan. 12:2) had a future meaning in the Old Testament, but have a present meaning since the New Testament (see, e.g. John 3:36; 5:24; 6:40, 47, 54: believers already *have* eternal life). According to Dodd, the parousia is included in the resurrection.[47] Therefore, there is no future parousia, and

---

45. See especially Dodd (1961); cf. Ridderbos (1962, xxxi–xxxii, 38–42).
46. The same objection applies to *realized millennialism*; see Adams (1970); A. A. Hoekema in Clouse (1977).
47. On the connection between resurrection and *parousia*, see

thus no kingdom in another, more glorious form to which we must look forward.

In the background lies a long-standing question (cf. §2.3): In the Bible, is the kingdom a present reality, or a future one, which will arrive only at the parousia?[48] Part of the discussion concerning this question turns on the meaning of the Greek word *ephthasen* (from the verb *phthanō*) in Matthew 12:28 and Luke 11:20 ("... has come upon you"). Does it mean that the kingdom of God (or of heaven) has "arrived" *or* that it "is near"?[49] Because of this and other biblical issues, many discussions have involved whether greater emphasis concerning God's kingdom is placed in the New Testament on in its present or on its future meaning.

The simple answer I have given in preceding chapters is: on both. Today, the kingdom exists in a hidden form, and one day, after the Messiahs's parousia, it will exist in power and glory. Starting from this insight, Werner G. Kümmel (1905–1995)[50] was one of the theologians who, as George R. Beasley-Murray put it,[51] have sought a real synthesis between the realized and the futuristic eschatology in Jesus' teaching.[52] Gerrit C. Berkouwer has argued that *realized eschatology* cannot be a sufficient description of the New Testament promise and expectation, but that it is good to take its "urgent warning"

---

Ridderbos (1962, 456–68).
48. See Ouweneel (2007b, §13.3.2).
49. See C. C. Caragounis in Green *et al.* (1992, 423).
50. Kümmel (1957).
51. Beasley-Murray (1954, 103).
52. On Schweitzer, Weiss, Dodd, and Kümmel, see Knight (2004, 16–26).

to heart "against any futuristic eschatology," that is, one that is exclusively focused on the future. First and foremost, we are dealing with the *presence* of salvation, of the kingdom of God, and even the presence of Christ himself through his Holy Spirit.[53]

### 11.5.2 A Delicate Balance

The view mentioned in 2 Timothy 2:18 that the resurrection has already occurred could, perhaps together with the denial of the resurrection as described in 1 Corinthians 15, be called a form of realized eschatology as well.[54] Adherents feel that they can appeal to Ephesians 2:6 and Colossians 2:12; 3:1 ("raised together with Jesus"—already now), ignoring the difference between the spiritual resurrection described there and the future physical resurrection: "For this perishable *body* must put on the imperishable, and this mortal *body* must put on immortality" (1 Cor. 15:53); ". . . the Lord Jesus Christ, who will transform our lowly *body* to be like his glorious *body*, by the power that enables him even to subject all things to himself" (Phil. 3:20-21). "If the Spirit of him who raised Jesus from the dead dwells in you, he who raised Christ Jesus from the dead will also give life to your *mortal bodies* through his Spirit who dwells in you" (Rom. 8:11).

Realized basileology/eschatology errs if it believes that *all* God's promises have already been realized. In opposition to this, one could imagine an equally objectionable eschatology consisting at most of the forgiveness of sins but for which all the rest is still future. These

---

53. Berkouwer (1972, 110).
54. Berkouwer (1972, 184-85).

are two extremes. The New Testament presents a delicate balance between the "already" and the "not yet" (see §5.2.3). There are many more things that belong to the "already" than some conservative Christians seem to believe. And there are many more things that belong to the "not yet" than some liberal Christians seem to believe. To the latter we say that at present, "we do not yet see everything in subjection" to Christ (Heb. 2:8), Jesus does not yet sit on the throne of his father David (Luke 1:32; cf. Rev. 3:21), and the earth is not yet full of peace and justice (Isa. 9:7; 11:4–5, 9). To the former—conservative Christians—we say that believers have tasted already now the "powers of the age to come" (Heb. 6:5), already now possess the "firstfruits of the Spirit" (Rom. 8:23), already now are seated "in Christ" in the heavenly places (Eph. 2:6), etc.

Oscar Cullmann speaks here of the anticipated deliverance of the human body.[55] Nowhere perhaps does this peace belonging to realized basileology come to light more strikingly than in miraculous physical healings,[56] and in the deliverance from demons who have taken possession of the body (see §2.3): "[I]f it is by the Spirit of God that I cast out demons, then the kingdom of God has come upon you" (Matt. 12:28). This is continued among believers: "[W]hoever believes in me will also do the works that I do; and greater works than these will he do" (John 14:12). "[T]hese signs will accompany those who believe: in my name they will cast out demons; . . . they will lay their hands on the sick, and they will recover" (Mark 16:17–18). Every miraculous healing and de-

---

55. Cullmann (1964).

56. See on this, remarkably enough, Berkouwer (1972, 199–202).

liverance is, as it were, an anticipation of the great miracle of the resurrection, which could be viewed as the ultimate healing of the entire body.

## 11.6 Transcendent/Existential Basileology
### 11.6.1 Barth, Bultmann, Moltmann

Our summary would not be complete without mentioning some more basileologies, such as the *transcendent* basileology of the young Karl Barth (1886–1968).[57] In his view, eschatology ought not to be a "short and perfectly harmless chapter" at the end of dogmatics.[58] All of Christianity, and thus of theology as well, is thoroughly eschatological in the sense that we are permanently confronted with eternity and the judgment of God. The point is not the *post* ("after" the present time) but the *trans* (that which transcends the present time). Here, "eschatological" means about the same as "existential," "transcendent," that which really matters and which necessarily surpasses our time and space.

In the case of Rudolf Bultmann (1884–1976), we do indeed speak of an *existential* basileology, which actually is a variety of the previous one.[59] Bultmann calls New Testament eschatology thoroughly mythical, and in this sense it has been done away with. No persons ascend and descend on clouds to or from the skies. However, the core of it, the actual *kerygma*, the "message" of the New Testament, is eternity as it is being realized within

---

57. See Barth (2010, especially III/2, III/4, and IV/1).
58. Barth (1968, 500: "adding at the conclusion of Christian Dogmatics a short and perfectly harmless chapter entitled—'Eschatology'").
59. E.g., Bultmann (1958).

the boundaries of the here and now. Within this kingdom of God, a person has to realize and experience his existentiality, interpreted by Bultmann in the sense of the philosopher Martin Heidegger (1889–1976).[60]

The similarity between the basileologies of, on the one hand, Weiss, Schweitzer, and Bultmann and, on the other hand, some conservatives is that both approaches begin from the view that the New Testament speaks of a literal kingdom of God, breaking into the course of the world by God's hand. According to Bultmann, Jesus and the apostles even expected this kingdom very soon (this is the idea of the *Naherwartung*, the imminent expectation). The difference between the two approaches is that, in the latter, the New Testament is viewed as binding, whereas in the former approach it is not—at best it is inspiring, directive.

In the "eschatology of hope" articulated by Jürgen Moltmann (b. 1926),[61] we find a reaction to the previous approaches in that he allows again for a certain futuristic dimension in the expectation of God's kingdom. However, this future remains quite vague. Again, the emphasis is on *our* eschatological acting here and now. This leads to, among other things, a politicized theology, in which Moltmann has been strongly inspired by the Jewish Marxist Ernst Bloch (1885–1977).[62]

## 11.6.2 Liberation Theology

Something similar is found in the—especially Latin American—liberation theology of Gustavo Gutiérrez (b.

---

60. See Heidegger (1996).
61. Moltmann (1993).
62. Bloch (1995).

1928), Leonardo Boff (b. 1938), and others.[63] Here, Jesus is not only the Savior of sinners but also the Deliverer of the oppressed. Liberation theology interprets Jesus' announcing the kingdom of God in terms of liberation and the introduction of social and political justice, with the help of arms, if necessary. The latter point is, among other things, based on Luke 22:36, "[L]et the one who has no sword sell his cloak and buy one." However, such a literalistic interpretation of this verse is made impossible by verses 49–51, where Jesus rebukes Peter who had cut off the ear of an opponent (cf. Matt. 26:52, "Put your sword back into its place. For all who take the sword will perish by the sword").[64] It is not the literal but the spiritual sword that is the weapon of the disciple: the "sword of the Spirit, which is the word of God" (Eph. 6:17; cf. Heb. 4:12, "the word of God is ... sharper than any two-edged sword").

The justice that Jesus preaches is not primarily a political but a moral righteousness (which, by the way, definitely has social and political consequences as well). Even less is it a justice of (semi-)Marxist orientation, but the characteristic righteousness of the kingdom of God (Matt. 6:33; Rom. 14:17). This is not a kingdom with a left-leaning government but with a Christ-like government; a kingdom based on God's laws, which may overlap left-leaning principles but does not coincide with them. The kingdom of God cannot be captured in ordinary, human categories (philosophies, ideologies): "My kingdom is not of this world," including the world of

---

63. Gutiérrez (1988); Boff (1984); see Ouweneel (2010c, §10.3.1) and the summary by Sauter (1996, 27–53).

64. Green (1997, 774–75).

philosophers and ideologists: "If my kingdom were of this world, my servants would have been fighting, that I might not be delivered over to the Jews. But my kingdom is not from the world" (John 18:36).

Please note that this does *not* necessarily mean spiritualizing the kingdom, or even spiritualizing it away. However, it does mean underscoring the other-worldliness of God's kingdom. This is the "not-*of*-this-world" aspect of the kingdom, which is just as important as its "*in*-this-world" aspect (cf. John 17:11, 14–18). The kingdom fully participates in the social-economic, judicial, and political life of this world, but starting from principles that are *not* of this world. Any view of the kingdom as it functions today should carefully preserve the balance between the fully being "*in* the world" (against all Pietist isolation) and not being "*of* the world" (against all Marxist or other secularization): "[T]hat way of life is nothing like what you learned when you came to know Christ" (Eph. 4:20 ERV).

## 11.7 Newer Views
### 11.7.1 The Jesus Seminar

Let us finally look at three different views that are very much in vogue today. We may compare these three somewhat colloquially as follows. The first says, There will be no future Messianic kingdom; all we have is the here and now. The second says, There will be a future Messianic kingdom (before the parousia), and God will place it in *our* (Reformed, Presbyterian) hands: we Christians will rule the world according to the Mosaic Law. The third says, There may be a future Messianic kingdom (before or after the parousia) but we are not very

## Later History of Kingdom Theology

interested in it because, through the Holy Spirit, Jesus Christ exhibits its power already now in granting us health and wealth. The first and second views put great emphasis on human effort, whereas the third emphasizes God's power. The first and third views put great emphasis on the here and now, whereas the second one looks forward to the future. The second and third views both believe in a future Messianic kingdom, whereas the first rejects this idea.

First, in the most recent stage in theological reflection on the kingdom of God, many are denying a basileology that refers to a future kingdom to be founded by Christ. I mention here John Dominic Crossan (b. 1934) and Marcus J. Borg (1942–2015), two prominent leaders associated with the Jesus Seminar.[65] One of their main arguments is that the New Testament hope is supposedly strongly connected to the figure of the "Son of Man" (cf. Dan. 7), but Jesus' statements about the Son of Man are not authentic. They are supposedly inventions of the early church, reflecting her dreams rather than giving us authentically divine utterances. Here we encounter the well-known circular argument: Jesus' statements about the Son of Man *cannot* be authentic because of the prejudices of the theologians concerned.

Time and again, this is the core of the matter: according to liberal basileologies, the statements about the parousia and the coming Messianic kingdom in power and glory tell us more about the eschatological visions of—partly Jesus himself and especially—the early church, *not* necessarily anything about a present or future kingdom of God. The basic presup-

---

65. Crossan (1995); Borg (2006).

position here is a form of anti-supernaturalism: a miraculous parousia on the clouds of heaven, interrupting (or even putting to an end to) the course of world history, is simply inconceivable.

In opposition to this, we find the traditional view, which in my opinion has not at all lost its power. If the prophets were able to predict in dozens of prophecies the birth, life, work, death, resurrection, and ascension of Jesus Christ, I do not see why they could not have predicted the parousia of the Messiah on the clouds of heaven, and the establishment of his kingdom. Apart from liberal prejudices, no strictly exegetical argument invalidates the view that the New Testament statements about parousia and kingdom are both authentic and divinely authoritative. We may therefore believe in their imminent fulfillment. It is excellent to carry on debates concerning the nature, the form, and the details of this literal-physical-historical parousia. But the matter itself stands, as long as there are no valid reasons to reject it.

### 11.7.2 Dominion Theology

The following type of basileology may be called conservative insofar as it does believe in a future Messianic kingdom brought about by Christ. It is *Dominion theology*, briefly mentioned earlier in §10.7.3. It is a form of "Kingdom Now" theology, just like the type of basileology mentioned hereafter—Charismatic basileology—but with a big difference. Dominion theology is thoroughly political, Charismatic theology is not. Dominion theology might even be called primarily a political ideology, with theological overtones.

Its basic view is, first, that the entire world ought be ruled by biblical norms, as interpreted by the adherents of this theology and strongly rooted in the Mosaic Law. To this end, Christians ought to participate actively in politics, especially with those who adhere to the same ideals. In Reformed and Presbyterian circles, these ideals are often described as "theocratic."[66] Usually this theology is linked with postmillennialism, that is, with the view that, before the parousia, God will restore all things on the natural, social-economic, political, and environmental levels. This theology is usually also supersessionist: the biblical world government as God will install it before the parousia will not be centered in earthly Jerusalem and a restored Israel but in what is called "spiritual Israel," the church.

The most important form of this theology seems to be Christian Reconstructionism, a Calvinist theocratic movement founded by Rousas J. Rushdoony (1916–2001).[67] Other important figures are Greg L. Bahnsen (1948–1995) and Gary K. North (b. 1942), Rushdoony's son-in-law.[68] The impact of this politically radical movement was significant in the 1980s, but began to dwindle in the 1990s, although its ideals are still being championed in various North American manifestations. In its most extreme form, Christian Reconstructionism advocates the death penalty for idolaters, adulterers, practicing homosexuals, and other sexual offenders, kidnappers, practitioners of occultism, false witnesses in capital cases, public blasphemers, etc.

The errors in this movement as I see them are manifold: (a) supersessionism is a grave mistake, rejected to-

---

66. A confusing term; see Ouweneel (2014a).
67. See Rushdoony (1973, 1984, 1986, 1991).
68. See Bahnsen (1991, 2002) and North (1990, 1991).

day by many conservative theologians; (b) postmillennialism has no support in Scripture; and (c) the Mosaic Law was explicitly and implicitly given to Israel alone, whatever Dominionists may say.[69] In addition to these theological objections, there are objections arising from a Christian view of the state: Dominion theology is not only radical, it is anti-democratic and an enemy of individual freedom.[70] The last thing I would wish is to live under this kind of dictatorial "theocracy" in which a group of Protestant radicals determines how we must live, think, and behave. Until the Messianic kingdom arrives, any form of democracy, in which the various branches of government keep each other's power in balance, will always be better than any "Christian" or other form of totalitarianism.

### 11.7.3 Prosperity Theology

The third movement we must mention is a very different form of "Kingdom Now" theology (see again §10.7.3). It is an Evangelical kingdom theology that strongly emphasizes the significance of signs and wonders today, but is *not* political: it does not strive for a radical-totalitarian (supposedly "theocratic") world government, that is, a political establishment of the millennial kingdom here and now. It is a Charismatic kingdom theology that can very well be premillennialist; Dominion theology, or Christian Reconstructionism, in its strict sense, is necessarily supersessionist and postmillennialist.

---

69. For a thorough and pointed refutation of these and other tenets of Christian Reconstructionism, see extensively, Ouweneel (2016c).
70. Cf. Ouweneel (2014a).

In §5.2.3, I have described two types of Christians with regard to the kingdom of God: "Gethsemane Christians" (Christians emphasizing the sufferings aspect of the kingdom) and "Tabor Christians" (Christians emphasizing the triumph aspect of the kingdom). The basileology that I am describing right now is especially the one of "Tabor Christians" because they emphasize the triumphant (signs and wonders) aspect of the kingdom in its present form. This view may even involve rather irreverently claiming God's miraculous power, especially in terms of health and material prosperity ("health and wealth gospel" or "prosperity theology").[71] Such Christians do know of persecutions, especially in remote countries. However, they argue that sickness, bondage, and poverty definitely do not belong to the suffering common to believers but are matters for which the unlimited power of Christ can be invoked.

Often, "Tabor Christians" do not seem to be very interested in the coming Messianic kingdom. They may even be rather uninterested in issues such as a-, pre- and postmillennialism because they think and live as if the parousia has already taken place and the age to come has already arrived when no inhabitant will still say, "I am sick" (Isa. 33:24). As I said before, "Gethsemane Christians" underestimate the power of the Holy Spirit, or limit his activity mainly to regeneration, or to the first, apostolic century. "Tabor Christians" overestimate the measure in which the Holy Spirit has been given to us now, as if already today we could receive everything

---

71. Ouweneel (2010c, §10.3.2).

in a fullness that in fact has been reserved for the Messianic kingdom of peace.[72]

Here again, the errors seem obvious: (a) Prosperity theology does not find any support in the New Testament (in spite of verses that are superficially applied, such as Matt. 25:14–30; John 10:10; Phil. 4:19; 3 John 1:2). (b) It focuses on material blessings instead of spiritual blessings (cf. Luke 16:10–13; 18:25 with Eph. 1:3–14). (c) It implicitly indicts the great majority of Christians, who live in poor countries (to say nothing of the poverty of Jesus himself as well as of his apostles). (d) It implicitly indicts those Christians who, in spite of much giving and fervent prayer, remain poor and/or sick. (e) It makes material blessing depend especially on giving (the so-called "Law of Compensation")—which in practice is beneficial mainly to the leaders of the movement. (f) It yields a poor soteriology, as if Jesus' work on the cross supplies health and wealth in the same way as it supplies forgiveness of sins. (g) It presents a basileology in which the "triumph" aspects are overemphasized at the expense of the "suffering" aspects.[73]

## 11.8 Basic Misunderstandings
## 11.8.1 Spiritualization

The dispensationalist-premillennialist Herman Hoyt has enumerated the greatest misunderstandings concerning the kingdom of God.[74] I offer a summary here, with my own arrangement (two groups:

---

72. Advocates of prosperity theology include Lindsay (1998); Osteen (2004); Ziglar (2012).
73. See, e.g., Jones and Woodbridge (2011).
74. H. A. Hoyt in Clouse (1977, 69–70).

## Later History of Kingdom Theology

spiritualized and secularized basileologies) and with my own comments.

The first group of misunderstandings involves various types of spiritualized basileologies. For instance, the expression "kingdom of heaven" (Luther: *Himmelreich*) has often led to equating the kingdom with heaven, or at least with God's rule in heaven. For instance, Matthew 19:23–24 ("[O]nly with difficulty will a rich person enter the kingdom of heaven. Again I tell you, it is easier for a camel to go through the eye of a needle than for a rich person to enter the kingdom of God") or 2 Peter 1:11 ("For in this way there will be richly provided for you an entrance into the eternal kingdom of our Lord and Savior Jesus Christ") is then explained in terms of going to heaven. This, indeed, was the view of many older expositors; a good example is Matthew Henry.[75]

However, in the Bible the "kingdom of heaven" in Matthew is fully identical with the "kingdom of God" in Mark and Luke (as many parallel passages prove, e.g., Matt. 3:2 and Mark 1:15, or Matt. 8:11 and Luke 13:29, or Matt. 13:11 and Mark 4:11 and Luke 8:10). Moreover, everywhere in Scripture the "kingdom of God" is a heavenly kingdom *on earth* (although it will have a heavenly "upper story," where Christ will rule with his own[76]). The kingdom is not "*of* (or from) here" (but "from above") but definitely "here" (cf. John 18:36; also see

---

75. http://biblehub.com/matthew/19-23.htm and http://biblehub.com/2_peter/1-11.htm.
76. Cf. Hill (2001), who contrasts the church fathers who believed in a *regnum caelorum terrestre* ("earthly kingdom of heaven") with those who believed in a *regnum caelorum caeleste* ("heavenly kingdom of heaven").

3:31; 8:23). It is a *heavenly* kingdom, but certainly *on earth*, as all the Old Testament prophecies concerning the Messianic kingdom show.

## 11.8.2 Kingdom and Church

The kingdom of God has often been spiritualized in yet another way, namely, by equating it with some "invisible" church (Protestants), or even the "visible church," that is, the Roman Catholic Church. (Some Protestant denominations, rejecting the notion of the "invisible church," have presented themselves as true representations, or even *the* true representation, of the *visible* church.)

This approach ignores at least two facts. First, it ignores the fact that the kingdom of God becomes manifest just as much in Christian marriages, families, states, schools, companies, etc., as in Christian denominations. Second, it ignores the fact that the church of God as the body of Christ includes only those who have been grafted into Christ by regeneration and faith, and that the church as the house or temple of God includes only those who have received the One who dwells in this house as dwelling in them as well, namely, the Holy Spirit. The kingdom of God, however, covers the entire world as the domain of God's rule, or, in a narrower sense, all those who in some way or another confess Christ as Lord. The church is the *dwelling place* of the Holy Spirit (1 Cor. 3:16; Eph. 2:22), the kingdom is the Spirit's (much wider) *sphere of operation*. The Spirit *dwells* in believers, but he *works* everywhere.

Now one may argue that the term "kingdom" sometimes has a narrower sense, including only the regenerate (cf. John 3:5), whereas the term "church" sometimes has a wider sense, including all Christ-confessors, whether true or false (cf. Rev. 2–3). However, even then the two terms are not necessarily identical. God's dominion over the entire world remains a wider concept than the totality of all Christ-confessors. The Spirit's sphere of operation is always wider than the Spirit's dwelling place.

Often, the kingdom is spiritualized in the sense that God's rule is limited to the human heart. The alleged proof text for this is Luke 17:21, "[T]he kingdom of God is within you" (NKJV, ASV, etc.; AMPC: "within you [in your hearts]"). But first, the proper translation of this verse is disputed (cf. "in your midst," NASB, NIV; ESV: "in the midst of you"). Second, if God's kingdom is a matter of the heart, we recall that from the heart "flow the springs of life" (NIV: "everything you do flows from it"; NLT: "it determines the course of your life") (Prov. 4:23). Thus, from the heart the kingdom necessarily comprises the entire human life, including our individual actions and the societal relationships in which confessors of Jesus function. If the kingdom governs our hearts, then it also governs our marriages, families, congregations, schools, companies, associations, etc.

### 11.8.3 The Parousia Already Fulfilled?

Of some interest is the view that the parousia has already occurred in AD 70 (the year of the Roman destruction of Jerusalem and the Second Temple) in a way that for us has remained invisible.[77] The first argument for

---

77. So, e.g., Bray (1996); cf. Kimball (1984) and Chilton (1987), who argues that the Great Tribulation is not future but took place in AD 66–70.

this view is that Jesus had announced that the parousia would take place before the death of some of his listeners (Matt. 16:28). Jesus' implicit announcement that the parousia would be within one generation (24:34) ties in with this. No other significant event could be mentioned that fulfilled these two predictions the way AD 70 does. I have dealt with this argument in §5.4 in connection with the so-called "imminent expectation" (*Naherwartung*) of Jesus and the early church. I have tried to explain how I read the passages mentioned. Moreover, I have pointed out that Jesus often implied that he would stay away for a long time: "My master is delayed" (Matt. 24:49; Luke 12:45), "As the bridegroom was delayed . . ." (Matt. 25:5), "Now after a *long time* the master of those servants came . . ." (v. 19). Jesus even contradicted such an imminent expectation: "As they heard these things, he proceeded to tell a parable, because he was near to Jerusalem, and because they supposed that the kingdom of God was to appear immediately" (Luke 19:11).

The second argument for the AD 70 parousia is that, in Matthew 24:15-31 (cf. Mark 13:14-27; Luke 21:20-28), the destruction of the temple, the Great Tribulation, and the parousia of the Son of Man are described as taking place within the same, short period. Given that, as the context demands, the destruction of the temple and the parousia must be kept together, not only the destruction of the temple but also the parousia must have taken place in AD 70. However, this is not the only way we can view the connection between the destruction of the temple, the Great Tribulation, and the parousia of the Son of Man. For instance, it is still possible that the destruction of the temple took place in AD 70, while the parousia is still future. One could refer here to Luke 21, where the destruction of the temple and the parousia are separated by what is called the "times of the Gentiles" (v. 24), which might last many centuries (as in fact they do). The main objection against both interpretations (claiming that Matt. 24:15 refers to AD 70)) is that there simply never was an "abomination of desolation" in the temple during AD 66-70 (in spite of inventive assertions of the contrary). In my view, *Matthew 24:15-31 does not refer to AD 70 at all.*

The main objection against the idea of a parousia in AD 70 is that, in my opinion, an invisible parousia cannot be reconciled with prophecies like these: "[A]s the lightning comes from the east and shines as far as the west, so will be the coming of the Son of Man" (Matt. 24:27). "This Jesus, who was taken up from you into heaven, will come in the same way as you saw him go into heaven" (Acts 1:11). "[T]he Lord Jesus is revealed from heaven with his mighty angels in flaming fire, inflicting vengeance on those who do not know God and on those who do not obey the gospel of our Lord Jesus. . . . [H]e comes on that day to be glorified in his saints, and to be marveled at among all who have believed, because our testimony to you was believed" (2 Thess. 1:7-10). "Behold, he is coming with the clouds, and every eye will see him, even those who pierced him" (Rev. 1:7). According to such passages, the parousia will be visible to all, and it is both miraculous and spectacular.

In my view, Matthew 24:15-31 is entirely eschatological.[78] That is, the passage refers to a time when Israel will be restored to its own land. They will have a temple

---

78. See extensively, Ouweneel (2012a, 271-77; cf. 261-64).

(cf. 2 Thess. 2:4, the Antichrist "takes his seat in the temple of God, proclaiming himself to be God"; Rev. 11:1–2, "Rise and measure the temple of God and the altar and those who worship there, but do not measure the court outside the temple; leave that out, for it is given over to the nations, and they will trample the holy city for forty-two months"). In this temple, at a given moment an "abomination of desolation" will be erected (cf. Rev. 13:11–15, there will be "an image for the beast that was wounded by the sword and yet lived. And it [i.e., the second beast] was allowed to give breath to the image of the [first] beast, so that the image of the beast might even speak and might cause those who would not worship the image of the beast to be slain"). This episode will end with the visible, miraculous, and spectacular parousia of Christ.

In Luke 21, the situation might be different; here the order seems to be: the destruction of the temple in AD 70, the "times of the Gentiles," and finally the parousia.

## 11.9 Materialist and Secularized Views
### 11.9.1 Material Aspects

No doubt there is a certain tension between, on the one hand, spiritualizing the kingdom and, on the other hand, overemphasizing the material aspects of it. Especially those who tend to overemphasize the spiritual aspects of the kingdom reject all (supposedly) "materialistic" and "carnal" expectations with regard to the kingdom of God. Their proof text is Romans 14:17, "[T]he kingdom of God is not a matter of eating and drinking but of righteousness and peace and joy in the Holy Spirit." In other words, the kingdom of God is not about material, this-worldly realities but about spiritual, other-worldly realities.

This is a typical example of taking a text out of its context. Paul argues against those who create dissensions in the church over matters such as what Christians are allowed to eat and drink (see vv. 1–6, 15, 20–23). But these are only secondary matters in the kingdom of God, where righteousness, peace, and joy in the Holy Spirit are far more important. Paul's point is not that the kingdom is spiritual, non-material, but rather that the material realities are always subservient to the spiritual realities.

In another sense, eating and drinking are definitely important in the kingdom of God as the (very literal) manifestation of the highest communion: "[P]eople will come from east and west, and from north and south, and recline at table in the kingdom of God" (Luke 13:29). "When one of those who reclined at table with him heard these things, he said to him, 'Blessed is everyone who will eat bread in the kingdom of God!'" (14:15). Jesus answered this with a parable, which, however, did not contradict the essence of what the person had asserted.

At the institution of the Lord's Supper Jesus said, "For I tell you I will not eat it until it is fulfilled in the kingdom of God" (22:16; cf. Matt. 26:29). But a little further: "I assign to you, as my Father assigned to me, a kingdom, that you may eat and drink at my table in my kingdom" (Luke 22:29–30). As the prophet of old had said, "On this mountain the Lord of hosts will make for all peoples a feast of rich food, a feast of well-aged wine, of rich food full of marrow, of aged wine well refined. And he will swallow up on this mountain the covering that is cast over all peoples, the veil that is spread over all nations. He will swallow up death forever; and the Lord God will wipe away tears from all faces, and the reproach of his people he will take away from all the earth, for the Lord has spoken" (Isa. 25:6-8). "They shall build houses and inhabit them; they shall plant vineyards and eat their fruit. They shall not build and another inhabit; they shall not plant and another eat; for like the days of a tree shall the days of my people be, and my chosen shall long enjoy the work of their hands. They shall not labor in vain or bear children for calamity, for they shall be the offspring of the blessed of the Lord, and their descendants with them" (65:21-23; cf. Mic. 4:3-4).

The spiritualizers cannot accept the idea of a Messianic kingdom after the parousia in which the numerous Old Testament material and physical promises concerning the kingdom of God will also be fulfilled. Part of their problem is the dangerous Greek dualism of spirit and matter in the sense that a kingdom of spiritual blessings supposedly excludes material blessings. People argue as if the only thing that matters is peace in one's heart (Phil. 4:7; Col. 3:15), as if the angels' "peace *on earth*" (Luke 2:14) has no significance. It will be the *earth* that the meek will inherit (Matt. 5:5; cf. Ps. 37:11), and it will be the *earth* that will be full of the Lord's steadfast love (Hebrew *chesed*) (Ps. 33:5), of his glory (Isa. 6:3), of his knowledge (11:9; Hab. 2:14), and of his praise (Hab. 3:3).

Karl Barth (1886-1968) and Emil Brunner (1889-1966) are the theologians who have elevated the kingdom of God far above events in our history, and have situated it in an eternity that belongs to God alone. Their view is far removed from the Old Testament prophecies describing a very earthly and material kingdom, and also from the premillennialist view of the early church that prevailed until the Constantinian turn. However, as I said before, why would we take Bethlehem Ephratha in Micah 5:2 literally, but not the eschatological "our land" in verses 5-6 and 11? Why take the birth of the divine Child in Isaiah 9:6 literally, but not the "throne of David" in verse 7? Why take the "colt, the foal of a donkey" in Zechariah 9:9 literally, but not the (eschatological) "Jerusalem" and "Zion" in verses 10 and 13?

### 11.9.2 Secularization

The spiritualized and the earthly-material views of the kingdom both look forward to the full realization of the kingdom. The earthly-material and the secularized views of the kingdom both believe in a kingdom here on earth. The spiritualized and the secularized views of the kingdom both believe in a kingdom that has nothing to do with some future heyday of ethnic Israel.

Many theologians have claimed that the Jews before and during the time of Jesus mistakenly believed in a kingdom of God that would be limited to Israel, or whose center would be Israel. It is argued that even the apostles believed this; hence (supposedly) their question in Acts 1:6, "Lord, will you at this time restore the kingdom to Israel?" Earlier (§6.5) I suggested that the question of the disciples was *not* mistaken: the Messianic kingdom *will* be given to Israel, "the people of the saints of the Most High" (Dan. 7:18, 27). The only thing hidden from the apostles was the time when this would occur (Acts 1:7).

By the way, as far as I am aware, no Jew has ever believed that this kingdom would be limited to Israel. The Old Testament makes clear that it will encompass all humanity, even though Jerusalem will be its center: "It shall come to pass in the latter days that the mountain of the house of the LORD shall be established as the highest of the mountains, and shall be lifted up above the hills; and all the nations shall flow to it, and many peoples shall come, and say: 'Come, let us go up to the mountain of the LORD, to the house of the God of Jacob, that he may teach us his ways and that we may walk in his paths.' For out of Zion shall go the law, and the word of the LORD from Jerusalem" (Isa. 2:2–3; cf. 51:4–5; 56:7; Mic. 5:1–5).

"In that day the root of Jesse, who shall stand as a signal for the peoples—of him shall the nations inquire, and his resting place shall be glorious" (11:10). "On this mountain the LORD of hosts will make for *all peoples* a feast of rich food, a feast of well-aged wine, of rich food full of marrow, of aged wine well refined. And he will swallow up on this mountain the covering that is cast over all peoples, the veil that is spread over *all nations*" (Isa. 25:6–7). "Behold my servant, whom I uphold, my chosen, in whom my soul delights; I have put my Spirit upon him; he will bring forth justice to *the nations*. . . . 'I am the LORD; I have called you in righteousness; I will take you by the hand and keep you; I will give you as a covenant for the people, a light for *the nations*'" (42:1, 6). "And *nations* shall come to your light, and kings to the brightness of your rising. . . Your gates shall be open continually; day and night they shall not be shut, that *people* may bring to you the wealth of the *nations*, with their kings led in procession" (60:3, 11).

"Peoples shall yet come, even the inhabitants of many cities. The inhabitants of one city shall go to another, saying, 'Let us go at once to entreat the favor of the LORD and to seek the LORD of hosts; I myself am going.' Many peoples and strong nations shall come to seek the LORD of hosts in Jerusalem and to entreat the favor of the LORD.... In those days ten men from the nations of every tongue shall take hold of the robe of a Jew, saying, 'Let us go with you, for we have heard that God is with you'" (Zech. 8:20-23). "Then everyone who survives of all the nations that have come against Jerusalem shall go up year after year to worship the King, the LORD of hosts, and to keep the Feast of Booths" (14:16).

### 11.9.3 The Premillennial View

There is a striking similarity between liberal eschatology ("there will be no literal parousia") and postmillennialism ("the parousia takes place after the Messianic kingdom"). Despite all their differences, both are focused upon the coming of the Messianic kingdom in the (near) future thanks to the efforts by Jesus' followers under God's blessing: global organization of humanity, worldwide social-economic improvement of humanity, worldwide preaching of the Christian message. The main difference is that liberal eschatology does not, and postmillennialism does, believe in a visible, one-time parousia of Christ.

The expectation of a kingdom here on earth built by human efforts, be it with the help of God, ignores the—in my view undeniable—fact that, in Revelation 19-20, the kingdom *follows upon* the parousia. There will be no Messianic kingdom in power and glory before the parousia of Christ. It is hardly defensible to argue that the events described in Revelation 19-21 are not chronological. Notice the following order of the three "I heard's" and the seven "I saw's" in these chapters:

(1) "After this I heard" (19:1): the announcement of the *eschaton*.
(2) "Then I heard" (19:6): the marriage supper of the Lamb.
(3) "Then I saw" (19:11): the parousia (the second coming of Christ).
(4, 5) "Then I saw .... And I saw" (19:17, 19): judgment on the hostile armies.
(6) "Then I saw" (20:1): the binding of Satan.
(7) "Then I saw" (20:4): the first resurrection; beginning of the "thousand years."
(8) "Then I saw" (20:11-12): after the "thousand years" the second resurrection.
(9) "Then I saw .... And I saw .... And I heard" (21:1-3): the arrival of the new heavens and the new earth.

Only prejudice can ignore the chronology presented here: the parousia—the "thousand years" of Christ's reign—the eternal state. Interestingly, no one less than Abraham Kuyper strongly argued that the "thousand years" are not *before* but *after* the parousia; in his view (and mine), Revelation 19-20 cannot possibly be read in any other way.[79] However, lest anyone think that Kuyper became a premillennialist, he *de facto* reduced the "thousand years" to zero, so that the eternal state follows almost immediately upon the parousia.[80] Kuyper

---

79. Kuyper (1931, 326); see also the quotation from Kuyper in Feinberg (1961, 169).
80. Kuyper (1931, 332-33; cf. 1934, 9).

## Later History of Kingdom Theology

clearly *saw* the chronological order of Revelation 19-21—in contrast to so many a- and postmillennialists—but his Augustinian, supersessionist prejudices hindered him from drawing the right conclusions from this.

Let me add here a few remarkable passages from the Old Testament prophecies.

(a) Isaiah 31-32 may have had a preliminary fulfillment in Hezekiah's time (the defeat of the Assyrians) but at a deeper level this passage is clearly eschatological. The prophet says that "the LORD of hosts will *come down* to fight on Mount Zion and on its hill. Like birds hovering, so the LORD of hosts will protect Jerusalem; he will protect and deliver it; he will spare and rescue it" (31:4-5). There is a hidden, yet evident reference to the parousia of the Messiah here. This is almost immediately followed by: "Behold, a king will reign in righteousness, and princes will rule in justice," etc. (32:1; read the entire chapter), which clearly describes the Messianic kingdom. That is, first the parousia, then the kingdom.

(b) "Behold, a day is coming for the LORD, when the spoil taken from you will be divided in your midst. For I will gather all the nations against Jerusalem to battle.... Then the LORD will go out and fight against those nations as when he fights on a day of battle. On that day *his feet shall stand on the Mount of Olives* that lies before Jerusalem on the east.... Then the LORD my God will come, and all the holy ones with him" (Zech. 14:1-5). Please note that this occurs *after* the Assyrian and Babylonian sieges of the city. Also note that, in Israel's final troubles, it is the LORD who personally intervenes. To this end, he descends on the Mount of Olives—a clear reference to the parousia of

Christ (cf. Luke 24:50-51; Acts 1:11). Note especially that, immediately after this descent and the destruction of enemies, we find a description of the Messianic kingdom (Zech. 14:6-21). Again it is first the parousia, then the kingdom, not the other way round.

(c) Perhaps some might doubt that Isaiah 31:4-5 and Zechariah 14:1-5 refer to the parousia of Christ, but there can be no doubt about Daniel 7:13, "[B]ehold, [One] like the Son of Man, coming with the clouds of heaven!" (NKJV; cf. Matt. 24:30; 26:64). Immediately after this we read: "And to him was given dominion and glory and a kingdom, that all peoples, nations, and languages should serve him; his dominion is an everlasting dominion, which shall not pass away, and his kingdom one that shall not be destroyed" (Dan. 7:14). Again, the message is: first the parousia, then the kingdom; it is the "Son of Man *coming in his kingdom*" (Matt. 16:28; or "into his kingdom" [Voice]). In summary, the idea of a Messianic kingdom arriving before the parousia is totally foreign to Scripture.

## 11.10 Summary of Dilemmas

Let me now summarize the dilemmas confronting all basileology and eschatology. In each case I briefly add my own view as I have expounded it thus far in the present volume, and as I have worked it out in my eschatological study.[81]

(a) *Is the kingdom of God God's world dominion, or specifically the kingdom of Christ?* It is both: God rules the world from the beginning to the end of history, but in addition has placed the world under the dominion of

---

81. Ouweneel (2012a).

humanity: initially, the first Adam and Eve, subsequently, the last Adam and Eve, that is, Christ and his church.

*(b) Is the kingdom of God primarily a spiritual kingdom, or a kingdom that is also of a material nature?* It is primarily a spiritual kingdom, existing in the hearts of people by the power of the Holy Spirit. But this does not excluded the earthly-material aspect; there is no room for some ancient-pagan dualism here. The kingdom encompasses the total lives of the people concerned, including their social-economic relationships, art, science, the judicial and political order, etc.

*(c) Is the kingdom of heaven a kingdom that must be situated primarily in heaven or on earth?* It is a kingdom that descends from heaven, as it were, that is, in which heaven rules over the earth explicitly and visibly in the person of Jesus Christ. Scripture does not know of a kingdom *in* heaven; on the contrary, it describes the Messianic kingdom in very earthly terms. However, already the Old Testament knows that in this earthly kingdom it is heaven that rules (cf. Dan. 4:26).

*(d) Is the kingdom of Christ primarily present or future?* Today, the kingdom of Christ already exists in a hidden form (in the hearts and the societal relationships of Christians), and further wherever the Holy Spirit is working. In the coming day, the kingdom will exist in a manifest, universal form: the Messianic kingdom. In its prophesied form, as a kingdom of worldwide peace and justice, it is necessarily still future.

*(e) Should the parousia be understood heavenly-spiritually or earthly-physically?* The parousia is earthly-physical, but we should not create any contrast here: it is also of a heavenly-spiritual nature. The earthly-physical na-

ture of the parousia comes to light, among other things, in its precise location (the Mount of Olives; cf. Zech. 14:1-5; Luke 24:50-51; Acts 1:11), which apparently must be taken literally; in the universal visibility of the parousia (Matt. 24:27, 30), which will even manifest Jesus' wounds (Zech. 12:10; Rev. 1:7); in the observable signs connected with the parousia (Luke 21:25-27); and in the tangible consequences of it (e.g., Matt. 16:27; Acts 17:31; Rev. 22:12).

(f) *Is the parousia past (AD 70) or future?* The divine intervention in AD 70 (the fall of Jerusalem) was of great significance, also prophetically, because at that time Israel's longest exile among the Gentiles began. The actual parousia, however, will take place, not at the beginning of the "times of the Gentiles" but at the end thereof (Luke 21:24), at the end of "this (present) age," which precedes the "age to come" (Matt. 12:32; 13:40; Mark 10:30; Luke 16:8; 18:30; 20:34-35; 1 Cor. 1:20; 3:18; 2 Cor. 4:4; Gal. 1:4; Eph. 1:21; 1 Tim. 6:17; 2 Tim. 4:10; Titus 2:12; Heb. 6:5), that is, the age of the Messianic kingdom of peace and justice. The signs of this parousia (see previous point) have not yet become manifest.

(g) *Will the Messianic kingdom arrive before or after the parousia?* Given the strictly logical order of Revelation 19-21, which, in the eyes of many, is also a strictly chronological order, there can be no reasonable doubt that the Messianic kingdom (20:16) will arrive only *after* the parousia (19:11-21).[82] This is also the picture supplied by Old Testament prophecy. This does not exclude the possibility, however, that even before the parousia the church may experience a heyday, a time of

---

82. See more extensively, Ouweneel (2012a, chapters 9 and 12-14).

## Later History of Kingdom Theology

revival and fruitfulness.[83] Postmillennialists erroneously view this heyday as the Messianic kingdom. However, as long as Jerusalem is not yet the center of the earth, this kingdom will not yet have arrived. God's earthly center for his kingdom is not Rome or Constantinople, nor is it Canterbury, Westminster, Wittenberg, or Dordrecht—it is Zion.

"Sing aloud, O daughter of Zion; shout, O Israel! Rejoice and exult with all your heart, O daughter of Jerusalem! The LORD has taken away the judgments against you; he has cleared away your enemies. The King of Israel, the LORD, is in your midst; you shall never again fear evil. On that day it shall be said to Jerusalem: 'Fear not, O Zion; let not your hands grow weak. The LORD your God is in your midst, a mighty one who will save; he will rejoice over you with gladness; he will quiet you by his love; he will exult over you with loud singing. I will gather those of you who mourn for the festival, so that you will no longer suffer reproach. Behold, at that time I will deal with all your oppressors. And I will save the lame and gather the outcast, and I will change their shame into praise and renown in all the earth. At that time I will bring you in, at the time when I gather you together; for I will make you renowned and praised among all the peoples of the earth, when I restore your fortunes before your eyes,' says the LORD" (Zeph. 3:14–20).

---

83. See Ouweneel (2010c: chapter 14).

# Chapter 12
# Early Dispensationalism and Kingdom Theology

*[God has] made known to us the
    mystery of His will,
    according to His good pleasure
    which He purposed in Himself,
that in the dispensation of the fullness
    of the times
In Him also we have obtained an
    inheritance,
    being predestined according to the
    purpose of Him
    who works all things according to
    the counsel of His will.*
              *Ephesians 1:9–11 (NKJV)*

*Now the salvation and the power and
    the kingdom of our God
    and the authority of his Christ
    have come.*
              *Revelation 12:10*

**Summary:** *This chapter offers an analysis of dispensationalism, and the underlying notion of "dispensation" (a redemptive-historical epoch with specific characteristics). In its strict form, dispensationalism arose no earlier than during the nineteenth century, although all of church history, including Protestantism, has exhibited many attempts of periodizing redemptive history. Depending on the preferred paradigm, we are living today either in the "third era" (here, the Dictum Eliae is important), the "fourth" or the "fifth era" (both have to do with the interpretation of Dan. 2 and 7), the "sixth era" (based on a typological approach to the days of creation), or the "seventh" or the "eighth" era (depending on one's interpretation of Rev. 17). In particular the links with kingdom theology are discussed: each paradigm has its own view of the kingdom of God.*

## 12.1 Terminology

### 12.1.1 Dispensation

AS WE HAVE SEEN, every investigation concerning the kingdom of God will sooner or later face the issue of the "millennial kingdom," that is, the battle between a-, pre- and postmillennialism. Usually—but certainly not always—the premillennialism that I defend stands within the wider framework of what is called dispensationalism.[1] People speak of "dispensationalist" premillenni-

---

1. For good representations of this view, see the following adherents as well as opponents: Savage (n.d.-a, n.d.-b); Berkhof (1996, 708–719); Froom (1954, 1203–1204, 1220–25); Bass (1960); Feinberg (1961, 222–32); Ryrie (1965, 1999); Fairbairn (1975); Hoekema (1979, 173–222); Chafer (1983, 1:40–41; 4:16–21); Crenshaw an Gunn (1985);Blaising and Bock (1992, 1993); Grenz (1992, chapter 4); Saucy(1993); Poytress(1994); Erickson (1999, 109-124); LaHaye and Jenkins (2000); Walvoord (2001); DeWitt (2002); Hoek (2004, 74–81).

## Early Dispensationalism and Kingdom Theology

alism as distinguished from what is called "historic" premillennialism, which is more of a federalist (covenantal) nature, as we will see in the next chapter.[2]

The word "dispensationalism" comes from the Latin *dispensatio*, which in the Vulgate occurs three times in Ephesians. First in 1:10 (NKJV: "the dispensation [ESV, etc.: plan] of the fullness of the times'; ESV, etc.: "a plan for the fullness of time"). Then in 3:2 (NKJV: "the dispensation [ESV, etc.: stewardship] of the grace of God") and in 3:9 (ASV: "the dispensation [ESV: plan; NASB: administration] of the mystery"). In Ephesians 1:10 it means something like "administration" (more or less as Americans speak of the "Reagan administration"), "order of things, arrangement." The Greek has *oikonomía*, which is literally "household" (cf. the cognate word "economy": state household). In English theology, "economy" is sometimes used in the sense of "dispensation," similar to *Haushalt* ("household") in German theology.

Dutch theologians, too, especially among the Cocceians, sometimes spoke of *Gods huishoudingen* ("God's households"). In 1709, Didericus van Batenburg, an opponent of the Cocceians, discerned several schools among them, among which were the *Oeconomize huishoudige Cocceanen* (the Cocceians distinguishing "economical households").[3] The common Dutch term for "dispensation" is *bedeling* (the verb *bedelen* means "to administer").

Dispensationalism entails the view that in redemptive history a number of dispensations must be distinguished. These are discontinuous redemptive-historical

---
2. On this distinction, see extensively, Ouweneel (2016b).
3. *Ouderlings Protest en Raed*, 16–28; quoted by Van Campen (2007, 280).

phases, each of which entails its own divine order of tings. Such an order of things involves a certain way God deals with people, each time with different rules, different promises and blessings, also different threats. Clearly there are universal foundations and principles in God's ways with humanity, which are valid for all dispensations. However, dispensationalism likes to emphasize the great *differences* that supposedly exist between the successive dispensations.

## 12.1.2 Dispensationalism

Dispensationalism as we know it today goes back especially to the Anglo-Irish John N. Darby (1800–1882), who used the term "dispensation" many times in his writings. He described a dispensation or "economy" literally as the "administration" (rule, order of things, arrangement) of a house, and from there as referring to every order of things that God has instituted.[4] Greek *nomos* (usually translated as "law") comes from the verb *nemō*, "to divide, to allot, to administer," in the middle voice: "to manage, to possess."

Thus, the *oikonomos* (cf. the English "economist") is the manager, administrator of the house, or the one who administers for the people in the household what they need (cf. Matt. 24:45). From this comes the common translation "steward," either literally (Rom. 16:23, also "treasurer"; Gal. 4:2, also "administrator, manager") or figuratively (Luke 12:42; 1 Cor. 4:1–2; Titus 1:7; 1 Pet. 4:10, also "[household] manager, dispenser, trustee, disposer"). Thus, *oikonomía* can be rendered as "stewardship" (1 Cor. 9:17; Eph. 3:2, 9; Col. 1:25; 1

---

4. Darby (CW 1, 288–89).

Tim. 1:4; also "dispensation, plan, administration"; CEB: "God's way of doing things"). When God has instituted a certain order of things on earth, people have developed the habit of calling this an economy or dispensation, such as the "Jewish dispensation," the "present dispensation," etc.[5]

At first glance, the term "dispensation" is not a temporal term at all but refers simply to a specific administration, a ministry, an order of things. However, as soon as people begin speaking of successive "dispensations," they mean epochs, such as the dispensation of the law, the dispensation of grace, or the dispensation of the millennial kingdom. In these cases, the term "dispensation" has acquired a temporal significance. This explains my description of a "dispensation" as a redemptive-historical phase (era, epoch).

## 12.2 Types of Dispensationalism
### 12.2.1 Biblical Hints

Terms like dispensationalism may be relatively new, but the underlying issues are as old as Christianity itself. Time and again, historians have felt the need to periodize secular history, that is, divide it into periods (eras, epochs). This is how, for instance, the terms "Middle Ages" and "medieval" arose, from Latin *medium aevum*, the "middle age." This is roughly the period (c. 500–c. 1500) between the fall of the (Western) Roman Empire, in which Western culture was to some extent cut off from ancient (Greco-Roman) culture, and the period of the Renaissance ("re-birth"), the revival of ancient culture in the West. From the seven-

---
5. Darby (CW 1, 289).

teenth century (Christoph Keller, Georg Horn) it became customary to describe this period as the Middle Ages. Terms such as Antiquity, Middle Ages, New Era, Modern Era, help us to deepen our understanding of history. At the same time, however, they can imply value judgments: the "dark" Middle Ages constituted the time of the decline of Greco-Roman culture. It would be senseless to try to get rid of the term, so we still speak of the Middle Ages. But we no longer accept the original pejorative element in this term.

In a similar way, church historians and theologians have felt the need to acquire a deeper insight into redemptive history by dividing it into periods.[6] Scripture points the way, for instance, in Daniel 2 and 7, where history from the fall of Jerusalem (586 BC) until the end time is divided into four epochs. These eras correspond with the four successive world empires, followed by the fifth empire, that of the Messiah. Another example is Revelation 17:7-9, where the seven heads of the beast are called seven kings. In the opinion of many expositors, it is most obvious that these seven kings are seven personified empires: from Egypt to the Roman Empire in its ultimate form.[7] As I have explained elsewhere, the anti-Christian empire in Revelation 17:11 is the eighth empire.[8] Those who see the power of the Antichrist looming today might argue that we already live on the threshold of the eighth epoch. This is followed by the ninth epoch, although it is not called this in Revelation 17; this is the age to come, the age of the Messianic kingdom.

---

6. See Ouweneel (2001a; 2015).
7. Ouweneel (2016d, 12-21, and references).
8. Ouweneel (2016d, chapter 9).

I wish to emphasize here that Revelation 17:9-11 is in fact the *only* passage in Scripture that—if we understand the passage correctly—gives a hint of some comprehensive periodization: there are eight successive kings, that is, kingdoms, world empires, which last until the parousia of him whom I have referred to as the Ninth King.[9]

Following Jewish apocalyptic, the New Testament teaches a modest periodization by distinguishing between, on the one hand, "this age" (Matt. 12:32; 13:40; Luke 16:8; 20:34; 1 Cor. 1:20; 3:18; 2 Cor. 4:4; Eph. 1:21), or "the present age" (1 Tim. 6:17; 2 Tim. 4:10; Titus 2:12), or "the present evil age" (Gal. 1:4), and, on the other hand, the "age to come" (Mark 10:30; Luke 18:30; 20:35; Eph. 1:21; Heb. 6:5). Paul uses this same differentiation: the New Testament believers are not (or no longer) "under the law" but "under grace" (Rom. 6:14), that is, there is an epoch of "the law" (from Moses to Christ) and an epoch of "(the) faith" (from Christ onward), as he explains in Galatians 3:23-4:7. The references to the two successive old and new covenants (Gal. 4:24-31; Heb. 8-10) are in fact also examples of periodization. Thus we may distinguish three epochs with Paul, three dispensations, if you will: the former age of the law, the present age of faith (which, seen from below, is an evil age, Gal. 1:4), and the age to come of the Messiah.

## 12.2.2 Forms of Dispensationalism

In this wider sense of the term, every theologian is in fact a dispensationalist, that is, someone who inevitably distinguished between various epochs in redemptive

---

9. Ouweneel (2016d).

history (see the next section). In the more limited sense, considering the fact that we are dealing with a real "-ism" here, a dispensationalist is someone who makes a rigid *system* of not just two or three but a large number (preferably seven) dispensations (see the next chapter). Moreover, he is someone who has a tendency to exaggerate the (supposed) *differences* between the successive dispensations. Federalists (Reformed or Presbyterian), for instance, exhibit instead a tendency to exaggerate the *similarities* between the successive epochs of redemptive history as being phases within the framework of the one covenant of grace.[10]

Some may argue that any theologian who rejects supersessionism may be called a dispensationalist because of the distinction he makes between (Old Testament) Israel and the (New Testament) *ekklesia,* and thus also between the dispensation of (Old Testament) Israel and the dispensation of the (New Testament) church. I would call myself an anti-supersessionist, but at the same time I am closer to being a moderate dispensationalist rather than a classical (traditional, consistent) dispensationalist. In addition to these, we will meet varieties, such as progressive dispensationalists and ultra-dispensationalists. Not everyone who emphasizes the differences between the Old and the New Testament is necessarily a (classical) dispensationalist.

### 12.2.3 Periodizing Is Unavoidable

Let us first give some more attention to the matter of periodizing as such. This is a basileological issue *par excellence,* because it (also) concerns the (supposedly) var-

---

10. See Ouweneel (2016b).

ied forms of the kingdom in successive dispensations (cf. in §2.4.1 the seven phases of the kingdom of God that I distinguish there: creation – fall – David – Christ's birth – his ministry – his glorification – his parousia – end of millennial kingdom).

On the one hand, we find that Scripture is not all that helpful to us when it comes to periodizing, because it gives us very few hints. On the other hand, it is equally true that no theological system investigating redemptive history can avoid a certain measure of periodizing. We might say that each theological system in fact entails its own dispensationalism, even if it perhaps does not distinguish seven but only four (the patriarchal, the Mosaic, the ecclesiastical, and the eschatological dispensation), or three (law, grace, kingdom), or even only two dispensations (Old and New Testament). The principle remains the same: no theologian can avoid periodizing, that is, distinguishing within redemptive history various successive phases that are discontinuous and that to some extent differ as to the order of things that God has instituted in each of these various stages for (a part of) humanity.

At best, we may have different opinions on the number of dispensations as well as on the measure of (dis)continuity between the successive dispensations. Concerning the latter point we notice that *all* orthodox theological systems acknowledge a certain measure of continuity because they all acknowledge the same moral principles of God throughout time (cf. James 1:17), or the one salvation in Christ alone (cf. Acts 4:12), or the fact that all post-Abrahamic believers are "sons of Abraham" (cf. Gal. 3:7), etc. And *all* orthodox theological systems also acknowledge a certain measure of discontinuity because they all distinguish between God's ways before and after the patriarchs, before and after the law-giving, before and after the cross, or before and after the parousia. Therefore Gordon Spykman is exaggerating when he says that dispensationalists "drive a wedge" between the Old and the New Testament.[11] They do indeed make a strong distinction between the Old and the New Testament, but they also acknowledge the continuity between them (although I have to admit that among some exponents this is more evident than in others).

The greatest danger of dispensationalism is the same as that of federalism, namely, a "theoreticalizing" of Scripture to such an extent that the resulting theological system begins to govern Bible interpretation tightly.[12] It imposes a certain thought system upon Scripture, and it manages to do so in such a neat way that eventually adherents begin to believe that such a system is taught directly by Scripture itself. However, the Bible directly teaches neither federalism, nor dispensationalism, nor any "-ism" whatsoever. Theologians themselves invent such systems with the intention of accounting as carefully as possible for the Scriptural data. These data are fixed (if, for a moment, we are allowed to make such a simplistic distinction between "fact" and "theory"). But the theories are invented by the theologians in order to account for the facts.

This is the path that *all* scientists and scholars follow.[13] It is not wrong; in fact, we have no other option. But scholars must remain conscious of the nature of this pro-

---

11. Spykman (1992, 537).
12. See Ouweneel (2016b).
13. See Ouweneel (2014b, 2015).

cedure. Theological theories are auxiliary constructs, not divinely revealed truth. And if, moreover, auxiliary constructs are in fact rather arbitrary, one may quietly wonder how "auxiliary" (helpful) they really are.

## 12.3 Are We Living in Some "Third Era"?
### 12.3.1 Many Calculations

According to one form of periodizing we are now living in some "Third Era." The idea of such a Third Epoch fits very well into the common anti-dispensationalist or amillennialist view of eschatology. For instance, Floyd E. Hamilton distinguished three epochs: the pre-Mosaic, the Mosaic, and the post-Mosaic (New Testament) era.[14] In this way, he followed church father Irenaeus, who spoke of three covenants, one made with Adam, one made with Moses, and one made with Christ.[15] The first covenant was characterized by the law written in the hearts (i.e., before Sinai; cf. Rom. 2:15), the second, by the law as an external commandment given at Sinai, and the third, by the law restored to the heart through the operation of the Holy Spirit (cf. 5:12–21). Augustine adhered to the same tripartite theory.[16]

Similarly, Johannes Cocceius distinguished three dispensations within the one covenant of grace,[17] the first *ante legem* ("before the law [was given]"), the second *sub lege* ("under the law"), and the third *post legem* ("after the law").[18] As opposed to this, other Reformational theologians, such as Louis Berkhof, preferred to distinguish only

---

14. Hamilton (1942, 26–27).
15. *Adversus Haereses* IV.38.
16. *Enchiridion* 118; *M.P.L.* 40, 287.
17. For this expression see extensively, Ouweneel (2016b).
18. See Berkhof (1996, 292).

two dispensations, those of the Old Testament and the New Testament.[19] William à Brakel distinguished three epochs in a different way: the Old Testament period (again divided into three epochs: Adam – Abraham – Sinai – Christ), the New Testament period (the time of Jesus and the apostles), and church history.[20] Here again, the third epoch is the one in which we are still living today.

The arrangement of three dispensations became especially interesting when some theologians began to link it with three historical periods of two thousand years each. This view was associated with a very common idea in church history, namely, that the Old Testament period lasted four thousand years. The English bishop James Ussher (1581–1656) calculated that the creation had occurred in the night preceding the 23rd of October in the year 4004 BC.[21] This date was even included in the margin of many editions of the KJV. If we assume that Christ was born in the fourth year before the Christian era, then there were precisely four thousand years between the creation and the birth of Christ. Other Reformational writers arrived at slightly different numbers, such as Martin Luther (3961 BC), Philipp Melanchthon (3964 BC), Johannes Kepler (3984 or 3993 BC?), Joseph B. Lightfoot (3960 BC), John Playfair (4008 BC), Joseph Scaliger (3950 BC), Johann A. Bengel (3943 BC).[22] With some satisfaction, Luther stated that the calculations by Melanchthon and himself differed very little.[23] However this may be, all the numbers near

---

19. Berkhof (1996, 293–301).
20. Van Campen (2007, 194).
21. See his *Annals of the World* (1650).
22. Bavinck (2004, 2:520–23); Morris (1976, 45).
23. Luther, WA, 55:23.

3965 BC point to a period of about four thousand years between the creation and Jesus' first public appearance.

Even in the twentieth century, we still encounter similar numbers. The Dutch theologian Johannes C. Sikkel (†1920) assumed that Adam was created in 4220 BC.[24] Herman Bavinck mentioned attempts to extend the time period of the Old Testament by a few thousand years, but saw no difficulty in assuming that Noah's flood occurred in 2348 BC, implying that Adam might have been created in 1,656 years earlier, or in 4004 BC. (When one adds the numbers in Gen. 5, 1,656 is the number of years between Adam's creation and Noah's flood.)[25]

### 12.3.2 The *Dictum Eliae*

Luther assumed that Abraham was born around 2000 BC, which divided the four thousand years of Old Testament history neatly into two equal parts.[26] In 1532, German astrologer and historian Johannes Carion (1499-1537) published a chronicle that largely depends on the lectures given by Luther's co-worker, Philipp Melanchthon (1497-1560). This chronicle distinguishes three epochs of two thousand years each: Adam – Abraham – Christ – parousia.[27] Interestingly, this division was based upon the so-called *Traditio Domus Eliae*, or the *Dictum Eliae*, that is, a proverb from the purported "school of Elijah," which in fact stemmed from the Talmud.[28]

---

24. Sikkel (1923, 33, 249–50)..
25. Bavinck (2004, 2:523).
26. Hartvelt (1977, 24).
27. Quoted by Hartvelt (1977, 18); see this work for further references.
28. Sanhedrin 97a and Aboda Sara 9a; also see the discussion between Rab Hanan and Rab Joseph (Sanhedrin 97b).

## THE ETERNAL KINGDOM: LIVING UNDER CHRIST

In 1531, Melanchthon wrote that the *Dictum Eliae* was very famous among the rabbis, and was generally accepted by the Jews.[29] Both Luther and Melanchthon referred to Paul of Burgos (1353–1435), a converted Spanish Jew, who quoted the *Dictum Eliae* from rabbinic sources. The *Dictum* was also quoted by Italian philosopher Giovanni Pico della Mirandola (†1494) and German theologian Andreas Osiander (†1552).[30] It says:

> *Sex millia annorum mundus, et deinde conflagratio [or, destructio].*
> *Duo millia inane [or, sine lege],*
> *Duo millia lex,*
> *Duo millia Messiae.*
> *Et propter peccata nostra, quae multa et magna sunt, deerunt anni qui deerunt.*[31]

The world consists of 6,000 years, and then the conflagration.
Two thousand are empty [or, without the law],
two thousand are the law,
two thousand the days of the Messiah.
And on account of our sins, which are many and great,
years will be lacking which will not be fulfilled.[32]

---

29. Cf. Luther, WA, 53:22.
30. For references, see Hartvelt (1977, 21, 95) and Froom (1948, 298–99).
31. For references and textual variants, see Hartvelt (1977, 93–94 n55).
32. Wengert (2005, 22; punctuation modified).

That is, world history will last six thousand years, namely, two thousand "empty" years (that is, without law), two thousand years under the law, and the subsequent two thousand years are the epoch of the Messiah. Because of our many and great sins, says the proverb in Melanchthon's version, a number of years will be lacking. That is, Christ was supposed to come again before the year 2000. In the Talmud's version, however, the words imply that the Messianic era should have started already, but it was postponed because of "our many and great sins." This suggests that these Talmudic words were probably first expressed shortly after AD 240, when, according to Jewish calculation, the four thousand years since creation were fulfilled. I will come back to this notion of six thousand years of world history when I return to the idea of a "Sixth Era."

## 12.4 Other Views

### 12.4.1 Playing with Numbers

It may sound strange that Melanchthon based such an important view concerning the tripartite nature of world history on a single extra-biblical—though Jewish—source. However, he believed he also found some support for his view in Daniel. In Daniel 12:11–12, two periods are mentioned, one of 1,290 days and one of 1,335 days. Like so many, Melanchthon was convinced that these "days" must be viewed as years, that the two numbers must be added, and that the total number refers to the end of time. Thus, he believed that 2,625 years would elapse between Daniel and the end time. Between Daniel and the birth of Christ was about six hundred years, leaving two thousand years for the period between

Christ's birth and his parousia.[33] This exegesis was rejected by Calvin,[34] although he too made the remark that the world was heading toward its end and had not yet reached six thousand years.[35]

In my view, interpreting these "days" as years, in both Daniel and in Revelation, is altogether mistaken. The period of 1,290 days is the first part of the 1,335 days (thus, the numbers must not be added), and is a bit longer than the 1,260 years in Revelation 11:2 and 12:6, which make $1,260 / 30 = 42$ months (11:2; 13:5), that is, a "time" (i.e., year), times (i.e., two years) and a "half time," which together makes three and a half years (12:14; cf. Dan. 7:25; 12:7). In *all* of these cases we are dealing with the second half of the last "week" (better: "seven," i.e., a period of seven years), that is, the last three and a half years of Daniel 9:24–27. To me, this is sufficient evidence that the periods of 1,260, 1,290, and 1,335 days must be taken literally, just as the seventy "sevens" (490 years) must be taken literally.[36]

Some time after Melanchthon and Calvin, the German theologian Andreas Musculus (1514–1581), in his tract *Vom jüngsten Tage* ("Concerning the Last Day," 1587), also referred to the *Dictum of Elijah* as a proof that the world would not exist any longer than six thousand years. He added that, because the world had existed al-

---

33. CR (*Melanchthonis Opera*), 13:977–978.
34. CR (*Calvini Opera*), 41:303.
35. Calvin, *Institutes*, 1.14.1.
36. See more extensively, Ouweneel (2012c, 255-65); the interpretation that I follow here assumes a large gap between the 69th and the 70th "weeks." The first 69 "weeks" (483 years) are roughly from 457 BC to AD 27, the beginning of Jesus' public ministry.

ready for 5,556 years, it should continue for some five hundred more years, according to Elijah's prophecy. So apparently Musculus, too, expected the end of world history around the year 2000. During the same time, the English theologian Hugh Latimer (c. 1487–1555) defended the six-thousand-years theory, and thus, writing in 1552, stated that there was no more than four hundred forty-eight years remaining, that is, until 2000, although he believed that the time would be shortened.[37] One and a half centuries later, Robert Fleming (c. 1660–1716), a Scotsman who pastored in the Dutch cities of Leyden and Rotterdam, wrote that he expected the destruction of the "Papal Kingdom" in the year 2000.[38] In that year, Christ would return and the world would enter upon that glorious "sabbatical millenary," when "the saints shall reign on the earth, in a peaceable manner for a thousand years more."[39]

### 12.4.2 Joachim of Fiore

The best known tripartite outline of history was designed by the monk Joachim of Fiore (c. 1135–1202).[40] He claimed that on a certain night of Easter he had received a vision in which God had unfolded to him his plan for history.[41] After the empire of the Father (that of

---

37. *Sermons on the Lord's Prayer*, 3rd sermon (www.katapi.org.uk/LordsPrayer/LatimerLP/Ch3.htm).
38. *The Rise and Fall of the Papacy* (1701).
39. Quoted in Froom (1948, 372, 646); he also mentions (330, 338) the German David Chytraeus (†1600) and the Swiss Theodor Bibliander (†1564).
40. See especially his *Expositio in Apocalypsim* (printed as late as 1527).
41. Cf. Lindeboom (1929, 112–39); Grundmann (1966); Hartvelt

the law, i.e., from Abraham to Christ) and that of the Son (the empire of the gospel), he saw a third empire rising, the millennial kingdom of the Holy Spirit, the kingdom of love and freedom, in which the corrupt church was to be restored in its original purity. In Joachim's view, the time unit of these epochs is the generation. Matthew 1:17 shows that forty-two generations had elapsed between Abraham and Christ; Joachim believed that the second epoch would encompass the same number of generations.

Joachim did not venture to calculate the beginning of the Third Epoch, but his zealous followers did. Assuming thirty years for a generation, they expected the kingdom of the Holy Spirit to arrive in the year 1260 (= 42 x 30). Of course, the numbers 42 and 1,260 alert us immediately (see above); the Joachimites turned the 1,260 days of Revelation into 1,260 years. They linked this with the Holy Roman Emperor Frederick II (1212–1250), who was exceptionally gifted both politically and scientifically, called the "emperor of peace" (the German name Friedrich comes from *Friede*, "peace"!), whom they nevertheless regarded as the Antichrist.

This astonishing person, called *stupor mundi* ("the amazement of the world"), indeed exhibited a kind of "end time" character. This came to light in, among other things, his intense conflict with pope Gregory IX, in which each of them depicted the other as the Antichrist. When, after Frederick's death, the Third Era had apparently not commenced, some Joachimites came to believe that the start of this Third Epoch should be enforced

---

(1977, 30-49); especially Tuveson (1964, 19-20), whose study also describes many other ancient millennial views.

with violence. One of the most famous of these fanatics was the monk Fra Dolcino, who shortly after 1300 announced the "church of the Spirit," implying the end of the "church of the flesh," and, hidden in the mountains with his followers, awaited the appearance of a saving emperor and a holy pope. (To be sure, Fra Dolcino himself worked with a blueprint of four epochs, assuming the Third Era to have begun with emperor Constantine the Great and pope Silvester I.) In 1307 Dolcino and his followers were all killed in a most cruel way.[42]

Later German philosophers, such as the Enlightenment thinker Gotthold E. Lessing (1729-1781), and the German philosopher Friedrich Schelling (1775-1854), each in his own way toyed with the notion of a Third Empire. Lessing found the idea of a triple empire not unattractive, but blamed Joachim and his followers for having proclaimed the Third Empire as being so near.[43] Schelling saw, after a *Petrine* (Roman Catholic) and a *Pauline* (Germanic Protestant) empire, a third, *Johannine* empire rising, which would allow only one world religion, a religion of love.

With his dialectic of *thesis, antithesis,* and *synthesis,* the German philosopher Georg W. F. Hegel (1770-1831) inspired quite a few philosophers of history. Thus, Norwegian playwright Henrik Ibsen (1826-1906) spoke of a Third Empire that was to be a synthesis of ancient culture (thesis) and Christianity (antithesis),[44] and Russian writer Dmitry R. Mereshovski (1865-1941) saw a Third

---

42. Umberto Eco's novel, *The Name of the Rose* (1980), contains many references to Fra Dolcino.
43. Lessing (1967, §86 etc.).
44. See on this Johnston (1980).

Empire as a synthesis of religion and science. With Russian novelist Fyodor M. Dostoyevski (1821–1881) and German philosopher of history Oswald Spengler (1880–1936)[45] we encounter similar notions.

In the twentieth century, the idea of a Third Era became well-known through the Third Reich of German National-Socialism. This was a third empire after the first one, the Holy Roman Empire of the German nation, and the second one, the Little German empire of the German emperors of the nineteenth and twentieth centuries. The person who inadvertently most influenced the national-socialist idea of the Third Empire was the German political writer Arthur Moeller van den Bruck (1876–1925). In 1923 he published his book, *Das dritte Reich* ("The Third Empire").[46] He too interpreted the notion of a Third Empire in a Hegelian-dialectical sense, namely, as an eschatological-millennialist synthesis of the Holy Roman Empire (thesis) and the "second" German empire (antithesis). In this sense, the term was adopted by National-Socialism, even though the latter gave it a form very different from what the writer had intended. The Nazis meant by the "Third Reich" the "millennial empire" (compare Joachim!), which after the first and the second empires was founded by Nazism in 1933—and ultimately would last only twelve years.

## 12.5 Are We Living in Some "Fourth" or "Fifth Era"?
### 12.5.1 The "Fourth Era"
In the nineteenth and early twentieth centuries, several Anglo-Saxon theologians and Bible teachers described a

---

45. Spengler (1991).
46. Moeller van den Bruck (1923).

view in which the seven days of creation were considered to be types of the seven epochs of redemptive history. These writers included Andrew Jukes (†1901), Frederick W. Grant (†1902), William Tytler (†1930), Albert E. Booth (†1950), Philip Mauro (†1952), and Algernon J. Pollock (†1957).[47] A somewhat similar view had been presented earlier, but then in the form of seven epochs within church history. We find this with Reformed writers in the Netherlands: Jacobus Koelman (†1695) and Pierre Jurieu (†1713, of French descent). Koelman interpreted the seventh day as the eternal rest of the new creation, whereas Jurieu, in a postmillennialist way, interpreted it as the supposed future heyday of the church.[48]

In the dispensationalist view of Jukes and the other authors mentioned, the fourth day, on which the celestial bodies were created, represents the present epoch of grace, that is, the era of the Christian church, the "heavenly" people of God. Christ is the sun of righteousness (Mal. 4:2), the light that came into the world (John 12:4, 6). As long as this light was in the world, it was "day," says Jesus in John 9:4–5. After a glorious "sunset" (so to speak), the "night" came, in which the light had to come from the moon and the stars. The church has no light of itself but, just as the moon reflects the light of the sun, the church spreads the divine light that it receives from Christ (cf. Matt. 5:14; 2 Cor. 3:18; Eph. 5:8; 1 Thess. 5:4–5). In Philippians 2:15, Christians are compared to celestial bodies, which must provide light in the darkness.

---

47. Jukes (1875, 5–58); Grant (n.d., 23–30); Mauro (1908, 24–55); Booth (1999); Tytler (n.d.); Pollock (n.d.:43–64).
48. Van Campen (2007, 179).

At this point, I would turn instead to Daniel 2 and 7 to investigate a bit further in what era of redemptive history we may be living. In these Bible chapters, we find the history of the four world empires: from the Babylonian to the Roman Empire, succeeded by a fifth empire, that of the Messiah. For many centuries, the nature of this fifth empire has been debated.[49] According to the context, it must be an "inner-temporal" kingdom, which in world history follows upon the previous four world empires. It cannot be the "Christian" empire that arose in Europe after the Constantinian turn, nor the "Christian" empire that has existed in numerous forms since the fall of the West-Roman Empire (AD 476). It is a future kingdom, which will arise either before the parousia (postmillennialism), or after it (premillennialism).

To premillennialists the matter is clear. According to Daniel 7:13–14, in comparison with 2:44–45, it is no one less than the Son of Man, the One who comes on the clouds of heaven, who puts a *radical* and *sudden* end to the fourth empire. Immediately after this empire, he erects the fifth and last inner-temporal empire: the Messianic kingdom. If we consider this, it must be crystal clear that the fourth empire—the Roman Empire—has not yet ended, and the empire of the Son of Man will arrive only at his parousia (cf. §12.5.2); this was the view of all Greek and almost all Latin fathers, even Augustine.[50] Taken in this sense, we must say that we are living during the time of the fourth empire; more precise-

---

49. See Ouweneel (2016d, 5–7).

50. See Kocken (1935, 6–72); Adamek (1938, 36–51).

ly: during the time between the apparent fall of the Roman Empire and its revival in the last days.

## 12.5.2 The "Fifth Era"

To repeat the question of the previous section: In what era are we living today? In the "fourth era" (thus especially premillennialists), or in the "fifth era" (thus many amillennialists, implicitly or explicitly). Let us now look a bit more closely at the latter view, namely, that of Calvin and other amillennialists.

The interpretation of John Calvin (1509-1564) concerning the fifth empire in Daniel 2 and 7 was totally different from that of the millennialists. According to him, the four world empires have basically reached their end—though in a very gradual way—not at the second, but at the first coming of Jesus Christ. Thus, since that event, we have been living in the fifth empire, the ecclesiastical empire of Jesus Christ, as he put it.[51] It is no wonder that outside Calvinist circles this interpretation has hardly received any following because of the exegetical contortions it involves.

First, the stone in Daniel 2 destroys the Roman Empire with one blow, whereas at the birth or the ascension of Christ, or at the day of Pentecost (Acts 2), the Roman Empire did not fall at all. It did not fall before Christianity; on the contrary, during the fourth century it assumed a Christian character, and survived this way for one and a half centuries. For the Western part of the empire, more than four centuries passed (until AD 476), and for the Eastern part more than fourteen centuries passed (until 1453), before they fell.

---

51. CR, 40:607.

Second, the ideal of a "Roman" Empire in Europe has never fully died out, also after it had turned Christian: it then simply became the Christian Roman Empire, or even the *Holy* Roman Empire, which formally lasted until 1806 when Napoleon forced the Austrian emperor Francis II to dissolve the empire after the Battle of Austerlitz.

Third, a world empire that was truly ruled according to the mind of Christ has simply never existed in church history, in no part of the world, not even during the best times of the Christian world.

Fourth, even the West-Roman Empire was not destroyed by orthodox Christianity, but by pagan or Arian Germanic tribes (AD 476). The East-Roman Empire was brought to an end by Turkish Muslims (1453). We could never assert that Christian orthodoxy has politically prevailed in the domain of the former Roman Empire (apart from the enormous political power of popes such as Innocent III around 1200, and a few similar popes).

Fifth, no matter how heavenly and spiritual the "fifth empire" of Christ may be, in the line of Daniel 2 and 7 it must be viewed, too, as an earthly, inner-temporal, political empire, and cannot be viewed as a spiritual, religious, supratemporal empire over against the four earthly, inner-temporal, political empires.

Sixth, in Daniel 7:13 the Messianic Kingdom clearly arrives, not at the birth or ascension of the Messiah, but at his coming on the clouds of heaven (cf. Matt. 24:30; 26:64; Mark 13:26; 14:62; 1 Thess. 4:17; Rev. 1:7).

Therefore, only one conclusion is possible; Calvin was wrong, and the majority of expositors have been and are right: the fifth empire, that of the Messiah, begins only at the parousia of Jesus Christ.

## 12.6 Are We Living in Some "Sixth Era"?
### 12.6.1 The "Friday" of Redemptive History

When we think of a Sixth Era, we might think again of the *Dictum Eliae*. Earlier I provided Melanchthon's version of it, which says that, because of our many and great sins, a number of years would be lacking. Instead of these lines, we find in the version supplied by Martin Luther the following:

> *Isti sunt Sex dies hebdomadae coram Deo,*
> *Septimus Dies Sabbatum aeternum est.*[52]

Here, the purported six thousand years of redemptive history are compared with the "six weekdays before God," that is, the days of creation, followed by the seventh "day" of God's eternal rest. Luther quoted Psalm 90:4 ("a thousand years in your sight are but as yesterday when it is past") and 2 Peter 3:8 ("with the Lord one day is as a thousand years, and a thousand years as one day") as evidence for his claim that, as God had created the world in six days, the history of the world was going to last six millennia in which God guides creation to its consummation. Of course, the references do not say this at all.

First, they do not say that we are free to interpret certain "days" in Scripture as periods of thousand years. The two passages quoted have nothing to do with our interpretation of biblical days but only with

---

52. Quoted in Warburg (1920, 72).

God's *experience* of our common, earthly days, since God is beyond time as we know it.

Second, the principle is not applied consistently. If the seven days of Genesis 1 must be taken to be seven periods of a thousand years each, why not the seven days of Genesis 7:4, 10 or 8:10, 12?

Third, Psalm 90:4 in fact says the opposite: not, one day is a thousand years, but: a thousand years are one day. 2 Peter 3:8 says both. Again, who would be foolish enough to interpret any period of a thousand years in the Bible as one day?

Nevertheless, in Luther's time, the one-day-is-a-thousand years idea was already very old. It occurs already in the Slavonic book of Enoch (32:2; 33:1-2), where God is claimed to say mysteriously, "I blessed the seventh day, which is the Sabbath, on which [Adam] rested from his works. And I appointed the eighth day also, that the eighth day should be the first-created after my work, and that the first seven revolve in the form of the seventh thousand, and that at the beginning of the eighth thousand there should be a time of not-counting, endless, with neither years, nor months nor weeks nor days nor hours." This seems to point to six thousand years of labor and toil until the judgment, followed by a millennial kingdom of rest and blessedness, and afterward the eighth, that is, the eternal day (2 Pet. 3:18, the "day of eternity").

The notion recurred in later rabbinic writing, such as that of Abraham bar Hiyya Hanasi (c. 1100) and that of Nachmanides (or Ramban, c. 1250). Both rabbis asserted that the Messiah would come at the end of the six thousand years. The same idea was found in the *Zohar*, the famous Cabbalistic work of Moses de León (thirteenth century; supposedly going back upon Rabbi Shimon bar Yochai, second century).[53] However, whether the idea comes from Jews or from Christians, it stands on shaky exegetical ground.

### 12.6.2 Early Millennialism

This millennialist six-days view crept into Christian thinking at an early stage. In the Epistle of Barnabas (c. AD 100) it is said: "Note, children, what this 'He was ready in six days' implies. It means: the Lord will complete all in six days. With the Lord, one day means thousand years. Thus, all will be completed in six days, that is, in six thousand years, children. And he rested at the seventh day. That means, when his Son is come and the time of lawlessness is finished, and he will judge the wicked and will change the sun, the moon and the stars, then he will certainly rest at that day" (15:3-5).

Similarly, Irenaeus wrote in his *Adversus Haereses*, "If the days of the Lord are as thousand years, and creation is completed in six days, then apparently its completion is the year 6000."[54] And a little later: "For the righteous, he will let arrive the times of the empire, that is, the rest, the holy seventh day."[55] The same view is encountered in the writings of church fathers such as Hippolytus, Lactantius, Hilary, Cyprian, Ambrose, Jerome, and Augustine. They expected a millennial period of peace and righteousness, although they had no place in it for ethnic Israel, and often took the seventh

---

53. See Froom (1948, 211, 216).
54. *Adversus Haereses* V.28.3 (http://www.newadvent.org/fathers/0103528.htm).
55. *Adversus Haereses* V.30.4; cf. 33.2.

"thousand" to mean "everlasting" (cf. again 2 Pet. 3:18, the "day of eternity").

Obviously, the comparison to the six days of creation not only suggested that world history would last seven thousand years, but also that world history could be neatly divided into seven periods of a thousand years each. Thus, the Christian scholar Sextus Julius Africanus (c. 160–c. 240) wrote a five-volume *Chronographia*, in which he attempted to synchronize sacred and profane history, and to divide history into six periods of a thousand years each.[56] Precisely in the middle of the six thousand years, that is, in the 3,000th year after creation, he placed the death of Peleg (Gen. 10:25); the name Peleg, probably meaning "division," was even interpreted to mean *to hēmisy*, "the half."

Just like several church fathers, Sextus Julius Africanus believed that Christ was born in the 5,500th year after creation—a number based on Septuagint chronology—which left precisely one twelfth of world history remaining. Origen found support for this idea in, for example, the parable of the vineyard in Matthew 20:1–16. The twelve hours of the "day" mentioned there are taken to represent the totality of world history. The "last hour," the hour of grace (Matt. 20:6, 9), had begun with the coming of Christ (1 John 2:18).[57] Therefore, several fathers expected the parousia of Christ in AD 500. This meant that, just as the rabbis had been on high alert

---

56. Regarding Julius Africanus and his calculations, see Hartvelt (1977, 26), and references there.
57. See his Commentary on Mattew, ad loc. (http://www.newavent.org/fathers/1016.htm).

around AD 240 (see above), tensions arose among some fathers as the year 500 approached.

### 12.6.3 Augustine

A wiser approach was followed by Aurelius Augustine.[58] He abandoned the idea of six periods of precisely a thousand years each. However, he did retain the interpretation of the days of creation as epochs of world history, though assuming that each epoch was of a different length.[59] Thus, he considered the first of the seven periods to encompass the 1,656 years between Adam's creation and Noah's flood. He arrived at roughly the same outline that John A. Savage followed many centuries later (see above): Adam – Noah – Abraham – David [Savage: Moses] – Babylonian captivity – Christ – the *eschaton*.

The greatest difference with the later dispensationalists was that, for Augustine, the seventh "day" was the "eternal state" (the new heavens and the new earth), whereas for the dispensationalists this "day" was the millennial Messianic kingdom, followed by a new, eighth "day," the "day of eternity" (2 Pet. 3:18), the eternal state.

Augustine found the basis for this division partly in the genealogy of Matthew 1, which is divided into three parts: from Abraham to David, then to the captivity, then to Christ. He explicitly stated: *Sexta nunc agitur nullo generationum numero metienda propter id quod dic-*

---

58. See his work, The Literal Meaning of Genesis (http://college.holycross.edu/faculty/alaffey/other_files/Augustine-Genesis1.pdf).
59. De civitate Dei, XXII.30 (https://en.wikisource.org/wiki/TheCity_of_God/Book_XXII/Chapter_30).

*tum est: Non est vestrum scire tempora, quae Pater posuit in sua potestate*, "Now this [present] age is the sixth, to be measured by no number [of years], because of that which is spoken: 'It is not for you to know the seasons, which the Father has placed in His own power' [cf. Acts 1:7]."[60]

The fact that he rejected the idea of six epochs of precisely a thousand years each had the advantage that it underscored the impossibility of calculating the year of Christ's parousia. Augustine quoted Acts 1:7 to show that such a calculation is neither possible nor desirable: the times and seasons are known to the Father alone, and that is in everyone's interest. We may add Mark 13:32 to this: "[C]oncerning that day or that hour, no one knows, not even the angels in heaven, nor the Son, but only the Father." Just as it is very good that we do not know the hour of our death, it is good that we do not know the time of the parousia. Be ready every minute, and work as if it might still be many years off.

We conclude that, according to Augustine but also according to some premillennialist dispensationalists, we are still living in the sixth epoch. Augustine's views received a fairly large following in late antiquity and the early Middle Ages. Paul Orosius, the fifth-century Christian historian, assumed them in his *Adversum Paganos* ("Against the Pagans"). The Spanish Isidore of Seville (†636) did so in his *Etymologiarum sive originum libri viginti* ("Twenty Books of Etymologies or Origins"). And the eighth-century English historian, Beda Venerabilis, did the same in his *De sex aetatibus* ("On the Six Epochs") and his *De ratione temporum* ("On the Reckoning of the Times"). Through-

---

60. See previous note (trans. Marcus Dods).

out the Middle Ages, the notion of the *aetates mundi* ("epochs of the world") as based upon the days of creation remained a well-known theme.⁶¹

## 12.7 Periodizing in the Reformed Tradition
### 12.7.1 Cocceius

The theme of how to divide redemptive history into a number of distinct epochs, in connection with intensive discussions about a possible millennial kingdom, has played a great role in the Reformed theological world of the Netherlands in the seventeenth and eighteenth centuries. I am again following the dissertation of M. ("Theo") van Campen, who refers to other important present-day writings of, among others, Willem J. van Asselt (†2014), Jan van den Berg, Roelof Bisschop, Teunis Brienen, Henk Florijn, Cornelis Graafland (†2004), Willem J. op 't Hof, Simon van der Linde (†1995), Doede Nauta, Willem van 't Spijker, and Ernestine G. E. van der Wal. These Dutch theologians often referred to the British Puritans.⁶²

The great pioneer in Reformed theology of the Netherlands in the field of periodizing was Johannes Cocceius (1603–1669, of German descent) in his *Summa Theologiae*. He was inspired by the *Dictum Eliae* as well as by the periodizing of Augustine and Joachim of Fiore. Earlier I mentioned Cocceius' distinction between three dispensations within the one covenant of grace: the first *ante legem*, the second *sub lege*, and the third *post legem* (§12.3.1). In addition, he concentrated especially on church history, that is, the development of the kingdom

---

61. See the helpful article by Schmidt (1955/56).
62. See Van Elderen (1992).

of God within the framework of the covenant of grace. In this development, he distinguished seven successive periods, seven *aetates ecclesiae* ("epochs of the church"), which he viewed as parallel with the seven letters, seven seals, seven trumpets, and seven bowls in the book of Revelation.[63] It is quite fascinating—but also rather speculative—that he thought these very same periods are prefigured in the book of Acts.[64]

Naturally, every periodizer is confronted with the task of properly fitting the "thousand years" of Revelation 20:1-6 somewhere into his model. He may argue the passage away, as Abraham Kuyper did, but he cannot ignore the passage. It is not easy to determine exactly how Cocceius understood this passage.[65] On the one hand, he believed that the millennial kingdom was in the past; he called those who thought differently "Thousand Years Chasers" (*Duisent Jaar-dryvers*). On the other hand, he did believe in a future blessed heyday for the church, including the restoration of Israel. This is a kind of postmillennialism after all, as we would say today (§11.2.1). In this kind of view, we occasionally find something that might be called a "double millennium," that is, a Messianic kingdom in the past or present, and one in the future. Adherents of this position are following the British Puritan, Thomas Brightman (†1607).[66]

---

63. See Van Campen (2007, 282, 293-95); cf. Ouweneel (2010b, §1.5).
64. Thus also the Coccerians Henricus Groenewegen and Fredericus van Leenhof, according to Van Campen (2007, 294-95, 406-407, 449).
65. Van Campen (2007, 295-97).
66. Van Campen (2007, 294-96, 577).

## 12.7.2 Sibersma and Van der Groe

Following Cocceius, Hero Sibersma (†1728) also distinguished seven periods in church history, which he called the "seven times of the Gentiles" (cf. Luke 21:24). In his view, he himself was living during the sixth epoch, so that he was expecting the seventh epoch—before the parousia—which would be a time of peace and justice, to which both Jews and Gentiles look forward.[67] In this sense, Sibersma may be called a postmillennialist as well. Please note that those who make such a clear-cut distinction between a sixth and a seventh epoch can hardly believe that the Messianic kingdom—the heyday of the church—will come in a very gradual way. It must have quite a marked beginning, some kind of divine intervention, so that the seventh epoch can be clearly distinguished from the previous, sixth epoch.

Other Cocceians adhered to some form of postmillennialism, too, such as Henricus Groenewegen (†1692), Campegius Vitringa (†1722), and Friedrich Adolph Lampe (†1729, of German descent), who appeal to Revelation 2-3 as well.[68] In contrast with Cocceius, Vitringa and Lampe located the millennial kingdom explicitly in the seventh phase of church history. Only after this will the eternal state arrive. This view led Lampe to the wonder whether one should not actually distinguish eight epochs, the eighth of which lasts eternally.

Among the Voetians, we encounter far fewer attempts to divide redemptive history into distinct epochs. In fact, we find this only with Theodore van de

---

67. Van Campen (2007, 349-50).
68. Van Campen (2007, 405-410, 463, 497-98, 505).

Groe (†1784), who in this respect was probably influenced by the Cocceians. This presumption is supported by his typically Cocceian appeal to Proverbs 9:1, "Wisdom has built her house; she has hewn her seven pillars,"[69] to underscore the meaning of the number seven. However, his way of periodizing is different from the others. In the Old Testament he distinguished four epochs: Adam – Noah – Abraham – Moses – Christ. In this view, the fifth epoch is from the Day of Pentecost to the entrance of the "fullness of the Gentiles" (Rom. 11:25), that is, the epoch in which we are still living today. The sixth period is that of the conversion of the Jews and their restoration in their own land until the end of the world, that is, including the Messianic kingdom. The seventh epoch is the eternal state.

Van der Groe associated the sixth epoch with the "glorious state of the church," whereby he, like so many other Reformed theologians of his time, advocated a postmillennial view according to the broad definition of the term that I have given. It is useful to identify someone as a postmillennialist if he believes in a *future* Messianic kingdom on earth, *before* the parousia, irrespective of his interpretation of Revelation 20:1–6.

## 12.8 Are We Living in Some "Seventh" or "Eighth Era"?
### 12.8.1 The "Seventh Era"

Let us now return for a moment to the matter of the four world empires. Not every author has viewed the empires after the fall of the West-Roman Empire as varieties of that Roman Empire. The "monk of St. Gall," an anonymous medieval chronicler (usually identified

---

69. Van Campen (2007, 237–41).

with Notker Balbulus, "the Stammerer," †912), saw, as it were, a new succession of empires arising after Rome. About the image that Nebuchadnezzar saw (Dan. 2) he wrote: "When the Almighty, who governs all and determines the destiny of kingdoms and epochs, had broken the feet of iron and clay of that wondrous image, that is, the Romans, he erected in the land of the Franks, by means of the renowned Charles, another, no less wondrous image with a head of gold."[70]

Such a *translatio imperii* ("transfer of the empire") had taken place earlier, when Constantine transferred the Roman empire to the Greeks (that is, at Constantinople, the "New Rome"). Five centuries later, the pope, on the basis of an authority supposedly founded on the Roman see and the tomb of Peter, transferred the empire from the Greeks (that is, the still extant East-Roman Empire) to the Franks (AD 800). This was called a *renovatio imperii Romani*, "renewal of the Roman Empire" (as Charlemagne wrote in his imperial bull), this time under Frankish authority.

Charlemagne (742–814) was seen to be a new golden head! But could a Christian such as this Sangallensic monk have wished to contradict Daniel 2? After the Roman Empire, the kingdom of the Son of Man arrives; that is certain from the outset. And thus, a new image of which Charlemagne would be the golden head is conceivable only *within* the framework of the Roman Empire as it survived in different (Christianized) varieties.

Many authors throughout church history have thought of such a solution. Thus, Otto bishop of Freising (†1158) distinguished not only the four

---

70. Pertz (1829, 731).

world empires, but also four epochs in world history, in such a way that the four world empires together form the first epoch of world history, the period until the birth of Christ.[71] Since then, three epochs supposedly have followed, of which the fourth and last—or, in the total series, the seventh empire—was supposed to have begun with the emperor Theodosius I, who on November 8, 392, elevated (Roman Catholic) Christianity to be the status of state religion, and soon after this forbade all pagan worship (§10.2.1).[72] However, the latter epochs, too, actually involve nothing but stages of the Roman Empire. This empire in its fourth and last stage has become a "Christian" empire, which supposedly will last until the parousia.

The question I posed for the monk is relevant for the bishop as well. Will the "Christian" empire really last until the second coming? Is there not, just before the parousia, an anti-Christian empire on earth, that is, the kingdom of the Antichrist? And when will that *anti*-Christian empire begin, or did it begin already today in the Islamic world? Or in resurging Russia? Or in China, or, more generally, in Asia? Or—most likely—in secularized, humanist, apostate Europe and North America? Many have loved to speak of a "Christian" empire since AD 392 (or a comparable year). But could we not, with equal validity, defend the thesis that the Western world, which today is so hostile to God, in fact already began with the purported "Christianization" of the Roman Empire, with its the blending of church and state (to the detriment of the

---

71. See Van Schelven (1944, 94–95); cf. Kocken (1935, 112–16, 145–54).
72. *Codex Theodosianus* 16, 10, 10–12 (http://ancientrome.ru/ius/library/codex/theod/liber16.htm#10).

church)? This too is a question of essential significance for any Christian view of history, one that I have discussed extensively in my book, *The Ninth King*.

This matter of the spiritual evaluation of the "Christianized" Roman Empire constitutes a question of eminent importance for any Christian view of history, and in fact for basileology as well. Must our evaluation be positive, that is, has the Christianized empire always been, and is it still, a presage of the Messianic kingdom? Or must our evaluation be negative, that is, has the Christianized empire always been, and is it today more than ever, a presage of the kingdom of the Antichrist? Or is it something in between?

### 12.8.2 The "Eighth Era"

It is very interesting to see how, each time when, in European history, an important empire was approaching its end, this kind of eschatological question emerged. When in 1254 the house of the Holy Roman Staufen emperors died out with Conrad IV (1228–1254), many voices were raised in Germany warning that with the fall of the empire—in this case the Staufen empire—the empire of the Antichrist would arrive.[73] And just as it was believed that in the year 1000, history would come to its end and Christ would return, the same rumors arose everywhere in the Christian world when humanity was facing the year 2000. Again, the question arose: Is our time a presage of the approaching kingdom of Christ, or of the approaching kingdom of the Antichrist?

In Revelation 17:10–14, we hear about the beast, ~~ich~~ is the eighth world empire, as well as the head of

~ann (1984, 424).

that empire, but which is a revival of one of the previous seven empires. It will ultimately perish, and that by the hand of the Lamb, who is the King of kings. After the well-known series of seven empires, there is an eighth empire, namely, that of the Antichrist, who will persecute God's people in a way that has hardly occurred before. The Ninth King is he who, a few verses later, in verse 14, is called "the Lamb" and "Lord of lords and King of kings." Only under him will all of Israel's exiles and tribulations, as well as all false kingdoms and empires, come to an end.

The idea that in history there are several successive world empires is deeply rooted in European history. As I said earlier, this phenomenon is traditionally called the *translatio imperii*, the "transference of the world empire [from one nation to another]." As far as can be ascertained, the idea of the transition of one empire to the other was expressed first in a writing ascribed to Demetrius of Phaleron (c. 300 BC). He presumed that the idea of four world empires was first launched by Greek politician and historian Zenon of Rhodos, shortly after the battle of Magnesia (190 BC). Already then, the fourth empire was thought to be the Roman one.

What we find today is the eighth empire, the empire of the Antichrist. Will it be a (pseudo)Christian empire? Or a Jewish empire? Or an Islamic empire? Or an empire of many political powers combined? Or an empire of the economic powers? This is not the place for speculations.[74]

Some who see the power of Antichrist looming might argue that we are already living in the eighth era, or that we are on the brink of it. If this is true, we have all the

---

74. See again extensively, Ouweneel (2012a).

more reason to look forward to the imminent coming of the Ninth King. In the nineteenth century, new interest in prophetic epochs and dispensations arose, as we will see in the next and last chapter. However, already at this point I would caution that we would be wise not to be carried away by speculations. Christians who looked forward to the Lord's coming have always clung to his word: "Behold, I am coming soon!" (Rev. 22:7, 12, 20).

# Chapter 13
# Later Dispensationalism and Kingdom Theology

> *Then comes the end, when he delivers the kingdom to God the Father after destroying every rule and every authority and power.*
> *For he must reign until he has put all his enemies under his feet.*
> *The last enemy to be destroyed is death.*
> *For "God has put all things in subjection under his feet."*
> *But when it says, "all things are put in subjection,"*
> *it is plain that he is excepted who put all things in subjection under him.*
> *When all things are subjected to him, then the Son himself will also be subjected to him*
> *who put all things in subjection under him,*
> *that God may be all in all.*
>
> — 1 Corinthians 15:24–28

***Summary:*** *Dispensationalism has gone through its own historical development. In "classical dispensationalism," the boundaries between Israel and the church were still very sharp; it necessitated, among other things, the doctrine of the secret rapture. In "ultradispensationalism," a sharp line is drawn between the earlier church and the later (post-Acts 28) church. The same line is drawn in cessationism ("the gifts of the Spirit have ceased since the apostolic era"). Newer forms of dispensationalism include "revised" and "progressive dispensationalism"; "classical dispensationalism" has simply been rendered obsolete by the historical facts. In the second half of the chapter, I offer diagrams of the seven stages in the history of the kingdom, and of the nine world empires of history. This half also deals with earlier "millenniums" in history, and concludes by pointing to the Solomonic kingdom as the great model for the Messianic kingdom.*

## 13.1 Classical Dispensationalism

### 13.1.1 John N. Darby

JOHN N. DARBY (†1882) has often been called the father of dispensationalism.[1] As we have seen, he was not the first to periodize redemptive history. But he certainly is the founder of that characteristic form of periodizing that we refer to as *dispensationalism*, because of Darby's own frequent use of the term "dispensation." As dispensationalism views them, the dispensations typically differ significantly from each other. Each dispensation supposedly has its own character. At the same time, Darby was interested in what all the dispensations had in com-

---

1. For a description (by an opponent) of him and the development of his thought system, see Efird (1986, 17-37).

mon, the "dispensational" character of each redemptive-historical epoch, those features that stamp each of them as a "dispensation."

Darby never presented an extensive and schematized system of dispensations. What comes closest to this is not a mature study at all, but an article from his early years.[2] Here, he views the dispensations in the proper sense as starting with Noah. Without numbering them, he mentions the following dispensations: (a) from Noah to the patriarchs, (b) then Israel under the law, (c) then the "royal dispensation" (from David onward), (d) then the Christian dispensation, (e) then the Messianic kingdom of peace.[3] His actual theme in this article is not so much dispensations as such but rather the fact that *each* dispensation apparently ends with decline, judgment on the majority of the people (humanity, Israel, the Christian world), and salvation of a faithful remnant.

At this point Darby is still developing his terminology. Thus he speaks of the "church dispensation," whereas later he claimed that "the church" because of its "heavenly character" is actually not a dispensation because it is not part of the earthly things.[4] Nonetheless, there is an order of things connected with it during its life on earth—an order of things whose existence is linked with the church's responsibility. We might put it this way: there *is* a dispensation of Christianity but, strictly speaking, not a dispensation of "the church" in its transcen-

---

2. Efird (1986, 124–30, where he refers to Darby's work, "*The Apostasy of the Successive Dispensations*".
3. *Contra* Hoek (2004, 300), who believes that Darby taught three dispensations.
4. Darby (CW 4:328; cf. 5:15 note).

dent-universal sense.[5] This is related to Darby's peculiar view that the church forms a "parenthesis," a kind of interim period in the ways of God with the earth.[6] Since the Exodus, Israel is the center of these divine ways but, during the parenthesis of the church, Israel has been temporarily set aside. However, after the rapture of the church (when it will be snatched up from the earth supposedly before the Great Tribulation; cf. 1 Thess. 4:13–18), God picks up the thread with Israel again.

Of course, this idea of a parenthesis is not meant in a deprecating way. On the contrary, for Darby, the church is the highest good that the counsel of God has ever produced, and that world history has ever manifested. Darby's point is only that, in his view, God's ways with Israel have been temporarily interrupted. To be sure, the term "parenthesis" does not necessarily imply a dispensationalist viewpoint. Gerrit C. Berkouwer used the term extensively for the period between the first coming of Christ (or his ascension) and his second coming (the parousia).[7] Apart from any dispensationalist model, the meaning of the parenthesis is just as evident: the parousia is delayed in order that as many people as possible may be saved. God is patient toward humanity not wishing that any should perish, but that all people should be saved (1 Tim. 2:4; 2 Pet. 3:9). The parenthesis is needed so that *all nations* may be reached with the gospel, "and then the end will come" (Matt. 24:14; cf.

---

5. Cf. Ouweneel (2010b, 39).
6. Darby (CW 1:93–94; 13:155; 26:248; also see 1:124–30, 169–86, 288–90; 2:53–63, 89–121, 374–76; 8:25–27, 227–29; 13:152–66).
7. Berkouwer (1972, chapter 4: "The Meaning of the 'Time Between'").

28:19). The parenthesis will come to an end when "the fullness of the Gentiles has come in" (Rom. 11:25); that moment coincides with the parousia. This "fullness" implies a mass of believers "from *every* tribe and language and people and nation" (Rev. 5:9; 7:9). As long as there are no dedicated believers among every tribe and nation, the parousia cannot occur.

### 13.1.2 Cyrus I. Scofield

The publication of the *Scofield Reference Bible* (1909) marked the first appearance of the best known and most schematized version of dispensationalism, which in several respects departed from the suggestions mentioned by Darby. Cyrus I. Scofield (†1921), who interestingly enough was not a Plymouth Brother (an Evangelical *avant la lettre*) like Darby but a Presbyterian, distinguished the following seven dispensations. I enumerate them here, indicating at the same time their potential importance for basileology.[8]

(1) The dispensation of *innocence*, that is, the (presumably very short) period from the creation of humanity until its fall into sin, governed by this one law: the prohibition to eat from the tree of knowledge of good and evil (Gen. 2:16–17). For basileology it is important that God entrusted the rule over his creation to the first pair of humans. At their fall into sin, Adam and Eve handed world dominion over into the hands of Satan, as it were (cf. Luke 4:5–6; Matt. 12:26), but

---

8. Distinguishing "dispensations" is an invitation to design "prophetic charts"; I only mention Neuffer (1913); Sauer (1955); Booth (1999); Burridge (n.d.); Ritchie (n.d.); Savage (n.d.-b); LaHaye and Ice (2001).

ultimately the world will return to Paradise, on the new earth (cf. Rev. 22:1-5).

(2) The dispensation of *conscience*, that is, the period from Adam's fall until Noah's flood, governed by this one law: the "law" of conscience awakened by the Fall, since the Mosaic Torah had not yet been given (cf. Rom. 2:12-16). For basileology it is important that, in the end, all those who have accepted the gospel (or have not known it but have sought God uprightly and humbly) will share in the blessings of the Messianic kingdom (vv. 6-16; cf. Matt. 25:31-46; Rom. 2:6-10; Acts 10:34-35; 17:27; Heb. 11:6).[9]

(3) The dispensation of *human government*, that is, the period from Noah's flood to the patriarchs; here, too, the Mosaic Law was still absent but, in addition to the individual conscience, in principle human jurisdiction, and thus human government, is instituted in Genesis 9:5-6 ("*by* man shall his [i.e., the murderer's] blood be shed"). For basileology it is important that all human government is supposed to be a reflection of the divine rule (cf. Rom. 13:1-7; 1 Pet. 2:13-14) and, in the end, will debouch in the perfect rule of the Son of Man during the seventh dispensation.

(4) The dispensation of *promise*, that is, the period from the patriarchs until the lawgiving to Moses on Mount Sinai. The new element here is God's unconditional promises to the patriarchs (cf. Heb. 6:17) and, through them, to all humanity. For basileology it is important that these promises will be completely fulfilled no earlier than in the seventh dispensation, that is, in Christ and in his blessed kingdom of peace.

---

9. See Ouweneel (2009a, 283-95).

(5) The dispensation of the *law*, that is, the period from the lawgiving on Sinai until Christ, or, the era of the Old (Sinaitic) Covenant, the time in which Israel stood in a conditional relationship toward God: "Do this, and you will live" (Luke 10:28; Rom. 10:5; Gal. 3:12; cf. Lev. 18:5; Ezek. 20:11, 13). Basileologically this implies the ultimate judgment on the majority of Israel and blessing of the "remnant chosen by grace" (cf. Rom. 11:5). In my view, this concerns not only those Jews who have consciously known and accepted the gospel, but also those Jews who still have the "veil over their hearts" (2 Corinthians 3:14–15) but who live like Zechariah and Elizabeth, being "righteous before God, walking blamelessly in all the commandments and statutes of the Lord" (Luke 1:6). In the end, the veil is taken away, and they will recognize Christ.

(6) The dispensation of *grace*, that is, the period from the first coming of Christ until his parousia, that is, the dispensation of the *church*, a heavenly people, sharply distinguished from the earthly people of Israel. Basileologically this implies that, during the Messianic kingdom, the church will have her place with Christ in heaven, and the restored Israel will be with Christ on earth. According to this view, we are living today in the Sixth Era (cf. §12.6).

(7) The dispensation of the *kingdom*, that is, the period from the parousia until the end of Christ's millennial kingdom of peace and justice, the eschatological "fullness of the times" (Eph. 1:10 NKJV, Greek *plērōma tōn kairōn*), in which all earlier "times" (*kairoi*) come to full blossom. Basileologically,

the Messianic kingdom is the age in which all earlier dispensations find their fulfillment.

After the completed "week" of "seven days," there will be an "eighth day," which at the same time will be a "first day," a new beginning. This will be the "day of eternity," the eternal state, which involves new heavens and a new earth (2 Pet. 3:13, 18; Rev. 21:1; cf. Isa. 65:17; 66:22).

### 13.1.3 Comments

That this arrangement is rather relative becomes obvious when we read other authors who have invented quite different arrangements. Thus, John A. Savage, too, sees the present dispensation as the Sixth Era but he begins his series at the Fall, and splits Scofield's dispensation of the law into two parts: from Moses to the Babylonian exile, and from the exile to Christ.[10] In the previous chapter, we considered other divisions into seven epochs, including seven epochs within church history. No two systems are identical. The more we delve into dispensationalism, the more we discover this intrinsic weakness: every author designs his own system.

For dispensationalism's rival, federalism, the same is true: no two federalists come up with the same arrangement of covenants. Here, we encounter the same weakness: consistent dispensationalists as well as federalists easily get caught in their respective theological paradigms, of which the inner logic enables all kinds of mutually exclusive interpretations. No longer do we encounter exegesis of Scriptural data, but different paradigmatic consequences, which far surpass actual biblical interpretation. This going adrift, severed from

---

10. Savage (n.d.-b, chapters 7–8).

## Later Dispensationalism and Kingdom Theology

exegesis, constitutes perhaps the greatest temptation for the dogmatician: his ingeniously construed system begins to live a life of its own, having become more important than the original text.

Dispensationalism clearly suffers from the beauty of the "sacred" number seven. One may drop a dispensation here, split up a dispensation there, but most authors apparently seek to end up with the number seven. This is odd, for there is no reason why, for instance, the number could not be doubled, since two times seven is also beautiful. I mention this here without claiming any theological authority for the following outline; it is just an example of what the impulse to divide up redemptive history may lead to.

(1) "Innocence": from Adam's creation to his fall.
(2) "Conscience": from the Fall to Noah's flood.
(3) From the flood to the tower of Babel (where the people were definitively dispersed, and thus for the first time it became possible to speak of "peoples," and thus afterwards also of the one "chosen people").
(4) From the tower of Babel to Abraham (from the dispersion of the peoples to the chosen people).
(5) "Promise": from Abraham to Sinai (or, from the promise to the law).
(6) From Sinai to David (from Moses to the first true king, presaging the Messiah).
(7) The time of the Davidic kingship: from David to the Babylonian exile.
(8) From the exile (no David kingship) to the birth of Jesus.

(9) From the birth of Jesus to emperor Constantine the Great (the transition from the pagan to the "Christian" Roman Empire).
(10) From Constantine to the fall of Rome (AD 476), that is, to the end of the "Christian" [West-]Roman Empire.
(11) From the fall of Rome to the Schism (AD 1054), that is, to the end of the leadership of the Christian world by a single head.
(12) From the Schism to the Reformation, that is, to the end of the unity of the Christian Western world.
(13) From the Reformation to the parousia.
(14) The Messianic kingdom of peace and justice.

Obviously such dividing cannot continue endlessly, but it is certainly possible to point out important differences between these fourteen phases as to the way God deals with humanity or with his people. The system that appeals to me most—if any—is what I might call a moderate dispensationalism. This is one that in particular makes those distinctions made by the New Testament itself: the distinction between the time of the law and the time of faith, between Israel and the church, and between "this (or, the present) age" and the "age to come" (see §4.4.2). By distinguishing dispensations on such a limited scale, the differences with an equally moderate federalism become rather inconspicuous.[11] For instance, it is important to see that, contrary to what is often thought, premillennialism is

---

11. Cf. Ouweneel (2016b).

not necessarily bound to dispensationalism, and a- or postmillennialism are not necessarily linked with federalism. Today I know of federalist premillennialists, and I could very well imagine dispensationalist postmillennialists.

## 13.2 Deviant Forms of Dispensationalism
### 13.2.1 Ultradispensationalism

Classical dispensationalism must be distinguished from so-called ultradispensationalism, especially as developed by Ethelbert W. Bullinger (†1913).[12] In this view, the New Testament church did not begin on the Day of Pentecost (Acts 2) but with Paul's statement (Acts 28:28), "Therefore let it be known to you that this salvation of God has been sent to the Gentiles; they will listen"—in contrast with Israel. The church as we know it today—the body of the glorified Christ—occurs supposedly only in Paul's so-called prison letters, especially Ephesians and Colossians, which deal with the church as a "mystery" (Eph. 1:9; 3:3-4, 9; 5:32; 6:19; Col. 1:26-27; 2:2; 4:3). The book of Acts and Paul's earlier letters supposedly deal only with the "Jewish" or "bridal" church, which is viewed as closing Israel's prophesied history. Since Ephesians and Colossians do not speak of (water) baptism and the Lord's Supper, and the earlier letters do, these "Jewish" institutions supposedly no longer have any significance for the post-Acts 28 church, the body of Christ.

Bullinger distinguished three different phases: (a) the Gospels, in which Christ offers the kingdom to the people; entering it occurred through water baptism; (b)

---

12. See especially Bullinger (1972); critiqued by Ironside (1938).

the book of Acts and Paul's early letters, in which the apostles offered to the Jews a share in the "bridal church," for which two baptisms were needed: water baptism and Spirit baptism (transitory period); and (c) the unity of believing Jews and believing Gentiles in the one body of Christ; admission to it is exclusively on the basis of Spirit baptism. Thus, in this view, water baptism was only of passing significance.

This extremely speculative view rests on the weak suggestion that, at the end of Acts, a new dispensation began, which supposedly differed essentially from the previous one. Of course, there is no question of such a transition in Acts 28. Paul was merely explaining that, as the Jews reject the gospel of Jesus, the Gentiles enter the picture in increasing number—but this was the case already in Acts 13: "[W]hen the Jews saw the crowds, they were filled with jealousy and began to contradict what was spoken by Paul, reviling him. And Paul and Barnabas spoke out boldly, saying, 'It was necessary that the word of God be spoken first to you. Since you thrust it aside and judge yourselves unworthy of eternal life, behold, we are turning to the Gentiles. For so the Lord has commanded us, saying, "I have made you a light for the Gentiles, that you may bring salvation to the ends of the earth."' And when the Gentiles heard this, they began rejoicing and glorifying the word of the Lord, and as many as were appointed to eternal life believed" (vv. 45–48).

Ultradispensationalism is not based on any reasonable argument whatsoever, and therefore can hardly be refuted. It is ultradispensationalists who should supply evidence indicating that there are two "churches": the bridal church and the body of Christ; or that the body of Christ does not administer water baptism and the Lord's Supper anymore (although Eph. 4:5 and Col. 2:11-12 do refer to water baptism); or that there is an essential doctrinal gap between Paul's earlier and later letters. Such evidence cannot be given. I mention ultradispensationalism only to show to what excesses the strong impulses of an adopted theological system may lead. I therefore want to emphasize that, in my entire basileology and eschatology, dispensationalism hardly plays any role—unless one wishes to call the (anti-supersessionist) distinction between Israel and the church, or premillennialism as such, forms of dispensationalism. That is a matter of definition. In such a view, supersessionism and dispensationalism are mutually exclusive.

## 13.2.2 Cessationism

Interestingly, some have argued that even many federalists have fallen into the snare of dispensationalism by creating a cleft between the apostolic and the post-apostolic eras.[13] Such federalists do so in order to prove why, in the post-apostolic period, we may no longer expect prophecies, glossolalia, miraculous healings, etc. We call this "cessationism," the view that, after the apostles died, miracles ceased as well. It is called a form of dispensationalism because the apostolic and the post-apostolic periods are viewed here as two epochs with some very different characteristics: the presence of prophecies, glossolalia, and miraculous healings *versus* the absence of these.

---

13. Examples of cessationism are Masters and Whitcomb (1988); MacArthur (1992); Thomas (1999); Mayhue (2009); for an explanation of various views, see Grudem and Gaffin (1996).

One of the most common arguments for this distinction is that the continuation of prophecy in the post-apostolic church would undermine the sufficiency and completeness of the biblical canon. Thus, the end of the apostolic period coincides with the completion of the New Testament canon. As long as this canon was not finished, the word of the apostles had to be supported by miracles: "[T]he Lord worked with them [i.e., the apostles] and confirmed the message by accompanying signs" (Mark 16:20). "The signs of a true apostle were performed among you with utmost patience, with signs and wonders and mighty works" (2 Corinthians 12:12). The gospel "was declared at first by the Lord, and it was attested to us by those who heard [i.e., the apostles], while God also bore witness by signs and wonders and various miracles and by gifts of the Holy Spirit distributed according to his will" (Heb. 2:3–4).

Cessationists like to point out that in all such passages it is the apostles as well as the generation directly following them that performed the miracles. In order words, miracles belonged to the apostolic dispensation. We have no promise that miracles would occur *after* the apostolic age, with the exception of *false* miracles (Matt. 24:24; 2 Thess. 2:9; Rev. 13:13–14). After the canon had been completed, any miraculous confirmation of the apostolic word was thought to be no longer necessary. Today, we appeal to Scripture, no longer to miracles, as evidence to support preaching. Scripture can speak for itself; it does not need the signs and wonders as corroboration.

In this context some like to refer to 1 Corinthians 13, "As for prophecies, they will pass away; as for tongues, they will cease; as for knowledge, it will pass away. For we know in part and we prophesy in part, but when the perfect comes, the partial will pass away" (vv. 8-10). Some cessationists refer to this passage because they believe that "the perfect" here refers to the "perfection" (completion) of the canon. In other words, when the canon will have been "perfected," prophecies will pass away, tongues will cease, (miraculous) knowledge will pass away.

### 13.2.3 Refutation of Cessationism

The arguments against cessationism seem rather obvious. There is not the slightest basis in 1 Corinthians 13 for suggesting that "the perfect" here refers to the completion of the canon. The notion of a completed canon is totally absent in the New Testament. It is far more obvious to think in 1 Corinthians 13 of the future glory; compare especially verse 12, "For now we see in a mirror dimly, but then *face to face*. Now I know in part; then I shall know fully, even as I have been fully known."

Moreover, the entire reasoning behind this argument is mistaken. The *preached* word of the apostles, confirmed by divine signs, is called "Word of God" (1 Thess. 2:13). Why would the *written* word of the apostles, which is also "Word of God," not need the confirmation by divine signs just as much? Even Jesus said, "[T]he works that the Father has given me to accomplish, the very works that I am doing, bear witness about me that the Father has sent me" (John 5:36; cf. 10:25, 37-38; 14:10-11). And Peter said about him, ". . . Jesus of Nazareth, a man attested to you by God with mighty works and wonders and signs that God did through him in your midst, as you yourselves know" (Acts 2:22)—how much more do his followers need their words to be thus attested. Did these signs and wonders "undermine the sufficiency and completeness" of Jesus' message? On the contrary.

The miracles *always* have been, and remain, necessary as a legitimization of the preaching. They are not a kind of "added value," a kind of surplus, which could be left out as the case may be. No, the miracles are a part of the preaching itself, they themselves are proofs that convey the message.[14] The divinely inspired words spoken by Moses were supported by many signs and wonders. And when the Torah was completed, the miracles did not stop. The preaching of that other great Old Testament prophet, Elijah, was confirmed by signs and wonders as well. Such corroboration never undermines the authority of the preached Word as such; on the contrary, it undergirds it. Even today, by far the most people who come to Christ every day, especially in Asia, Africa, and South America, are convinced not by the preaching only but also by signs and wonders.

Why would the written or preached Word of God as such be more convincing than signs and wonders? Is the Word of God not convincing exclusively through the operation of the Holy Spirit (cf. Rom. 8:16)? But why would the Spirit, who speaks through the Word, no longer speak through miracles? The New Testament claims no such thing. The *main* reason why so many theologians think otherwise seems to be that they have not experienced any miracles themselves. They do not see them, or they mistrust what are presented as miracles today, or have been frightened away by what they view as fake miracles. Therefore, they try to come up with a

---

14. Paul (1997, 32).

theological reason for this alleged absence of true miracles instead of humbling themselves before God because of this lack of miracles. Paul speaks of "what Christ has accomplished through me to bring the Gentiles to obedience—by word and deed, by the power of signs and wonders, by the power of the Spirit of God" (Rom. 15:18-19). He told the Corinthians: "my speech and my message were not in plausible words of wisdom, but in demonstration of the Spirit and of power, so that your faith might not rest in the wisdom of men but in the power of God" (1 Cor. 2:4-5). What reason does the New Testament give us to believe that it would be any different today?

If signs and wonders were intended only for the apostolic period, then why do we have testimonies of miracles in the time of the church fathers?[15] Has there ever been a time in church history that was completely void of signs and wonders, not only on the mission field but also in Western countries? Why do some claim that God can no longer give us signs and wonders, supposedly because of the weak spiritual condition of his people? If that were true, why did God give miracles in a period as dark as that of the Old Testament prophets Elijah and Elisha? Some argue that God limits his signs and wonders to the mission field. Such people forget that the most important mission field at present is none other than Western Europe (and soon North America as well).

Others argue that the miracles are signs only for unbelievers—forgetting that we find at least four New Testament cases in which believers were miraculously healed through the Lord's servants: Saul of Tarsus be-

---

15. See Ouweneel (2005a, chapter 2).

came blind on the road to Damascus but was healed through Ananias (Acts 9:8-9, 17-18). Aeneas, one of the saints at Lydda who was paralyzed, was healed through Peter (vv. 9:32-34). The disciple Dorcas died of a disease but was raised by Peter (vv. 36-41). Eutychus, who belonged to the church in Troas, dropped dead but was restored to life by Paul (20:9-10). None of these healings was primarily intended as a testimony to unbelievers (as some have claimed). Jesus healed people, not just to prove that he was the Messiah, but because he was moved with compassion (Matt. 14:14; 20:34; Mark 1:41; Luke 7:13-15; also cf. Matt. 9:36; 15:32). Also in the case of Dorcas, the first motive for her healing seems to have been God's compassion (cf. Acts 9:39b). This is also why he healed brother Epaphroditus: "Indeed he was ill, near to death. But God had mercy on him" (Phil. 2:27).

I will leave the matter here; elsewhere I have written much more extensively on these subjects.[16] The point I wish to make right now is this: there is no basis for any dispensationalism when it comes to the apostolic and the post-apostolic times. Cessationism has no exegetical basis.

## 13.3 Newer Forms of Dispensationalism

### 13.3.1 "Revised" and "Progressive Dispensationalism"

The dispensationalism of John N. Darby, Cyrus I. Scofield, and also Lewis Sperry Chafer,[17] is sometimes called "classical" (or rather, "traditional") dispensationalism.[18]

---

16. See Ouweneel (2005a).
17. Chafer (1983, 4 and 6).
18. en.wikipedia.org/wiki/Progressive_dispensationalism. This view has become very well-known through the bestseller by Hal Lindsey (1970)—on this see Carroll *et al.* (2000, 193-95)—and

That of John F. Walvoord and Charles C. Ryrie has been called "revised dispensationalism," and rather recently a new school split off from this: the "progressive dispensationalism" of Craig A. Blaising, Darrell L. Bock, and Robert L. Saucy,[19] which has met with acceptance. The term "progressive" has no political-ideological implications but refers to the idea that the successive dispensations exhibit a certain progression. Progression means that redemptive history is basically linear: it follows the CCC-line from Creation through the Cross to the Consummation. Dispensationalism may never be taken to suggest that redemptive history is circular (a succession of circles, each moving from a good beginning to decline and judgment, followed by a new beginning).

The viewpoint that I defend in this chapter is actually a form of progressive dispensationalism. This view forms a bridge between historical and traditional dispensationalism. At any rate, we find that many theologians who began as classical dispensationalists have exchanged this view for a much more moderate form, or have even rejected it altogether. See, for instance, Curtis I. Crenshaw and Grover E. Gunn, two former dispensationalists of Dallas Theological Seminary, who have returned to the idea of the church as the spiritual Israel.[20]

It is characteristic of all dispensationalists to interpret the Old Testament prophecies literally, to believe in the essential difference between Israel and the church,

---

especially the series of novels (plus the film version) of *Left Behind* by Tim Lahaye and Jerry Jenkins (2010), critiqued by Blomberg and Chung (2009).

19. Blaising and Bock (1992, 1993); Saucy (1993).
20. Crenshaw and Gunn (1985).

in a future Great Tribulation during the last "seven" (i.e., seven years) of Daniel 9:24–27, and in premillennialism: the belief in a millennial Messianic kingdom after the parousia and before the eternal state. Now what are some of the main theological *differences* between traditional and progressive dispensationalism? Let me try to formulate my own response to this question.

As we have seen, traditional dispensationalism views the present dispensation as a kind of parenthesis (interim period), that is, between God's earlier ways with Israel (which at the Day of Pentecost gave way to his totally new ways with the church) and his future ways with Israel. After the rapture of the church (supposedly before the Great Tribulation) "God will pick up the thread with Israel again," as the saying goes. This means that the boundaries between the dispensations are rather sharp. On the traditional dispensationalist standpoint, it is inconceivable that God would pick up the thread with Israel again as long as the church is still on earth. Therefore, traditional dispensationalism believed that the return of Israel to its land, the establishment of the state of Israel, and the formation of the Messianic remnant of Israel would all necessarily occur *after* the rapture of the church.[21] Thus, in traditional dispensationalism, pretribulationalism (the doctrine that the church is taken up into heaven before the Great Tribulation) was an essential element.

However, today everybody knows *that* Israel has returned to its land, has established its own state (1948), and that the formation of the believing Jewish remnant (Messianic Judaism) has begun, especially after the con-

---

21. Thus, e.g., still very clearly in Voorhoeve (1866).

quest of old Jerusalem (1967). It is therefore an undeniable fact that God already *has* "picked up the thread with Israel again"—presuming he had let this thread slip out of his hand in the first place. Moreover, we all know that the church has not yet been raptured. The conclusion must be obvious: something must be utterly wrong with traditional dispensationalism.

### 13.3.2 Traditional Dispensationalism Outdated

The points just mentioned do not in themselves prove that revised or progressive dispensationalism is faring any better. But let me add the following arguments.

(a) In progressive dispensationalism, the transitions are much more fluid as far as both the time of Acts and the end time are concerned. In Acts 2, the history of the New Testament church on earth does start but the thread with Israel has not yet been dropped. There are several specific appeals to Israel (2:14-42; 3:12-26; 4:8-12; 5:29-32; 7:2-53; 9:20; 13:15-41; 17:2-3, 10-12; 22:1-21; 23:6; 26:1-23; 28:17-20). At the same time, there are several (temporary) farewells to Israel (13:46-47; 18:6; 28:25-28). In the same way, we could easily imagine a similar kind of transitional period at the end of the present dispensation, which, as in Acts, might last several decades. Again, there is a Messianic (i.e., Jesus-believing) kind of Judaism in the land of Israel, just as in Acts (cf. 21:20), and worldwide, especially in the so-called Third World, we are seeing a restoration of the signs and miracles of the Holy Spirit, just as in Acts. Apart from purely exegetical objections to pretribulationalism,[22] these events rob this school of its dogmatic foundation.

---

22. See Ouweneel (2012a, chapter 10).

(b) Progressive dispensationalism acknowledges that the members of Christ's body are sons of Abraham, too, and have been welcomed under the roof of the New Covenant, which is made with Israel. According to traditional dispensationalism, the church has "nothing to do with the New Covenant,"[23] and according to revised dispensationalism, there are *two* New Covenants: one for the church and one for Israel (Walvoord, Ryrie). According to progressive dispensationalism, however, there is only one New Covenant, with a present-day preliminary fulfillment, and a future complete fulfillment for Israel.

(c) Another example: according to traditional dispensationalism, the Sermon on the Mount (Matt. 5–7), the Olivet Discourse (Matt. 24–25), and the Great Commission of Matthew 28:18–20 are in fact intended for (the faithful remnant of) Israel only, whereas the church has nothing to do with the "gospel of the kingdom" (Matt. 4:23; 9:35; 24:14; Mark 1:15).[24] According to progressive dispensationalism, however, the church has everything to do with the "gospel of the kingdom." It places great emphasis on the significance of the kingdom of God in its present form. In this way, too, Israel and the church—no matter how different in many other respects—have much more in common than is accepted in traditional dispensationalism.

(d) This also means that, when Old Testament prophecies are quoted in the New Testament with regard to the church, we do not have to think of some application only, as does traditional dispensationalism. Rather, we are allowed to think of a true fulfillment, though it

---

23. See, e.g., Darby (CW 27:380–81).
24. See, e.g., Kelly (1896, ad loc.); Gaebelein (1910, ad loc.).

is a preliminary, incomplete one. In this way, new insight has been acquired into the significance that Old Testament prophecies have for the church as well, without first having to declare the church to be some spiritual Israel.

Today, all these insights have been communicated so widely that it becomes increasingly difficult to find a thoroughgoing traditional dispensationalist theologian. More and more, the sharp edges of dispensationalism have been smoothed. The essential differences between Israel and the church are maintained, but there is much more insight into the similarities.[25] There is more continuity between the dispensations, also very concretely between the Old and the New Testament.[26] To some extent, this means that it becomes less meaningful to keep using the term "dispensationalism." However, if dispensationalism still means that (a) Christ's *ekklesia* did not begin in Paradise but in Acts 2, that (b) she is not some spiritual Israel but there are essential differences between Israel and the church, and that (c) there will be a millennial Messianic kingdom after the parousia, in which the church will be in heaven and Israel will be the center on earth, then I myself am still a dispensationalist. "What's in a name?"

## 13.4 The Stages of the Kingdom
### 13.4.1 The First Four Stages

If, in the framework of my basileology, I were to design my own dispensational system, I would like to divide the history of God's kingdom into seven stages in the

---

25. Cf. Ouweneel (2010b, 93-98).
26. See the essays in Feinberg (1988) and the work of Poythress (1994).

following way. In doing so, I bring together various lines that have been dealt with in previous chapters, which may function as a theological basis for this survey.

(1) *Theocracy:* the universal divine rule before the creation of humanity, that is, without a special position of the pre-incarnate Christ, the Son of God (although we should keep in mind that the universally ruling God is always the Triune God: Father, Son, and Holy Spirit). Of this eternal theocracy the poets have spoken: "Your throne is established from of old; you are from everlasting" (Ps. 93:2). "Your throne, O God, is forever and ever" (45:6); "you, O Lord, reign forever; your throne endures to all generations" (Lam. 5:19). There is an eternal throne of God, and thus there is a divine rule from eternity to eternity. In fact, this remains true, also during the next stages: this theocracy is the kingdom of God in its widest and most fundamental meaning.

(2) *Rule of the First Adam:* "Then God said, 'Let us make man in our image, after our likeness. And let them have dominion over the fish of the sea and over the birds of the heavens and over the livestock and over all the earth and over every creeping thing that creeps on the earth. . . . Be fruitful and multiply and fill the earth and subdue it, and have dominion over the fish of the sea and over the birds of the heavens and over every living thing that moves on the earth" (Gen. 1:26, 28). In fact, this is also the content of Psalm 8, even though, since the fall into sin, the situation has fundamentally changed: "[W]hat is a human being that you are mindful of him, a son of man that you care for him? You have made him a little lower than the angels and crowned him with glory and honor. You made him ruler over the

works of your hands; you put everything under his feet" (vv. 4–6 NIV note). In this formulation, God's intention concerning the kingdom comes to light: it is *his* kingdom, but from the start it was his will to put all that he had created under the feet of a Man: first under those of the first Adam, and when he failed, under the feet of the second Man, the last Adam (1 Cor. 15:45–47), the Son of Man (as the text says), *the* Man *par excellence*, and alongside him the "last Eve," God's church.

(3) *Light versus Darkness:* since Adam's fall into sin, Satan is the "prince of the world" (John 12:31; 14:30; 16:11), the "god of this world" (2 Cor. 4:4); he represents the "power of darkness" (Luke 22:53; also cf. Eph. 2:2; 6:12). But this does not mean that the world has been hopelessly abandoned to Satan's mercy. Over against his tyranny there is this counterbalance:

(a) The universal rule of God, who grants no more room to Satan than his sovereign will allows him (the chariots of the powers move freely, but then only between two "mountains of bronze"; Zech. 6:1).

(b) The promise of the kingdom of God in its Messianic form. Let me limit myself here to quotations from the Torah: since the Fall, God's people live by the promise that, one day, the "woman's offspring" will bruise the head of the "serpent's offspring" (Gen. 3:15, the so-called *protevangelium*). One day, all nations will have been brought under the dominion of Shiloh (49:10 ESV note). One day, the Lamb of God will bring the definitive deliverance from bondage (Exod. 12). One day, the Day of Atonement will come for Israel and the world, at which time definitive atonement will be accomplished (Lev. 16; cf. Dan. 9:24). One day, the star shall come out of Jacob, the scepter shall rise out of Israel (Num. 24:17). One day, the Prophet will be raised to whom Israel shall listen (Deut. 18:15-19).

(c) The great types of the King (§2.2) also speak a clear language. Every type of the Messiah is at the same time a promise, which keeps God's people anticipating the Messianic kingdom. Moses subdued the Egyptians, David and Solomon subdued the neighboring nations, Cyrus did so with the Babylonian Empire, and Mordecai with the Amalekite Haman. Similarly, the Messiah will subdue all his enemies (Ps. 45:5; 72). Encouraged by these examples, God's people keep longing for the complete deliverance from Satan's tyranny, and the establishment of God's kingdom under the guidance of his Anointed One.

(4) *The Davidic Government*, that is, the rule by David and his descendants on the throne of David. In fact, there is a difference with the previous stage insofar as God's people still live by the unfulfilled promise of the "woman's offspring," that is, the Messiah, the anointed King of Israel, the Son of Man as well as the Son of God has not yet come. There are, however, new elements in this stage; they are these:

(a) In the entire Old Testament history of Israel, no person is such a clear type and such a striking foreshadowing of the Messiah as David, or actually I should say, the double type David-Solomon.[27] This foreshadowing goes so far that the Messiah himself is sometimes referred to as "David" (Ezek. 34:23-24; 37:24-25; Hos. 3:4-5). Various Psalms that primarily refer to David or Solo-

---

27. See chapter 11, n13.

## Later Dispensationalism and Kingdom Theology

mon have an obviously Messianic dimension (Ps. 2, 18, 20, 21, 22, 24; etc.; see further §13.7).

(b) The second point is an immediate effect of the previous one: from now on, Messianic prophecy is narrowed down to the descendants of David. One day, *the* Son of David shall sit on the throne of David (Luke 1:32; cf. Ps. 132:11; Isa. 9:6; Jer. 33:17), and rule over het kingdom of David-Solomon (cf. Gen. 15:18 with 1 Kgs. 4:21, Ps. 72:8 and Zech. 9:10; geographical keyword: "the River," i.e., the Euphrates). A beautiful example of the parallels between the David-Solomon dominion and the Messianic rule is found in the parallels between Psalm 72 and Isaiah 60 (see §13.7).

### 13.4.2 The Fifth Stage

(5) *Light versus Darkness:* with the first coming of Christ, and specifically at his resurrection and ascension, the kingdom of God has arrived in a tangible way, with two particular characteristics.

(a) It exists today in a hidden form, at least insofar as the King is still hidden (cf. Col. 3:3). However, it becomes manifest wherever people or societal relationships consciously and visibly submit to the rule of Christ in their individual and collective lives (for this present meaning of the kingdom in the letters, cf. especially: Rom. 14:17; 1 Cor. 4:20; Col. 1:13).

(b) In the present dispensation, the kingdom permanently stands in opposition to, and is in conflict with, the kingdom of evil: the "power of darkness" (Luke 22:53; cf. Acts 26:18) stands in opposition to the "kingdom of the Son of his [i.e., the Father's] love" (Col. 1:13).

The "kingdom of Satan" (Matt. 12:25-26) stands in opposition to the "kingdom of the Son of Man" (13:41).

Thus, the kingdom of God has acquired an ambiguous character: to some extent it *has* arrived, but not in the fullness intended and originally announced by God. Therefore, at times Jesus speaks of the kingdom as something that is near, but, as this term suggests, apparently still future (Matt. 4:17; 6:10; 10:7). At other occasions he speaks of it as a present reality (the so-called "presence passages," *Gegenwartstellen*):[28] "But if it is by the Spirit of God that I cast out demons, then the kingdom of God *has* come upon you" (Matt. 12:28; cf. Luke 11:20); "behold, the kingdom of God *is* [right now] in the midst of you" (Luke 17:21). Together with the King, the kingdom has arrived too.[29] However, the kingdom in power and majesty is still future (see stage 6, §13.4.3). In Christ, the kingdom has unmistakably arrived in a certain form but it will break through in its fullness only at the parousia.[30]

It is striking that so much theological debate has occurred as to whether the kingdom was proclaimed by Jesus as present or future (see §2.3).[31] The simple answer is that Jesus did both; at certain times he spoke of the present hidden kingdom, at other times about the fu-

---

28. Cf. Ridderbos (1962, 36-60, 104-106); Meier (1994, chapter 16); Stein (1996, 125-31); Bock (2002, 574-79); Theissen and Merz (1998, 252-78) on the present and the future aspect of the kingdom.
29. Origen spoke of *autobasileia*: Christ is the kingdom in his own person (Ratzinger (2007, 49).
30. Ratzinger (2007, 72).
31. Cf. Knight (2004, 15-26, 105-111).

ture kingdom, appearing in glory. *Both* lines are firmly present in the Synoptic Gospels and permeate them.[32]

The hiddenness of the kingdom refers to the proper nature of the kingdom during a time when it has not yet been revealed in majesty and splendor.[33] In other words, one day the kingdom *will* arrive in power and glory, but already today it has entered into the world in order to work in secret among the people (cf. Mark 4:26–29). Thus, Jesus announced a kingdom that ultimately would satisfy the hopes of the Old Testament prophets, but first presented it in a hidden form that *hardly* fulfilled Old Testament hopes. "Hardly" means that the majority of Old Testament predictions concerning the kingdom have yet to be fulfilled; this will happen only at, and after, the parousia. Therefore, especially the Jews had great difficulty believing that, in spite of the invisibility of its King, the King *had* come and the kingdom *had* arrived. In 1 Peter 1:3–13, Peter describes this problem in a splendid way: "Though you have not seen him [i.e., Jesus], you love him. Though you do not now see him, you believe in him and rejoice with joy that is inexpressible and filled with glory" (v. 8)—but also: "[S]et your hope fully on the grace that will be brought to you at the revelation [i.e., parousia] of Jesus Christ" (v. 13).

Please note that the hidden character of the kingdom does not imply that the *disciples* of the kingdom are hidden, or must remain hidden, or are allowed to remain hidden. On the contrary, they must be very manifest in this world, otherwise the kingdom could never expand. Jesus told his followers, precisely in

---

32. Dunn (2005, 72).
33. Ladd (1974b, 222, 225).

their quality as disciples of the King and subjects of the kingdom: "You are the light of the world. A city set on a hill cannot be hidden" (Matt. 5:14; cf. Luke 8:16; 11:33). One day, the "sun of righteousness" will rise (Mal. 4:2; cf. Matt. 17:2) and the day will dawn (Rom. 13:12; 2 Pet. 1:19). At present, it is night, but not a night without light: ". . . children of God without blemish in the midst of a crooked and twisted generation, among whom you shine as lights [CJB, NIV, etc.: stars] in the world" (Phil. 2:15; cf. Eph. 5:8–10).

### 13.4.3 The Last Two Stages

(6) *Rule of the Last Adam:* this is the dominion of the Son of Man mentioned in Daniel 7:13–14, "I saw in the night visions, and behold, with the clouds of heaven there came one like a son of man [i.e., the Son of Man], and he came to the Ancient of Days [i.e., God] and was presented before him. And to him was given dominion and glory and a kingdom, that all peoples, nations, and languages should serve him; his dominion is an everlasting dominion, which shall not pass away, and his kingdom one that shall not be destroyed."

This is the kingdom of which Israel will constitute the center. Paul says, "[A] partial hardening has come upon Israel, until the fullness of the Gentiles has come in. And in this way [TLB, NLV, WE: then] all Israel will be saved, as it is written, 'The Deliverer will come from Zion, he will banish ungodliness from Jacob'; 'and this will be my covenant with them when I take away their sins'" (Rom. 11:25–27; cf. Ps. 14:7; Isa. 27:9; Jer. 31:31–34). "The kingdom of the world has become the kingdom of our Lord and of his Christ, and he shall reign forever and ever"

(Rev. 11:15). "And I heard the number of the sealed, 144,000, sealed from every tribe of the sons of Israel" (7:4). "Then I looked, and behold, on Mount Zion stood the Lamb, and with him 144,000 who had his name and his Father's name written on their foreheads" (14:1).

(7) *Theocracy:* at the end of Christ's millennial rule, together with his own (Rev. 20:1-6), Satan is definitively overcome, and then follows the judgment of the wicked who have died (vv. 7-15). After this, a new heaven and a new earth will arrive (21:1-8). The last enemy that is destroyed is death, as Revelation 20:14 tells us, and this corresponds with 1 Corinthians 15:24-28, "Then comes the end, when he [i.e., Christ] delivers the kingdom to God the Father after destroying every rule and every authority and power. For he must reign until he has put all his enemies under his feet [Ps. 110:1]. The last enemy to be destroyed is death. For 'God has put all things in subjection under his feet.' [8:6] But when it says, 'all things are put in subjection,' it is plain that he is excepted who put all things in subjection under him. When all things are subjected to him, then the Son himself will also be subjected to him who put all things in subjection under him, that God may be all in all."

## 13.5 Chiastic Structure
### 13.5.1 First Similarity

In the system presented in §13.4 we may recognize a clear chiastic structure, that is, a symmetric relationship between the first three and the last three stages.

The *first* similarity is between the first and the last (seventh) stages, both characterized by the term "theocracy." It is the universal rule of God, which is not yet, or no longer, characterized by the rule of the Son of Man. This does not mean that Christ has nothing to do with it.

(a) As far as the past is concerned, just as God created the world in and through and for Christ, he also preserves the world in and through and for him (John 1:1-3; Col. 1:15-17; Heb. 1:1-3).

(b) As far as the future is concerned: to Christ has been given an "everlasting dominion" (Dan. 7:14)—although the Aramaic word *'alam* could be taken here to mean the Messianic "age" (the "age to come"; see §4.4.2). At the same time, the universal rule of God is always being exercised by the Triune God: Father, Son, and Holy Spirit. In 1 Corinthians 15:24-28 (see at the close of the previous section), this becomes immediately clear: the *Man* Christ delivers the kingdom to God the *Father*, the *Son* subjects himself to him, in order that *God*—that is, God the Father, God the Son, and God the Holy Spirit—may be "all in all."[34]

### 13.5.2 Second Similarity

The *second* similarity is between the second and the sixth stages: the rule of the first and of the last Adam, respectively. I already pointed out how strikingly this parallelism comes to light in Psalm 8: "When I consider your heavens, the work of your fingers, the moon and the stars, which you have set in place, what is a human being that you are mindful of him, a son of man that you care for him? You have made him a little lower than the angels and crowned him with glory and honor. You made him ruler over the works of your hands; you put every-

---

34. Ouweneel (2007b, 103, 292).

thing under his feet, all flocks and herds, and the animals of the wild, the birds in the sky, and the fish in the sea, all that swims the paths of the seas" (vv. 3-8 NIV note).

If we considered this psalm on its own, we would not easily come to see it as a Messianic psalm. However, this is precisely the use that Hebrews 2:5-9 makes of it,[35] by viewing the rule of the last Adam as it were on the same line as that of the first Adam: "For it was not to angels that God subjected the world to come, of which we are speaking. It has been testified somewhere, 'What is man, that you are mindful of him, or the son of man, that you care for him? You made him for a little while lower than the angels; you have crowned him with glory and honor, putting everything in subjection under his feet.' Now in putting everything in subjection to him, he left nothing outside his control. At present, we do not yet see everything in subjection to him. But we see him who for a little while was made lower than the angels, namely Jesus, crowned with glory and honor because of the suffering of death, so that by the grace of God he might taste death for everyone."

In this way, the parallelism between the second and the sixth stages has been clearly identified. The rule of the first Adam is ultimately followed by the rule of the last Adam, as a continuation, and at the same time as a contrast: where the first Adam failed, the last Adam will triumph.

## 13.5.3 Third Similarity

The *third* similarity is between the third and the fifth stages. In both stages, there is a battle between light (life,

---

35. See Ouweneel (1982, 1, ad loc.).

love) and darkness (death, hatred). The kingdom of Satan (of darkness, death, hatred) has made its appearance, and opposes the people of God. In both stages, this is an expectant people, that is, awaiting the first and the second coming of the Messiah, respectively.

In stronger terms: in both stages, the third and the fifth, Gods people are waiting for the Messianic kingdom of power and glory, universal peace and justice. In the third stage, God's people lived out of the promises made by the prophets with regard to the coming kingdom. In the fifth stage, God's people live out of the promises made by Christ himself, plus those of the apostles, with regard to that same kingdom.

To be sure, there is a difference: in the third stage, the kingdom has not yet arrived at all, whereas in the fifth stage, it *has* arrived, though not yet in the form that the Old Testament prophets had announced. Hence the similarity: in both stages believers are looking forward to the kingdom in power and glory.

In the chiastic structure, the middle one of the seven stages, namely, the Davidic kingdom, necessarily occupies a unique place. Just as in the third stage, during this stage the Messianic kingdom has not yet arrived, but at the same time it does exist already in the form of typological foreshadowing. In the figure of David, the true "David" clearly comes to light. This stage shares with the third stage the ardent expectation of the Messiah, but at the same time there is a tinge of fulfillment. That is to say, never in redemptive history did the Messianic kingdom acquire a more manifest form—though only typologically—than under David and especially under Solomon (see further in §13.7).

## 13.6 The Nine World Empires
### 13.6.1 Framework

We have now considered seven redemptive-historical stages (§13.4) as well as eight world empires (§12.2.1), including the four special world empires of Daniel 2 and 7. All of these empires are portents of, and also contrasts to, the Messianic kingdom. Taking all these aspects together, I have developed the following framework:

*First stage: from eternity to Adam's creation*
*Second stage: from Adam's creation to his fall*
*Third stage: from the Fall to David;* in this:
    First empire: Egyptian
*Fourth stage: from David to Christ;* in this:
    Second empire: Neo-Assyrian (700–605 BC)
    Third empire: (Neo-)Babylonian = first empire of Daniel (605–540 BC)
    Fourth empire: Medo-Persian = second empire of Daniel (540–331 BC)
    Fifth empire: Greek-Macedonian = third empire of Daniel (331–146 BC)
    Sixth empire: Roman = fourth empire of Daniel (146–c. 5 BC)
*Fifth stage: from Christ' first to his second coming;* in this:
    Continuation of the Roman Empire = fourth empire of Daniel
- the pagan empire (c. 5 BC–AD 324)
- the Christianized empire (324–parousia); in this:
  - the Holy Roman Empire (843–1806)
  - the Second German Empire (1871–1918)

    Seventh empire: a peculiar revival of the Roman

Empire shortly before the end times
- possibly the Third Reich (1933–1945)

Eighth empire: revived Roman Empire = kingdom of the Antichrist (end time)

*Sixth stage*: from Christ's parousia to the "eternal state"

Ninth empire: the Messianic millennial kingdom

*Seventh stage*: the "eternal state"

## 13.6.2 Earlier Millennial Kingdoms

The Holy Roman Empire of the German Nation was an exact millennial kingdom, which began at February 6, AD 806, when emperor Charlemagne divided his empire among his sons (*Divisio regnorum*). (I admit, though, that it is more common to take the year 843 as the Empire's beginning: the year of the Treaty of Verdun, when the empire of Louis the Pious was divided among *his* sons.) It ended on August 6, 1806, when Napoleon forced the German-Austrian emperor Francis II to abdicate; on December 2, 1804, he had already put the crown of a new empire on his own head.[36] Even more than this event, the formation of the separate Confederation of the Rhine on July 12, 1806, by sixteen German princes, signified *de facto* the end of the Holy Roman Empire, or what was left of it.

Another millennial kingdom in history was the Christian East-Roman or Byzantine Empire.[37] After the death of its great opponent, Attila, king of the Huns, in March, AD 453, this kingdom managed for the first time to really flourish. On February 7, AD 457, Leo I the Thracian was the first East-Roman emperor to receive his imperial digni-

---

36. Regarding this empire, see Herbers and Neuhaus (2005).
37. Cf. Beck (1994); more recently, Shepard (2008).

ty from the hands of the patriarch of Constantinople, the "Second Rome." In this way, for the first time the Christian character of this kingdom was formally confirmed. After AD 476, the year of the fall of Rome, and thus of the West-Roman Empire, it was now the East-Roman Empire that carried the torch of the Christian-Roman Empire. It kept the Roman ideal alive, particularly under emperor Justinian II (527–565), until the fall of Constantinople, the capital of the Byzantine Empire, on May 29, 1453. It was exactly one thousand years after Attila's death.

Christianity was officially introduced to Russia in AD 988 by grand prince Vladimir the Great (958–1015) at Kiev. After the fall of Constantinople (1453), the Russian Orthodox Church considered itself to be the successor of the Byzantine Church. Thus, a new spiritual empire emerged. In 476, Rome had been forced to pass the torch to Constantinople, *nova Roma*, the "New (Second) Rome." Almost one thousand years later, in 1453, Constantinople was forced to pass the torch to Moscow, which, after Rome and Constantinople, was called the "Third Rome." In 1988, Russia celebrated the thousandth anniversary of the birth of Russian Christianity, three years before the collapse of the Soviet Union, the empire whose new czar had been the atheist Communist party leader.

Of course, the actual millennial kingdom, namely, that of the Bible (Rev. 20:1-6), is a very different matter. In spite of their Christian confessions, figures such as the emperors Charlemagne and Justinian could in many respects almost be called antitypes of Christ. There have been quite a few unsuccessful millennial empires. Thus, after 1806, the Holy Roman Empire was succeeded by the Second Empire of the German emperors (1871–

1918), which lasted only 47 years. This was succeeded by the Third Reich of Nazi Germany, which loved to characterize itself as a millennial empire, but then a thoroughly pagan one. On September 1, 1933, Adolf Hitler announced officially that the state ruled by him was a third empire, which was to last a thousand years.[38]

Heinrich Himmler (1900-1945), leader of the SS (*Schutzstaffel*, "Protection Squadron") and head of the German police during the Nazi era, was an occultist, who seriously viewed himself as the reincarnation of the German king Henry I the Fowler (876-936). On July 2, 1936, he proudly celebrated the thousandth anniversary of the death of this first German king. He also announced that the Third Reich would rule another thousand years.[39] Hitler and Himmler did not know that it would be less than nine years when, following the First and the Second *Reich*, this third one would collapse as well. Hitler committed suicide on April 30, 1945, and Himmler on May 23 of that year, the very day of the dissolution of the Third Reich.

## 13.7 The Middle Stage

### 13.7.1 The Old Testament Solomon

Nothing is left of the magnificence either of the National-Socialist (Nazi) empire (1933-1945), or of the Communist empire in Europe (1922-1991). *Sic transit gloria mundi*, "Thus passes the glory of the world." Christians are waiting for the *gloria* of the only genuine millennial kingdom, a glory that is linked with that of the King of kings and the Lord of lords himself. Not one of the millennial kingdoms

---

38. Wippermann (2007, 479-80); see extensively, Ouweneel (2016d, chapter 8).
39. de.wikipedia.org/wiki/Drittes_Reich.

that people have celebrated in world history is even remotely similar to it. The *only* kingdom in history that has constituted a genuine and fair reflection of the coming Messianic kingdom of peace has been the kingdom of king Solomon, which lasted about forty years (c. 970-931 BC). Perhaps even more so than David, king Solomon, the son of David, is *the* Old Testament type of the Messiah.[40]

The name Solomon (Hebrew *Shelomoh*) is generally viewed as derived from Hebrew *shalom*, "peace." King Solomon "had peace on all sides around him" (1 Kgs. 4:24b). This reminds us, for instance, of Isaiah 9:7, where we read of the Messiah: "Of the increase of his government and of peace there will be no end, on the throne of David and over his kingdom, to establish it and to uphold it with justice and with righteousness from this time forth and forevermore." After David himself, Solomon was the first to sit on the "throne of David" (1 Kgs. 1:13; 2:12, 24; 3:6; 5:5; Ps. 132: 11; cf. 1 Chron. 29:23). "The mountains will bring peace to the people, and the little hills, by righteousness. . . . In His days the righteous shall flourish, and abundance of peace" (Ps. 72:3, 7 NKJV).

If the Messiah is called the "Son of David" (Matt. 1:1; 21:9, 15; 22:42),[41] we remember that Solomon is the "son of David" in the primary and literal sense. Although he was David's tenth son—if this calculation is correct (cf. 1 Chron. 3:1-9)—he nevertheless was the first in rank among these sons (in spite of 1 Chron. 3:1, where Amnon is called the "firstborn"). His kingship was explicitly linked with the title "son of David" (1 Chron. 29:22; 2 Chron. 1:1; 30:26; 35:3; Prov. 1:1). Notice especially the

---

40. See Ouweneel (2007b, chapter 5).
41. See D. R. Bauer in Green *et al.* (1992, 766-69).

prophecy of Nathan, given to David (2 Sam. 7:12-16), in which we hear Messianic overtones in the references to David's "son." This does not follow only from Hebrews 1:5, but also Rabbi Samuel Goldman says on this passage: "[T]his promise of an everlasting kingdom of the house of David powerfully influenced the development of the Messianic hope in Israel."[42] And Adam S. van der Woude says, "[A]lthough this prophecy, viewed by itself, was originally not a Messianic promise, under certain conditions the Messianic expectation did sprout from it."[43]

We may safely conclude that there is indeed a Messianic perspective embedded in these verses. However, this perspective unfolds only in the ongoing divine revelation. Therefore, Albert H. Edelkoort went too far in asserting that David "was allowed to learn here that the Messiah would originate from his posterity."[44] Yet, the *root* of the Messianic hope in Israel can certainly be found here (cf. Ps. 89:19-29; 132:11).[45]

There has been some discussion about whether David's "offspring" in 2 Samuel 7:12 refers to Solomon alone, or to every Davidic king.[46] In both cases, the warning is understandable, which certainly is *not* applicable

---

42. Goldman (1983, 229).
43. Van der Woude (1973, 5-6).
44. Edelkoort (1941, 162).
45. Brown (1994, 130, 156-60). He sees a second stage in the Messianic hope in, e.g., Isa. 7:14; 9:5-6; 11:1-5; Mic. 5:1; Jer. 23:5; 30:9; Ezek. 17:23; 34:23-24; 37:24-5, and a third, postexilic stage in, e.g., Zech. 9:9-10, the Psalms of Solomon, the Dead Sea Scrolls, and 1 Henoch.
46. Goslinga (1962, 139-40); H. G. L. Peels in Knevel and Paul (1995, 45).

to the Messiah: "When he commits iniquity, I will discipline him with the rod of men, with the stripes of the sons of men" (v. 14). But verse 16 ("your house and your kingdom shall be made sure forever before me. Your throne shall be established forever") does find its ultimate fulfillment in the Messiah. If the passage refers primarily to Solomon, the literal son of David, he is here a type of the Messiah (see §2.2).

### 13.7.2 The Glory of Solomon

The scope of Solomon's kingdom was truly prophetic: "Solomon ruled over all the kingdoms from the Euphrates [lit., the River] to the land of the Philistines and to the border of Egypt" (1 Kgs. 4:24). The words remind us of the great promise of Genesis 15:18, "On that day the LORD made a covenant with Abram, saying, 'To your offspring I give this land, from the river of Egypt to the great river, the river Euphrates.'" Psalm 72 says, "He shall have dominion also from sea to sea, and from the River [i.e., Euphrates] to the ends of the earth" (v. 8 NKJV). And the prophet says, "Rejoice greatly, O daughter of Zion! Shout aloud, O daughter of Jerusalem! Behold, your king is coming to you; righteous and having salvation is he, humble and mounted on a donkey, on a colt, the foal of a donkey. I will cut off the chariot from Ephraim and the war horse from Jerusalem; and the battle bow shall be cut off, and he shall speak peace to the nations; his rule shall be from sea to sea, and from the River to the ends of the earth" (Zech. 9:9–10).

The tributes of Solomon were impressive: "They brought tribute and served Solomon all the days of his life. . . . [H]e had dominion over all the region west of the Euphrates from Tiphsah to Gaza, over all the kings west of the Euphrates" (1 Kgs. 4:21, 24). "The kings of Tarshish and of the isles will bring presents; the kings of Sheba and Seba will offer gifts. . . . And He [i.e., the Messiah] shall live; and the gold of Sheba will be given to Him; prayer also will be made for Him continually, [and] daily He shall be praised" (Ps. 72:10, 15 NKJV). "And nations shall come to your light, and kings to the brightness of your rising. . . . A multitude of camels shall cover you, the young camels of Midian and Ephah; all those from Sheba shall come. They shall bring gold and frankincense, and shall bring good news, the praises of the LORD. . . . [T]he coastlands shall hope for me, the ships of Tarshish first, to bring your children from afar, their silver and gold with them, for the name of the LORD your God, and for the Holy One of Israel, because he has made you beautiful" (Isa. 60:3, 6, 9).

"And Judah and Israel lived in safety, from Dan even to Beersheba, every man under his vine and under his fig tree, all the days of Solomon" (1 Kgs. 4:25). This reminds us of this prophetic word: "It shall come to pass in the latter days that the mountain of the house of the LORD shall be established as the highest of the mountains, and it shall be lifted up above the hills; and peoples shall flow to it, and many nations shall come, and say: 'Come, let us go up to the mountain of the LORD, to the house of the God of Jacob, that he may teach us his ways and that we may walk in his paths.' For out of Zion shall go forth the law, and the word of the LORD from Jerusalem. He shall judge between many peoples, and shall decide for strong nations far away; and they shall beat their swords into plowshares, and their spears into pruning hooks; nation shall not lift up sword against nation, neither shall they learn war anymore; but they shall sit every man under his vine and under his fig tree, and no one shall make them afraid, for the mouth of the LORD of hosts has spoken" (Mic. 4:1–4).

Psalm 72 offers a picture of the ideal Davidic king, with its strong emphasis on justice and peace, as we encounter often in Messianic prophecies.[47] Rabbinic tradition, too, finds in this Psalm a Messianic tone, as is clear from Targum and Talmud.[48] Rashi interpreted the Psalm as David's prayer for his son Solomon; compare the starting term *lishelomoh*, which may mean either "Of Solomon" (ESV, EXB, [N]KJV, NCV, NIV, OJB, RSV; or "By Solomon," NOG, WEB, YLT) *or* "For Solomon" (BRG, JUB, NET; or "To Solomon," ERV, WYC). In my view, the second interpretation fits better with the Messianic application: "for Solomon" means as much as "in view of the Messiah." If this is the correct approach, it is better to render the Psalm in the indicative form (v. 2, "He shall judge . . .," KJV, JUB, OJB, etc.) than in the conjunctive form ("May he judge . . .," ESV, NASB, RSV, NIV, etc.).

### 13.7.3 The New Testament and the Future Solomon

Jesus said, "The queen of the South will rise up at the judgment with this generation and condemn it, for she came from the ends of the earth to hear the wisdom of Solomon, and behold, something greater than Solomon is here" (Matt. 12:42). This "greater than" does not imply contrast but what the rabbis called a *kal vechomer* argument: if A is such, then B is all the more so (*a fortiori*). As

---

47. Van Gemeren (1991, 469).
48. Cohen (1985, 227).

the queen of the South came to Solomon, so *all* the "ends of the earth" will come to hear the wisdom of the greater-than-Solomon. Compare the prayer by Jeremiah, "O LORD, my strength and my stronghold, my refuge in the day of trouble, to you shall the nations come from the ends of the earth" (16:19).

The Old Testament verse most quoted in the New Testament is Psalm 110:1, "The LORD says to my Lord: 'Sit at my right hand, until I make your enemies your footstool'" (see, e.g., Matt. 22:44; 26:64; Luke 20:42–43; Acts 2:34–35; 7:49; 1 Cor. 15:25; Eph. 1:20; Heb. 1:13; 10:12–13). Just like Psalm 2, for instance, Psalm 110 is not primarily Messianic, but may be applied to every Davidic king, beginning with Solomon.[49] The Psalm refers to the priesthood of the Davidic king because of verse 4, "The LORD has sworn and will not change his mind, 'You are a priest forever after the order of Melchizedek'" (cf. Heb. 5:6, 10; 6:20; 7:11, 17, which apply this verse to Christ). This priesthood was clearly manifested in David, who was clothed like a priest, brought sacrifices, and placed a priestly blessing on the people (2 Sam. 6:14, 17–18). Solomon, too, brought sacrifices and blessed the people (1 Kgs. 8:14, 55, 62–64), while even the high priest stood under his authority (2:27, 35).

In the Messianic interpretation of Psalm 110, as unfolded in the New Testament (especially with regard to vv. 1 and 4), the typological significance of Solomon comes to light—implicitly but clearly. What was true of the literal son of David will one day be true of the greatest Descendant of David. "[A] throne will be established

---

49. See Van Gemeren (1991, 696–700); Hengel (1995, chapter 3).

in steadfast love, and on it will sit in faithfulness in the tent of David one who judges and seeks justice and is swift to do righteousness" (Isa. 16:5). "Behold, the days are coming, declares the Lord, when I will raise up for David a righteous Branch, and he shall reign as king and deal wisely, and shall execute justice and righteousness in the land" (Jer. 23:5). "In those days and at that time I will cause a righteous Branch to spring up for David, and he shall execute justice and righteousness in the land" (33:15). "My servant David shall be king over them, and they shall all have one shepherd. They shall walk in my rules and be careful to obey my statutes" (Ezek. 37:24).

Let me close with this reference to the Messianic kingdom: "In that day I will raise up the booth of David that is fallen and repair its breaches, and raise up its ruins and rebuild it as in the days of old" (Amos 9:11). In the version and interpretation of the apostle James: "God showed his love for the non-Jewish people. For the first time, God accepted them and made them his people. The words of the prophets agree with this too: '"I will return after this. I will build David's house again. It has fallen down. I will build again the parts of his house that have been pulled down. I will make his house new. Then the rest of the world will look for the Lord God—all those of other nations who are my people too." The Lord said this. And he is the one who does all these things.' 'All this has been known from the beginning of time'" (Acts 15:14–18 ERV).

Salvation will go out to all nations, and all the saved ones, from Israel and the Gentiles, will eventually be brought together under the headship of the great Son of

# Bibliography

Aalders, G. C. 1925. *De Klaagliederen.* KV. Kampen: Kok.
———. 1948. *Het boek de Prediker.* COT. Kampen: Kok.
Adamek, J. 1938. *Vom römischen Endreich der mittelalterlichen Bibelerklärung.* Würzburg: Stürtz.
Adams, J. E. 1970. *The Time Is at Hand.* Nutley, NJ: Presbyterian and Reformed Publishing Company.
Allis, O. T. 1945. *Prophecy and the Church.* Philadelphia: Presbyterian and Reformed Publishing Company.
Arthur, A. 1999. *The Tailor-King: The Rise and Fall of the Anabaptist Kingdom of Münster.* New York: St. Martin's Press.
Augustine. 1998. *The City of God Against the Pagans.* Translated by R. W. Dyson. New York: Cambridge University Press.
———. N.d. *De civitate Dei.* https://en.wikisource.org/wiki/The_City_of_God/Book_XXII/ Chapter_30.
———. N.d. *The Literal Meaning of Genesis.* http://college.holycross.edu/faculty/alaffey/other_files/Augustine-Genesis1.pdf.
Baarslag, D. J. 1940. *Gelijkenissen des Heeren.* 2 Vols. Baarn: Bosch and Keuning.
Bahnsen, G. L. (1977) 2002. *Theonomy in Christian Ethics.* Nacogdoches, TX: Covenant.
———. 1991. *By This Standard: The Authority of God's Law Today.* Tyler, TX: Institute for Christian Economics.
Barclay, W. 1999. *The Parables of Jesus.* Louisville, KY: Westminster John Knox Press.

Barrett, C. K. 1968. *A Commentary on the First Epistle to the Corinthians.* New York: Harper and Row.

Barth, K. 1968. *The Epistle to the Romans.* Translated by E. C. Hoskyns. Oxford: Oxford University Press).

Barth, K. 2010 (repr.). *Church Dogmatics*, 14 vols. Peabody, MA: Hendrickson.

Bass, C. B. 1960. *Backgrounds to Dispensationalism: Its Historical Genesis and Ecclesiastical Implications.* Grand Rapids, MI: Baker Books.

Bauckham, R. 2005. *God Will Be All in All: The Eschatology of Jürgen Moltmann.* Edinburgh: T. and T. Clark.

Bauckham, R. and P. F. Guttesen. 2009. *Leaning into the Future: The Kingdom of God in the Theology of Jürgen Moltmann and the Book of Revelation.* Edinburgh: T. and T. Clark.

Bauckham, R. and T. Hart. 1999. *Hope Against Hope: Christian Eschatology at the Turn of the Millennium.* London: Darton, Longman and Todd.

Bavinck, H. 2002–2008. *Reformed Dogmatics.* Edited by John Bolt. Translated by John Vriend. 4 vols. Grand Rapids: Baker Academic.

Beasley-Murray, G. R. 1954. *Jesus and the Kingdom of God.* London: Macmillan.

Beck, H.-G. 1994. *Das Byzantinische Jahrtausend.* München: C. H. Beck.

Berger, K. 2004. *Jesus.* München: Pattloch.

Berkhof, H. 1979. *Christian Faith: An Introduction to the Study of the Faith.* Translated by S. Woudstra. Grand Rapids, MI: Eerdmans.

———. 2004 (repr.). *Christ the Meaning of History.* Eugene, OR: Wipf and Stock.

Berkhof, L. (1938) 1996. *Systematic Theology*. Grand Rapids, MI: Eerdmans.

Berkouwer, G. C. 1972. *The Return of Christ*. Edited by M. J. Van Elderen. Translated by J. Van Oosterom. Studies in Dogmatics. Grand Rapids, MI: Eerdmans.

Betz, O. and W. Grimm. 1977. *Wesen und Wirklichkeit der Wunder Jesu*. Frankfurt: Peter Lang.

Bivin, D. and R. B. Blizzard. 1984. *Understanding the Difficult Words of Jesus*. Shippensburg, PA: Destiny Image Publishers.

Blackburn, J. S. 1978. *Seek Ye First: A Study of the Kingdom of God*. Wooler: Central Bible Hammond Trust.

Blaising, C. A. and D. L. Bock. 1992. *Dispensationalism, Israel and the Church: The Search for Definition*. Grand Rapids, MI: Zondervan.

———. 1993. *Progressive Dispensationalism*. Wheaton, IL: BridgePoint.

Bloch, E. 1995. *The Principle of Hope*, 3 vols.. Cambridge, MA: MIT Press.

Bloesch, D. G. 2004. *The Last Things: Resurrection, Judgment, Glory*. Downers Grove: InterVarsity Press.

Blomberg, C. L. and S. W. Chung, eds. 2009. *Premillennialism: An Alternative to 'Left Behind' Eschatology*. Grand Rapids, MI: Baker Academic.

Blum, E. A. 1981. *1,2 Peter, Jude*. EBC 12. Grand Rapids, MI: Zondervan.

Blum, G. G. 1981. "Chiliasmus II. Alte Kirche." In *Theologische Realenzyklopädie* 7:729–732. Berlin/New York: Walter de Gruyter.

Bock, D. L. 2002. *Jesus According to Scripture*. Grand Rapids, MI: Baker Academic.

Bockmuehl, M. 1994. *This Jesus: Martyr, Lord, Messiah.* Downers Grove, IL: InterVarsity Press.

Boettner, L. (1957) 1990. *The Millennium.* Phillipsburg, NJ: Presbyterian and Reformed Publishing Company.

Boff, L. 1984. *Church: Charism and Power.* London: SCM.

Boice, J. M. 1986. *Christ's Call to Discipleship.* Chicago: Moody.

Bonhoeffer, D. (1959) 1995. *The Cost of Discipleship.* New York: Simon and Schuster.

Booth, A. E. 1999 (repr.). *The Course of Time from Eternity to Eternity: Chart.* Neptune, NJ: Loizeaux Brothers.

Borg, M. J. 2006. *Jesus: Uncovering the Life, Teachings, and Relevance of a Religious Revolutionary.* San Francisco: HarperSanFrancisco.

Bornkamm, G., G. Barth, and H. J. Held, eds. 1963. *Tradition and Interpretation in Matthew.* Philadelphia: Westminster.

Bouma, C. 1937. *De brieven van den apostel Paulus aan Timotheus en Titus.* KV. Kampen: Kok.

Brakel, W. à. (orig. Dutch ed. 1700) 1992–1995. *The Christian's Reasonable Service.* Edited by J. R. Beeke. Translated by B. Elshout. 4 vols. Grand Rapids, MI: Reformation Heritage Books.

Bratt, J. D., ed. 1998. *Abraham Kuyper: A Centennial Reader.* Grand Rapids, MI: Eerdmans

Bray, J. L. 1996. *Matthew 24 Fulfilled.* Lakeland, FL: John L. Bray Ministries.

Brienen, T. et al., eds. 1986. *De Nadere Reformatie: Beschrijving van haar voornaamste vertegenwoordigers.* 's-Gravenhage: Boekencentrum.

Bright, J. 1953. *The Kingdom of God.* New York: Abingdon Press.

Brouwer, C. [1953]. *Het Koninkrijk Gods in gelijkenissen.* Baarn: Bosch and Keuning.

Brower, K. E. and M. W. Elliott, eds. 1997. *Eschatology in Bible and Theology: Evangelical Essays at the Dawn of a New Millennium.* Downers Grove, IL: InterVarsity.

Brown, R. E. 1994. *An Introduction to New Testament Christology.* New York: Paulist Press.

Bruce, A. B. 1979. *The Synoptic Gospels.* EGT 1. Grand Rapids, MI: Eerdmans.

Bruce, F. F. 1988. *The Book of the Acts, Revised Edition.* NICNT. Grand Rapids, MI: Eerdmans.

Bryan, S. M. 2002. *Jesus and Israel's Traditions of Judgement and Restoration.* Cambridge: Cambridge University Press.

Bullinger, E. W. 1972 (repr.). *The Foundations of Dispensational Truth.* London: Samuel Bagster and Sons.

Bultmann, R. 1962. *History and Eschatology.* New York: Harper and Row.

Bunyan, J. (1669) 2003. *The Pilgrim's Progress.* Mineola, NY: Dover Publications.

Burridge, J. H. N.d. *God's Prophetic Plan: A Comprehensive View of God's Dealings with Man from Creation to the New Heavens and New Earth.* London etc.: Marshall, Morgan and Scott.

Calvin, J. 1960. *The Institutes of the Christian Religion.* Edited by John T. McNeill. Translated by Ford Lewis Battles. Library of Christian Classics. Vol. XX. Philadelphia: Westminster Press.

Capon, R. F. 2002. *Kingdom, Grace, Judgment: Paradox, Outrage, and Vindication in the Parables of Jesus.* Grand Rapids, MI: Eerdmans.

Capp, B. S. 1972. *The Fifth Monarchy Men: A Study in Seventeenth-Century English Millenarianism.* London: Faber.

Carroll, J. T. et al. 2000. *The Return of Jesus in Early Christianity.* Peabody, MA: Hendrickson.

Carson, D. A. 1984. *Matthew.* EBC 8. Grand Rapids, MI: Zondervan.

Chafer, L. S. 1983. *Systematic Theology.* 15th ed. 8 vols.. Dallas: Dallas Seminary Press.

Chia, R. 2005. *Hope for the World: A Christian Vision of the Last Things.* Downers Grove, IL: IVP Academic.

Chilton, D. 1987. *The Great Tribulation.* Fort Worth, TX: Dominion Press.

Clouse, R. G., ed. 1977. *The Meaning of the Millennium.* Downers Grove, IL: InterVarsity Press.

Coates, C. A. 1922. *An Outline of the Book of Leviticus.* Kingston-on-Thames: Stow Hill Bible and Tract Depot.

———. 1931. *An Outline of Luke's Gospel.* Kingston-on-Thames: Stow Hill Bible and Tract Depot.

Cohen, A., ed. 1980 (repr.). *The Twelve Prophets.* SBB. London: Soncino.

———. 1983. *The Soncino Chumash.* SBB. London: Soncino.

Cohen, A. and A. J. Rosenberg. 1985. *Proverbs.* SBB. London: Soncino.

Cohn, N. (1957) 1970. *The Pursuit of the Millennium: Revolutionary Millenarians and Mystical Anarchists of the Middle Ages.* New York: Oxford University Press.

Cole, R. A. 1961. *The Gospel According to St. Mark.* TNTC. Grand Rapids, MI: Eerdmans.

Collins, A. Y. 1976. *The Combat Myth in the Book of Revelation.* Diss. in Religion 9. Cambridge, MA: Harvard University.

Crenshaw, C. I. and G. E. Gunn III. 1985. *Dispensationalism Today, Yesterday, and Tomorrow.* Memphis, TN: Footstool Publications.

Crossan, J. D. 1995. *Jesus: A Revolutionary Biography.* San Francisco: HarperSanFrancisco.

Cullmann, O. 1941. *Königsherrschaft Christi und Kirche im Neuen Testament.* Zollikon-Zürich: Evangelischer Verlag.

———. 1964. *Christ and Time: The Primitive Christian Perception of Time.* Translated by F. V. Filson. Louisville, KY: Westminster John Knox.

Darby, J. N. N.d.. *The Collected Writings of J.N. Darby.* Kingston-on-Thames: Stow Hill Bible and Tract Depot.

De Jong, J. A. 1970. *As the Waters Cover the Sea: Millennial Expectations in the Rise of Anglo-American Missions 1640–1810.* Kampen: Kok.

Demarest, B. 1997. *The Cross and Salvation: The Doctrine of Salvation.* Wheaton, IL: Crossway Books.

Den Hertog, G. C. 2003. *Hoop die leven doet: Over de samenhang van eschatologie en ethiek.* Apeldoorn: Theologische Universiteit.

Den Heyer, C. J. 2003. *Van Jezus naar christendom: De ontwikkeling van tekst tot dogma.* Zoetermeer: Meinema.

DeWitt, D. S. 2002. *Dispensational Theology in America During the Twentieth Century: Theological Development and Cultural Context.* Grand Rapids, MI: Grace Bible College.

Dibelius, M. 1953. *Paul.* Philadelphia: Westminster.

Dodd, C. H. 1903. *New Testament Studies.* Manchester: Manchester University Press.

———. (1935)1961. *The Parables of the Kingdom.* London: Clowes.

Douma, J. 2008. *Christenen voor Israël? Verantwoording van een politieke keus.* Barneveld: De Vuurbaak.

Doyle, R. C. 1999. *Eschatology and the Shape of Christian Belief.* Carlisle: Paternoster Press.

Duffield, G. P. and N. M. Van Cleave. (1987) 2008. *Foundations of Pentecostal Theology.* Lake Mary, FL: Creation House.

Dumbrell, W. J. 1994. *The Search for Order: Biblical Eschatology in Focus.* Grand Rapids, MI: Baker Books.

Dunn, J. D. G. 2005. *A New Perspective on Jesus: What the Quest for the Historical Jesus Missed.* Grand Rapids, MI: Baker Academic.

Edelkoort, A. H. 1941. *De Christusverwachting in het Oude Testament.* Wageningen: H. Veenman and Zonen.

Edersheim, A. (1883) 1979. *The Life and Times of Jesus the Messiah.* Grand Rapids, MI: Eerdmans.

Efird, J. M. 1986. *End-Times: Rapture, Antichrist, Millennium.* Nashville, TN: Abingdon Press.

Eggenberg, Th. 2010. *Kirche als Zeichen des Reiches Gottes: Eine Studie zur Bedeutung des Reiches Gottes für die Kirche in Auseinandersetzung mit Küng, Moltmann, Pannenberg und Hauerwas.* Diss. Heverlee: Evangelische Theologische Faculteit.

Erickson, M. J. 1998 (rev. ed.). *Christian Theology.* Grand Rapids, MI: Baker Book House.

———. 1999. *A Basic Guide to Eschatology: Making Sense of the Millennium.* 2nd ed. Grand Rapids, MI: Baker Books.

Erlemann, K. 1999. *Gleichnisauslegung: Ein Lehr- und Arbeitsbuch.* Tübingen/Basel: A. Francke Verlag.

Fairbairn, P. (1845) 1975. *The Typology of Scripture, Viewed in Connection with the Whole Series of the Divine Dispensations.* Grand Rapids, MI: Baker Book House.

Fee, G. D. 1987. *The First Epistle to the Corinthians.* NICNT. Grand Rapids, MI: Eerdmans.

Feinberg, C. L. 1961. *Premillennialism or Amillennialism? The Premillennial and Amillennial Systems of Biblical Interpretation Analyzed and Compared.* New York: American Board of Missions to the Jews.

Feinberg, J. S., ed. 1988. *Continuity and Discontinuity: Perspectives on the Relationship Bewteen the Old and New Testaments.* Wheaton, IL: Crossway Books.

Flusser, D. 1981. *Die rabbinischen Gleichnisse und der Gleichniserzähler Jesus.* Bern: Lang.

———. 2001. *Jesus.* 3rd ed. Jerusalem: Magnes Press.

France, R. T. 2007. *The Gospel of Matthew.* NICNT. Grand Rapids, MI: Eerdmans.

Froom, L. E. 1946–1954. *The Prophetic Faith of Our Fathers: The Historical Development of Prophetic Interpretation.* 4 vols. Washington, DC: Review and Herald.

Gaebelein, A. C. 1910. *The Gospel of Matthew,* 2 vols. Wheaton, IL: Van Kampen Press.

Geldenhuys, N. 1983 (repr.). *Commentary on the Gospel of Luke.* NICNT. Grand Rapids, MI: Eerdmans.

Gerlach, F. 1920. *Der Kommunismus als Lehre vom tausendjährigen Reich.* München: Hugo Bruckmann.

Gibbs, J. A. 2001. *Jerusalem and Parousia: Jesus' Eschatological Discourse in Matthew's Gospel.* St. Louis, MO: Concordia Academic Press.

Goldman, S., ed. 1983 (repr.). *Samuel.* SBB. London: Soncino.

Goslinga, C. J. 1962. *Het tweede boek Samuël.* COT. Kampen: Kok.

Graafland, C. 1973. *Waarom nog gereformeerd?* Kampen: Kok.

Grant, F. W. 1897. *The Numerical Bible: The Gospels.* New York: Loizeaux Brothers.

———. 1901. *The Numerical Bible: Acts to 2 Corinthians.* New York: Loizeaux Brothers.

———. N.d. *Genesis in the Light of the New Testament.* New York: Loizeaux Brothers.

Green, J. B. 1997. *The Gospel of Luke.* NICNT. Grand Rapids, MI: Eerdmans.

Green, J. B., S. McKnight, and I. H. Marshall. 1992. *Dictionary of Jesus and the Gospels.* Downers Grove, IL: InterVarsity Press.

Greijdanus, S. 1922. *De brief van den apostel Paulus aan de Galaten.* KV. Kampen: Kok.

———. 1931. *1 en 2 Peterus.* KV. Kampen: Kok.

———. (1941) 1955. *Het evangelie naar Lucas.* 2nd ed. 2 vols. KV. Kampen: Kok.

Grenz, S. J. 1992. *The Millennial Maze: Sorting Out Evangelical Options.* Downers Grove, IL: InterVarsity Press.

Grosheide, F. W. 1954. *Het heilig evangelie volgens Mat-*

*theüs*. 2nd ed. Commentaar op het Nieuwe Testament. Kampen: Kok.

———. 1962. *De Handelingen der Apostelen*. Vol. 1: Chapters 1-14. KV. Kampen: Kok.

Grudem, W. and R. B. Gaffin, eds. 1996. *Are Miraculous Gifts for Today? Four Views*. Grand Rapids, MI: Zondervan.

Grundmann, H. (1927) 1966. *Studien über Joachim von Fiore*. 2nd ed. Darmstadt: Wissenschaftliche Buchgesellschaft.

———. 1984. "Die Grundzüge der mittelalterlichen Geschichtsanschauungen." In *Geschichtsdenken und Geschichtsbild im Mittelalter*, ed. by W. Lammers, 418-29. Darmstadt: Wissenschaftliche Buchgesellschaft.

Guthrie, D. 1981. *New Testament Theology*. Leicester: IVP Academic.

Gutiérrez, G. 1988. *A Theology of Liberation*. Maryknoll, NY: Orbis Books.

Habershon, A. R. (1957) 1967. *The Study of the Types*. Grand Rapids, MI: Kregel.

Hall, S. 1992. *Doctrine and Practice of the Early Church*. Grand Rapids, MI: Eerdmans.

Hamilton, F. E. 1942. *The Basis of Millennial Faith*. Grand Rapids, MI: Eerdmans.

Hamilton, N. Q. 1957. "The Holy Spirit and Eschatology in Paul." *Scottish Journal of Theology Occasional Papers* 6. Edinburgh: Oliver and Boyd.

Hamilton, V. P. 1990/95. *The Book of Genesis*, 2 vols. NICOT. Grand Rapids, MI: Eerdmans.

Harnisch, W. 2001. *Die Gleichniserzählungen Jesu: Eine hermeneutische Einführung*. 4th ed. Göttingen: Vandenhoeck and Ruprecht.

Hartley, J. E. 1988. *The Book of Job.* NICOT. Grand Rapids, MI: Eerdmans.

Hartvelt, G. P. 1977. *Het gebinte van de tijd: Een historische studie over constructies van de geschiedenis, met name in de tijd der Reformatie.* Kampen: Kok.

Hays, J. D., J. S. Duvall, and C. M. Pate. 2007. *Dictionary of Biblical Prophecy and End Times.* Grand Rapids, MI: Zondervan.

Heering, G. J. (1928) 1972. *The Fall of Christianity: A Study of Christianity, the State, and War.* Dissertations-G. Orig. 1930. London: Allen and Unwin.

Heidegger, M. (1927) 1996. *Being and Time.* Albany, NY: State University of New York Press.

Hengel, M. 1995. *Studies in Early Christology.* Edinburgh: T. and T. Clark.

Herbers, K. and H. Neuhaus, eds. 2005. *Das Heilige Römische Reich: Schauplätze einer tausendjährigen Geschichte (843–1806).* Köln/Weimar: Böhlau-Verlag.

Heyns, J. A. 1988. *Dogmatiek.* Pretoria: NG Kerkboekhandel.

Hill, C. E. 2001. *Regnum Caelorum: Patterns of Millennial Thought in Early Christianity.* 2nd ed. Grand Rapids, MI: Eerdmans.

Hodges, Z. C. 1989. *Absolutely Free!*, Dallas: Redencion Viva.

Hoek, J. 2004. *Hoop op God: Eschatologische verwachting.* 2nd ed. Zoetermeer: Boekencentrum.

Hoekema, A. A. 1979. *The Bible and The Future.* Grand Rapids, MI: Eerdmans.

Horton, M. S., ed. 1992. *Christ the Lord: The Reformation and Lordship Salvation.* Grand Rapids, MI: Baker.

Hultgren, A. J. 2002. *The Parables of Jesus: A Commentary.* Grand Rapids, MI: Eerdmans.

Ironside, H .A. 1938. *Wrongly Dividing the Word of Truth.* Neptune, NJ: Loizeaux Brothers.

Jeremias, J. 2003. *The Parables of Jesus.* London: SCM.

Johnston, B. 1980. *To the Third Empire: Ibsen's Early Drama.* Minneapolis: University of Minnesota.

Jones, D. and R. Woodbridge. 2011. *Health, Wealth and Happiness: Has the Prosperity Gospel Overshadowed the Gospel of Christ?* Grand Rapids, MI: Kregel Publications.

Jones, P. R. 1999. *Studying the Parables of Jesus.* Macon, GA: Smyth and Helwys.

Jukes, A. 1875. *The Types of Genesis Briefly Considered.* London: Longmans, Green and Co.

Jülicher, A. 1910. *Die Gleichnisreden Jesu.* 2nd ed. 2 vols. Tübingen: Mohr (Siebeck).

Kaiser Jr., W. C. 1990. *Exodus.* EBC 2. Grand Rapids, MI: Zondervan.

Kallas, J. 1961. *The Significance of the Synoptic Miracles.* London: SPCK.

Kee, H. C. 1983. *Miracle in the Early Christian World.* New Haven: Yale University Press.

Kelly, W. 1896 (new ed.). *Lectures on the Gospel of Matthew.* London: A. S. Rouse.

———. (1898) 1966. *An Exposition of the Gospel of John.* London: C. A. Hammond.

Kelsey, M. 1973. *Healing and Christianity.* New York: Harper and Rowe.

Kersten, G. H. 1947. *De gereformeerde dogmatiek voor de gemeenten toegelicht.* 2 vols. Utrecht: De Banier.

Kimball, W. R. 1984. *What the Bible Says about the Great*

*Tribulation*. Phillipsburg, NJ: Presbyterian and Reformed Publishing Company.

Kittel, G. et al., eds. 1964–1976. *Theological Dictionary of the New Testament*. Translated by G. W. Bromiley. 10 vols. Grand Rapids, MI: Eerdmans.

Knevel, A. G. and M. J. Paul, eds. 1995. *Verkenningen in de oudtestamentische messiasverwachting*. Kampen: Kok Voorhoeve/Hilversum: Evangelische Omroep.

Knight, J. 2004. *Jesus: An Historical and Theological Investigation*. London: T. and T. Clark.

Knowling, R. J. 1979 (repr.). *The Acts of the Apostles*. EGT 2. Grand Rapids, MI: Eerdmans.

Kocken, E. 1935. *De theorie van de vier wereldrijken en van de overdracht der wereldheerschappij tot op Innocentius III*. Nijmegen: Berkhout.

Kreck, W. 1961. *Die Zukunft des Gekommenen: Grundprobleme der Eschatologie*. München: Chr. Kaiser.

Kruse, H. 1977. Das Reich Satans. *Biblica* 58:29–61.

Kümmel, W. G. 1957. *Promise and Fulfillment: The Eschatological Message of Jesus*. Translated by D. M. Barton. Norcross, GA: Trinity Press.

Küng, H. 2001. *The Church*. Translated by R. and R. Ockenden. New York: Bloomsbury Academic.

Kuyper, A. 1931. *Van de voleinding*. Vol. 4. Kampen: Kok.

———. 1934. *Chiliasm or the Doctrine of Premillennialism*. Grand Rapids, MI: Zondervan.

———. (1898) 2009. *Lectures on Calvinism: Six Lectures from the Stone Foundation: Lectures Delivered at Princeton University*. CreateSpace Independent Publishing Platform.

Ladd, G. E. (1959) 1964. *The Gospel of the Kingdom:*

*Popular Expositions on the Kingdom of God.* Grand Rapids, MI: Eerdmans.

———. 1974a. *A Theology of the New Testament.* Grand Rapids, MI: Eerdmans.

———. 1974b. *The Presence of the Future: The Eschatology of Biblical Realism.* Grand Rapids, MI: Eerdmans.

LaHaye, T. and T. Ice. 2001. *Chartering the End Times: A Visual Guide to Understanding Bible Prophecy.* Eugene, OR: Harvest House Publishers.

LaHaye, T. and J. B. Jenkins. 2000. *Are We Living in the End Times?* Wheaton, IL: Tyndale House.

———. (1995–2007) repr. 2010. *Left Behind.* 4 vols. Carol Stream, IL: Tyndale House Publishers.

Lambrecht, J. 1992. *Out of the Treasure: The Parables in the Gospel of Matthew.* Grand Rapids, MI: Eerdmans.

Landgrebe, W. 1986. *Dietrich Bonhoeffer: Wagnis der Nachfolge.* 6th ed. Gießen/Basel: Brunnen Verlag.

Lane, W. L. 1974 (repr. 1979). *The Gospel of Mark.* NICNT. Grand Rapids, MI: Eerdmans.

Lee, F. N. 2006. *Always Victorious! The Earliest Church not Pre- but Postmillennial.* www.dr-fnlee.org/docs5/postmill/postmill.html.

Lessing, G. E. 1967. *Die Erziehung des Menschengeschlechts. Lessing Werke, Schriften* II. Frankfurt: Insel Verlag.

Lewis, G. R. and B. A. Demarest. 1996. *Integrative Theology: Historical, Biblical, Systematic, Apologetic, Practical.* 3 vols. Grand Rapids, MI: Zondervan.

Liefeld, W. L. 1984. *Luke.* EBC 8. Grand Rapids, MI: Zondervan.

Lierman, J. 2004. *The New Testament Moses: Christian Perceptions of Moses and Israel in the Setting of Jewish Religion.* Tübingen: Mohr (Siebeck).

Lindeboom, J. 1929. *Stiefkinderen van het Christendom.* 's-Gravenhage: Martinus Nijhoff.

Lindsay, G. (1960) 1998. *God's Master Key to Prosperity.* Dallas, TX: Christ for the Nations.

Lindsey, H. 1970. *The Late Great Planet Earth.* Grand Rapids, MI: Zondervan.

Linnemann, E. (1961) 1982. *Parables of Jesus: Introduction and Exposition.* 6th ed. London: SPCK.

———. 1999. *Original oder Fälschung: Historisch-kritische Theologie im Licht der Bibel.* Bielefeld: CLV.

———. 2007. *Was ist glaubwürdig – die Bibel oder die Bibelkritik?* Nürnberg: VTR-Verlag.

Lockyer, H. 1988. *All the Parables of the Bible.* Grand Rapids, MI: Zondervan.

Lohfink, G. 1998. *Braucht Gott die Kirche? Zur Theologie des Volkes Gottes.* 3rd ed. Freiburg: Herder.

Longenecker, R. N., ed. 2000. *The Challenge of Jesus' Parables.* Grand Rapids, MI: Eerdmans.

Longman III, T. 1998. *The Book of Ecclesiastes.* NICOT. Grand Rapids, MI: Eerdmans.

Luce, H. K. 1933. *The Gospel According to St. Luke.* Cambridge: Cambridge University Press.

Luther, M. 1883. *Werke,* Vol. XXIV. Weimar: Metzler Verlag.

MacArthur, J. F. 1992. *Charismatic Chaos.* Grand Rapids, MI: Zondervan.

McClain, A. J. 1959. *The Greatness of the Kingdom.* Grand Rapids, MI: Zondervan.

McDowell, J. 1972. *Evidence That Demands a Verdict.* San Bernardino, CA: Campus Chrusade for Christ.

McGrath, A. E. 2010. *Christian Theology: An Introduction.* Hoboken, NJ: Wiley-Blackwell.

Marshall, I. H. 1978. *The Gospel of Luke.* NIGTC. Grand Rapids, MI: Eerdmans.

Masters, P. and J. C. Whitcomb. 1988. *The Charismatic Phenomenon.* London: Wakeman Trust.

Mauro, P. 1908. *Man's Day: The World and Its God.* London: Morgan and Scott.

———. 1919. *God's Present Kingdom.* Boston: Hamilton Bros.

Mayhue, R. 2009. *The Healing Promise: Is It Always God's Will to Heal?* San Clemente, CA: Mentor.

Meier, J. P. 1994. *A Marginal Jew: Rethinking the Historical Jesus.* Vol. 2: *Mentor, Message, and Miracles.* New York: Doubleday.

Meinhold, A. 1991. *Die Sprüche.* 2 vols. Zurcher Bibelkommentare. Zürich: Theologischer Verlag.

Metzger, B. M. 1975. *A Textual Commentary on the Greek New Testament.* 2nd ed. London/New York: United Bible Societies.

Moeller van den Bruck, A. 1923. *Das dritte Reich.* Berlin: Ring-Verlag.

Moerkerken, A. 2004. *Ons troostboek: Verklaring van de Heidelbergse Catechismus.* Houten: Den Hertog.

Moffatt, J. 1979. *The First and Second Epistle to the Thessalonians.* EGT 4. Grand Rapids, MI: Eerdmans.

Moltmann, J. 1975. *The Church in the Power of the Spirit: A Contribution to Messianic Ecclesiology.* London: SCM.

———. 1976. *Im Gespräch mit Ernst Bloch: Eine theologische Wegbegleitung.* München: Kaiser.

———. 1993. *Theology of Hope.* Minneapolis: Fortress.

Moo, D. J. 1996. *The Epistle to the Romans.* NICNT. Grand Rapids, MI: Eerdmans.

Moore, R. D. 2004. *The Kingdom of Christ: The New Evangelical Perspective.* Wheaton, IL: Crossway Books.

Morphew, D. 2011. *Breakthrough: Discovering the Kingdom.* Cape Town: Derek Morphew Publishing.

Morris, H. M. 1976. *The Genesis Record: A Scientific and Devotional Commentary on the Book of Beginnings.* San Diego, CA: Creation-Life Publishers.

Morris, L. 1959. *The First and Second Epistles to the Thessalonians.* Grand Rapids, MI: Eerdmans.

———. 1974. *The Gospel According to St. Luke.* TNTC. Grand Rapids, MI: Eerdmans.

Müller, P. et al. 2002. *Die Gleichnisse Jesu: Ein Studien- und Arbeitsbuch für den Unterricht.* Stuttgart: Calwer Verlag.

Münch, C. 2004. *Die Gleichnisse Jesu im Matthäusevangelium: Eine Studie zu ihrer Form und Funktion.* Neukirchen-Vluyn: Neukirchener Verlag.

Neuffer, E. 1913. *Prophetische Karte: Des Menschen Tun und Gottes Wege.* Wuppteral: R. Brockhaus.

Noordegraaf, A. 1980. *Gods bouwwerk: Aspecten van het gemeente-zijn in bijbels-theologisch licht.* 's-Gravenhage: Boekencentrum.

Noordmans, O. 1935. *Dingen die verborgen waren.* Zeist: Ploegsma.

North, G. 1990. *Tools of Dominion: The Case Laws of Exodus.* Tyler, TX: Institute for Christian Economics.

———. 1991. *Theonomy: An Informed Response.* Tyler, TX: Institute for Christian Economics.

Odendall, D. H. 1970. *The Eschatological Expectation of*

*Isaiah 40-66 with Special Reference to Israel and the Nations*. Philadelphia: Presbyterian and Reformed Publishing Company.

Origen. N.d. *Commentary on Mattew*. http://www.newadvent.org/fathers/1016.htm.

Osteen, J. 2004. *Your Best Life Now: 7 Steps to Living at Your Full Potential*. New York: FaithWords.

Oswalt, J. N. 1986. *The Book of Isaiah Chapters 1-39*. NICOT. Grand Rapids, MI: Eerdmans.

Ouweneel, W. J. 1981. *Glaube und Werke: Eine Auslegung des Jakobusbriefes*. Schwelm: Heijkoop Verlag.

———. 1982. *"Wij zien Jezus": Bijbelstudies over de brief aan de Hebreeën*. 2 vols. Vaassen: Medema.

———. 1998. *De zevende koningin: Het eeuwig vrouwelijke en de raad van God*. Metahistorische triologie. Vol. 2. Heerenveen: Barnabas.

———. 2000. *Het Jobslijden van Israël: Israëls lijden oplichtend uit het boek Job*, Vaassen: Medema.

———. 2001a. "The Year 2000 and the Epochs of World History." *Tydskrif vir Christelike Wetenskap* 37:99-115.

———. 2001b. *Hoogtijden voor Hem: De bijbelse feesten en hun betekenis voor Joden en christenen*. Vaassen: Medema.

———, ed. 2003. *F. M. Dostojevski: De groot-inquisiteur: Christus door de Kerk verworpen*. Soesterberg: Aspekt.

———. (2003) 2005a. *Geneest de zieken! Over de bijbelse leer van ziekte, genezing en bevrijding*. 4th ed. Vaassen: Medema.

———. 2005b. *De God die is, of: Waarom ik geen atheïst ben*. Vaassen: Medema.

———. 2007a. *De Geest van God: Ontwerp van een pneumatologie*. EDR 1. Vaassen: Medema.

———. 2007b. *De Christus van God: Ontwerp van een christologie*. EDR 2. Vaassen: Medema.

———. 2008a. *De schepping van God: Ontwerp van een scheppings-, mens- en zondeleer*. EDR 3. Vaassen: Medema.

———. 2008b. *Het plan van God: Ontwerp van een voorbeschikkingsleer*. EDR 4. Vaassen: Medema.

———. 2008c. *Geloof, zekerheid, groei*. Vaassen: Medema.

———. 2009a. *Het zoenoffer van God: Ontwerp van een verzoeningsleer*. EDR 5. Vaassen: Medema.

———. 2009b. *Vijf olifanten in de porseleinkast: Vijf brandende onderwerpen waarover christenen verdeeld zijn*. Heerenveen: Medema.

———. 2010a. *Het heil van God: Ontwerp van een soteriologie*. EDR 6. Heerenveen: Medema.

———. 2010b. *De kerk van God I: Ontwerp van een elementaire ecclesiologie*. EDR 7. Heerenveen: Medema.

———. 2010c. *De kerk van God II: Ontwerp van een historische en praktische ecclesiologie*. EDR 8. Heerenveen: Medema.

———. 2010d. *Hoe word ik vervuld met de Heilige Geest?* Harderwijk: Highway Media/Rock Publications.

———. 2011a. *Het verbond en het koninkrijk van God: Ontwerp van een foederologie en basileologie*. Heerenveen: Medema.

———. 2012a. *De toekomst van God: Ontwerp van een eschatologie*. Heerenveen: Medema.

———. 2014a. *Power In Service: An Introduction to Christian Political Thought*. Jordan Station, ON: Paideia Press.

———. 2014b. *Wisdom For Thinkers: An Introduction to Christian Philosophy*. Jordan Station, ON: Paideia Press.

———. 2016. *Probing The Past: An Introduction to Christian Historical Science*. Jordan Station, ON: Paideia Press.

———. 2016a. *The Heidelberg Diary: Daily Devotionals on the Heidelberg Catechism*. Jordan Station, ON: Paideia Press.

———. 2016b. *The Eternal Covenant: An Evangelical Theology of Living With God*. Vol 2, An Evangelical Introduction to Reformational Theology. Jordan Station, ON: Paideia Press.

———. 2016c. *The Eternal Torah: An Evangelical Theology of Living Under God*. Vol. 1, An Evangelical Introduction to Reformational Theology. Jordan Station, ON: Paideia Press.

———. 2016d. *The Ninth King: The Last of the Celestial Empires: The Triumph of Christ over the Powers*. Jordan Station, ON: Paideia Press.

———. N.d. *Het boek Esther*. Alblasserdam: Stg. Boeken bij de Bijbel.

Packer, J. I. 1970. *Evangelism and the Sovereignty of God*. Downers Grove, IL: InterVarsity.

Pannenberg, W. 1977. *Jesus—God and Man*. Translated by L. L. Wilkins and D. A. Priebe. 2nd ed. Philadelphia: Westminster Press.

———. 1998. *Systematic Theology*. Translated by G. W. Bromiley. Vol. 3. Grand Rapids, MI: Eerdmans.

Paul, M. J. 1997. *Vergeving en genezing: Ziekenzalving in de christelijke gemeente*. Zoetermeer: Boekencentrum.

Pentecost, J. D. (1958) 1964. *Things to Come: A Study in Biblical Eschatology*. Grand Rapids, MI: Academie Books.

———. 1998. *The Parables of Jesus: Lessons in Life from the Master Teacher*. Grand Rapids, MI: Kregel.

Perrin, N. 1963. *The Kingdom of God in the Teaching of Jesus*. Philadelphia: Westminster Press.

Pertz, G. H., ed. 1829. *Monachus Sangallensis: De gestis Karoli Magni imperatoris*. Hannover: Hahn.

Pesch, R. 1976/77. *Das Markusevangelium*. 2 vols. Herders Theologischer Kommentar zum Neuen Testament. Freiburg: Herder.

Peters, G. N. H. (1884) 1952. *Theocratic Kingdom*. 3 vols. Grand Rapids, MI: Kregel.

Petzoldt, M. 1984. *Gleichnisse Jesu und christliche Dogmatik*. Göttingen: Vandenhoeck and Ruprecht.

Plummer, A. 1922. *Gospel According to St. Luke*. 5th ed. International Critical Commentary. Edinburgh: T&T Clark.

Pollock, A. J. N.d. *Genesis I and II, Historically and Typically Considered*. London: Central Bible Truth Depot.

Porter, J. R. 1963. *Moses and Monarchy: A Study in the Biblical Tradition of Moses*. Oxford: Basil Blackwell.

Poythress, V. (1986) 1994. *Understanding Dispensationalists*. 2nd ed. Phillipsburg, NJ: Presbyterian and Reformed Publishing Company.

Ratzinger, J. (Benedict XVI). 2007. *Jesus of Nazareth: From the Baptism in the Jordan to the Transfiguration. Jesus of Nazareth*. Translated by A. J. Walker. Vol. 1. San Francisco: Ignatius Press.

Ridderbos, H. N. 1962. *The Coming of the Kingdom*. Edited by R. O. Zorn. Translated by H. de Jongste.

Nutley, NJ: Presbyterian and Reformed Publishing Company.

———. (1965) 1970. *Het evangelie naar Mattheüs.* 2 vols. KV. Kampen: Kok.

———. 1997. *Paul: An Outline of His Theology.* Translated y J. R. De Witt. Grand Rapids, MI: Eerdmans.

———. (1989) 1995. "The Kingdom of God and Our Life in the World." In *Confessing Christ in Doing Politics: Essays on Christian Political Thought and Action,* edited by B. Van der Walt and R. Swanepoel, 10-24. Potchefstroom: Potchefstroom University for Christian Higher Education.

Ridderbos, J. 1955. *De psalmen.* Vol. 1: *Psalm 1-41.* COT. Kampen: Kok.

———. 1958. *De psalmen.* Vol. 2: *Psalm 42-106.* COT. Kampen: Kok.

Ridderbos, S. J. 1947. *De theologische cultuurbeschouwing van Abraham Kuyper.* Kampen: Kok.

Ritchie, J. N.d. *The Second Advent of the Lord Jesus, with Subsequent Events in Heaven and on Earth.* Kilmarnock: The Young Watchman Office.

Rogers, P. G. 1966. *The Fifth Monarchy Men.* London: Oxford University Press.

Ross, A. P. 1991. *Proverbs.* EBC 5. Grand Rapids, MI: Zondervan.

Rushdoony, R. J. 1973. *The Institutes of Biblical Law.* Nutley, NJ: Presbyterian and Reformed Publishing Company.

———. 1984. *Law and Liberty.* Vallecito, CA: Ross House Books.

———. 1986. *Christianity and the State.* Vallecito, CA: Ross House Books.

———. 1991. *The Roots of Reconstruction.* Vallecito, CA: Ross House Books.

Ryrie, C. C. 1953. *The Basis of the Premillennial Faith.* Neptune, NJ: Loizeaux Brothers.

———. 1965. *Dispensationalism Today.* Chicago: Moody Press.

———. 1969. *Balancing the Christian Life.* Chicago: Moody.

Sailhamer, J. H. 1990. *Genesis.* EBC 2. Grand Rapids, MI: Zondervan.

Saucy, M. R. 1997. *The Kingdom of God in the Teaching of Jesus in 20th Century Theology.* Dallas etc.: Word Publishing.

Saucy, R. L. 1993. *The Case for Progressive Dispensationalism: The Interface Between Dispensational and Non-Dispensational Theology.* Grand Rapids, MI: Zondervan.

Sauer, E. 1955. *Gott, Menschheit und Ewigkeit.* 2nd ed. Wuppertal: R. Brockhaus.

Sauter, G. 1996. *Eschatological Rationality: Theological Issues in Focus.* Grand Rapids, MI: Baker Books.

Savage, J. A. N.d.-a. *The Kingdom of God and of Heaven.* London: G. Morrish.

———. N.d.-b. *The Scroll of Time, or, Epochs and Dispensations of Scripture.* London: A. S. Rouse.

Schaeffer, F. A. 1982. *A Christian View of the Bible As Truth. The Complete Works: A Christian Worldview.* Vol. 2. Westchester, IL: Crossway Books.

Schaff, P. 1910. *History of the Christian Church.* Vol. 2. Peabody, MA: Hendrickson.

Schippers, R. 1962. *Gelijkenissen van Jezus.* Kampen: Kok.

Schmidt, K. L. 1964. "*Basileia.*" In *Theological Dictionary of the New Testament.* Edited by G. Kittel et al. Translated by G. W. Bromiley. Grand Rapids, MI: Eerdmans. 1:579 –90.

Schmidt, R. 1955/56. "Aetates Mundi: Die Weltalter als Gliederungsprinzip der Geschichte." *Zeitschrift für Kirchengeschichte* 67:288–317.

Schneider, R. (1947) 1979. *Das Vaterunser.* 6th ed. Freiburg: Herder.

Schoeps, H. J. 1961. *Paul: The Theology of the Apostle in the Light of Jewish Religious History.* Philadelphia: Westminster.

Schottroff, L. 2005. *Die Gleichnisse Jesu.* Gütersloh: Gütersloher Verlagshaus.

Schuyler English, E. 1986. *The Rapture.* 2nd ed. Neptune, NJ: Loizeaux Brothers.

Schwarz, H. 2000. *Eschatology.* Grand Rapids, MI: Eerdmans.

Schweitzer, A. (1914) 1985. *The Mystery of the Kingdom of God: The Secret of Jesus' Messiahship and Passion.* Amherst, NY: Prometheus Books.

———. (1910) 2001. *The Quest of the Historical Jesus: A Critical Study of Its Progress From Reimarus To Wrede.* Minneapolis, MN: Augsburg Fortress.

Schwemer, D. 2001. *Die Wettergottgestalten Mesopotamiens und Nordsyriens im Zeitalter der Keilschriftkulturen: Materialien und Studien nach den schriftlichen Quellen.* Wiesbaden: Harrassowitz.

Scofield, C. I. (1909) 1967. *The New Scofield Reference Bible.* New York: Oxford University Press.

Scott, B. B. 1989. *Hear Then the Parable: A Commentary on the Parables of Jesus.* Minneapolis: Fortress.

Shepard, J., ed. 2008. *The Cambridge History of the Byzantine Empire, c. 500–1492*. Cambridge: Cambridge University Press.

Sigal, Phillip. 1987. *The Halakah of Jesus of Nazareth According to the Gospel of Matthew*. Philadelphia: Fortress.

Sikkel, J. C. 1923. *Het boek der geboorten: Verklaring van het boek Genesis*. 2nd ed. Amsterdam: H. A. van Bottenburg.

Simonetti, M. 1992. "Millenarism." In *Encyclopedia of the Early Church*. Edited by A. Di Bernadino. Translated by A. Walford. New York: Oxford University Press. 1:560.

Smits, P. 1959. "Waarvóór stierf Jezus?" *Kerk en Wereld* 51/7:1 and further.

Snodgrass, K. R. 2008. *Stories with Intent: A Comprehensive Guide to the Parables of Jesus*. Grand Rapids, MI: Eerdmans.

Spengler, O. 1991. *The Decline of the West*. New York: Oxford University Press.

Spykman, G. J. 1992. *Reformational Theology: A New Paradigm for Doing Dogmatics*. Grand Rapids, MI: Eerdmans.

Stein, R. H. 1996. *Jesus the Messiah: A Survey of the Life of Christ*. Downers Grove, IL: InterVarsity Press.

Stern, D. H. 1992. *Jewish New Testament Commentary*. Clarksville, TN: Jewish New Testament Publications.

———. 1997. *Messianic Jewish Manifesto*. 3rd ed. Clarksville, TN: Jewish New Testament Publications.

Stilley, K. 1996. "Edwards, Jonathan." In *Dictionary of Premillennial Theology*, 100. Edited by M. Couch. Grand Rapids, MI: Kregel.

Stott, J. R. W. 1959. "Yes." *Eternity*. Sept. 1959.

Strack, H. L. and P. Billerbeck. (1922–1928) 1986–1997. *Kommentar zum Neuen Testament aus Talmud und Midrasch*. 6 vols. München: Beck.

Swete, H. B. (1906) 1951. *The Apocalypse of St. John*. Grand Rapids, MI: Eerdmans.

Tasker, R. V. G. 1961. *The Gospel According to St. Matthew*. TNTC. Grand Rapids, MI: Eerdmans.

Theissen, G. and A. Merz. 1998. *The Historical Jesus: A Comprehensive Guide*. Minneapolis: Fortress.

Theodosius. N.d. *Codex Theodosianus*. http://ancientrome.ru/ius/library/codex/theod/liber16.htm#10.

Thielicke, H. 2015. *The Waiting Father: Sermons on the Parables of Jesus*. Cambridge: Lutterworth Press.

Thiselton, A. C. 2000. *The First Epistle to the Corinthians*. NIGTC. Grand Rapids, MI: Eerdmans.

Thomas, R. L. 1999. *Understanding Spiritual Gifts*. Grand Rapids, MI: Kregel.

Towner, P. H. 2006. *The Letters to Timothy and Titus*. NICNT. Grand Rapids, MI: Eerdmans.

Tozer, A. W. 1991. *I Call It Heresy*. Edited by G. B. Smith. Camp Hill, PA: Christian Publications.

Tukker, C. A. 1981. *Het Chiliasme van Reformatie tot Réveil*. Apeldoorn: Willem de Zwijgerstichting.

Tuveson, E. L. (1949) 1964. *Millennium and Utopia: A Study in the Background of the Idea of Progress*. New York: Harper.

Tytler, W. N.d. *Plain Talks on prophecy, or, The Great Prophetic Cycles of Time*. London etc.: Pickering and Inglis.

Van Campen, M. 2007. *Gans Israël: Voetiaanse en coccejaanse visies op joden gedurende de zeventiende en achttiende eeuw.* 2nd ed. Zoetermeer: Boekencentrum.

Van der Woude, A. S. 1973. "De oorsprong van Israëls messiaanse verwachtingen in het Oude Testament en in de vroeg-joodse traditie." *Kerk en Theologie* 24 (1973):1-11.

Van Elderen, R. J. 1992. *Toekomst voor Israël: Een theologie-historisch onderzoek naar de visie op de bekering der Joden en de toekomst van Israël bij Engelse protestanten in de periode 1547-1670, tegen de achtergrond van hun eschatologie.* Kampen: Dissertatie-uitgeverij Mondiss.

Van Gemeren, W. A. 1991. *Psalms.* EBC 5. Grand Rapids, MI: Zondervan.

Van Genderen, J. and W. H. Velema, eds. 2008. *Concise Reformed Dogmatics.* Translated by G. Bilkes and E. M. van der Maas. Phillipsburg, NJ: Presbyterian and Reformed Publishing Company.

Van Leeuwen, J. A. C. 1928. *Het evangelie naar Markus.* KV. Kampen: Kok.

Van 't Spijker et al., eds. 1999. *Eschatologie: Handboek over de christelijke toekomstverwachting.* Kampen: De Groot Goudriaan.

Van Schelven, A. A. 1944. "Otto, bisschop van Freising's denkbeelden over den zin der geschiedenis." In *De zin der geschiedenis.* Edited by Z. W.Sneller et al. Wageningen: Zomer and Keuning.

Verkuyl, J. 1992. *De kern van het christelijk geloof.* Kampen: Kok.

Versteeg, J. P. 1969. *Het heden van de toekomst.* Kampen: Kok.

Von Rad, G. 1964. "*Melek* and *malkut.*" In *Theological Dictionary of the New Testament.* Edited by G. Kittel et al. Translated by G. W. Bromiley. Grand Rapids, MI: Eerdmans. 1:565–71.

Voorhoeve, H. C. (1866) 1922. *De toekomst onzes Heeren Jezus Christus en de daarmee in verband staande gebeurtenissen.* 8th ed. 's-Gravenhage: J. N. Voorhoeve.

Vos, G. 1903. *The Teaching of Jesus Concerning the Kingdom of God and the Church.* New York: American Tract Society.

———. 1912. "The Eschatological Aspect of the Pauline Conception of the Spirit." *Biblical and Theological Studies*, 209–259.

Wagner, C. P. 2008. *Dominion: How Kingdom Action Can Change the World.* Grand Rapids, MI: Chosen Books.

Waltke, B. K. 2004. *The Book of Proverbs.* Vol. 1: *Chapters 1–15.* NICOT. Grand Rapids, MI: Eerdmans.

Walvoord, J. F. 1974. *Matthew: Thy Kingdom Come.* Chicago: Moody Press.

———. 2001. *Prophecy in the New Millennium.* Grand Rapids, MI: Kregel.

Warburg, A. 1920. *Heidnisch-antike Weissagung in Wort und Bild zu Luthers Zeiten.* Heidelberg: C. Winter.

Weber, O. 1981. *Foundations of Dogmatics.* Translated by D. L. Guder. 2 vols. Grand Rapids, MI: Eerdmans.

Weiss, J. 1892. *Die Predigt Jesu vom Reiche Gottes.* Göttingen: Vandenhoeck and Ruprecht.

Wengert, T. J. 2005. "Philip Melanchthon on time and history in the Reformation." *Consensus.* 30.2:9–33. Available at: http://scholars.wlu.ca/consensus/vol30/iss2/2.

Wenham, D. 1989. *The Parables of Jesus.* Downers Grove, IL: InterVarsity Press.

———. (1984) 2003. *The Rediscovery of Jesus' Eschatological Discourse.* Series *Gospel Perspectives,* 2nd ed. Vol. 4. Eugene, OR: Wipf and Stock.

Werner, M. 1941 (repr. 1959). *Die Entstehung des christlichen Dogmas.* Kamen: Hartmut Spenner.

Wessell, W. W. 1984. *Mark.* EBC 8. Grand Rapids, MI: Zondervan.

White, N. J. D. 1979 (repr.). *The First and Second Epistles to Timothy and the Epistle to Titus.* EGT 4. Grand Rapids, MI: Eerdmans.

Willis, W., ed. 1987. *The Kingdom of God in Twentieth-Century Interpretation.* Peabody, MA: Hendrickson.

Wippermann, W. 2007. "Drittes Reich." In *Enzyklopädie des Nationalsozialismus.* Edited by W. Benz, H. Graml, and H. Weiß. 5th ed. Stuttgart: Klett-Cotta.

Witherington III, B. 1992. *Jesus, Paul, and the End of the World: A Comparative Study in New Testament Eschatology.* Downers Grove, IL: InterVarsity Press.

Wolters, A. M. 1985. *Creation Regained: Biblical Basics for a Reformational Worldview.* Grand Rapids, MI: Eerdmans.

Wood, A. S. 1978. *Ephesians.* EBC 11. Grand Rapids, MI: Zondervan.

Wood, L. J. 1985. *Hosea.* EBC 7. Grand Rapids, MI: Zondervan.

Wrede, W. 1901. *Das Messiasgeheimnis in den Evangelien: Zugleich ein Beitrag zum Verständnis des Markusevangeliums.* Göttingen: Vandenhoeck and Ruprecht.

Wright, C. J. H. 2006. *The Mission of God: Unlocking the Bible's Grand Narrative.* Downers Grove, IL: IVP Academic.

Wright, J. S. 1991. *Ecclesiastes.* EBC 5. Grand Rapids, MI: Zondervan.

Wright, N. T. 2003. *The Resurrection of the Son of God.* London: SPCK.

———. 2008. *Surprised by Hope: Rethinking Heaven, the Resurrection, and the Mission of the Church.* New York: HarperOne.

Young, B. H. 1998. *The Parables: Jewish Tradition and Christian Interpretation.* Peabody, MA: Hendrickson.

Ziglar, Z. and T. Ziglar. 2012. *Born to Win: Find Your Success Code.* Dallas: Success Media.

Zimmermann, R., ed. 2008. *Hermeneutik der Gleichnisse Jesu: Methodische Neuansätze zum Verstehen urchristlicher Parabeltexte.* Tübingen: Mohr (Siebeck).

Zorn, R. O. 1962. *Church and Kingdom.* Philadelphia: Presbyterian and Reformed Publishing Company.

Zwiep, A. 2003. *Jezus en het heil van Israëls God: Verkenningen in het Nieuwe Testament.* Zoetermeer: Boekencentrum.

# Scripture Index

**OLD TESTAMENT**
**Genesis**
1           16, 18,
            30, 31,
            554, 557
1:3         307
1:16–18     34
1:26        31, 89,
            141, 592
1:26–27     141
1:28        89, 300,
            592
1:31        5
2:2         467
2:7         398
2:8–9       16
2:11–12     33
2:16–17     573
2:18–25     300
3:5         34, 593
3:15        36, 53,
            54, 78,
            91, 293
3:20        35
4:8         25
5:24        394
7:4         554
9:5–6       574
10:10       16
10:25       556
11:1–9      176
11:3–4      27
13:13       131
14:18       97
14:19       13
14:22       13
15:18       595, 609
17:1        373
18:6        176
18:17       254
18:20–21    254
18:22–32    254
18:23       168
18:25       168
22:11       348
24:3        29
37:8        31
38:17–20    325
41:40       18
41:40–41    63
41:45       64
49          395, 399
49:10       11
49:18       11, 394

**Exodus**
3:4         348
3:14–15     370
4:20        67
5:1         29, 97
6:23        414
7:4         151
11:9        24
12          593
12:41       151
14:21       24
15          95, 97
15:14–16    106
15:18       13, 89,
            94, 97,
            373
16:36       176
17:9        67
17:11       203
19:6        18, 366
20:3        14
20:12       258
24:6        42, 360
28:36–38    375
29:40       145
32:9–10     254
32:11–14    254
33:11       254
34:29–30    421

**Leviticus**
2:11        177
4:3         53
7:13        176
11          174
13–14       82
16          593
18:3        42
18:5        575
19:18       259, 361
23:15–18    176
26          107, 441
26:45       106

**Deuteronomy**
4:19        41
4:25        14

| | | | | | |
|---|---|---|---|---|---|
| 4:34–35 | 24 | 7:12 | 608 | 29:23 | 22, 23, 382, 607 |
| 5:16 | 258 | 7:12–16 | 608 | | |
| 10:17 | 14 | 7:14 | 61 | | |
| 12:5 | 96 | 7:14–16 | 358 | **2 Chronicles** | |
| 13:5 | 167 | 12:24–25 | 65 | 1:1 | 607 |
| 14 | 174 | 14:24 | 375 | 1:4 | 96 |
| 14:1 | 42 | 15:31 | 94 | 3:1 | 96 |
| 14:34–35 | 24 | 15–18 | 358 | 6:10 | 382 |
| 16:16 | 97 | 16:16 | 253 | 6:42 | 53 |
| 17:14–15 | 19 | 17–18 | 612 | 13:8 | 22 |
| 18:15–19 | 594 | 19:23 | 37 | 18:18 | 23 |
| 21:15 | 258 | 23:3 | 31 | 20:6 | 364 |
| 27:15–26 | 441 | 23:3–4 | 57 | 20:7 | 254 |
| 28 | 107, 441 | 24:17 | 255 | 24:20–21 | 146 |
| 32:8–9 | 42 | | | 30:26 | 607 |
| 32:39 | 14 | | | 35:3 | 607 |
| 32:43 | 457 | **1 Kings** | | | |
| 33 | 107 | 1:13 | 607 | | |
| 33:4–5 | 68 | 2:12 | 23, 382 | **Ezra** | |
| 33:6 | 19 | 4:20–25 | 65 | 1:3 | 159 |
| | | 4:21 | 32, 595, 610 | 6:7–10 | 168 |
| **Joshua** | | | | 6:20 | 168 |
| 3:11 | 29 | 4:24 | 30, 607, 609 | 7:12 | 365 |
| 7:11 | 176 | | | 7:16 | 159 |
| 12:5 | 31 | 4:24b | 607 | 7:25 | 159 |
| 22:22 | 14 | 4:25 | 610 | 7:26–44 | 427 |
| | | 5:18 | 37 | 12:25 | 168 |
| | | 8:14 | 612 | 14:10 | 168 |
| **Ruth** | | 8:20 | 382 | | |
| 4:18–22 | 55 | 8:32 | 168 | | |
| | | 8:53 | 106 | **Esther** | |
| | | 9:5 | 382 | 1:14 | 375 |
| **1 Samuel** | | 11:14 | 37 | 6:7–9 | 66 |
| 1:24 | 176 | 18 | 393, 595 | 10:3 | 18 |
| 3:10 | 348 | | | | |
| 4:4 | 23 | 19:16 | 54 | **Job** | |
| 6:21 | 96 | 22:19 | 23 | 1 | 37, 42 |
| 7:1–2 | 96 | 23 | 37 | 1:6–8 | 37 |
| 8:7 | 19 | 25 | 37, 382 | 1:12 | 129 |
| 9:2 | 367 | | | 2 | 37, 42 |
| 9:3–5 | 55 | **2 Kings** | | 2:1–7 | 37 |
| 9:20 | 55 | 1:2 | 194 | 2:6–7 | 39 |
| 12:3 | 53 | 2:11 | 394 | 12:10 | 15 |
| 12:5 | 53 | 17:24–41 | 270 | 24:7–10 | 360 |
| 13:14 | 24, 254 | 19:15 | 23 | 26:12 | 16 |
| 18:13 | 252 | | | 29:4 | 253 |
| 18:16 | 252 | | | 38:4–11 | 16 |
| 24:6 | 55 | **1 Chronicles** | | 38:7 | 41 |
| 29:4 | 37 | 3:1 | 607 | 39:27 | 174 |
| | | 3:1–9 | 607 | 42:6 | 235 |
| | | 13:5–6 | 96 | | |
| **2 Samuel** | | 17:14 | 22 | | |
| 1:16 | 55 | 21:1 | 37 | **Psalm** | |
| 5:7 | 96 | 21:17 | 255 | 1:1 | 131 |
| 6:14 | 61, 612 | 27:33 | 253 | 1:5–6 | 168 |
| 6:17 | 20 | 29:12 | 24 | 2 | 55, 90, 595 |
| 7:1–17 | 96 | 29:22 | 607 | | |

## Scripture Index

| | | | | | | |
|---|---|---|---|---|---|---|
| 2:1–6 | 22 | 43 | 237 | 110:1 | 57, 86, 142, 214, 295, 599 |
| 2:2 | 40, 54, 90 | 45 | 23 | | |
| | | 45:5 | 594 | 110:2 | 68 |
| 2:2–9 | 91 | 45:6 | 357 | 116 | 347 |
| 2:5–7 | 62 | 45:9–11 | 33 | 118:22–23 | 147 |
| 2:7 | 61, 88, 462 | 46 | 444 | 118:26 | 159 |
| | | 47:6–7 | 28 | 119:136 | 236 |
| 2:9 | 368 | 48:2 | 20 | 132 | 96 |
| 5:2 | 20 | 50:1 | 14 | 132:1–5 | 96 |
| 8 | 370, 592, 600 | 51:10 | 222 | 132:10 | 53 |
| | | 55:13–14 | 253 | 132:11 | 595, 607 |
| 8:4 | 83, 87 | 66:3–4 | 28 | 132:15 | 72 |
| 8:4–6 | 61, 9 | 67:2–4 | 28 | 132:17 | 12 |
| 8:5–8 | 33–34 | 68:32–33 | 28 | 133:3 | 328, 497 |
| 8:6 | 49, 333 | 69:5 | 53 | 144:3 | 83 |
| 8:6–7 | 89 | 71:13 | 36 | 145:13 | vii, 24, 363 |
| 9:11 | 96 | 72 | 595 | | |
| 10:16 | 20, 364 | 72:3 | 507, 607 | 149:2 | 20 |
| 11:9 | 24 | 72:7 | 507, 607 | | |
| 14:7 | 598 | 72:7–11 | 32 | **Proverbs** | |
| 15 | 82, 610 | 72:8 | 31, 32, 595 | 1:1 | 607 |
| 16:8–11 | 62 | | | 3:1 | 244 |
| 18 | 595 | 72:8–17 | 65 | 3:1–4 | 410 |
| 18:11–12 | 85 | 72:10 | 610 | 3:33 | 168 |
| 18:13–15 | 16 | 73 | 399 | 4:2 | 244 |
| 18:45 | 155 | 73:24 | 396 | 4:23 | 513 |
| 19:1–2 | 29 | 73:24b | 397 | 6:20 | 244 |
| 19:4–6 | 141 | 74:9–11 | 493 | 7:2 | 244 |
| 19:12 | 133 | 74:14 | 16 | 8:22–31 | 443 |
| 20 | 595 | 78:2 | 112 | 8:30–31 | 400 |
| 20:2 | 96 | 78:12 | 24 | 9:1 | 562 |
| 21 | 595 | 80:1 | 23 | 14:21 | 237 |
| 21:2 | 68 | 80:9–16 | 146 | 14:32 | 397 |
| 22 | 595 | 82:1 | 34 | 18:10 | 144 |
| 22:18 | 94 | 84:7 | 207 | 19:12 | 102 |
| 22:27–28 | 28 | 89:10 | 16 | 20:26 | 38 |
| 22:28 | 31, 364 | 89:19–29 | 608 | 21:1 | 307, 315 |
| 23:5 | 347 | 89:20 | 55 | 22:11 | 253 |
| 24 | 595 | 90:4 | 221, 553, 554 | 23 | 244 |
| 24:1 | 308 | | | 28:13 | 133, 352 |
| 24:3–4 | 238 | 91:1 | 65 | 30:8–9 | 415 |
| 24:7–10 | 159, 360 | 93:2 | 592 | | |
| 25:14 | 253 | 95:3 | 14 | **Ecclesiastes** | |
| 26:9 | 131 | 97:5 | 29 | 3:39 | 466 |
| 29:9 | 97 | 98:4–6 | 28 | 4:12 | 385 |
| 29:10 | 13 | 99:1 | 23 | 7:6 | 418 |
| 33:5 | 518 | 99:1–2 | 18 | 12:5–7 | 398 |
| 33:6 | 212 | 102:25–27 | 61 | | |
| 33:8 | 28 | 103:20 | 25 | **Isaiah** | |
| 37:11 | 236, 327, 518 | 104 | 15 | 6 | 20, 62 |
| | | 104:15 | 145 | 6:1–3 | 213 |
| 37:25 | 386 | 104:29 | 15 | 6:5 | 15 |
| 38:20 | 36 | 104:35 | 131 | 9:1–2 | 94 |
| 40:8 | 245 | 105:15 | 53 | 9:6 | 462, 463, |
| 41:9 | 94 | 109:6 | 37 | | |
| 42:2 | 237 | 110 | 97 | | |

649

|         |          |          |              |            |            |
|---------|----------|----------|--------------|------------|------------|
|         | 519      | 33:11    | 56           |            | 563        |
| 9:6–7   | 51       | 33:17    | 358, 595     | 2:34–35    | 428, 447   |
| 9:7     | 23, 607  | 48:17    | 68           | 2:37       | 365        |
| 10:5–15 | 24, 29   | 49:34    | 16           | 2:43       | 308–309    |
| 14:12–15| 45       |          |              | 2:45       | 428, 447   |
| 24:23   | 16, 21   | **Lamentations** | | 2:47 | 14 |
| 24–27   | 426      | 3:44     | 85           | 4:3        | vii        |
| 25      | 21       | 4:20     | 65           | 4:11–12    | 173        |
| 26:19   | 80       | 5:19     | 592          | 4:17       | 90         |
| 27:1    | 16       |          |              | 4:21       | 173        |
| 29:18   | 80       |          |              | 4:26       | 9, 9–10,   |
| 31:4–5  | 524      | **Ezekiel** | |            | 525        |
| 31–32   | 523      | 1:15–25  | 102          | 4:35       | 25         |
| 32      | 435      | 1:26     | 23           | 4:46       | 69         |
| 32:14–16| 180      | 7:10     | 68           | 5:23       | 15         |
| 33:22   | 20       | 9:4      | 236          | 6:27       | 24         |
| 35      | 844      | 11:19    | 148          | 7          | 84, 114,   |
| 35:4–6  | 80       | 12:21–28 | 493          |            | 371, 431,  |
| 35:5    | 80       | 13:9     | 226          |            | 440, 495,  |
| 37:16   | 23       | 15:1–8   | 146          |            | 505, 530,  |
| 40:13–14| 25       | 17:23    | 65, 608      |            | 551, 552   |
| 41:21   | 18       | 19:11    | 68           | 7:9        | 213        |
| 42:6–7  | 27       | 19:14    | 68           | 7:9–10     | 212        |
| 42:18   | 80       | 20:11    | 575          | 7:13       | 83, 85,    |
| 51:9    | 16       | 20:13    | 575          |            | 86, 214,   |
| 52:5    | 28       | 20:40    | 56           |            | 524, 552   |
| 53:4–5  | 80       | 21:27    | 180          | 7:13–14    | 214, 357,  |
| 57:15   | 227      | 26:7     | 365          |            | 376, 425,  |
| 60      | 448, 595 | 28:13–19 | 45           |            | 550, 598   |
| 61:1–2  | 80       | 29:15    | 31           | 7:14       | 274, 363,  |
| 62:1    | 180      | 31:6     | 173          |            | 470, 524,  |
|         |          | 32:2     | 102          |            | 600        |
| **Jeremiah** | |     32:7 | 211–212      | 7:18       | 444, 519   |
| 3:17    | 22       | 34:4     | 131          | 7:22       | 213        |
| 4:23    | 17       | 34:20–31 | 24           | 7:25       | 544        |
| 5:21    | 112      | 34:23–24 | 24, 594,     | 7:27       | vii, 431,  |
| 5:31    | 226      |          | 608          |            | 519        |
| 6:9     | 146      | 36       | 326          | 7–12       | 426        |
| 8:13    | 146, 179 | 36:20–23 | 28           | 8:10       | 212        |
| 10:7    | 13, 364  | 36:25–27 | 222, 321     | 8:17       | 84, 426    |
| 10:10   | 14       | 36:26    | 233          | 8:19       | 426        |
| 12:7    | 160      | 37:24    | 613          | 9:19       | 159        |
| 16:19   | 612      | 37:24–25 | 24, 52,      | 9:24       | 593        |
| 17:9    | 120      |          | 608          | 9:24–27    | 46, 495,   |
| 17:12   | 189      | 39:29    | 321          |            | 544, 588   |
| 21:11–14| 25       | 40–44    | 96, 451,     | 9:25–26    | 54         |
| 22:2    | 23       |          | 458          | 9:26       | 426        |
| 23:5    | 608, 613 | 40–48    | 453          | 10         | 426        |
| 24:10   | 179      | 43:7     | 22           | 10:13      | 42         |
| 26:1    | 16       |          |              | 10:20      | 42         |
| 27:1    | 16       | **Daniel** |            | 10:21      | 42         |
| 28:1    | 16       | 1:2      | 176          | 11:27      | 426        |
| 30:9    | 608      | 2        | 63, 440,     | 11:35      | 426        |
| 31:15   | 62       |          | 495, 530,    | 11:36      | 14         |
| 31:31–34| 598      |          | 534, 550,    | 11:40      | 426        |
| 31:34   | 72       |          | 551, 552,    | 11:45      | 426        |

# Srcipture Index

| | | | | | |
|---|---|---|---|---|---|
| 12:1 | 42 | 4:3-4 | 518 | 14:6-21 | 523 |
| 12:1-3 | 328 | 4:4 | 65 | 14:8-9 | 59 |
| 12:2 | 406, 497 | 5:1 | 608 | 14:9-11 | 21 |
| 12:3 | 92 | 5:1-5 | 520 | 14:16 | 59 |
| 12:4 | 426 | 5:2 | 93, 462, 463, 519 | 14:16-17 | 15, 16 |
| 12:6 | 426 | | | | |
| 12:7 | 544 | 6:8 | 422 | **Malachi** | |
| 12:9 | 426 | 7:18-20 | 72 | 1:14 | 14 |
| 12:11-12 | 543 | 7:20 | 81 | 3:16 | 272 |
| 12:13 | 426 | | | 4:2 | 57, 301, 549, 598 |
| | | **Habakkuk** | | | |
| **Hosea** | | 1:2 | 493 | | |
| 1:9 | 159 | 1:6 | 151 | **NEW TESTAMENT** | |
| 1:10 | 42 | 1:6-11 | 29 | | |
| 1:11 | 62 | 2:3 | 493 | **Matthew** | |
| 2:23 | 159 | 2:4b | 383 | 1 | 557 |
| 3:4-5 | 56, 594 | 2:14 | 308, 518 | 1:1 | 83 |
| 3:5 | 24 | 3:3 | 518 | 1:1-21:9 | 607 |
| 4:1 | 422 | 3:11 | 212 | 1:15 | 607 |
| 5:15 | 180 | | | 1:17 | 546 |
| 6:11 | 181 | **Zephaniah** | | 1:20 | 83 |
| 9:10 | 146, 179 | 1:7-16 | 497 | 1:22-23 | 93 |
| 10:1 | 146 | 3:12 | 235 | 2 | 281 |
| 14:7 | 65 | 3:12-17 | 59 | 2:1-11 | 93 |
| | | 3:14-17 | 190 | 2:2 | 72 |
| **Joel** | | 3:14-20 | 527 | 2:11 | 124 |
| 1:7 | 146, 179 | 3:15 | 16, 18 | 2:15 | 62 |
| 2:14 | 145 | 3:17 | 400 | 2:18 | 62 |
| 2:28-32 | 321 | 3:18 | 236 | 3:2 | 7, 69, 70, 82, 255, 511 |
| 2:31 | 212, 343 | 3:19 | 236 | | |
| 3 | 448 | | | 3:4 | 119 |
| | | **Zechariah** | | 3:7-10 | 256 |
| **Amos** | | 1-6 | 426 | 3:8 | 362 |
| 1:6 | 132 | 2:8 | 397 | 3:11 | 322 |
| 3:7 | 254 | 3:1 | 36, 37 | 3:12 | 155, 235 |
| 5:26 | 41 | 3:1-2 | 37 | 3:17 | 336, 409 |
| 8:3 | 97 | 5:5-11 | 176 | 4:1 | 37 |
| 8:11-14 | 237 | 6:1 | 307, 593 | 4:1-11 | 39, 200 |
| 9:7 | 29 | 6:5 | 29 | 4:8-9 | 487 |
| 9:11 | 613 | 6:12-13 | 98 | 4:10 | 37, 375 |
| 9:11-12 | 57 | 7:9-10 | 422 | 4:15-16 | 93 |
| 9:11-15 | 57 | 8:20-23 | 521 | 4:17 | 7, 69, 351 |
| | | 8:23 | 431 | 4:18 | 269 |
| **Jonah** | | 9:9 | 84, 90, 94, 462, 463, 519 | 4:23 | 7, 256, 317, 338, 384, 590 |
| 1:4 | 129 | | | | |
| | | 9:9-10 | 608, 609 | 5 | 162, 226, 252 |
| **Micah** | | 9:10 | 595 | | |
| 1:2-3 | 29 | 10:9 | 495 | 5-7 | 79, 105, 590 |
| 2:3 | 198, 252 | 12:10 | 321, 526 | | |
| 3:8 | 388 | 13:1 | 72 | 5:1-2 | 113 |
| 4 | 448 | 14 | 435 | 5:3 | 162, 188, 199, 227, 235 |
| 4:1-2 | 431 | 14:1-5 | 523, 524, 526 | | |
| 4:1-4 | 59, 611 | | | | |
| 4:1-5 | 435 | 14:6 | 459 | | |

651

## THE ETERNAL KINGDOM: LIVING UNDER CHRIST

| | | | | | | |
|---|---|---|---|---|---|---|
| 5:3–9 | 330 | 8:31 | 257 | | | 110, 112, |
| 5:3–12 | 235 | 9:2 | 390, 407 | | | 116, 158, |
| 5:4 | 236 | 9:13 | 131 | | | 159, 160, |
| 5:5 | 236, 327, 518 | 9:22 | 384, 390, 407 | | | 161, 163, 172, 176, 212, 372 |
| 5:6 | 237 | 9:25 | 7 | 13:1 | | 160 |
| 5:7 | 237, 419 | 9:27 | 65 | 13:3 | | 115 |
| 5:8 | 82, 237, 238 | 9:28–29 | 390 | 13:10–17 | | 111 |
| | | 9:29 | 384 | 13:11 | | 254, |
| 5:9 | 162, 238 | 9:35 | 256, 384, 419, 590 | 407, | | 511 |
| 5:10 | 162 | | | | | |
| 5:10–12 | 283 | 9:36 | 81, 586 | 13:13–15 | | 113 |
| 5:11–12 | 239 | 10 | 106 | 13:14 | | 535 |
| 5:13–14 | 304 | 10:3 | 203 | 13:17 | | 113 |
| 5:14 | 549, 598 | 10:7 | 69 | 13:18 | | 308 |
| 5:16 | 330 | 10:7–8 | 73, 91, 256, 338 | 13:18–23 | | 114 |
| 5:17 | 441 | | | 13:19 | | 115 |
| 5:19–20 | 223, 257 | 10:18 | 110 | 13:24 | | 74, 106, 121 |
| 5:20 | 123 | 10:23 | 86, 218, 492 | 13:24–30 | | 74, 165, 491 |
| 5:22 | 155 | | | | | |
| 5:29–30 | 155 | 10:24–25 | 127, 181, 241, 242 | 13:27 | | 117, 145, 181, 242 |
| 5:34 | 69 | | | | | |
| 5:35 | 20, 90 | 10:25 | 117, 245 | | | |
| 5:45 | 29, 168 | 10:28 | 155 | 13:27–28 | | 127 |
| 6:1–5 | 224 | 10:39 | 258 | 13:29 | | 242 |
| 6:1–18 | 239 | 10:42 | 130 | 13:31 | | 74, 106, 121 |
| 6:7 | 110 | 11–12 | 159, 175 | | | |
| 6:10 | 90, 214 | 11:1 | 123 | 13:32 | | 123, 392 |
| 6:13b | 372 | 11:3 | 88 | 13:33 | | 74, 106, 121, 123, 172, 174 |
| 6:19–21 | 124 | 11:11–12 | 118 | | | |
| 6:30 | 385 | 11:12 | 123, 197 | | | |
| 6:33 | 69, 123, 385, 407, 503 | 11:12–13 | 196 | 13:34–35 | | 111 |
| | | 11:16 | 106 | 13:35 | | 299 |
| | | 11:20–24 | 119 | 13:36–43 | | 74, 114, 165, 491 |
| 7:11 | 80 | 11:25 | 130 | | | |
| 7:12 | 415 | 11:28 | 230 | 13:38 | | 123, 303, 314, 321, 389 |
| 7:13 | 123 | 12 | 73 | | | |
| 7:13–14 | 198 | 12:1–8 | 82 | | | |
| 7:21 | 123, 408 | 12:24 | 194 | 13:38a | | 169 |
| 7:21–23 | 165, 225, 348 | 12:25–26 | 36, 40, 47, 195 | 13:39 | | 39 |
| | | | | 13:39–40 | | 189, 446 |
| 7:22 | 343 | 12:26 | 573 | 13:39–43 | | 167 |
| 7:24 | 106 | 12:27 | 226 | 13:40 | | 92, 526 |
| 7:24–27 | 114 | 12:28 | 69, 70, 72, 74, 80, 91, 256, 294, 321, 384, 498, 500, 596 | 13:40–41 | | 214 |
| 7:26 | 106 | | | 13:41 | | 86, 225 |
| 7:28 | 105 | | | 13:42 | | 155 |
| 8 | 160 | | | 13:43 | | 90, 92, 407 |
| 8–9 | 79 | | | | | |
| 8:2–3 | 82 | | | | | |
| 8:5–13 | 388 | | | 13:44 | | 116 |
| 8:10 | 384 | | | 13:44–45 | | 74, 107, 121 |
| 8:11 | 511 | 12:29 | 46, 200 | | | |
| 8:12 | 155, 316 | 12:32 | 168, 446, 526, 535 | 13:46 | | 116 |
| 8:13 | 390 | | | 13:47 | | 74, 107, 121, 160, 177 |
| 8:17 | 80 | 12:35 | 124 | | | |
| 8:20 | 360 | 12:42 | 30, 611 | | | |
| | | 13 | 74, 106, | 13:47–50 | | 74 |

652

## Scripture Index

| | | | | | | | |
|---|---|---|---|---|---|---|---|
| 13:48 | 189 | 18:12 | 123 | | | 21:23 | 140 |
| 13:49 | 67 | 18:14 | 130 | | | 21:23–27 | 140 |
| 13:50 | 155 | 18:15–20 | 166, 271 | | | 21:28–32 | 139, 141 |
| 13:52 | 107, 117, 124, 145, 251 | 18:17 | 172, 299 | | | 21:31 | 69, 116 |
| | | 18:18–20 | 271 | | | 21:31–32 | 138 |
| | | 18:21–35 | 114, 132 | | | 21:32 | 351 |
| 13:53 | 106 | 18:23 | 74, 90, 107, 121, 172, 181, 242 | | | 21:33 | 117, 125, 145 |
| 13:58 | 390 | | | | | 21:33–41 | 144 |
| 14:14 | 419, 586 | | | | | 21:33–46 | 141 |
| 14:19 | 72 | | | | | | |
| 14:25 | 217 | 18:23–33 | 127 | | | 21:34 | 181 |
| 15:4 | 258 | 18:24 | 189, 242 | | | 21:34–36 | 242 |
| 15:14 | 119 | 18:25 | 125 | | | 21:35–39 | 142 |
| 15:14–16 | 301 | 18:32–33 | 416 | | | 21:37–39 | 146 |
| 15:15 | 119 | 18:34 | 124 | | | 21:41–43 | 144 |
| 15:15–20 | 114 | 18:35 | 135 | | | 21:42 | 117 |
| 15:17 | 120 | 19:12 | 257 | | | 21:42–43 | 257 |
| 15:22–28 | 389 | 19:14 | 299 | | | 21:43 | 147 |
| 15:28 | 384 | 19:16 | 406 | | | 21:45 | 112 |
| 15:30 | 419 | 19:19 | 258 | | | 22:1–14 | 110, 124, 141 |
| 15:36 | 72 | 19:20 | 247 | | | | |
| 16:6 | 175 | 19:21 | 124, 247 | | | 22:2 | 74, 107, 121 |
| 16:11–12 | 175 | 19:23–24 | 123, 228, 257, 511 | | | 22:3 | 181 |
| 16:16 | 175, 381 | | | | | 22:3–10 | 127, 242 |
| 16:17 | 200 | 19:24 | 69, 86 | | | 22:5–6 | 150 |
| 16:18 | 128, 148, 172, 289, 290, 292, 293, 298, 299 | 19:28 | 189, 204, 433 | | | 22:6 | 90, 142 |
| | | 19:29 | 327, 406 | | | 22:7 | 151, 152 |
| | | 19:30 | 162 | | | 22:8–10 | 153 |
| | | 20:1 | 74, 107, 117, 121, 136 | | | 22:9 | 124 |
| 16:19 | 172, 268, 289, 298 | | | | | 22:9–10 | 153 |
| | | | | | | 22:11–14 | 155 |
| 16:21 | 142, 205, 210 | 20:1–2 | 144 | | | 22:13 | 155, 316 |
| | | 20:1–16 | 110, 136, 556 | | | 22:15–22 | 141 |
| 16:24 | 205 | | | | | 22:16 | 90 |
| 16:25 | 258 | 20:2 | 134, 190 | | | 22:23–33 | 141 |
| 16:27–28 | 86 | 20:3 | 124 | | | 22:25–40 | 249 |
| 16:28 | 210, 215, 218, 492, 514, 524 | 20:6 | 556 | | | 22:34–40 | 142 |
| | | 20:9 | 556 | | | 22:41 | 142 |
| | | 20:10 | 144 | | | 22:42 | 607 |
| 17:1–8 | 214, 215 | 20:11 | 117, 145 | | | 22:42–45 | 57 |
| 17:2 | 301, 598 | 20:16 | 136 | | | 22:44 | 612 |
| 17:5 | 336 | 20:19 | 110 | | | 23:4 | 269 |
| 17:20 | 378, 392 | 20:25 | 40, 67, 110 | | | 23:8 | 88 |
| 17:22–23 | 210 | | | | | 23:10 | 88 |
| 17:23 | 142 | 20:27 | 181 | | | 23:23 | 421 |
| 18 | 106, 110, 298 | 20:28 | 249 | | | 23:23–24 | 341 |
| | | 20:34 | 419 | | | 23:29–31 | 146 |
| 18–23 | 257 | 21–22 | 141 | | | 23:33 | 155 |
| 18:3 | 123 | 21:1–9 | 94 | | | 23:34 | 146 |
| 18:3–4 | 172, 226 | 21:1–11 | 159 | | | 23:35 | 146 |
| 18:4–5 | 130 | 21:3 | 343 | | | 23:37 | 146, 150 |
| 18:6 | 130, 228 | 21:12–15 | 140 | | | 23:38–39 | 158 |
| 18:8–9 | 155 | 21:16 | 130 | | | 24 | 426 |
| 18:10 | 130, 375 | 21:18–20 | 179 | | | 24–25 | 107, 145, 590 |
| 18:10–14 | 130 | 21:21 | 378 | | | | |

653

| | | | | | | |
|---|---|---|---|---|---|---|
| 24:3 | 446 | 25:31 | 189, 213, 369 | 6:5 | 390 | |
| 24:4-28 | 219 | | | 7:17 | 119 | |
| 24:9 | 110 | 25:31-34 | 189 | 8:12 | 219 | |
| 24:14 | 7, 353, 494, 572, 590 | 25:31-46 | 179, 574 | 8:15 | 175 | |
| | | 25:33-36 | 143 | 9:1 | 372 | |
| | | 25:34 | 192, 327, 406 | 10:17 | 327 | |
| 24:15 | 515 | | | 10:29 | 92 | |
| 24:15-21 | 495 | 25:41 | 39, 477 | 10:31 | 62 | |
| 24:15-31 | 514, 515 | 25:46 | 406, 477 | 10:37-40 | 433 | |
| 24:24 | 582 | 26:22 | 165 | 10:46 | 247 | |
| 24:27 | 114, 486, 515, 526 | 26:25 | 165 | 10:52 | 390 | |
| | | 26:28 | 4 | 12:1-11 | 144 | |
| 24:27-30 | 212 | 26:29 | 90, 343, 517 | 13:14-27 | 514 | |
| 24:30 | 85, 297, 524, 526, 552 | | | 13:26 | 552 | |
| | | 26:35-46 | 206 | 13:28-29 | 179 | |
| | | 26:52 | 503 | 13:32 | 276, 558 | |
| 24:32 | 179 | 26:63-68 | 87 | 14:24 | 4 | |
| 24:32-33 | 179 | 26:64 | 85, 125, 552 | 14:25 | 347 | |
| 24:34 | 218, 219 | | | 14:62 | 87 | |
| 24:36 | 343 | 27:19 | 246 | 15:43 | 10, 404, 414 | |
| 24:37-39 | 212 | 27:29 | 303 | | | |
| 24:43 | 117, 145 | 27:57 | 414 | 16:16 | 256 | |
| 24:45 | 145, 181, 532 | 28:18 | 70, 78, 91, 163, 200, 208, 280, 294, 383, 484 | 16:17-18 | 279, 500 | |
| | | | | 16:19 | 343 | |
| 24:45-50 | 127 | | | 16:19-20 | 384 | |
| 24:45-51 | 181, 184, 242 | | | 16:20 | 582 | |
| 24:45-25:30 | 189 | | 386 | **Luke** | | |
| 24:48 | 210, 216, 491 | 28:18-19 | 251, 267, 279, 590 | 1:6 | 575 | |
| | | 28:18-20 | | 1:32 | 23, 83, 132, 212, 358, 369, 382, 500, 595 | |
| 24:49 | 188 | 28:19 | 243, 256, 352 | | | |
| 24:51 | 155 | | | | | |
| 25 | 145, 178, 330 | 28:19-20 | 241 | | | |
| | | 28:20 | 272 | 1:43 | 345 | |
| 25:1 | 106, 121, 124 | | | 1:68 | 29, 159 | |
| 25:1-13 | 124, 185 | **Mark** | | 1:68-75 | 12 | |
| 25:1-30 | 74, 127 | 1:4 | 256 | 2:1 | 279 | |
| 25:5 | 514 | 1:8 | 322 | 2:14 | 518 | |
| 25:9 | 188 | 1:15 | 1, 69, 351, 511, 590 | 2:25 | 10, 404 | |
| 25:14 | 116, 125, 144, 145, 162, 181 | | | 2:37 | 375 | |
| | | 1:22 | 79 | 2:42 | 97 | |
| | | 1:41 | 81, 419, 586 | 3:3 | 256 | |
| 25:14-30 | 242, 510 | | | 3:16 | 322 | |
| 25:15 | 175, 190 | 2:10 | 72 | 3:23-28 | 35 | |
| 25:19 | 490 | 3:1-6 | 80 | 4:5-6 | 43, 573 | |
| 25:20 | 165 | 3:24-26 | 195 | 4:14 | 234 | |
| 25:20-23 | 189 | 3:27 | 200 | 4:18-21 | 322 | |
| 25:22 | 165 | 4:3-9 | 163 | 5:8 | 235 | |
| 25:22-36 | 143 | 4:11 | 511 | 5:27-29 | 264 | |
| 25:24 | 165, 190 | 4:26-29 | 15, 116, 597 | 5:32 | 351 | |
| 25:25-28 | 193 | | | 6:12 | 255 | |
| 25:26 | 189 | 4:30-32 | 172 | 6:35 | 323 | |
| 25:27 | 191 | 4:39 | 129 | 6:36 | 419 | |
| 25:30 | 191, 316, 382 | 5:36 | 350, 384, 391 | 6:40 | 246 | |
| | | | | 7:13 | 81, 343, | |

*Scripture Index*

| | | | | | | | |
|---|---|---|---|---|---|---|---|
| | 419 | 13:25 | 187 | 22:20 | 4 | | |
| 7:13–15 | 586 | 13:29 | 511 | 22:29–30 | 204, 517 | | |
| 7:31–32 | 118 | 13:29–30 | 161 | 22:30 | 190 | | |
| 7:35 | 119 | 13:30 | 162 | 22:31 | 38, 348 | | |
| 7:47 | 133 | 14:16–24 | 149 | 22:36 | 503 | | |
| 7:50 | 390 | 14:21 | 153 | 22:53 | 199, 203, | | |
| 8:2 | 256 | 14:26 | 258 | | 593, 595 | | |
| 8:4–8 | 163 | 14:26–27 | 242, 346 | 22:69 | 297 | | |
| 8:5 | 115 | 14:27 | 260 | 22:70 | 87 | | |
| 8:12 | 39 | 14:28–33 | 262 | 23:39–43 | 330 | | |
| 8:16 | 598 | 14:33 | 262 | 23:42 | 200, 232 | | |
| 8:22–25 | 392 | 15:1–2 | 130 | 23:42–43 | 402, 432 | | |
| 8:41 | 388 | 15:3–7 | 130 | 23:50 | 414 | | |
| 8:50 | 350 | 15:7 | 131 | 24:3 | 343 | | |
| 9:2 | 338 | 15:11–32 | 140 | 24:26 | 88 | | |
| 9:11 | 338 | 15:18 | 69 | 24:31 | 113 | | |
| 9:23 | 260 | 15:25 | 119 | 24:40–41 | 89 | | |
| 9:27–36 | 381 | 16:1 | 38 | 24:44 | 117 | | |
| 9:28–36 | 206 | 16:8 | 168, 526, | 24:47 | 279, 352 | | |
| 9:52–53 | 277 | | 538 | 24:50–51 | 524, 526 | | |
| 10:8–9 | 73 | 16:10–13 | 510 | | | | |
| 10:9–10 | 384 | 16:14–18 | 422 | **John** | | | |
| 10:12 | 343 | 16:16 | 196, 197, | 1:1–3 | 600 | | |
| 10:18 | 45, 46, | | 263 | 1:12–13 | 233 | | |
| | 465 | 16:19–31 | 401, 414 | 1:26 | 75 | | |
| 10:23–24 | 113 | 17:4 | 132 | 1:33 | 322 | | |
| 10:24 | 116 | 17:12–17 | 82 | 1:41 | 53 | | |
| 10:25 | 327 | 17:19 | 390 | 3:1 | 40 | | |
| 10:25–37 | 248 | 17:21 | 74, 92, | 3:1–5 | 111 | | |
| 10:28 | 575 | | 294, 513, | 3:3 | 303 | | |
| 10:33 | 419 | | 596 | 3:3–5 | 211, 269 | | |
| 10:41 | 348 | 18:9–14 | 135 | 3:5 | 120, 136, | | |
| 11:2 | 214 | 18:11–12 | 137 | | 177, 222, | | |
| 11:13 | 80, 188 | 18:13 | 137 | | 233, 314, | | |
| 11:17–18 | 295 | 18:18–30 | 247 | | 316, 323, | | |
| 11:20 | 72, 76, | 18:24–25 | 414 | | 326, 513 | | |
| | 80, 498, | 18:30 | 168, 310, | 3:20 | 132 | | |
| | 596 | | 406, 535 | 3:35 | 409 | | |
| 11:21 | 200, 418 | 18:36 | 237 | 3:36 | 355, 497 | | |
| 11:22 | 201 | 18:43 | 247 | 4:1–30 | 351 | | |
| 11:42 | 412 | 19:11 | 214, 217 | 4:9 | 248, 277 | | |
| 12:4 | 254 | 19:12 | 109, 116, | 4:25–26 | 88 | | |
| 12:21 | 263 | | 125, 484 | 4:39 | 351 | | |
| 12:32 | 234, 358 | 19:14 | 152, 259 | 4:47–49 | 388 | | |
| 12:35 | 187 | 19:27 | 152 | 5:1–18 | 80 | | |
| 12:38 | 216, 491, | 19:29 | 92 | 5:25 | 466 | | |
| | 492 | 20:9–18 | 144 | 5:27 | 297 | | |
| 12:42 | 181, 532 | 20:16 | 138, 147, | 5:36 | 583 | | |
| 12:42–48 | 181 | | 148 | 6:60–66 | 164 | | |
| 12:45 | 514 | 20:34–35 | 446 | 6:70 | 39 | | |
| 13:6–9 | 179 | 20:36 | 162 | 7:7 | 259 | | |
| 13:18–19 | 172 | 20:42–43 | 612 | 7:38 | 295 | | |
| 13:19 | 173 | 21:24 | 495, 526, | 7:38–39 | 413 | | |
| 13:20–21 | 172, 174 | | 561 | 8:23 | 168 | | |
| 13:24 | 122, 198, | 21:29–31 | 179 | 8:31 | 246 | | |
| | 228, 229 | 21:31 | 70 | 8:33 | 223 | | |

655

| | | | | | | |
|---|---|---|---|---|---|---|
| 8:44 | 35 | | 383 | | | 195, 371, 372 |
| 8:48 | 248 | 1:7 | 519, 558 | | | |
| 9:4–5 | 549 | 1:7–8 | 202 | 11:28 | 280 | |
| 9:24 | 131 | 1:8 | 234, 388, 420 | 12:22 | 345 | |
| 10:10 | 510 | | | 13:19 | 329 | |
| 10:11 | 210 | 1:8b | 202 | 13:22 | 254 | |
| 10:27–28 | 353 | 1:11 | 515, 524, 526 | 13:28 | 152 | |
| 10:36–37 | 112 | | | 13:45 | 147 | |
| 11:1–44 | 80 | 1:15 | 268 | 14:9–10 | 391 | |
| 11:49–52 | 200 | 1:21 | 343 | 14:12 | 285 | |
| 12:25 | 258 | 2:22 | 583 | 14:17 | 29 | |
| 12:31 | 40 | 2:23 | 152 | 14:22 | 9, 199, 205, 231, 368, 377 |
| 12:41 | 382 | 2:25–31 | 62 | | | |
| 12:43 | 224 | 2:33 | 295 | | | |
| 13:7 | 116 | 2:34–35 | 612 | 15:2 | 272 | |
| 13:13 | 165 | 2:36 | 342 | 15:14–18 | 613 | |
| 13:14 | 88 | 2:38 | 351 | 15:16–17 | 57 | |
| 13:18 | 94 | 2:42 | 272 | 15:28–29 | 441 | |
| 13:34–35 | 248 | 3:14 | 246 | 16:7 | 250 | |
| 14:1 | 380 | 3:16 | 384 | 17:6–7 | 279 | |
| 14:3 | 403 | 3:17–26 | 25 | 17:28 | 332 | |
| 14:12 | 500 | 3:21 | 211 | 17:30–31 | 332 | |
| 14:15 | 267 | 4:13 | 269 | 17:31 | 526 | |
| 15:4 | 247 | 4:25–26 | 54 | 19:2 | 325 | |
| 15:5 | 250 | 4:26 | 64 | 20:24 | 353 | |
| 15:8 | 250 | 5:30–31 | 11 | 20:25 | 319 | |
| 15:10 | 249 | 5:32 | 355 | 20:28–30 | 166 | |
| 15:12–13 | 418 | 5:41 | 331 | 20:32 | 329 | |
| 15:14 | 253 | 6:3 | 203 | 20:36 | 255 | |
| 15:15b | 243 | 6:5 | 385 | 21:23–26 | 441 | |
| 15:24 | 150 | 7:9–38 | 61 | 22:8 | 346 | |
| 15:25 | 94 | 7:35 | 65 | 23:6 | 406 | |
| 16:8–11 | 385 | 7:38 | 294 | 23:6–8 | 175 | |
| 16:28 | 296 | 7:49 | 294 | 23:11 | 407 | |
| 16:33 | 386 | 7:51–52 | 150, 151 | 24:14 | 375 | |
| 17:3 | 292 | 7:51–53 | 151 | 24:15 | 404 | |
| 17:5 | 386 | 7:52 | 146 | 25:26 | 343 | |
| 17:11 | 305, 504 | 7:56 | 381 | 26:6–7 | 435 | |
| 17:24 | 65 | 7:59 | 184 | 26:18 | 36, 39, 198, 335, 595 |
| 18:5–6 | 203 | 8:5–8 | 277 | | | |
| 18:36 | 77, 136, 430, 504, 511 | 8:6 | 322 | | | |
| | | 8:9 | 226 | 28:20 | 435 | |
| | | 8:12 | 277, 322 | 28:23 | 319 | |
| 18:36–37 | 136 | 8:12–13 | 337 | 28:23 | 319 | |
| 18:37 | 86 | 8:27 | 97 | 28:28 | 579 | |
| 19:7 | 87 | 9:2 | 9 | 28:30–31 | 353 | |
| 19:15 | 152 | 9:4 | 348 | 28:31 | 319 | |
| 19:38 | 414 | 9:4–7 | 381 | | | |
| 20:28 | 345 | 9:8–9 | 586 | **Romans** | | |
| 21:22–23 | 491 | 9:10 | 381 | 1:5 | 344, 355 | |
| | | 9:20 | 9 | 1:8 | 345 | |
| | | 9:22 | 43 | 1:9–10 | 255 | |
| **Acts** | | 9:36 | 266 | 1:20 | 18 | |
| 1:6 | 79, 322, 432, 519 | 9:39b | 586 | 2:5 | 380 | |
| | | 10:34–35 | 574 | 2:6–10 | 574 | |
| 1:6–7 | 433 | 10:38 | 39, 187, | 2:12–16 | 574 | |
| 1:6–8 | 79, 337, | | | | | |

## Scripture Index

| | | | | | | | |
|---|---|---|---|---|---|---|---|
| 2:15 | 539 | | | 460 | | 2:6 | 42 |
| 2:16 | 343 | 11:26-36 | | 458 | | 2:7-8 | 360 |
| 2:17-24 | 28 | 11:27 | | 8 | | 2:8 | 40, 42 |
| 2:28-29 | 441 | 11:29 | | 442 | | 2:9 | 336 |
| 3:8 | 355 | 12 | | 416 | | 2:13 | 129 |
| 3:20 | 356 | 12:1 | | 375, 455 | | 2:14 | 259 |
| 3:27-28 | 356 | 12:4-5 | | 292 | | 2:16 | 250 |
| 3:28 | 232 | 12:6 | | 391 | | 3:1-3 | 227 |
| 4:4 | 136 | 12:18 | | 127, 340 | | 3:16 | 293, 296, |
| 4:13 | 325 | 13:1-7 | | 574 | | | 303, 321, |
| 4:17-18 | 410 | 13:4 | | 315 | | | 512 |
| 4:18 | 406, 418 | 13:9 | | 259 | | 4:1-2 | 532 |
| 5:1 | 232 | 13:11 | | 220 | | 4:7 | 190 |
| 5:2 | 405, 406 | 13:11-14 | | 127 | | 4:8 | 209 |
| 5:3-4 | 368 | 13:12 | | 187, 301, | | 4:19-20 | 336 |
| 5:5 | 248, 413, | | | 598 | | 4:20 | 8, 79, |
| | 421 | 13:12-14 | | 182 | | | 202, 278, |
| 5:8 | 131, 208 | 14 | | 126, 127, | | | 372, 383, |
| 5:14 | 60 | | | 416 | | | 387, 420 |
| 5:19 | 131 | 14:4-9 | | 345 | | 5:5 | 39 |
| 6:14 | 535 | 14:8-9 | | 353 | | 5:6 | 77 |
| 6:17 | 344 | 14:11 | | 303 | | 5:6-7 | 175 |
| 6:22 | 251 | 14:16-19 | | 475 | | 5:11 | 303 |
| 8:1-11 | 233 | 14:17 | | 8, 149, | | 5:13 | 167 |
| 8:2 | 250 | | | 190, 236, | | 6:2 | 331, 485 |
| 8:9 | 250, 323 | | | 304, 321, | | 6:9 | 330 |
| 8:11 | 499 | | | 323, 338, | | 6:9-10 | 328, 360 |
| 8:14 | 323, 420 | | | 503, 516, | | 6:19 | 233, 323, |
| 8:16 | 584 | | | 595 | | | 324 |
| 8:17 | 204, 237, | 14:17-18 | | 338 | | 7:5 | 39 |
| | 261, 324, | 14:18 | | 341 | | 7:14 | 299 |
| | 325, 360, | 15:4 | | 60 | | 7:29 | 220, 229 |
| | 368 | 15:7 | | 418 | | 7:30-31 | 228 |
| 8:19 | 324, 405 | 15:13 | | 233 | | 7:31 | 264 |
| 8:20 | 43, 44 | 15:14 | | 60 | | 7:39 | 331 |
| 8:23 | 322, 325, | 15:18 | | 344, 355 | | 8:3 | 187 |
| | 500 | 15:18-19 | | 337, 585 | | 9:2 | 244, 267, |
| 8:28 | 336, 361 | 15:19 | | 233 | | | 351, 381, |
| 8:34 | 255 | 15:30 | | 412 | | | 415 |
| 8:37 | 207 | 15:33 | | 238 | | 9:17 | 532 |
| 8:38-29 | 34 | 16:2 | | 331 | | 9:21 | 244, 267, |
| 9:4 | 8, 375 | 16:19 | | 344 | | | 351, 415 |
| 9:6 | 441 | 16:20 | | 220 | | 10:26 | 308 |
| 10:1 | 255 | 16:23 | | 532 | | 11:1 | 266, 346 |
| 10:4 | 245 | 16:26 | | 344, 355 | | 11:25 | 8 |
| 10:5 | 575 | | | | | 11:26-27 | 380 |
| 10:9-10 | 165, 343 | **1 Corinthians** | | | | 12:3 | 165, 344 |
| 10:16 | 344, 355 | 1:4 | | 345 | | 12:9 | 378, 392 |
| 11 | 449, 450 | 1:7 | | 380, 405 | | 12:12-13 | 294 |
| 11:5 | 154, 160, | 1:8 | | 343 | | 12:12-27 | 292 |
| | 575 | 1:20 | | 168, 526, | | 13:13 | 378, 379 |
| 11:17 | 441 | | | 535 | | 15:12 | 477 |
| 11:25 | 562, 573 | 1:29 | | 235 | | 15:13 | 478 |
| 11:25-27 | 598 | 2:4 | | 234, 388, | | 15:23-28 | 333 |
| 11:26 | 456 | | | 585 | | 15:24 | 246 |
| 11:26-27 | 449, 451, | 2:4-5 | | 585 | | 15:24-28 | 49, 569, |

657

# THE ETERNAL KINGDOM: LIVING UNDER CHRIST

| | | | | | | |
|---|---|---|---|---|---|---|
| | 599, 600 | 3:12 | 575 | 2:20–22 | 293, 303 |
| 15:25 | 295 | 3:15 | 9 | 2:22 | 296, 321, |
| 15:25–28 | 49 | 3:23–4:7 | 535 | | 512 |
| 15:27 | 89 | 4:2 | 532 | 3:2 | 532 |
| 15:28 | 163 | 4:5–6 | 323 | 3:11 | 290 |
| 15:45 | 30, 48, | 4:6 | 250, 324 | 3:16–19 | 250 |
| | 53, 89 | 4:7 | 360 | 4:1 | 331 |
| 15:45–47 | 593 | 4:9 | 287 | 4:4–6 | 348 |
| 15:47 | 48, 53 | 4:19 | 423 | 4:5 | 581 |
| 15:48–49 | 84 | 4:24 | 535 | 4:11–16 | 272 |
| 15:50–55 | 333 | 4:24–31 | 535 | 4:13 | xxv |
| 15:51–52 | 220 | 4:25–26 | 374 | 4:14 | 227 |
| 15:53 | 499 | 4:26 | 435 | 4:20 | 504 |
| 16:22 | 336 | 5:5 | 405 | 4:24 | 84 |
| | | 5:6 | 232, 354 | 4:26–27 | 39 |
| **2 Corinthians** | | 5:14 | 259 | 4:32 | 134 |
| 1:3 | 235 | 5:16–18 | 116, 233, | 4:32–5:2 | 134 |
| 1:14 | 343 | | 250 | 5:2 | 249, 258, |
| 1:20–22 | 325 | 5:19–21 | 328 | | 412, 421 |
| 1:21–22 | 187, 323 | 5:20 | 340 | 5:5 | 9, 231, |
| 1:22 | 372 | 5:21 | 9, 231, | | 329, 422 |
| 4:4 | 42, 168, | | 360 | 5:8 | 549 |
| | 526, 535, | 5:22 | 356 | 5:8–10 | 598 |
| | 593 | 5:22–23 | 419 | 5:9 | 251 |
| 4:5 | 353 | 5:24 | 260 | 5:18 | 188, 233, |
| 4:13 | 85 | 6:2 | 244, 267, | | 422 |
| 4:18–5:8 | 401 | | 351, 415, | 5:18–20 | 420 |
| 5:1–2 | 490 | 6:10 | 416 | 5:25 | 258 |
| 5:1–10 | 220 | 6:14 | 261 | 6:2 | 258 |
| 5:15 | 346 | 6:16 | 449 | 6:4 | 299 |
| 5:21 | 177 | | | 6:11 | 39, 393 |
| 6:17–18 | 324 | **Ephesians** | | 6:11–12 | 40 |
| 8:9 | 122 | 1:3–14 | 510 | 6:12 | 283, 286 |
| 9:10 | 251 | 1:9 | 579 | 6:17 | 503 |
| 11:14 | 39, 166, | 1:9–11 | 325 | 6:18 | 420 |
| | 226 | 1:10 | 575 | 6:24 | 336, 361 |
| 11:15 | 138 | 1:10–14 | 325 | | |
| 11:26 | 303 | 1:13–14 | 277 | **Philippians** | |
| 12:7 | 40 | 1:15–17 | 255 | 1:3 | 345 |
| 12:9 | 200 | 1:18 | 111, 113 | 1:3–5 | 255 |
| 13:4 | 199 | 1:20 | 612 | 1:6 | 343 |
| 13:5 | 355 | 1:20–21 | 196, 230 | 1:11 | 251 |
| 13:7 | 255 | 1:20–23 | 297 | 1:23 | 220, 401, |
| | | 1:20–2:6 | 293 | | 490 |
| **Galatians** | | 1:21 | 34, 310, | 1:27 | 331 |
| 1:4 | 168, 249, | | 355, 526, | 2:5 | 246 |
| | 360, 526, | | 535 | 2:6–11 | 206 |
| | 535 | 1:22 | 89, 335 | 2:9–11 | 342 |
| 1:6–9 | 350 | 2:2 | 41, 43, | 2:10 | 303 |
| 2:7–8 | 268 | | 168, 296, | 2:15 | 187, 308, |
| 2:9 | 380 | | 321, 355, | | 598 |
| 2:15 | 131 | | 512, 593 | 2:16 | 301 |
| 2:16 | 232 | 2:5–6 | 466 | 2:17 | 145 |
| 2:20 | 250, 412 | 2:6 | 500 | 2:27 | 586 |
| 3:7 | 537 | 2:8–10 | 356 | 3:3 | 250, 375 |
| | | 2:12 | 9 | 3:8 | 345 |

# Scripture Index

| | | | | | |
|---|---|---|---|---|---|
| 3:10–11 | 205, 261 | 2:12 | 9, 231, 234, 330, 334 | 4:8 | 343 |
| 3:19 | 229, 263 | | | 4:10 | 168, 353, 526 |
| 3:20–21 | 405, 499, 533 | 2:14–15 | 150, 152 | 4:18 | 342 |
| | | 2:15 | 146 | | |
| 3:21 | 324 | 2:18 | 39 | **Titus** | |
| 4:4 | 127 | 3:11 | 370 | 1:2 | 406 |
| 4:5 | 220, 492 | 4:13–18 | 333, 572 | 1:7 | 532 |
| 4:7 | 518 | 4:15 | 220 | 2:12 | 168, 526, 535 |
| 4:9 | 238 | 4:15–17 | 347 | | |
| 4:19 | 379, 510 | 4:17 | 403, 552 | 2:13 | 380, 405 |
| | | 5:2 | 343 | 2:14 | 249 |
| | | 5:4 | 493 | 3:3 | 355 |
| **Colossians** | | 5:4–5 | 187, 549 | 3:7 | 360, 406 |
| 1:3 | 255 | 5:23 | 238 | | |
| 1:5 | 405 | | | | |
| 1:12–13 | 329 | **2 Thessalonians** | | **Philemon** | |
| 1:13 | 9, 47, 198, 234, 259, 361, 409, 595 | 1:5 | 9, 231 | 1:4 | 255, 345 |
| | | 1:7–10 | 515 | | |
| | | 1:8 | 353 | **Hebrews** | |
| | | 2:8 | 380 | 1:1–3 | 600 |
| 1:15–17 | 600 | | | 1:2 | 146, 446 |
| 1:16 | 34, 45, 196, 281, 335 | **1 Timothy** | | 1:3 | 15, 25, 213 |
| | | 1:9 | 131, 168 | | |
| 1:17 | 15, 25 | 1:15 | 353 | 1:5 | 65, 88 |
| 1:18 | 295 | 1:17 | 13, 364 | 1:8–9 | 23 |
| 1:25 | 532 | 1:20 | 39 | 1:10–12 | 62 |
| 1:26–27 | 579 | 2:4 | 572 | 1:13 | 612 |
| 1:27 | 405 | 2:6 | 249 | 1:14 | 328, 360 |
| 2:6 | 355 | 3:7 | 39 | 2:3–4 | 582 |
| 2:8 | 129 | 4:4–5 | 229 | 2:5 | 83, 90, 310 |
| 2:11–12 | 581 | 6:6–10 | 229 | | |
| 2:12 | 466 | 6:13–15 | 200 | 2:5–9 | 370, 601 |
| 2:15 | 36, 195 | 6:14 | 380 | | |
| 3:1–3 | 126 | 6:15 | 365 | 2:6–8 | 62 |
| 3:2 | 229, 300 | 6:17 | 13, 168, 526 | 2:6–9 | 90 |
| 3:3 | 116, 595 | | | 2:7 | 34 |
| 3:9–11 | 84 | 6:17–19 | 263 | 2:8 | 89, 500 |
| 3:12–14 | 419 | | | 2:14 | 36, 42, 46, 47, 199 |
| 3:12–17 | 251 | **2 Timothy** | | | |
| 3:13 | 134 | 1:3 | 255 | 2:14–15 | 195 |
| 3:15 | 518 | 1:5 | 362 | 2:17 | 367 |
| 3:18–20 | 301 | 1:12 | 343 | 2:18 | 255 |
| 3:19 | 258 | 2:11–12 | 205 | 3:1 | 235 |
| 3:20 | 300 | 2:12 | 261 | 4:6 | 355 |
| 3:24 | 346 | 2:18 | 499 | 4:12 | 503 |
| 4:1 | 331 | 2:26 | 39 | 5:6 | 97, 612 |
| 4:11 | 334 | 3:8 | 166 | 5:10 | 97, 612 |
| | | 3:10–11 | 267 | 5:12–13 | 227 |
| | | 3:12 | 199 | 6:1 | 351 |
| **1 Thessalonians** | | 3:15 | 117 | 6:5 | 79, 202, 276, 278, 310, 323, 337, 387, |
| 1:2 | 255 | 4:1 | 9, 168, 380 | | |
| 1:5 | 202, 234, 388 | | | | |
| | | 4:1–2 | 9 | | |
| 1:6 | 346 | 4:6 | 145, 220 | | |
| 1:10 | 405 | | | | |

659

| | | | | | | | |
|---|---|---|---|---|---|---|---|
| | | 1:8–9 | 233 | 3:5 | 177 | | |
| | 500, 526, 535 | 1:13 | 405 | 3:8 | 36, 39, 46, 195 | | |
| 6:17 | 574 | 2:9 | 36, 47, 198, 335, 366, 485 | 3:10 | 35, 223 | | |
| 7:1–3 | 61 | | | 3:11–12 | 35 | | |
| 7:1–4a | 63 | | | 3:16 | 418 | | |
| 7:2 | 360 | 2:21 | 346 | 4:8 | 237 | | |
| 9:1 | 375 | 2:22 | 211 | 4:16 | 271 | | |
| 9:6 | 375 | 3:14 | 239 | 4:19 | 412, 415 | | |
| 9:9 | 375 | 3:15 | 165, 352 | 4:20–21 | 336, 361, 416 | | |
| 10:12–13 | 404 | 3:18 | 246 | | | | |
| 10:37 | 220, 492 | 3:21 | 60 | | | | |
| 11:1 | 380 | 3:21–22 | 196 | 5:3 | 411 | | |
| 11:5 | 394 | 3:22 | 212 | 5:4 | 386 | | |
| 11:6 | 574 | 4:6 | 326 | 5:20 | 292 | | |
| 11:8 | 329 | 4:7 | 220, 492 | | | | |
| 11:10 | 329 | 4:10 | 532 | **2 John** | | | |
| 12:1 | 228 | 4:13 | 204, 262 | 1:6 | 411 | | |
| 12:1–2 | 262 | 4:16 | 266 | | | | |
| 12:2 | 198, 202 | 4:18 | 168 | **3 John** | | | |
| 12:5 | 206 | 5:1–4 | 166 | 1:2 | 510 | | |
| 12:7 | 324 | 5:3 | 182 | 1:6 | 331 | | |
| 12:11 | 251 | 5:8 | 39, 226 | | | | |
| 12:14 | 238, 340 | | | | | | |
| 12:23 | 290 | **2 Peter** | | **Jude** | | | |
| 12:28 | 409 | 1:10–11 | 361 | 1:14 | 95 | | |
| 12:28–29 | 357 | 1:11 | vii, 511 | 1:15 | 131 | | |
| | | 1:16–18 | 215 | 1:20 | 420 | | |
| **James** | | 1:16–19 | 381 | | | | |
| 1:17 | 361, 537 | 1:19 | 217, 301, 598 | **Revelation** | | | |
| 2:1 | 360 | | | 1:5 | 67 | | |
| 2:5 | 336, 359, 361, 377 | 2:12 | 179 | 1:5–6 | 365 | | |
| | | 3:2 | 267 | 1:8 | 371, 373 | | |
| 2:8 | 259, 267, 286, 361, 415 | 3:3 | 184 | 1:9 | 205, 367 | | |
| | | 3:3–4 | 221, 492, 493 | 2–3 | 561 | | |
| 2:8–13 | 409 | 3:8 | 468, 553, 554 | 3:10 | 280 | | |
| 2:17 | 232, 330 | | | 4:7 | 102 | | |
| 2:19 | 354 | 3:9 | 572 | 4:8 | 374 | | |
| 2:23 | 254 | 3:10 | 343 | 7 | 449 | | |
| 4:7 | 39 | 3:12 | 405, 489, 494 | 7:4 | 449 | | |
| 4:8 | 131 | | | 11:2 | 544 | | |
| 5:6 | 246 | 3:13 | 155, 576 | 11:8 | 371 | | |
| 5:8–9 | 220 | 3:15–16 | 356 | 11:15 | 599 | | |
| 5:15 | 384 | 3:18 | 554, 556, 557 | 11:15–18 | 369, 372 | | |
| 5:15–16 | 133 | | | 11:17 | 370 | | |
| | | | | 12 | 444 | | |
| **1 Peter** | | **1 John** | | 12:6 | 495 | | |
| 1:1 | 380 | 1:5 | 235, 261 | 12:7–18 | 46 | | |
| 1:2 | 380 | 1:5–7 | 187 | 12:9 | 279 | | |
| 1:3–5 | 405 | 1:9 | 133 | 12:10 | 371, 372, 529 | | |
| 1:3–13 | 597 | 2:1 | 246 | | | | |
| 1:4 | 125, 324 | 2:3–4 | 351 | 13:1 | 495 | | |
| | | 2:15–17 | 229 | 13:18 | 434 | | |
| 1:5–9 | 379 | 2:18 | 556 | 14:6–7 | 28 | | |
| 1:7 | 380 | 3:2–3 | 238 | 15:3 | 13 | | |
| | | | | 17–18 | 287 | | |

| | |
|---|---|
| 17:10–14 | 565 |
| 17:11 | 534 |
| 18:2 | 173 |
| 19–20 | 521, 522 |
| 19:6 | 372, 373 |
| 19:16 | 367 |
| 20:1–6 | 367, 447, 465, 483, 560, 599, 605, 662 |
| 20:1–7 | 358, 453, 464 |
| 20:4 | 464 |
| 20:4–6 | 367, 465 |
| 20:14 | 599 |
| 21:9 | 374 |
| 22:3–5 | 374, 375 |
| 22:5 | 470 |

# Subject Index

## A

Aalders, Gerhard C
 65, 398, 615
Aaron 104, 501, 502, 619
Abraham 12, 54, 60, 61, 63, 81, 161, 223, 254, 293, 300, 324, 348, 389, 406, 450, 537, 540, 541, 546, 554, 557, 562, 577, 590
Abram 609
Adam 2, 17, 24, 25, 30, 31, 32, 33, 35, 43, 44, 47, 48, 49, 52, 53, 55, 60, 78, 89, 90, 370, 448, 450, 525, 539, 540, 541, 554, 557, 562, 573, 574, 577, 592, 593, 598, 600, 601, 603, 608
Adamek, Josef 430, 550, 615
Adams, Jay E. 497, 615
Adonai 20, 22, 57, 198, 213, 253, 370, 371, 373
Adversaries 222, 223, 224, 226, 229, 230, 236, 237, 238, 239, 281, 282
Allis, Oswald T. 469, 615
Ambrose 439, 445, 467, 555
Amillennialism 168, 184, 469, 485, 539
Anabaptists 170, 171, 302, 435
Ancient of Days 84, 212, 213, 371, 425, 598
Angels 14, 15, 17, 34, 39, 46, 47, 87, 130, 151, 161, 166, 167, 169, 178, 189, 192, 196, 210, 212, 375, 396, 426, 515, 518, 558, 592, 600, 601
Anglican 429, 459
Anointed One 86, 90, 91, 342, 372, 373, 594
Antichrist 73, 516, 534, 546, 564, 565, 566, 604, 622
Antiquity 534
Apocalypse 452, 468, 477, 641
Peter vii, xiv, xv, xvii, 7, 8, 38, 88, 119, 124, 132, 152, 195, 205, 206, 215, 217, 219, 220, 221, 233, 239, 266, 268, 269, 270,

663

|  |  |  |  |
|---|---|---|---|
| | 271, 273, 289, 292, 295, 298, 332, 342, 345, 355, 361, 379, 380, 381, 387, 388, 405, 440, 443, 447, 451, 452, 472, 492, 493, 503, 511, 553, 554, 563, 583, 586, 597, 617 | | 140, 141, 142, 146, 182, 190, 196, 201, 202, 208, 225, 251, 267, 268, 269, 270, 271, 274, 276, 279, 280, 295, 297, 299, 333, 334, 355, 364, 368, 371, 372, 383, 386, 430, 484, 496, 497, 529, 563, 569, 577, 584, 599, 612 | | 616, 618 |
| Apostles | xv, 186, 271, 628 | | | Basileology | 2, 5, 6, 30, 426, 433, 435, 448, 455, 486, 487, 488, 489, 490, 497, 499, 500, 501, 505, 506, 509, 510, 524, 565, 573, 574, 581, 591 |
| Apostolic Fathers | 469 | | | Bass, Charlie B. | 530, 616 |
| Asaph | 396, 399 | | | Bauckham, Richard | 401, 616 |
| Ascension | 70, 71, 116, 145, 150, 154, 191, 210, 215, 276, 295, 343, 381, 386, 394, 506, 551, 552, 572, 595 | | | Bavinck, Herman | 306, 307, 312, 431, 432, 540, 541, 616 |
| | | **B** | | Beatitudes | 131, 227, 235, 237, 239 |
| | | Baarslag, Dirk J. | 103, 615 | Beck, Hans-Georg | 604, 616, 641 |
| | | Babylon | 14, 45, 173, 176, 185, 399, 462 | Beelzebul | 36, 159, 193, 194 |
| Asia Minor | 286, 469 | Babylonian Captivity | 461, 462, 557 | Belgic Confession | 172, 292, 294, 448 |
| Athanasius | 439 | Bahnsen, Greg L. | 507, 615 | Berger, Klaus | 290, 616 |
| Atonement | 411, 457, 593 | Baptism | xxiv, 60, 243, 256, 270, 271, 287, 339, 348, 349, 579, 580, 581 | Berkhof, Hendrikus | 493 |
| Augsburg Confession | 429, 477 | | | Berkhof, Louis | 313, 539 |
| Augustine | xviii, xxi, 98, 170, 171, 302, 426, 439, 440, 445, 446, 447, 448, 450, 468, 469, 470, 472, 473, 539, 550, 555, 557, 558, 559, 615 | | | Berkouwer, Gerrit C. | 209, 210, 218, 411, 487, 491, 492, 493, 498, 499, 500, 572, 617 |
| | | Baptist theology | 243 | | |
| | | Barclay, William | 103, 113, 615 | | |
| | | Barrett, Charles K. | 337, 616 | Betz, Otto | 80, 617 |
| | | Barth, Karl | 493, 501, 518 | Beza, Theodore | 450, 451 |
| Authority | 2, 12, 17, 32, 39, 43, 70, 72, 77, 78, 84, 90, 91, 125, | Barth, Markus | 215, 493, 501, 518, | Bible | 1, 3, 13, 29, 38, 43, 63, 83, 131, 232, |

664

236, 285, 293, 297, 395, 402, 403, 409, 412, 418, 429, 442, 448, 455, 466, 479, 498, 511, 538, 548, 550, 554, 573, 605, 617, 619, 620, 621, 624, 626, 627, 629, 630, 631, 639, 645
Biblical Canon
  582
Bivin, David
  268, 617
Blackburn, John S.
  115, 617
Blaising, Craig A.
  530, 587, 617
Bloch, Ernst
  401, 502, 617, 631
Bloesch, Donald G.
  464, 617
Blomberg, Craig L.
  466, 587, 617
Blum, Edwin A.
  617
Blum, Günther G.
  467
Bock, Darrell L.
  71, 215, 219, 530, 587, 596, 617
Bockmuehl, Markus
  218, 491, 618
Boettner, Loraine
  464, 618
Boff, Leonardo
  503, 618
Boice, James M.
  344, 618
Bonhoeffer, Dietrich
  356, 618, 629

Booth, Abraham E.
  549, 573, 618
Borg, Marcus J.
  505, 618
Bornkamm, Günther
  79, 618
Bouma, Clarence
  10, 618
Brakel, Wilhelmus à
  xviii, 452, 454, 455, 456, 457, 461, 480, 482, 540, 618
Bratt, James D.
  307, 618
Bray, John L.
  218, 513, 618
Bright   3, 6, 618
Brouwer, C  619
Brower, K. E.
  619
Brown, R.E.  619
Bruce, A. B.  619
Bruce, F.F.  619
Bryan   219, 619
Bultmann, R.
  xix, 104, 501, 502, 619
Byzantine Empire
  604, 605, 640

## C

Caesaropapism
  437
Caiaphas  86, 200, 213
Calvinist Theologians
  451, 460
Calvin, John
  170, 171, 184, 302, 311, 447, 448, 449, 450, 460, 477, 478, 544, 551, 552, 619
Carson, Don
  175, 219

Cessationism
  xxi, 581, 583, 586
Charismatic Basileology
  506
Chiastic Structure
  599
Christianity
  126, 266, 267, 339, 427, 436, 439, 501, 533, 547, 551, 552, 564, 571, 605, 620, 626, 627, 637
Christianization
  443, 564
Christian Reconstructionism
  472, 507, 508
Church   6, 26, 46, 86, 106, 133, 148, 154, 158, 166, 167, 170, 171, 172, 173, 175, 176, 183, 184, 185, 186, 243, 264, 271, 272, 273, 289, 290, 291, 292, 293, 294, 295, 296, 297, 298, 299, 300, 301, 302, 303, 304, 305, 306, 307, 308, 310, 311, 312, 313, 314, 315, 316, 320, 321, 335, 339, 341, 342, 347, 349, 374, 378, 406, 413,

416, 421, 426, 428, 436, 437, 438, 440, 441, 442, 443, 445, 446, 447, 448, 449, 450, 453, 454, 455, 456, 457, 458, 462, 465, 466, 468, 469, 471, 472, 473, 476, 477, 478, 481, 482, 483, 486, 487, 491, 493, 497, 505, 507, 511, 512, 513, 514, 517, 519, 525, 526, 530, 534, 536, 539, 540, 546, 547, 549, 552, 555, 556, 559, 560, 561, 562, 563, 564, 565, 570, 571, 572, 575, 576, 578, 579, 580, 581, 582, 587, 588, 589, 590,

Church Fathers
   466
church history
   183, 185, 186, 302, 450, 477, 478, 530, 540, 549, 552, 559, 561, 563, 576, 585

Classical Dispensationalism
   xxi, 570

Cocceius, Johannes
   457, 459, 461, 482, 559

Constantine
   183, 436, 437, 438, 440, 443, 444, 467, 547, 563, 578

Constantinople
   443, 496, 527, 563, 605

Covenant 4, 5, 7, 8, 12, 23, 81, 96, 98, 180, 243, 339, 340, 358, 366, 458, 520, 536, 539, 560, 598, 609

Cranmer, Thomas
   479

Cromwell, Oliver
   433

# D

Daniel vii, 9, 54, 69, 83, 84, 85, 90, 92, 114, 212, 213, 214, 274, 371, 425, 426, 428, 431, 440, 444, 447, 469, 470, 481, 483, 495, 524, 534, 543, 544, 550, 551, 552, 563, 588, 598, 603

Darby, John N.
   xxi, 99, 484, 532, 570, 586

David 2, 12, 21, 22, 23, 24, 25, 30, 51, 52, 53, 54, 55, 56, 57, 58, 61, 64, 65, 68, 78, 81, 83, 90, 93, 94, 96, 126, 127, 142, 155, 200, 206, 212, 252, 253, 254, 255, 274, 275, 282, 347, 358, 369, 380, 381, 382, 427, 451, 457, 462, 463, 464, 480, 482, 500, 519, 537, 545, 557, 571, 577, 594, 595, 602, 603, 607, 608, 609, 611, 612, 613

Davidic Government
   594

Davidic kings
   2, 90

Day of Pentecost
   8, 152, 215, 289, 293, 337, 342, 562, 579, 588

Disciples ix, xiv, xv, xxxi, 242, 243, 245, 247, 249, 250, 251, 253, 255, 257, 259, 261, 263, 264, 265, 267, 269, 271, 273, 275, 277, 279, 281, 283, 285,

Dispensationalism
   25, 452,

## Subject Index

530, 531, 532, 533, 537, 538, 570, 573, 576, 578, 579, 581, 586, 587, 588, 589, 590, 591
Dominion theology 471, 472, 506, 508
Dooyeweerd, Herman 344
Dostoyevsky, Fyodor M. 184

## E

Edersheim, Alfred 272, 622
Efird, James M. 570, 571, 622
Eggenberg, Theodor 311, 315, 622
Ekklesia 441, 536, 591
Elijah 198, 392, 393, 394, 541, 544, 545, 584, 585
Enlightenment 486, 488, 547
Erickson, Millard J. 218, 314, 464, 487, 530, 622
Erlemann, Kurt 104, 623
Eschaton 5, 48, 332, 522, 557
Eternity 5, 12, 24, 64, 155, 296, 297, 299, 318, 334, 373, 386, 396, 456, 501, 518, 554, 556, 557, 576, 592, 603

Evangelical Basileology 486
Evangelical Kingdom Theology 471, 508
Eve 17, 31, 32, 33, 35, 43, 47, 78, 525, 573, 593
Ezra 68, 159, 168, 365, 397, 427, 430

## F

Fairbairn, Patrick 60, 466, 530, 623
Faith xxv, 4, 14, 110, 160, 161, 183, 204, 220, 229, 231, 232, 233, 234, 246, 261, 267, 270, 283, 284, 285, 292, 329, 330, 331, 336, 344, 345, 346, 348, 349, 350, 351, 352, 353, 354, 355, 356, 359, 360, 361, 362, 377, 378, 379, 380, 381, 383, 385, 386, 387, 388, 389, 390, 391, 392, 393, 395, 406, 408, 413, 414, 416, 421, 438, 439, 468, 473, 476, 512, 535, 578, 585

Fee, Gordon D. 336, 485, 623
Feinberg, C. L. 623
Feinberg, J. S. 623
Fig tree 59, 107, 109, 179, 180, 181, 610, 611
Forgiveness 72, 108, 132, 133, 135, 138, 269, 270, 279, 280, 298, 335, 352, 390, 419, 499, 510

## G

Garden of Eden 33, 397
Geneva Study Bible 395
Gentiles 27, 28, 40, 42, 67, 93, 102, 108, 109, 110, 134, 137, 138, 141, 144, 148, 149, 154, 157, 161, 162, 223, 243, 244, 270, 337, 389, 441, 448, 449, 455, 456, 457, 458, 459, 465, 483, 495, 515, 516, 526, 561, 562, 573, 579, 580, 585, 598, 613
Gideon 19, 176
Gill, John 44, 68, 395, 396, 397, 406
Gospel xxiv, xxv,

667

Grace  1, 7, 28,
29, 77,
106, 110,
122, 135,
194, 208,
215, 218,
230, 232,
265, 270,
277, 278,
279, 281,
282, 283,
284, 305,
317, 318,
320, 331,
332, 337,
338, 344,
345, 346,
349, 350,
351, 353,
354, 356,
357, 384,
419, 494,
509, 515,
546, 572,
574, 575,
580, 582,
590

Grace 26, 99,
108, 110,
122, 134,
135, 136,
137, 138,
139, 151,
153, 160,
162, 190,
192, 194,
221, 230,
232, 234,
247, 278,
279, 293,
317, 331,
332, 339,
344, 351,
353, 354,
355, 356,
357, 378,
387, 391,
392, 531,
533, 535,
536, 537,
539, 549,
556, 559,
560, 575,
597, 601

Great Commission
279, 352,
590

Great Tribulation
513, 514,
572, 588,
620, 627

Greco-Roman culture
534

Grenz, Stanley J.
464, 530,
624

## H

Halakhah 242, 266,
267, 268,
269, 271,
272, 273

Heidelberg Catechism
xxviii, 71,
208, 292,
320, 350,
448, 635

Herod 72, 73, 281
Herodians 175
Heyns, Johan
305, 314
Hezekiah 523
Holy Eucharist
169
Holy Roman Empire
437, 496,
548, 552,
603, 604,
605

Holy Spirit 7, 8, 26,
52, 79, 80,
111, 116,
126, 127,
150, 165,
169, 187,
188, 194,
195, 196,
202, 208,
209, 222,
233, 234,
241, 242,
248, 250,
251, 256,
258, 269,
272, 274,
276, 279,
289, 293,
294, 295,
296, 303,
304, 316,
317, 318,
320, 321,
322, 323,
325, 326,
329, 330,
337, 338,
340, 344,
348, 351,
371, 372,
378, 383,
384, 385,
387, 391,
407, 408,
412, 413,
415, 418,
420, 421,
422, 423,
475, 499,
505, 509,
512, 516,
517, 525,
539, 546,
582, 584,
589, 592,
600, 625

Horton, Michael S.
354, 626

## I

Inner sincerity
225, 233
Irenaeus 442, 445,
466, 468,
539, 555
Isaac 54, 161,
389
Israel x, xii,
xviii, xix,
xxiv, 2, 4,
8, 9, 10,
12, 13, 14,
16, 18, 19,
20, 21, 22,
23, 24, 26,
27, 28, 29,
30, 41, 42,
52, 55, 56,
57, 59, 60,
61, 64, 66,
67, 68, 73,
74, 75, 78,
86, 87, 90,
93, 94, 95,
96, 97,
102, 104,
106, 108,

*Subject Index*

109, 110,
113, 125,
131, 134,
137, 139,
141, 144,
145, 146,
147, 148,
149, 150,
151, 152,
153, 154,
155, 157,
158, 159,
160, 161,
162, 176,
178, 179,
180, 184,
202, 204,
206, 218,
224, 246,
254, 269,
270, 274,
275, 276,
278, 292,
294, 327,
366, 382,
383, 388,
389, 395,
396, 400,
401, 404,
406, 421,
425, 426,
427, 428,
429, 430,
431, 432,
434, 435,
437, 441,
442, 443,
448, 449,
450, 451,
452, 453,
454, 455,
456, 457,
458, 459,
460, 461,
465, 468,
481, 483,
484, 495,
497, 507,
508, 515,
519, 520,
523, 526,
527, 536,
555, 560,
566, 570,
571, 572,
575, 578,
579, 581,
587, 588,
589, 590,
591, 593,
594, 598,
599, 608,
610, 613,
617, 619,
630, 633

## J

Jacob    x, 11, 18,
20, 42, 52,
54, 56, 58,
68, 81, 96,
161, 275,
348, 389,
394, 395,
396, 399,
463, 470,
520, 594,
598, 610

Jerusalem    10, 20, 21,
22, 23, 54,
58, 59, 66,
70, 82, 94,
95, 96, 97,
98, 150,
151, 152,
154, 159,
180, 204,
215, 217,
218, 219,
265, 270,
274, 275,
277, 282,
359, 371,
374, 381,
382, 383,
400, 404,
435, 436,
444, 447,
453, 454,
457, 459,
460, 463,
467, 481,
495, 507,
513, 514,
519, 520,
521, 523,
526, 527,
534, 589,
609, 610,
623, 624

Jesus Christ    xxiii, xxiv,
xxv, 8, 9,
25, 84, 93,
102, 177,
196, 203,
215, 233,
250, 261,
265, 269,
270, 277,
284, 292,
295, 317,
318, 329,
332, 336,
342, 343,
353, 355,
360, 361,
370, 379,
382, 386,
405, 455,
499, 505,
506, 511,
525, 551,
553, 597

Jesus Seminar    504, 505

John the Baptist    7, 70, 82,
88, 118,
196, 198,
255

Josiah    52, 65
Judaism    27, 244,
428, 461,
588, 589
Judgmen    xiii, 151,
171, 429,
478, 617,
619
Justin Martyr    442, 445,
466, 468

## K

Kempis, Thomas à    393
kingdom of God    1, 2, 3, 4,
5, 7, 9, 10,
22, 23, 36,
40, 48, 49,
60, 65, 69,
70, 71, 72,
74, 76, 78,
79, 80, 82,
86, 89, 90,
91, 92, 93,

669

99, 101,
105, 109,
111, 113,
115, 116,
118, 119,
120, 122,
123, 124,
125, 126,
127, 132,
133, 135,
136, 137,
138, 139,
147, 148,
149, 152,
154, 156,
157, 158,
160, 161,
162, 163,
167, 168,
171, 173,
174, 177,
178, 179,
181, 188,
191, 193,
194, 195,
197, 198,
199, 201,
202, 203,
204, 205,
211, 217,
219, 221,
222, 224,
228, 229,
230, 231,
232, 233,
234, 235,
239, 242,
243, 244,
251, 252,
255, 257,
259, 260,
261, 262,
263, 264,
265, 268,
269, 270,
271, 273,
274, 276,
277, 278,
279, 283,
284, 289,
291, 294,
297, 298,
299, 300,
301, 302,
303, 304,
308, 309,
310, 311,
313, 314,
315, 316,
319, 320,
321, 322,
326, 327,
328, 329,
330, 331,
334, 335,
336, 337,
338, 340,
342, 346,
347, 348,
349, 361,
362, 365,
372, 374,
376, 377,
378, 379,
380, 381,
383, 384,
385, 386,
387, 388,
391, 400,
402, 404,
407, 410,
413, 414,
415, 417,
418, 419,
420, 422,
423, 427,
433, 434,
442, 443,
454, 456,
458, 473,
475, 485,
487, 488,
497, 498,
499, 500,
502, 503,
505, 509,
510, 511,
512, 513,
514, 516,
517, 518,
519, 524,
525, 530,
537, 559,
590, 592,
593, 595,
596

Kingdom of heaven
    3, 7, 9, 10,
    69, 70, 73,
    74, 76, 77,
    101, 111,
    116, 123,
    124, 125,
    131, 161,
    162, 164,
    165, 174,
    175, 176,
    196, 199,
    223, 225,
    226, 227,
    228, 235,
    251, 252,
    254, 256,
    268, 289,
    298, 299,
    338, 348,
    359, 384,
    388, 389,
    408, 511,
    525

Kingdom theology
    401, 425,
    426, 471,
    472, 476,
    508, 530

Küng, Hans 302, 311,
    315, 431,
    432, 433,
    489, 622,
    628

Kuyper, Abraham
    26, 300,
    307, 471,
    522, 560,
    618, 628,
    637

Kuyperian theology
    300

# L

Ladd, George
    314
LaHaye, Timothy
    530, 573,
    629
Lane, William L.
    201, 215,
    260, 629
Latin    2, 105,
    141, 242,
    345, 369,
    374, 419,
    464, 502,
    531, 533,
    550
Law    xviii, 60,
    196, 197,

*Subject Index*

229, 245,
265, 319,
415, 420,
441, 504,
507, 508,
510, 574,
615, 637
Liberal basileology
486, 487,
488, 490
Liberation Theology
502
Longenecker, Richard N.
103, 104,
630
Longman III, Tremper
630
Luther, Martin
34, 69,
166, 184,
285, 447,
448, 449,
460, 477,
511, 540,
541, 542,
553, 554,
630

# M

MacArthur, John F.
346, 581,
630
Marxism
400, 488
Mashiach 53, 54
Matthew Henry
394, 396,
511
McGrath, Alister E.
209, 631
Meinhold, Arndt
397
Melchizedek
52, 61, 62,
63, 97,
357, 612
Messiah x, xi, 2, 8,
9, 11, 21,
23, 24, 30,
32, 33, 35,
36, 52, 53,
54, 55, 56,
57, 61, 62,
64, 68, 79,
83, 84, 85,
86, 87, 88,
89, 98,
109, 110,
115, 116,
118, 128,
142, 148,
159, 160,
168, 180,
189, 198,
214, 269,
270, 274,
277, 342,
345, 368,
372, 373,
380, 381,
382, 383,
385, 395,
396, 397,
402, 426,
427, 428,
432, 435,
456, 462,
463, 466,
506, 523,
534, 535,
542, 543,
550, 552,
553, 554,
577, 586,
594, 602,
607, 608,
609, 610,
611, 618,
622, 640
Messianic hope
53, 608
Messianic kingdom
5, 8, 10,
21, 24, 32,
56, 58, 62,
74, 78, 81,
97, 115,
118, 127,
155, 158,
163, 181,
183, 188,
189, 191,
199, 209,
230, 235,
236, 237,
238, 240,
261, 276,
282, 318,
321, 323,
325, 326,
327, 328,
332, 357,
358, 359,
360, 367,
368, 372,
373, 379,
381, 382,
384, 394,
395, 396,
397, 400,
401, 402,
403, 404,
406, 425,
426, 427,
428, 429,
430, 431,
432, 434,
436, 440,
443, 444,
446, 462,
464, 466,
470, 471,
472, 482,
484, 485,
486, 488,
490, 491,
492, 494,
495, 504,
505, 506,
508, 509,
510, 512,
518, 519,
521, 523,
524, 525,
526, 527,
534, 550,
557, 560,
561, 562,
565, 570,
571, 574,
575, 576,
578, 588,
591, 594,
602, 603,
607, 613
Messianic Torah
102, 108,
118, 120,
128, 132,
133, 135,
222, 223,
226, 227,
234, 243,
245, 248,
267, 272,
331, 422
Middle Ages 473, 476,

533, 534, 558, 559, 620
Millennial Kingdom 445, 466, 467, 471, 472, 473, 479, 480, 482, 483, 484, 508, 530, 533, 537, 546, 554, 559, 560, 561, 575, 604, 605, 606
Miracles 24, 72, 76, 79, 80, 81, 82, 91, 165, 203, 207, 208, 284, 337, 391, 392, 420, 438, 581, 582, 584, 585, 589
*missio Dei* 26, 27, 28
Moo, Douglas J. 44
Moses xi, 19, 52, 61, 67, 68, 96, 105, 107, 128, 166, 206, 249, 253, 254, 265, 319, 348, 421, 443, 535, 539, 554, 557, 562, 574, 576, 577, 584, 594, 630, 636
Mount of Olives 523, 526
Mount Zion 21, 427, 523, 599

# N

Nations 4, 13, 14, 18, 19, 20, 21, 26, 28, 29, 30, 33, 41, 42, 45, 57, 58, 59, 65, 84, 91, 98, 106, 110, 153, 154, 155, 160, 178, 189, 214, 241, 243, 274, 275, 279, 352, 353, 363, 364, 368, 369, 401, 425, 435, 447, 459, 462, 494, 496, 516, 518, 520, 521, 523, 524, 572, 593, 594, 598, 609, 610, 612, 613
Nebuchadnezzar 9, 68, 90, 173, 365, 440, 563
Netherlands xxvii, 6, 311, 434, 450, 452, 455, 457, 461, 473, 482, 483, 549, 559
New Covenant 590
New Jerusalem 374, 444, 447
New Testament x, xv, xvii, 3, 5, 7, 8, 18, 27, 37, 39, 53, 60, 61, 62, 63, 64, 87, 117, 131, 147, 148, 163, 168, 174, 187, 213, 221, 233, 243, 247, 255, 257, 258, 264, 265, 267, 268, 273, 274, 289, 290, 292, 293, 295, 297, 308, 320, 323, 329, 342, 343, 348, 356, 361, 365, 367, 371, 400, 401, 403, 404, 426, 428, 438, 446, 449, 455, 457, 459, 467, 481, 486, 491, 492, 493, 497, 498, 500, 501, 502, 505, 506, 510, 535, 536, 537, 538, 539, 540, 578, 579, 582, 583, 584, 585, 589, 590, 591, 611, 612, 619, 622, 624, 625, 628, 629, 630, 631, 639, 640, 643,
Nicene Creed 470
Noah 5, 212, 541, 557, 562, 571, 574, 577
North America 311, 564, 585

# O

Old Testament 5, 12, 21, 22, 26, 27, 32, 52, 53,

# Subject Index

54, 55, 56, 58, 60, 61, 62, 63, 67, 68, 72, 79, 81, 83, 93, 109, 114, 115, 117, 118, 145, 151, 168, 176, 184, 187, 205, 206, 238, 246, 253, 254, 321, 326, 327, 342, 343, 365, 366, 367, 371, 393, 394, 399, 400, 401, 402, 426, 427, 428, 433, 443, 444, 448, 450, 451, 457, 458, 460, 461, 464, 469, 485, 493, 495, 497, 512, 518, 519, 520, 523, 525, 526, 536, 540, 541, 562, 584, 585, 587, 590, 591, 594, 597, 602, 606, 607,

Olivet Discourse xiii, 88, 107, 109, 179, 194, 211, 590

Origen 76, 171, 439, 468, 470, 556, 596, 633

# P

Pannenberg, Wolfhart 209, 314, 315, 401, 493, 622, 635

Pannenber, Wolfhart 314, 401, 493

Parables of the Kingdom 101, 103, 105, 107, 109, 111, 113, 115, 117, 119, 121, 123, 125, 127, 129, 131, 133, 135, 137, 139, 141, 143, 145, 147, 149, 151, 153, 155, 157, 159, 161, 163, 165, 167, 169, 171, 173, 175, 177, 179, 181, 183, 185, 187, 189, 191, 622

Paradise 11, 48, 99, 125, 211, 359, 397, 399, 401, 402, 403, 406, 432, 574, 591

Parousia 9, 11, 58, 70, 71, 79, 91, 92, 99, 109, 114, 115, 116, 145, 154, 158, 159, 168, 181, 183, 184, 186, 194, 208, 210, 214, 217, 218, 219, 220, 276, 291, 320, 334, 368, 369, 372, 378, 380, 383, 402, 403, 404, 405, 436, 438, 442, 445, 447, 454, 456, 459, 462, 463, 464, 465, 466, 469, 471, 476, 481, 482, 483, 484, 485, 486, 490, 491, 492, 493, 494, 495, 496, 497, 498, 504, 505, 506, 507, 509, 513, 514, 515, 516, 518, 521, 522, 523, 524, 525, 526, 535, 537, 538, 541, 544, 550, 553, 556, 558, 561, 562, 564, 572, 573, 575, 578, 588, 591, 596, 597, 603, 604

Paul (The Apostle) 255, 263, 290, 322, 378

Pentecost 8, 103, 152, 154, 176, 209, 210, 215, 289, 293, 337, 342, 551, 562, 579, 588, 636

Peter (The Apostle) 7, 8, 38, 88, 119, 124, 132, 152, 195, 206, 215, 217, 219,

220, 221, 239, 268, 269, 270, 271, 273, 289, 292, 295, 298, 332, 342, 345, 355, 379, 380, 381, 387, 388, 405, 440, 443, 447, 451, 452, 472, 492, 493, 503, 511, 553, 554, 563, 583, 586, 597, 617
Pharisees 75, 130, 131, 142, 144, 156, 164, 174, 223, 224, 226, 252, 269, 341, 412, 421
Philosophy 300
Pilgrim xii, 98, 99, 363, 619
Postmillennialism 463, 481
Premillennialism 25, 452, 464, 466, 467, 469, 470, 471, 472, 473, 476, 530, 531, 550, 578, 581, 588
Progressive Dispensationalism 586, 617, 638
Prophets 196, 197, 229, 265, 319, 415, 620
Prosperity Theology 508
Protestant 157, 158, 232, 311, 329, 350, 429, 473, 476, 479, 481, 508, 512, 547
Puritans 449, 451, 452, 459, 559

# R

Realized Eschatology 498, 499
Reformational 476, 539, 540, 635, 640, 644
Reformed theology 243, 559
Regeneration 77, 120, 125, 148, 208, 211, 222, 223, 226, 227, 232, 233, 256, 269, 320, 326, 447, 466, 509, 512
Religion 129, 157, 183, 280, 421, 436, 453, 547, 548, 564
Resurrection 7, 88, 91, 141, 142, 162, 202, 205, 210, 211, 215, 218, 261, 273, 280, 324, 343, 363, 378, 381, 393, 399, 401, 402, 404, 405, 406, 429, 445, 447, 465, 466, 467, 468, 477, 486, 497, 499, 501, 506, 522, 595

Ridderbos, Herman 2, 4, 6, 76, 112, 291, 306
Righteousness 8, 12, 23, 29, 51, 58, 61, 63, 66, 126, 127, 128, 131, 138, 156, 157, 180, 194, 196, 199, 223, 224, 227, 233, 235, 237, 239, 245, 251, 252, 257, 275, 280, 297, 301, 304, 323, 328, 330, 332, 338, 340, 341, 357, 360, 380, 385, 386, 405, 418, 464, 475, 503, 516, 517, 520, 523, 549, 555, 598, 607, 613
Roman Catholicism 157, 169, 302, 310, 311, 431, 447, 471, 473, 512, 547, 564
Roman Empire 279, 280, 281, 282, 284, 287, 428, 429, 434, 436, 437, 440, 443, 446, 495, 496, 497, 533, 534, 548, 550, 551, 552, 562, 563, 564,

## Subject Index

Rushdoony, Rousas J. 565, 578, 603, 604, 605
507
Ryrie, Charles
349, 476

## S

Sabbath
80, 98, 441, 467, 554
Sadducees 175
Salvation 5, 11, 12, 20, 29, 77, 90, 94, 149, 156, 175, 180, 207, 209, 210, 264, 280, 292, 324, 328, 343, 347, 349, 350, 351, 352, 356, 362, 371, 379, 394, 395, 396, 406, 407, 499, 529, 537, 571, 579, 580, 609
Satan x, xi, 2, 6, 17, 27, 30, 33, 34, 35, 36, 37, 38, 39, 40, 41, 42, 43, 44, 45, 46, 47, 49, 73, 77, 78, 81, 129, 155, 164, 166, 193, 194, 195, 198, 200, 201, 279, 280, 281, 287, 308, 318, 335, 409, 440, 447, 465, 483, 522, 573, 593, 594, 596, 599, 602
Satanolog 2, 194
Schaeffer, Francis A. 35, 638
Scofield Reference Bible 573, 639
Scolastisim 4, 14, 110, 160, 161, 183, 204, 220, 229, 231, 232, 233, 234, 246, 261, 267, 270, 283, 284, 285, 292, 329, 330, 331, 336, 344, 345, 346, 348, 349, 350, 351, 352, 353, 354, 355, 356, 359, 360, 361, 362, 377, 378, 379, 380, 381, 383, 385, 386, 387, 388, 389, 390, 391, 392, 393, 395, 406, 408, 413, 414, 416, 421, 438, 439, 468, 473, 476, 512, 535, 578, 585
Scripture 3, 4, 5, 30, 33, 84, 93, 118, 129, 152, 169, 175, 258, 322, 340, 350, 351, 363, 377, 393, 398, 409, 413, 420, 441, 453, 477, 484, 508, 511, 524, 525, 534, 535, 537, 538, 553, 582, 617, 623, 638
Second Millennial Kingdom 483
Secularism 476
Septuagint 34, 37, 42, 57, 84, 85, 92, 198, 212, 343, 370, 398, 556
Sermon on the Mount 79, 105, 112, 118, 128, 142, 252, 385, 590
Sexual immorality 120, 177, 328, 329
Sinai 18, 105, 145, 539, 540, 574, 575, 577
Solomon 20, 22, 30, 32, 52, 65, 78, 95, 96, 97, 206, 227, 253, 358, 396, 443, 448, 594, 595, 602, 606, 607, 608, 609, 610, 611, 612
Solomonic kingdom 570
Son of David 83, 358, 382, 595, 607, 613
Son of God 9, 61, 63, 86, 87, 88, 89, 102, 147, 195, 201, 215, 250, 297, 357, 381, 382, 448, 592, 594,

Son of Man  645, 72, 82, 83, 84, 85, 86, 87, 90, 102, 125, 161, 163, 166, 167, 171, 189, 210, 211, 212, 213, 214, 215, 218, 264, 274, 294, 297, 327, 363, 370, 371, 372, 373, 382, 431, 484, 505, 514, 515, 524, 550, 563, 574, 593, 594, 596, 598, 600
Soteriology  5, 476, 510
Soviet Union  605
Spiritualism  184, 186, 428, 448, 458, 460, 470, 472, 473
Supersessionism  440
Synoptic Gospels  597, 619

## T

Talmud  84, 174, 243, 266, 272, 427, 541, 543, 611, 641
Tertullian  75, 439, 442, 445, 466, 468
Theocracy  592, 599
Theology  2, 5, 85, 243, 244, 300, 301, 401, 421, 425, 426, 437, 441, 442, 471, 472, 476, 487, 491, 501, 502, 503, 506, 507, 508, 509, 510, 530, 531, 559
The Pilgrims' Progress  393
Third Era  539, 546, 547, 548
Throne of David  51, 58, 65, 83, 126, 127, 200, 212, 274, 275, 358, 368, 380, 381, 382, 427, 463, 464, 519, 594, 595, 607
Totalitarianism  508
Tozer, Aiden W.  354, 641
Transfiguration  206, 214, 215, 381
Tribulation  164, 205, 211, 242, 367, 407
Triune God  15, 25, 334, 373, 592, 600
tsaddiq  245, 246, 330, 386
Typology  60, 623

## U

Ultradispensationalism  579, 580

## V

Vertical Love  411
Virgin Birth  35, 486
Virgin Mary  339, 443
Vos, Geerardus  307
Vos, Geerhardus  307, 321, 643

## W

Walvoord, John F.  69, 103, 121, 172, 174, 180, 186, 218, 530, 587, 590, 643
Western Culture  533
Western Europe  452, 480, 585
William Perkins  451
Wolters, Al  307, 308, 644
Worship  26, 28, 29, 59, 148, 285, 287, 357, 363, 374, 375, 406, 420, 455, 459, 487, 516, 521, 564
Wright, John Stafford  398
Wright, N. T.  344

## Z

Zechariah  12, 21, 37, 84, 146, 426, 435, 459, 462, 463, 519, 524, 575
Zwingli, Ulrich  447

www.ingramcontent.com/pod-product-compliance
Lightning Source LLC
Chambersburg PA
CBHW072114050526
44107CB00127BA/1483/J